WordPerfect®: Secrets, Solutions, Shortcuts

Series 5 Edition

Nov 1992

WordPerfect®: Secrets, Solutions, Shortcuts
Series 5 Edition

Mella Mincberg

Osborne **McGraw-Hill**
Berkeley, California

Osborne **McGraw-Hill**
2600 Tenth Street
Berkeley, California 94710
U.S.A.

For information on translations and book distributors outside of the U.S.A., write to Osborne **McGraw-Hill** at the above address.

A complete list of trademarks appears on page 1051.

WordPerfect®: Secrets, Solutions, Shortcuts, Series 5 Edition

234567890 DODO 898

ISBN 0-07-881359-X

Contents

Acknowledgments

I wish to thank Osborne/McGraw-Hill editor-in-chief Cindy Hudson for backing me up when I needed it most; associate editor Ilene Shapera, who kept the pieces together and kept me marching forward with her sympathetic ear and good humor; project editor Dusty Bernard, whose attention to detail is impressive and much appreciated; technical reviewers Stuart Osser and Bill Usim for making sure that what I wrote was, in fact, true and accurate; copy editor Martha Free, who often had to deduce what I was trying to say and make my words clearer; and the staff at WordPerfect Corporation in Orem, Utah, who found the time to answer my many—and usually obscure—questions.

I am grateful to Cathy Wild, David Cohen, Cliff Mazer, and Scott Johnson for their love and support during the arduous writing process, and also to Scott for helping me escape at critical times. YTAC.

Finally, I appreciate all the kind words from readers of my first few computer books. It's reassuring to know that you're actually out there.

Introduction

WordPerfect is one of the most sophisticated and intelligent word processing packages ever written for the personal computer. It is fast. It is powerful. It is packed with advanced features. And it is easy to learn. It is no surprise, then, that by 1986 WordPerfect had become a best-seller in the U.S., in Canada, and in Europe.

Refusing to rest on its laurels, WordPerfect Corporation released an upgrade in May 1988—WordPerfect version 5.0. Major modifications were made and new features were added. Version 5.0 has been praised as enthusiastically as its predecessors.

If you want to learn how best to use WordPerfect version 5.0—whether you're a beginning or experienced user, or if you're switching from an earlier version of WordPerfect—this book is for you. It provides a comprehensive explanation of all of WordPerfect's superior features.

The book's 28 chapters are grouped into two parts. Part I (Chapters 1 through 15) focuses on basic word processing with WordPerfect: typing and editing text, controlling the layout on a page, storing documents, and printing. Part II (Chapters 16 through 28) covers WordPerfect's complementary features—those that surpass routine word processing needs—including the speller, the thesaurus, columns, footnotes, merging, and macros.

In every chapter, you'll find step-by-step instructions for performing a particular word processing task. These instructions are followed by Tips to make you proficient in completing that task and Traps to warn you about potential pitfalls along the way. From the Tips and Traps, you will learn *secrets* that you won't find in the WordPerfect documentation, *solutions* to program limitations, and *shortcuts* to save you time. A Tips and Traps Summary concludes each chapter.

How to Use This Book

What's the wisest method for tackling this book? That depends on your level of experience with WordPerfect.

Beginning users will want to read all of Part I to become comfortable with the WordPerfect basics. At a minimum, go through Chapters 1 through 5 on startup, typing a document, and text editing, Chapter 8 on format changes (such as altering your document's left and right margins), Chapter 9 on page breaks, Chapter 11 on storing documents for future use, and Chapter 14 on printing. Read the main text in each chapter to become comfortable with the step-by-step procedures and then peruse the Tips and Traps for a deeper understanding of each feature. After you master the basics, proceed to Part II.

More *experienced WordPerfect version 5.0 users* may wish to skip the step-by-step information in Part I, but they should at least skim the Tips and Traps to enrich their understanding of the basics. They may then move on to Part II. Because each chapter covers a narrow set of WordPerfect features, this book serves as an effective reference guide; use the table of contents and the index to find the chapters covering those topics you want to learn about.

WordPerfect users who are upgrading to version 5.0 will want to discover how WordPerfect has changed. For that reason, special Tips are provided. Look to the last Tip in each chapter section— the one marked "When upgrading from 4.2." You'll find a synopsis of version 5.0 changes to the feature under discussion. (The "upgrading" Tip is omitted only in sections discussing features that are brand new.) Then look to the surrounding Tips and Traps for further details. You'll learn that, among the many modifications since version 4.2, significant ones include the following:

- New startup options have been added, and WordPerfect now requires more memory in order to run.
- Seven function keys have been renamed or assigned new tasks.
- The status line, as well as margins, tabs, and other format settings, displays in inches (although other units of measure are available).

- Text and codes can now be inserted while on the Reveal Codes screen.
- Font changes can be made either by altering the base font used in a document or by selecting an attribute (such as italics or large print) for a particular base font, and margins and line height adjust automatically based on a font change.
- Printing now takes full advantage of your printer's capabilities, including font cartridges, printing in color, and graphics.
- Macros can be edited and can be defined using advanced programming commands.
- Many advanced features have been added. Table I-1 (at the end of this introduction) lists these new features along with the chapter where each feature is covered, so that you know where to turn for more information.

Make the Most of WordPerfect

Don't let the power of WordPerfect intimidate you. Once you have a solid understanding of WordPerfect's basics, challenge yourself to explore some of its more specialized capabilities. You will discover more efficient methods for completing your work and will save yourself time (and potential headaches).

What specialized features should you investigate? That will depend on the types of documents you wish to produce. Here are some suggestions:

- **To take advantage of desktop publishing so that you can create professional-looking documents and combine pictures with your words** Review font changes (Chapter 7), document formatting (Chapter 8), styles (Chapter 10), and how to add graphics images to your text (Chapter 18). You may also wish to learn about line draw (Chapter 17) and, if you plan to produce newsletters or similar publications, text columns (Chapter 19).
- **To complete books, reports, or other long documents** Read about establishing headers, footers, and page numbers (Chapter 9), master documents (Chapter 12), creating automatic references (Chapter 21), generating lists, indexes, and tables of contents (Chapter 22), and footnotes and endnotes (Chapter 23). The Sort feature (Chapter 26) is useful for reorganizing lists and paragraphs alphabetically or numerically.
- **To type and edit legal briefs, depositions, and contracts** Learn about redline and strikeout (Chapter 5), combining standard paragraphs into one

document (Chapter 12), text columns (Chapter 19), paragraph numbering (Chapter 21), creating tables of contents and authorities (Chapter 22), and footnotes and endnotes (Chapter 23). Also, refer to the discussion on special characters (Chapter 17) for inserting such symbols as the section or paragraph symbol into your document, and on merging (Chapter 25) if you wish to create a sophisticated system for assembling paragraphs.

- **To create tables of text or numbers** Find out how to align text on tab stops (Chapter 7), how to set tab stop locations (Chapter 8), or, depending on your needs, how to establish text columns (Chapter 19). Also, look to WordPerfect's match capabilities (Chapter 20) for totaling columns of numbers.
- **To produce repetitive documents** Discover how to combine text into one document (Chapter 12) and, if you wish to personalize letters with variable information (such as names on a mailing list), learn about the Merge feature (Chapters 24 and 25). Chapter 25 also describes how to produce multiple envelopes or mailing labels.
- **To design and/or fill out standard forms** Review the Advance feature (Chapter 7), line draw (Chapter 17), graphics lines (Chapter 18), and merging with the keyboard (Chapter 24).
- **To exchange documents between software packages, such as from WordStar to WordPerfect or from WordPerfect version 4.2 to version 5.0** Turn to the discussion on converting your files (Chapter 28).
- **To complete quickly any document or set of documents in which certain tasks are continual and tedious** Take another look at styles (Chapter 10), which can save you considerable time in embellishing your text, and at macros (Chapter 27), which can transform a long series of WordPerfect commands into a one-keystroke process.

Book Notation

A specific notation is used throughout this book to indicate what keys you press to execute a certain WordPerfect command. All keys are shown in SMALL CAPITALS. A plus (+) sign between two keys indicates they must be pressed simultaneously. A comma (,) between two keys indicates they must be pressed sequentially. Here are examples:

PGUP	Press the PGUP key

CTRL + END	While holding down the CTRL key, press END. Now release both keys
HOME, UP ARROW	Press HOME and release it. Then press UP ARROW and release it

WordPerfect assigns a one- or two-word name to commands involving function keys. These, too, are listed in SMALL CAPITALS, and the keystrokes are provided in parentheses following the name. Here are examples:

EXIT (F7)	The command is called "exit" and is executed by pressing the F7 function key
PRINT (SHIFT + F7)	The command is called "print" and is invoked by holding down the SHIFT key and, while holding it down, pressing the F7 function key. Then release both keys
SPELL (CTRL + F2)	The command is called "spell" and is executed by holding down the CTRL key and, while holding it down, pressing the F2 function key. Then release both keys

The keystrokes provided are based on the version of WordPerfect created for IBM personal computers and compatibles. If you are using a version for another type of computer, then the key combination you press may differ slightly. Check your manual for details.

Also, the keystrokes are based on the first release of version 5.0. Should a Tip or Trap work differently for you than specified in this book, keep in mind that WordPerfect Corporation continues to improve its product; there may be minor distinctions between WordPerfect version 5.0 program disks that have different release dates.

A Final Note

Whatever your level of experience with WordPerfect, *WordPerfect: Secrets, Solutions, Shortcuts* is sure to help you become a skillful (or more skillful) WordPerfect user. And, you'll enjoy the process of discovering more features and more efficient ways to do your work.

Table I-1. Summary of Features Added to WordPerfect Version 5.0

New Feature	Chapter (or Appendix)	Description
Automatic Reference	21	Ties a reference to a page, paragraph number, footnote, endnote, or graphics box, and updates the reference after the text is edited
Cartridges and Fonts	A	Marks a font cartridge, print wheel, or downloadable font for use with your printer
Colors/Fonts/Attributes	B	Determines how text is displayed on screen—which depends on your monitor and graphics card
Compose	17	Allows you to insert any of over 1500 different special characters in a document
Cursor Speed	B	Increases or decreases key repetition speed
Display Pitch	7	Sets the amount of horizontal space one character occupies on screen
Document Initial Codes	8	Allows default initial codes to be altered for a particular document while reducing the clutter at the top of a document
Document Compare	12	Compares the contents of a document on disk to a document on screen
Endnote Placement	23	Enables endnotes to be compiled anywhere in a document
Fast Save	11	Allows a document to be saved quickly, without being formatted
Force Odd/Even Page	9	Ensures that a particular page is numbered with an even or odd number
Forms	A	Defines the type, size, and location of forms you plan to use with your printer (such as standard paper, envelopes, labels, and so on)
Graphics	18	Combines graphics images with text in a document
Initialize Printer	14	Sends downloadable fonts to your printer
Kerning	7	Reduces the amount of white space between particular letter pairs
Keyboard Layout	B	Assigns a WordPerfect feature, a special character, or a macro to any key on your keyboard
Language	8, 16	Tells WordPerfect which Speller, Thesaurus, and/or Hyphenation files to use—a convenience when creating multilingual documents

Table I-1. Summary of Features Added to WordPerfect Version 5.0 (continued)

New Feature	**Chapter (or Appendix)**	**Description**
Line Height	8	Determines the amount of vertical space assigned to one line; normally, it is adjusted automatically by WordPerfect based on font size
Location of Auxiliary files	B	Tells WordPerfect where certain files (such as the speller dictionary) can be found
Master Document	12	Creates a main document, consisting of one or more subdocuments, to help manage large document files
Paper Size/Type	8	Specifies the form on which the document will print
Style	10	Controls the format of certain elements in a document with a combination of formatting codes and text
Units of Measure	B	Determines the units used in the status line and for commands that require measurements
Word/Letter Spacing	7	Determines the amount of space allowed between words and/or letters on the printed page
Word Spacing Justification Limits	8	Adjusts the amount of space between words when right justification is active

I

WordPerfect Basics

1

Starting and Ending WordPerfect

Suppose that you're ready to produce a report, a letter, or a newsletter article. You're ready to take advantage of WordPerfect's myriad features. This chapter describes how to begin a basic WordPerfect session and explains startup options available to make your work session as productive as possible. Also explained is a topic of equal importance—how to clear your computer of WordPerfect when you're done for the day. You should acquire the habit of always exiting WordPerfect before you turn off your machine.

If you have just purchased the WordPerfect package, be sure to turn to Appendix A, "Installing WordPerfect." Appendix A describes how you prepare WordPerfect to work with your computer hardware, and how, if you choose, you can write what's called a batch file to make the process of starting WordPerfect quicker. Once you have installed WordPerfect, read on.

Starting WordPerfect

When you work with WordPerfect, you are also working with another program, called DOS, or disk operating system. If your computer is not equipped with a hard disk, then after you install WordPerfect to work with your computer hardware (Appendix A), both DOS and WordPerfect are housed on the WordPerfect 1 disk. If your computer is equipped with a hard disk, then after you install WordPerfect (Appendix A), both DOS and WordPerfect are housed on the hard disk.

You begin a WordPerfect session by loading both DOS and WordPerfect. This means that you notify the computer to put a copy of DOS and the WordPerfect program instructions into random-access memory (RAM). RAM is a computer's workspace; it is to a computer what your desktop is to you. The computer must place instructions into RAM before it can process words, just as you must place files on your desktop before you can begin your work.

All information stored in RAM is temporary and disappears as soon as electricity stops flowing into the computer. You must thus load DOS and WordPerfect into RAM at the beginning of each work session.

When loading WordPerfect, there are two keys on the keyboard that you should know about:

- **ENTER** Used before and as you load WordPerfect to send a command to the computer. The ENTER key is marked on the keyboard with the word "ENTER" or "RETURN" or with a symbol of a bent arrow pointing to the left (↵).

- **BACKSPACE** Used to erase mistakes as you type, deleting the character to the left of the cursor, which is the flashing light that serves as your pointer on the screen. The BACKSPACE key is marked on the keyboard with the word "BACKSPACE" or with a symbol of a long arrow pointing to the left (⟵). BACKSPACE is often located above the ENTER key.

Also, you should know that how you load WordPerfect determines the default drive or directory to start the computer session. The default drive or directory is where WordPerfect assumes you wish to store your documents on disk, and it is where WordPerfect looks to find a document that you wish to retrieve from disk for editing. You do not want to establish the default as the same drive or directory where the WordPerfect program is housed—but on another disk drive (drive B) if you're a floppy disk user, and on another drive or another directory (such as \WPER\DATA) if you're a hard disk user. By keeping the actual WordPerfect program separate from your data files (documents), you won't inadvertently erase or corrupt a program file, and you will have a clean, uncluttered space just for your documents. As you'll learn in Chapters 11 and 13, the default drive or directory can be changed, but typically it is more convenient to set an appropriate default when you first load the program. That way you are ready to work on your documents as soon as WordPerfect is loaded.

The step-by-step procedure for loading depends on (1) whether or not your computer is equipped with a hard disk, and (2) whether or not you have written a batch file (a set of DOS instructions, described in Appendix A, to automatically load WordPerfect and set the proper drive or directory as the default).

For those of you using a floppy disk system only who have written a batch file as described in Appendix A:

1. Insert your WordPerfect 1 disk in drive A (the drive on the left or on top), and insert the floppy disk, where you will store your documents, in drive B (the drive on the right or on the bottom).

2. Turn on the computer, and, if your computer is not equipped with an internal clock, enter the current date and time when prompted to do so. (Refer to the Tip that follows this discussion if you have never typed the date and time.)

3. Because of the automatically activated batch file, WordPerfect immediately loads the computer's operating system (DOS) and begins loading WordPerfect for you. For 5 1/4-inch floppy disk users, a WordPerfect screen appears, with this message:

   Insert diskette labeled "WordPerfect 2" and press any key

4. Take out your WordPerfect 1 disk from drive A, place it back in its protective envelope, and insert your WordPerfect 2 disk in drive A.

5. Press ENTER to continue loading WordPerfect.

For those of you using a floppy disk system only who have not written a batch file:

1. Insert your WordPerfect 1 disk in drive A (the drive on the left or on top), and insert the floppy disk, where you will store your documents, in drive B (the drive on the right or on the bottom).

2. Turn on the computer, and if your computer is not equipped with an internal clock, enter the current date and time when prompted to do so. (Refer to the Tip that follows this discussion if you have never typed the date and time.)

The computer's disk operating system (DOS) is now in RAM. This DOS prompt appears on the screen:

A>

This means that you are operating from disk drive A.

3. Type **B:**. The screen looks like this:

A>B:

This switches the default drive—the drive for storing and retrieving documents—to drive B.

4. Press ENTER. DOS responds with:

B>

5. Type **A:WP** (either uppercase or lowercase letters can be used) at the DOS prompt. The screen looks like this:

B>A:WP

This tells the computer to search the disk in drive A for the WordPerfect program.

6. Press ENTER to load WordPerfect. For 5 1/4 ″ floppy disk users, a WordPerfect screen appears, with the following message:

Insert diskette labeled ″WordPerfect 2″ and press any key

7. Take out your WordPerfect 1 disk from drive A, place it back in its protective envelope, and insert your WordPerfect 2 disk in drive A.
8. Press ENTER to continue loading WordPerfect.

For those of you using a hard disk system who have written a batch file as described in Appendix A:

1. Turn on the computer and, if your computer is not equipped with an internal clock, enter the current date and time. (Refer to the Tip that follows this discussion if you have never typed the date and time.)

   The computer's disk operating system (DOS) is now in RAM. The DOS prompt on your screen should look like:

C>

or

C:\>

This means that you are operating from disk drive C, the hard disk drive.

2. Type **WP5** (either uppercase or lowercase letters can be used), which is the name of the batch file, and press ENTER.
3. Because of the batch file, WordPerfect is automatically loaded for you.

For those of you using a hard disk system who have not written a batch file:

1. Turn on the computer and, if your computer is not equipped with an internal clock, enter the current date and time. (Refer to the Tip that follows this discussion if you have never typed the date and time.)

   The computer's operating system (DOS) is now in RAM. The DOS prompt on your screen should look like:

   C>

   or

   C:\>

   This means that you are operating from disk drive **C**, the hard disk drive.

2. Issue the CD (Change Directory) command to switch to the hard disk directory that you want to establish as the default— the directory for saving and retrieving files. Suppose, for example, that the WordPerfect program is housed in \WPER and you store files in a separate subdirectory named \WPER\DATA, as suggested in Appendix A.

   Note: If you used the Auto-Install program as described in Appendix A to install WordPerfect, then the WordPerfect directory is instead named \WP50, and you may have created a separate directory named \WP50\DATA to store files. If this is the case, substitute WP50 wherever you read WPER.

   At the DOS prompt, you would type **CD \WPER\DATA**. The screen will look like this:

   C>CD \WPER\DATA

   or

   C:\>CD \WPER\DATA

3. Press ENTER to change directories. The screen shows

   C>

   or

   C:\WPER\DATA>

4. If you use DOS version 3.0 or higher, and assuming that the WordPerfect program is housed in the \WPER directory, type **\WPER \WP** at the DOS prompt. The screen shows the following:

   C>\WPER\WP

   or

   C:\WPER\DATA>\WPER\WP

   If you use a lower DOS version (such as 2.0 or 2.1), type **WP** at the DOS prompt. The screen shows the following:

   C>WP

   or

   C:\WPER\DATA>WP

5. Press ENTER to load WordPerfect.

   Note to DOS version 2.0 or 2.1 users: If the computer responds with a message such as "Bad command or file name," then start again at step 2, but this time change to the hard disk directory where the WordPerfect program is housed. For example, if the program is stored in \WPER, you would enter **CD \WPER** and then continue with steps 2 through 5. The default when you load WordPerfect would be the directory where the WordPerfect programs are stored, so you would then want to change the default; refer to Chapter 11. Also, refer to Appendix A so that you can write what's called a *path command,* so that the next time WordPerfect will not respond with "Bad command or file name," but will find and load the WordPerfect program.

Whether you are a floppy disk or a hard disk user, you will know that you have started WordPerfect successfully when, after a few seconds, you see WordPerfect copyright information on your screen. After another few seconds, your screen becomes blank except for a line of writing in the lower right-hand corner of the screen, as shown in Figure 1-1. You are viewing the WordPerfect Typing screen, which means that WordPerfect now resides in RAM; the computer is ready to process words for you. WordPerfect remains in memory until you exit the program or until the computer's power is shut off.

Be aware that you have the ability to load WordPerfect in a slightly different way in order to activate options that might make your WordPerfect session more productive. See the following section, "Startup (Slash) Options," for details.

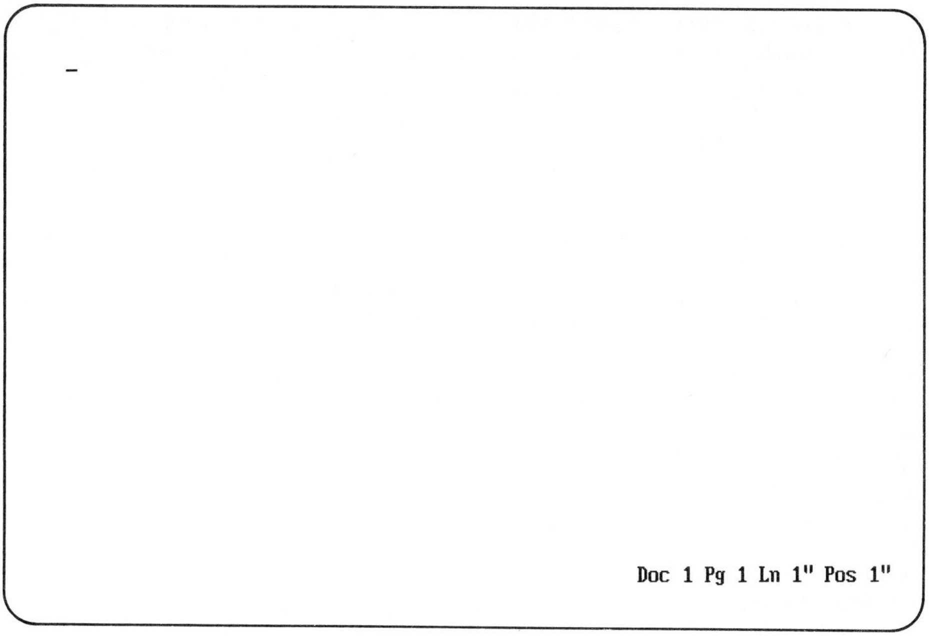

Figure 1-1. WordPerfect Typing screen

Tip: *Enter the correct date and time at the beginning of a WordPerfect session.*

If the correct date and time flash momentarily each time you turn on your computer, then your computer is equipped with an internal clock. Internal clock owners can ignore the following discussion.

If the date is not correct, the screen may provide the following message:

Current date is Tues 1-01-1980
Enter new date:_

Or you can display that message by typing **DATE** (either uppercase or lowercase letters can be used) at the DOS prompt. Then you respond to the message by typing the month, day, and year, separated by slashes (/) or hyphens (-). For example, assume today's date is December 31, 1988. You could type either

12-31-88

or

12/31/88

You must use numbers, not letters. For example, don't type a lowercase letter l instead of a 1 (one) or an uppercase letter O instead of a 0 (zero). (If you make a typing mistake, erase it by pressing BACKSPACE, the key labeled with a large arrow pointing left and located above ENTER.) Press ENTER after you have entered the date.

The computer also requests the correct time at the start of a session, as shown:

Current time is 0:00:55.90
Enter new time:_

Or you can display that message by typing **TIME** (either uppercase or lowercase letters can be used) at the DOS prompt. The computer works with a 24-hour clock, like the military does. The computer's clock refers to 6 A.M. as 6:00 and to 6 P.M. as 18:00. You enter the hours, minutes, seconds, and even tenths of a second. It is easiest simply to type the hours and minutes. At 4:31 P.M., for example, you can type

16:31

(Remember to use numbers, not letters, when typing 1 and 0.) Then press ENTER.

When you first turn on the computer, you can bypass the date and time messages, if they appear, by pressing ENTER only. That, however, is a bad idea; you will lose out on a number of WordPerfect features (such as the ability to have WordPerfect automatically insert the current date and time in a document for you, as described in Chapter 8). So take a moment at the outset of a session to set the computer's clock.

Trap: *Don't use the original WordPerfect disks to load WordPerfect.*

Your WordPerfect package includes twelve 5 1/4-inch (or six 3 1/2-inch) floppy diskettes: WordPerfect System disks 1 and 2, Thesaurus disk, Speller disk, Learning disk, Fonts/Graphics disk, Conversion disk, Printer disks 1, 2, 3, and 4, and PTR Program disk. None are indestructible. You could accidentally lose a disk or bend it, or a disk could just refuse to work one day. See Appendix A if you haven't already made working copies of your original WordPerfect disks—either on another set of floppies or on your hard disk.

Trap: *DOS is missing when either the date or the DOS prompt doesn't appear on screen.*

The computer's disk operating system (DOS) must be placed into RAM even before WordPerfect is loaded. On a hard disk system, this is already accomplished, because DOS is already on the hard disk; the computer finds DOS and places it into memory when you turn on the computer. (If DOS is missing from your hard disk, refer to your computer manual.)

On a floppy disk system, you must place a portion of the DOS instructions, along with WordPerfect files, onto the working copy of the WordPerfect 1 disk. In that way, when you place the working copy in drive A, the computer places DOS in memory immediately. If, however, DOS is absent from the disk in drive A, you will see the following message, after turning on the computer:

Non-system disk or disk error
Replace and strike any key when ready

Appendix A describes how to place WordPerfect and a portion of DOS together on the same disk.

Trap: *WordPerfect can't load unless you have sufficient memory and at least DOS version 2.0.*

WordPerfect version 5 requires an IBM or compatible and approximately 384K (kilobytes) of free RAM; a machine with at least 512K is recommended. If your computer is equipped with less memory, when you attempt to load WordPerfect, the program will respond with the message:

Insufficient memory to load WordPerfect

You will be returned to DOS. If this happens, talk to a computer vendor about purchasing additional memory for your computer.

In addition, you must have DOS version 2.0 or a later version (2.1, 3.1, 3.2, and so on) to work with WordPerfect. If you do not, you must purchase a more recent version of DOS.

Trap: *Don't load WordPerfect without first having created a CONFIG.SYS file.*

WordPerfect requires that you set up your computer so that a DOS file named CONFIG.SYS contains a statement such as:

files=20

This tells DOS how many files can be open at one time. If this is not done, then when you are loading WordPerfect, you will get an error message, such as:

Insufficient file handles to load WordPerfect

WordPerfect will be unable to operate properly. Refer to Appendix A for the procedure to create or modify your CONFIG.SYS file. This file should be set up before you can begin working in WordPerfect.

Trap: *The computer can't find the WordPerfect instructions on a hard disk unless you indicate the correct subdirectory.*

If you're a hard disk user, assume that you're at the DOS prompt C> and you type **WP** in an attempt to load WordPerfect. But then, you see the following message:

Bad command or file name

This could mean that the WordPerfect program files have not been copied onto the hard disk; refer to Appendix A for assistance.

Or this message could mean that the computer does not know which subdirectory houses the WordPerfect files. You have several alternatives to let DOS know where the files are stored. You can write a DOS batch file to load WordPerfect for you automatically, as described in Appendix A. Or, if you don't elect to use a batch file to load WordPerfect, you have other options. First, if you work with DOS version 3.0 or higher, you can type the directory name followed by WP, such as typing **\WPER\WP** at the DOS prompt. Second, you can include that directory in your computer's path command (as described in Appendix A), so that the computer knows where to look for the WordPerfect program files when you type **WP**. Third, you can use the CD (Change Directory) command to switch to the directory where WordPerfect is stored before typing **WP** at the DOS prompt.

Trap: *In some cases, you can't load WordPerfect unless you use a special startup option.*

There may be certain cases in which WordPerfect conflicts with your computer hardware or with a TSR (terminate and stay resident) software package that you load before WordPerfect. If this is the case, then WordPerfect may not load, or the program may lock (the computer keyboard freezes) if it does load. To get around these problems, you can start up WordPerfect with special startup options. See the following section, "Startup (Slash) Options," for details.

Trap: *When you load WordPerfect, don't begin typing a document until you define and select a printer.*

When you first open the WordPerfect package and install WordPerfect in your computer, it is critical that you also define your printer. Your printer and WordPerfect will work effectively together only after you've indicated to WordPerfect which brand of printer (or printers) you use. You can define many printers; you should define and select at least one.

If you haven't yet defined a printer, then after you load WordPerfect, refer to Appendix A for the details on defining your printer to work with WordPerfect.

Tip: *When you plan to store documents on floppy disks, remember to have a formatted disk available before you load WordPerfect.*

Floppy disk users always store their files on floppy disks, while hard disk users have a choice. They can store documents on the hard disk or, if certain documents are personal or confidential, these can be stored on floppies.

Assuming that you plan to store your documents on a floppy disk, you should place a formatted disk in the unoccupied disk drive (drive B for floppy disk users, drive A or B for hard disk users) so that it is available when you're ready to store documents. A *formatted disk* is a disk that has been prepared by the computer to accept files. It is through DOS that you format disks, so format a disk (if you haven't already) before you load WordPerfect. Turn to Appendix A if you are unfamiliar with the format procedure.

Tip: *You can change the character used as your cursor.*

The flashing line that serves as your pointer on the screen is called the cursor. If you dislike the flashing line or if you find it to be too small, you can use a different symbol or a larger one. Or, if the cursor dash is distracting, you can use a smaller dash. The following steps show how to alter the appearance of the cursor.

1. You must be in DOS and the DOS prompt must be on the screen. Floppy disk users should see the DOS prompt A> on screen; place the Conversion disk in drive A. Hard disk users should change to the directory to which the files on the Conversion disk have been copied.
2. Type **CURSOR** (either uppercase or lowercase letters can be used). Press ENTER. In a few moments a matrix of letters appears on the screen. Your cursor is positioned at the intersection of the first letter G and the second letter H.
3. Move the cursor by pressing the arrow keys, and the cursor character will change in shape and size. For instance, at the intersection of the first letter A and second letter G, the cursor is shaped like a tall rectangle. (You can press the SPACEBAR to see the cursor on a line of text.)
4. When you find a cursor size to your liking, press ENTER. The DOS prompt appears again.

5. Load WordPerfect. The cursor character you have chosen is in effect until you turn off the computer.

Once you become familiar with the matrix of letters, you can change the cursor size without viewing the matrix. For instance, if you want the cursor to become the size indicated by the intersection of the first letter A and the second letter G, then at the DOS prompt, type **CURSOR/AG** (instead of typing **CURSOR**) and press ENTER. The cursor size will change, and you will now be ready to load WordPerfect. (In fact, you can include a command such as CURSOR/AG in your WordPerfect batch file so that the cursor size is automatically changed just before WordPerfect is loaded.)

Tip: *(When upgrading from 4.2.) Because it offers more features than ever before, WordPerfect now occupies more disks.*

Version 5 of WordPerfect offers more features than before. Therefore, the program alone is now housed on two disks (disks 1 and 2), rather than on one disk. To use version 5, WordPerfect Corporation recommends 512K of memory, rather than the 256K which was required in version 4.2. If you have insufficient memory, then you must purchase additional memory for your computer. In addition, WordPerfect now requires that you create (or edit) a DOS file named CONFIG.SYS to run WordPerfect properly (Appendix A explains how to do this).

You'll notice when you load WordPerfect that the Typing screen's status line is different in version 5: it displays units of measure in inches rather than in lines and columns, as in version 4.2. Refer to Chapter 3 for a discussion of this new status line. Chapter 3 also explains that you can, if you prefer, change the status line to version 4.2 units—lines and column positions.

Startup (Slash) Options

Depending on your equipment and needs, it may be advantageous to load WordPerfect in a slightly different way. If you don't load WordPerfect using a batch file, then instead of typing **WP** to load WordPerfect, you can add the slash symbol (/), followed by various letters, to activate options that might make a session more productive for you. The options take effect until the next time you load Word-

Perfect. Or you can include these options in your batch file, so that they are activated *each time* you load WordPerfect (the procedure to write a batch file is discussed in Appendix A). The options are described below.

Option 1: Speed Up the Program by Using Expanded Memory or Inhibit the Use of Expanded Memory

As you now know, WordPerfect is loaded into RAM before you begin a working session; the file that is loaded is named WP.EXE. Yet the computer must still refer to a WordPerfect file named WP.FIL on disk from time to time. You can tell when the computer is referring to a disk drive—the red light on your disk drive illuminates. One reason that WordPerfect refers to the disk is that some detailed program instructions are *not* loaded into RAM when you type **WP** at the DOS prompt. The computer thus refers to the disk periodically for further information, which slows down the processing time of the computer.

Both hard and floppy disk users can avoid this slowdown—if, and only if, your computer's RAM is large enough. If your computer is equipped with *expanded* memory, and at least 300K is unused, then you can load into RAM even the more detailed instructions, housed in the file named WP.FIL. To do so, instead of typing **WP** at the DOS prompt to load WordPerfect, you can invoke what is called the /R (pronounced "slash R") option by typing (in either uppercase or lowercase letters) the following:

WP/R

This loads about 300K of menus, error messages, and overlay files found in WP.FIL.

Conversely, if you wish to inhibit the use of expanded memory when using WordPerfect, then use the /NE option. At the DOS prompt, type

WP/NE

Option 2: Redirect Temporary Files

WordPerfect often creates temporary overflow and buffer files as you make requests and type long documents, and it stores those temporary files on whatever disk or directory the WordPerfect program file WP.EXE is stored on. These files have names such as WP}WP{.BV1 or WP}WP{.TV1, and are necessary for WordPerfect's own internal housekeeping functions. As a result, floppy disk users must still keep the WordPerfect disk in drive A, even after exercising the /R option.

You can direct WordPerfect to perform housekeeping functions on another drive or directory, however, by using the /D option. To use this option, type **WP/D-** and then the new drive and directory. For example, assume that you wanted to redirect housekeeping to drive B. To load WordPerfect, you would type

WP/D-B:

If you redirect the temporary files to drive B, make sure that the disk in drive B has enough room to store those temporary files. 64K is usually sufficient. Also, make sure that you keep the same disk in drive B for the entire working session or you'll get a message prompting you to do so, such as "Put WordPerfect disk back in drive."

A floppy disk user who employs the /D option in conjunction with the /R option can remove the WordPerfect 2 disk from drive A for most of the working session. This cuts down on constant disk swapping. For example, you can then keep the Speller disk in drive A, to check your spelling at any time without needing to change disks before initiating a spelling check (a feature described in Chapter 16).

Option 3: Load WordPerfect and a Commonly Used File Simultaneously

Assume that you're working on the same document every day for a week. You can specify the document's filename so that the document and WordPerfect are loaded together. If your document is in a file called JONES, then, at the DOS prompt, type the following:

WP JONES

(Notice that no slash is typed here.) After WordPerfect is loaded, the file named JONES is automatically retrieved to the Typing screen for editing.

Option 4: Load WordPerfect and a Commonly Used Macro Simultaneously

A *macro* is a fast way to store phrases or to execute keystrokes that you use often (the Macro feature is explained thoroughly in Chapter 27). If you wish to start a macro as soon as you load WordPerfect, then specify that macro as you load. Type **WP/M**, followed by a hyphen, and then type the macro name. If your macro is named TOC, for example, then, at the DOS prompt, type the following:

WP/M-TOC

The macro is activated as soon as WordPerfect appears on the screen.

Option 5: Improve WordPerfect's Performance on Certain Computer Equipment or in Conjunction with Certain Software

Use the /I option if you are running WordPerfect under DOS version 2.0 or 2.1 and if WordPerfect cannot find the program file named WP.FIL. At the DOS prompt, type

WP/I

Use the /NC option if you wish to disable the Cursor Speed feature (as described in Appendix B). This is necessary if you are using certain equipment or a TSR software package that conflicts with this feature. Sometimes WordPerfect won't load at all unless you use this option. At the DOS prompt, type

WP/NC

Use the /NF (Non-flash) option if your screen goes blank periodically or if you use windowing programs (other than Topview) along with WordPerfect. At the DOS prompt, type

WP/NF

Use the /NK option to disable enhanced keyboard commands that are unable to be recognized by certain equipment or TSR software packages. Sometimes

WordPerfect will load and then lock up (the keyboard freezes) unless you use this option. At the DOS prompt, type

WP/NK

Use the /SS (Screen Size) option to set the screen size of your monitor. The standard monitor displays 25 rows and 80 columns. If your monitor is a different size (as is the Genius monitor, for example), and WordPerfect does not detect the correct size, then type **WP/SS**, followed by a hyphen, the rows that your screen supports, a comma, and the columns that your screen supports. For example, for the Genius monitor, try typing the following at the DOS prompt:

WP/SS-66,80

Be sure to set the screen to its actual size or the screen display will not operate correctly.

Option 6: Return to the Default Settings

When you purchase WordPerfect, certain settings are provided as defaults by WordPerfect Corporation. For example, one default setting calls for left/right margins of one inch. Another calls for printing documents with justification set to "on" (meaning that the right margin will be even).

Realizing that individuals have different needs, the WordPerfect designers also provided the means to change those defaults permanently via the Setup menu. Using the Setup menu (described in Appendix B), you can change any or all of the defaults as set up by WordPerfect Corporation, to permanently tailor the program to your needs. For example, if you always use a left margin of 0.75 inch for your documents, you can establish .75" as your new default left-margin setting.

However, if you wish to load WordPerfect and restore the original default settings (as defined by WordPerfect Corporation) for a particular working session, then employ the /X option. At the DOS prompt, type

WP/X

WordPerfect will then be loaded with the original default settings. When you exit WordPerfect, the previous changes that you initiated using the Setup menu will be restored.

Tip: *You can combine more than one startup option.*

You can combine two or more of the options mentioned previously. For example, assume that you use a floppy disk system with expanded memory, which means that you have enough memory to exercise the /R option. You also decide to redirect all temporary files to the disk in drive B so that you can place the Speller disk in drive A. To load WordPerfect, you would type the following, at the DOS prompt:

WP/R/D-B:

Trap: *The startup options take effect only until you exit WordPerfect.*

Startup options load WordPerfect in a certain way, but only for the current working session. When you exit WordPerfect and, at a later time, wish to activate those startup options, you cannot simply type **WP** to load WordPerfect; you must load WordPerfect along with the startup options.

See the following Tip if you wish to activate the same startup options each time you load WordPerfect.

Tip: *You can automatically load WordPerfect with all the options you desire.*

It can become time consuming to type in the command to load WordPerfect if you have many startup options you wish to activate. A *batch file,* which is a set of DOS instructions, can be a handy tool for simplifying this task. In fact, you can quickly write a batch file so that at the beginning of every session, all you need to do is enter the correct date and time (if necessary) and press only a few keys; WordPerfect will load automatically for you, with the startup options you desire. See Appendix A for directions on creating batch files.

Tip: *A RAM drive provides several advantages in WordPerfect when used in conjunction with startup options.*

A *RAM drive* (sometimes called a virtual drive) is a portion of RAM that is partitioned to act like a disk drive. RAM works more quickly than a disk can, so that RAM drives speed up computer operations, especially on computers with no hard disks. You have access to a RAM drive provided that you use DOS 3.0 or a later version, that your computer has extended memory, or that your computer is equipped with a multifunction board. See your DOS manual or your user's manual if you are unfamiliar with the procedure for establishing a RAM drive.

RAM disk users will find no advantage in loading the WordPerfect program into the RAM disk. That's because the /R option (discussed at the beginning of this chapter section) loads all of the WordPerfect instructions into RAM anyway.

A RAM disk is useful, however, for directing overflow files to that disk—especially if your computer is not equipped with a hard disk. If you redirect temporary files to a RAM drive, you don't have to worry about reserving room on a data disk in drive B for temporary storage, and yet, if you also use the /R option, you can still remove the WordPerfect 2 disk from drive A while editing. To do so, set up your RAM drive. Usually 64K is sufficient space. Then, assuming that the RAM drive is referred to as drive D, for example, type the following to load WordPerfect and to be able to remove the WordPerfect disk from drive A:

WP/R/D-D:

A RAM disk can also hold other files, such as the Thesaurus or the Speller. For example, when the Thesaurus is copied into RAM, WordPerfect's ability to find alternative words speeds up, and floppy disk users don't need to insert the Thesaurus disk in a disk drive to perform that function. You will need to set the size of your RAM disk to accommodate the files to be copied there; the Thesaurus, for example, occupies 362K of space in a RAM disk. If you do load the Thesaurus or the Speller into a RAM drive, you must indicate this to WordPerfect by using the Location of Auxiliary Files option on the Setup menu (as described in Appendix B).

Tip: *(When upgrading from 4.2.) WordPerfect now offers new startup options.*

WordPerfect has added several startup options to its repertoire so that it can work more effectively with your equipment—including the /NC option to disable the new Cursor Speed feature, the /NK option to turn off enhanced keyboard commands, and the /SS option to set the screen size of your monitor if different from the standard size.

In addition, the /R option has been altered. You need approximately 392K of *expanded* RAM (above and beyond the 640K of conventional RAM) to use the /R option; in version 4.2, you needed only 384K of *conventional* RAM to take advantage of this option.

The /S option has been eliminated in version 5. The Setup menu, which allows you to change default settings for every document, is no longer accessed when you start up WordPerfect. Instead of the /S option (version 4.2), you display the Setup menu from within WordPerfect by pressing the SETUP (SHIFT + F1) key. A full description of the Setup menu is provided in Appendix B.

Another startup option that has been eliminated is /B (Timed Backup), which offered protection against a power failure. In version 4.2, you could turn on the Timed Backup feature in one of two ways: either when loading WordPerfect using /B or via the Setup menu. In version 5, Timed Backup can be activated only from the Setup menu (as described in Appendix B).

Ending a WordPerfect Session

With many software packages, all you do to end a session is turn off the computer. Not so with WordPerfect. You must exit the program properly so that WordPerfect can complete its own internal file management before you touch the power switch. Otherwise, you could, over time, harm the WordPerfect program disk—losing disk space to what is referred to as "lost clusters."

Suppose you've had a productive day. You've typed two memos, three reports, and four letters. You are ready to exit WordPerfect until tomorrow. The EXIT (F7) key, located on your function keypad, takes you out of WordPerfect. You can exit WordPerfect properly, as follows:

1. Press EXIT (F7). The following prompt appears on screen:

   Save Document? (Y/N) Yes

   WordPerfect is prompting you to decide whether or not you wish to save the document currently on the screen before exiting WordPerfect. This prompt is a handy reminder; if you don't store a document onto either a hard or a floppy disk, it resides only in RAM, and thus disappears when you clear the screen. "(Y/N)" indicates that WordPerfect is waiting for a yes or no answer.

2. Type **N** to erase the document from the screen without saving it to disk, or type **Y** or press ENTER to erase the document only after saving it as a file. If you choose to save the file, WordPerfect will request a filename. (Refer to Chapter 11 for a complete discussion on saving documents to disk.) The following prompt appears next:

   Exit WP? (Y/N) No

3. Type **Y** to exit the program. (Or type **N** or press ENTER if you change your mind and wish to remain in WordPerfect.) If you're a 5 1/4-inch floppy disk user, WordPerfect may prompt, asking you to place the disk containing COMMAND.COM in your computer. In that case, place the WordPerfect 1 disk in drive A and press ENTER to complete the exit procedure.

The DOS prompt returns to the screen in a few moments. You have now properly exited WordPerfect. At this point you are free to either load another software package or, if your work is done, to turn off the computer.

Trap: *If you forget to exit properly, or if you experience a power failure, you'll need to answer questions the next time you load WordPerfect.*

Suppose that you turn off your computer without properly exiting WordPerfect. Or suppose that you're in the middle of typing a letter and the power fails, clearing both your letter and WordPerfect from the screen. In either case, you will have to answer several prompts when reloading.

When you type **WP** (or **WP** with various options) to reload WordPerfect, a question, such as the following, appears on the screen in a few moments:

Are other copies of WordPerfect currently running? Y/N

The message indicates that WordPerfect had no chance to close its own internal files before the power went off. Type **N**, telling WordPerfect to clear those files and begin again. You would type **Y** only if you wished to run two copies of the WordPerfect program at once (which is a possibility, if you have a large amount of expanded memory and are using WordPerfect Library or a windowing program). WordPerfect will now load.

Presuming that you activated the Timed Backup option during the session in which the power went off, WordPerfect will provide a second prompt as you begin working in WordPerfect with Timed Backup again activated:

Old Timed Backup file exists: 1 Rename **2** Delete

As discussed in Appendix B, if you exercise the Timed Backup option, WordPerfect periodically saves a copy of the text on the screen to the file called WP{WP}.BK1 or WP{WP}.BK2. WordPerfect prompts you to decide whether or not to clear that file. Choose 1, Rename, if the power went off before you saved your document on disk. You can then rename the file (see Chapter 11 for naming conventions) and retrieve that file to the screen for further editing. Or, choose 2, Delete, if you don't need the information that WordPerfect stored in the backup file.

Trap: *The message "WP DISK FULL" might appear on the WordPerfect screen if WordPerfect is exited improperly one too many times.*

If your building is prone to power outages or if your computer is continually turned off before WordPerfect is exited, the WordPerfect program can be damaged.

An indication of this is a message that could one day appear at the bottom of the WordPerfect Typing screen:

WP DISK FULL

If that message should appear, exit WordPerfect so that the DOS prompt is on the screen. You can correct the problem by using the DOS command CHKDSK, which can repair damage to the program.

Floppy disk users should keep the WordPerfect disk in drive A, place the DOS disk in drive B, and enter

B:CHKDSK A:/F

Then type **N** if asked a question about converting lost chains into clusters. When the DOS prompt reappears, reload WordPerfect.

Hard disk users, at the DOS prompt, should enter

CHKDSK/F

Answer no to any prompts by typing **N**. Reload WordPerfect when the DOS prompt reappears.

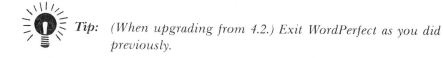

Tip: *(When upgrading from 4.2.) Exit WordPerfect as you did previously.*

The method for exiting WordPerfect has not changed in version 5.

Tips and Traps Summary

Starting WordPerfect

Tip: Enter the correct date and time at the beginning of a WordPerfect session.

Trap: Don't use the original WordPerfect disks to load WordPerfect.

Trap: DOS is missing when either the date or the DOS prompt doesn't appear on screen.

Trap: WordPerfect can't load unless you have sufficient memory and at least DOS version 2.0.

Trap: Don't load WordPerfect without first having created a CONFIG.SYS file.

Trap: The computer can't find the WordPerfect instructions on a hard disk unless you indicate the correct subdirectory.

Trap: In some cases, you can't load WordPerfect unless you use a special startup option.

Trap: When you load WordPerfect, don't begin typing a document until you define and select a printer.

Tip: When you plan to store documents on floppy disks, remember to have a formatted disk available before you load WordPerfect.

Tip: You can change the character used as your cursor.

Tip: (When upgrading from 4.2.) Because it offers more features than ever before, WordPerfect now occupies more disks.

Startup (Slash) Options

Tip: You can combine more than one startup option.

Trap: The startup options take effect only until you exit WordPerfect.

Tips and Traps Summary (*continued*)

Tip: You can automatically load WordPerfect with all the options you desire.

Tip: A RAM drive provides several advantages in WordPerfect when used in conjunction with startup options.

Tip: (When upgrading from 4.2.) WordPerfect now offers new startup options.

Ending a WordPerfect Session

Trap: If you forget to exit properly, or if you experience a power failure, you'll need to answer questions the next time you load WordPerfect.

Trap: The message "WP DISK FULL" might appear on the WordPerfect screen if WordPerfect is exited improperly one too many times.

Tip: (When upgrading from 4.2.) Exit WordPerfect as you did previously.

2

Selecting Features and Getting Help

In WordPerfect, the keyboard's function keys control most of the program's special features—everything from moving a paragraph to changing margin settings, and from checking the spelling in a document to creating automatic footnotes. Because of this function key orientation, the Typing screen remains free of distracting messages.

This chapter explains how the function keys operate, so that you will be prepared to use WordPerfect's many features. You will learn what to expect on screen after you press a function key, how to respond, and how to get a helping hand right on the screen.

Features, Function Keys, and Codes

Depending on your keyboard, the function keypad is located either on the left, with keys labeled F1 through F10, or at the top, with keys labeled F1 through F12. Each of the first ten function keys—F1 through F10—controls four sets of features, depending on whether you press the function key alone, or whether you hold down ALT, SHIFT, or CTRL while you press a function key. For example, you can press F1 on its own. Or you can press the ALT key and, while holding it down, also press F1 (denoted as ALT + F1). Or you can press SHIFT + F1. Or you can press CTRL + F1. Each key combination invokes a different command. Thus, there are 40 separate commands at your fingertips on the function keypad.

To remind you of which function key performs which command, two plastic templates are supplied with the WordPerfect package. One template is supplied for those of you with function keys on the left side of the keyboard, while the other is for those who have function keys on the top of the keyboard. (Templates for other styles of keyboards are also available from WordPerfect Corporation.) A template indicates—by means of one- or two-word key names—the features that each key controls. With more than 40 commands, a template is a critical aid, freeing you from having to memorize key combinations. *You should place the template appropriate for your keyboard next to your function keys before you start typing (see Figure 2-1).* Also, you can refer to Table 2-1 for a convenient alphabetical list of function key names.

Each template is color-coded. The key names that are written in black are accessed by pressing the function key alone; names in blue are accessed by pressing ALT + the function key; in green, by pressing SHIFT + the function key; and in red, by pressing CTRL + the function key.

When you press a function key to select a command, what occurs generally falls into one of the following categories:

- WordPerfect displays a prompt that asks for further information. For example, press the RETRIEVE (SHIFT + F10) key and WordPerfect prompts

  Document to be retrieved:

  Wordperfect is asking that you type in a filename and press ENTER so that file can be retrieved.

- WordPerfect displays a prompt, asking for a yes or a no response. WordPerfect waits for you to type **Y** for Yes or **N** for No, and always suggests a response. This suggestion is usually the more conservative one—the one that will cause the least amount of damage if chosen accidentally. You reject a yes by typing **N**. You reject a no by typing **Y**. You accept the suggestion by pressing any other key, such as a letter key or the ENTER key.

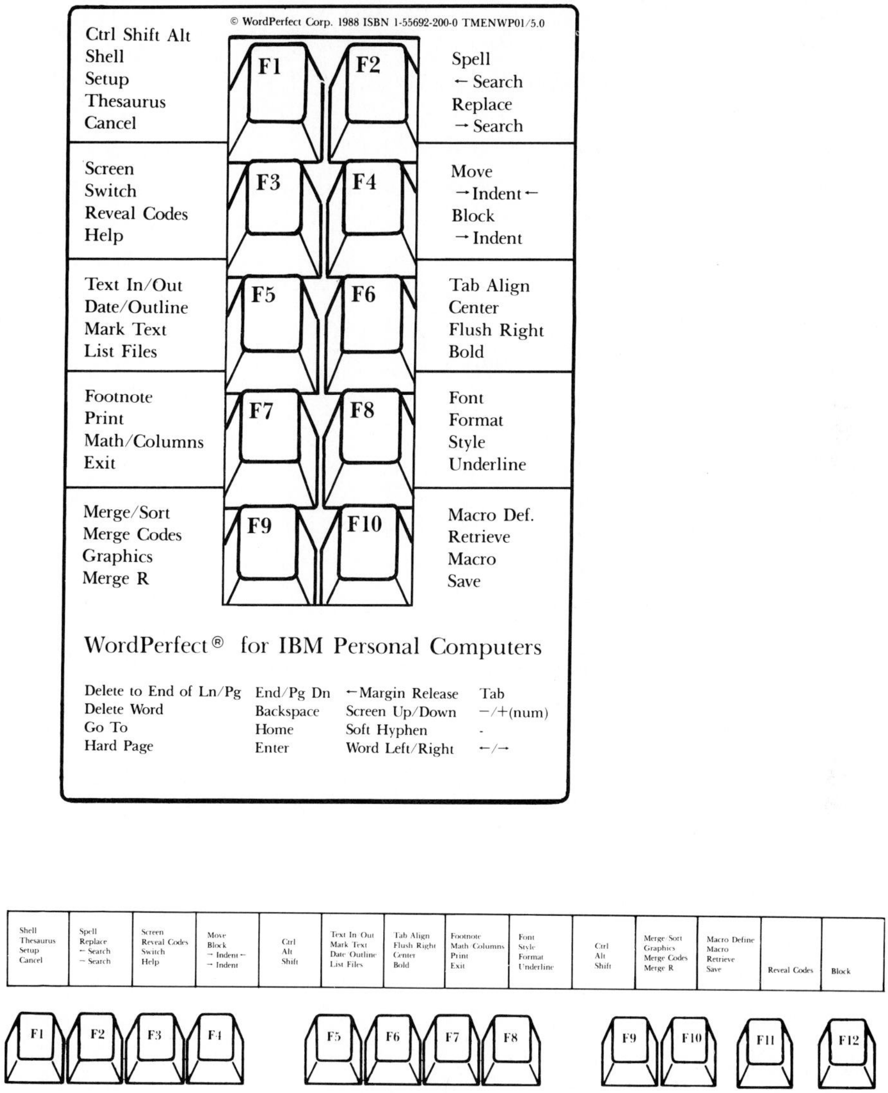
© WordPerfect Corp. 1988 ISBN 1-55692-200-0 TMENWP01/5.0
Ctrl Shift Alt
Shell
Setup
Thesaurus
Cancel
F1
F2
Spell
← Search
Replace
→ Search
Screen
Switch
Reveal Codes
Help
F3
F4
Move
→Indent←
Block
→Indent
Text In/Out
Date/Outline
Mark Text
List Files
F5
F6
Tab Align
Center
Flush Right
Bold
Footnote
Print
Math/Columns
Exit
F7
F8
Font
Format
Style
Underline
Merge/Sort
Merge Codes
Graphics
Merge R
F9
F10
Macro Def.
Retrieve
Macro
Save
WordPerfect® for IBM Personal Computers
Delete to End of Ln/Pg End/Pg Dn
Delete Word Backspace
Go To Home
Hard Page Enter
←Margin Release Tab
Screen Up/Down −/+(num)
Soft Hyphen -
Word Left/Right ←/→
Shell Thesaurus Setup Cancel
Spell Replace ← Search → Search
Screen Reveal Codes Switch Help
Move Block → Indent ← → Indent
Ctrl Alt Shift
Text In/Out Mark Text Date/Outline List Files
Tab Align Flush Right Center Bold
Footnote Math/Columns Print Exit
Font Style Format Underline
Ctrl Alt Shift
Merge/Sort Graphics Merge Codes Merge R
Macro Define Macro Retrieve Save
Reveal Codes
Block
F1
F2
F3
F4
F5
F6
F7
F8
F9
F10
F11
F12

Figure 2-1. Function key templates for two different keyboard styles

Table 2-1. Alphabetical List of WordPerfect Function Key Names and Equivalents

Function Key Name	Key Combination
BLOCK	ALT + F4
BOLD	F6
CANCEL	F1
CENTER	SHIFT + F6
DATE/OUTLINE	SHIFT + F5
EXIT	F7
FLUSH RIGHT	ALT + F6
FONT	CTRL + F8
FOOTNOTE	CTRL + F7
FORMAT	SHIFT + F8
GRAPHICS	ALT + F9
HELP	F3
→INDENT	F4
→INDENT←	SHIFT + F4
LIST FILES	F5
MACRO	ALT + F10
MACRO DEFINE	CTRL + F10
MARK TEXT	ALT + F5
MATH COLUMNS	ALT + F7
MERGE CODES	SHIFT + F9
MERGE R	F9
MERGE/SORT	CTRL + F9
MOVE	CTRL + F4
PRINT	SHIFT + F7

Table 2-1. Alphabetical List of WordPerfect Function Key Names and Equivalents (continued)

Function Key Name	Key Combination
REPLACE	ALT + F2
RETRIEVE TEXT	SHIFT + F10
REVEAL CODES	ALT + F3
SAVE TEXT	F10
SCREEN	CTRL + F3
→SEARCH	F2
←SEARCH	SHIFT + F2
SETUP	SHIFT + F1
SHELL	CTRL + F1
SPELL	CTRL + F2
STYLE	ALT + F8
SWITCH	SHIFT + F3
TAB ALIGN	CTRL + F6
TEXT IN/OUT	CTRL + F5
THESAURUS	ALT + F1
UNDERLINE	F8

For example, when you press the EXIT (F7) key, WordPerfect responds with a yes/no prompt:

Save document? (Y/N) Yes

The cursor rests on the Y. WordPerfect thus suggests Y for yes, the more conservative approach, because it is better to save a document you don't need than to erase a document you do need. Press any other key, including **Y** or ENTER, to accept the suggestion to save the document currently on screen. Type **N** to reject WordPerfect's assumption, meaning that you do not wish to save the document.

- WordPerfect offers a menu of choices at the bottom of the Typing screen. For example, when you press the DATE/OUTLINE (SHIFT + F5) key, the following menu, called a line menu, appears at the bottom of the screen:

  1 Date Text; 2 Date Code; 3 Date Format; 4 Outline; 5 Para Num; 6 Define: 0

  The cursor remains at the end of the menu, waiting for you to choose from the options available, and it suggests a response. Usually the response is "0," which means that if you press ENTER, the menu clears without your having made a selection. When you make a menu selection, sometimes a new menu of items appears.

- WordPerfect temporarily replaces the Typing screen with a full-screen menu of choices. For example, when you press the FORMAT (SHIFT + F8) key, the menu shown in Figure 2-2 appears. The cursor remains at the bottom of the menu, on the zero, waiting for you to choose from the options available. If you select an item, you may be presented with a new menu.

- WordPerfect turns a feature or a mode on or off. For example, when you press the UNDERLINE (F8) key, WordPerfect switches on the Underline feature, and will underline all text you type until you press UNDERLINE a second time. The UNDERLINE key is one example of a toggle switch. Like a light switch, the toggle is pressed once to turn the feature on and a second time to turn it off.

  As another example, when you press REVEAL CODES (ALT + F3), you toggle into the Reveal Codes screen. Press REVEAL CODES a second time to toggle back to the Typing screen.

After you respond to all prompts and menus, the feature you requested is activated and all the prompts and menus clear from the Typing screen. You can continue to type, or you can press another function key.

Often when you employ the function keys to activate a command, WordPerfect places symbols called *codes* in the text of your document. Codes are used by word processors to dictate how your text will be displayed on the screen, how it should be printed, or both. In WordPerfect, codes are represented as words or

```
Format

     1 - Line
              Hyphenation                        Line Spacing
              Justification                      Margins Left/Right
              Line Height                        Tab Set
              Line Numbering                     Widow/Orphan Protection

     2 - Page
              Center Page (top to bottom)        New Page Number
              Force Odd/Even Page                Page Numbering
              Headers and Footers                Paper Size/Type
              Margins Top/Bottom                 Suppress

     3 - Document
              Display Pitch                      Redline Method
              Initial Codes/Font                 Summary

     4 - Other
              Advance                            Overstrike
              Conditional End of Page            Printer Functions
              Decimal Characters                 Underline Spaces/Tabs
              Language

Selection: 0
```

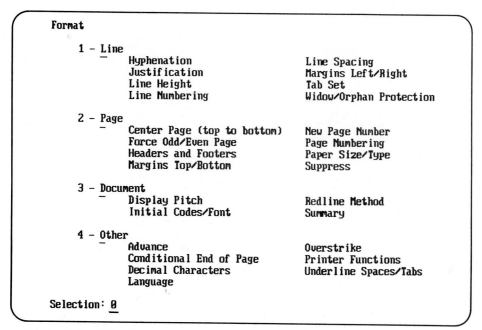

Figure 2-2. *The Format menu*

phrases, in abbreviated form, enclosed in square brackets [ ]. But codes are concealed (they "hide" behind your text) so as not to clutter the Typing screen, and so that your text will appear on screen much like it will appear when printed.

There are two types of codes: paired codes and open (or single) codes. Paired codes include a beginning or an "On" code, and an ending or an "Off" code. For example, suppose you press the UNDERLINE (F8) key, type the phrase "as soon as possible", and press UNDERLINE again to turn the feature off. WordPerfect inserts a matched pair of codes around the phrase you typed, as follows:

[UND]as soon as possible**[und]**.

These two codes affect only the text between them, serving to keep the phrase underlined. (Underlining is discussed in Chapter 7.)

Open codes consist of only a beginning code, and affect the text from the point at which they appear until the end of the document, or until the next code of that type appears. For instance, suppose you press the FORMAT (SHIFT + F8) key to change your left/right margins. WordPerfect will insert a single code in the text, such as: **[L/R Mar: 2", 2"]**. This code dictates margins to the right of where it appears and downward to the end of the document, or until another **[L/R Mar:]** code is encountered farther on in the document. (Margins are discussed in Chapter 8.)

There is a method for revealing these hidden codes in their hiding places—by pressing the REVEAL CODES (ALT + F3) key, which switches the display from the Typing screen to the Reveal Codes screen. (Chapter 3 describes the Reveal Codes screen in detail.)

Tip: *The template for one keyboard style is position-coded, in addition to being color-coded.*

When the function keys are located on the left side of a keyboard, CTRL is located above SHIFT, which is located above ALT. The WordPerfect template used with that keyboard style lists command names in that same order. In other words, the CTRL combination is listed on top of the template, followed by the SHIFT combination, followed by the ALT combination, followed by the single-key command.

For example, the top template in Figure 2-1 lists the names for the F3 function key from top to bottom, in the following order: Screen, Switch, Reveal Codes, and Help. Since Screen is the top command name, you can tell that the key combination to press for the SCREEN key is CTRL + F3. Similarly, the key combination for the SWITCH key is SHIFT + F3, while the key combination for the REVEAL CODES key is ALT + F3. Realizing that the command names are positioned in this way can help you become comfortable with the template quickly.

Tip: *If your keyboard has function keys F11 and F12, then WordPerfect offers you a shortcut.*

On keyboards equipped with 12 function keys, F11 and F12 have been assigned for your convenience. Pressing F11 is identical to pressing ALT + F3—the REVEAL CODES key. Pressing F12 is just like pressing ALT + F4—the BLOCK key.

Try the F11 and F12 keys on your keyboard to see if they operate for you. As you work with WordPerfect, you'll find that Reveal Codes and Block are two of the features you use constantly—and F11 and F12 can make it easier to access them.

Trap: *Don't hold a function key down too long.*

When you press a function key combination, it takes a certain touch—or you won't activate the feature you meant to. Hold down CTRL, ALT, or SHIFT firmly, and keep holding it down until you've pressed a function key. But hold a function key down for only a moment, using a quick, solid stroke. Don't hold a function key down too long or the result will be as if you pressed it twice, and you're liable to accidentally cancel the command.

Tip: *Try pressing CANCEL (F1) if you need to clear an unwanted message from the screen.*

If you press a function key inadvertently and a menu or prompt appears, you will want to back out of that feature. Several keys allow you to do this, but it becomes good habit to rely on one key to help you out of trouble. CANCEL (F1) works the best. Pressing CANCEL is like putting your car in reverse; it takes you back, one menu at a time, until all messages are cleared from the screen. You may have to press CANCEL more than once to completely clear out that command or feature.

A word of caution when using this function key: sometimes pressing CANCEL brings up a menu. This is because CANCEL serves a second purpose; in addition to backing you out of features that display a message, CANCEL recovers text that you delete by accident (a feature discussed in Chapter 5). So if you press CANCEL one too many times and a new menu appears at the bottom of the screen that begins with the word "Undelete," simply press CANCEL one additional time to clear that Undelete menu.

Another caution is that there are several circumstances in which the CANCEL key won't back you out of a command. First, CANCEL won't work if you press a function key that acts like a toggle switch. For instance, if you press REVEAL CODES (ALT + F3) to view codes hidden in your document, you can't press CANCEL (F1) to return to the Typing screen; you must again press REVEAL CODES. Or, if you press UNDERLINE (F8) to begin underlining a section of text, you must press UNDERLINE, and not CANCEL, to stop the underlining.

Moreover, CANCEL won't work if you're viewing a screen that has a message at the bottom, such as "Press Exit when done." This message appears, for example, when you use the FOOTNOTE (CTRL + F7) key and WordPerfect displays a screen so that you can type in your footnote. The message indicates that the only way to return to the Typing screen is to press EXIT (F7) (which then preserves the effects of the command you invoked), and you cannot use the CANCEL key to back out of the command. (However, once you press EXIT to return to the Typing screen, you can always undo what you've just done—such as delete a footnote—by deleting the resulting code.)

Trap: *Don't press ESC to cancel a command.*

In many software packages, it is the ESC (ESCAPE) key that backs you out of a feature and saves you from trouble. This is not the case in WordPerfect, however, so rely instead on the CANCEL (F1) key to void commands.

In WordPerfect, the ESC key controls the Repeat feature, whereby you can repeat a character, or the actions of certain cursor movement keys or certain deletion keys, a specified number of times (as described in Chapter 3). If you press ESC by accident, a prompt, such as **"Repeat Value = 8"** appears at the bottom of the screen; simply press CANCEL (F1) to clear that prompt.

Tip: *Try pressing BACKSPACE if your text shifts unexpectedly or looks awkward after you press a function key.*

If you accidentally press a function key and your words move into an odd configuration, chances are that you inserted a hidden code. You need to erase this hidden code. To do this, try pressing BACKSPACE one time.

For example, if you press the →INDENT (F4) key in the middle of a line, the text you type afterward will have odd margins because you have just inserted the code [**→Indent**], which attempts to indent a paragraph for you (as described in Chapter 7). Press BACKSPACE to delete this hidden code.

If BACKSPACE doesn't help, then the hidden code is located somewhere other than just to the left of the cursor, so you will need to track down and delete that hidden code. (Chapter 5 describes how to delete characters and codes from your text.)

Tip: *Menu items can be selected in either of two ways.*

When you press a function key that displays a menu—whether it is a line menu at the bottom of the screen or a full-screen menu—you have two options for selecting an item. First, and more obviously, you can type the number, shown at the left of the item, that corresponds to your selection. Or, second, you can type the mnemonic character that corresponds to your selection— which is indicated as the only boldfaced letter for that menu item. For example, when you press the MOVE (CTRL + F4) key, the following line menu appears

Move: 1 Sentence; **2 P**aragraph; **3** P**a**ge; **4 R**etrieve: **0**

If you wish to select the Sentence option, for example, you would type **1**, or instead, you could type **S**.

Be warned that the mnemonic character is not necessarily the first letter of the menu option. For instance, to select the Page option, you would type **3** or **A** (but not **P**).

You have the option of displaying the mnenomic character in a manner other than boldface, such as in underline, for example, in which case the Move menu would appear

Move: 1 Sentence; **2** Paragraph; **3** Page; **4** Retrieve: **0**

(In fact, mnemonic characters are *underlined,* rather than boldfaced, throughout this book to emphasize them as a distinct way to select a menu item.) If you wish, you can change the display of the mnemonic character by using the Display option on the Setup menu (described in Appendix B).

Trap: *It is all too easy to insert extraneous codes in your text.*

It is very easy to press the wrong function key by mistake and accidentally insert a hidden code in the text. If you're viewing the Typing screen, you may not realize that you inserted an unneeded code that could cause problems later, as you attempt to print out your document. It is good practice, especially for beginning users, to periodically reveal codes in order to check for extraneous codes in the text. (Chapter 3 further describes how to reveal codes.)

Tip: *Use the Keyboard Layout feature to assign features to the key combination of your choice.*

Although WordPerfect assigns features to specific keys, you can change these key assignments. You can even write a whole routine, called a macro, that is carried out by pressing a simple key combination. This is all possible with the Keyboard Layout feature. You can assign features and macros not only to function key combinations (such as F3 or CTRL + F3), but to other combinations as well (such as ALT + 5 or CTRL + R).

For instance, you can reverse the usual duties of the F1 and F3 keys, so that the F3 key functions as the CANCEL key and the F1 key activates the Help facility (which you may desire because software packages other than WordPerfect provide help via the F1 key rather than the F3 key). Or you can direct WordPerfect to print out five copies of the document that is on screen when you press CTRL + 5. (For more information on the powerful Keyboard Layout feature, which is accessed from the Setup menu, refer to Appendix B.)

Tip: *(When upgrading from 4.2.) Some of the function keys have been given new duties in version 5.*

In version 5, seven function keys have each been assigned a new key name—and thus a new mission. These changes are shown in Table 2-2. Notice that the largest modification involves the format commands, which in version 5 are housed under the SHIFT + F8 key, to make way for additional features; in version 4.2, they were separated under three disparate function key combinations.

Although you could previously use your keyboard's top row of numbers, rather than the function keys in combination with the CTRL or ALT key, to activate certain features and commands, you can no longer do so. The numbers are no longer predefined to control certain commands, as they did in version 4.2.

In version 5 you can select a menu item either by typing the item number or by typing the mnemonic character. By typing a letter, your fingers won't need to stretch quite as far when you select certain options.

A dramatic addition in version 5 is the ability to reassign features to any key of your choosing by using the Keyboard Layout feature (Appendix B covers this feature in greater detail).

Table 2-2. Version 5 Versus 4.2: Function Key Differences

Version 5 Key Name	Function Key	Version 4.2 Key Name
SETUP	SHIFT + F1	SUPER/SUBSCRIPT
DATE/OUTLINE	SHIFT + F5	DATE
FORMAT	SHIFT + F8	LINE FORMAT
STYLE	ALT + F8	PAGE FORMAT
FONT	CTRL + F8	PRINT FORMAT
MERGE CODES	SHIFT + F9	MERGE E
GRAPHICS	ALT + F9	MERGE CODES

The HELP Key

If you want a quick refresher on how to activate a specific feature, help is literally at your fingertips. Help is available any time you are typing or editing a document—whether you've just started a WordPerfect session or you're viewing a 20-page document that was typed earlier. Just press the HELP (F3) key to get your on-line reference. Then you press a *function key* combination to read about the capabilities of that key combination, a *letter key* to view the portion of WordPerfect's Help index that starts with that letter of the alphabet, or a *cursor movement or editing key* to learn about that key's capabilities.

Assume, for example, that you forget how to create endnotes (discussed in Chapter 23). For a quick reminder, you can

1. Press the HELP (F3) key. The screen shown in Figure 2-3 appears.
2. Type **E**, the first letter of the word "endnote." WordPerfect provides a list of features that begin with the letter E, as shown in Figure 2-4.
3. Discover by reading down the list that CTRL + F7 controls the creation of endnotes and that the function key name is FOOTNOTE.
4. Press CTRL + F7 for more information, as shown in Figure 2-5. You can then press 1 or 2 for additional help on the menu options.

```
Help                                                    WP 5.0   05/05/88

     Press any letter to get an alphabetical list of features.

          The list will include the features that start with that letter,
          along with the name of the key where the feature is found.  You
          can then press that key to get a description of how the feature
          works.

     Press any function key to get information about the use of the key.

          Some keys may let you choose from a menu to get more information
          about various options.  Press HELP again to display the template.

     Press Enter or Space bar to exit Help.
```

Figure 2-3. The main Help menu

Key	Feature	Key Name
Ctrl-F5	Encrypt a Document	Text In/Out,2
F9	End of Field	Merge R
End	End of Line	End
Ctrl-End	End of Line, Delete to	Del EOL
Ctrl-PgDn	End of Page, Delete to	Del EOP
Shft-F9	End of Record	Merge E
Ctrl-F7	Endnote	Footnote
Ctrl-F7	Endnote Placement	Footnote
Shft-F1	Enhanced Keyboard Definition	Setup,6
Alt-F8	Enter, Define for Styles	Style
Alt-F10	Execute Macro	Macro
Ctrl-F9	Execute Merge	Merge,1
F7	Exit	Exit
Alt-F5	Expand Master Document	Mark Text,6
Ctrl-V	Extended Characters	Compose
Home F2	Extended Forward Search	Home, -> Search
Home Shft-F2	Extended Backward Search	Home, <- Search
Home Alt-F2	Extended Search & Replace	Home, Replace
Ctrl-F8	Extra Large Print	Font,1

Figure 2-4. The Help index, starting with E

```
Footnote/Endnote

     Allows you to create and edit footnotes and endnotes as well as determine
     where endnotes will be placed.

     WordPerfect automatically numbers the footnotes and endnotes, placing the
     footnotes on the same page as the note number and compiling endnotes at a
     place of your choice in the document.

     1 - Footnote/Endnote:  Choosing Footnote or Endnote will display the
          following options ("note" refers to both footnotes and endnotes):

          Create:  Create the text of the note.
          Edit:  Edit any note.  Type the number of the note you want to edit
               and press Enter.
          New Number:  Renumbers all the notes located after the cursor,
               starting with the number you enter.
          Options:  Changes the printed appearance of notes.

     2 - Endnote Placement:  Allows you to choose where endnotes will be
          printed.

                    Type a menu option for more help: 0
```

Figure 2-5. Help on the FOOTNOTE *key*

For information on other features, you can continue to press letter, function, cursor movement, or editing keys. When you wish to exit the Help facility and return to your document, simply press the SPACEBAR or the ENTER key.

Tip: *Floppy disk users will need to place the Help disk in drive A to get help.*

WordPerfect's Help facility is stored on the original WordPerfect 1 disk in two files called WPHELP.FIL and WPHELP2.FIL. Appendix A suggests that, when you install WordPerfect to work on your computer, you copy these two files to a separate disk, which you label the "Help" disk.

When you press the HELP (F3) key, WordPerfect checks the disk drives to find those help files. If the Help disk (or the original WordPerfect 1 disk) is not in one of the floppy drives, you will see the following message on the Help menu:

WPHELP.FIL not found. Insert disk and press drive letter:

Remove the disk from drive A, insert the Help disk (or the original WordPerfect 1 disk if you did not create a Help disk) in its place, and type **A**. Now you have access to Help. Don't forget to exchange disks after you exit the Help facility.

Tip: *Hard disk users should store the Help facility alongside the WordPerfect program.*

WordPerfect's Help facility is stored in two files called WPHELP.FIL and WPHELP2.FIL. When you want to access Help and you press HELP (F3), WordPerfect looks in the same directory where the WordPerfect program is stored in a file called WP.EXE. Therefore, keep the help file alongside the WordPerfect program file on your hard disk. (For more information on copying files to the hard disk, refer to Appendix A.)

Trap: *The Help facility is not context-sensitive.*

When you're in the midst of executing a feature and you ask for on-line help, some software packages display a Help menu related to the particular feature you are using. In those cases, help is said to be "context-sensitive." WordPerfect cannot evaluate the situation for you, however. When you press HELP, WordPerfect will always display the main Help menu. You must then indicate the topic of interest by pressing a letter or a function key.

Tip: *The Help menu lists your software's release date.*

WordPerfect Corporation continually revises its product. You can determine the release date of your copy of WordPerfect by checking the upper right-hand corner of the main Help menu. If you're having problems with the program and you call WordPerfect Corporation (their phone number is provided in Appendix C), one of the first questions you may be asked is the release date of your program.

Tip: *With the HELP key you can produce a copy of the function key template.*

What happens if your WordPerfect template is somehow lost or disappears? Here's one solution, if you need help remembering the function key names. Simply press the HELP (F3) key twice (floppy disk users, make sure the Help or original WordPerfect 1 disk is in drive A when you do so). The screen displays a template listing the function keys in two rows, based on the keyboard configuration with function keys on the left side.

You can even print out that screen template by turning on your printer and pressing SHIFT + PRTSC. A copy of the template is printed out for you. Then press the SPACEBAR or the ENTER key to clear the template from the screen and return to your document. You now have another template, albeit one that won't fit around the function keys. (If your function keys are across the top of the keyboard, this key template might prove a bit awkward to use.)

Trap: *The one time you can't press CANCEL to back out of a command is while using the Help facility.*

Typically, CANCEL (F1) saves you from peril by clearing all prompts and messages from the screen. Press CANCEL while using the Help facility, however, and WordPerfect will describe CANCEL's purpose rather than exit the Help facility. Instead, press the SPACEBAR or ENTER to clear the Help menu.

Tip: *There's more help available.*

See Appendix C for other sources of assistance when you need more specific help than the Help facility offers.

Tip: *(When upgrading from 4.2.) The Help facility operates as it did previously.*

Help works the same in version 5 as it did in version 4.2, but the information offered on the help screens is different, of course, to reflect the changes and enhancements to WordPerfect.

Tips and Traps Summary

Features, Function Keys, and Codes

Tip: The template for one keyboard style is position-coded, in addition to being color-coded.

Tip: If your keyboard has function keys F11 and F12, then WordPerfect offers you a shortcut.

Trap: Don't hold a function key down too long.

Tip: Try pressing CANCEL (F1) if you need to clear an unwanted message from the screen.

Trap: Don't press ESC to cancel a command.

Tip: Try pressing BACKSPACE if your text shifts unexpectedly or looks awkward after you press a function key.

Tip: Menu items can be selected in either of two ways.

Trap: It is all too easy to insert extraneous codes in your text.

Tip: Use the Keyboard Layout feature to assign features to the key combination of your choice.

Tip: (When upgrading from 4.2.) Some of the function keys have been given new duties in version 5.

The HELP Key

Tip: Floppy disk users will need to place the Help disk in drive A to get help.

Tip: Hard disk users should store the Help facility alongside the WordPerfect program.

Trap: The Help facility is not context-sensitive.

Tip: The Help menu lists your software's release date.

Tips and Traps Summary (*continued*)

Tip: With the HELP key you can produce a copy of the function key template.

Trap: The one time you can't press CANCEL to back out of a command is while using the Help facility.

Tip: There's more help available.

Tip: (When upgrading from 4.2.) The Help facility operates as it did previously.

3

Typing a Document

Those of you who have used other word processing packages might be pleasantly surprised at the uncluttered appearance of the WordPerfect screen. Nothing interferes with you and your words. All you see as you start to type a document is the *cursor,* a flashing line that serves as your pointer on the screen, and the *status line,* a single row that contains information about the precise location of the cursor.

This chapter explains how to interpret the status line and how to type your documents on the Typing screen. You will learn about word wrap, which frees you from having to end each line of text manually. The chapter also discusses the concept of codes, and how to view them on the Reveal Codes screen. And, you will learn about two special features that enhance your ability to produce a document: the Repeat Value feature, which repeats a character a specified number of times, and the Document Comments feature, which are notes to yourself within a document that are displayed on the screen but not on the printed page.

Typing on the Typing Screen

Figure 3-1 shows the clear WordPerfect Typing screen. Before you start to type, the cursor blinks in the upper left-hand corner of the screen and the status line reads

Doc 1 Pg 1 Ln 1″ Pos 1″

Doc 1 informs you that document 1 is currently on the screen. (You can also work with a document 2—a second document— simultaneously, a feature described in Chapter 12.) **Pg 1** indicats that the cursor is on page 1 of the document. **Ln 1 ″** tells you that the vertical position of the cursor is one inch from the top of the page. Because WordPerfect assumes a top margin of one inch when a document is printed (as described in Chapter 8), this implies that the cursor is located on the very first text line of the page. **Pos** 1″ informs you that the horizontal position of the cursor is one inch from the left edge of the page. Because WordPerfect assumes a left margin of one inch (as described in Chapter 8) when a document is

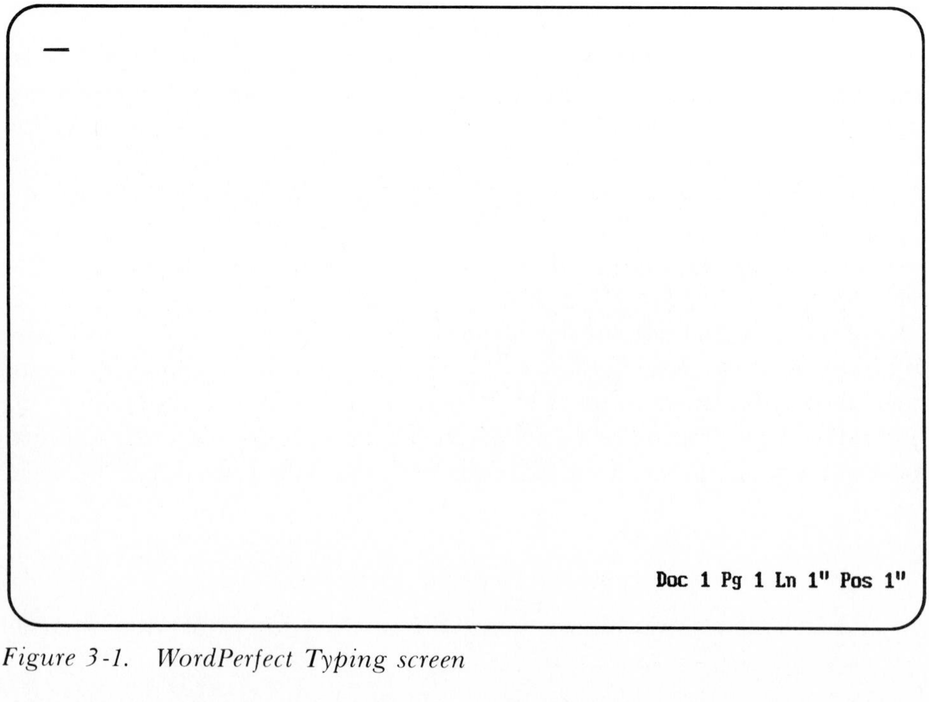

Figure 3-1. WordPerfect Typing screen

printed, this implies that the cursor is located flush against the left margin. Once you see this screen, you can begin typing your document.

Figure 3-2 shows examples of the two basic keyboard styles—the IBM standard and enhanced computer keyboards. Although some of the keys on your keyboard may be located in different places than in those shown in Figure 3-2, the keys will work just the same.

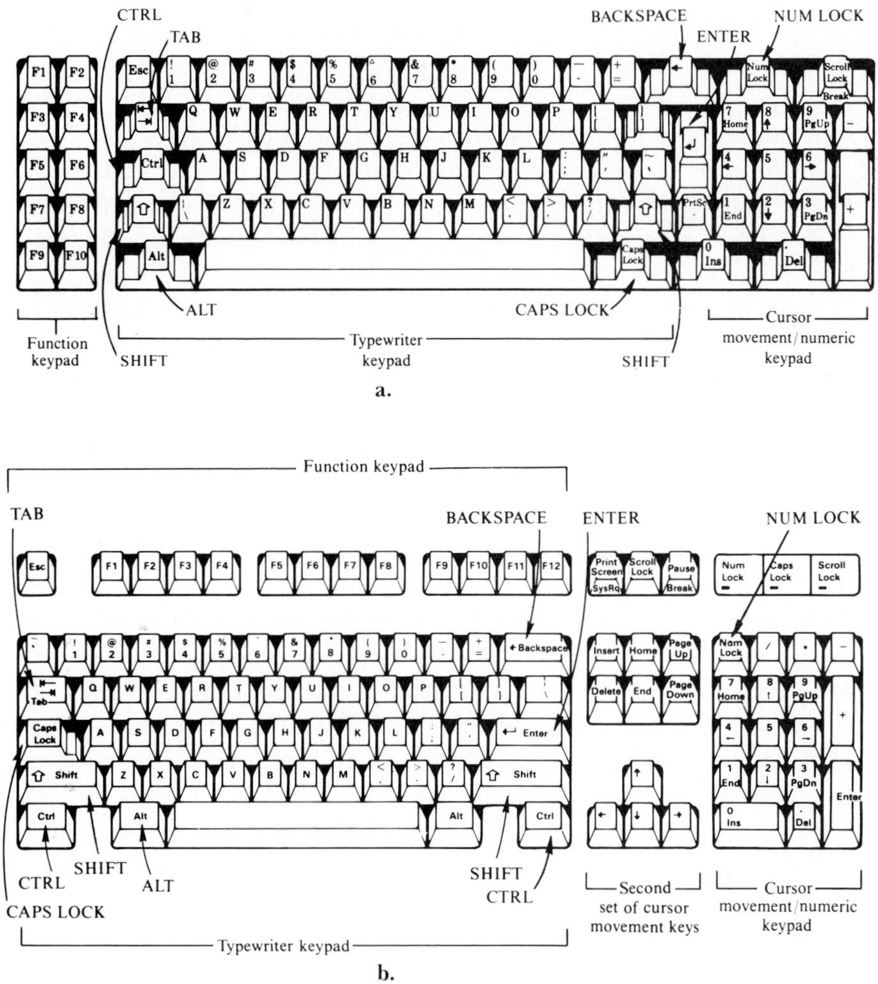

Figure 3-2. The IBM standard (a) and enhanced (b) keyboards

The letter keys on the typewriter keypad maintain their usual function in WordPerfect. WordPerfect puts the letters you type into lowercase on screen. To type in uppercase, such as at the beginning of a sentence, hold down SHIFT and then press a letter key, just as you do on a typewriter.

Numbers can be typed using the row above the letter keys. To produce the symbols that appear on those same keys—such as the asterisk (*), the dollar sign ($), or the exclamation point (!)—you must hold down SHIFT and then type a key on that top row.

Even the best typist hits the wrong key once in a while. To erase a character you just typed, press BACKSPACE, which is usually located above the ENTER key and labeled with a large arrow pointing left. Your cursor moves to the left, erasing the character. (Many other ways to edit your typing are described in Chapter 5.)

With each character you type, the cursor moves to the right and the status line "Pos" number changes to reflect that horizontal movement. When the cursor reaches the right margin (initially set as a one-inch right margin), WordPerfect wraps the cursor, along with any words that can't fit inside the margin, down to the beginning of the next line and the status line "Ln" number changes to reflect that vertical movement. This capability, known as *word wrap,* keeps text inside the right margin. Thus, word wrap helps you gain typing speed. Because of this feature, WordPerfect also is able to readjust text to fit within the margins when you later edit your text (see Chapter 5).

In addition to letters, numbers, and symbols, another category of character inserted into the text as you type is codes. You learned in Chapter 2 how all word processors use codes. They are commands that tell the word processor and your printer what to do. In WordPerfect, codes are represented by phrases enclosed in square brackets [ ]. They are hidden on the Typing screen—tucked behind letters, numbers, and symbols—so as not to distract you while you type. Providing a clutter-free screen is the basic philosophy behind the design of the WordPerfect Typing screen.

Four codes that are inserted (but remain hidden) in almost every page that you type are **[SRt]**, **[HRt]**, **[SPg]**, and **[TAB]**. **[SRt]** is called the *soft return,* a code inserted by WordPerfect at the end of each line where word wrap takes effect. Thus, in a paragraph, a *soft return code* ends each line of a paragraph controlled by word wrap. The return is "soft" because it will relocate or disappear if text is readjusted on a line.

[HRt], which represents a *hard return code,* is a code inserted by you whenever you press the ENTER key as you type. It is "hard" because, since the code is inserted by you, it will not disappear as you edit. Press ENTER only when you wish to do one of the following:

- End a paragraph
- End a short line of text
- Insert a blank line

Otherwise, let word wrap work for you.

Another code inserted by WordPerfect is **[SPg]**, which represents a *soft page.* After you fill a page with text, WordPerfect displays a dashed line and inserts a soft page to indicate the start of a new page. Figure 3-3 shows what the Typing screen looks like when WordPerfect indicates a new page. Notice that the status line says **Pg 2** because the cursor is below the dashed line. Like a soft return code at the end of a line, a soft page code at the end of a page adjusts automatically when new lines are added or old lines are deleted. That's why it's referred to as soft. (Chapter 9 discusses page breaks in detail.)

Finally, **[TAB]** is inserted by you whenever you press TAB, the key labeled with two arrows pointing in opposite directions. The TAB key is commonly used to indent the first line of a paragraph or to align items on tab stops, as shown here:

Sam Morris	6/16/88	$50
Peter Collins	1/20/89	$65

Each time you press TAB and insert a code, your cursor jumps to the next tab stop. Tab stops are initially set in your document every half inch. (Chapter 8 describes how to reset tab stops.)

```
     Bookkeeping is the recording of income and expenses in
journals.  You can keep a record of your financial transactions in
a notebook, but you will soon outgrow this method.  It is best,
---------------------------------------------------------------------
from the outset, to organize your transactions effectively.  The
proven method is with double-entry bookkeeping, where each
transaction is recorded twice -- as a debit and as a credit item.
Your books are in balance when you record both parts of the same
transaction._

                                  Doc 1 Pg 2 Ln 1.66" Pos 2.2"
```

Figure 3-3. Dashed line indicates the bottom of a page

Trap: *If you hold a key down too long as you type, you'll get extra characters.*

Most keys on your keyboard have what is called an autorepeat feature. Press and hold down the SPACEBAR, for example, and you'll insert a row of spaces. Press and hold the 5 key and you'll produce a trail like this: 555555555555. That's good news if you wish to repeat a character, but bad news if what you want is ABC and what you get is AABBCC all the time. Hold keys down if you want them to repeat, but press keys sharply when you wish to avoid extra, unwanted characters.

Keys on the keyboard that commonly do not repeat when held down include CTRL, ALT, SHIFT, CAPS LOCK, and NUM LOCK.

Tip: *The easiest way to type a whole string of letters in uppercase is to press CAPS LOCK.*

The CAPS LOCK key is handy for typing text entirely in uppercase letters. Rather than pressing down on the SHIFT key and typing letters, simply press CAPS LOCK. Now, every letter you subsequently type appears in uppercase.

CAPS LOCK is a toggle switch—press once to turn it on, a second time to turn it off. Check the status line to see whether CAPS LOCK is activated. When it is on, the position indicator appears in all capital letters.

Doc 1 Pg 1 Ln 1" POS 1"

When it is off, the position indicator shows an uppercase P and lowercase "os".

Doc 1 Pg 1 Ln 1" Pos 1"

CAPS LOCK affects only letters; to type the symbols that appear on the same keys as the numbers on the top row of the keyboard, you must still press SHIFT.

Be warned that with CAPS LOCK on, the SHIFT key has the opposite effect on letters than with CAPS LOCK off—it shifts letters into lowercase. If you hold down on the shift key, type a letter, and it appears in lowercase, you'll know that CAPS LOCK is active.

Tip: *WordPerfect can reverse uppercase letters and lowercase letters.*

You can switch upper- and lowercase letters without retyping your text. This feature, accessed with the SWITCH (CTRL + F3) key, is described in Chapter 5.

Trap: *Don't type letters to substitute for numbers.*

One of the hardest habits for many new computer users to break is the way in which they type numbers. Unlike a typewriter, a computer won't accept a lowercase l for a 1 (one). Likewise, don't substitute an uppercase O for 0 (zero). The computer must recognize the difference between letters and numbers so that WordPerfect's Math feature, as well as other features, work properly.

Tip: *A convenient way to type a whole group of numbers is to use the NUM LOCK key.*

The NUM LOCK key, located in the right-hand section of the keyboard, is handy if you're comfortable with a calculator's ten-key pad. Instead of using the top row on the typewriter keypad to enter numbers, press NUM LOCK; the right side of the keyboard can now be used to type numbers instead of functioning as a keypad that moves the cursor around the screen. Press NUM LOCK a second time to turn off the feature and to return the keypad to its original function.

Generally, you can tell whether NUM LOCK is on or off by checking the status line: **Pos** blinks when NUM LOCK is on and shines steadily when NUM LOCK is off. Be warned, however, that when you press specific keys—the SCREEN (CTRL + F3) key, the ENTER key, the CANCEL (F1) key, or function keys that display a menu—**Pos** stops blinking even though NUM LOCK is still on.

Those of you with the standard keyboard will find that you must switch between the cursor movement and numeric keys, since they are shared on one keypad. Those of you who have the enhanced keyboard may wish to keep NUM LOCK activated all the time, since you have a second cursor movement keypad for moving the cursor around the screen.

Trap: *Don't press the SPACEBAR to indent the first line of a paragraph.*

If you press the SPACEBAR rather than TAB to indent the beginning of a paragraph, the indentation may disappear when you edit your text. Also, using the SPACEBAR may cause uneven spacing when you print out your document. Instead, rely on the TAB key to indent paragraphs. Pressing TAB inserts a code to keep a line indented to a specific tab stop, eliminating the problem of uneven spacing.

Trap: *You can't turn off word wrap, but you can change the place where text is wrapped to a new line.*

WordPerfect determines the length of each line in your document, and therefore where to wrap words to the next line, based on your selection for three format settings:

- **Paper size** The dimensions of the paper on which the document will print. The default setting is for Standard size (8 1/2 by 11 inches), so that the page is 8.5 inches wide.
- **Left margin** The quantity of white space at the left edge of a page when printed. The default setting is for a left margin of 1″.
- **Right margin** The quantity of white space at the right edge of a page when printed. The default setting is 1″.

Assuming the default paper size and margin settings, WordPerfect will insert a **[SRt]** code and wrap text to the next line after 6.5 inches of text have been typed (paper width of 8.5 inches minus 2 inches for left and right margins). Since the status line measures the cursor's horizontal position from the left edge of the page, this means that WordPerfect will break to a new line when the "Pos" number on the status line reaches approximately 7.5″.

Depending on the document you are typing, you may wish to change where WordPerfect inserts soft return codes to break to a new line. For instance, if you are typing a table, you may need to increase the length of each line; in this case, you can reduce left or right margins and/or increase the width of your paper should you decide to print on wider paper. Conversely, to reduce the length of each line, you can increase margins and/or decrease the width of your paper. You will thus have altered your line length to something other than 6.5 inches. Look to Chapter 8 for directions on how to alter paper size and margins.

Moreover, there is another alternative for changing where WordPerfect wraps text: you can change the document's font, meaning the style, type, or size of characters on the printed page. WordPerfect assumes that you wish to use a certain font to print your document (based on how you defined your printer, as discussed in Appendix A). If you use a different font, the line length will not change (it will still be 6.5 inches), but now a different number of characters may fit on that 6.5-inch line. For instance, suppose that you originally typed a document with a 10-pitch font, meaning that ten characters fit in one horizontal inch. Then you change to a 12-pitch font, so that characters are packed more tightly. As a result, more characters will fit across one line, and WordPerfect will adjust the line breaks accordingly. Look to Chapter 7 for a discussion of how to make font changes in your document.

Tip: *You can type a hard space to stop word wrap from separating two words or a hyphen character to stop it from separating a hyphenated word.*

Often it is important to treat two words, or other elements in a phrase, as a single unit. For instance, you may wish to make sure that the date "March 25, 1989" remains on one line. However, if this date falls at the end of a line, then word wrap will split it, perhaps as follows:

Mr. Jones signed the legal contract on March
25, 1989

To protect against such a split, you can place a code called a *hard space* in your text. To do so, press HOME, SPACEBAR when inserting spaces between "March", "25", and "1989. That is, (1) type **March**, (2) press HOME, SPACEBAR, (3) type **25**, (4) press HOME, SPACEBAR, and (5) type **1989**. In a sense, all three elements become glued together; they won't ever be split between lines. WordPerfect inserts the hidden code [ ] between each word or element to be kept together. (The [ ], which represents a hard space, can be seen on the Reveal Codes screen.) Now the text reads

Mr. Jones signed the legal contract on
March 25, 1989.

In a similar way, you can prevent a hyphenated word from being split between two lines. Instead of typing a regular hyphen, insert a *hyphen character* by pressing HOME, HYPHEN. An example would be when you're typing the phrase "open-ended" and you want to prevent it from being split between two lines. To do so, (1) type **open**, (2) press HOME, HYPHEN, and (3) type **ended**. WordPerfect inserts the hidden code **-** between "open" and "ended" and treats it as one word to be kept together. If you type a regular hyphen, the hidden code **[-]** is inserted, while a hyphen character simply inserts a hyphen, or **-**.

Finally, if you want to insert a dash (—) and prevent the two hyphens that represent a dash from being separated, then press HOME, HYPHEN, HYPHEN. The codes inserted are **-[-]**.

Trap: *Pressing ENTER at the end of each line causes word wrap to be inoperative.*

If you press ENTER at the end of every line, you will forfeit the convenience of word wrap; WordPerfect will be unable to reformat your text within the margins as you edit your text later on. You will have to readjust the text yourself, a time-consuming and unnecessary procedure. It is advisable to take full advantage of the word wrap feature and press ENTER only in limited circumstances: at the end of a paragraph, at the end of a line that should end before it reaches the right margin, or at the beginning of a line that you want left blank.

If you wish to double space your document, the same rule applies: don't press ENTER between lines. Instead, refer to Chapter 8 for a discussion of the line spacing feature.

Tip: *Hard returns can be represented by a specific character on the Typing screen.*

If you've worked with other word processors, you may have grown accustomed to seeing a character that represents a hard return appear every time you press ENTER. While WordPerfect assumes that you don't wish to clutter the screen with extra characters, this feature is available. For instance, if you select > as the character, then your text might read as follows:

Mr. John Smith>
335 Mission Street>
San Francisco, CA 94334>
>
Dear John:>

You can select the character to represent hard returns by using the Display option on the Setup menu. (See Appendix B for more on the Setup menu.)

Tip: *WordPerfect has a useful feature for typing the date and time in your text.*

When you want to insert today's date or the current time, you can do so with only a few keystrokes. Refer to Chapter 8 for more on the DATE/OUTLINE (SHIFT + F5) key.

Trap: *What you see on the screen is not equivalent to one page of text.*

Most computer screens allow you to view 25 lines at a time, although some screens are larger and others are smaller. If your screen shows 25 lines (as do IBM PCs, XTs, ATs, and compatibles), then you can see 24 lines of text on WordPerfect's Typing screen; one line is occupied by the status line. But since a standard 8 1/2- by 11-inch page holds 66 lines of text, you cannot see the text of a whole page at once. You must become accustomed to viewing only a "screenful" of text at a time and watching for the dashed line that indicates the page end.

Trap: *If you accidentally press certain function keys, you can move text out of sight or produce odd results.*

Sometimes when typing you might accidentally press a key and erase all that you've typed. Generally, the text is still there; it has just disappeared from view. A hidden code is often the culprit. If you are working at the top of a document, for example, and your finger is resting firmly on the ENTER key, your text will drift downward and out of sight. Has your document disappeared? No. The text drifts down because you inserted hidden return codes and thus numerous blank lines.

Other hidden codes may cause problems in your text as well. Typically, when your text goes awry, a code is to blame. For example, you are typing along, you press a key inadvertently, and suddenly your text won't wrap back to the left margin. It looks out of alignment, as in Figure 3-4. What's going on? Most likely you pressed the →INDENT (F4) key in the middle of a line, inserting the **[→Indent]** code, so that the rest of the paragraph is now indented to the next tab stop.

If these types of problems occur, the easiest solution is to reveal codes to find the culprit. The next section in this chapter, "Typing on the Reveal Codes Screen," describes how to switch to and work on the Reveal Codes screen.

Finally, text may disappear if you accidentally press the SWITCH (SHIFT + F3) key. WordPerfect has not erased your first document; it is still in memory. If this is the case, the status line reads **Doc 2**. Just switch back to document 1 by pressing the SWITCH (SHIFT + F3) key again. (Chapter 12 explains how to switch between documents.)

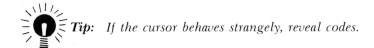

Tip: *If the cursor behaves strangely, reveal codes.*

Sometimes key combinations that position text on a line—such as the CENTER or the FLUSH RIGHT key—cause text to overlap. As a result, the cursor jumps back and forth on the overlapping text. You can detect and solve this problem by

```
     Bookkeeping is the recording of income and expenses in
journals.  You can keep a record of your financial transactions in
a notebook, but you will soon outgrow this method.  It is best,
from the outset, to      organize your transactions effectively.
                         The proven method is with double-entry
                         bookkeeping, where each transaction is
                         recorded twice -- as a debit and as a
                         credit item.  Your books are in balance
                         when you record both parts of the same
                         transaction.

                                        Doc 1 Pg 1 Ln 3.66" Pos 3.5"
```

Figure 3-4. Misaligned text—the result of an errant code

revealing codes, a process described in the next section, "Typing on the Reveal Codes Screen."

Trip: *The status line works in increments depending on the font used.*

WordPerfect assumes that you wish to use a specific printer and a specific font—the style, type, and size of characters—to print your documents. (The process for defining your printer is discussed in Appendix A.) The increments with which the "Ln" and "Pos" numbers on the status line change as you type depend on your printer and font. For instance, if that font is 10-pitch, meaning that ten characters fit across one horizontal inch, then as you are typing text, the "Pos" number on the status line would increase by 0.1″ increments. (See Chapter 7 for more on selecting and changing fonts for your printer.)

Tip: *You can alter the units of measure used in the status line.*

When you first start up WordPerfect, the status line reports the cursor's vertical and horizontal position on the page in inches, with the unit of measure represented by a double quotation mark (″). You can instead represent the unit of measure with a lowercase "i," so that, with the cursor at the top of a document, the status line would read

Doc 1 Pg 1 Ln 1i Pos 1i

Further, the program offers you the flexibility of displaying the cursor's position using three other units of measure—centimeters, points, or version 4.2 units (lines and columns). Using centimeters will be convenient if you're more accustomed to that unit of measure than to inches. The status line would look as follows:

Doc 1 Pg 1 Ln 2.54c Pos 2.54c

Using points will be convenient for graphic artists or printers or people familiar with desktop publishing. The status line would appear as follows:

Doc 1 Pg 1 Ln 72p Pos 72p

Using version 4.2 units may be your selection if you're upgrading from version 4.2 and feel more familiar with the lines and columns orientation. It may also be your choice if you have used another software package and prefer to think of the vertical position as the actual text line number starting just below the top margin and the horizontal position as the column (character) number starting at the left margin. The status line would read

Doc 1 Pg 1 Ln 1 Pos 10

Should you decide to work with the status line in version 4.2 units, you must keep in mind that the "Ln" number indicates a distance from the top *margin,* while for the other units of measure, "Ln" indicates a distance from the top *edge of the page.*

You change the status line appearance using the Units of Measure option on the Setup menu. (Refer to Appendix B for details.)

Tip: *Color monitor owners can select the display colors and/or appearance of characters on screen.*

If you have a color monitor, you may not like the color choices that have been provided for you by WordPerfect Corporation. Depending on the type of monitor you have, you can select from a rainbow of foreground and background colors.

If your monitor has graphics capabilities, you may also be able to select from a variety of fonts (such as italics or small caps) for the characters that appear on screen. This all depends on your monitor and display card. The screen options you select have no effect on how your documents look when printed. (For more on screen options, refer to Appendix B, which discusses the Setup menu.)

Tip: *(When upgrading from 4.2.) New options have been added to change the look of the Typing screen.*

The basic way that you enter text remains unchanged in version 5. What has changed is that the status line displays the cursor's vertical position as inches from the top of the page and its horizontal position as inches from the left edge of the page. This can, however, be changed. If you prefer, you can alter the status line so that the cursor's position is shown in familiar version 4.2 units (lines from the top margin and columns from the left edge). You can also use centimeters or points as your unit of measure.

You may wish to start out using inches and then remain with inches if you get accustomed to this unit of measure or change to version 4.2 units otherwise. If you do use version 4.2 units, be warned that because WordPerfect now automatically adjusts margins as you change your font (as discussed in Chapters 7 and 8), the horizontal position of the cursor will now be based on that font. For example, if you type a document with a 10-pitch font, when the cursor is at the left margin (and assuming a left margin of 1 inch), then the status line will indicate **Pos** 10. If you switch to a 12-pitch font, then with the cursor at the left margin, the status line will instead indicate **Pos** 12.

The ability to change the status line, along with new features allowing you to quickly and easily select the background and foreground colors used on the Typing screen (for color monitor users), are found on the Setup menu (described in Appendix B).

Typing on the Reveal Codes Screen

There is an alternative to typing your documents on the Typing screen. You can also type while on the Reveal Codes screen. But why use the Reveal Codes screen? Because it enables you to see the commands that determine how your document is printed. You can delete a code you no longer want or one that is sabotaging a document's appearance. Being able to uncover codes is an advantage of WordPerfect, because it gives you complete control over your final printed product.

You can access the Reveal Codes screen by pressing the REVEAL CODES (ALT + F3) key. The screen splits into two windows, which represent two different perspectives on the same text. Examine the windows one at a time, and you will become comfortable with and appreciative of all the information they provide.

Figure 3-5 shows a clear Reveal Codes screen. The screen is split in half by the ruler line, a solid bar on which triangles represent tab settings and curved braces { } represent the left or right margin where a tab also is located. (Square brackets [ ] represent the left and right margins where no tab is located, a situation not shown in Figure 3-5.) Margins are at 1 inch, while tabs are located every 0.5 inch—the initial WordPerfect settings. The window above the ruler line is reserved for displaying text as it appears on the Typing screen, with all the codes hidden. The window is small, enabling you to view (at one time) only ten lines of text plus the status line. The bottom window is reserved for displaying the same

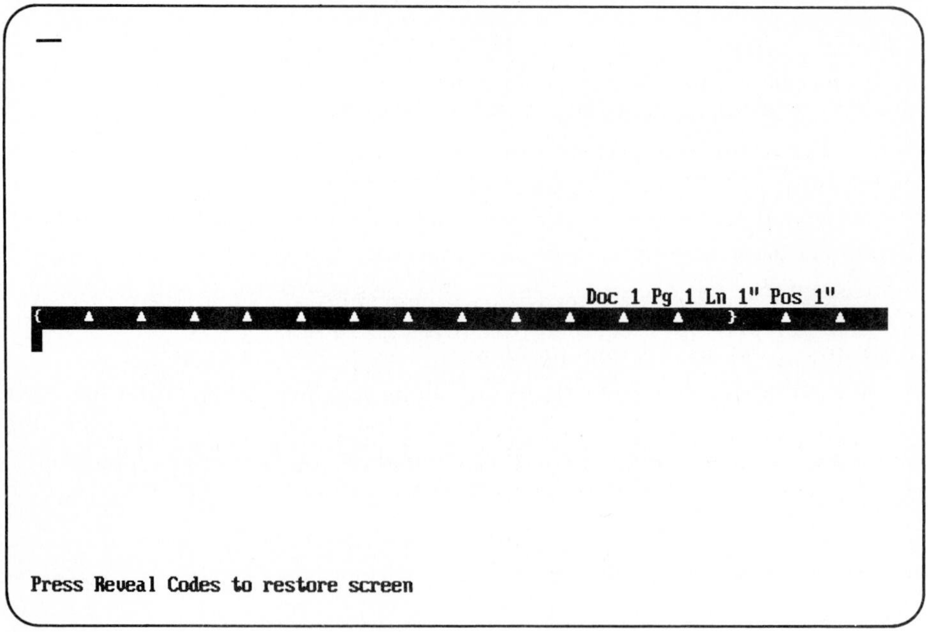

Figure 3-5. Reveal Codes screen

ten lines of text with codes in full view. The cursor's position is shown in both the top and bottom windows. In the bottom, it is represented as a highlighted block that is the same height as a standard character.

Figure 3-6 shows a Reveal Codes screen filled with text. In the bottom window notice that **[SRt]** codes appear at the end of every line where word wrap took effect within a paragraph. **[HRt]** codes are revealed at the end of paragraphs, where a short line of text ends, and on the blank line separating paragraphs. A tab code, **[TAB]**, precedes the first character of both paragraphs. Finally, you can see that WordPerfect considers a hyphen to be a code, with **[-]** shown on the bottom screen in several places. Also notice that when the cursor is on a code, the entire code is highlighted by the cursor in the bottom window. In this case, the cursor is on the **[TAB]** code.

Figure 3-7 shows a Reveal Codes screen after several uncommon codes have been inserted. A **[Tab Set:1″. . . .]** code in the bottom window indicates where tabs have been reset for this document; notice that the ruler line has changed to reflect the change in tab stops. (Remember that the square bracket represents a right

```
    _Bookkeeping is the recording of income and expenses in
journals.  You can keep a record of your financial transactions in
a notebook, but you will soon outgrow this method.  It is best,
from the outset, to organize your transactions effectively.

     The proven method is with double-entry bookkeeping, where each
transaction is recorded twice -- as a debit and as a credit item.
Your books are in balance when you record both parts of the same
transaction.


                                        Doc 1 Pg 1 Ln 1" Pos 1"
{ ▲ ▲ ▲ ▲ ▲ ▲ ▲ ▲ ▲ ▲ ▲ ▲ } ▲ ▲
[Tab]Bookkeeping is the recording of income and expenses in[SRt]
journals.  You can keep a record of your financial transactions in[SRt]
a notebook, but you will soon outgrow this method.  It is best,[SRt]
from the outset, to organize your transactions effectively.  [HRt]
[HRt]
[Tab]The proven method is with double[-]entry bookkeeping, where each[SRt]
transaction is recorded twice [-][-] as a debit and as a credit item. [SRt]
Your books are in balance when you record both parts of the same[SRt]
transaction.[HRt]


Press Reveal Codes to restore screen
```

Figure 3-6. Codes and text on the Reveal Codes screen

margin without a tab stop.) Also notice in the bottom window that the first line of text wraps around to a second line, providing space to display the **[Tab Set:]** code. (Since the Reveal Codes screen contains codes, text doesn't wrap the same way as on the Typing screen.) **[BOLD]** and **[bold]** codes surround a portion of text that will appear in boldface when printed, "organize your transactions effectively".

Because the Reveal Codes screen is visible, you are informed about your codes. You know precisely where the **[TAB]**, the **[HRt]**, and other codes are located, in case you decide to delete or to move them. You know exactly where new tab set codes will take effect, and exactly where the printer will switch to boldface. You therefore know precisely how the document will appear when printed.

When on the Reveal Codes screen, you can type text and select features just as you do on the Typing screen. All the Tips mentioned previously that are related to the Typing screen apply equally to the Reveal Codes screen. Be aware that if you press a function key to display a line menu, the menu will appear in the top window, rather than the bottom window, of the Reveal Codes screen.

```
        _Bookkeeping is the recording of income and expenses in
journals.  You can keep a record of your financial transactions in
a notebook, but you will soon outgrow this method.  It is best,
from the outset, to organize your transactions effectively.

        The proven method is with double-entry bookkeeping, where
each transaction is recorded twice -- as a debit and as a credit
item.  Your books are in balance when you record both parts of the
same transaction.


                                        Doc 1 Pg 1 Ln 1" Pos 1"
[Tab Set:1",2",3.5",4.5",6",6.5",7"][Tab]Bookkeeping is the recording of income
and expenses in[SRt]
journals.  You can keep a record of your financial transactions in[SRt]
a notebook, but you will soon outgrow this method.  It is best,[SRt]
from the outset, to [BOLD]organize your transactions effectively[bold].  [HRt]
[HRt]
[Tab]The proven method is with double[-]entry bookkeeping, where[SRt]
each transaction is recorded twice [-][-] as a debit and as a credit[SRt]
item.  Your books are in balance when you record both parts of the[SRt]
same transaction.[HRt]

Press Reveal Codes to restore screen
```

Figure 3-7. Additional codes added on the Reveal Codes screen

To again hide the codes and return to the Typing screen, press REVEAL CODES (ALT + F3). In fact, note the message at the bottom of Figure 3-7 which reminds you of that fact: **Press Reveal Codes to restore screen.** The REVEAL CODES key is like a toggle switch, taking you in and out of the Reveal Codes screen.

Table 3-1 provides a list of all the codes used in WordPerfect that you are likely to encounter as you type on the Reveal Codes screen. These codes are inserted as you activate various features and commands. You will learn how to use the full range of WordPerfect features throughout the remaining chapters in this book. For instance, in Chapter 7 you will learn how to insert **[BOLD]** codes to boldface portions of text. In Chapter 8 you will learn how to insert a **[Tab Set]** code to alter tab stops. Refer to Table 3-1 when you find a code on the Reveal Codes screen with which you're unfamiliar, so that you can look up the associated feature, understand how it will affect the text when printed, and decide whether you want that code to remain in the text.

Table 3-1. WordPerfect Codes

-	Soft Hyphen
^M	Merge (M=merge code letter, as in ^E or ^R)
[/]	Cancel Hyphenation
[-]	Hard Hyphen
[ ]	Hard Space
[+]	Subtotal Calculation (Math)
[=]	Total Calculation (Math)
[*]	Grand Total Calculation (Math)
[!]	Formula Calculation (Math)
[N]	Calculation treated as negative (Math)
[t]	Total Entry (Math)
[AdvDn:]	Advance Down
[AdvLft:]	Advance Left
[AdvRgt:]	Advance Right
[AdvToPos:]	Advance to Position
[AdvToLn:]	Advance to Line
[AdvUp:]	Advance Up
[Align] [C/AFlrt]	Tab Align (begin and end)
[Block]	Beginning of Block (in Reveal Codes)
[Block Pro:On] [Block Pro:Off]	Block Protection (begin and end)
[BOLD] [bold]	Bold (begin and end)
[Box Num]	Caption in Graphics Box
[C/A/Flrt]	End of Center, Tab Align, or Flush Right
[Center Pg]	Center Page Top to Bottom
[Cntr] [C/A/Flrt]	Center (begin and end)
[Cndl EOP:]	Conditional End of Page
[Col Def:]	Text Columns Definition
[Col Off]	Text Columns Off (end)
[Col On]	Text Columns On (begin)
[Comment]	Document Comment
[Color:]	Print Color
[Date:]	Date
[DBL UND][dbl und]	Double Underline (begin and end)
[Decml/Algn Char:]	Decimal Align and Thousands' Separator Characters
[Def Mark:Index]	Index Definition
[Def Mark:List,n]	List Definition (n=list number)
[Def Mark:ToA,n]	Table of Authorities Definition (n=section number)
[Def Mark:ToC,n]	Table of Contents Definition (n=ToC level)
[DSRt]	Deletable Soft Return

Courtesy of WordPerfect Corporation

Table 3-1. WordPerfect Codes (continued)

[End Def]	End of Index, List, or Table (after generation)
[End Mark:List,n]	End marked text for List (n=list number)
[End Mark:ToC,n]	End marked text for Table of Contents (n=ToC level)
[End Opt]	Endnote Options
[Endnote:n;[Note Num] text]	Endnote (n=note number)
[Endnote Placement]	Endnote Placement
[EXT LARGE] [ext large]	Extra Large Print (begin and end)
[Figure:n;;]	Figure Box (n=box number)
[Fig Opt]	Figure Box Options
[FINE] [fine]	Fine Print (begin and end)
[Flsh Rt] [C/A/Flrt]	Flush Right (begin and end)
[Footnote:n;[Note Num] text]	Footnote (n=note number)
[Font:]	Base Font
[Footer N:n;text]	Footer (N=type, A or B) (n=frequency)
[Force:]	Force Odd or Force Even
[Ftn Opt]	Footnote Options
[Header N:n;text]	Header (N=type, A or B) (n=frequency)
[HLine:]	Horizontal Line
[HPg]	Hard Page
[HRt]	Hard Return
[Hyph Off]	Hyphenation Off
[Hyph On]	Hyphenation On
[HZone:n,n]	Hyphenation Zone (n=left,right)
[→Indent]	Indent
[→Indent←]	Left/right Indent
[Index:heading;subheading]	Index Entry
[ISRt]	Invisible Soft Return
[ITALC] [italc]	Italics Print (begin and end)
[Just Off]	Right Justification Off
[Just On]	Right Justification On
[Just Lim:]	Justification Limits for Word Spacing
[Kern:Off]	Kerning Off
[Kern:On]	Kerning On
[L/R Mar:]	Left and Right Margins
[Lang:]	Language (for Speller, Thesaurus, Hyphenation module)
[LARGE] [large]	Large Print (begin and end)
[Ln Height:]	Line Height
[Ln Num:Off]	Line Numbering Off
[Ln Num:On]	Line Numbering On
[Ln Spacing:]	Line Spacing

Courtesy of WordPerfect Corporation

Table 3-1. WordPerfect Codes (continued)

[←Mar Rel]	Left Margin Release
[Mark:List,n] [End Mark:List,n]	List Entry Mark (n=list number) (begin and end)
[Mark:ToC,n] [EndMark:ToC,n]	Table of Contents Entry Mark (n=ToC level) (begin and end)
[Math Def]	Math Columns Definition
[Math Off]	Math Columns Off (end)
[Math On]	Math Columns On (begin)
[New End Num:]	New Endnote Number
[New Fig Num:]	New Figure Box Number
[New Ftn Num:]	New Footnote Number
[New Tab Num:]	New Table Number
[New Txt Num:]	New Text Box Number
[New User Num:]	New User-Defined Box Number
[Note Num]	Footnote/Endnote Reference Number
[Open Style:name]	Open Style (n=style name)
[OUTLN] [outln]	Outline Attribute (begin and end)
[Ovrstk:]	Overstrike
[Paper Sz/Typ:]	Paper Size and Type
[Par Num:Auto]	Paragraph Number, Automatic
[Par Num:n]	Paragraph Number (n=paragraph level)
[Par Num Def]	Paragraph Numbering Definition
[Pg Num:]	New Page Number
[Pg Numbering:]	Page Numbering Position
[Ptr Cmnd:]	Printer Command
[REDLN] [redln]	Redline (begin and end)
[Ref(name) t]	Automatic Reference (name=target name) (t=what reference is tied to)
[SHADW] [shadw]	Shadow (begin and end)
[SM CAP] [sm cap]	Small Caps (begin and end)
[SMALL] [small]	Small Print (begin and end)
[SPg]	Soft Page
[SRt]	Soft Return
[STKOUT] [stkout]	Strikeout (begin and end)
[Style On:name] [Style Off:name]	Paired Style (begin and end) (name=style name)
[Subdoc:]	Subdocument in a Master Document
[Subdoc Start:] [Subdoc End:]	Subdocument after Master Document generated (begin and end)
[SUBSCPT] [subscpt]	Subscript (begin and end)
[SUPRSCPT] [suprscpt]	Superscript (begin and end)
[Suppress:]	Suppress Page Format Options
[T/B Mar:]	Top and Bottom Margins

Courtesy of WordPerfect Corporation

Table 3-1. WordPerfect Codes (continued)

[Tab]	Tab
[Tbl Opt]	Table Box Options
[Tab Set:]	Tab Set
[Table:n;;]	Table Box (n=box number)
[Target(name)]	Target for Automatic Reference (name=target name)
[Text Box:n;;]	Text box (n=box number)
[ToA:;text]	Table of Authorities Short Form (text=text of Short Form)
[ToA:n;text;Full Form]	Table of Authorities Full Form (n=section number) (text=text of Short Form)
[Txt Opt]	Text Box Options
[UND] [und]	Underlining (begin and end)
[Undrln:]	Underline Spaces and/or Tabs
[Usr Box:n;;]	User-Defined Box (n=box number)
[Usr Opt]	User Defined Box Options
[VLine:]	Vertical Line
[VRY LARGE] [vry large]	Very Large Print (begin and end)
[Wrd/Ltr Spacing:]	Word and Letter Spacing
[W/O Off]	Widow/Orphan Off
[W/O On]	Widow/Orphan On

Courtesy of WordPerfect Corporation

Trap: *The two windows on the Reveal Codes screen don't move in synch as you type.*

When you use the Reveal Codes screen, the cursor in the *top* window moves in the same way as it does on the Typing screen. That is, the cursor moves to the bottom of the window and then the window begins scrolling upward so you can view your text as you type.

On the other hand, the cursor in the *bottom* window attempts to remain in the middle (on line three, to be more precise); the window scrolls constantly so that the cursor can maintain that position. At first, you may find the dissimilar movement of the cursor in the two windows disconcerting. Just realize that you're getting two separate perspectives on the same line of text, which is marked by the cursor.

Tip: *The Reveal Codes screen gives a clear view of which codes dominate which portions of the text.*

When you reveal codes, you can see precisely where a code's dominance starts and stops. There are two types of codes: those that travel in pairs, and those that work on their own to indicate where a specific feature takes effect.

Code pairs clearly mark the beginning and the endpoint of the text they enhance. When you boldface a sentence, for example, **[BOLD]** is placed in front of the sentence and **[bold]** is placed at the end of the sentence.
Examples of code pairs include

[Align] [C/A/Flrt]	Tab align
[BOLD] [bold]	Bold
[BlockPro:On] [BlockPro:Off]	Block protection
[Cntr][C/A/Flrt]	Center
[Flsh Rt] [C/A/Flrt]	Flush right
[REDLN] [redln]	Redline
[STKOUT] [stkout]	Strikeout
[SM CAP] [sm cap]	Small caps
[SUBSCPT] [subscpt]	Subscript
[UND] [und]	Underlining

Conversely, a single code dominates text from that point forward, either to the end of a document or until the next code of its type occurs (farther on in the text) that can override it—whichever comes first. Change left and right margins, for example, and a **[L/R Mar:]** code is embedded at the cursor's position; all text from that code forward readjusts for the new margin settings until the next margin code appears farther forward in the text. If you find no other margin code, then that one code will apply for all remaining document pages.

Remember that a complete list of codes is provided in Table 3-1.

Tip: *Some codes offer much information and are quite detailed.*

It is likely that you will find some codes that are quite long. Read a code's contents and you will know the exact function of that code. A tab set code, for example, provides the location of each tab stop. If you set six tab stops, for instance, the tab code will include a long list of all of their locations.

[Tab Set:1″,2″,4″,5″,6″,L7″]

A header/footer code indicates which choices you made on the Header/Footer menu, and the text of your header or footer (or the first 50 characters of text, if the header or footer is a long one).

[Header A:2;ABC CORPORATION   FEBRUARY 1, 1989]

A:2 indicates the choices made on the Header/Footer menu: header A is to be printed on every page. The code also contains up to the first 50 characters in the header or footer.

A code can thus provide fairly detailed information on the feature which that code represents.

Trap: *When you reveal codes, you may find your document crowded.*

It is easy to insert codes without even realizing it. Often this occurs when you mistakenly press the wrong key combination and, seeing little or no change on the screen, you try again and again, thus inserting multiple codes. For example, suppose you try to center a title, but by accident you press the BOLD (F6) key, then CENTER (SHIFT + F6), and BOLD (F6) again. With a slight slip of the fingers, you've inserted a trail of unneeded codes.

[BOLD][Cntr][bold][BOLD][bold]

Another way unwanted codes are inserted is if you change your mind about a setting. For example, say you change to double spacing, then change your mind, and then change your mind a third time. Only the third code—the one farthest along in the document (that is, farthest to the right)—has an effect on text, although the other margin codes remain.

[Ln Spacing:2][Ln Spacing:1][Ln Spacing:1.5]

As a rule, you should use the least number of codes possible in a document. Unwanted codes take up space and can cause problems later on, when you attempt to edit or print, so they should be deleted. Codes are deleted in the same way as regular text (see Chapter 5 for a complete discussion of how to edit text and codes in your document).

Tip: *Rely on the Reveal Codes screen if the cursor or your text is acting inconsistently.*

If you find that your text looks misaligned or that your cursor jumps oddly from place to place, the Reveal Codes screen can help you detect the problem. For instance, suppose that the cursor behaves oddly and different letters appear and disappear near "n Tuesday" in the following awkward sentence:

We'll be returning after n Tuesday. Jaclyn Brown, Marketing Dept.

Reveal codes and the screen might look like that shown in Figure 3-8. Notice how the bottom window indicates the problem: half the text starts at the left margin, while half the text is flush right against the right margin (a feature described in Chapter 7), and is enclosed in a pair of codes, **[Flsh Rt]** and **[C/A/Flrt]**. In the middle the two phrases overlap, so the cursor jumps between the two. Delete one code in the pair of flush right codes and the problem is solved.

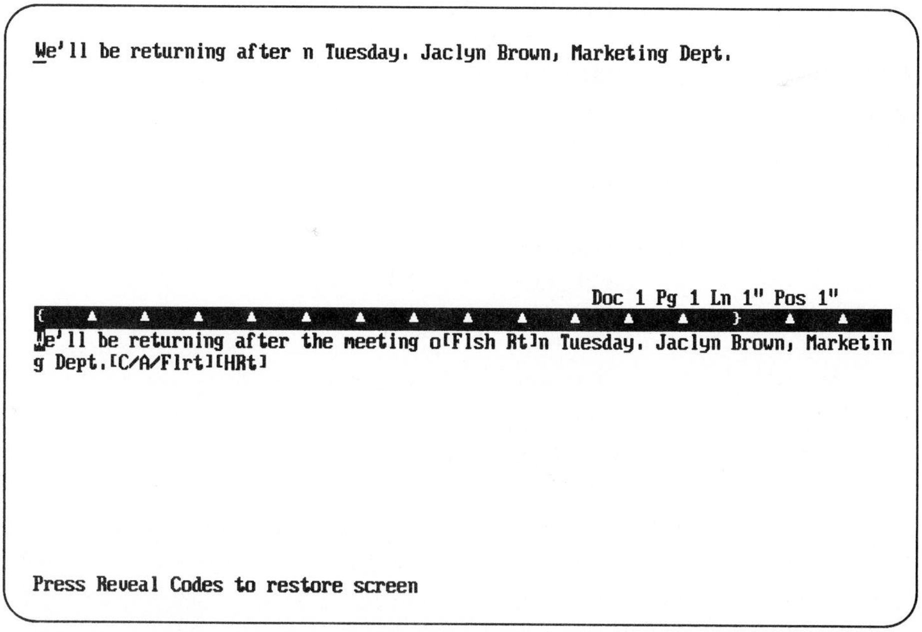
We'll be returning after n Tuesday. Jaclyn Brown, Marketing Dept.
Doc 1 Pg 1 Ln 1" Pos 1"
We'll be returning after the meeting o[Flsh Rt]n Tuesday. Jaclyn Brown, Marketin
g Dept.[C/A/Flrt][HRt]
Press Reveal Codes to restore screen
Figure 3-8. Overlapping text exposed on the Reveal Codes screen

We'll be returning after the meeting on Tuesday. Jaclyn Brown, Marketing Dept.

It would be much more difficult to figure out the cause of the problem on the Typing screen. So, switch to the Reveal Codes screen when a problem arises in the text.

Tip: *(When upgrading from 4.2.) You can now type your documents on the Reveal Codes screen.*

A major change in version 5 enables you to type, add to, and edit your text on the Reveal Codes screen. You can remain in Reveal Codes as you type, edit, save, print, and so on. Although you may find this distracting, in some cases it is a useful option. Because all the features on Reveal Codes work in the same way as they do on the Typing screen, you can no longer press CANCEL (F1), the SPACEBAR, or a number of other keys to return to the Typing screen. You must now press REVEAL CODES (ALT + F3) to do so.

In addition, some of the codes are different. For instance, the begin and end underline codes used to be **[U]** and **[u]**, whereas that code pair is now **[UND]** and **[und]**. Refer to Table 3-1 for a list of the codes in version 5.

Finally, if the cursor on the bottom window in Reveal Codes rests on a code, the cursor stretches to highlight the entire code, regardless of the code's length. This makes it quite easy to see your exact cursor location.

Duplicating a Character

The ESC key, usually located in the upper left-hand corner of the computer keyboard, helps you gain typing speed in WordPerfect. This key provides access to the Repeat Value feature so that you can repeat a character a specific number of times. The repeat value is initially set for eight repetitions.

Suppose you are typing a form and need to show the plus (+) sign 40 times across the screen. Instead of pressing the PLUS key 40 times, proceed as follows:

1. Move your cursor to the spot where you would like the plus signs to begin.
2. Press ESC. WordPerfect responds with the following message at the bottom of the screen:

   Repeat Value = 8

3. Type **40**. The message now reads

   Repeat Value = 40

4. Press the PLUS key (+) once. The following appears on the screen:

   ++

This method for repeating a character is faster and more precise than simply holding a key down because you can't be sure how many times that key will repeat.

Trap: *Don't press ESC to cancel a command.*

For many computer users, pressing ESC is almost automatic because some other software programs rely on the ESC key to abort commands. In WordPerfect, rely instead on the CANCEL (F1) key to void commands. If you do press ESC by accident so that the repeat prompt appears, simply press CANCEL (F1) to clear it from the screen. Or you can press ESC a second time to clear the ESC prompt.

Tip: *You can change the repeat value's initial setting.*

Suppose that during a specific working session you must draw 45 equal signs across the screen in separate sections of a document. You can reset the repeat value to 45 for the entire working session. Press ESC and, at the prompt, type 45. Press ENTER. Until you exit WordPerfect or change the value again, each time you press ESC, the prompt will read

Repeat Value = 45

You can also change the repeat value on a more permanent basis. The Setup menu (described in Appendix B) has a selection under the Initial Settings option for permanently changing the repetition value. If you changed the repeat value to 45 in the Setup menu, the ESC prompt would suggest **Repeat Value = 45** the first time you pressed it in every working session.

Tip: *(When upgrading from 4.2.) The Repeat Value feature operates basically the same in version 5.*

The procedure for using the ESC key is the same in version 5 as it was in version 4.2. However, the prompt now reads **Repeat Value = 8** rather than **n = 8**, and is thus more descriptive.

Inserting Document Comments

The Document Comment feature enables you to insert comments into a document that appear only when the document is on screen, but not when the document is printed. Therefore, document comments are helpful as you type when you wish to insert a reminder to yourself or a note to another person who reads the document on screen.

When you insert a comment, it appears on screen in a double-line box. Up to 1157 characters can be typed into the comment box. Figure 3-9 illustrates a comment inserted into a document. Each time you wish to insert a comment:

1. Move the cursor to the line above where you want the comment to appear. (For example, to insert the comment shown in Figure 3-9, the cursor was located at the end of the first paragraph.)

```
                         MEMORANDUM

TO: Real Estate Committee                  FROM:  Jean Lazurus

RE: Status Report                          DATE:  June 1, 1989

     Currently, all units in the building on State Street are
occupied.  On August 1st, however, two units will be vacated.  I
suggest that we advertise for new tenants immediately.  Regarding
that same building, before next winter we must address the problem
of the inadequate heating system.  Most of the tenants in the
building have complained.

  Call Mr. Margolis to find out about the heating system.  Should we
  consider installing a new one?  Can the old one be repaired?  Who should
  gather estimates?  Insert the findings into this section of the report.

     In another matter, R&R Realty has for sale two buildings on
Polk Avenue.  I have attached a description of the properties for
your consideration.

                                      Doc 1 Pg 1 Ln 1" Pos 1"
```

Figure 3-9. Comment in the document

2. Press the TEXT IN/OUT (CTRL + F5) key. WordPerfect responds with the following menu:

   1 Dos Text; 2 Password; 3 Save Generic; 4 Save WP 4.2; 5 Comment: **0**

3. **Press Comment (5 or C). Another menu appears:**

   Comment: 1 Create; 2 Edit; 3 Convert to Text: **0**

4. Press Create, (1 or C). Your document disappears temporarily, as WordPerfect displays an empty comment box for you to fill in. This is shown in Figure 3-10.

5. Type the comment and press the EXIT (F7) key to exit (as noted at the bottom of Figure 3-10).

The comment appears at the current cursor position on screen. The code **[Comment]** is inserted at the same spot in the document. If the cursor is just before or after the comment box, press the RIGHT or LEFT ARROW key to move past the Comment box in one keystroke.

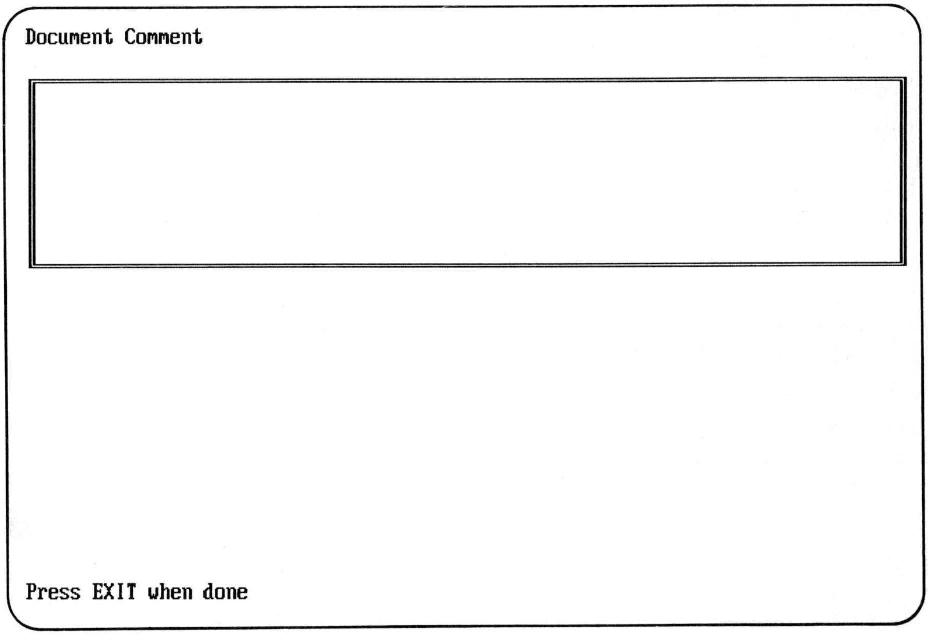

Figure 3-10. An empty document comment box

Trap: *Don't rely on the visual representation of your text on screen if document comments are interspersed in your text.*

Each comment can be many lines long. Since comments aren't printed by WordPerfect, the lines they occupy are ignored when printed. Therefore, refer to the status line to keep track of where text will appear on the printed page.

The screen can be especially deceiving if you insert a comment in the middle of a line of text. For example, the comment in Figure 3-11 was inserted after the phrase "that same building,". Notice how it appears that the comment splits up the rest of that line of text. However, the entire line will be unbroken when printed.

Trap: *The only text enhancements that can be included in a document comment are underline and boldface.*

As described in Chapter 7, there are a myriad of ways to enhance your text by changing the size, position, or appearance of characters. In a comment, you are

```
                          MEMORANDUM

TO: Real Estate Committee                     FROM:  Jean Lazurus

RE: Status Report                             DATE:  June 1, 1989

     Currently, all units in the building on State Street are
occupied.  On August 1st, however, two units will be vacated.  I
suggest that we advertise for new tenants immediately.  Regarding
that same building,
 ┌──────────────────────────────────────────────────────────────┐
 │Call Mr. Margolis to find out about the heating system.  Should we
 │consider installing a new one?  Can the old one be repaired?  Who should
 │gather estimates?  Insert the findings into this section of the report.
 └──────────────────────────────────────────────────────────────┘
                    before next winter we must address the problem
of the inadequate heating system.  Most of the tenants in the
building have complained.
     In another matter, R&R Realty has for sale two buildings on
Polk Avenue.  I have attached a description of the properties for
your consideration.


                                         Doc 1 Pg 1 Ln 1" Pos 1"
```

Figure 3-11. Document comment inserted mid-line

limited to the underline and boldface features. Also, these features must be used while you're typing the text, not with already-existing text in the body of a comment.

Tip: *To erase a comment already created, you must erase its hidden code.*

When you create a comment, WordPerfect inserts a **[Comment]** code in the text. You can locate and erase the corresponding code. On the Reveal Codes screen, simply position the cursor to the right of the code and press BACKSPACE, or position the cursor on the code and press DEL. On the Typing screen, with the cursor on the left margin just below the comment, press BACKSPACE. WordPerfect asks for verification of your decision to erase the code: **Delete [Comment]? (Y/N) No.** Type **Y** and the comment disappears. (Erasing codes is explained further in Chapter 5.)

Tip: *Document comments can be edited.*

If you wish to edit a comment, there's no need to erase the original and type a new one. Instead, WordPerfect can edit the comment. First, position the cursor farther forward in the text. You must do this because WordPerfect always looks backward from the cursor position to the first comment it can find.

Next, press the TEXT IN/OUT key, select Comment (5 or C), and select Edit (2 or E). WordPerfect searches backward and displays the first comment it meets. Edit the text (most of the editing features described in Chapter 5 operate in comments) and press EXIT (F7).

Tip: *An option allows you to hide the screen display of all comments.*

WordPerfect assumes that you want comments displayed on the screen. If they prove distracting, you can hide them from view by using the Display option on the SETUP (SHIFT + F1) key (see Appendix B). Once you turn off the display of comments, they will remain off in documents that you work on in the future. You can change your mind at any time, however, and view the comments by using the same option on the SETUP key.

Tip: *You can change a comment to text and vice versa.*

To print out a comment in WordPerfect, you must change that comment to text. There is a quick way to do this: (1) Position the cursor forward in the text from the comment you wish to change, (2) press the TEXT IN/OUT (CTRL + F5) key, (3) select Comment (5 or C), and (4) select Convert to text (3 or T). In an instant the entire text of the comment is converted to standard text, whether or not the comment had been displayed (see the previous Tip).

Moreover, WordPerfect offers the ability to change a portion of text to a comment: (1) use the BLOCK (ALT + F4) key (as described in Chapter 4) to highlight the text you want converted to a comment, and (2) press the TEXT IN/OUT (CTRL + F5) key. When WordPerfect asks you, **Create a comment (Y/N)? No**, (3) press **Y** to place the highlighted text into a comment box. Type **N** or any character other than Y, or press ENTER, to abort the operation.

With the ability to switch in and out of comments, you can switch to text, print out your notes, and then quickly switch the text back into a comment.

Tip: *If you wish to print a document comment, you can also bypass WordPerfect with the PRINT SCREEN key.*

The document comments never print during the normal WordPerfect process unless switched to text. You can, however, bypass WordPerfect by pressing the PRINT SCREEN key, which on some keyboards is labeled as PRTSC. This key directs the computer to print an exact copy of the screen—status line, comment box, and all.

Turn on your printer. Position the cursor so that your screen displays the comment you wish to print. Next, press PRTSC (often, you must hold the SHIFT key down to activate PRTSC). You can continue using WordPerfect when the printer stops.

Tip: *(When upgrading from 4.2.) The Document Comment feature now contains more options.*

WordPerfect has the added ability to change from standard text to a comment, and vice versa, in version 5. As a result, you can now print the contents of a comment once it's converted to text.

The code inserted when you create a comment has changed. The new code is a short one: **[Comment]**. You can no longer use Reveal Codes to view the first 50 characters of the comment within the code.

Incidentally, you may be wondering about the Document Summary feature, which in version 4.2 was housed alongside the Document Comment feature on the TEXT IN/OUT key. You'll now find that feature on the FORMAT (SHIFT + F8) key, under the Document option (the Document Summary feature is discussed in Chapter 11).

Tips and Traps Summary

Typing on the Typing Screen

Trap: If you hold a key down too long as you type, you'll get extra characters.

Tip: The easiest way to type a whole string of letters in uppercase is to press CAPS LOCK.

Tip: WordPerfect can reverse uppercase letters and lowercase letters.

Trap: Don't type letters to substitute for numbers.

Tip: A convenient way to type a whole group of numbers is to use the NUM LOCK key.

Trap: Don't press the SPACEBAR to indent the first line of a paragraph.

Trap: You can't turn off word wrap, but you can change the place where text is wrapped to a new line.

Tip: You can type a hard space to stop word wrap from separating two words or a hyphen character to stop it from separating a hyphenated word.

Trap: Pressing ENTER at the end of each line causes word wrap to be inoperative.

Tips and Traps Summary (*continued*)

Tip: Hard returns can be represented by a specific character on the Typing screen.

Tip: WordPerfect has a useful feature for typing the date and time in your text.

Trap: What you see on the screen is not equivalent to one page of text.

Trap: If you accidentally press certain function keys, you can move text out of sight or produce odd results.

Tip: If the cursor behaves strangely, reveal codes.

Tip: The status line works in increments depending on the font used.

Tip: You can alter the units of measure used in the status line.

Tip: Color monitor owners can select the display colors and/or appearance of characters on screen.

Tip: (When upgrading from 4.2.) New options have been added to change the look of the Typing screen.

Typing on the Reveal Codes Screen

Trap: The two windows on the Reveal Codes screen don't move in synch as you type.

Tip: The Reveal Codes screen gives a clear view of which codes dominate which portions of the text.

Tip: Some codes offer much information and are quite detailed.

Trap: When you reveal codes, you may find your document crowded.

Tip: Rely on the Reveal Codes screen if the cursor or your text is acting inconsistently.

Tip: (When upgrading from 4.2.) You can now type your documents on the Reveal Codes screen.

Tips and Traps Summary (*continued*)

Duplicating a Character

Trap: Don't press ESC to cancel a command.

Tip: You can change the repeat value's initial setting.

Tip: (When upgrading from 4.2.) The Repeat Value feature operates basically the same in version 5.

Inserting Document Comments

Trap: Don't rely on the visual representation of your text on screen if document comments are interspersed in your text.

Trap: The only text enhancements that can be included in a document comment are underline and boldface.

Tip: To erase a comment already created, you must erase its hidden code.

Tip: Document comments can be edited.

Tip: An option allows you to hide the screen display of all comments.

Tip: You can change a comment to text and vice versa.

Tip: If you wish to print a document comment, you can also bypass WordPerfect with the PRINT SCREEN key.

Tip: (When upgrading from 4.2.) The Document Comment feature now contains more options.

4

Moving the Cursor, Searching, and Blocking Text

Once you've typed some text, you will move the cursor constantly as you reread, rewrite, or edit what you've typed. This chapter describes how to move the cursor quickly between lines, between screens, and between pages. The cursor movement choices are so numerous that you may decide to focus on a limited number.

This chapter also presents two unique ways to maneuver through a document. The Search command is popular among experienced word processors because it quickly moves the cursor to a word or phrase you specify. The Block command marks a section of text—whether it is 3 words, 2 lines, 1 sentence, or 18 paragraphs—as you move the cursor, and designates that portion of text for special treatment. It is a prominent and frequently used command in WordPerfect, and in this chapter you'll learn the various methods for blocking text like an expert.

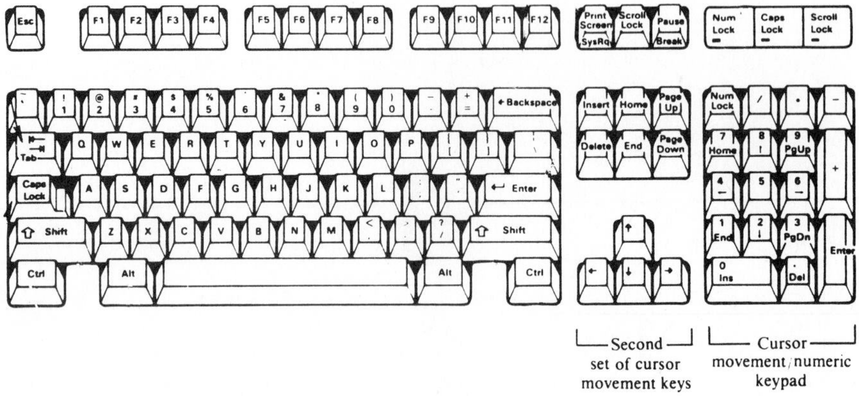

Figure 4-1. Cursor movement keys on the IBM enhanced keyboard

Traveling Between Characters, Words, and Lines

Depending on the computer keyboard you use, you have access to either one or two keypads that enable you to move the cursor. The basic keyboard styles are the standard and the enhanced. On the standard keyboard, there is one cursor movement keypad, which also serves as a numeric keypad. (Chapter 3 describes how the NUM LOCK key controls whether that keypad is used for cursor movement or for entering numbers.) On the enhanced keyboard (Figure 4-1), there are two sets of cursor movement keypads—one just like on the standard keyboard and another set that has no other function but to move the cursor. Enhanced keyboard users therefore have access to both a numeric keypad and a cursor movement keypad at the same time, without having to continually press NUM LOCK to switch back and forth. If you use the enhanced keyboard, you can use either of your cursor movement keypads, since both perform identically (when NUM LOCK is off).

The directional arrow keys on the cursor movement keypad—the LEFT, RIGHT, UP, and DOWN ARROW keys—are used to move the cursor short distances. They also can be used in combination with other keys to move more quickly between characters, words, and lines. These keys work the same whether you're on the Typing screen or the Reveal Codes screen.

- To move *character by character* to the left or right, press the LEFT ARROW or the RIGHT ARROW key.
- To move *word by word* to the left or right, press the appropriate arrow key in combination with the CTRL key. CTRL + LEFT ARROW moves the cursor one word to the left, while CTRL + RIGHT ARROW moves the cursor one word to the right.
- To move *line by line* up or down, press the UP ARROW or the DOWN ARROW key.
- To move to the *left or right end of the line,* press the appropriate arrow key in combination with the HOME key. HOME, HOME, LEFT ARROW moves the cursor to the left end, while HOME, HOME, RIGHT ARROW moves the cursor to the right end of the line. Or, to save keystrokes, press the END key to perform the same operation as performed by HOME, HOME, RIGHT ARROW.

  Note: If the lengths of the lines of your document are narrower than the screen, you can press HOME once rather than twice. See the next section, "Traveling Between Screens," for details.

Table 4-1 summarizes movement between characters, words, and lines. For easy reference, these cursor movements are also summarized on the command card at the back of this book.

Trap: *Don't press the SPACEBAR to move through already existing text.*

If you're used to typing on a typewriter, you're in the habit of pressing the SPACEBAR to move through text. This is a habit you must break, because with a computer, each time you press the SPACEBAR, a space is inserted. That space occupies a position just like any letter or number. Therefore, use the cursor movement

Table 4-1. Cursor Movement Between Characters, Words, and Lines

Key Combination	**Cursor Movement**
LEFT ARROW	One character to the left
RIGHT ARROW	One character to the right
UP ARROW	One line up
DOWN ARROW	One line down
CTRL + LEFT ARROW	One word to the left
CTRL + RIGHT ARROW	One word to the right
HOME, HOME, LEFT ARROW	Left end of line
HOME, HOME, HOME, LEFT ARROW	Left end of line before any codes
END or HOME, HOME, RIGHT ARROW	Right end of line
ESC, #, LEFT ARROW	Specific number of characters to the left
ESC, #, RIGHT ARROW	Specific number of characters to the right
ESC, #, UP ARROW	Up a specific number of lines
ESC, #, DOWN ARROW	Down a specific number of lines
ESC, #, CTRL + LEFT ARROW	Specific number of words to the left
ESC, #, CTRL + RIGHT ARROW	Specific number of words to the right

keys—not the SPACEBAR—to move across a line already occupied by text (unless you want to insert spaces).

Tip: *Take advantage of word wrap when moving the cursor.*

If your cursor is at the *end* of one line and you wish to move it to the *beginning* of the next, just press RIGHT ARROW. WordPerfect will wrap the cursor to exactly where you wish, just like it wraps words as you type. This feature works in reverse as well. If your cursor is at the beginning of one line but you wish to move to the end of the previous line, just press LEFT ARROW.

Trap: *The cursor moves through existing text and codes only.*

The farthest character that you type from the top of a document determines the document's end—the cursor cannot move beyond that. For instance, suppose you have typed as far as line 21 in a document. If no text or codes are located below line 21, then pressing DOWN ARROW will not move the cursor down any farther. You can press ENTER to insert a hard return, which extends the length of the document. Or, you can continue to type text on line 21 until the cursor wraps down to the next line. Now the document ends at line 22 and the cursor can be moved with the cursor movement keys down to and within line 22.

Trap: *Sometimes pressing a cursor movement key can insert a number in the text instead of moving the cursor.*

In Chapter 3 you learned about the NUM LOCK key, which turns the right side of the keyboard into a ten-key numeric keypad. If you press a cursor movement key and find that a number appears instead, you're undoubtedly working on the numeric keypad. Simply press NUM LOCK to switch back to the cursor movement keypad. (Generally, you can tell whether the numeric keypad is active by checking the status line. When it is active, the position indicator **Pos** blinks on the screen.) If you are using an enhanced keyboard, you can press keys on the other cursor movement keypad.

Tip: *Press HOME an extra time to move to the beginning of a line before any codes.*

You now know that HOME, HOME, LEFT ARROW moves the cursor to the left end of a line of text. However, when certain codes are located at the left margin (such as a tab set code), the cursor stops just to the right of the codes. If you wish to move the cursor to the left end of a line of text *and* all codes, then press HOME one extra time—that is, press HOME, HOME, HOME, LEFT ARROW. This is a quick way to properly position the cursor in front of codes that you may wish to delete, move, or copy.

Tip: *The directional arrow keys have an autorepeat feature.*

Just as with character keys, when you press a directional arrow key and keep holding it down, the key repeats until you release it. Continuing to press down on a key is a much faster way to move 20 spaces or lines than pressing a key 20 times.

Tip: *The speed with which your cursor moves can be changed.*

WordPerfect offers the ability to control the speed of your cursor on the screen and the speed of the autorepeat feature. The rate can vary from 10 characters per second (cps) to 50 cps. You also can set the speed to normal and then use a utility such as Repeat Performance or kbfix to control speed. (See Appendix B for information on the SETUP key, which houses the Cursor Speed feature.)

Tip: *You can press ESC to move the cursor a specific number of times.*

In Chapter 3 you learned about the Repeat Value feature, which enables the ESC key to insert a character across the screen a specific number of times. The ESC key works with the directional arrow keys as well. To move five spaces to the right, for example, press ESC, 5, RIGHT ARROW. To move 15 words to the right, press ESC, 15, CTRL + RIGHT ARROW. To move eight lines down, press ESC, 8, DOWN ARROW.

Trap: *There are times when pressing a directional arrow key mid-document appears to do nothing on the Typing screen.*

On the Typing screen, codes are hidden from view, concealed behind text characters. At times you may press the RIGHT ARROW or the LEFT ARROW key while viewing the Typing screen and find that the cursor remains in the same spot. Actually, the cursor has moved to the opposite side of a concealed code. This is quite subtle, but if you move the cursor around codes when on the Reveal Codes screen, you'll be able to see the cursor actually maneuvering around codes.

Trap: *The two windows move in different ways on the Reveal Codes screen.*

On the Reveal Codes screen, the top and bottom windows operate differently as you move the cursor. In the bottom window, where codes are displayed, the cursor *always* remains on the third line (except at the very top of a document). Thus, the window must shift up or down every time you press UP ARROW or DOWN ARROW. On the other hand, the cursor in the top window has no such restriction and can appear on any line. The window scrolls up and down less frequently. (See Chapter 3 for background on the Reveal Codes screen.)

As a result of the different ways the windows function, you'll often find that you're viewing different lines of text in the two windows. For instance, if the cursor is on line 12, you may be viewing lines 3 through 13 in the top window, and lines 10 through 20 in the bottom window. This takes some getting used to.

Tip: *(When upgrading from 4.2.) In version 5, cursor movement between words and lines has not changed.*

You can move the cursor in version 5 just as you did in version 4.2. On the Reveal Codes screen, however, you will need to become accustomed to the fact that the cursor in the bottom window always stays on line 3, while in the top window it can appear on any line. (In version 4.2, the cursor in both windows remained on line 4, so that the windows moved at the same time.)

An addition to version 5 is the Cursor Speed feature; you now have the ability to move about a document much faster than you could in version 4.2.

Traveling Between Screens

The standard-size computer monitor shows just 24 lines of text on the Typing screen (and 11 lines on the Reveal Codes screen) at any one time. Therefore, unless you have a full-page monitor, you must move through approximately 2 1/2 screens to read a full page of single-spaced text on the Typing screen. WordPerfect makes it easy to move quickly within and between screens.

- To move to the *top line* of the current screen, press HOME, UP ARROW. If the cursor is already at the top of the screen, press HOME, UP ARROW to move your cursor up one full screen (which equals 24 lines on the Typing screen or 11 lines on the Reveal Codes screen).

- To move to the *bottom line* of the current screen, press HOME, DOWN ARROW. If the cursor is already at the bottom of the screen, the cursor will move down one full screen (which equals 24 lines on the Typing screen or 11 lines on the Reveal Codes screen).
- To move to the *right or left edge* of the current screen, press HOME, RIGHT ARROW or HOME, LEFT ARROW.

Table 4-2 summarizes the methods for moving the cursor between screens. For easy reference, these cursor movements are also summarized on the command card at the back of this book.

Tip: *The PLUS and MINUS keys on the numeric keypad are useful shortcuts.*

The MINUS (−) key, situated on the far right side of the IBM keyboard, performs the same function as HOME, UP ARROW. The PLUS key (+), which is just below the MINUS key, performs the same function as HOME, DOWN ARROW. These keys thus save a keystroke when you move to the top or bottom of a screen.

The MINUS and PLUS keys also can be used in combination with the Repeat Value feature (ESC key). You can use them to move up or down a specific number of

Table 4-2. Cursor Movement Between Screens

Key Combination	**Cursor Movement**
HOME, UP ARROW or MINUS (numeric keypad)	Top of screen
HOME, DOWN ARROW or PLUS (numeric keypad)	Bottom of screen
HOME, LEFT ARROW	Left end of screen
HOME, RIGHT ARROW	Right end of screen
ESC, #, MINUS (numeric keypad)	Specific number of screens up
ESC, #, PLUS (numeric keypad)	Specific number of screens down

screens. For example, move up three screens by pressing ESC, 3, MINUS. The ESC key is described in more detail in Chapter 3. (HOME, UP ARROW and HOME, DOWN ARROW do not work in conjunction with the Repeat Value feature.)

Tip: *Screen movement keys are extremely effective for reading through a document.*

A quick, easy way to peruse a document on screen is to read a screen, press HOME, DOWN ARROW (or the PLUS key), read the next screen, and so on.

Trap: *There are distinctions in cursor movement horizontally across a line depending on your line length.*

In this section you learned that HOME, LEFT ARROW moves the cursor to the left edge of the *screen*. You learned in the previous section of this chapter that HOME, HOME, LEFT ARROW moves the cursor to the left edge of the *line*. This is a subtle difference, but an important one if your line length is wider than what can be displayed on screen.

As discussed in Chapter 3, the number of characters that fit on a line depends on your paper size, left/right margins, and font selection. (In that way, WordPerfect displays on screen the number of characters that will actually be printed per line.) When paper size, margin, and font settings are such that a full line of text can be displayed across the computer screen, you can always press HOME, LEFT ARROW as a shortcut, rather than HOME, HOME, LEFT ARROW, to move to the left edge of the line.

However, suppose you alter your paper size, margins, or font so that there are 100 characters on a line. These are more characters than can be displayed across the screen at once. In this case, these cursor movement keystrokes produce different results. With the cursor at the right margin, HOME, HOME, LEFT ARROW shifts across the entire line so that the cursor is at the left margin. But HOME, LEFT ARROW moves the cursor only to the left edge of the current screen, which is not the same as the left end of the line. You would need to press HOME, LEFT ARROW once again to move to the left end of the line.

The same distinction applies when pressing HOME, HOME, RIGHT ARROW (or END) versus pressing HOME, RIGHT ARROW.

Tip: *(When upgrading from 4.2.) In version 5, cursor movement between screens has not changed.*

Move the cursor between screens in version 5 just as you did in version 4.2.

Traveling Between Pages

The computer monitor displays information screen by screen, but most users are oriented toward pages. WordPerfect provides the ability to advance page by page through a document, or to move to a specific page number.

- To move to the *top or bottom of the current page,* press the arrow keys in combination with the GOTO (CTRL + HOME) key. CTRL + HOME, UP ARROW moves the cursor to the top of the page on which the cursor is currently located, while CTRL + HOME, DOWN ARROW moves to the bottom of the page.
- To move to the *top of a specific page,* press CTRL + HOME, then the desired page number, and ENTER. For example, to relocate to page 2, press CTRL + HOME. A prompt appears on the status line at the lower left-hand corner of the screen:

  Go to

  Type 2 and press ENTER. The cursor moves to the very top of page 2.
- To move to the *top of the previous or following page,* press PGUP to move the cursor to the top of the prior page, or PGDN to move to the top of the next page.
- To move to the *beginning or end of the document,* press HOME, HOME, UP ARROW or HOME, HOME, DOWN ARROW.

Table 4-3 summarizes movement between pages. For easy reference, cursor movement between pages is also summarized on the command card at the back of this book.

Tip: *The ESC key works in combination with PGUP and PGDN.*

Table 4-3. Cursor Movement Between Pages

Key Combination	**Cursor Movement**
CTRL + HOME, UP ARROW	Top of current page
CTRL + HOME, DOWN ARROW	Bottom of current page
CTRL + HOME, #	Top of specific page number
PGUP	Top of previous page
PGDN	Top of next page
HOME, HOME, UP ARROW	Beginning of document
HOME, HOME, HOME, UP ARROW	Beginning of document before any codes
HOME, HOME, DOWN ARROW	End of document
ESC, #, PGUP	Up a specific number of pages
ESC, #, PGDN	Down a specific number of pages
CTRL + HOME, CTRL + HOME	Cursor position before last cursor movement command

The PGUP and PGDN keys can be used in combination with the Repeat Value feature (ESC key). You can thus move up or down a specific number of pages. To move down three pages, for example, press ESC, 3, PGDN.

Tip: *The GOTO key can quickly return the cursor to its previous location.*

It is not uncommon to press the wrong key by mistake—such as the PGDN key when you meant to press DOWN ARROW, or END when you wanted to press LEFT ARROW. You can return the cursor to its previous position by pressing the GOTO (CTRL + HOME) key twice in a row. Just hold down on the CTRL key and press HOME twice. This double GOTO sequence works after you press PGDN, PGUP, GOTO, or any of the screen movement keys.

Tip: *Press HOME an extra time to move to the beginning of a document before any codes.*

You now know that HOME, HOME, UP ARROW moves the cursor to the top of a text document. However, when certain codes are located at the top of the document, the cursor stops just to the right of the codes.

If instead you wish to move the cursor to the top of the document before text *and* all codes, then press HOME one extra time—that is, press HOME, HOME, HOME, UP ARROW. This is a quick way to properly position the cursor in front of codes that you wish to delete, move, or, copy.

Tip: *(When upgrading from 4.2.) In version 5, cursor movement between pages has not changed.*

Move the cursor in version 5 just as you did in version 4.2.

Searching for Character Strings

Moving the cursor is fast and easy if you know the line, screen, or page on which you would like to locate the cursor. But what if you don't know the precise line and page to which you want to move the cursor? For example, assume you want to find the portion of your 22-page document that describes a new branch office in Africa. Reading through each page to find it is time-consuming. Instead, you can ask WordPerfect to find the reference by using the Search feature.

You can search for any character string of 59 characters or fewer. You also can search forward or backward in the text. WordPerfect will stop just past the first occurrence of the desired search string. All you need to know to find the portion of the document on Africa, for example, is whether it precedes or follows the cursor's current position.

To look forward, press the →SEARCH (F2) key. To look backward, press the ←SEARCH (SHIFT + F2) key. Both are executed the same way, and you can work on either the Typing or Reveal Codes screen when you execute a search.

1. Press →SEARCH (F2) for a forward search and WordPerfect responds

   → Srch:

   or press ←SEARCH (SHIFT + F2) for a reverse search and WordPerfect responds

   ← Srch:

   Note: If you wish to change the direction of the search *after* WordPerfect prompts for a search string, press UP ARROW to search backward or DOWN ARROW to search forward from the cursor.

2. Type **Africa**. *Africa* is the character string to be searched for. For a forward search, the message now reads

   → Srch: Africa

3. Press either the →SEARCH (F2), ←SEARCH (SHIFT + F2), or the ESC key to execute the search in either direction.

If the search string is found, the cursor will stop just to the right of *Africa*. If the character string is not found, WordPerfect will display this message:

*** Not Found ***

Trap: *Don't press ENTER unless you wish to include the hard return in a search string.*

Keep in mind that in WordPerfect the SEARCH (F2) and ESC keys, *but not the ENTER key,* begin a search execution. What if you press ENTER? In a search, WordPerfect treats a hard return code as part of a character string.

For instance, suppose that in initiating a search, you type **Africa** and then press ENTER. You'll see the following:

→ Srch: Africa**[HRt]**

[HRt] is the hard return code. WordPerfect will find only the character string *Africa* followed by a hard return. If you press ENTER inadvertently, press BACKSPACE to erase the code before beginning the search.

Tip: *To move the cursor to the next occurrence of a specific character, you can also use the GOTO key.*

Although less powerful than the Search feature, the GOTO (CTRL + HOME) key is an alternative when you wish to move the cursor to a specific character. GOTO takes you to a *single* letter or punctuation mark within the next 2000 characters, but only in the forward direction. When used for punctuation marks, GOTO is quite convenient. Suppose, for example, that the cursor is at the top of a page and you wish to move to the end of the first sentence. Press GOTO (CTRL + HOME). WordPerfect responds with the prompt:

Go to

Type a period (**.**). The cursor relocates just to the right of the period.

The GOTO key also moves the cursor quickly between two paragraphs. Since a hard return ends paragraphs that you type, press GOTO and then press ENTER. The cursor quickly locates itself just past the next hard return—at the end of a paragraph.

Tip: *With the Search feature, make sure you're searching in the correct direction.*

If the Search command returns with the message * **Not Found** *, but you're sure that the character string exists in your text, then perhaps you searched in the wrong direction. After you type in a search string but before you initiate the search, always check the direction of the arrow in the WordPerfect search prompt. If you wish to search in the opposite direction, press UP ARROW or DOWN ARROW. Now initiate the search.

Another possibility for a * **Not Found** * message is that you typed the character string entirely in uppercase. If so, the next Tip should prove useful.

Tip: *The search is case-significant if you specify uppercase letters.*

Lowercase letters in the Search command match both lower- and uppercase letters in the document. But uppercase letters match only uppercase letters in the document. If you type **africa** at the search prompt, the cursor will stop at the first occurrence of "AFRICA", "Africa", or "africa". If you type **Africa**, the cursor will stop at either "AFRICA", or "Africa". If you type **AFRICA**, WordPerfect will find only "AFRICA". Therefore, you can type a search string in lowercase letters and be unconcerned about its case in the text.

Tip: *WordPerfect remembers the last string you searched for.*

If you've already executed a search and then begin a new search, WordPerfect suggests the previous string on the prompt line. This enables you to keep searching for the same string everywhere it occurs in the text without retyping it. For example, suppose you've already searched for the string "Africa". If you wish to find the next occurrence of the string, then simply press →SEARCH (or ←SEARCH) twice in a row.

When you wish to search for a new character string, simply press the →SEARCH (or ←SEARCH) key and, when WordPerfect suggests the old string, you have two options. If the new string is completely different, then start typing over the suggestion; WordPerfect will erase the previous string as you begin typing the new one. But, if the new string is similar to the old (perhaps you now wish to search for "African", for example), then use the cursor movement, and editing keys to edit the string. Now press →SEARCH or ESC to initiate the search for that new string.

Tip: *You can use the Search feature to create stop markers.*

Suppose you are typing a document in which three paragraphs, each on a different page, cannot be completed without information you don't yet have. You can write the rest of the document today and, in place of each of those three paragraphs, type an unusual character string—like **** or **ZZZ**—that would not otherwise appear in the text. You have thus inserted three temporary stop markers. When you obtain the needed information, you can rapidly locate the first stop marker with the Search feature. Erase the marker, write the paragraph, and then search for the next marker. This saves time, especially in long documents.

Trap: *Use spaces cautiously in a character string.*

You can use spaces preceding and following a search string to designate it as a separate word. For example, when searching for the string *car,* WordPerfect will also stop at *carpet* and *incarcerate* unless you surround the string with spaces.

Working with spaces in a character string can be tricky, however, because words at the beginning of paragraphs or at the end of sentences are not surrounded by spaces. When *Car* starts a paragraph, a hard return or a tab precedes it. When *car* ends a sentence, a period or other punctuation mark follows it. Therefore, inserting spaces in the string does not always guarantee that you will find all instances of that string.

Tip: *The Search feature can also seek out hidden codes.*

In the same way that you search for character strings containing text, you can also search for those strings that contain codes or a combination of text and codes. After you press the →SEARCH (F2) or ←SEARCH (SHIFT + F2) key, the keystrokes that typically insert a code into your document can now include that code in a character string.

For example, suppose you wish to position the cursor at the beginning of the next paragraph that is indented with a TAB. Press →SEARCH and then press the TAB key. WordPerfect displays the following on the prompt line:

→ Srch: [TAB]

Press →SEARCH again and the cursor will move to the right of the next tab code, just at the first character of the first word of that paragraph.

For a more complicated example, suppose you wish to move to the location of a date code (this feature, described in Chapter 8, can automatically insert today's date for you). It would be time-consuming to turn on the Reveal Codes screen and look through screen after screen for this code. As you'll see in Chapter 8, the keystrokes used to place a date code in the text are the DATE/OUTLINE (SHIFT + F5) key and to select option 2, Date Code. In the present example, however, you wish to search for the code, not insert it, in the document. To do so, you would

1. Press →SEARCH (F2). WordPerfect responds

   → Srch:

2. Press the DATE/OUTLINE (SHIFT + F5) key, since this is the key that was originally used to insert the date code. Now, WordPerfect responds with the following menu:

   1 Date Code; **2** Paragraph Number; **3** Paragraph Number Definition: **0**

   WordPerfect is providing the opportunity to indicate which of the three codes—which can be inserted when you use the DATE/OUTLINE key—you wish to hunt for.

3. Select Date Code (1 or C). Now, the search string reads

   → Srch: [Date]

4. Press either →SEARCH (F2) or ESC to execute the search. The cursor moves just to the right of the first **[Date]** code it reaches (or, if no **[Date]** code exists in the text, WordPerfect responds with * **Not Found** *). If you are viewing the Reveal Codes screen, you will see the code just to the left of the cursor.

You can always combine codes and characters in the same search string. For example, suppose you are looking for an occurrence of the phrase, "It is important," but only where that phrase is underlined. Press →SEARCH, and at the search prompt, press UNDERLINE (F8). Now type the phrase **It is important**. The search string appears as follows:

→ Srch: [UND]It is important

WordPerfect finds that phrase only if it is preceded by an underline code.

To insert the second code of a code pair in a search string, press the function key for that code twice. Then delete the first code in the pair. For instance, press UNDERLINE (F8) twice. The search string reads "[UND][und]". Now delete the [**UND**] code.

You can also search for soft returns, soft pages, or special control characters. When WordPerfect prompts for the search string, press HOME, ENTER to insert

[ISRt] as part of the search string. To insert other special codes in the search screen, press CTRL + V. The following appears in place of the search prompt:

key =

Press CTRL + K to insert **[SPg]** in the search string; or press CTRL + M to search for an **[SRt]** code. Press CTRL + another letter to insert a special control character. (Sometimes when you convert files from other programs to WordPerfect, a procedure described in Chapter 28, codes such as ^H are inserted. You can use the Search feature to move to those errant codes.)

In addition, you can search for a special character by pressing COMPOSE (CTRL + 2) and entering the corresponding WordPerfect character number. (For more on special characters and the Compose feature, refer to Chapter 17.)

Tip: *WordPerfect can be set to sound a beep each time your search string is not found.*

By selecting item 5, Initial Settings, in the Setup menu, you can turn on or turn off the sound of a beep if a search string is not found. (It is initially set to "off." See Appendix B for further details.)

Tip: *You can return the cursor to its previous location after a search.*

Once a search is complete, you can return to the previous cursor position—the position before you began the search—by pressing GOTO, GOTO. Suppose, for example, that the cursor is on page 6 of a document and you perform a search. When the search is complete, you can bring the cursor back to its original position on page 6 by pressing GOTO, GOTO (CTRL + HOME, CTRL + HOME).

Tip: *You can use wild card characters in search strings.*

A wild card is available that can be substituted for any character or for a space. The wild card key combination is CTRL + V, CTRL + X.

Suppose you wish to search for a reference to a client named Mr. Smith, whom you referred to in your document by first name only. But is his first name Dan or Don? When you enter the search string, (1) type **D**, (2) hold down CTRL and type **V** (you'll see a prompt that reads **Key** =), (3) hold down CTRL and type **X**, and (4) type **n**. The string reads

→ **Srch:** D^**X**n

Now WordPerfect will search for any three-character string starting with D and ending with n.

Two restrictions apply to the use of the wild card character: it cannot be the first character in the string, and it cannot substitute for a code.

Tip: *The HOME key can extend a search beyond the standard text.*

You can search for character strings not only in standard text, but also within headers, footers, footnotes, endnotes, graphics box captions, and graphics text boxes. To activate the Extended Search feature, press the HOME key before pressing →SEARCH (F2) or ←SEARCH (SHIFT + F2). If the cursor moves to a header, footer, footnote, endnote, or graphics box screen as a result of the search, then you can press EXIT (F7) to return to the standard Typing screen. Or you can continue the search by pressing HOME, →SEARCH or HOME, ←SEARCH again.

Tip: *A search can be restricted to just a portion of text.*

You can narrow down your search to a specific section of text. For example, suppose you wish to search for a character string within the first three pages of your document. First, designate that three-page section by using the Block feature, and then follow the same search procedures as for an entire document. The following section explains how to use the Block command.

Tip: *(When upgrading from 4.2.) In version 5, the Search feature has not changed.*

The Search feature operates basically the same in version 5 as it did in version 4.2 except that now, when WordPerfect prompts for a search string, you can press UP ARROW or DOWN ARROW to change the search direction.

Blocking a Section of Text

Blocking out a section of text is a useful step in performing various word processing tasks. By turning on the Block feature and then marking off text, you're able to isolate that text for special treatment. For example, you might want to mark three sentences for underlining. Or, you might want to specify four words to be centered. You also might want to mark a page and a half of your document for printing, or a paragraph for deletion.

In WordPerfect, such a section of text—whether one character or 700 characters—is referred to as a *block.* Three letters can equal a block; a sentence can be a block; two paragraphs together can equal a block; or a page and a half of text can be a block. The block can be comprised of only text, only codes, or a combination of both.

You specify a block by using the BLOCK (ALT + F4) key.

1. Position the cursor on the first character you want to include in the block of text.
2. Press the BLOCK (ALT + F4) key. WordPerfect responds by repeatedly flashing the following message in the lower left-hand corner of the screen:

   Block on

   Now you have turned on the Block feature.
3. Move the cursor (using any of the cursor movement key combinations) just past the last character to be included in the block. You must move one

```
Part of this paragraph has been marked as a block.  It was
highlighted by locating the cursor on the "P" in "Part", pressing
BLOCK (ALT + F4), and then moving the cursor to the space just past
the exclamation point!  This part of the paragraph was not included
in the block, and therefore is not highlighted in reverse video.



Block on                                  Doc 1 Pg 1 Ln 1.5" Pos 3.2"
```

Figure 4-2. Highlighting a block of text

character beyond the last character you want included in the block. WordPerfect responds by highlighting the block of text in reverse video, as shown in Figure 4-2.

4. Press a function key that corresponds to the task you wish to accomplish within that block. For instance, you can underline it by pressing the UNDERLINE (F8) key.

5. When the operation is complete, the Block feature is automatically turned off. The cursor will remain just past the last character in the recently defined block.

Numerous features work with the BLOCK key to provide great control over your text. You can delete, center, move, boldface, print, or save a block. You can include it in an index, check its spelling, or search through it. References to features that work in conjunction with the BLOCK key are made throughout this book.

Tip: *Many shortcuts can be used when defining a block.*

It is easy to define a block of text in just seconds because there are numerous options available for indicating the end (the last character) of a block. First, you can define a block backward as well as forward. Move the cursor one character past the last character wanted in the block, press the BLOCK key, and highlight text by using the UP ARROW and LEFT ARROW keys.

Other arrow keys and key combinations also work to highlight text. For example, you can block a full line of text by (1) positioning the cursor at the left margin, (2) pressing BLOCK, and (3) pressing HOME, RIGHT ARROW. Another quick way to define the boundaries of a line once you activate the Block feature is to press the DOWN ARROW key; this highlights every character up to the cursor.

However, you don't necessarily need to use the cursor movement keys to define the block's endpoint. You can mark a block up to and including a specific character by (1) positioning the cursor at the beginning of the block, (2) pressing BLOCK, and (3) pressing that single character. For example, start with the cursor on the first character of the block, press BLOCK, and then type **J** to define the block up to the first uppercase J. Or, type a period (**.**) to mark text to the end of a sentence. Or, press ENTER to mark to the end of a paragraph.

Finally, the Search command can aid you in marking a block of text. Suppose, for example, that you wish to define a block starting at the top of a document and up to and including the heading *Consumer Spending,* which is located mid-document. To do so, (1) move the cursor to the top of the document, (2) press BLOCK, (3) press →SEARCH, (4) type **Consumer Spending**, and (5) press →SEARCH or ESC to execute the search. WordPerfect highlights the text up to and including *Consumer Spending.* Your task is complete.

Trap: *Don't press the BLOCK key until the cursor is on the first character in the block (or one place past the last character in the block).*

WordPerfect assumes that when you press BLOCK, the cursor is on the first or one past the last character in that block. If not, you must press CANCEL (F1) or press BLOCK (ALT + F4) a second time to abort the Block command. Now reposition the cursor, and begin again.

Tip: *Highlight a block on the Reveal Codes screen if the section of text is surrounded by or includes codes.*

The Block feature works on both the Typing screen and the Reveal Codes screen. If codes are in the vicinity of the text that you are blocking, then it is advantageous to block on the Reveal Codes screen. When you activate Block on, WordPerfect places the temporary code **[Block]** at the current cursor position. On the Reveal Codes screen, this **[Block]** code, along with all other codes, is visible, so that you can see exactly which codes are being included in the section of text you are blocking.

There are times when it is appropriate to include codes in a block. For example, you may wish to move a table from one location to another, along with the **[Tab Set]** code preceding the table, which sets the proper tab stops. In this case, you will want to include the **[Tab Set]** code as part of the block.

Other times, it is appropriate to exclude codes from a block. For instance, you may wish to omit a **[Margin Set]** code that precedes a paragraph when you block off that paragraph for deletion, so that the margins remain in effect after the paragraph is deleted. If you use the Block feature on the Reveal Codes screen, there's no guesswork; you know which codes are being included or excluded from the block.

Tip: *You can quickly mark a block twice in a row.*

Assume that you have marked a block of text by underlining it. Now you wish to designate the same block for boldfacing. Marking it the second time is very easy: (1) press BLOCK (ALT + F4), and (2) press GOTO, GOTO (CTRL + HOME, CTRL + HOME). WordPerfect will highlight the same block again, so that you can perform another task on that block of text.

Tip: *You can position the cursor at the beginning of the most recently defined block.*

Once the Block feature is turned off, the cursor is relocated just past the end of the block. You can then press GOTO, BLOCK (CTRL + HOME, ALT + F4) to position the cursor at the beginning of the most recently defined block. Thus, GOTO, BLOCK is especially useful when you have just defined a block, the Block feature is off, and you want to move the cursor back up to the first character of the block.

Trap: *When **Block on** is flashing, certain commands will not execute while others will operate differently.*

Certain function keys, such as EXIT (F7), are inoperative when the Block feature has been turned on. Other function keys work differently with Block on than with Block off. For example, if you press SWITCH (SHIFT + F3) with Block off, the cursor switches to a second document in the computer's memory (as described in Chapter 12). If you press SWITCH with Block on, the following message appears:

1 Uppercase; 2 Lowercase: **0**

This provides the opportunity to switch the case of letters within the designated block. If you don't first turn on Block and mark off a section of text, this feature is unavailable. As discussed in various chapters, other keys that display different menu items with Block on than with Block off include FONT, FORMAT, MARK TEXT, PRINT, MOVE, and TEXT IN/OUT.

Tip: *(When upgrading from 4.2.) In version 5, the Block feature turns off when a task is complete.*

In version 4.2, you had to remember to turn off Block after performing tasks like switching between upper- and lowercase letters or appending a block of text to another document. This is no longer the case; Block is always turned off by WordPerfect 5 after a task is executed.

Another change in version 5 enables you to complete a block function on the Reveal Codes screen, in addition to the Typing screen.

Tips and Traps Summary

Traveling Between Characters, Words, and Lines

Trap: Don't press the SPACEBAR to move through already existing text.

Tip: Take advantage of word wrap when moving the cursor.

Trap: The cursor moves through existing text and codes only.

Trap: Sometimes pressing a cursor movement key can insert a number in the text instead of moving the cursor.

Tip: Press HOME an extra time to move to the beginning of a line before any codes.

Tip: The directional arrow keys have an autorepeat feature.

Tip: The speed with which your cursor moves can be changed.

Tip: You can press ESC to move the cursor a specific number of times.

Trap: There are times when pressing a directional arrow key mid-document appears to do nothing on the Typing screen.

Trap: The two windows move in different ways on the Reveal Codes screen.

Tip: (When upgrading from 4.2.) In version 5, cursor movement between words and lines has not changed.

Traveling Between Screens

Tip: The PLUS and MINUS keys on the numeric keypad are useful shortcuts.

Tip: Screen movement keys are extremely effective for reading through a document.

Tips and Traps Summary (*continued*)

Trap: There are distinctions in cursor movement horizontally across a line depending on your line length.

Tip: (When upgrading from 4.2.) In version 5, cursor movement between screens has not changed.

Traveling Between Pages

Tip: The ESC key works in combination with PGUP and PGDN.

Tip: The GOTO key can quickly return the cursor to its previous location.

Tip: Press HOME an extra time to move to the beginning of a document before any codes.

Tip: (When upgrading from 4.2.) In version 5, cursor movement between pages has not changed.

Searching for Character Strings

Trap: Don't press ENTER unless you wish to include the hard return in a search string.

Tip: To move the cursor to the next occurrence of a specific character, you can also use the GOTO key.

Tip: With the Search feature, make sure you're searching in the correct direction.

Tip: The search is case-significant if you specify uppercase letters.

Tip: WordPerfect remembers the last string you searched for.

Tip: You can use the Search feature to create stop markers.

Trap: Use spaces cautiously in a character string.

Tip: The Search feature can also seek out hidden codes.

Tip: WordPerfect can be set to sound a beep each time your search string is not found.

Tips and Traps Summary (*continued*)

Tip: You can return the cursor to its previous location after a search.

Tip: You can use wild card characters in search strings.

Tip: The HOME key can extend a search beyond the standard text.

Tip: A search can be restricted to just a portion of text.

Tip: (When upgrading from 4.2.) In version 5, the Search feature has not changed.

Blocking a Section of Text

Tip: Many shortcuts can be used when defining a block.

Trap: Don't press the BLOCK key until the cursor is on the first character in the block (or one place past the last character in the block).

Tip: Highlight a block on the Reveal Codes screen if the section of text is surrounded by or includes codes.

Tip: You can quickly mark a block twice in a row.

Tip: You can position the cursor at the beginning of the most recently defined block.

Trap: When **Block on** is flashing, certain commands will not execute while others will operate differently.

Tip: (When upgrading from 4.2.) In version 5, the Block feature turns off when a task is complete.

5

Editing Text and Codes

One major advantage of a word processor over a typewriter is that as you type the computer stores characters electronically rather than as marks on paper. Revisions both large and small can be made right on the screen, without having to retype the entire document. As you edit, WordPerfect automatically readjusts the remaining text to fit properly on the page.

This chapter describes the techniques for inserting and deleting characters in your document—whether you wish to edit just one character or twenty pages of text. You also are shown how to restore text with the marvelous Undelete command, and how to mark editing changes with redline and strikeout, techniques commonly used in legal offices or by writers and editors who need to keep track of editing changes as a document is revised.

Inserting Text

You can insert characters and edit your text while working on either the Typing screen or the Reveal Codes screen. WordPerfect is defaulted to what is called Insert mode, which means that you can add characters or codes of any length anywhere in the document without destroying already existing text; existing text merely shifts over and reformats within the current margin, tab, and other settings to accommodate the insertion. Just locate the cursor where you want the new text to appear and start typing. (When you wish to insert text just before an already existing code, on the Reveal Codes screen, place the cursor on the existing code. WordPerfect will insert to the left of the code the characters you type.)

For instance, suppose you want to insert the word "Wednesday" and a comma before the word "February" in the following sentence:

I met with Ms. Wood on February 4th.

To insert the change, (1) place the cursor on the F (as indicated), (2) type **Wednesday**, and (3) press the SPACEBAR to insert a space between the two words. The text now reads

I met with Ms. Wood on Wednesday, February 4th.

Or suppose you want to insert the item "cherries" before "bananas" in the following list:

apples
pineapples_
bananas

To make the insertion, (1) position the cursor just to the right of the "s" in "pineapples" (as indicated), (2) press ENTER to insert a **[HRt]** code and thus a blank line, and (3) type **cherries**. The text now reads

apples
pineapples
cherries
bananas

Although WordPerfect is initially set for Insert mode, at times it may be faster to edit text by replacing rather than inserting characters. An option that allows you to replace characters is available if you switch from Insert mode to what is referred to as Typeover mode. Press the INS key (sometimes marked as INSERT) on your cursor movement keypad to turn on Typeover. (Refer to Figure 3-2 in Chapter 3 if you need to locate the cursor movement keypad on your keyboard.) The following message appears on the left edge of the status line:

Typeover

Now position the cursor where you wish to type over the existing text and begin typing. The new characters you type will replace the existing characters. Press INS a second time to turn off Typeover; you are returned to Insert mode, and the Typeover message disappers from the status line.

Typeover performs two duties at once: it inserts a new character and simultaneously deletes the character it is replacing. Likely candidates for Typeover are words or numbers in which you transpose characters. For example, assume you typed "srtehtc," when you really meant to type "stretch". Correct the error quickly: (1) press the LEFT ARROW key to move the cursor under the "s" in "srtehtc," (2) press INS to switch into Typeover mode, and (3) type **stretch**. You then can remain in Typeover mode or you can press INS a second time to switch back to Insert mode.

Trap: *Sometimes you must move the cursor before text is readjusted.*

When you use the Insert mode to insert numerous words or sentences, occasionally you might find that the existing text seems to disappear at the right margin. If this happens, just keep on typing, and then press a cursor movement key, such as the DOWN ARROW key. This reformats the text so that the words reappear and the entire text is adjusted properly to fit within the current margins.

Tip: *If you prefer, you can inhibit WordPerfect from automatically reformatting your document as you edit.*

WordPerfect is set up so that text is readjusted on screen as you edit. Changes are made immediately, or as soon as you press the DOWN ARROW key (see the previous Trap). However, you can request that WordPerfect stop automatic reformatting of text, a feature that is most useful if you frequently work with newspaper or parallel columns (using columns is discussed in Chapter 19). You turn off the Automatic Reformat and Rewrite feature by using the Display option on the SETUP key (refer to Appendix B for further information). Once rewrite is set to "off," you direct WordPerfect to reformat the screen by pressing the SCREEN (CTRL + F3) key and selecting Rewrite (0 or R), or by moving the cursor, for instance, by continuing to press DOWN ARROW down to the bottom of the screen.

Trap: *The TAB and BACKSPACE keys work differently in Typeover mode than in Insert mode.*

In Insert mode, pressing the TAB key inserts a tab code. In Typeover mode, the TAB key moves the cursor to the next tab stop without inserting a tab (unless the cursor is at the end of a line). And if you press SHIFT + TAB, the cursor moves back to the previous tab stop. Further, the BACKSPACE key in the Insert mode erases the character to the left of the cursor. In Typeover mode, BACKSPACE moves the cursor one character to the left and replaces that character with a space.

Trap: *You can't overwrite codes in Typeover mode.*

Be aware that WordPerfect won't overwrite codes, even in Typeover mode. If you switch to Typeover and come across a code while typing, the code will shift to the right and you will begin inserting text, just as when you're in Insert mode. For example, when the cursor meets a hard return, that hard return, along with the words that follow it will not be typed over.

Tip: *The SWITCH key can reverse upper- and lowercase letters faster than Typeover mode can.*

Have you ever typed a title in lowercase letters and then decided that it should be all uppercase? Or perhaps you've glanced up at your screen after typing a page only to discover that CAPS LOCK was on so that all your words are in uppercase instead of lowercase? You could switch to Typeover mode, put your cursor back to the beginning of the text, and retype. But a time-saving alternative is to use the SWITCH key. The SWITCH key enables you to switch the case of a block of text. To do so:

1. Mark the text that you wish to convert to uppercase or lowercase by using the BLOCK (ALT + F4) key. (If you need a refresher on the Block feature, review the discussion in Chapter 4.)

2. Press SWITCH (SHIFT + F3). The following menu appears:

   1 Uppercase; **2** Lowercase: **0**

3. Select Uppercase (1 or U), or select Lowercase (2 or L). WordPerfect will reverse the case accordingly and automatically turn off the Block feature.

When switching to lowercase, WordPerfect leaves the beginning of a sentence capitalized if you include the punctuation mark from the preceding sentence in the block. For instance, block a sentence like this:

```
I will work on the charts on Saturday.  THEREFORE, I WILL
HAVE THE REPORT ON YOUR DESK BY MONDAY MORNING.
```

When you switch to lowercase, you'll get this:

```
I will work on the charts on Saturday.  Therefore, I will
have the report on your desk by monday morning.
```

Then, as a slight adjustment, you can position the cursor in the "m" in "monday" and change it to read "Monday".

Make sure that you turn on the Block feature before pressing the SWITCH key; otherwise, you'll switch to a second Typing screen (a feature described in Chapter 12) instead of switching between upper- and lowercase.

Tip: *You can insert the entire text of a file stored on disk into the document currently on screen.*

Suppose that you wish to insert into your document a set of boilerplate paragraphs that are housed in a file on disk. Position the cursor where you wish to insert those paragraphs, press the RETRIEVE (SHIFT + F10) key, type in the name of the file containing the paragraphs, and press ENTER. The paragraphs will be brought into the document on screen. (Refer to Chapter 12 for more on combining the text of two or more documents.)

Tip: *WordPerfect can be forced into either Insert or Typeover mode.*

You can require that WordPerfect change to either Typeover or Insert mode regardless of the current setting. The keystrokes for Forced Typeover mode are HOME, INSERT. The keystrokes for Forced Insert mode are HOME, HOME, INSERT. The ability to force Typeover or Insert is most important when defining a macro, which is described in Chapter 27.

Tip: *(When upgrading from 4.2.) In version 5, you can now insert as well as delete text in Reveal Codes.*

The major change in the editing functions in version 5 as compared with 4.2 is that you can now insert characters—both text and codes—while on the Reveal Codes screen. Previously, you could only delete characters or move the cursor on the Reveal Codes screen; if you pressed a letter, a number, or most of the function keys, WordPerfect would revert to the Typing screen.

There are slight differences, as well, in version 5. One is that when you use the SWITCH key to change text between uppercase and lowercase, the Block feature is automatically turned off after the case conversion is complete. The other difference is the new Forced Typeover/Insert feature, which is described in a previous tip.

Deleting Characters and Words

You have various options for erasing text and/or codes from your document. You can erase on either the Typing screen or the Reveal Codes screen. However, when you wish to erase codes, it is advisable (especially for beginning users) to switch to the Reveal Codes screen, where codes are no longer hidden. This way, you'll be able to determine a code's exact location without guesswork.

If you wish to delete a single character, the position of the cursor determines which key you press.

- Press BACKSPACE (sometimes marked on the keyboard as a long arrow pointing to the left) to erase a character or code when the cursor is just *to the right of a character* you wish to erase. For example, if the cursor is positioned like this:

nicer_

then press BACKSPACE to erase the "r". (Backspace is useful when you wish to erase a character you just typed.)

- Press DEL (sometimes marked on the keyboard as DELETE) on the cursor movement keypad to erase a character when the cursor is located *on that character.* For example, if the cursor is positioned like this:

  nicer

  then press DEL to erase the "r". (DEL is useful when you wish to make corrections to the text during later editing.)

WordPerfect recognizes as a word any group of characters (including periods, exclamation points, or other punctuation marks) bordered by spaces. This distinction allows you to delete words and parts of words quickly and easily (without deleting any codes that may be present):

- Press CTRL + BACKSPACE to erase *a whole word,* including the space (or spaces) following the word. Your cursor must be on any character in the word or on the space just to the right of the word. For example, if the cursor is on the "a" in "larger", press CTRL + BACKSPACE to delete the entire word.
- Press HOME, BACKSPACE to erase *characters to the left of the cursor* up to the space preceding the word. For example, if the cursor is on the "c" in "incomplete," press HOME, BACKSPACE to erase "in". Now the word becomes "complete".
- Press HOME, DEL to erase the *characters to the right of the cursor,* including the character at the cursor and the space or spaces following the word. For example, if the cursor is on the first "e" in "whatever" press HOME, DEL to delete "ever".

***Tip:** The deletion keys have an autorepeat feature.*

In Chapter 3 you learned how to type a character numerous times simply by holding that key down. The same applies when deleting characters. For instance, erase a group of characters to the left of the cursor by pressing and holding down BACKSPACE, or a group of characters to the right of the cursor by pressing and holding down DEL. Or, you can erase a number of words to the right of the cursor by pressing and holding down CTRL + BACKSPACE.

Tip: *You can combine most deletion keys with ESC for power deleting.*

In Chapter 3 you learned about the ESC key and the Repeat Value feature, which duplicates a key a specific number of times. The same applies when you wish to repeat certain deletion keys. Combine ESC with DEL to erase a specific number of letters, or combine ESC with CTRL + BACKSPACE to erase a specific number of words. To erase ten words, for example, (1) position the cursor on the first word to the left that you wish to erase, (2) press ESC, (3) type **10**, and (4) press CTRL + BACKSPACE.

Tip: *Use BACKSPACE or DEL to delete a blank line.*

If you want to erase a blank line, you must delete the hard return code, **[HRt]**, that occupies the line. You can move the cursor to the blank line and press DEL. Or, move the cursor to the following line's left margin and press BACKSPACE.

For example, assume you want to bring the following sentences closer together.

You might be interested in a phone call I received today.

Mr. Jonas called about the property on Main Street.

Position the cursor at the left margin on the second sentence, as shown. Press BACKSPACE. This deletes a hard return and thus the sentence moves up one line. Press BACKSPACE a second time to move the sentence higher still.

Note: If you're editing on the Reveal Codes screen, you can view the **[HRt]** codes as you erase them.

***Tip:** As you press* DEL *or* BACKSPACE *on the Typing screen, a prompt might appear on the status line as you are about to erase hidden codes.*

As you're editing on the Reveal Codes screen, you can erase a code just like you can erase any other character. That is, press DEL to erase the code that the cursor is on, and press BACKSPACE to erase the code to the left of the cursor.

As you're editing on the Typing screen, common codes, such as **[HRt]** and **[TAB]** can be erased in the same manner.

Because codes are hidden on the Typing screen, WordPerfect requires confirmation when you are about to erase the less frequently found codes. This prevents the inadvertent erasure of one of those codes. For example, if the code to the left of the cursor is a Right Justification Off code and you press BACKSPACE, a prompt will appear which reads

Delete [Just Off]? (Y/N) No

Type **Y** to delete the code. Press any other key (such as N, ENTER, or BACKSPACE) and the code remains.

***Tip:** With code pairs, you need only delete one of the matched set.*

As described in Chapter 3, certain codes travel in pairs to mark the beginning and end of the text that they affect. For instance, an underlined word will appear as follows on the Reveal Codes screen:

[UND]word**[und]**

If you wish to delete the pair of codes (and thus delete the underlining for that word), you can erase just *one* of the pair; the other will disappear immediately (or as soon as you move the cursor to update the screen).

***Trap:** Don't try to delete soft codes.*

[SRt] and **[SPg]** are two codes that WordPerfect automatically inserts to wrap words to a new line or a new page. Don't attempt to erase either the soft return or the soft page code; if you try, you'll most likely erase a space or another character instead.

Tip: *(When upgrading from version 4.2.) In version 5, you erase characters and words as before.*

Erase characters and words in version 5 just as you did in version 4.2. Only now, because the cursor on the Reveal Codes screen highlights an entire code, deleting with the DEL key is more apparent than before.

Deleting Large Amounts of Text

It is time-consuming to delete a chunk of text by pressing DEL or BACKSPACE, but not so if you take advantage of the Block feature. The steps for a block delete are as follows:

1. Position the cursor and use the BLOCK (ALT + F4) key to highlight the text to be deleted. (The Block feature is described in Chapter 4.)
2. Press BACKSPACE or DEL. WordPerfect prompts

   Delete Block? (Y/N) No

   so you can verify your decision.
3. Press Y to delete the marked block. Press N or ENTER, or any key other than Y, to abort the command and leave the text intact. (If you choose not to delete the block, then Block remains on, so press CANCEL (F1) or again press BLOCK (ALT + F4) to turn Block off.)

Table 5-1 summarizes the various deletion options in WordPerfect. For easy reference, this summary is also included on the command card at the back of this book.

Table 5-1. Options for Deleting Text

Key Combination	**Text Deleted from Screen**
BACKSPACE	Character left of the cursor position
DEL	Character at the cursor
ESC, #, DEL	Specified number of characters at and to the right of the cursor
CTRL + BACKSPACE	Word at the cursor
ESC, #, CTRL + BACKSPACE	Specified number of words at and to the right of the cursor
HOME, BACKSPACE	Characters left of the cursor to the word boundary
HOME, DEL	Characters right of the cursor to the word boundary
CTRL + END	Characters right of the cursor to line end
ESC, #, CTRL + END	Specified number of lines at and below the cursor
CTRL + PGDN	Characters right of the cursor to page end
BLOCK (ALT + F4), DEL or BACKSPACE	Characters in a marked block
MOVE (CTRL + F4)	One entire sentence, paragraph, or page
EXIT (F7)	Entire document from screen
CANCEL (F1)	Restore a previous deletion

***Trap:** A code in a block marked for deletion will be deleted as well.*

Tabs, hard returns, and other codes can be erased like any character. Include a code in a block marked for deletion and the code will be deleted as well. The difficult part is knowing whether you've included codes in a block when editing on the Typing screen—after all, they are hidden from view. Thus you may wish to reveal codes before you mark a block for deletion; that way, you won't accidentally erase a code or a group of codes.

Tip: *To quickly erase text to the end of a line, use the DELETE EOL key.*

If the text you wish to erase is a line, you can use the DELETE EOL (End Of Line) key, which is the key combination CTRL + END. This deletes from the current cursor position to the end of the line. For example, to erase a whole line of text, start with the cursor at the left margin and press CTRL + END. The text is erased, but if the line ends with a **[HRt]** code, that code remains intact in the document.

DELETE EOL works in combination with the ESC key so you can delete a specific number of lines at once. This is useful for deleting a specific number of lines within a paragraph.

Tip: *To quickly erase text to the bottom of a page, use the DELETE EOP key.*

If the text you wish to erase is the bottom part of a page, you can use the DELETE EOP (End Of Page) key, which is the key combination CTRL + PGDN. This deletes from the current cursor position to the end of a page of text. You must verify your decision with a WordPerfect prompt.

For example, suppose you wish to erase the last three paragraphs on a page. Place the cursor at the beginning of the first of the three paragraphs. Press CTRL + PGDN. WordPerfect responds with:

Delete Remainder of Page? (Y/N) No

Type **Y** to delete the final three paragraphs on the page (that is, all the way to the dotted line that indicates a page end). Type **N** or any key other than Y, or press ENTER, to abort the deletion.

Tip: *Use a shortcut if you wish to erase a whole sentence, paragraph, or page of text.*

WordPerfect recognizes three common units of text: a sentence is text that ends with a period (.), a question mark (?), or an exclamation point (!), followed by a space; a paragraph is text that ends with a hard return code; a page is text that ends with a page-break code and the accompanying dotted line. If the text you wish to delete falls into one of these three categories, then you can bypass the Block function. WordPerfect can mark the text for you. The steps are

1. Position the cursor *anywhere* within the sentence, paragraph, or page you wish to delete.
2. Press the MOVE (CTRL + F4) key. WordPerfect responds with a menu.

   Move: 1 Sentence; **2** Paragraph; **3** Page; **4** Retrieve: **0**

3. Type the number (or mnemonic) key corresponding to the unit of text to be deleted. For instance, select 2 or P if you wish to delete a paragraph. WordPerfect responds with a second prompt:

   1 Move; **2** Copy; **3** Delete; **4** Append: **0**

4. Select Delete (3 or D). WordPerfect erases that unit of text. (Technically, you can also select Move (1 or M) and then press CANCEL to erase the following prompt.)

Trap: *Sometimes you must move the cursor before text will readjust after a deletion.*

If you delete a large block of text and the remaining words seem unaligned, simply press a cursor movement key, such as the DOWN ARROW. WordPerfect will readjust the text for you.

Tip: *WordPerfect provides the ability to delete a column or a rectangular portion of text.*

The Block command typically marks the first character to the last (this includes, of course, all characters in between), line by line. It also gives you the flexibility to isolate an individual column or rectangle as a block. The distinctions between the standard, column, and rectangle blocks are shown in Figure 5-1. Notice in the figure that by using the Column or Rectangle Block feature, you can isolate just a

STANDARD BLOCK
Entire table marked for deletion

Dpt.	Employee	Rank
333	Silver	GS-5
991	Stevens	GS-3
333	Underwood	GS-13
446	Cohen	GS-5
991	Tang	GS-12

COLUMN BLOCK
Second column marked for deletion

Dpt.	Employee	Rank
333	Silver	GS-5
991	Stevens	GS-3
333	Underwood	GS-13
446	Cohen	GS-5
991	Tang	GS-12

RECTANGLE BLOCK
Portion of table shaped like a rectangle marked for deletion

Dpt.	Employee	Rank
333	Silver	GS-5
991	Stevens	GS-3
333	Underwood	GS-13
446	Cohen	GS-5
991	Tang	GS-12

Figure 5-1. Types of blocks that can be deleted

portion of each line for deletion. A column block is handy when you wish to erase one tabular column. But for a column block to work properly, each item in the column must be aligned on a tab stop, at the left margin, or with hard returns. A rectangle deletion is useful for erasing two or more columns at once, part of a column, part of a line drawing, or part of a statistical equation.

You access the column or rectangle deletion by first pressing the BLOCK (ALT + F4) key to highlight the text, use the MOVE (CTRL + F4) key to specify the block as a column or rectangle, and then choose to delete that block. Chapter 6 describes the MOVE key in detail and discusses how to move and/or copy a column or a rectangle; that same basic procedure applies for a deletion as well.

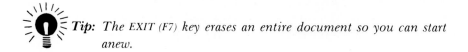

Tip: *The EXIT (F7) key erases an entire document so you can start anew.*

Erase an entire document from the screen as follows (be sure that you want to clear the screen of all pages that you have typed):

1. Press the EXIT (F7) key. WordPerfect provides the following prompt:

   Save Document? (Y/N) Yes

2. Type **N** to clear the screen without saving the document. Type **Y** or any key other than N, or press ENTER, to save the document and then clear the screen, in which case WordPerfect requests a filename. (The Save feature is described in detail in Chapter 11. You *must* save a document on disk before you erase the screen if you want WordPerfect to be able to bring that document back on screen at a later time.) The following prompt appears next:

   Exit WordPerfect? (Y/N) No

3. Type **N** or any key other than Y, or press ENTER to remain in WordPerfect. The screen is erased, the cursor moves back to page 1 and line 1″ at the left margin, and you are ready to start a new document.

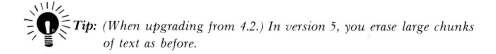

Tip: *(When upgrading from 4.2.) In version 5, you erase large chunks of text as before.*

Erase blocks of text in version 5 just as in version 4.2, except that now you can use quick delete methods, such as DELETE EOL or block delete, to erase on the Reveal Codes screen. Previously, using these methods popped you out of Reveal Codes and back to the Typing screen.

Recovering Deleted Text

Have you ever deleted a word and then wished you hadn't? Or a whole paragraph? Or a whole page? Fortunately, WordPerfect enables you to "undelete" already erased text or codes by using the CANCEL (F1) key.

WordPerfect keeps track of your last three deletions, where a deletion is considered to be a series of characters and/or codes erased consecutively before you moved the cursor or resumed typing. There's no limit to the number of characters in one deletion. WordPerfect saves the deletions in a portion of memory called the *delete buffer,* which is like an electronic holding tank. Examples of deletions that are held in the delete buffer are as follows:

- You press DEL one time to erase a hard return code and then move the cursor to the left margin—the **[HRt]** is considered one deletion.
- You highlight four sentences using the Block feature, delete that block of text, and resume typing—those four sentences constitute another deletion.
- You press CTRL + BACKSPACE six times in a row to erase "If it is acceptable to you," and then move your cursor to the top of the document—those six words constitute the third and most recent deletion.

The delete buffer will maintain three deletions, such as the ones described above, until: (1) you delete again, in which case the oldest deletion gets booted out of the buffer to make room for the most recent one; (2) you exit WordPerfect; or (3) the computer's power is turned off.

To bring a deletion stored in the buffer back into your document:

1. Position the cursor where you would like the recovered text to reappear in your document.
2. Press the CANCEL (F1) key. The most recent deletion appears highlighted at the current cursor position and WordPerfect responds with the Undelete menu:

   Undelete: 1 Restore; **2** Previous deletion: **0**

   An example of this is shown in Figure 5-2, where the most recent deletion is the phrase, "If it is acceptable to you,".
3. To recover the most recent level, type **1** or **R**. Your text is restored. Or to recover one of the two older deletions, type **2** or **P**—once to view the second deletion, twice to view the third deletion. After the correct deletion appears highlighted on screen, type **1** or **R** to restore it.

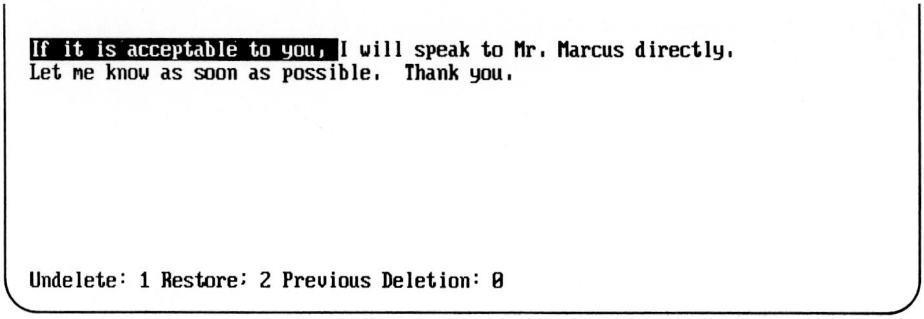

If it is acceptable to you, I will speak to Mr. Marcus directly.
Let me know as soon as possible. Thank you.
Undelete: 1 Restore; 2 Previous Deletion: 0

Figure 5-2. Highlighted text to be restored with the Undelete menu

The Undelete feature will restore your deletions, no matter which method you used to delete the characters in the first place. In fact, even when you switch to the Typeover mode to type over existing text, that text is saved as a deletion that can be undeleted. The one exception involves the EXIT (F7) key; when you press EXIT and clear the screen, you cannot restore the whole screen with CANCEL. That's why it's critical to save a document on disk if you wish to later use that document again (see Chapter 11).

Trap: *Undelete won't work if prompts or menus are currently on the screen.*

The Undelete feature becomes operational only after prompts, messages, or menus are cleared from the Typing or the Reveal Codes screen. Chapter 2 describes the CANCEL key's other responsibility, which is to allow you to abort a command in case you inadvertently press a function key. If you're viewing a WordPerfect prompt or menu and you wish to undo a deletion, you must first clear the screen of all prompts and menus. Either make your selection on the menu to complete the procedure, or press CANCEL to terminate the procedure. Then, when all prompts and menus are cleared, press CANCEL again to initiate the Undelete menu. (If at any time you decide to abort the Undelete feature, you would again simply press CANCEL.)

Tip: *You can use directional arrow keys to view a previous deletion level.*

When in the Undelete menu, you can use the directional arrow keys as an alternative to choosing Previous deletion (2 or P). The UP ARROW key displays one of the previous levels, and DOWN ARROW displays the other.

Trap: *CANCEL will be unable to restore text erased using the Move/Copy options on the MOVE key.*

In addition to the delete buffer, WordPerfect also reserves a separate place in memory for the *move buffer,* which is a holding tank for characters that you wish to move or copy. Text is placed in the move buffer whenever you use the MOVE (CTRL + F4) key and select the Move or Copy option.

As described in an earlier section of this chapter, "Deleting Large Amounts of Text," the MOVE key is a shortcut when erasing a sentence, a paragraph, or a page. But if you choose the Move or Copy option rather than the Delete option on the MOVE key, pressing CANCEL will not restore the text because it is in the move buffer, not the delete buffer. Refer to Chapter 6, which fully describes the move/copy process, to learn how to bring text back into a document from the move buffer.

Trap: *Watch out for running out of space in the deletion buffer.*

Sometimes there may not be any room left in your computer's memory or on disk to save a deletion in the delete buffer. This depends on the amount of memory in your computer, disk availability, and the size of the deletion. If no more space exists, then when you attempt to delete, WordPerfect will warn you with the prompt:

Delete without saving for Undelete? (Y/N) No

Press **Y** if you wish to delete the text even though you will be unable to restore it later. Press N or ENTER, or any character other than Y, to cancel the deletion.

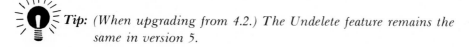

Tip: *(When upgrading from 4.2.) The Undelete feature remains the same in version 5.*

Use the CANCEL key to undelete, just as you did when working with version 4.2.

Redline and Strikeout

The Redline and Strikeout features enable you to edit a document without losing the original. Redline marks text that could be added to a document. It does this by showing a change in the text's appearance or color, or with a symbol that appears in the left margin of the lines where the text is to be added. Strikeout marks text that could be deleted from a document. It does this by showing a line of hyphens that strike over the text to be deleted. Figure 5-3 provides an example of how these features could look on a printed page. Notice that redline appears with a shadowed background, while strikeout appears as a solid line.

A document with redline and strikeout serves as a record of revisions made since an earlier draft. Changes are emphasized so that the parties working on the document can discuss the alterations. These features are popular with writers and editors and in legal offices, where a one-sentence change can give an entirely different meaning to a 50-page contract.

You can mark text for redline or strikeout either as you type the text or after typing it. If you are about to insert text that you also want to mark for redline or strikeout, then proceed as follows:

1. Press the FONT (CTRL + F8) key. WordPerfect responds with the Font menu:

   1 Size; **2** Appearance; **3** Normal; **4** Base Font; **5** Print Color: **0**

2. Select Appearance (2 or A). WordPerfect responds with the Appearance menu:

   1 Bold **2** Undrln **3** Dbl Und **4** Italc **5** Outln **6** Shadw
   7 Sm Cap **8** Redln **9** Stkout: **0**

3. Select Redline (8 or R). Or, select Strikeout (9 or S).

4. Type the text that you want marked for redline or strikeout.

Text before changes

```
If the premises are damaged by fire or from any other cause, then
either party can terminate this lease as of the date on which the
damages occur.  If the lease is not terminated, then Owner will
repair said premises and reduce Tenant's rent by a proportional
amount until the premises are repaired and ready for the Tenant's
return.
```

Text after changes are marked with redline and strikeout

If the premises are damaged by fire~~ or from any other cause~~, then either party can terminate this lease as of the date on which the damages occur. Notice of intent must be given within thirty (30) days after the occurrence of damage. If the lease is not terminated, then Owner will repair said premises~~ and reduce Tenant's rent by a proportional amount~~ until the premises are repaired and ready for the Tenant's return.

Figure 5-3. Redline and strikeout on a printed document

5. Turn off the Redline or Strikeout feature in one of three ways:
   - Press RIGHT ARROW to position the cursor to the right of the redline or strikeout code (the quickest option), or
   - Repeat steps 1 through 3 above, or
   - Press the FONT (CTRL + F8) key and select Normal (3 or N).

If you wish to mark for redline or strikeout on already existing text, then the BLOCK key comes into play. Proceed as follows:

1. Use the BLOCK (ALT + F4) key to highlight the text intended for redline or strikeout.

2. Press the FONT (CTRL + F8) key. With Block on, the following menu appears:

   Attribute: 1 Size; **2** Appearance: **0**

3. Select Appearance (2 or A). Now WordPerfect responds with:

   1 Bold **2** Undrln **3** Dbl Und **4** Italc **5** Outln **6** Shadw **7** Sm Cap
   8 Redln **9** Stkout: **0**

4. Select Redline (8 or R). Or, select Strikeout (9 or S). The text is marked, and WordPerfect automatically turns off the Redline, Strikeout and the Block features.

WordPerfect designates the text for redline or strikeout by enclosing the text within a pair of codes, as in the following examples:

[REDLN]This is text marked for redline.**[redln]**
[STKOUT]This is text marked for strikeout.**[stkout]**

When viewing the Reveal Codes screen, you can see these codes bordering the text.

Tip: *How redline and strikeout appear on the Typing screen depends on your computer monitor and display card.*

You will not see the actual redline or strikeout marks on the Typing screen; they will appear when printed. WordPerfect knows it should print these marks because of the code pair that surrounds the text.

However, you can indicate redline or strikeout on the Typing screen in various ways, depending on your monitor and display card. If you have a color monitor, you can indicate how WordPerfect should show redline and strikeout on the screen by selecting a specific color (and/or a specific font if your monitor has graphics capabilities) for redline and another for strikeout. If you have a monochrome monitor (such as green or amber characters only on a black background), you can choose to show redline or strikeout as any combination of a blinking, underlined, boldfaced, or reverse video display of text. This is accomplished with option 3, Display, from the Setup menu. (For more information on the Setup menu, refer to Appendix B.)

Tip: *How redline and strikeout appear on the printed page depends on your printer.*

All printers operate differently, so that how redline and strikeout appear when printed depends on your printer. Redline is set up for a change in the appearance of the text, but that change is different from printer to printer. For example, redline text on an HP LaserJet series II (with no cartridges or downloaded fonts) will normally print with the background shaded (as shown in Figure 5-3), but may appear in italics or with another font change. Similarly, text marked for strikeout will appear with a solid line through the middle of the characters on the LaserJet (also shown in Figure 5-3), but may appear with a broken line through the characters on another printer.

You must test your printer to see exactly how redline and strikeout are handled. To do so, you can place redline and strikeout codes in any document you are working on and then print the document. You also can print out a file named PRINTER.TST, which is provided with WordPerfect. Refer to Chapter 15 for more on PRINTER.TST, a file that tests various features of your printer. By testing your printer, you'll learn the basic way in which your printer manages redline and strikeout.

Also, see the next Tip for information on changing the Redline option for your printer.

Tip: *You can change the way text marked for redline is printed with the Document Format menu.*

WordPerfect provides the ability to change the way in which your printer denotes redline. By testing your printer (see the previous Tip), you'll uncover the basic option. But, depending on your printer's capabilities, you have other choices as well.

To alter Redline:

1. Press the FORMAT (SHIFT + F8) key. The Format menu, shown in Figure 5-4, appears.
2. Select Document (3 or D). The Document Format menu, shown in Figure 5-5, appears.
3. Select Redline (4 or R). The Redline menu appears at the bottom of the screen as follows:

Redline Method: 1 Printer Dependent; **2** Left; **3** Alternating: **1**

The choices available to you are as follows:

- **Printer Dependent (1 or P)** This choice prints the redline text in whichever font has been set up as the basic Redline option for your printer. This is the default setting. Notice on the Document Format menu in Figure 5-5 that the setting next to Redline reads **Printer Dependent**, which indicates the default selection. (For instance, for the HP LaserJet series II, the default provides a shaded background.)
- **Left (2 or L)** This prints a specific character in the left margin. You can choose any character you desire. WordPerfect prompts

  Redline character: ¦

  Press ENTER to select ¦, or type in a new redline character, such as + or <. Suppose you selected ¦ as the character. Then, the setting next to Redline on the Document Format menu changes to read "¦ Left."
- **Alternating (3 or A)** This prints a specific character in the left margin of odd pages and in the right margin of even pages (this is especially useful for documents that will be copied double-sided so that text appears on both sides of a page). You can choose any character you desire.

```
Format

     1 - Line
              Hyphenation                      Line Spacing
              Justification                    Margins Left/Right
              Line Height                      Tab Set
              Line Numbering                   Widow/Orphan Protection

     2 - Page
              Center Page (top to bottom)      New Page Number
              Force Odd/Even Page              Page Numbering
              Headers and Footers              Paper Size/Type
              Margins Top/Bottom               Suppress

     3 - Document
              Display Pitch                    Redline Method
              Initial Codes/Font               Summary

     4 - Other
              Advance                          Overstrike
              Conditional End of Page          Printer Functions
              Decimal Characters               Underline Spaces/Tabs
              Language

Selection: 0
```

Figure 5-4. The Format menu

```
Format: Document

     1 - Display Pitch - Automatic      Yes
                         Width          0.1"

     2 - Initial Codes

     3 - Initial Font                   Courier 10 pitch (PC-8)

     4 - Redline Method                 Printer Dependent

     5 - Summary










Selection: 0
```

Figure 5-5. The Document Format menu

WordPerfect prompts

Redline character: ¦

Press ENTER to select ¦, or type in a new redline character, such as + or <. Suppose you selected ¦ as the character. Then, the setting next to Redline on the Document Format menu changes to read "¦ Alternating."

4. Press the EXIT (F7) key to return to the Typing screen. Or, press ENTER to return to the Format menu.

When you change the Redline option, no code is inserted into the text, but the redline is changed for that one document. When you clear the screen and begin working on a new document, the Redline option will revert to the default setting (printer dependent).

Tip: *Preview how redline and strikeout will appear before you print.*

WordPerfect offers a feature called View Document, whereby you can view how text will actually appear when printed. Using this feature, you can (depending on your monitor) see where the redline and strikeout characters will appear in the printed text. (For more on View Document, refer to Chapter 14.)

Trap: *Not all printers support the Redline and Strikeout features.*

You must try Redline and Strikeout with your printer to see whether those features are fully supported. If Redline doesn't seem to work, try to alter the redline method (as described in a previous Tip), and see if it works then.

Trap: *You must change the definition of your printer if you wish to alter the strikeout character.*

Most printers are defined in such a way that the strikeout character is the hyphen (-). However, you can change the character used in the Strikeout feature. For example, perhaps you prefer that the strikeout character be the slash (/). Changing this character is more difficult than changing the Redline option, but it can be done by altering how your printer has been defined by using a file named PTR.EXE. Refer to Chapter 15 for more on the PTR.EXE program, which enables you to change the way in which your printer and WordPerfect work together.

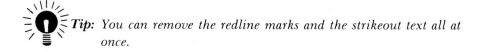

Tip: *You can remove the redline marks and the strikeout text all at once.*

You can turn your original draft containing redline and strikeout into a final document in seconds. WordPerfect offers the ability to eliminate the redline markings and erase the text defined for strikeout all at once. To do so:

1. Make sure the document is on screen.

2. Press the MARK TEXT (ALT + F5) key to display the Mark Text menu:

   1 Auto Ref; **2** Subdoc; **3** Index; **4** ToA Short form; **5** Define;
   6 Generate: **0**

3. Select Generate (6 or G). The full-screen menu appears, as shown in Figure 5-6.

4. Select Remove redline markings and strikeout text from document (1 or R). To verify, WordPerfect prompts with the following:

   Delete redline markings and strikeout text? (Y/N) No

5. Type **Y**, and in moments the document will be in final form. All redline marks will be gone. All strikeout text will be deleted.

   Or, type **N**, or any character other than Y, to abort the operation, or press ENTER.

```
Mark Text: Generate

     1 - Remove Redline Markings and Strikeout Text from Document

     2 - Compare Screen and Disk Documents and Add Redline and Strikeout

     3 - Expand Master Document

     4 - Condense Master Document

     5 - Generate Tables, Indexes, Automatic References, etc.



Selection: 0
```

Figure 5-6. The Generate Mark Text menu

Tip: *You can be selective in the redline and strikeout text you eliminate by using other WordPerfect features.*

You can be discerning about which text marked with redline you choose to insert in a final document and which strikeout text you choose to delete. Handy methods for doing this involve the use of either the Search or the Replace feature (discussed in Chapters 4 and 6, respectively).

For instance, suppose you choose to delete only certain portions of text marked with strikeout. You can use the Search feature in this case. Position the cursor at the top of the document and press the →SEARCH (F2) key. Now select the keys you would normally press to insert the **[STKOUT]** code; that is, (1) press the FONT (CTRL + F8) key, (2) select Appearance (2 or A), and (3) select Stkout (9 or S). The search prompt now reads

→ Srch: [STKOUT]

Press →SEARCH or ESC to move the cursor to the first strikeout code in the text. You can now either delete the text marked for strikeout using the Block feature or leave the text intact and simply press BACKSPACE to delete the **[STKOUT]** code. (WordPerfect will automatically delete the **[stkout]** code that is part of the pair when you erase the **[STKOUT]** code.) Continue searching until all the text marked for strikeout has been found and acted upon.

In addition to Search and Replace, another aid in quickly deleting selected redline and strikeout text is found by defining a macro to do this. A macro allows you to record repetitive keystrokes and to play the keystrokes back at your command. (Refer to Chapter 27 for more information on defining macros.)

Tip: *The Document Compare feature can insert redline and strikeout codes for you automatically.*

Redline and strikeout are useful features when you are comparing two documents. Wherever the first document has additional text that is not contained in the second document, this text can be marked with redline, and wherever the first document lacks text contained in the second, text is copied to the first document and is marked with strikeout.

WordPerfect can insert redline and strikeout for you with the Document Compare feature. A document on screen is contrasted with a second document on screen. (For more information on this feature, refer to Chapter 12.)

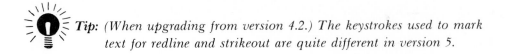

Tip: *(When upgrading from version 4.2.) The keystrokes used to mark text for redline and strikeout are quite different in version 5.*

In version 5, the Redline and Strikeout features have moved to the FONT key, and the set of keystrokes used to access these features is quite distinct from the ones in version 4.2.

In addition, redline and strikeout offer more options than before. You can now do the following: choose to have redline and strikeout text displayed differently on screen than normal text (depending on your monitor); select an alternative redline character without having to tamper with the printer program (PTR.EXE); use the Document Compare feature to have WordPerfect insert redline and strikeout for you; and use the View Document feature to see not only the redline but the strikeout characters as well. (The View Document feature was referred to as "Preview" in version 4.2.) All of these changes are discussed in the last section of this chapter, "Redline and Strikeout."

Tips and Traps Summary

Inserting Text

Trap: Sometimes you must move the cursor before text is readjusted.

Tip: If you prefer, you can inhibit WordPerfect from automatically reformatting your document as you edit.

Trap: The TAB and BACKSPACE keys work differently in Typeover mode than in Insert mode.

Trap: You can't overwrite codes in Typeover mode.

Tip: The SWITCH key can reverse upper- and lowercase letters faster than Typeover mode can.

Tips and Traps Summary (*continued*)

Tip: You can insert the entire text of a file stored on disk into the document currently on screen.

Tip: WordPerfect can be forced into either Insert or Typeover mode.

Tip: (When upgrading from 4.2.) In version 5, you can now insert as well as delete text in Reveal Codes.

Deleting Characters and Words

Tip: The deletion keys have an autorepeat feature.

Tip: You can combine most deletion keys with ESC for power deleting.

Tip: Use BACKSPACE or DEL to delete a blank line.

Tip: As you press DEL or BACKSPACE on the Typing screen, a prompt might appear on the status line as you are about to erase hidden codes.

Tip: With code pairs, you need only delete one of the matched set.

Trap: Don't try to delete soft codes.

Tip: (When upgrading from 4.2.) In version 5, you erase characters and words as before.

Deleting Large Amounts of Text

Trap: A code in a block marked for deletion will be deleted as well.

Tip: To quickly erase text to the end of a line, use the DELETE EOL key.

Tip: To quickly erase text to the bottom of a page, use the DELETE EOP key.

Tip: Use a shortcut if you wish to erase a whole sentence, paragraph, or page of text.

Tips and Traps Summary (*continued*)

Trap: Sometimes you must move the cursor before text will readjust after a deletion.

Tip: WordPerfect provides the ability to delete a column or a rectangular portion of text.

Tip: The EXIT (F7) key erases an entire document so you can start anew.

Tip: (When upgrading from 4.2.) In version 5, you erase large chunks of text as before.

Recovering Deleted Text

Trap: Undelete won't work if prompts or menus are currently on the screen.

Tip: You can use directional arrow keys to view a previous deletion level.

Trap: CANCEL will be unable to restore text erased using the Move/Copy options on the MOVE key.

Trap: Watch out for running out of space in the deletion buffer.

Tip: (When upgrading from 4.2.) The Undelete feature remains the same in version 5.

Redline and Strikeout

Tip: How redline and strikeout appear on the Typing screen depends on your computer monitor and display card.

Tip: How redline and strikeout appear on the printed page depends on your printer.

Tip: You can change the way text marked for redline is printed with the Document Format menu.

Tips and Traps Summary (*continued*)

Tip: Preview how redline and strikeout will appear before you print.

Trap: Not all printers support the Redline and Strikeout features.

Trap: You must change the definition of your printer if you wish to alter the strikeout character.

Tip: You can remove the redline marks and the strikeout text all at once.

Tip: You can be selective in the redline and strikeout text you eliminate by using other WordPerfect features.

Tip: The Document Compare feature can insert redline and strikeout codes for you automatically.

Tip: (When upgrading from 4.2.) The keystrokes used to mark text for redline and strikeout are quite different in version 5.

6

Moving, Copying, and Replacing Text

If you write like most of us, you change your mind constantly as you formulate words and produce documents. During this process, you may decide to rearrange the sequence of your text. Should the third paragraph be moved up in the text? Should the table on page 2 be duplicated on page 14 for quick reference? WordPerfect makes it easy to make such changes and rearrange your text with the MOVE key. You can "cut and paste" paragraphs together in a different order or copy text from one page to another.

At other times, you may decide to alter the choice of words in a document. Should the phrase "unfortunate mistake" be changed to "costly error" throughout the document? Should the client be referred to as "Dan" rather than "Mr. Janowitz" in this letter? WordPerfect provides you with the ability to change such word choices with the REPLACE key, substituting new phrases for old ones automatically. The powerful MOVE and REPLACE keys are described in this chapter.

Moving and Copying Text

The MOVE key has a misleading name; not only does it offer features to move text, but it can also copy, delete, or append text. The distinction is that in a move, text actually disappears from one place and is relocated in another place. In a copy, text remains at its present location and is also placed in another location. In a delete, the text is simply erased. (The ability to delete text is explained in Chapter 5.) In an append, the text remains at its present location and is also copied to a file stored on disk. (The Append feature is explained in Chapter 12, as it relates more to working between documents.)

You can move/copy a block of text of any size, whether it is made up of six pages, five words, eight numbers, or one code. There are two distinct parts to the move/copy process. First, you indicate which text you wish to move/copy; WordPerfect places that text in a move buffer, which is like a temporary holding tank. Second, you indicate where you want that text to be repositioned; WordPerfect retrieves that text from the move buffer and puts it in the spot that you indicated. The move/copy buffer is distinct from the delete buffer, which (as described in Chapter 5) is where deleted text is stored.

At first glance, the move/copy process may seem confusing: several steps are involved, the Move menu changes depending on whether you have Block on or Block off, and the menu is harder to decipher than most other WordPerfect menus. But once you become accustomed to the procedure and learn the shortcuts, text can be relocated in seconds. The basic method is as follows:

1. Position the cursor on the first character to be copied or moved.
2. Designate the text to be copied or moved by pressing the BLOCK (ALT + F4) key and positioning the cursor on the last character. WordPerfect highlights the text in reverse video and the message **Block on** flashes on the screen. (For a review of the Block command, see Chapter 4.)
3. Press MOVE (CTRL + F4). With the Block feature on, WordPerfect responds with the following menu:

   Move: 1 Block; **2** Tabular Column; **3** Rectangle: **0**

4. Select Block (1 or B). WordPerfect responds

   1 Move; **2** Copy; **3** Delete; **4** Append: **0**

5. To move the block, select Move (1 or M). The block disappears from the screen and is placed in the move buffer. The **Block on** message clears.

Or, to copy the block, press Copy (2 or C). The block *remains* on the screen. WordPerfect places a copy of the block in the move buffer, and the **Block on** message clears.

A new message appears at the bottom of the Typing screen:

Move cursor; press **Enter** to retrieve.

6. Position the cursor at the spot where you want the block to reappear.
7. Press ENTER.
8. If the text needs adjustment to fit within the margins, simply press the DOWN ARROW key.

Tip: *Use a shortcut if you wish to copy or move a whole sentence, paragraph, or page of text.*

WordPerfect recognizes these common units of text: a sentence is text that ends with a period (.), a question mark (?), or an exclamation point (!), which is followed by a space; a paragraph is text that ends with a hard return code; a page is text that ends with a page break code. If the block you wish to move or copy falls into one of these three categories, then you can bypass the Block feature. WordPerfect marks the text for you. The steps are

1. Position the cursor anywhere within the sentence, paragraph, or page that you wish to copy or move.
2. Press MOVE (CTRL + F4). With Block off, WordPerfect displays the following menu:

   Move: 1 Sentence; **2** Paragraph; **3** Page; **4** Retrieve: **0**

3. Press the number (or mnemonic) key corresponding to the unit of text to be copied or moved. For instance, type **2** or **P** to choose "Paragraph" and WordPerfect responds by highlighting the whole paragraph and prompting

   1 Move; **2** Copy; **3** Delete; **4** Append: **0**

4. Choose Move (1 or M), if you want to move (that is, "cut and paste") text. Choose Copy (2 or C) to copy the text. A new message appears at the bottom of the Typing screen:

   Move cursor; press **Enter** to retrieve.

5. Position the cursor at the spot where you want the block to reappear.
6. Press ENTER.
7. If the text needs to be adjusted to fit within the margins, simply press DOWN ARROW.

Note that the last four steps above are the same as for the method presented previously, wherein you block a section of text before initiating the move or copy. The advantage to the method described here is that if the block is a sentence, paragraph, or page, you save time because WordPerfect defines the boundaries of the block for you.

Tip: *You don't have to retrieve a block immediately after moving or copying it.*

Sometimes you may wish to perform other tasks between the time that you place a block in the move buffer and the time that you retrieve that block for placement in a new location. This is possible. When the message "Move cursor; press **Enter** to retrieve" appears on screen, you can move the cursor anywhere and still perform many tasks, such as pressing a number or letter key, centering a title, saving a document, or clearing the screen. Thus, you can press ENTER to retrieve the block after pressing other function keys.

The MOVE key, however, will not operate when the message "Move cursor; press **Enter** to retrieve" is on screen. And, if you forget about the message, start typing, and press ENTER, you'll find that the block reappears unexpectedly.

There is a better strategy if you wish to delay the retrieval of a block. After moving/copying the block so that it is in the move buffer, simply press the CANCEL (F1) key. The message "Move cursor; press **Enter** to retrieve" disappears. The block is still in the move buffer, however, so that whenever you're ready to retrieve the block, you have two choices. The first choice is to use the MOVE key:

1. Position the cursor in the location to which you wish to retrieve the block.
2. Press MOVE (CTRL + F4). WordPerfect displays the following menu:

   Move: 1 Sentence; **2** Paragraph; 3 Page; **4** Retrieve: **0**

3. Select Retrieve (4 or R). WordPerfect displays another menu:

    Retrieve: 1 Block; **2** Tabular Column; **3** Rectangle: **0**

4. Select Block (1 or B).

The second choice for retrieving a block uses the RETRIEVE key. Typically, the Retrieve command fetches a file from storage (as explained in Chapter 11). But it also can be used to retrieve text from the move buffer, provided that you indicate no filename when WordPerfect asks for the file to be retrieved:

1. Position the cursor where you wish the retrieved block to be located.
2. Press RETRIEVE (SHIFT + F10). WordPerfect responds

    Document to be retrieved:

3. Press ENTER.

Using the RETRIEVE key saves you several keystrokes. Try both the MOVE and RETRIEVE keys and see which set of keystrokes you prefer.

Tip: *When you place a block in the move buffer, it can be inserted an unlimited number of times into many documents.*

Once a block of text is in the move buffer, it remains there until (1) you move or copy a new section of text (see the following Trap), (2) you exit WordPerfect, or (3) the computer's power goes off. Therefore, you can insert whatever is in the move buffer into a document numerous times.

For instance, suppose you are typing a legal document and place in the move buffer a sentence that reads: "Plaintiff gave no response to that question." Now you can keep inserting that sentence over and over, everywhere else it applies, as follows. The first time, simply press ENTER to retrieve it, as the prompt at the bottom of the screen indicates. For each additional time you wish to retrieve the block, follow the directions described above, that is: (1) reposition the cursor, (2) press the MOVE (CTRL + F4) key, (3) select Retrieve (4 or R), and (4) select Block (1 or B). Or, an alternative is to (1) reposition the cursor, (2) press the RETRIEVE (SHIFT + F10) key, and (3) press ENTER. Repeat as many times as you desire.

You can even retrieve text contained in the move buffer and put it in other documents. This is because the text remains in the buffer even when you clear the screen to work on another document.

Trap: *You can't move or copy two separate blocks at once.*

WordPerfect has room for only one block at a time in its move buffer. Therefore, if you move or copy a block, whatever its length, remember to retrieve that text into the new document location before you move or copy a second block. Be aware that it is especially easy to forget about a block if you press CANCEL (F1) midway through the Move or Copy command, so that the "Move cursor; press **Enter** to retrieve" prompt disappears.

Tip: *As an alternative set of keystrokes, you can delete and then undelete as a means of moving text.*

Since WordPerfect has a delete buffer in addition to a move buffer, another alternative for relocating text is to delete it and then undelete it. You can delete a block of text in any of the ways described in Chapter 5. Next, move your cursor to the location where you wish to insert the block. Press the CANCEL (F1) key and then select Restore (1 or R) to reinstate the text from the delete buffer.

Tip: *WordPerfect gives you the ability to move or copy a tabular column.*

The Block command typically marks the first character through the last character and all characters in between—all the way from the left margin to the right. But what if you want to move or copy an individual column, perhaps a column in a table? This is possible in WordPerfect. The column must be aligned on tab stops, at the left margin, or with hard returns. You first define a standard block and then specify that block as a column.

For example, suppose you set tabs for each column and typed the table shown in Figure 6-1. Each column entry is thus lined up on a tab stop. You now

Here are the April figures for all Account Executives:

No.	Executive	Volume	Goal	Earnings
1.	S. Thomas	8 clients	$2000	$2200
2.	P. Peters	4 clients	$1200	$1000
3.	L. Berger	9 clients	$3500	$4150
4.	J. Johnson	7 clients	$1900	$2500
5.	M. Wurman	9 clients	$4500	$5000

Figure 6-1. *Example of a table created on tab stops, in which a column will be moved*

wish to move the second column, titled "Executive," to the right of all the other columns:

1. Position the cursor anywhere on the first line of the "Executive" column.
2. Press BLOCK (ALT + F4) and DOWN ARROW until the cursor is positioned anywhere on the last line of the "Executive" column. WordPerfect highlights every character.

No.	Executive	Volume	Goal	Earnings
1.	S. Thomas	8 clients	$2000	$2200
2.	P. Peters	4 clients	$1200	$1000
3.	L. Berger	9 clients	$3500	$4150
4.	J. Johnson	7 clients	$1900	$2500
5.	M. Wurman	9 clients	$4500	$5000

3. Press MOVE (CTRL + F4).
4. Select Tabular column (2 or C). WordPerfect highlights only the one column, along with the **[TAB]** codes that precede it, and prompts for a move, copy, or delete instruction.

No.	Executive	Volume	Goal	Earnings
1.	S. Thomas	8 clients	$2000	$2200
2.	P. Peters	4 clients	$1200	$1000
3.	L. Berger	9 clients	$3500	$4150
4.	J. Johnson	7 clients	$1900	$2500
5.	M. Wurman	9 clients	$4500	$5000

1 Move; 2 Copy; 3 Delete; 4 Append: 0

5. Select Move (1 or M). WordPerfect erases that one column only, placing it in the move buffer, and moves the remaining columns to the left. The result is illustrated in Figure 6-2. WordPerfect prompts

   Move cursor; press **Enter** to retrieve.

6. Locate the cursor on the top line in the column to the left of where you want to insert the moved column. In this case, that's just to the right of the "s" in "Earnings." This is where you wish to insert the column that is now contained in the column buffer.

7. Press ENTER. The "Executive" column is retrieved from the buffer and is positioned at the far right, as shown in Figure 6-3.

If you press the CANCEL (F1) key so that the "Move cursor; press **Enter** to retrieve" message disappears, then to retrieve that column, locate the cursor, and then:

1. Press MOVE (CTRL + F4).

Here are the April figures for all Account Executives:

No.	Volume	Goal	Earnings
1.	8 clients	$2000	$2200
2.	4 clients	$1200	$1000
3.	9 clients	$3500	$4150
4.	7 clients	$1900	$2500
5.	9 clients	$4500	$5000

Figure 6-2. "Executive" column cut from the table

Here are the April figures for all Account Executives:

No.	Volume	Goal	Earnings	Executive
1.	8 clients	$2000	$2200	S. Thomas
2.	4 clients	$1200	$1000	P. Peters
3.	9 clients	$3500	$4150	L. Berger
4.	7 clients	$1900	$2500	J. Johnson
5.	9 clients	$4500	$5000	M. Wurman

Figure 6-3. "Executive" column moved to the far right

2. Select Retrieve (4 or R). WordPerfect displays the following:

   Retrieve: 1 Block; **2** Tabular Column; **3** Rectangle: **0**

3. Select Tabular Column (2 or C).

If the cursor is at the far right as you retrieve, the other columns remain at their present location. If the cursor is between columns, other columns accommodate by moving one tab stop to the right. Before you start moving or copying, be sure that tab stops have been set so that the columns are wide enough to accommodate the insertions. Because it is a bit tricky at first to become accustomed to moving/copying columns, play it safe by saving a copy of your document on disk before you attempt to use the MOVE key in columns.

Note: This method for moving/copying tabular columns is entirely separate from WordPerfect's newspaper column and parallel column features, which are described in Chapter 19. You should not use the procedure just described when working with newspaper or parallel columns (unless text is aligned on tab stops within those columns).

Tip: *WordPerfect gives you the ability to move or copy a rectangular block of text.*

In addition to defining a standard block and a column block (see the previous Tip), you can also define a rectangular block in WordPerfect. This provides you with the flexibility to move or copy whole chunks of text rather than just whole lines. Your ability to define a rectangular block is not dependent on tabs, as it is for moving/copying columns. You first define a standard block and then specify it as a rectangle. The first and last characters in the marked block form the rectangle's opposite borders.

```
This is an example of two sentences marked as a standard block.
Notice how WordPerfect highlights every character, from first to
last, and all characters in between.
```

```
This is an example of two sentences marked as a rectangle.  Notice
how WordPerfect highlights only that rectangular section of text
defined by the first character and the last.
```

As an example, suppose you typed the table shown in Figure 6-4. You now decide to remove the first and second columns and place them below the rest of the columns. If you want to move both columns at once, you can use the rectangular move/copy feature as follows:

1. Position the cursor on the first character of the first column, which is the E in "Executive".
2. Press BLOCK (ALT + F4) and mark all the text until the cursor is positioned one past the last character of the second column, which is just on the P in "Planter." By moving all the way to the third column, WordPerfect will also cut from the table the **[TAB]** codes that precede column three.

Executive	Office	Account	Volume
S. Thomas	San Francisco	ABC Company	$32.5
P. Peters	Pittsburgh	Trader Magazine	60.8
L. Berger	St. Louis	J.J Henson	55.4
J. Johnson	Chicago	Mertek Corp.	90.8
M. Wurman	Newark	J&B Limited	9.0
S. Malcolm	Chicago	XYZ, Inc.	55.7
R. Charles	San Francisco	Planter Shoes	34.4

3. Press the MOVE (CTRL + F4) key.

ACCOUNTS

Executive	Office	Account	Volume
S. Thomas	San Francisco	ABC Company	$32.5
P. Peters	Pittsburgh	Trader Magazine	60.8
L. Berger	St. Louis	J.J Henson	55.4
J. Johnson	Chicago	Mertek Corp.	90.8
M. Wurman	Newark	J&B Limited	9.0
S. Malcolm	Chicago	XYZ, Inc.	55.7
R. Charles	San Francisco	Planter Shoes	34.4

Figure 6-4. Example of a table in which a rectangle will be moved

4. Select Rectangle (3 or R). WordPerfect highlights only the rectangle defined by the first and last characters.

Executive	Office	Account	Volume
S. Thomas	San Francisco	ABC Company	$32.5
P. Peters	Pittsburgh	Trader Magazine	60.8
L. Berger	St. Louis	J.J Henson	55.4
J. Johnson	Chicago	Mertek Corp.	90.8
M. Wurman	Newark	J&B Limited	9.0
S. Malcolm	Chicago	XYZ, Inc.	55.7
R. Charles	San Francisco	Planter Shoes	34.4

1 Move; 2 Copy; 3 Delete; 4 Append: 0

5. Select Move (1 or M). WordPerfect erases that rectangular area, moving the remaining columns to the left. (Note that the columns moved to the left because you cut the **[TAB]** codes along with the text.)
6. Position the cursor below the remaining columns, at the left margin of the line on which you want to retrieve the two columns.
7. Press ENTER. The rectangle of text is relocated, as shown in Figure 6-5.

If you press the CANCEL (F1) key so that the "Move cursor; press **Enter** to retrieve" message disappears, then to retrieve that rectangle, locate the cursor and then

ACCOUNTS

Account	Volume
ABC Company	$32.5
Trader Magazine	60.8
J.J Henson	55.4
Mertek Corp.	90.8
J&B Limited	9.0
XYZ, Inc.	55.7
Planter Shoes	34.4

Executive	Office
S. Thomas	San Francisco
P. Peters	Pittsburgh
L. Berger	St. Louis
J. Johnson	Chicago
M. Wurman	Newark
S. Malcolm	Chicago
R. Charles	San Francisco

Figure 6-5. Two columns shaped like a rectangle moved onto separate lines

1. Press MOVE (CTRL + F4).
2. Select Retrieve (4 or R). WordPerfect displays the following:

   Retrieve: 1 Block; **2** Tabular Column; **3** Rectangle: **0**

3. Select Rectangle (3 or R).

In addition to moving or copying multiple columns, the rectangular move/copy feature is also handy for just part of a column, as shown here:

Executive	Office
S. Thomas	San Francisco
P. Peters	Pittsburgh
L. Berger	St. Louis
J. Johnson	Chicago
M. Wurman	Newark
S. Malcolm	Chicago
R. Charles	San Francisco

This feature also enables you to move/copy part of a statistical equation or a corner of a line drawing. Because it is a bit tricky at first to become accustomed to moving/copying rectangles, play it safe by saving a copy of your document on disk before you attempt to use the MOVE key for a rectangular block of text.

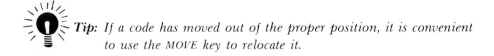

Tip: *If a code has moved out of the proper position, it is convenient to use the MOVE key to relocate it.*

In Chapter 5, you learned that codes can be deleted like any other character. Similarly, they can be moved or copied like any other character. Include the **[TAB]** code in a block when moving a paragraph, for example, and the first line of the paragraph, in its new location, will remain indented.

You can also move/copy one code by itself. Sometimes you may find that after extensive editing of a document, a code may be in the wrong location. Perhaps you find that a **[Tab Set]** code has wound up below, rather than above, a table of information. Instead of erasing the code and inserting a new one in the correct location, you can move the code. Move it just as you would move one character of text, but make sure that you do so on the Reveal Codes screen so that you can view the code as you block it and place a copy in the move buffer. Similarly, you can copy a code to a different location in a document, or even to another document.

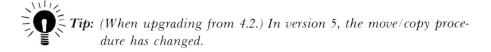

Tip: *(When upgrading from 4.2.) In version 5, the move/copy procedure has changed.*

The version 5 procedure for moving/copying text has been changed so that it is easier to retrieve text immediately after it is placed in the move buffer. If you've grown so accustomed to the keystrokes for moving/copying that you press keys automatically, you'll have to slow down to adjust to the new version 5 keystroke sequence.

Remember that you can now remain on the Reveal Codes screen to move/copy codes, which you could not do previously. This makes it easier than before to locate and therefore to move/copy codes.

Replacing Text

What happens if you type a 20-page document only to realize that you misspelled someone's name throughout? Or what if you wish to use a proposal you wrote last year for a new client this year? Or what if you decide to delete a certain phrase everywhere it occurs in a report? Without WordPerfect's Replace feature, you would have to move through the document, find every instance in which you typed in that name or client or phrase, and manually correct it. With WordPerfect's Replace feature, text that occurs repeatedly in a document can be changed in seconds. (The Replace feature is sometimes referred to in other word processing software as "global search and replace.")

Replace finds specific words or phrases just like the Search feature does, a procedure that was explained in Chapter 4. But the Replace command goes further; it deletes a phrase each time it occurs in a document, and in its place inserts a new phrase. A phrase, referred to as a character string, can be up to 59 characters in length.

You can use the Replace command in either of two ways. First, you can direct WordPerfect to substitute character strings automatically, without prompting you beforehand. The automatic replace is fast and easy when you want every occurrence of a phrase replaced with a new one. The alternative is to have WordPerfect stop after finding a string and prompt you for a confirmation before making the swap. With confirmation you have the option to replace phrases only in selected circumstances. Whichever method you choose, you must press REPLACE (ALT + F2) to begin the process.

Figure 6-6 shows a section of a document in which the name "Smith" appears six times. But suppose "Smith" must be replaced with the name "Jones". Here is the procedure:

1. Move the cursor to the top of the document (or just above the text you want the Replace command to operate on).
2. Press REPLACE (ALT + F2). WordPerfect responds with the following prompt in the lower left-hand corner of the screen:

   w/Confirm? (Y/N) No

3. If you want confirmation before WordPerfect makes a substitution, type **Y**. If you do not want confirmation, type **N** or any key other than Y, or press ENTER.

   In either case, WordPerfect displays another prompt:

MEMO

TO: Donna Wong, Legal Department

SUBJECT: Meeting with Jacob Smith

DATE: 9/17/88

I met with Mr. Jacob Smith last Friday. As you know, Mr. Smith is a partner in the law firm of Barnes, Jacoby and Smith. He has numerous years of experience with insurance cases such as the one we find ourselves immersed in.

Mr. Smith posed several questions which must be answered before he can provide us with any advice whatsoever. He first asked us to assess the extent of our loss. Mr. Smith also must know precisely when the loss occurred.

Figure 6-6. Text before "Smith" is replaced

→ **Srch:**

4. Type **Smith**. The prompt reads

   → **Srch:** Smith

5. Press REPLACE (ALT + F2), →SEARCH (F2), or ESC to register the search string of characters. WordPerfect displays the prompt:

   Replace with:

6. Type **Jones**. The prompt reads

   Replace with: Jones

7. Press REPLACE, →SEARCH, or ESC to register the replace string of characters. The following prompt appears:

   *** Please Wait ***

If you declined confirmation, WordPerfect carries out the Replace command to the end of the document. The job is completed in moments. The results are shown in Figure 6-7.

MEMO

TO: Donna Wong, Legal Department

SUBJECT: Meeting with Jacob Jones

DATE: 6/17/88

I met with Mr. Jacob Jones last Friday. As you know, Mr. Jones is a partner in the law firm of Barnes, Jacoby and Jones. He has numerous years of experience with insurance cases such as the one we find ourselves immersed in.

Mr. Jones posed several questions which must be answered before he can provide us with any advice whatsoever. He first asked us to access the extent of our loss. Mr. Jones also must know precisely when the loss occurred.

Figure 6-7. Text after "Smith" is replaced with "Jones"

If you choose confirmation, however, WordPerfect positions the cursor just past the first occurrence of "Smith" and provides the following message at the bottom of the screen:

Confirm? (Y/N) No

8. Type **Y** to replace "Smith" with "Jones". Or type **N** or any key other than Y, or press ENTER, to leave the name as "Smith". WordPerfect proceeds to the next occurrence of the word and again prompts for confirmation. This continues until WordPerfect has paused at each occurrence.

With the Replace feature, you can also eliminate a specific phrase each time it occurs in a document. Just leave the replace string empty when WordPerfect prompts for one with the prompt "**Replace with:**." Simply press REPLACE, →SEARCH, or ESC to begin the Replace procedure. WordPerfect will find each occurrence of the search string and replace it with nothing, effectively deleting that search string throughout the document.

Tip: *The Replace feature can operate in either the forward or the backward direction.*

When you use the Replace feature, WordPerfect assumes that you wish to proceed in a forward direction—searching for the character string from the current cursor position to the right and downward. However, you can also proceed in a backward direction. When WordPerfect prompts for the search string, press UP ARROW to search backward from the cursor, or DOWN ARROW to search forward.

For example, suppose your cursor is at the end of a document when you press the REPLACE (ALT + F2) key. WordPerfect prompts with:

w/Confirm? (Y/N) No

Once you respond by typing **Y** or **N**, WordPerfect asks for the search string with the prompt:

→ Srch:

WordPerfect is assuming a search in the forward direction. Since the cursor is located at the end of the document, you want to search in the opposite direction. So, press UP ARROW, and the prompt changes to read

← Srch:

Now WordPerfect will perform the search in the backward direction. (Or, press DOWN ARROW if you change your mind and again wish to search forward.) Now proceed with the operation as previously described.

Tip: *The Replace command adjusts automatically for differences in length between the search string and the replace string.*

Your search string and replace string can be of different sizes. You can, for example, look for "Smith" and replace it with "Leibernisky, Jr." WordPerfect automatically readjusts the text to fit within the margins.

Tip: *Speed up your typing by using abbreviations for frequently used words or phrases in combination with the Replace command.*

The Replace command can save keystrokes. You can insert an abbreviation in your document and later spell out that abbreviation by using the Replace feature. Suppose, for example, that you work for The Marrinoko Corporation and you're typing a document in which the company name appears many times. While you're working on the document, you insert the name as "TMC". When you've completed the document, use the REPLACE key to substitute "The Marrinoko Corporation" for all occurrences of "TMC".

Tip: *The CANCEL key cancels the Replace command.*

You can press CANCEL (F1) at any time to abort a replace, even while WordPerfect pauses with a prompt before making a substitution.

Trap: *An uppercase search string cannot match lowercase text.*

An uppercase search string matches only uppercase, while lowercase will match either. Thus, if the search string is "SMITH", the cursor will stop only at the occurrence of "SMITH" in the document. If the string is "Smith", it will stop at "SMITH" or "Smith". If the string is "smith", it will stop at "SMITH", "Smith", or "smith". Therefore, to find all occurrences, irrespective of case, type the search string in lowercase letters.

Trap: *WordPerfect inserts the replace string in the text exactly as typed, regardless of the capitalization of the phrase you are replacing.*

A replace string is inserted in a document just as you typed it, whether the phrase to be replaced is typed in upper- or lowercase letters. For instance, suppose you are searching for "large" to replace it with "big". It doesn't matter if the word in the text is typed in as "large", "Large", or "LARGE"; it will be replaced with "big" in lowercase letters, because that's how the replace string was typed.

As a result, follow a certain procedure if you wish to maintain the case of letters as they exist in the text. First, type both the search string and the replace string in uppercase ("BIG" and "LARGE"). Perform the replace. Only those occurrences with all uppercase letters will be found and replaced (see the previous Trap for an explanation). Then, on the next replace, type both the search and the replace string in proper case ("Big" and "Large"). Perform one more replace, where you type both the search and the replace string in lowercase ("big" and "large"). This way, wherever you placed uppercase characters in the document, uppercase will be maintained when replaced with the new phrase.

Follow a different procedure if you want to ensure that a certain phrase is consistently capitalized in the document. Suppose you want *every* occurrence of the word "Canada" to start with a capital C. The problem is that many times you typed "CANADA", or even "canada"—but WordPerfect can fix this for you. Just search for "canada" and replace with "Canada". Because of the way WordPerfect treats capital letters, it changes all occurrences so that only the first letter is uppercase.

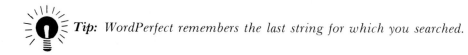

Tip: *WordPerfect remembers the last string for which you searched.*

If you've already executed a replace and then begin a new one, WordPerfect will suggest the previous search string on the prompt line. To change it, simply begin typing, and WordPerfect erases the previous string. Or, you can edit the search string using cursor movement and editing keys.

Trap: *Use spaces cautiously in a character string.*

You can use spaces preceding and following a search string to designate it as a separate word. For example, when searching for the string "use", WordPerfect also stops at "abuse" and "cause" unless you surround the string with spaces. Working with spaces in a character string can be tricky, however, because words at the beginning of a paragraph or at the end of sentences are not surrounded by spaces. When "Use" starts a paragraph, a hard return or a tab precedes it. When "use" ends a sentence, a period or another punctuation mark follows it. Therefore, inserting spaces in the string does not always work. You may have to specify each condition in a search string.

Trap: *If you request an automatic replace on a common character string, you could get unexpected results.*

Obviously, replace with confirmation is necessary when you want to switch phrases only some of the time. For example, to swap "error" for "mistake" in limited instances, you want the Replace command with confirmation; this gives you the opportunity to trade or not to trade with each occurrence of "error".

In addition, confirmation is also important when the search string is a common one that appears in the text in many contexts. For example, suppose you write a letter that mentions due dates in May. Later you realize that the project will take an additional month, so you replace the word "May" with "June" throughout the text. Figure 6-8 shows the last paragraph of the original letter. Figure 6-9 shows the version after an automatic replace. Notice the awkward result, "*June* I call you next week..." instead of "*May* I call you next week...." And then there's "*Junebe* we can meet...," instead of "*Maybe* we can meet...." That's not a letter you want to send!

The lesson here is that confirmation is unnecessary if you're sure you want all the occurrences replaced, and you're sure that the search string is not found in other contexts in the text. Otherwise, the wise approach is to request confirmation.

Tip: *Take advantage of the Replace feature to erase or insert codes.*

In the same way that you search for and replace character strings which contain text, you can also perform those functions on strings that contain codes or a combination of text and codes. To include a code in a string, press the same keystrokes that typically place that code in your document. You can search for text and/or specific codes for replacement with another code or a combination of text/codes. Or, if you specify an empty replace string, you can effectively erase a code throughout a document.

For example, suppose you created your own page breaks in a document by inserting numerous **[HPg]** codes (described in Chapter 9). But now, you decide to

```
As I mentioned, the report must be submitted in May.  May I call
you next week to set up an appointment?  I believe your input will
be valuable.  Maybe we can meet when you return from Chicago.

                                             Sincerely,

                                             May Jordan
```

Figure 6-8. Text before "May" is replaced

```
As I mentioned, the report must be submitted in June.  June I call
you next week to set up an appointment?  I believe your input will
be valuable.  Junebe we can meet when you return from Chicago.

                                             Sincerely,

                                             June Jordan
```

Figure 6-9. Text after "May" is replaced by "June" without confirmation

change the way you paginated the document. To delete all the hard page break codes that you previously inserted:

1. Move the cursor to the top of the document (or just above the text you want the Replace feature to operate on).
2. Press REPLACE (ALT + F2). WordPerfect responds with the following prompt in the lower left-hand corner of the screen:

   w/Confirm? (Y/N) No

3. For confirmation before WordPerfect makes a substitution, type **Y**. For no confirmation type **N** or any key other than Y. In either case, WordPerfect displays another prompt:

   → **Srch:**

4. Press HARD PAGE (CTRL + ENTER), which is the set of keystrokes that normally inserts a hard page code into a document. The prompt now reads

   → **Srch: [HPg]**

5. Press REPLACE (ALT + F2), →SEARCH (F2), or ESC to register the search string of characters. WordPerfect displays the prompt:

   Replace with:

   You want to delete the code. Therefore, do not respond to this prompt.

6. Instead, press REPLACE, →SEARCH, or ESC. The following prompt briefly appears:

   *** Please Wait ***

   If you decline confirmation, WordPerfect carries out the Replace command to the end of the document. All hard page break codes are erased in moments.

   Or, if you choose confirmation, WordPerfect positions the cursor just to the right of the first hard page break code and provides the following message:

   Confirm? (Y/N) No

7. Type **Y** to delete the code. Type **N** or any key other than Y, or press ENTER to retain the code. WordPerfect proceeds to the next occurrence of the code and again asks for confirmation. This continues until all occurrences have been found.

As another example, suppose you want to insert codes to boldface every occurrence of the phrase "XYZ Company" in your document. You can combine codes and characters in the same Replace command. The search string will read

→ **Srch:** XYZ Company

In the replace string you must insert the boldface symbol both before and after the phrase. When WordPerfect prompts for a replace string, press BOLD (F6), type **XYZ Company**, and press BOLD again. (For code pairs such as **[BOLD][bold]**, press the appropriate key once to insert the beginning code, and another time to insert the ending code.) Now, the replace string will read

Replace with: [BOLD]XYZ Company**[bold]**

In this way, WordPerfect will boldface every occurrence of the phrase "XYZ Company".

If you wish to insert the end code of a code pair in a search string or replace string, insert both codes in the pair and then delete the first code. For instance, when WordPerfect prompts for a search string, press the BOLD (F6) key twice. WordPerfect inserts

→ Srch: [BOLD] [bold]

Now you can position the cursor and delete the **[BOLD]** code. WordPerfect will search for only the end bold code **[bold]**.

You can also search for soft returns, soft pages, or special control characters. When WordPerfect prompts for the search string, press HOME, ENTER, to insert **[ISRt]** in the search string, or CTRL + V, in which case WordPerfect prompts

key =

Now press CTRL + K to insert **[SPg]** as part of the search string. Or press CTRL + M to search for a **[SRt]** code. Or press CTRL + another character to insert a special control character. (Sometimes when you convert files from other programs to WordPerfect, a procedure described in Chapter 28, control codes such as **^H** are inserted. You can use the Replace feature to delete those errant codes and clear your document of them.)

In addition, you can search for a special character by pressing COMPOSE (CTRL + 2) and typing the corresponding WordPerfect character number. (For more on special characters and the Compose feature, refer to Chapter 17.)

Although any WordPerfect code can be part of a search string, there's no way to specify a particular parameter within a code. For instance, you can search for a left/right margin code, but not for only those left/right margin codes with a left margin of 0.5 inch and a right margin of 1.5 inches.

Moreover, codes that require the specification of exact parameters should not be included in a replace string. WordPerfect will seem to accept such codes in the replace string, but will ignore the codes during the actual operation. For instance, WordPerfect will not replace with a left/right margin code because it is impossible to specify the left/right margin parameters that you desire (such as a left margin of 1 inch and a right margin of 1.5 inches). The features that can be used in a replace string include

Center
Center Page
Columns On/Off
Flush Right
Font Appearance
Font Size
Hard Page
Hard Space
Hyphen
Hyphenation Cancel
→Indent
→Indent←
Justification On/Off
Margin Release
Math On/Off
Math Operators
Merge Codes
Soft Hyphen
Tab
Tab Align
Widow/Orphan On/Off

Trap: *Don't press* ENTER *unless you want it to be included in a character string.*

The REPLACE (ALT + F2), →SEARCH (F2), or ESC keys begin a replace execution, whereas the ENTER key does not. What if you press ENTER to begin a Replace command? WordPerfect treats a hard return as part of a character string.

For instance, suppose in the replace string you type "Jones" and then press ENTER. The following appears on the screen:

→ **Srch:** Jones**[HRt]**

[HRt] is the hard return code. WordPerfect replaces the search string with "Jones" followed by a hard return. If you press ENTER inadvertently, press BACKSPACE to erase the code from the replace string.

Tip: *WordPerfect can sound a beep each time a search string is not found.*

By selecting Initial Settings, item 5 in the Setup menu, you can turn on or turn off the sound of a beep if a search string is not found. It is initially set to "off" (see Appendix B for details).

Tip: *You can return the cursor to its previous location after a replace.*

Once a replace is complete, you can return to the previous cursor position—the position the cursor was in before you began the replace procedure—by pressing GOTO, GOTO. Suppose, for example, that the cursor is in the middle of page 1 of your document when you initiate a replace. Immediately after the replace is complete, you can bring the cursor back to the middle of page 1 by pressing GOTO, GOTO (CTRL + HOME, CTRL + HOME).

Tip: *You can use wild cards in a character string.*

In Chapter 4, you learned about a wild card that can be substituted for any character in a search string. You can use that same wild card in a search string during a replace. The wild card is the key combination CTRL + V, CTRL + X; this inserts the characters ^X into the search string to represent any character or a space.

Several restrictions apply to the use of the wild card character: it cannot be the first character in the string and it cannot substitute for a code. In addition, it makes no sense to include the wild card in a replace string, since all you'll get is ^X wherever you insert it in the string.

Tip: *The HOME key can extend a replace beyond the standard text.*

You can search for character strings not only in standard text, but also within headers, footers, footnotes, endnotes, graphics box captions, and graphics text boxes. To activate the Extended Replace feature, press the HOME key before pressing REPLACE (ALT + F2). If you requested no confirmation and the cursor moves inside a header, footer, footnote, endnote, or graphics box screen during the search, then you can press EXIT (F7) to return to the standard Typing screen. If you requested confirmation and the cursor pauses on one of these screens, type **Y** or **N** to continue the replace procedure, or press CANCEL (F1) to abort the procedure and return to the typing screen. Or continue by pressing REPLACE again.

Tip: *The Replace feature can be restricted to just a portion of a document.*

You can narrow down the Replace feature so it operates on only one section of text. First, mark that section by using the BLOCK (ALT + F4) key and then follow the same replace procedures as for an entire document.

Be sure to use only the forward replace even if your cursor is at the end of the block. That's because a forward replace always searches forward from the *start* of the block. A backward replace will not work *at all* with blocked text.

Tip: *(When upgrading from 4.2.) In version 5, the Replace feature has been enhanced in several ways.*

Version 5 makes the Replace feature more powerful than before. First of all, you can now perform a replace in either the forward or backward direction simply by using the UP ARROW or DOWN ARROW key when prompted for the search string.

Second, the way in which the replace string works with uppercase letters is more logical. In version 4.2, if the phrase being searched for in the text was in uppercase letters, then the replace string would be substituted in proper case even when typed in lowercase letters. For instance, suppose you were searching for "large" and replacing it with "big". If the word in the text was typed as either "Large" or "LARGE", then it would be replaced with "Big". In Version 5, the replace string is always inserted in the text exactly as typed (for example, "big"), regardless of the capitalization in the text. This causes less confusion.

Third, the codes for features such as indent, left/right indent, flush right, and center can now be included in a replace string. This was not previously possible and will be a welcome addition for many version 4.2 users.

Tips and Traps Summary

Moving and Copying Text

Tip: Use a shortcut if you wish to copy or move a whole sentence, paragraph, or page of text.

Tip: You don't have to retrieve a block immediately after moving or copying it.

Tips and Traps Summary (*continued*)

Tip: When you place a block in the move buffer, it can be inserted an unlimited number of times into many documents.

Trap: You can't move or copy two separate blocks at once.

Tip: As an alternative set of keystrokes, you can delete and then undelete as a means of moving text.

Tip: WordPerfect gives you the ability to move or copy a tabular column.

Tip: WordPerfect gives you the ability to move or copy a rectangular block of text.

Tip: If a code has moved out of the proper position, it is convenient to use the MOVE key to relocate it.

Tip: (When upgrading from 4.2.) In version 5, the move/copy procedure has changed.

Replacing Text

Tip: The Replace feature can operate in either the forward or the backward direction.

Tip: The Replace command adjusts automatically for differences in length between the search string and the replace string.

Tip: Speed up your typing by using abbreviations for frequently used words or phrases in combination with the Replace command.

Tip: The CANCEL key cancels the Replace command.

Trap: An uppercase search string cannot match lowercase text.

Trap: WordPerfect inserts the replace string in the text exactly as typed, regardless of the capitalization of the phrase you are replacing.

Tip: WordPerfect remembers the last string for which you searched.

Trap: Use spaces cautiously in a character string.

Tips and Traps Summary (*continued*)

Trap: If you request an automatic replace on a common character string, you could get unexpected results.

Tip: Take advantage of the Replace feature to erase or insert codes.

Trap: Don't press ENTER unless you want it to be included in a character string.

Tip: WordPerfect can sound a beep each time a search string is not found.

Tip: You can return the cursor to its previous location after a replace.

Tip: You can use wild cards in a character string.

Tip: The HOME key can extend a replace beyond the standard text.

Tip: The Replace feature can be restricted to just a portion of a document.

Tip: (When upgrading from 4.2.) In version 5, the Replace feature has been enhanced in several ways.

7

Positioning and Enhancing Text

A memo or a report can be commonplace or it can sparkle with enhancements that really grab your reader's attention. Even the positioning of words on a page—a centered title, a date flush against the right margin, a word raised slightly above the line—can help focus the reader's attention. Words also can be made to stand out by using special effects such as boldfacing or underlining, a contrasting type style such as italic, and proportional spacing.

This chapter presents various methods for embellishing text. You first learn how to arrange text on the page—whether centered, aligned flush right, aligned in various ways on a tab stop, or positioned horizontally and/or vertically with the Advance and the Superscript and Subscript features. You then discover how to enhance your text by using techniques such as underlining and boldfacing, as well as font changes, which alter a character's typeface, pitch, horizontal spacing, size, and/or appearance. You'll see that many of the options available to you for positioning and enhancing text in your document depend on your printer's capabilities.

Centered and Flush Right Text

As you type a standard line of text, the line begins flush against the left margin. With WordPerfect you can center a line of text between the left and right margins. Also, you can align text flush against the right margin.

FLUSH LEFT

CENTER

FLUSH RIGHT

The procedure is the same, whether text you are about to type will be centered or positioned flush right on the page:

1. Position the cursor at the left margin.
2. Press the CENTER (SHIFT + F6) key and the cursor jumps to the middle of the page. Or press the FLUSH RIGHT (ALT + F6) key and the cursor jumps to the right margin.
3. Type your text and notice how it is automatically positioned for you.
4. Press ENTER to end the line of text and move to the left margin of the next line down. (If the line you are on already ends with a hard return, you can press DOWN ARROW rather than ENTER.) Or, if you centered text, you can press TAB to move to the following tab stop.

What if you wish to center or position flush right a line of text that you've already typed which rests against the left margin? Move the cursor to that line's first character at the left margin. Press the CENTER or the FLUSH RIGHT key. The cursor jumps to the center or to the right margin, pushing the text with it. Then press DOWN ARROW so that the text is repositioned properly.

WordPerfect designates the text for centering or flush right by enclosing the text within a pair of codes, as in the following examples:

[Cntr]Centered text**[C/A/Flrt]**

[Flsh Rt]Text aligned flush right**[C/A/Flrt]**

These codes ensure that the text stays in the location you specified—even if you edit the text within the codes, or even if you change the margins of your document.

Tip: *WordPerfect can center or set flush right many lines of text at once.*

With the Block feature, you can center or set flush right a group of lines:

1. Type the lines of text. Each line should be short, and should end with a hard return.
2. Use the BLOCK (ALT + F4) key to block the lines (if you need a review of the Block command, refer to Chapter 4).
3. Press the CENTER key, in which case WordPerfect responds with a message verifying the Center command:

   [Cntr?] (Y/N) No

   Or press the FLUSH RIGHT key, in which case WordPerfect responds with a message verifying the Flush Right command:

   [Flsh Rt?] (Y/N) No

4. Type **Y** for Yes. Each line of text in the highlighted block is repositioned on the page; the pair of center or flush right codes is inserted, with one at the beginning and one at the end of each line.

   Or type **N** or press ENTER, in which case the command is canceled.

Figure 7-1 shows three blocks of text, each positioned differently: one typed at the left margin, one centered, and a third aligned against the right margin.

Tip: *You can have flush left, centered, and flush right text all on the same line.*

Flush left
We are all accustomed to text that looks just like this. It is flush left, meaning that the first character of every line sits on the left margin.

Centered
You will notice with centered text how the left margin becomes as ragged as the right. That's because each line is centered between the margins.

Flush right
You will notice with right flush text how the last character of every line sits at the right margin. It is the left margin that looks ragged.

Figure 7-1. Three types of text alignment

As long as phrases are short enough, two or three can be positioned differently on the same line. Type a phrase. Press CENTER and type the next phrase. Then press FLUSH RIGHT and type the third phrase. The results will be similar to this:

Left Center Right

Or place just two phrases on a line. At the top of a page, for example, type your company name, press FLUSH RIGHT, and type your division, to produce a format similar to this:

ABC Company Sales Division

Tip: *The Flush Right command is convenient in correspondence.*

It is typical in correspondence to type the date in the upper right-hand corner. Use the Flush Right command to position the date just where you want it to be. (Also see the section of the next chapter, titled "Date and Time Format," to learn how to get WordPerfect to insert the date for you.)

Tip: *To reposition centered or flush right text, you must erase the accompanying codes.*

When you change your mind and want to place at the left margin text that has already been positioned in the center or at the right margin, you must erase the pair of codes surrounding that text. You need to erase only one of the pair; the other code is deleted automatically by WordPerfect.

The codes can be erased either on the Typing screen or on the Reveal Codes screen by using the DEL or the BACKSPACE key. For instance, suppose you wish to delete the centering around a title. On the Reveal Codes screen, you can position the cursor on the **[Cntr]** code that precedes the title or on the **[C/A/Flrt]** code that follows it, and press DEL. On the Typing screen, you can position the cursor on the first character in the title and press BACKSPACE.

Note that when you're on the Typing screen and you press DEL or BACKSPACE to erase a **[Cntr]** or a **[Flsh Rt]** code, WordPerfect erases the code immediately. However, if you attempt to erase the **[C/A/Flrt]** code, which marks the end of centered text or text aligned flush right, WordPerfect prompts for confirmation, asking:

Delete [C/A/Flrt]? (Y/N) No

Type **Y** to delete the code. Or type **N** or press ENTER to abort the command.

Trap: *Within center or flush right codes, don't type more text than can fit on a line.*

When using the Center or the Flush Right command, you might accidentally type more characters than can fit within the margins. For example, suppose you type a short sentence and press CENTER or FLUSH RIGHT, then type additional text. Part of the text may disappear and then reappear erratically, and the cursor may dart back and forth inconsistently. This is because some centered words or words aligned flush right overlap with other words that were aligned at the left margin. To alleviate the problem of text that disappears and reappears erratically, you can switch to the Reveal Codes screen to figure out where the problem lies. Then you can delete words that overlap, or you can delete the center or the flush right code from the line.

Trap: *You cannot center text on a line if the command is preceded by a tab or by more than one space.*

There are two instances in which the CENTER key does not center text between the left and right margins. The first is when you press TAB and then press CENTER; WordPerfect centers the text around the tab stop. The second is when you press the SPACEBAR two or more times in a row and then press CENTER; WordPerfect centers the text around the current cursor position.

Tip: *You can also center text or make it flush right on a tab stop location.*

In addition to centering text or making it flush right in relation to the margins, WordPerfect offers the ability to center text or to make it flush right on tab stops. This can enhance your work with tables, as in the following example:

CENTERED ON A TAB STOP	FLUSH RIGHT ON A TAB STOP
John Smith	March 25
Paulette Jamison	November 31
Scott Witcome	May 3

See the next section of this chapter, "Text Aligned on a Tab Stop," for more information on this procedure.

Tip: *Besides centering text horizontally, WordPerfect can also center text vertically on a page.*

WordPerfect gives you the ability to center a short page of text vertically on a page when it is printed. This is convenient when printing a short letter or a title page for a report (refer to Chapter 9 for details of the procedure).

Tip: *(When upgrading from 4.2.) The CENTER and FLUSH RIGHT keys have not changed.*

Use the CENTER and the FLUSH RIGHT keys as you did before. But be aware that the hidden codes inserted in the text have been changed, as described in a previous Tip. In addition, if you attempt to delete a beginning center or flush right code while on the Typing screen, WordPerfect will no longer prompt to ask for confirmation.

Text Aligned on a Tab Stop

WordPerfect is initially set with tab stops every 0.5 inch, beginning at the left edge of the paper (Chapter 8 describes how to change the tab stop locations). Various keys operate to align text on a tab stop, and can thus enhance the appearance of paragraphs of text or of text typed in a table. As shown in Figure 7-2, each key produces a slightly different effect:

- TAB inserts the code **[TAB]**, and aligns text flush left against the code, operating for only the current line. TAB is commonly used to indent the first line of a paragraph.
- →INDENT (F4) inserts the code **[→Indent]**, and aligns text flush left against the code, operating until it encounters a hard return. Therefore, it essentially creates a new, temporary left margin and is used frequently to indent an entire paragraph of text. If you press →INDENT and then TAB, you create a paragraph in which every line is indented, with the first line of the paragraph indented one extra time.
- →INDENT← (SHIFT + F4) inserts the code **[→Indent←]**, which pushes lines in at both ends. It indents the beginning of each line to the next tab stop and the end of each line by an equal number of spaces. It stops affecting text when a hard return is encountered. →INDENT← can ensure proper format for a long quotation.

THE RECONSTRUCTION PERIOD

TAB

The Civil War ended, but there were a number of aftereffects. The most obvious was the abolition of slavery. Other effects included:

→INDENT

The power of the national government increased, at the expense of states' rights. For example, the national banking system remained even after the war ended.

The fundamental structures of the Southern economy and Southern society were virtually destroyed.

And, what truly happened to the former slaves? How did they adjust to their newfound freedom? According to Mr. Don Samuelson:

→INDENT←

There was mass confusion. Even though Congress set up a Freedman's Bureau in March of 1865, exploitation of the freed slaves did not stop. In most cases, it became worse.

Who oversaw the country during the turbulent years that followed?

←MARGIN RELEASE

Andrew Johnson ascended to the presidency after the shocking assassination of Abraham Lincoln on April 14, 1865. He continued Lincoln's basic policies.

Ulysses S. Grant was elected President in 1868, when the country was in the midst of massive change and reconstruction.

Hayes, the governor from Ohio, succeeded Grant as another Republican president in 1876. He was capable, yet unpopular during his time in office.

For a detailed 30-page report that includes these facts and more on the United States after the Civil War, prices are:

CENTER

Quantity	Price per copy
1 to 19 copies	$2.25 each
20 to 49	1.80
50 to 99	1.35
100 to 499	.95
500 to 999	.80

TAB ALIGN

Figure 7-2. Tab stop keys and their effect

- ←MARGIN RELEASE (SHIFT + TAB) inserts the code **[←Mar Rel]**, pushing one line to the next tab stop to the *left.* It is the mirror image of the TAB key. If you first press →INDENT and then press ←MARGIN RELEASE, you create a hanging paragraph, in which the first line of the paragraph starts at the tab stop to the left of the other lines in the paragraph.
- TAB ALIGN (CTRL + F6) positions text with a specific character (the Decimal/Align alignment character) on the next tab stop, surrounding the text with two hidden codes, **[Align]** and **[C/A/Flrt]**. It is often used in a table to line up a column of numbers on their decimal points.
- CENTER (SHIFT + F6) centers text around a tab stop. WordPerfect surrounds text typed on that tab stop with two codes, **[Cntr]** and **[C/A/Flrt]**.

You can use these keys either while you type the text or after you have typed it. For example, to indent an entire paragraph while you type it:

1. Position the cursor on the line where you wish the text to appear.
2. Press →INDENT until the cursor jumps to the tab stop you desire.
3. Type the paragraph and press ENTER at the end of the paragraph, which ends the indent.

Or, to indent an entire paragraph *after* you have typed it:

1. Position the cursor at the left margin, on the first character of the paragraph you wish to indent.
2. Press →INDENT until the cursor jumps to the tab stop you desire.
3. Press DOWN ARROW to readjust the text.

The TAB ALIGN key differs from the other keys that align text on a tab stop in that a message appears as you press that key:

Align char =.

For example, when you wish to align a number on the decimal point and haven't yet typed the number:

1. Position the cursor on the line where you wish the text to appear.
2. Press TAB ALIGN until the cursor jumps to the tab stop you desire. The following message appears at the bottom of the screen:

   Align char = .

3. Type the number, including the decimal point (period). The message disappears as soon as you type the decimal point; WordPerfect aligns the decimal point at the tab setting.

To cancel the effect of using the Tab, Indent, Margin Release, Center, or Tab Align features, you must delete the codes that you inserted. You can do so on the Typing screen or on the Reveal Codes screen. For example, to cancel the effect of indenting a paragraph when on the Typing screen, position the cursor on the first character in the paragraph and press BACKSPACE to delete the **[→Indent]** code. Or, on the Reveal Codes screen, position the cursor on the **[→Indent]** code and press DEL. Although the Center and the Tab Align features insert a pair of codes to align the text—rather than just one code—you need only erase one of the pair; WordPerfect erases the second code automatically.

Trap: *You can't center on a tab stop until you position the cursor on that tab stop with the TAB key.*

The CENTER key must be used in conjunction with the TAB key to center on a tab stop. First you press the TAB key, to position the cursor on the appropriate tab stop, before you press the CENTER key. For example, to center text on a tab stop, assuming you haven't yet typed the text:

1. Position the cursor on the line where you wish the text to appear.
2. Press TAB to move to the tab stop you desire.

3. Press CENTER.
4. Type the text and press ENTER to end the centering. The cursor moves down to the next line.

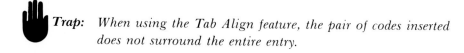

Trap: *When using the Tab Align feature, the pair of codes inserted does not surround the entire entry.*

When you use the Tab Align feature, WordPerfect inserts tab align codes around the text or around the number that *precedes* the decimal point, but not around the entire entry. For example, if you press TAB ALIGN and type **122.44**, the hidden codes inserted are as follows:

[Align]122**[C/A/Flrt]**.44

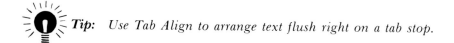

Tip: *Use Tab Align to arrange text flush right on a tab stop.*

The Tab Align feature can align text flush right on a tab stop if you don't type a decimal point as part of the entry. For example, press TAB ALIGN and then type the date **December 31**. Now press ENTER to move down to the next line. The date will be aligned with the *last* character (the number "1") aligned on the tab stop. On the Reveal Codes screen, the text will appear as follows:

[Align]December 31**[C/A/Flrt]**

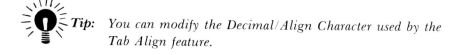

Tip: *You can modify the Decimal/Align Character used by the Tab Align feature.*

Although the Tab Align feature is set, by default, with the Decimal/Align Character as a decimal point, it can be used to align text not only on a decimal point, but also on any letter, number, or symbol, such as %, :, =, or $. For example,

Figure 7-3 shows a memo in which two different decimal/align characters were used. The alignment character was set as the colon (:) for the top half and as the dollar sign (**$**) for the bottom of the page.

You can change the Decimal/Align Character via the Format menu, as follows:

1. Move the cursor to where you want the new alignment character to take effect.
2. Press FORMAT (SHIFT + F8) to display the Format menu.
3. Select Other (4 or O) to display the Other Format menu, as shown in Figure 7-4.

Report Date:	February 14
Topic:	Outstanding Balances
To:	Peter Michels
From:	Collections

==

Status report for the week is as follows:

Total Owed $

Collected in the Current Week $

Outstanding $

Goal for the Coming Week $

Figure 7-3. *Using : and $ as the alignment character*

```
Format: Other

     1 - Advance

     2 - Conditional End of Page

     3 - Decimal/Align Character          .
         Thousands' Separator             ,

     4 - Language                         EN

     5 - Overstrike

     6 - Printer Functions

     7 - Underline - Spaces               Yes
                     Tabs                 No




Selection: 0
```

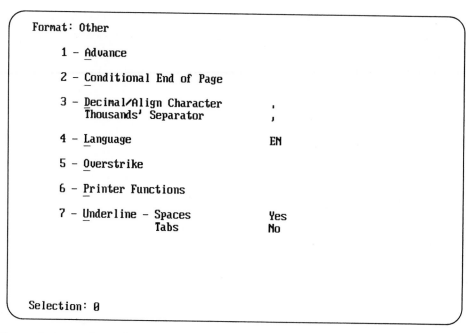

Figure 7-4. The Other Format menu

4. Select Decimal/Align Character (3 or D). The cursor moves to the decimal point.
5. Type in the character that will be used as the new alignment character. The cursor moves to the heading "Thousands' Separator" (the Thousands' Separator is used in conjunction with the Math feature, and is therefore described in Chapter 20).
6. Press ENTER, and then press EXIT (F7) to return to the document.

WordPerfect inserts a code in the text. For example, if the new Decimal/Align

Character is the dollar sign, the hidden code reads **[Decml/Align Char:$,,]**. From that point on until the end of the document (or until the next decimal/align code appears), all text positioned with the TAB ALIGN key aligns to that new character and not to a period. WordPerfect reminds you of this. If you subsequently press TAB ALIGN, WordPerfect responds

Align Char =$

You can change the tab alignment character as many times as you wish in a document. Be sure to position the cursor where you want the change to take effect before pressing FORMAT.

Tip: *WordPerfect enables you to set tab stops with different styles.*

Chapter 8 describes how you can reset tab stops at any location you desire. You also learn that you can set many tab stop styles, so that text is automatically centered, tab aligned, or aligned flush right merely by using the TAB key. In this way, you can avoid using the TAB ALIGN or the CENTER key when typing tabular columns.

Tip: *(When upgrading from 4.2.) Align text on a tab as you did previously.*

Use the TAB, →INDENT, →INDENT←, ←MARGIN RELEASE, TAB ALIGN, and CENTER keys as in version 4.2. Be aware that some of the codes have changed. Another change is that WordPerfect will no longer prompt for confirmation when you wish to erase any of the codes inserted. (In version 4.2, WordPerfect would prompt for confirmation when, on the Typing screen, you attempted to delete codes for margin release, tab align, or center.)

Positioning Text with Advance and Superscript or Subscript

The Advance feature enables you to position text or graphics at a specific location on the page—either vertically or horizontally. You can use Advance Up or Down to position the cursor up or down a certain number of inches. The amount you advance up or down is relative to the cursor position. Or, you can use Advance to Line to position the cursor vertically an exact distance from the top of the page, independent of the current cursor position. For example, suppose that your cursor is located four inches from the top of the page. If you choose to Advance Up one inch, text that follows the advance-up code will print three inches from the top of the page. However, if you choose Advance to Line one inch, text that follows the advance-to-line code will print one inch from the top.

Similarly, you can select Advance Left or Right to position the cursor left or right a certain number of inches. The amount you advance left or right is relative to the cursor position. Or, you can use Advance to Position to locate the cursor horizontally an exact distance from the left edge of the page, independent of the current cursor location. For example, suppose that your cursor is located four inches from the left edge of the page. If you choose to Advance Left 1.5 inches, text that follows the advance-left code will print 2.5 inches from the left edge. However, if you choose Advance to Position 1.5 inches, text that follows the advance-to-position code will print 1.5 inches from the left edge.

The Advance feature enables you to avoid inserting numerous hard returns or spaces when you want text printed at a certain spot on the page. Also, advance code measurements are absolute, so that text is placed at the same spot on the page even if you use a larger or smaller font. While the status line reflects the change in position, the cursor will not move. The visual result happens only at the printer. Use the Advance feature as follows:

1. Move the cursor to where you want the advance to begin.
2. Press the FORMAT (SHIFT + F8) key to view the Format menu.
3. Select Other (4 or O) to display the Other Format menu (as in Figure 7-4).

4. Select Advance (1 or A). WordPerfect prompts

Advance: 1 Up; **2** Down; **3** Line; **4** Left; **5** Right; **6** Position: **0**

5. Choose an item and then enter a distance, either in inches (such as 0.5, which WordPerfect assumes is in inches), centimeters (such as 2c), points (such as 10p) or version 4.2 units (such as 5v for vertical units measured as lines when advancing up or down, or 10h for horizontal units measured as column positions when advancing left or right). WordPerfect converts the entry to inches, if you use a unit of measure other than inches.
6. Press EXIT (F7) to return to the document.

When you select the Advance feature, codes you insert in the text are as follows:

Advance Up	**[AdvUp:]**
Advance Down	**[AdvDn:]**
Advance to Line	**[AdvToLn:]**
Advance Left	**[AdvLft:]**
Advance Right	**[AdvRgt:]**
Advance to Position	**[AdvToPos:]**

The distance that you specified will also appear in the code, following the colon (:). For example, if you advanced up one inch, then the code reads **[AdvUp:1″]**. Any text after such a code will abide by the distance you specified.

For positioning characters slightly above or below a line, use the Superscript or Subscript features, rather than the Advance feature. With Superscript and Subscript, characters are automatically moved up or down by approximately one-third of a line (although this depends on your printer). Thus, you need not bother calculating a distance, as you would with the Advance feature.

When you superscript characters, you position them slightly above the other characters in that line. For example:

X^{14} A word moves ^{up} slightly.

When you subscript, you position characters slightly below the standard line. For example:

H_2O A word moves $_{down}$ slightly.

You can indicate that characters are to be superscripted or subscripted either as you type the text or after typing. If you are about to insert text that is to be superscripted or subscripted, then proceed as follows:

1. Press the FONT (CTRL + F8) key. WordPerfect responds with the Font menu:

   1 Size; **2** Appearance; **3** Normal; **4** Base Font; **5** Print Color: **0**

2. Select Size (1 or S). WordPerfect responds with the Size menu:

   1 Suprscpt; **2** Subscpt; **3** Fine; **4** Small; **5** Large; **6** Vry Large; **7** Ext Large: **0**

3. Select Suprscpt (1 or P). Or select Subscpt (2 or B).
4. Type the text that you want to superscript or subscript.
5. Turn off the Superscript or Subscript feature in one of three ways:
   - Press RIGHT ARROW to position the cursor to the right of the superscript or subscript code (the quickest method).
   - Repeat steps 1 through 3 above.
   - Press the FONT (CTRL + F8) key and select Normal (3 or N), which turns off all font attributes, including superscript or subscript.

If you wish to mark already existing text for superscript or subscript, then the BLOCK key comes into use. Proceed as follows:

1. Press the BLOCK (ALT + F4) key and highlight the text intended for superscript or subscript.
2. Press the FONT (CTRL + F8) key. With **Block on** flashing, the following menu appears:

   Attribute: 1 Size; **2** Appearance: **0**

3. Select Size (1 or S). WordPerfect responds with

    1 Suprscpt; **2** Subscpt; **3** Fine; **4** Small; **5** Large; **6** Vry Large;
    7 Ext Large: **0**

4. Select Suprscpt (1 or P). Or select Subscpt (2 or B). The text is marked, and WordPerfect automatically turns off the Superscript or Subscript and the Block features.

WordPerfect designates the text for superscript or subscript by enclosing the text within a pair of codes, as in the following examples:

[SUPRSCPT]This is text to be printed above the line.**[suprscpt]**
[SUBSCPT]This is text to be printed below the line.**[subscpt]**

When viewing the Reveal Codes screen, you can see these codes surrounding the text.

Trap: *The SPACEBAR is much less reliable for positioning text horizontally than Advance.*

It may seem easier to position text left or right by using the SPACEBAR. However, depending on your printer and how you are formatting a document, the spacing may adjust so that you have more space or less space once the document is printed. For example, when you choose right justification (see Chapter 8), WordPerfect may insert more space between characters on the printed page. Or, if you select a font that uses proportional spacing (described in the last section of this chapter, "Font Changes in the Text"), WordPerfect may insert less space between characters on the printed page. Therefore, use the Advance feature when you want text positioned at a precise location.

Tip: *Select the opposite direction to return to the original line or column position.*

Suppose you use the Advance feature to instruct the printer to print text at a specific location. When you want to return to the original position, you have two choices. First, you can select the opposite direction and enter the appropriate distance. For instance, after selecting Advance Up one inch and typing a short line of text, select Advance Down one inch. As an alternative, you can also use the Advance to Line or Advance to Position option and enter the original line or column value.

Tip: *When measuring for Advance to Line, the measurement should not include the line of text to be printed.*

The Advance to Line feature positions the cursor at a specific location from the top of the page. You should take into account the line height when employing this feature, excluding the line of text that will be printed. For instance, suppose that a blank line on a form is 3.16 inches from the top of the form. Assuming a 12-point font, which means that a line of text has a line height of approximately 0.16 inch, the correct Advance to Line measurement would be 3 inches. (Chapter 8 discusses the Line Height feature.)

Tip: *Advance is useful when positioning text on a preprinted form.*

If you want to use WordPerfect to insert text on a preprinted form, the Advance feature can assist you. Use a ruler to measure exactly where on the form the blanks that you wish to fill in are located. Then use the Advance feature, as you type the information, to fill in the blanks. For example, suppose you discover that the place to insert a person's name is located two inches from the top of the form, and 1.5 inches from the right edge. On the Typing screen, use Advance to Line to move the cursor two inches from the top. Then use the Advance to Position feature to move the cursor 1.5 inches from the right edge of the page. Now type a name. Press ENTER to move down to a new line, and continue until you've inserted advance codes and have typed in all the pertinent information. You're then ready to insert the form into your printer and begin printing.

If you frequently use the same preprinted form, you can create a file that contains nothing but Advance codes and comments (see Chapter 3 for details on the Comment feature) to tell you what information goes on which line. That way, you'll be able to fill out the form quickly.

Tip: *Use the Advance feature to print twice in the same location.*

Laser printers have the ability to print anywhere on a page before ejecting that page of text from the printer. As a result, you can take advantage of the Advance feature to print twice in the same location. This enhances your ability to work with certain WordPerfect features. For example, you can type a full page of text starting at the top of the page, use the Advance feature to advance back up to the top of the same page, and then use the Line Draw feature (Chapter 17) to draw a large box. When the text is printed, there will be a border (or box) around the text. Or you can type text with double spacing, use the Advance feature to advance back to the top of the page, and then use the Line Numbering feature (Chapter 21) to number lines in single spacing. When the text is printed, line numbers will appear at the left margin of each line, while the text will appear on every other line. Because of an advance code in the text, the printer prints twice on the same page.

If your printer prints only top to bottom, and therefore can't move back up to the top of the page to print additional text before ejecting the page, then the Advance feature won't be useful in conjunction with features such as Line Draw or Line Numbering; instead, you will actually have to print two times on the same piece of paper to achieve this effect.

Tip: *How superscript and subscript appear on the Typing screen depends on your computer display.*

You will not actually see the superscript or subscript text as being above or below the standard line; the effect will appear when printed. WordPerfect knows that text should be superscripted or subscripted because of the pair of codes that surround the text.

However, you can indicate superscript or subscript on the Typing screen in various ways, depending on your monitor and display card. If you have a color monitor, you can indicate how WordPerfect should show these features on the screen by selecting a specific color (and/or a specific font if your monitor has graphics capabilities) for superscript and another for subscript. If you have a monochrome monitor (such as green or amber characters only on a black background), you can select any combination of boldface, blink, underline, or blocked (reverse video). This is accomplished with option 3, Display, on the Setup menu (for more on the Setup menu, refer to Appendix B).

Tip: *Preview how text will be positioned before you print.*

Remember that while the status line will reflect a change in position caused by Advance, the text you type following the advance code will not show the change; the result takes place at the printer.

Similarly, you can't actually view the superscript or subscript characters as being above or below the standard line of text when typing a document. The characters are raised or lowered in relation to the rest of the line only on the printed document.

However, WordPerfect offers a feature called View Document (discussed in Chapter 14), whereby you can see how text will actually appear when printed. Using this feature, you can (depending on your monitor) see where the text positioned with Advance Up or Down or with Superscript or Subscript will print on the page. (See Chapter 14 for further discussions on the View Document features.)

Tip: *Superscript or subscript may cause the size of characters to change.*

Depending on your printer, you may find that superscripted or subscripted characters are smaller in height than the normal text. This often makes text more readable.

Trap: *Not all printers support the Superscript or Subscript command or the Advance command.*

Some printers do not respond to Superscript and Subscript commands. If you try to print superscript or subscript and the printer doesn't respond, then try using Advance. If the Advance command does not work, then your printer cannot place characters above or below the standard line of text.

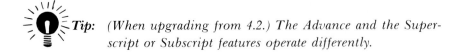

Tip: *(When upgrading from 4.2.) The Advance and the Superscript or Subscript features operate differently.*

The Advance feature has been enhanced in version 5. Not only can you position text vertically on the page, but horizontally as well. The distance can be indicated in inches, centimeters, or points, or in version 4.2 units. The Advance feature is accessed with the FORMAT key, rather than what was called the SUPER/SUBSCRIPT key in version 4.2.

Superscript and Subscript are now accessed with the FONT key. Also, these features no longer operate on a single character. Instead, once you activate Superscript or Subscript, the feature remains in effect until you turn it off.

Underlined and Boldfaced Text

As you type, you can underline, so that a solid line is placed just below the text, or you can boldface, so that text is printed darker than it normally is. When you underline or boldface, WordPerfect places a pair of hidden codes on both sides of the text to mark the enhancement: **[UND]** and **[und]** for underlined text, and **[BOLD]** and **[bold]** for boldfaced text.

Underlining is controlled by the UNDERLINE (F8) key. Similarly, boldfacing is controlled by the BOLD (F6) key. If you are about to type text that you want underlined or boldfaced, keep in mind that the UNDERLINE and BOLD keys work like a toggle switch; press once to turn the feature on and a second time to turn the feature off. The procedure is the same for both:

1. Press the UNDERLINE (F8) key. An underscore appears underneath the status line's position number, indicating that the Underline feature is on. (With a color monitor, the position number changes color.)

   Or press the BOLD (F6) key. The status line's position number becomes as bold as the rest of the status line, indicating that the Bold feature is on. (With a color monitor, the position number changes color.)

2. Type the text you want underlined or boldfaced.
3. Press the UNDERLINE key a second time to turn off the Underline command. The status line returns to normal.

   Or press the BOLD key a second time to turn off the Bold command. The status line returns to normal.

With already existing text, the BLOCK key comes into use. Suppose that you've already typed some words and, as an afterthought, you realize that you'd like to underline or boldface them. To do this:

1. Position the cursor on the first character of the first word.
2. Mark the block with the BLOCK (ALT + F4) key. **Block on** flashes on the screen.
3. Press the UNDERLINE (F8) key. Or press the BOLD (F6) key.

When you use the BLOCK key, it is no longer necessary to turn off Underline or Bold; WordPerfect automatically starts these features at the beginning of the block and ends them after the last highlighted character.

If you wish to remove boldfacing or underlining, you must delete the codes that surround the text. You need to remove only one code from the pair of codes; the other is removed automatically by WordPerfect. On the Reveal Codes screen, position the cursor on the code and press DEL (or position it just to the right of the code and press BACKSPACE). If you're viewing the Typing screen and press DEL or BACKSPACE to erase a code, WordPerfect prompts for verification. For example, if it's a bold code you're deleting, the prompt reads

Delete [bold]? (Y/N) No

Type **Y** to delete boldfacing. Or type **N**, or press any other key, to leave the bold code in your document.

Tip: *If boldfaced text looks no different from standard text on a monochrome screen, adjust the brightness and contrast.*

Like a television set, a monochrome monitor can be adjusted for contrast and brightness. Some monitors provide one knob for both, while others have a separate knob for contrast (often labeled with a picture of a half-moon) and another for brightness (often labeled with a picture of the sun). Sometimes you must adjust the knobs in order to see boldfaced text.

On a monitor with two knobs, try the following: (1) boldface a portion of text on the screen; (2) turn down the contrast and brightness knobs until the text disappears; (3) turn up the brightness knob until the boldfaced text is bright (but the background stays black); and (4) turn up the contrast knob until all the text is displayed. You can now distinguish bold text from standard text.

Tip: *How bold and underline appear on the Typing screen depends on your computer display.*

You can indicate how bold and underline display on the Typing screen in various ways, depending on your monitor and display card. If you have a color monitor, you can indicate how WordPerfect should show these features on the screen by selecting a specific color (and/or a specific font if your monitor has those graphics capabilities) for underline, and another for bold. On EGA and VGA monitors, you can even select an underlining font, so that you can see underlining on screen.

If you have a monochrome monitor (such as green characters on a black background), then you may be able to indicate underline or bold with any combination of blink, bold, blocked, underline, or normal. (On some monochrome monitors, you are unable to alter the way bold or underlined text is displayed on screen.)

Change the way Bold and Underline appear on screen by using option 3, Display, on the Setup menu (for more on the Setup menu, refer to Appendix B).

Trap: *Some monitors may not show underlining as it will appear when printed.*

On certain color monitors (such as CGA), you cannot see underlining on the screen; instead, the text is displayed in different colors.

Even on color monitors for which an underlining font is available, you might see the underlining in a manner that is different from the result at the printer. For instance, some monitors will show no underlining of spaces, even though the result at the printer will have spaces underlined:

> Display on the screen
> Result at the printer

Tip: *Try a shortcut if you forget to turn off the Bold or Underline features.*

You'll have pages of boldfaced or underlined text if you turn on Bold or Underline and then forget to turn off the toggle switch. Suppose you press UNDERLINE and type a sentence. You continue for an entire page before you realize that Underline is still on. There are several ways to fix the text so that only the first sentence is underlined. Here's the basic method:

1. At the bottom of the page, when you realize you haven't yet turned off Underline, press DEL. The cursor should encounter the hidden underline code, in which case (if you're on the Typing screen) WordPerfect prompts

   Delete [und]? (Y/N) No

   (If you don't encounter the underline code and pressing DEL begins to erase your text, then the underline code is located elsewhere. Reveal codes, find the underline code, and delete it.)
2. If you're on the Typing screen, type **Y**. The underscore disappears from the entire page. (If you're on the Reveal Codes screen, WordPerfect doesn't prompt for confirmation.)
3. Use the directional arrow keys to move back to the beginning of the sentence that you wish to underline, then use the BLOCK key in conjunction with the UNDERLINE key to do so.

Here's a shortcut for underlining only one sentence (when you've typed a whole page with Underline on), which circumvents the need to use the BLOCK key:

1. Position the cursor one character past the period that ends the sentence that should remain underlined.

2. Press UNDERLINE (F8). WordPerfect assumes that you wish to end and then begin Underline again, and so inserts **[und][UND]**.
3. Press DEL to delete the **[UND]** code (and type **Y** if prompted to do so). Only the sentence preceding the cursor remains underlined.

Tip: *Moving the cursor through text turns off Underline and Bold.*

If you press the UNDERLINE or the BOLD key to turn on one of these two features, you actually insert both the beginning and end code at the same time—such as **[UND]** and **[und]**. When you press UNDERLINE or BOLD to turn the feature off, the cursor actually jumps just to the right side of the **[und]** or the **[bold]** code. These features can also be switched off automatically when you stop typing and press a directional arrow key or another key combination to move the cursor. For example, press BOLD, type some text, and then press RIGHT ARROW, instead of BOLD, to end the boldfacing.

Tip: *You can underline and boldface the same section of text.*

Underline and boldface at once as you type: press UNDERLINE, press BOLD, and type the text. Then press UNDERLINE and press BOLD to turn off both features. You can also underline and boldface already existing text, but you must do so in two steps. First, mark the text with the BLOCK key and press UNDERLINE. Then mark the text a second time with BLOCK and press BOLD.

Tip: *Underline and Bold are also located on the FONT (CTRL + F8) key.*

Underlining and boldfacing are also located on the FONT (CTRL + F8) key. Rather than using BOLD (F6) or UNDERLINE (F8), you can:

1. Press the FONT key. WordPerfect responds with the Font menu:

   1 Size; **2** Appearance; **3** Normal; **4** Base Font; **5** Print Color: **0**

2. Select Appearance (2 or A). The following menu appears

   1 Bold; **2** Undrln; **3** Dbl Und; **4** Italc; **5** Outln; **6** Shadw; **7** Sm Cap; **8** Redln; **9** Stkout: **0**

3. Select Bold (1 or B). Or select Undrln (2 or U).
4. Type the text that you want boldfaced or underlined.
5. Turn off the Bold or Underline in one of three ways:
   - Press RIGHT ARROW to position the cursor to the right of the final underline or boldface code.
   - Repeat steps 1 through 3 above.
   - Press the FONT (CTRL + F8) key and select Normal (3 or N), which turns off all font utilities, including bold and underline.

If you wish to underline or boldface already existing text, then the BLOCK key can be used in combination with the FONT key.

While use of the FONT key can be cumbersome, there is at least one instance in which it can be convenient: if you've changed the appearance of the text in more than one way and you wish to turn off *all* the enhancements. For example, suppose that you've chosen to redline, underline, and boldface a piece of text. (Redline is an editing tool that is described in Chapter 5.) To turn off all three features at once, you can press the FONT key and then select Normal (3 or N). That selection cancels all size or appearance changes that you made. Thus, you end the redlining, underlining, and boldfacing all at once.

Another enhancement you can request is double underlining, but you can request it only with the FONT key (see the following Tip).

Tip: *You can underline with a double underscore rather than a single underscore.*

When you use the UNDERLINE (F8) key, WordPerfect assumes that you wish to underline with a single underscore. When you use the FONT (CTRL + F8) key, however, you also have the option of a double underscore as you underline.

1. Press the FONT key. WordPerfect responds with the Font menu.
2. Select Appearance (2 or A). The following menu appears :

   1 Bold; **2** Undrln; **3** Dbl Und; **4** Italc; **5** Outln; **6** Shadw; **7** Sm Cap; **8** Redln; **9** Stkout: **0**

3. Select Dbl Und (3 or D).
4. Type the text that should have a double underline.
5. Turn off the Double Underline feature in one of three ways:
   - Press RIGHT ARROW to position the cursor to the right of the final underline code (the quickest alternative).
   - Repeat steps 1 through 3 above.
   - Press the FONT (CTRL + F8) key and select Normal (3 or N).

As with a single underline, you can use the Setup menu to determine how double underlining is displayed on screen.

Be aware that some printers do not support WordPerfect's Double Underline feature. Instead, these printers either ignore the double underline request or print a choppy underline instead of a smooth, solid one. The easiest way to see whether your printer supports Double Underline is to experiment: type and underline some words using the double underline, and print the page.

Trap: *You cannot use boldface with certain printers unless you change the cartridge or the print wheel.*

Some printers do not have the capacity to boldface unless you change their cartridge or print wheel. Experiment with your printer to see whether a different cartridge or print wheel is required to boldface text.

Tip: *You can specify whether spaces and tabs are underlined.*

You can choose whether or not WordPerfect underlines spaces and tabs (in addition to characters) in the text. The default setting is to underline spaces but not that portion of your document that follows a character and precedes a **[TAB]** code. The alternatives are shown in Figure 7-5.

You can change the default underline style as follows:

1. Move the cursor to where you want the underline style to change.
2. Press the FORMAT (SHIFT + F8) key to view the Format menu.
3. Select Other (4 or O) to display the Other Format menu, shown in Figure 7-4.

Spaces underlined

Please call me as soon as possible.

Spaces not underlined

Please call me as soon as possible.

Tabs and spaces underlined

Name	Current Address	City
Smith	229 Dickson Drive	Baltimore

Tabs and spaces not underlined

Name	Current Address	City
Smith	229 Dickson Drive	Baltimore

Figure 7-5. Alternative underline style choices

4. Select Underline—Spaces/Tabs (7 or U).
5. Type **Y** or **N** to indicate whether you wish to underline spaces.
6. Type **Y** or **N** to indicate whether you wish to underline tabs.
7. Press EXIT to return to the document.

When you make an underline style change, a code is inserted at the current cursor position in the text which indicates whether you chose to underline spaces and/or tabs. For instance, if you chose to underline both, then the code reads **[Undrln:Spaces,Tabs]**. Or, if you chose to underline neither spaces nor tabs, the code simply reads **[Undrln:]**. The code takes effect from that point forward in the text (or until the next **[Undrln]** code appears). Therefore, you must position the cursor before pressing FORMAT. You can choose various styles for different portions of the text by inserting underline codes throughout the text.

Tip: *(When upgrading from 4.2.) Although the basics of underlining and boldfacing are the same, a few commands have changed.*

Underline and boldface as you did previously—by using the UNDERLINE and BOLD keys, respectively. There's now also a second method for underlining and boldfacing—using the FONT key. Be aware that the codes you insert are different than in version 4.2.

In version 5 you have the option of underlining tabs (which replaces the version 4.2 concept of continuous and non-continuous underline), and also canceling the underlining of spaces. Previously, you had to continually turn on and off UNDERLINE to avoid underlining spaces. These options are now found on the Other Format menu, accessed via the FORMAT key.

If you wish to use a double underscore, you can do so by selecting Double Underlining via the FONT key. In version 4.2, you selected double underscore by changing the underline style.

Font Changes in the Text

In WordPerfect, altering the *font* means that you alter some or all of the following characteristics, which determine the look of printed text:

- **Typeface** The general design or style category of characters. For example, books are often published in Times Roman type. A standard typewriter produces lettering in Courier. Words are often emphasized in Helvetica.
- **Pitch** The density of characters per inch (CPI) on a line. Ten characters per inch is referred to as 10-pitch (pica), 12 characters per inch equal 12-pitch (elite), and so on. The larger the pitch size, the smaller or more tightly packed the characters.
- **Horizontal spacing** How characters are spaced on a line. Standard text is *monospaced,* that is, each character occupies the same amount of space. For example, monospaced 10-pitch letters each take up one-tenth of an inch. The alternative is *proportional spacing,* wherein each character occupies a different amount of space in proportion to its width. For example, narrow letters like "i" take up less space than wider letters like "m," so that all the letters are equidistant from one another. Although the difference is subtle, proportional spacing gives documents a more polished, "typeset" look than does monospacing.
- **Character set** The specific set of symbols that can be printed when using a font. These have names such as U.S. ASCII, Roman Eight, Legal and Math, and Line Draw.
- **Type style or appearance** The specific style of characters available to add emphasis or contrast—such as italic, bold, shadow, or small caps. The term type style applies to a particular typeface. (You learned about bold, along with underline, in the previous section of this chapter, "Underlined and Boldfaced Text.")
- **Type size** The size or height of characters. Type is measured in points, and

there are approximately 72 points per vertical inch. It is most common for standard text to print in 8-, 10-, or 12-point.

Figure 7-6 shows some font examples. Some printers support few fonts, while others support many. Still others use a different print wheel or cartridge to do so.

The default setting for your current font depends on which initial font you chose when designating your printer. As you select your printer (see Appendix A for a discussion of selecting a printer), WordPerfect offers a choice of those fonts that your printer will support; you select one as your initial font. For instance, when selecting the HP LaserJet Series II as your printer, you may have chosen as your initial font: Courier, 12-point, 10-pitch, PC-8 character set. Or, when selecting the Okidata 192, you could have chosen near-letter-quality, Pica 10-pitch. For daisy wheel printers, more fonts are available to choose from if you purchase additional print wheels. For laser printers, more fonts are available if you purchase cartridges or downloadable fonts.

There are three different ways to change a font in your document: by changing the initial font for an entire document, by changing the base font for a section of your text, or by changing a font attribute for a section of your text.

When you wish to display your initial font and/or change that font for an entire document, you use the Initial Font option via the FORMAT key:

1. The cursor can be positioned anywhere in your document.
2. Press the FORMAT (SHIFT + F8) key.
3. Select Document Format (3 or D). Figure 7-7 shows the Document Format menu. Notice that option 3 indicates that the initial font for this particular example is Courier, 10-pitch, using the PC-8 character set.
4. If you do not wish to alter the initial font, then simply press EXIT (F7) to return to your document.

   Or, if you wish to change the initial font, then:

   Select Initial Font (3 or F). WordPerfect displays the Document Initial Font screen, which indicates the fonts currently available for your printer. For example, Figure 7-8 shows this screen for an HP LaserJet Series II printer with two cartridges present (the B and the R cartridges). The current initial font is preceded by an asterisk.

```
Courier font, monospaced, 10-pitch, 12-point.  Courier is used as
the basic, standard typeface.
```

Times Roman, a proportionally spaced font, 10-point. Notice that the 10-point type size is smaller in height that the 12-point type shown above (in the Courier font). Also notice the professional look of this typeface when it is proportionally spaced.

Times Roman font, also 10-point, with italic. Letters are slanted to provide a cursive effect.

PRESENTATION FONT, 8.1-PITCH, 16-POINT, BOLDFACED. WITH A PITCH OF 8.1, FEWER CHARACTERS CAN FIT ACROSS ONE LINE. AND, WITH 16-POINT TYPE SIZE, THE CHARACTERS ARE LARGER IN HEIGHT.

Figure 7-6. *Examples of different fonts*

```
Format: Document

     1 - Display Pitch - Automatic        Yes
                         Width            0.1"

     2 - Initial Codes

     3 - Initial Font                     Courier 10 pitch (PC-8)

     4 - Redline Method                   Printer Dependent

     5 - Summary




Selection: 0
```

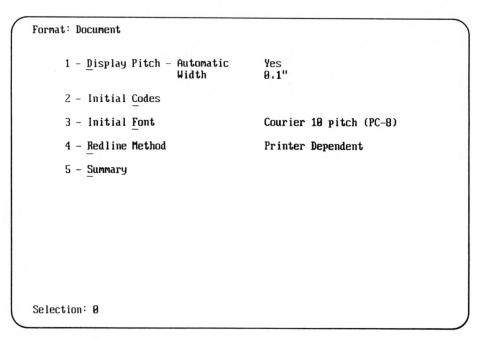

Figure 7-7. *The Document Format menu*

Press the UP ARROW or the DOWN ARROW key until the cursor is positioned on the font you wish to select.

Or, select **N**, Name search, and then begin to type the name of the font that you wish to select until the cursor is positioned on that font. Then press ENTER or EXIT (F7) to end the name search.

Choose Select (1 or S) to select that font. The asterisk moves in front of that font, and you are returned to the Document Format menu. The change you made is reflected next to item 3, Initial Font.

Press EXIT (F7) to return to your document.

When you change the initial font for a document, no code is inserted in the text. Instead, that initial font change is stored as part of the invisible packet of information (prefix) that is saved along with the document. That initial font remains unless you again use the FORMAT key to change it.

In addition to changing the initial font for an entire document, you can also

```
Document: Initial Font

* Courier 12pt 10 pitch (PC-8)
  Courier 12pt 10 pitch (Roman-8)
  Courier 12pt Bold 10 pitch (PC-8)
  Courier 12pt Bold 10 pitch (Roman-8)
  Helv 14.4pt Bold
  Letter Gothic 14pt 10 pitch
  Line Printer 08.5pt 16.66 pitch (PC-8)
  Line Printer 08.5pt 16.66 pitch (Roman-8)
  Presentations 14pt Bold 10 pitch
  Presentations 16pt Bold 8.1 pitch
  Presentations 18pt Bold 6.5 pitch
  Tms Rmn 08pt
  Tms Rmn 10pt
  Tms Rmn 10pt Bold
  Tms Rmn 10pt Italic






1 Select; N Name search: 1
```

Figure 7-8. A Document Initial Font screen for the HP LaserJet Series II and several cartridges

modify that font for *a particular section of text* in the document. You do so by using the Base Font option via the FONT key:

1. Position the cursor in your document where you want a change in the current font to occur. For example, to change the font beginning with the text on page 3, position the cursor at the top of page 3.
2. Press the FONT (CTRL + F8) key. WordPerfect displays the Font menu:

   1 Size; **2** Appearance; **3** Normal; **4** Base Font; **5** Print Color: **0**

3. Select Base Font (4 or F). WordPerfect displays a Base Font screen, which lists the available fonts for your printer. The screen is identical to the Initial Font screen (an example of which is shown in Figure 7-8), except that the heading reads "Base Font" rather than "Document: Initial Font." An asterisk appears next to the current font.

4. Press the UP ARROW or the DOWN ARROW key until the cursor is positioned on the font that you wish to select.

   Or press **N**, Name search, and then begin to type the name of the font that you wish to select until the cursor is positioned on that font. Then press ENTER or EXIT (F7) to end the name search.

5. Choose Select (1 or S) to select that font. The asterisk moves in front of that font, and you are returned to the Typing screen.

A **[Font:]** code is inserted in the text which changes the base font from that point forward in the text (or until you select another base font). For example, suppose you select a Courier, 12-point, 10-pitch font using the Roman-8 character set. Then the code inserted is **[Font:Courier 12pt 10 pitch (Roman-8)]**. If you then wish to change back to the original font, reposition the cursor farther forward in the text and follow the steps outlined above.

Even after you change your font—your initial font for an entire document and/or your base font for a specific section of text—you still have another option. You can maintain the same font, but alter only a specific *font attribute for a section of text.* In WordPerfect, a font attribute refers to a particular type size or appearance characteristic of your font. For instance, you can select to print using the same font, but by selecting very large as your size, you are increasing the pitch and/or height of characters (depending on your printer). Or you can select to print using the same font, but by selecting italic you are causing the characters to be slanted, as they are in italic type styles.

You can change a font attribute either while you type or after you type the text for which you wish to change the attribute (just as you can underline a section of text while you type or after you type that text). To change an attribute while you type the text:

1. Position the cursor where you want a change in size or appearance to occur.

2. Press the FONT (CTRL + F8) key. WordPerfect displays the Font menu:

   1 Size; **2** Appearance; **3** Normal; **4** Base Font; **5** Print Color: **0**

3. Select Size (1 or S), in which case the following menu appears:

    1 Suprscpt; **2** Subscpt; **3** Fine; **4** Small; **5** Large; **6** Vry Large; **7** Ext Large: **0**

    Or select Appearance (2 or A) from the Font menu, in which case this menu appears:

    1 Bold; **2** Undrln; **3** Dbl Und; **4** Italc; **5** Outln; **6** Shadw; **7** Sm Cap; **8** Redln; **9** Stkout: **0**

4. Select a size or appearance attribute. (Refer to previous sections in this chapter for specifics on superscript and subscript, bold, underline, and double underline; refer to Chapter 5 for details on redline and strikeout.)

5. Type the text that should have the attribute you selected.

6. Turn off the attribute in one of three ways:

    - Press RIGHT ARROW to position the cursor to the right of the end code.
    - Repeat steps 2 through 4 above.
    - Press the FONT (CTRL + F8) key and select Normal (3 or N), which turns off *all* font attributes.

If you wish to change an attribute for already existing text, then the BLOCK key is used. Proceed as follows:

1. Use the BLOCK (ALT + F4) key to highlight the text for which you wish to change the attribute.

2. Press the FONT (CTRL + F8) key. With **Block on** flashing, the following menu appears:

    Attribute: 1 Size; **2** Appearance: **0**

3. Select Size (1 or S). Or Select Appearance (2 or A).
4. Select an attribute. The text is changed, and WordPerfect automatically turns off the Attribute and the Block features.

WordPerfect designates the text for a different size or appearance attribute by enclosing the text within a pair of codes, as follows:

Size Attribute Codes	Appearance Attribute Codes
[FINE][fine]	[ITALC][italc]
[SMALL][small]	[OUTLN][outln]
[LARGE][large]	[SHADW][shadw]
[VRY LARGE][vry large]	[SM CAP] [sm cap]
[EXT LARGE][ext large]	

When viewing the Reveal Codes screen, you can see these codes surrounding the text.

Tip: *Your font choices depend on the fonts your printer has available.*

Each printer has its own set of allowable fonts. These fonts are shown when you view the Initial Font or Base Font screen for the currently selected printer. For printers that can print in either landscape or portrait orientation (laser printers), the fonts shown are only those available for the current orientation. The orientation is determined based on the paper type and size you selected for that document. (See Chapter 8 for more on paper size and type.)

For your printer, additional fonts may be available if you purchase additional print wheels, cartridges, or downloadable fonts. To choose from those additional fonts, you must inform WordPerfect that you have other cartridges and fonts available when you define your printer. See Appendix A for the procedure to do so.

Tip: *You can change the default setting for the intial font.*

The default initial font for a certain printer depends on how you defined your printer to work with WordPerfect. If you wish to use a font that is not the default setting in most of your documents, you can change your printer definition on the Printer Selection menu. (See Appendix A for a discussion on defining printers.) That way, you will need to change the initial font for a specific document only if it is different from the font that you typically use.

Tip: *A change in the initial font affects not only the font used for the body of the text, but the font for headers, footers, footnotes, and endnotes as well.*

Using the FORMAT key to change the initial font of the document alters the entire document, including the font used to print headers, footers, footnotes, and endnotes. Conversely, a change in the base font affects only text or header or footer codes following the base font code.

As an example, suppose that you change your initial font to Helvetica. Then, on page three of your document, you insert a base font code to change to a Courier font. The text of the first two pages, all footnotes and endnotes, and any headers or footers for which the codes are located on page one or two will be printed in Helvetica. The text starting at page three, including any headers and footers whose codes you insert in the text following the base font code, will be printed in Courier. (For more information on headers and footers, refer to Chapter 9, and for more on footnotes and endnotes, refer to Chapter 23.)

Tip: *How font changes are reflected on screen depends on your computer display.*

When you alter your initial or base font, you will see no change in the size or shape of your characters (but margins and line height may change—see the following Tip).

When you alter a font attribute, WordPerfect can show on screen only what is possible based on your monitor and your display card. For example, if you have a monochrome monitor with no graphics card, you will be unable to view any change in the size or style of your characters on screen. If you have an EGA or VGA monitor and a standard graphics card, you have the ability to view small caps or italic attributes. If you have a monochrome monitor and the Hercules Graphics Card Plus with Ramfont, you can view attributes, such as italic and extra large characters, on screen.

You can indicate how a font attribute will appear on screen by using the Setup menu. If you have a color monitor, you can indicate that certain attributes appear in a different color. If you have a monochrome monitor, you can indicate that certain attributes appear with a combination of blink, bold, block, or underline. In addition, depending on your graphics display, you may be able to indicate certain attributes with italic, small caps, and so on. (Refer to Appendix B for a discussion on selecting how font attributes are displayed on screen, which depends on your computer equipment.)

Tip: *When you alter a font or font attribute, WordPerfect adjusts the document's margins and line height automatically.*

When you change your initial font, base font, or font attribute, this may result in a change in pitch, so that more or fewer characters fit on a line. WordPerfect automatically readjusts margins for you. For example, suppose that left and right margins are both set at one inch (Chapter 8 describes how to change your margin settings). With 10-pitch, approximately 65 characters can fit across the width of the page (depending on your printer). If you then select a font that results in a change to 12-pitch, approximately 78 characters will fit across the width of the page. The text is readjusted on screen to reflect the fact that more characters can now fit across the printed page.

The "Pos" number on the status line works in increments depending on the font's pitch. For instance, if that font is 10-pitch, then the "Pos" number increases by 0.1-inch increments as you move the cursor horizontally.

Now a full line of text may no longer fit across the width of your screen. Thus you may need to press HOME, LEFT ARROW or HOME, HOME, LEFT ARROW to view the beginning of a line, and HOME, RIGHT ARROW, or HOME, HOME, RIGHT

ARROW, or END, to view the end of the line (refer to Chapter 4 for more on cursor movement keys).

Moreover, a change in font may result in a change in line height. For example, you may select an attribute such as extra large. If that attribute causes an increase in the size of the character (that is, a "taller" character), then the line height will be readjusted automatically; because fewer lines of text will fit on a page, WordPerfect will insert a soft page break earlier than if you had selected a "shorter" character.

The "Ln" number on the status line works in increments depending on the font's type size. For instance, if that font is 11-point, then the "Ln" number increases by 0.15-inch increments as you move the cursor vertically. If you change your font many times in one document, you may wish to select a fixed line height to maintain consistent spacing. (See Chapter 8 for more on line height and Chapter 9 for more on page breaks.)

Tip: *You can change more than one attribute for the same section of text.*

You can enhance a section of text in a variety of ways. For instance, you can choose that a sentence print simultaneously with underlining, very large type, and italic type. But select the three attributes before you type the sentence. Then, after typing the sentence, there is a quick way to turn off all three attributes at once: press the FONT key and then select Normal (3 or N) from the Font menu. That selection cancels all size or appearance changes that you made. Alternatively, you can select all three attributes for text already typed, but then you must block the sentence three separate times.

Tip: *Type sizes and styles are not necessarily available for each font.*

Each type of printer has a unique set of characteristics and, therefore, a unique set of font capabilities. Your font options are listed when you select Initial Font (3 or F) on the Document Format menu, or when you select Base Font (4 or F) on the Font menu.

Depending on the initial base font you've chosen, a change in type size or style may or may not result in a change on the printed page. For example, in one font, selecting fine, small, large, very large, and extra large may have no effect because that font offers no variation in type size. In another font, perhaps only selecting very large produces a larger type. One font may have the capacity for proportional spacing, while another works in monospacing. Or a certain printer may not have the capacity to print in italic no matter which font is chosen.

Obviously, there is great variety in the manner in which printers operate. The best way to uncover the talents and quirks of your particular printer is to experiment with how WordPerfect and your printer work together (see Chapter 15 for some specifics on doing this). Once you know what each font and attribute change represents for your printer, you have solid control over the look of characters on a printed page.

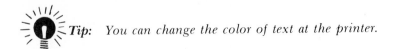

Tip: *You can change the color of text at the printer.*

If you have a printer that prints in color, then you have another option for embellishing your text—change the color of text at the printer. To print in a specified color:

1. Position the cursor where you want the color change to take effect at the printer.
2. Press the FONT (CTRL + F8) key.
3. Select Print Color (5 or C). The menu shown in Figure 7-9 appears.
4. Select a color by typing the corresponding number or letter. There are 11 predefined colors: Black, White, Red, Green, Blue, Yellow, Magenta, Cyan, Orange, Gray, and Brown. WordPerfect indicates the primary color mixture (the relative intensity of red, green, and blue) that creates the particular color you selected.
5. Press EXIT (F7) to return to the document.

WordPerfect inserts a code in the text to affect the color of printed text from that position forward. If you selected A, Gray, for example, then the code inserted is **[Color:Gray]**.

```
Print Color

                               Primary Color Mixture
                              Red       Green       Blue
```

	Red	Green	Blue
1 - Black	0%	0%	0%
2 - White	100%	100%	100%
3 - Red	67%	0%	0%
4 - Green	0%	67%	0%
5 - Blue	0%	0%	67%
6 - Yellow	67%	67%	0%
7 - Magenta	67%	0%	67%
8 - Cyan	0%	67%	67%
9 - Orange	67%	25%	0%
A - Gray	50%	50%	50%
N - Brown	67%	33%	0%
O - Other			
Current Color	0%	0%	0%

Selection: 0

Figure 7-9. *The Print Color menu*

When you wish to turn off the color and return to standard black text, follow steps 1 through 5 above, selecting 1, Black, as the printing color you desire.

If you are dissatisfied with the predefined colors, you can create a color of your own. From the Print Color menu, you can select O, Other, and then enter the new intensity percentage for Red, Green, and Blue in the Primary Color Mixture columns. (There is no need to type in the percentage sign—just type the amount; WordPerfect inserts the % for you.) Now press EXIT. A code such as the following will appear in the text: **[Color:20%,20%,100%]**.

Keep in mind that a color change takes effect at the printer, not on the Typing screen—even if you possess a color monitor. (To change the color of your text on screen, change the Display option on the Setup menu, which is discussed in Appendix B).

Tip: *WordPerfect offers the ability to kern letters or alter the spacing between words and letters.*

Two features are available to refine the horizontal spacing between characters on the printed page—Kerning and Word Spacing/Letter Spacing.

Kerning allows for reduction in space between specific pairs of letters, eliminating excessive white space between them. A classic example is the extra space between A and V, as in "AVA" or in "BRAVE." Kerning can enhance a person's ability to read large text, such as a headline, as distinct words rather than as individual letters.

Manual (but not automatic) kerning is available in WordPerfect. The letter combinations that are kerned depend on the kerning tables set up for your printer. By default, kerning is turned off. It is turned on by positioning the cursor where you want kerning to begin, and then proceeding as follows:

1. Press the FORMAT (SHIFT + F8) key to display the Format menu.
2. Select Other (4 or O) to display the Other Format menu, as shown in Figure 7-4.
3. Select Printer Functions (6 or P) to display the Printer Functions menu, as shown in Figure 7-10.
4. Select Kerning (1 or K).
5. Type **Y** to turn kerning on, or type **N** to turn kerning off.
6. Press EXIT (F7) to return to your document.

A **[Kern:On]** or **[Kern:Off]** code is inserted at the current cursor position, affecting text from that point forward in the document (not on screen, but at the printer).

The Kerning feature may or may not be available for your printer. Also keep in mind that certain fonts are defined with kerning tables, while others are not. Test the Kerning feature on your printer to see if it has an effect. (You can alter the kerning table using the Printer program, which is described in Chapter 15.)

The Word Spacing/Letter Spacing feature adjusts the spacing between neighboring words and letters. Depending on your printer, you may find that this enhances the readability of your text. To initiate this feature, position the cursor where you wish to change the word and/or letter spacing. Next, follow steps 1 through 3 as described above for kerning, and these additional steps:

4. Select Word Spacing/Letter Spacing (3 or W). WordPerfect displays the following Word Spacing menu:

   Word Spacing: 1 Normal; **2** Optimal; **3** Percent of Optimal; 4 Set Pitch: **2**

```
Format: Printer Functions

     1 - Kerning                              No

     2 - Printer Command

     3 - Word Spacing                         Optimal
         Letter Spacing                       Optimal

     4 - Word Spacing Justification Limits
           Compressed to (0% - 100%)          60%
           Expanded to (100% - unlimited)     400%












Selection: 0
```

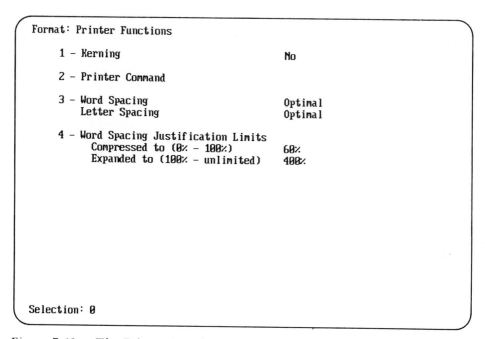

Figure 7-10. The Printer Functions menu

Your word spacing options are

- **Normal** The spacing that looks best according to the printer manufacturer.
- **Optimal** The spacing that looks best according to WordPerfect Corporation (which, for certain printers, is the same as the Normal option). Optimal is the default setting.
- **Percent of Optimal** Used to change spacing to a specific width of your own, which is a percentage of the Optimal setting. Using 100% is comparable to using the Optimal setting; numbers lower than 100% reduce the space, while numbers greater than 100% increase the space.

- **Set Pitch** Used to change spacing to an exact pitch (characters per inch, such as 10- or 12-pitch). The pitch you enter is converted into a percentage of the Optimal setting. This setting affects only the current font, and not other fonts you may select later in the document.

5. Select an option from the Word Spacing menu (and enter a width setting if you selected the Percent of Optimal or the Set Pitch option). WordPerfect next displays the Letter Spacing menu, with the same four options available.
6. Select an option from the Letter Spacing menu (and enter a width setting if you selected the Percent of Optimal or the Set Pitch option).
7. Press EXIT (F7) to return to the document.

WordPerfect inserts a width-adjustment code in the text which indicates the selections you made. For instance, suppose you selected word spacing as optimal and letter spacing as 84% of optimal. Then the code inserted is **[Wrd/Ltr Spacing: Optimal,84% of Optimal]**, which affects text from that point forward in the document.

The results of the Word Spacing/Letter Spacing feature appear on the printed page, but are not shown on the Typing screen. Test this feature on your printer for a given font to see if there's a particular spacing you prefer, rather than the default setting.

Tip: *You can specify that on-screen text be displayed with a specific pitch, regardless of the results at the printer.*

With the Display Pitch feature, you can change the amount of horizontal space that one character occupies on the screen. If you decrease the display pitch, a document expands in width; if you increase the display pitch, a document contracts in width. As a default, the display pitch is set to automatic so that WordPerfect will adjust the characters on screen to allow for small fonts. Tabs, indents, column margins, and other absolute measurements take up more space to prevent text from overlapping. You may wish to increase the display-pitch measurement so that the amount of space preceding a tab code will be less and columns will appear closer together. To change the display pitch:

1. Press the FORMAT (SHIFT + F8) key.
2. Select Document (3 or D) to display the Document Format menu, shown Figure 7-7.
3. Select Display Pitch (1 or D). The default settings are shown. For example, the settings in Figure 7-7 are for WordPerfect to adjust display pitch automatically, with a width of 0.1″.
4. Type **Y** so that WordPerfect continues to adjust display pitch automatically, or type **N** to set a display pitch of your own. (If you wish to increase the display pitch, then you must type **N**.)
5. Enter a display pitch.
6. Press EXIT (F7) to return to the document.

No code is inserted in the document. Instead, the new display-pitch setting is saved in an invisible packet of information (prefix), along with the document.

Remember that display pitch affects on-screen text, and has no relation to the pitch of text on the printed page.

Tip: *Bitstream Inc. and WordPerfect Corporation are offering fontware at no extra charge.*

If you have a Hewlett-Packard LaserJet Plus (and compatibles) or a PostScript PDL printer, you'll want to take advantage of an offer to receive the Bitstream Fontware Installation Kit for WordPerfect and nine Bitstream fonts—free of charge. The free typefaces included in the kit are Dutch and Swiss (Bitstream versions of Times Roman and Helvetica) in roman, italic, bold, and bold italic, as well as the roman weight of Bitstream Charter.

The kit for WordPerfect runs under PC or MS-DOS version 3.1 or later, and needs an IBM PC, AT, or compatible, at least 512K RAM, a hard disk, and a high-density or double-density drive. If your equipment meets these specifications, then order the kit from WordPerfect Corporation at (800) 222-9409, or from Bitstream Inc. at (617) 497-7512 or, outside Massachusetts, at (800) 522-3668. You can test these free fonts on your printer and, if you become hungry for more, you can purchase additional typefaces; Bitstream offers more than 120 typefaces.

Tip: *(When upgrading from 4.2.) The ability to print using different fonts has improved demonstrably with version 5.*

Fonts are no longer selected from the PRINT FORMAT key as in version 4.2. One default font (the "initial font") exists for each printer. If you wish to change the initial font for a document, you do so on the Document Initial Font screen. Or, to change the font for a section in the text, you do so on the Base Font screen. Unlike version 4.2, in version 5 you know exactly which font you're choosing because all the available fonts are listed on the Initial Font screen. In version 4.2, you selected a font number, and then tested your printer to see what resulted.

A major enhancement to version 5 is that once you select a font, you can then choose a different font attribute—type size or appearance—for that font. For example, you can choose very large type, italic, or shadow print. Also, you can now kern letters or alter the spacing between words and letters and can print in color (if your printer supports that feature).

The other major enhancement to version 5 is that you are no longer required to adjust margins and line height when you change your font. In version 4.2, you had to recalculate and reset these formats manually if a change in font resulted in a different pitch or type size. Because of this enhancement, you can now mix and match different fonts, type sizes, and styles within the same line, even if this results in changes in pitch or line height—WordPerfect handles these adjustments for you.

You no longer change the orientation of how text is printed (landscape versus portrait) by selecting a different font, but instead by selecting a different paper size and type (see Chapter 8).

Tips and Traps Summary

Centered and Flush Right Text

Tip: WordPerfect can center or set flush right many lines of text at once.

Tips and Traps Summary (*continued*)

Tip: You can have flush left, centered, and flush right text all on the same line.

Tip: The Flush Right command is convenient in correspondence.

Tip: To reposition centered or flush right text, you must erase the accompanying codes.

Trap: Within center or flush right codes, don't type more text than can fit on a line.

Trap: You cannot center text on a line if the command is preceded by a tab or by more than one space.

Tip: You can also center text or make it flush right on a tab stop location.

Tip: Besides centering text horizontally, WordPerfect can also center text vertically on a page.

Tip: (When upgrading from 4.2.) The CENTER and FLUSH RIGHT keys have not changed.

Text Aligned on a Tab Stop

Trap: You can't center on a tab stop until you position the cursor on that tab stop with the TAB key.

Trap: When using the Tab Align feature, the pair of codes inserted does not surround the entire entry.

Tip: Use Tab Align to arrange text flush right on a tab stop.

Tip: You can modify the Decimal/Align Character used by the Tab Align feature.

Tip: WordPerfect enables you to set tab stops with different styles.

Tip: (When upgrading from 4.2.) Align text on a tab as you did previously.

Tips and Traps Summary (*continued*)

Positioning Text with Advance and Superscript or Subscript

Trap: The SPACEBAR is much less reliable for positioning text horizontally than Advance.

Tip: Select the opposite direction to return to the original line or column position.

Tip: When measuring for Advance to Line, the measurement should not include the line of text to be printed.

Tip: Advance is useful when positioning text on a preprinted form.

Tip: Use the Advance feature to print twice in the same location.

Tip: How superscript and subscript appear on the Typing screen depends on your computer display.

Tip: Preview how text will be positioned before you print.

Tip: Superscript or subscript may cause the size of characters to change.

Trap: Not all printers support the Superscript or Subscript command or the Advance command.

Tip: (When upgrading from 4.2.) The Advance and Superscript or Subscript features operate differently.

Underlined and Boldfaced Text

Tip: If boldfaced text looks no different from standard text on a monochrome screen, adjust the brightness and contrast.

Tip: How bold and underline appear on the Typing screen depends on your computer.

Trap: Some monitors may not show underlining as it will appear when printed.

Tips and Traps Summary (*continued*)

Tip: Try a shortcut if you forget to turn off the Bold or Underline features.

Tip: Moving the cursor through text turns off Underline and Bold.

Tip: You can underline and boldface the same section of text.

Tip: Underline and Bold are also located on the FONT (CTRL + F8) key.

Tip: You can underline with a double underscore rather than a single underscore.

Trap: You cannot use boldface with certain printers unless you change the cartridge or the print wheel.

Tip: You can specify whether spaces and tabs are underlined.

Tip: (When upgrading from 4.2.) Although the basics of underlining and boldfacing are the same, a few commands have changed.

Font Changes in the Text

Tip: Your font choices depend on the fonts your printer has available.

Tip: You can change the default setting for the initial font.

Tip: A change in the initial font affects not only the font used for the body of the text, but the font for headers, footers, footnotes, and endnotes as well.

Tip: How font changes are reflected on screen depends on your computer display.

Tip: When you alter a font or font attribute, WordPerfect adjusts the document's margins and line height automatically.

Tips and Traps Summary (*continued*)

Tip: You can change more than one attribute for the same section of text.

Trap: Type sizes and styles are not necessarily available for each font.

Tip: You can change the color of text at the printer.

Tip: WordPerfect offers the ability to kern letters or alter the spacing between words and letters.

Tip: You can specify that on-screen text be displayed with a specific pitch, regardless of the results at the printer.

Tip: Bitstream Inc. and WordPerfect Corporation are offering fontware at no extra charge.

Tip: (When upgrading from 4.2.) The ability to print using different fonts has improved demonstrably with version 5.

8

Setting Margins, Tabs, and Other Formats

When you decide how a document will appear on the printed page, you are setting the format, or general makeup, of the document. As you begin typing a document on a clear Typing screen, WordPerfect assumes certain predefined format settings for you—such as margins, tabs, line height, and line spacing. While certain format settings are fine for some text, not all documents are the same. With WordPerfect you can modify some or all of the settings as often as necessary as you type or edit a document.

This chapter explains the initial format settings for each document. Then you learn how to change margins, tabs, line spacing and height, the justification of text on a page, and how to turn on hyphenation. You'll also discover the Date feature and how to alter the date format so that the date and time are automatically inserted in your text.

Initial Document Settings

WordPerfect's basic default settings (as set by WordPerfect Corporation) for how text appears on the printed page are shown in Figure 8-1. These settings, listed in alphabetical order, are

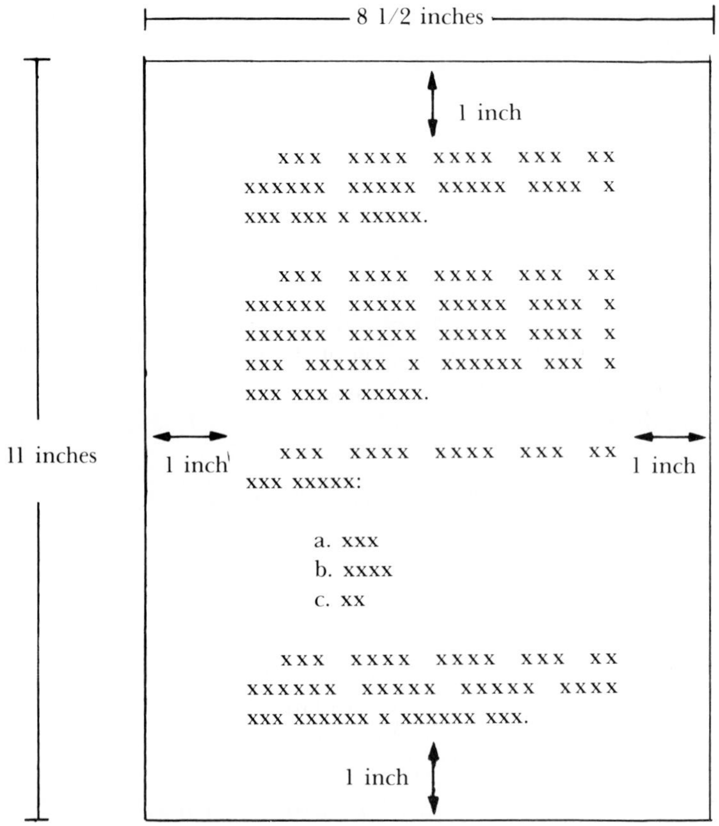

Figure 8-1. Default format settings

Hyphenation	Off
Hyphenation zone	10% left, 4% right
Justification	Yes (On)
Line height	Automatic
Line spacing	Single

Margins—left/right	1 inch
Margins—top/bottom	1 inch
Page size	8.5 inches by 11 inches
Paper type	Standard
Tab stops	Starting at 0 inches, every 0.5 inch

If you wish to change a default setting for a particular document, you insert into the document a format code that dictates the format change. The code overrides the default settings.

There are two places where you can insert a format code. The first is on the Document Initial Codes screen. You should place a format code on this screen if you wish to change a default setting starting at the top of the document. Codes inserted on the Initial Codes screen *are not shown* on the Reveal Codes screen. To access the Initial Codes screen:

1. With the cursor positioned anywhere in your document, press the FORMAT (SHIFT + F8) key to display the Format menu, shown in Figure 8-2.
2. Select Document (3 or D), to view the Document Format menu, shown in Figure 8-3.
3. Select Initial Codes (2 or C). WordPerfect displays a split document screen. The bottom window or screen is either blank, indicating that all the *original* WordPerfect default settings (as established by WordPerfect Corporation) are in effect, or it contains codes because you or someone else used the Setup menu to change the default settings for the WordPerfect program you are using (as described in Appendix B).
4. Insert or delete format codes as desired to change the default settings for that one document only. The codes will be displayed on only the bottom window on the screen.
5. Press EXIT twice to return to the Typing screen. The cursor is now repositioned at the top of the document.

The second place to insert a format code is in the document itself. For example, you can change margins on page 4 and on all succeeding pages by position-

```
Format

     1 - Line
              Hyphenation                        Line Spacing
              Justification                      Margins Left/Right
              Line Height                        Tab Set
              Line Numbering                     Widow/Orphan Protection

     2 - Page
              Center Page (top to bottom)        New Page Number
              Force Odd/Even Page                Page Numbering
              Headers and Footers                Paper Size/Type
              Margins Top/Bottom                 Suppress

     3 - Document
              Display Pitch                      Redline Method
              Initial Codes/Font                 Summary

     4 - Other
              Advance                            Overstrike
              Conditional End of Page            Printer Functions
              Decimal Characters                 Underline Spaces/Tabs
              Language

Selection: 0
```

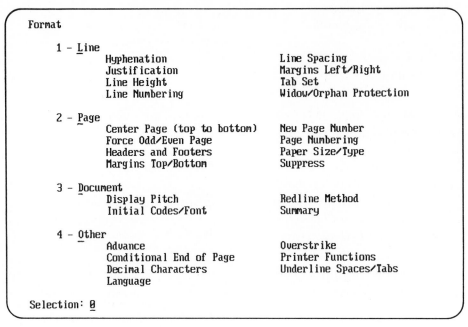

Figure 8-2. The Format menu

ing the cursor at the top of page 4 and then inserting a margin code. You can view any format code that you insert in this manner by switching to the Reveal Codes screen.

Read on to learn the specifics of inserting a format code in the text—either in the document itself or on the Initial Codes screen—in order to change the appearance of your document.

Tip: *Place codes on the Document Initial Codes screen to reduce the clutter at the top of a document.*

You can alter a setting for a whole document either by placing a code at the top of the document itself or by inserting a code on the Document Initial Codes screen. The advantage of the latter is that it reduces the potential jumble of codes at the top of a document, and it also protects those codes from being accidentally erased or moved as you edit the text.

```
Format: Document

     1 - Display Pitch - Automatic      Yes
                         Width          0.1"

     2 - Initial Codes

     3 - Initial Font                   Courier 10 pitch (PC-8)

     4 - Redline Method                 Printer Dependent

     5 - Summary




Selection: 0
```

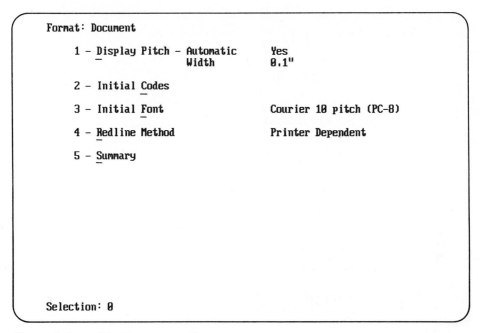

Figure 8-3. *The Document Format menu*

For example, suppose you insert a margin code at the top of a document. Later, you move back to the top of the document and insert several sentences in the text. If you happen to place the cursor *before* the margin code, then those sentences will be governed by the default margin settings, and they will not have the margins dictated by the margin code. However, if you insert the margin code on the Document Initial Codes screen, you needn't worry about the precise position of the cursor when you add text at the top of the document.

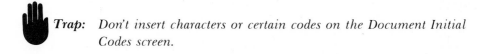

Trap: *Don't insert characters or certain codes on the Document Initial Codes screen.*

If you type letters or numbers on the Document Initial Codes screen, those characters will be ignored. In fact, if you exit the screen and then return, you'll find that those characters have been erased. In addition, certain features—such as tabs, indents, headers, footers, comments, styles, advance, center page top to bottom, and font attribute changes—cannot be created on the Document Initial Codes screen. Reserve this screen for inserting only basic format codes in order to change the appearance of a document starting at the top of that document.

Trap: *Codes inserted on the Document Initial Codes screen are not visible when you reveal codes.*

Codes inserted on the Document Initial Codes screen are shown only on that screen, and not when you display the Reveal Codes screen in your document. Thus, when editing a document that you typed earlier, or when editing a document originally typed by someone else, it is good practice to check the Document Initial Codes screen to see if any format changes have been made.

Tip: *Erase codes from the Document Initial Codes screen as you would on the Reveal Codes screen.*

When you insert format codes on the Document Initial Codes screen, they are displayed on the bottom window of the screen. If you change your mind and wish to erase a code, follow the same procedure as you would for the Reveal Codes screen. That is, position the cursor on the code and press DEL, or position it just to the right of the code and press BACKSPACE.

Tip: *A change on the Document Initial Codes screen affects not only the body of the text, but headers, footers, footnotes, and endnotes as well.*

Inserting a format code on the Document Initial Codes screen alters the format for the entire document, including the formats for headers, footers, footnotes, and endnotes. Conversely, a format code placed within the text affects only text following the format code.

As an example, suppose that on the Document Initial Codes screen, you insert a code to change margins to 1.5 inches. Next, on page three of your document, you insert a code to change margins to 2 inches. The text of the first two pages, all footnotes and endnotes, and any headers or footers whose codes are located on page one or two will be printed using 1.5-inch margins. The text starting at page three, including any headers and footers whose codes you insert in the text following the margin code, will be printed using 2-inch margins. (For more information on headers and footers, refer to Chapter 9, and for more on footnotes and endnotes, refer to Chapter 23.)

Tip: *You can move codes between the Document Initial Codes screen and the body of the document.*

WordPerfect conveniently allows you to move codes between the Document Initial Codes screen and the body of the document in the same way that you can relocate codes throughout your text. Suppose, for example, you place a margin change code in your document, and then realize that it is better placed on the Document Initial Codes screen. You would (1) highlight the code with the BLOCK (ALT + F4) key, (2) indicate that you wish to move the block containing the code via the MOVE (CTRL + F4) key, (3) display the Document Initial Codes screen, and (4) retrieve the code onto the screen. (The Move feature is described in Chapter 6.)

Tip: *When you insert codes on the Document Initial Codes screen, WordPerfect saves them as part of a document prefix.*

Every time you create a document, WordPerfect earmarks that document with information about that document's attributes, such as the printer you selected, the initial font you selected, graphics (if any), and the like. When you save your file, this invisible prefix of information is attached to the document.

Part of this packet stores the default format settings as well as any codes that you may have inserted on the Document Initial Codes screen to override the defaults. As a result, you can travel with any document to another computer system using WordPerfect, and the document's format will remain the same, even though there may be different default settings on the other system.

Trap: *Codes on the Document Initial Codes screen are in effect only if you retrieve a document onto a blank screen.*

Suppose you type a document, make a few basic format changes (such as widening margins) on the Document Initial Codes screen, and save the document to disk as a file named MEMO. When you retrieve MEMO onto a blank screen, the invisible prefix of information attached to that document, including formatting changes made on the Document Initial Codes screen, are intact.

However, when you retrieve MEMO onto a screen already containing text (whether the screen contains just one space, two characters, or five pages of text), then the Document Initial Codes for the document *on screen* are in effect. The format settings for the original document on screen take precedence, and those in MEMO's Document Initial Codes screen are essentially wiped out. On the other hand, any codes inserted directly into the text of MEMO are brought in along with the text of the document.

Thus, make sure that if you wish to work on a file in exactly the form in which you saved it, formatting changes made on the Document Initial Codes screen and all, then retrieve that document only after using the EXIT (F7) to clear the screen.

And, if text you are typing will be combined into other documents and you want the formatting of this document to remain intact, insert codes into the text itself, rather than on the Document Initial Codes screen.

Tip: *Consider using the Styles feature if you're making consistent format changes for similar documents.*

WordPerfect offers the Styles feature, whereby you can specify the appearance of certain document elements: for example, titles will be centered and followed by a blank line, and subtitles will be double spaced and underlined. You can then compose a style, which is a set of formatting codes and text, for each element. As a result, the Styles feature is a superb way to organize formats; you simply select a format style from a menu. (Refer to Chapter 10 for further information on this feature.)

Tip: *Change the default settings permanently by using the Setup menu.*

The default settings described at the beginning of this chapter are the original, predefined settings that WordPerfect has when you first install the program on your computer. You can, however, change any of these settings for the documents you create in WordPerfect by using the Setup menu. If you consistently change a format setting for virtually every document you type, then it is a good idea to change that setting permanently on the Setup menu. For example, you can turn off right justification, so that WordPerfect assumes you desire a ragged right margin *unless* you turn on that feature for a specific document on the Document Initial Codes screen or in the document itself. (Refer to Appendix B for more on the Setup menu.)

Tip: *(When upgrading from 4.2.) The Document Initial Codes screen is a new feature.*

In version 4.2, you had to insert codes at the top of a document in order to change the format settings for that document. As a result, there could be a long string of codes at the top of a document. In version 5, however, you can insert codes on the Document Initial Codes screen. This reduces the clutter at the top of the document, and protects against accidentally displacing a code when you edit text at the top of that document.

Another change is that in version 5, a document's default format settings and any codes on the Document Initial Codes screen are stored in an invisible prefix when the document is saved. As a result, a version 5 document will now maintain the same format even if you retrieve it into a copy of WordPerfect version 5 with different default settings. Conversely, when working in version 4.2, a document retrieved into another copy of WordPerfect would take on that other copy's default settings.

Paper Size and Type

WordPerfect assumes that when you print you will be using a *paper size* that is 8.5 inches wide by 11 inches deep. WordPerfect also assumes that you will be printing on a *paper type* termed Standard, which is the name of a basic type of form defined to work with your printer (you define additional forms when you select printers, as described in Appendix A). If you plan to print on a page that has other dimensions or is of a different type (such as an envelope, label, or transparency), then you must insert a paper size/type code, which takes effect from that page to the end of the document (or until the next size/type code appears later in the document). To change the code for the paper size/type:

1. Position the cursor on the Document Initial Codes screen to change the paper size or type starting with the first page of the document. Or position the cursor in the document itself, at the very top of the page for which you wish to change the paper size or type.
2. Press the FORMAT (SHIFT + F8) key to display the Format menu, shown in Figure 8-2.
3. Select Page (2 or P), to display the Page Format menu, shown in Figure 8-4. Notice in Figure 8-4 that WordPerfect shows the default settings for the paper size/type.
4. Select Paper Size/Type (8 or S). The Paper Size Format menu, shown in Figure 8-5, is displayed.

```
Format: Page

     1 - Center Page (top to bottom)    No

     2 - Force Odd/Even Page

     3 - Headers

     4 - Footers

     5 - Margins - Top                  1"
                   Bottom               1"

     6 - New Page Number                1
          (example: 3 or iii)

     7 - Page Numbering                 No page numbering

     8 - Paper Size                     8.5" x 11"
               Type                     Standard

     9 - Suppress (this page only)

Selection: 0
```

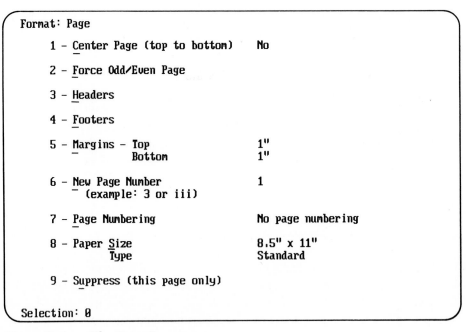

Figure 8-4. The Page Format menu

5. Type a number or a letter to select the appropriate paper size. For example, type **3** or **L** to select legal-size paper, which is 8.5 inches wide by 14 inches deep. The Paper Type Format menu shown in Figure 8-6 appears.
6. Type a number or a letter to select the appropriate paper type. For example, type **1** or **S** to choose the standard paper type. You are returned to the Page Format menu.
7. Press EXIT (F7) to return to the Document Initial Codes screen or to your document, depending on where you positioned the cursor in step 1.

A paper size/type code is inserted at the current cursor position in your document. For example, if you selected legal-size paper, standard type, then the code inserted is **[Paper Sz/Typ:8.5″ x 14″,Standard]**.

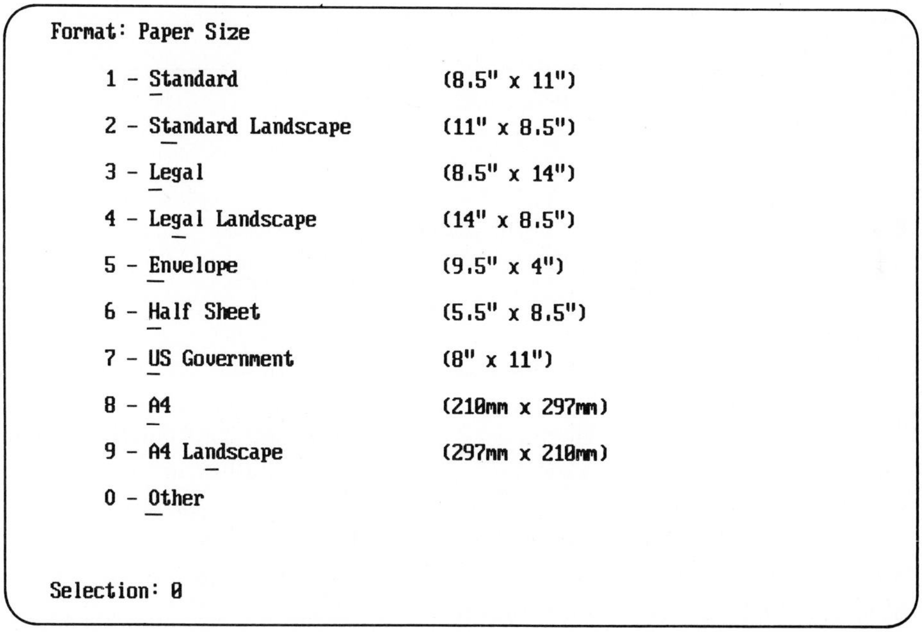

Format: Paper Size
1 - Standard (8.5" x 11")
2 - Standard Landscape (11" x 8.5")
3 - Legal (8.5" x 14")
4 - Legal Landscape (14" x 8.5")
5 - Envelope (9.5" x 4")
6 - Half Sheet (5.5" x 8.5")
7 - US Government (8" x 11")
8 - A4 (210mm x 297mm)
9 - A4 Landscape (297mm x 210mm)
0 - Other
Selection: 0

Figure 8-5. The Paper Size Format menu

```
Format: Paper Type

     1 - Standard

     2 - Bond

     3 - Letterhead

     4 - Labels

     5 - Envelope

     6 - Transparency

     7 - Cardstock

     8 - Other




Selection: 0
```

Figure 8-6. *The Paper Type Format menu*

Tip: *When you change your paper size, text on screen and at the printer is readjusted to maintain current margins.*

WordPerfect initially assumes one-inch left, right, top, and bottom margins. If you alter your paper size, then the text on screen readjusts to maintain these margins. For example, if you change your paper size to standard landscape, which means 11 inches *wide* by 8.5 inches *deep,* then text will adjust in two ways. First, the length of the lines across the screen will increase by 2.5 inches (because the width of the paper has increased from 8.5 to 11 inches). Second, the number of lines on a page will decrease by 2.5 inches (because the length of the paper has decreased from 11 inches to 8.5 inches).

Tip: *Laser printer owners can switch from portrait to landscape printing by changing the paper size.*

On dot matrix and daisy wheel printers, you can print sideways on a page by changing the paper size accordingly (that is, by changing it to 11 inches by 8.5 inches, for example) and then by simply inserting the paper sideways before you print.

On laser printers, however, you are unable to insert the paper sideways. Certain fonts are available to print in portrait mode, while others are available to print in landscape (or sideways) mode. LaserJet printer users will still change the paper size (by changing it to 11 inches by 8.5 inches, for example); then, the paper can be fed in the normal manner—either from the paper tray or manually. Only fonts that print in landscape will be allowed. But the paper size/type you specify must have been previously defined as available for landscape mode when you select your printer (see the section "Selecting Your Printer" in Appendix A).

Tip: *A change in paper type has an effect only at the printer.*

When you select a paper type, you are providing special instructions on how to print the form you selected. These instructions include

- The orientation in which the characters will print, such as landscape or portrait (see the preceding Tip)
- Whether the form is present in the printer or sheet feeder when you begin to print (if it is not, WordPerfect will stop the printing job and prompt you to insert the form)
- The location of the form, that is, whether it is fed continuously, fed manually, or fed from a specific bin in a sheet feeder
- Whether your form requires an offset because it is fed into the printer at different horizontal and vertical positions

For example, when you defined printers, you may have defined the form called "bond" as paper fed into the printer from sheet-feed bin No. 2. If you select Bond paper type, WordPerfect knows to feed the paper from bin No. 2. Or suppose that you defined the form called "envelope" as landscape orientation that would be manually fed. In this case, if you select Envelope paper type, WordPerfect will print lengthwise on the page and will wait until you hand-feed the form before printing.

All of these characteristics of your form take effect only when you print out your document. (Refer to Chapter 14 for information on printing your document; see Appendix A for information on defining the characteristics of the forms you use as you define your printer.)

Trap: *A specific paper size or type may be unavailable on your printer.*

When you insert a paper size/type code in the text, WordPerfect checks the form definitions available for your printer, which you designated when selecting your printer (see Appendix A). WordPerfect uses those definitions when you print a document. However, if there is no form type to match the paper size/type code you selected, then WordPerfect selects the closest match. In addition, an asterisk (*) and the message **Requested Form Unavailable** appear on the Page Format menu. The paper size/type code you insert will also contain asterisks to remind you of this fact.

If this situation occurs, you can attempt to print and see if the match WordPerfect made is appropriate. Or you can assign a new form definition to your printer by using the Select Printer option via the PRINT (SHIFT + F7) key (refer to Appendix A for the procedure to use when selecting printers).

Tip: *Change other format settings in addition to paper size/type to print out special documents, such as envelopes or mailing labels.*

When you change the paper size/type that you are printing on, it is often necessary to change other settings as well. Otherwise, the text won't print in the correct location on the page.

For example, suppose that you wish to print an envelope and so select an envelope as your paper size/type. If you then type an address (assuming that you have stationery with your company's return address already printed), where will the address appear on the printed envelope? Remember that the default is for one-inch margins; the address will print one inch from the top and one inch from the left, which produces awkward results.

Instead, when you print an address on an envelope, you will want to change your margins, in addition to changing your paper size/type, so that the address prints in the proper spot. Assuming a 9.5- by 4-inch envelope, you will typically want to print an address 2.5 inches from the top and 4.5 inches from the left edge of the envelope. (The method to change margins is discussed later in this chapter. The Advance feature is discussed in Chapter 7 and is a convenient way to ensure that the address starts on the proper line.) To print out an envelope, try these settings at the top of the page.

- **Paper Size/Type** Envelope size; Envelope type (see Appendix A for methods to define the envelope form for your printer)
- **Left margin** 4.5 inches
- **Right margin** 0 inches (to allow room for a lengthy line in an address)
- **Top margin** 0 inches (so that the Advance feature works properly. If the Advance feature doesn't operate on your printer, then set your top margin to 2.5 inches)
- **Bottom margin** 0 inches (to allow room for an address with numerous lines)
- **Advance: down** 2.5 inches (to start the address in the correct vertical position. If the Advance feature doesn't work on your printer, then set your top margin to 2.5 inches)

Once you insert these formatting codes into the text, you can type and print out the envelope. Save these codes in a document of their own, so that you can retrieve them quickly when you wish to print out an envelope.

As for envelopes, you must change the format settings when you wish to print out labels. For a 4- by 1 7/16-inch label, which is a standard size, try these settings:

- **Paper Size/Type** Other size; Labels type (see Appendix A for methods to define the label form for your printer)
- **Left margin** .5 inch
- **Right margin** 0 inches (to allow room for a lengthy line in an address)
- **Top margin** 0 inches (so that the Advance feature works properly; if the Advance feature doesn't work on your printer, then set your top margin to .25 inch)
- **Bottom margin** 0 inches (to allow room for a multi-line address)

- **Advance: down** .25 inch (if the Advance feature doesn't work on your printer, then set your top margin to .25 inch)

The label's height is less than the total of the default top and bottom margins. Thus, you must reset top and margin codes *before* inserting a paper size/type code for labels of this size.

For labels of other sizes, experiment with the labels and your printer to determine the appropriate settings. Even for labels of the size 4 by 1 7/16 inches, you will need to experiment a bit with your printer to see the best way to insert the label so that it prints correctly. Because labels are so close, you may need to make slight adjustments of these settings for your printer.

Note: Refer to Chapter 25 to learn about the Merge feature to aid in printing numerous envelopes and labels (whether one, two, or three labels across a page).

Tip: *(When upgrading from 4.2.) Paper Size/Type is a brand-new feature in version 5.*

In version 4.2, you changed your left and right margins and/or page length if you planned to print on a different size of paper. In version 5, you insert a paper size/type code to change your paper size and to indicate how and where paper will be inserted into the printer. Current margin settings are maintained unless you change them; they are automatically adjusted to conform to the new paper-size setting. Assuming that you have left/right/top/bottom margins of one inch, these margins remain intact when you select a new paper size. Because of the paper size/type feature, there is no longer a page-length setting in version 5.

Margins

A margin is measured as the number of inches from the edge of the paper inward. For example, the left margin is measured from the left edge of the paper inward, while the top margin is measured from the top edge of the paper downward. The initial settings are one inch on all sides, which produces one-inch borders on the printed page. The margins determine where text begins on the printed page. With a one-inch top margin, for example, WordPerfect rolls the paper up one inch before starting to print.

Margins take effect from your current cursor position forward—either to the end of the document or until the next margin code, whichever comes first. Insert a margin code on the Document Initial Settings screen to change margins starting at the beginning of the document. Or position the cursor at the upper left-hand corner of page 2 to change margins from page 2 forward. Or position the cursor at the beginning of a paragraph to change margins from that paragraph on.

Change left and right margins as follows:

1. Position the cursor on the Document Initial Codes screen to change the left/right margins starting at the top of the document. Or position the cursor in the document itself, to the left of the line on which you want a margin change to begin.
2. Press the FORMAT (SHIFT + F8) key to display the Format menu.
3. Select Line (1 or L), to display the Line Format menu, as shown in Figure 8-7. Notice that WordPerfect indicates the current left/right margin settings on this menu.

```
Format: Line

     1 - Hyphenation                          Off

     2 - Hyphenation Zone - Left              10%
                            Right             4%

     3 - Justification                        Yes

     4 - Line Height                          Auto

     5 - Line Numbering                       No

     6 - Line Spacing                         1

     7 - Margins - Left                       1"
                   Right                      1"

     8 - Tab Set                              0", every 0.5"

     9 - Widow/Orphan Protection              No


Selection: 0
```

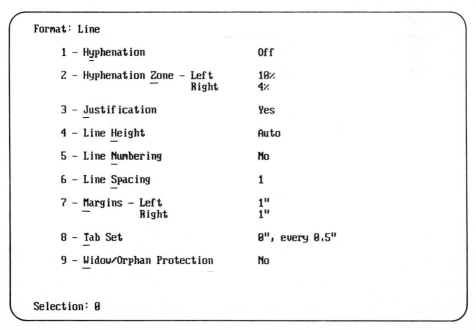

Figure 8-7. The Line Format menu

4. Select Margins Left and Right (7 or M).
5. Enter both your left and right margin settings. For instance, type **1.25** and press ENTER to indicate a left margin of 1 1/4 inches, and type **2** and press ENTER to indicate a right margin of two inches.
6. Press EXIT (F7) to return to the Document Initial Codes screen or your document, depending on where you positioned the cursor in step 1.

At your current cursor position, WordPerfect places a hidden code, such as **[L/R Mar:1.25″,2″]**. All text from that code forward readjusts for the new margin settings.

Change top and bottom margins as follows:

1. Position the cursor on the Document Initial Codes screen to change the top/bottom margins starting at the beginning of the document. Or position the cursor in the document itself, at the top of the page on which you want a margin change to begin.
2. Press the FORMAT (SHIFT + F8) key to display the Format menu.
3. Select Page (2 or P), to display the Page Format menu, shown in Figure 8-4. Notice that WordPerfect indicates the current top/bottom margin settings on this menu.
4. Select Margins Top and Bottom (5 or M).
5. Enter both your top and bottom margin settings. For instance, type **2.5** and press ENTER to indicate a top margin of 2 1/2 inches, and type **2** and press ENTER to indicate a bottom margin of two inches.
6. Press EXIT (F7) to return to the Document Initial Codes screen or your document, depending on where you positioned the cursor in step 1.

At your current cursor position, WordPerfect places a code, such as **[T/B Mar: 2.5″,2″]**. All text from that code forward readjusts for the new margin settings.

If you later change your mind and wish to return the entire document to the default margin settings, just erase the margin code you inserted.

Tip: *WordPerfect will assume default margins if you try to select invalid margins.*

If you try to set margins that are wider or narrower than your paper size will allow, WordPerfect will insert the default margins of one inch. You must then modify your paper size (as described in the previous section of this chapter, "Paper Size and Type") before you again try to use these margin settings.

Also, if you set margins that are narrower than your printer will allow, WordPerfect will insert the narrowest allowable margins. For instance, on an HP LaserJet Series II, if you attempt to set a left margin of 0", WordPerfect will change this setting to .25".

Trap: *Don't reset left/right margins when the cursor is within a line of text.*

If you press the FORMAT key to change left/right margins while the cursor is in the middle of a text line, WordPerfect inserts a hard return and wraps the margin code, along with the words that follow it, down to the next line. For example, if a margin change occurs right here,

then you can see what happens
to the text.

Instead, initiate a margin change when the cursor is at the left margin of a document (or on the Document Initial Codes screen).

Tip: *Make two left/right margin changes when a portion of a document should have margins different from the rest of the text.*

If you want a different margin setting for one portion of a document, then you must modify margins twice—once with the cursor positioned at the beginning of that section, and a second time with the cursor just below that section to change margins back to the original settings. The first margin code you insert will affect the text to the end of the document unless you insert a second code to override it.

However, if you wish to type just a few paragraphs with a new, temporary left or right margin located at a tab stop, then you can use the →INDENT (F4) key or the →INDENT← (SHIFT + F4) key without having to bother with a margin change (see Chapter 7 for details).

Trap: *Don't reset top/bottom margins when the cursor is in the middle of a page.*

If you press the FORMAT key to change top/bottom margins while the cursor is somewhere other than at the very top of a page, the new margins will properly take effect starting on the *next* page, rather than on the current page. Initiate a margin change only when the cursor is at the top of a page (or on the Document Initial Codes screen).

Tip: *WordPerfect gives you the ability to center a short page from top to bottom.*

You can override the current top/bottom margins for a specific page in order to center that page of text from top to bottom. For example, you may wish to vertically center the title page of a report (refer to Chapter 9 for details).

Tip: *You can check current margin settings at any time.*

It's easy to lose track of margins when you change them several times in one document. To examine left/right margin settings, place the cursor on the line for which you wish to check margins, press the FORMAT key, and then select Line (1 or L). The current margins are shown on the Line Format screen. To examine top/bottom margin settings, place the cursor on the page for which you wish to check margins, press the FORMAT key, then select Page (2 or P). The current margins are shown on the Page Format screen. Now press CANCEL (F1) until you return to your document. The menu clears and the margin settings remain intact.

Tip: *You can establish a ruler line to display left/right margin settings continuously on the screen.*

On a standard, 25-line screen display, WordPerfect reserves 24 lines as a window for your text. The twenty-fifth line is occupied by the status line. If you choose, you can reserve another line to display current margin and tab settings. But to provide this ruler line (also called a tab ruler), WordPerfect must reduce the window by one line. Create a ruler line by following these steps:

1. Press the SCREEN (CTRL + F3) key. A menu appears:

   0 Rewrite; **1** Window; **2** Line Draw: **0**

2. Select Window (1 or W). WordPerfect prompts you with the current number of lines in the window:

   Number of lines in this window: 24

3. Type **23** and press ENTER. The text window shrinks by one line and a ruler line appears at the bottom of the screen. The ruler line is a solid bar with triangles on it that represent tab settings, square brackets [ ] that represent the left or right margin, and curved braces { } that represent the left or right margin where a tab is also located.

If you prefer to see margins and tabs as you type, leave the window set at 23. If later you find the ruler line distracting, clear it by changing the window size back to 24 (windows are discussed in more detail in Chapter 12).

Trap: *It may appear that margins are changing when you alter your paper size or font.*

Margins will appear to change when you alter one of two settings: (1) paper size—the dimensions of the paper on which the document will print (described in the previous section of this chapter, "Paper Size and Type"), or (2) font—the appearance of the text when printed, including typeface, type size, and pitch, or characters per horizontal inch (all described in Chapter 7). In reality, WordPerfect is *maintaining* your margins; the program is actually adjusting the length of lines in order to do this.

Trap: *A full line of text may not be displayed at one time.*

If you change your paper size because you plan to print on wide paper, or if you choose a font with a small pitch, your text lines may be wider than can be displayed on screen. Simply use the directional arrow keys (described in Chapter 4) to move quickly from one end of the line to the other.

Tip: *Left/right margin settings require no special considerations if you plan to bind your document.*

Suppose you plan to print out a report, make two-sided copies, and bind the copies into a book. The right margins on even-numbered pages and the left margins on odd-numbered pages need to be wide enough to accommodate the binding. Fortunately, there's no need to adjust margins on each page; WordPerfect's Binding feature does it for you. You set the binding width just before you print, (as described in Chapter 14).

Tip: *You can set your margins in units other than inches.*

When you first start up WordPerfect, the program assumes that you wish to enter units of measurement in inches. Thus, if you enter a left margin setting of 1.5, WordPerfect assumes that you mean 1.5 inches. However, you can enter your margin settings in three other units of measure: centimeters, points, or version 4.2 units (horizontal or vertical). Type in the margin setting, followed by the letter that represents the unit of measure you desire. To enter a right margin setting of 5 centimeters, for example, type **5c**. To enter a top margin setting of 50 points, type **50p**. To enter a left margin setting of horizontal position fifteen (the version 4.2 unit of measure, which is the column position) type **15h**. WordPerfect converts your entry into inches.

If you desire, you can also request that WordPerfect assume a unit of measure other than inches. For instance, you can request that WordPerfect display all numbers for margins in points. WordPerfect thus converts your margin entries into points, rather than inches; even the margin code shows the setting in points. You can change the unit of measure on the Setup menu (described in Appendix B).

Tip: *It is possible to preview exactly how margins will appear on the printed page.*

A feature called View Document, accessed with the PRINT (SHIFT + F7) key, can show you how text, when printed, will be positioned on the page relative to your margin settings. This is only a preview; you cannot make editing changes on the View Document screen (Chapter 14 describes the feature in detail).

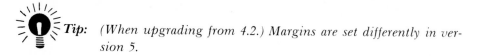

Tip: *(When upgrading from 4.2.) Margins are set differently in version 5.*

In version 5, left/right margins are no longer measured from the left edge of the paper, but rather from the outer edge inward. There's no longer a need to calculate your right margin based on a formula; set it just as you do your left margin. Also, the number of characters that fit on a line depends not only on your margin settings, but also on your paper size and font selection.

The bottom margin can now be set directly; previously, you set the bottom margin by changing either your top margin or your page length. Top and bottom margins are, in version 5, independent of each other.

Margins can be set in inches, points, or centimeters, or in version 4.2 horizontal and vertical units. Moreover, if you're more comfortable working with margins in 4.2 units or in points or centimeters, you can change WordPerfect's assumption for how you enter margins (and other format changes) into 4.2 units by using the Units of Measure option on the Setup menu (as described in Appendix B).

Tabs

Starting at position 0, tab stops are preset every 0.5 inch up to position 8.5 inches. Each time you press TAB, the cursor advances to the right to the next tab stop, inserting a **[TAB]** code at that tab stop to position text that follows.

You can change the location of tab stops to meet your needs by inserting a tab set code **[Tab Set]** in the text. Tab set codes take effect from the current cursor position forward, just as margin codes do. Position the cursor at the top of page 3 to change tab stops starting on that page. Position the cursor above where you plan to type a table to change tab stops for that table. Or position the cursor on the Document Initial Codes screen to change tab stops starting at the top of a document. Tabs can be spaced evenly or erratically—for example, at positions 2″, 3.5″, and 4.7″.

You have four tab styles to choose from when setting tabs:

- **Left-aligned** The default tab style. The left edge of the text will be positioned on the tab stop.
- **Right-aligned** The right side of the text will be positioned on the tab stop.
- **Center** The text will be centered around the tab stop.
- **Decimal** The decimal point within the text will be positioned on the tab stop.

These style variations are shown in Figure 8-8, in which a triangle (▲) represents a tab stop location. The right-aligned, center, and decimal tabs are helpful when typing tables. You can set up to 40 tab stops at one time, as follows:

1. Position the cursor on the Document Initial Codes screen to change tabs starting at the beginning of the document. Or position the cursor in the document itself, where you want new tab settings to begin.

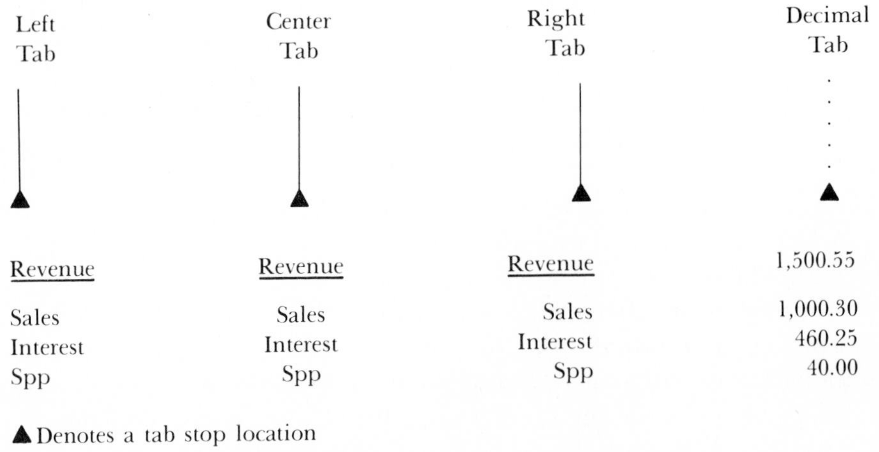

Figure 8-8. Different tab stop styles

2. Press the FORMAT (SHIFT + F8) key. WordPerfect displays the Format menu.
3. Select Line (1 or L), to display the Line Format menu, shown in Figure 8-7. Notice that WordPerfect indicates the current tab settings on this menu.
4. Select Tab Set (8 or T). A ruler line appears at the bottom of the screen, indicating your current tab settings. (If the cursor was located in the document itself in step 1, then the cursor on the ruler line is located in the same position as when you first pressed the FORMAT key.) This is the ruler line for the default tab settings:

```
L....L....L....L....L....L....L....L....L....L....L....L....L....L....L....L...
:    ^    :    ^    :    ^    :    ^    :    ^    :    ^    :    ^    :    ^
1"        2"        3"        4"        5"        6"        7"        8"
Delete EOL (clear tabs); Enter Number (set tab); Del (clear tab);
Left; Center; Right; Decimal; .= Dot Leader
```

   L stands for left-aligned tab. You can tell where each tab is located by the inch markers at the bottom of the ruler line. Also, a caret (^) indicates a half-inch location. You can view only a portion of the ruler line at one time, but you can move the cursor to the extreme left of the line by pressing HOME, HOME, LEFT ARROW, to the extreme right end by pressing END, or one screen's width to the left or right with HOME, LEFT ARROW or HOME, RIGHT ARROW. Or simply use the LEFT ARROW or the RIGHT ARROW key to move one character at a time.

5. To delete tab settings one by one, move the cursor to the tab you wish to erase and press DEL.

   Or, to delete all the tab settings at once (from the cursor position to the right), press the DELETE EOL (CTRL + END) key. For example, press HOME, HOME, LEFT ARROW and then press CTRL + END to delete all tab settings.

6. To set tabs one by one, you can type the position measurement where you want to place a left-aligned tab stop (such as **2.5** to insert a tab stop at position 2.5 inches) and press ENTER. Continue until you set all tabs.

   Or you can press LEFT ARROW or RIGHT ARROW to move the cursor to the position at which you want to locate a tab setting, and type **L** (left), **R** (right), **C** (center), or **D** (decimal), depending on the tab style you desire. Continue until you set all tabs.

To set evenly spaced, left-aligned tabs all at once, type the position measurement for the first tab stop, type a comma, type the tab stop increment, and then press ENTER. For example, to set tabs starting at position 1.5 inches and appearing every two inches after that, type **1.5,2** and press ENTER.

7. Press the EXIT (F7) key once to return to the Line Format menu, and press it again to return to the Document Initial Codes screen or your document, depending on where you positioned the cursor in step 1.

WordPerfect places a tab set code at the current cursor position. If tab stops are set at positions 2 inches and 3 inches, for example, then the code inserted is **[Tab Set:2″,3″]**. Or, if tab stops are set starting at position 1 inch and every 2.5 inches after that, then the code inserted is **[Tab Set:1″, every 2.5″]**. The code affects text from that point forward in the document.

When you press TAB to move the cursor to a left-aligned tab stop, the single code **[TAB]** is inserted in the text, preceding your entry. However, when you press TAB to move the cursor to a tab stop defined as a different style, then a pair of codes is inserted as you type your entry.

This shows characters positioned on a right-aligned tab stop:

[Align]xxxxxx**[C/A/Flrt]**.

This shows characters positioned on a decimal tab:

[Align]2222**[C/A/Flrt]**.222

(Notice that only the characters preceding the decimal point are within the code pair.)

This shows characters aligned on a center tab:

[Cntr]xxxxxxxxx**[C/A/Flrt]**

Trap: *Don't set tabs wider than the margins.*

Keep left/right margin settings in mind when you set tabs. Tab stops that fall outside the margins cannot be accessed. Also, be aware that center tab stops located too close to a margin may position text so that it extends outside the margins.

Trap: *Remember to erase old tab stops before setting new ones.*

When you set new tabs, WordPerfect does not automatically erase the old ones. Unless you delete old settings, they will remain.

Tip: *You can keep track of tab settings in two ways.*

You can change tabs as many times as necessary in one document. If you wish to check your tab stops on a certain line, move to that line. You have two alternatives. First, you can proceed as if changing tabs. Press FORMAT (SHIFT + F8), then select Line Format (1 or L), and then Tab Set (8 or T). The tab ruler line is displayed. Press CANCEL (F1) to clear the ruler line without altering the tabs.

Your second alternative is to shrink the screen window by one line in order to establish a permanent ruler line, which will show current tab locations as you move the cursor from line to line. The tab ruler does not, however, indicate which style is at each tab stop location. (The procedure for setting up the ruler line is described in the preceding section of this chapter, "Margins.")

Trap: *When you set evenly spaced tabs, WordPerfect assumes the left-aligned style unless you specify otherwise.*

If you wish to set evenly spaced tabs that are other than left-justified, you must indicate to WordPerfect that another tab style—not left-aligned tabs—is what you desire. To do this, you must type the style letter at the first position, then enter the position measurement, a comma, and the tab stop increment.

For example, suppose you wish to set *center* tabs starting at position 1 inch, and appearing every two inches thereafter. Proceed with steps 1 through 5 for setting tab stops, as described earlier in this section. Then, to set evenly spaced tabs, follow these additional steps:

6. Move the cursor to position 1 inch and type **C** to set a single center tab.
7. Type **1,2** and press ENTER.
8. Press EXIT twice to return to the document.

Because you placed an individual center tab at position 1 inch before setting the others, WordPerfect assumed all center tabs. If no tab style had been indicated at position 1 inch, WordPerfect would have assumed left-aligned tabs.

Trap: *Be careful when the position of the tab begins with a decimal point.*

Start your entry with a zero (0) if you wish to type a position measurement for a tab stop that starts with a decimal point. In other words, type **0.5** rather than .5 when setting a tab stop at position .5 inch. Or type **0.75,1** rather than .75,1 when setting tabs beginning at position .75 inch and appearing every one inch after that. If you start with a period, WordPerfect thinks in terms of a dot leader rather than a position measurement (see the following Tip for a discussion of dot leaders).

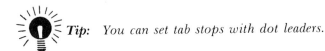

Tip: *You can set tab stops with dot leaders.*

Evenly spaced dot leaders carry your eye from column to column, making lists, charts, and tables of contents easier to read. WordPerfect can draw a line of dots (.) up to a left-aligned, right-aligned, center, or decimal tab stop:

.... Left Aligned
..................................Right Aligned
....Centered Text
....4,897.44

Specify the dot leader option by pressing the period key when setting a tab. For instance, to set a decimal tab with a dot leader, follow steps 1 through 5 for setting tab stops, as described earlier in this section. Then follow these additional steps:

6. Move the cursor to where you want to insert the decimal-style tab stop.
7. Type **D** for a decimal tab.
8. Type a period. The D displays in reverse image, signifying that the dot leader option is activated.

9. Press EXIT twice to return to the document.

(In fact, when setting a right-aligned tab with a dot leader, you can omit step 7; simply type a period, and WordPerfect assumes right-aligned with the dot leader.) Now, each time you press TAB so that the cursor jumps to that tab stop, dots appear on the line—starting from the location of the cursor when you pressed TAB and ending at the tab stop. Here's an example of numbers aligned on a decimal tab stop with a dot leader:

Sales	111,500.55
Interest	4,100.39
Spp	293,000.40

Tip: *Although it does not do so for other tab styles, WordPerfect prompts you at a decimal tab stop.*

Once you set a tab with a particular style, that style takes effect whenever you press TAB to reach it. For example, assume your first tab stop is a center tab at position 3 inches. The cursor is on the left margin. Press TAB and the cursor skips to position 3 inches. Start typing; WordPerfect centers the text for you. Press ENTER to end the text and move to the next line.

The decimal tab adds something extra; WordPerfect provides a prompt. For example, assume that your second tab stop is a decimal tab at position 5 inches. The cursor is on the left margin. Press TAB twice and the cursor skips to position 5 inches. At that second tab stop, WordPerfect displays the following prompt:

Align char = .

This message indicates that the cursor is on a decimal tab; you must type a period somewhere in this entry so it can be positioned on a decimal. (If you don't, the text is right-aligned on the tab stop.) As soon as you type a period (or press ENTER), the message disappears.

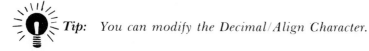

Tip: *You can modify the Decimal/Align Character.*

The decimal tab is, in some ways, a misnomer. It is more powerful than its name indicates. It could almost be called the "align-on-any-character" tab, because not only can you line up a column around a period, but also around any letter, number, or symbol—such as %, :, =, or $. The Decimal/Align Character is preset as the period. But just as you can change margins or tabs, you can modify this character by inserting a hidden code in the document.

To change the Decimal/Align Character:

1. Move the cursor to where you want the new alignment character to take effect.
2. Press FORMAT (SHIFT + F8) to display the Format menu.
3. Select Other (4 or O) to display the Other Format menu, shown in Figure 8-9.
4. Select Decimal/Align Character (3 or D). The cursor moves to the decimal point.

```
Format: Other

     1 - Advance

     2 - Conditional End of Page

     3 - Decimal/Align Character          .
         Thousands' Separator             ,

     4 - Language                         EN

     5 - Overstrike

     6 - Printer Functions

     7 - Underline - Spaces               Yes
                     Tabs                 No




Selection: 0
```

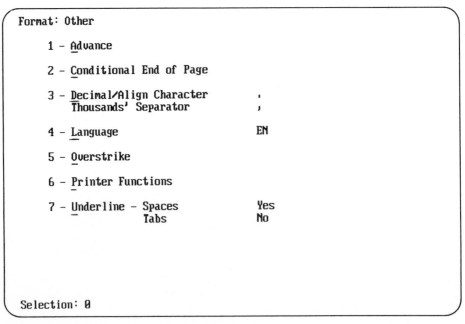

Figure 8-9. The Other Format menu

5. Type in the character that will be used as the new alignment character. The cursor moves to the heading "Thousands' Separator" (the Thousands' Separator is used in conjunction with the Math feature, and is therefore described in Chapter 20).
6. Press ENTER and then press EXIT to return to the document.

WordPerfect inserts a code in the text. For example, if the alignment character is the dollar sign, the hidden code reads **[Decml Char:$,,]**. From that point on to the end of the document (or until the next decimal/align character code appears), all text positioned on a decimal tab aligns to that new character and not to a period. WordPerfect reminds you of this. If you subsequently press TAB to move to a decimal tab, WordPerfect responds

Align Char = $

You can change the tab alignment character as many times as you wish in a document. Be sure to position the cursor where you want the change to take effect before pressing FORMAT.

Tip: *Even after you set tabs, you can create different tab styles with keys other than TAB.*

Once you've set your tabs and are ready to move from tab stop to tab stop, you are not limited to the TAB key. Five other keys work with tab stops as well. Each produces a slightly different effect.

- →INDENT (F4) starts lines at the next tab to the right until it encounters a hard return.
- →INDENT← (SHIFT + F4) indents the beginning of each line to the next tab stop to the right and the end of each line to the next tab stop to the left.
- MARGIN RELEASE (SHIFT + TAB) pushes one line to the next tab stop to the *left*.
- TAB ALIGN (CTRL + F6) lines up text on a specific character (the decimal/align character).
- TAB CENTER (SHIFT + F6) centers text around a left-aligned tab.

These keys are described in detail in Chapter 7. You will find that it doesn't matter which tab styles are already set—for all but the TAB CENTER key. The TAB CENTER key works only on a left-aligned tab (it is unnecessary on a center tab); but the other four keys temporarily override a tab of any style. For example, suppose the next tab stop is a decimal tab. If you press TAB, text will be aligned on a decimal point. If you press →INDENT, however, the decimal style is overridden; instead, text is indented. To cancel the effect of an indent, margin release, center, or tab align, you must delete the code that you inserted.

Tip: *You can set your tabs in units other than inches.*

When you first start up WordPerfect, the program assumes that you wish to enter tab stop locations in inches. However, you can enter your tab settings in three other units of measure: centimeters, points, or version 4.2 units. Type in the tab setting followed by a letter that represents the unit of measure you desire. To enter a tab stop at 15 centimeters, for example, type **15c**. To enter a tab stop at 100 points, type **100p**. To enter a tab stop at horizontal position 15 (which is the version 4.2 unit of measure), type **15h**. WordPerfect converts your entry into inches, and places the tab stop at the correct relative position on the tab ruler line.

If you desire, you can also request that WordPerfect assume a unit of measure other than inches. For instance, you can request that WordPerfect display the tab ruler line in centimeters. Then the ruler line would appear as:

```
L....L....L....L....L....L....L....L....L....L....L....L....L....L....L....L...
 ^    :    ^    :    ^    :    ^    :    ^    :    ^    :    ^    :    ^    :
      4c        6c        8c       10c       12c       14c   16c       18c       20c       22c
Delete EOL (clear tabs); Enter Number (set tab); Del (clear tab);
Left; Center; Right; Decimal; .= Dot Leader
```

WordPerfect then converts your tab stop entries into centimeters, rather than inches; even the tab code shows the settings in centimeters (you can change the unit of measure by using the Setup menu, as described in Appendix B).

Tip: *(When upgrading from 4.2.) The procedure for setting tabs is similar to what it was previously.*

In version 5, you still set tab stops on a ruler line. Now, however, tab stops can be set in terms of inches, points, or centimeters, or by using version 4.2 units. WordPerfect assumes inches. If you're more comfortable setting tabs as in version 4.2, and you wish to set a tab at position 20, for example, you would type **20h** on the tab ruler line. Or type **15h,10h** to set tabs beginning at position 15 and appearing every ten positions after that. WordPerfect converts your entry into inches.

Line Height

Line height is the amount of vertical space assigned to each line, and is measured from the baseline (bottom) of one line to the baseline of the next. A larger line height means there is more white space between lines. Line height is preset to be automatic; WordPerfect assigns a line height that is based on a combination of the printer, the font, and the font attributes you are using (see Chapter 7 for a discussion of fonts). For instance, if you print using the Courier, 12-point, 10-pitch font on the HP LaserJet Series II printer, and if you select no attributes (where an attribute might be something like extra large characters), then the automatic line height assigned to your document is 0.16 inch. Line height is automatically adjusted if you change the font or an attribute of your document.

If you wish to set a line-height measurement of your own which is evenly spaced regardless of the fonts or attributes you are using, then proceed as follows:

1. Position the cursor on the Document Initial Codes screen to change the line height starting at the top of the document. Or position the cursor in the document itself where you want a line-height change to begin.
2. Press the FORMAT (SHIFT + F8) key to display the Format menu.
3. Select Line (1 or L) to display the Line Format menu, shown in Figure 8-7. Notice that WordPerfect indicates the current margin settings on this menu.
4. Select Line Height (4 or H). WordPerfect provides the following menu:

   1 Auto; **2** Fixed: **0**

5. Select Fixed (2 or F). WordPerfect indicates the current line-height setting (such as **0.17″** or **0.16″**).
6. Type in a new line-height setting, such as **.2**.

7. Press EXIT (F7) to return to the Document Initial Codes screen or to your document, depending on where you positioned the cursor in step 1.

WordPerfect inserts a line-height code in your document, such as **[Ln Height:0.2″]**. This setting takes effect from that point on to the end of the document, or until another line-height code appears in the text.

Trap: *A change in line height is not reflected on the screen, although the number of lines on a page will adjust.*

If you change to a fixed line height, the printed page—but not the screen—will reflect the change. However, WordPerfect will adjust the number of lines that can fit on a page based on the new line-height setting (refer to Chapter 9 for more information on page breaks in a document).

Trap: *Be cautious when switching to a fixed line height.*

Remember that if you select a fixed line height, no adjustments will be made if you select different fonts and attributes throughout your document. As a result, certain lines may, to the eye, appear closer together than others, even though consistent spacing is maintained.

Also, be careful that you don't select a line-height setting that is so small that lines overlap.

Trap: *Not all printers can support the Line Height feature.*

Certain printers are able to print only at a specific line height, such as 0.1666 inch (six lines per vertical inch). Other printers support only one or two settings. Test the Line Height feature on your printer to determine the extent to which it is supported.

Tip: *You can set your line height in units other than inches.*

When you first start up WordPerfect, the program assumes that you wish to enter a line-height setting in inches. However, you can also enter your line height in three other units of measure: centimeters, points, or version 4.2 units (horizontal or vertical). Type in the line-height setting followed by a letter that represents the unit of measure you want to use. To enter a line height of 0.4 centimeter, for example, type **.4c**. To enter a line height of 13 points, type **13p**. To enter a line height of 1.5 vertical lines (which is the version 4.2 unit of measure), type **1.5v**. WordPerfect converts your entry into inches.

If you desire, you can also request that WordPerfect assume a unit of measure other than inches (you can change the unit of measure by using the Setup menu, as described in Appendix B).

Tip: *(When upgrading from 4.2.) The Line Height feature takes the place of the lines-per-inch setting.*

In version 4.2, the default setting was six lines per inch, and WordPerfect offered the opportunity to change to eight lines per inch. In version 5, the Line Height feature is the substitute for the lines-per-inch setting. Height is automatically adjusted for you if you change your font or an attribute in the middle of a document. Or, if you select a fixed setting, you can now enter a precise measurement.

Line Spacing

WordPerfect's initial setting is for single spacing, which can be changed in fractional increments. To change your line spacing:

1. Position the cursor on the Document Initial Codes screen to change the line spacing starting at the top of a document. Or position the cursor in the document itself at the left margin on the line where you want a line-spacing change to begin.
2. Press the FORMAT (SHIFT + F8) key to display the Format menu.
3. Select Line (1 or L) to display the Line Format menu, shown in Figure 8-7. Notice that WordPerfect indicates the current spacing setting on this menu.

4. Select Line Spacing (6 or S).
5. Type the number that represents the new spacing. For double spacing, type **2**. For 1 1/2-line spacing, type **1.5**. For 2 1/4-line spacing, type **2.25**. Then press ENTER.
6. Press EXIT to return to the Document Initial Codes screen or your document, depending on your cursor position in step 1.

A line-spacing code is inserted in the text, such as **[Ln Spacing:2]**. That code takes effect from that point to the end of the document or until the next line-spacing code appears in the text. WordPerfect multiplies the line-spacing number you enter by the current line height to calculate the new line spacing.

Trap: *WordPerfect may be unable to display line spacing on screen to reflect your setting.*

When you select spacing in whole-number increments, such as 2 for double spacing, or 3 for triple spacing, WordPerfect will display your line-spacing setting on screen. WordPerfect cannot, however, display line spacing in fractional increments; instead it displays the closest whole-number spacing, and anything above 0.5 will display as the next whole number. For example, if you select line spacing of 1.1 or 1.25, WordPerfect shows single spacing. If you select line spacing of 1.5 or 1.85, WordPerfect shows double spacing on screen.

For fractional line spacing, rely on the status line to determine your actual line position and how the text will print. For example, assume the cursor is on line 1. With 1.5 spacing and a line height of .16″, as you press DOWN ARROW the status line reads **Ln 1.25″**. Press DOWN ARROW again and it reads **Ln 1.5″**.

Trap: *Not all printers can support fractional line spacing.*

Certain printers are able to print spacing in whole-number increments only. Therefore, as with line height, you'll have to test line spacing on your printer to determine the extent to which it is supported.

Tip: *A line-spacing change won't affect text in footnotes and endnotes.*

In general, a format code inserted on the Document Initial Codes screen alters the format for the entire document, including the formats within headers, footers, footnotes, and endnotes. A Line Spacing code, however, has no effect on footnotes and endnotes; the spacing with and between footnotes and endnotes is set separately (as described in Chapter 23).

Tip: *(When upgrading from 4.2.) Line spacing can now be set more specifically.*

The Line Spacing feature replaces version 4.2's Spacing feature, and allows you to set spacing in precise increments—such as 1.25 spacing, or 2.1 spacing. Previously, you could set spacing in only half- or whole-line increments.

Another change in version 5 is that the line-spacing setting is multiplied by line height to determine the new spacing between lines. In version 4.2, line spacing was considered in relation to six or eight lines per inch. Thus, you are now allowed greater variance in your document's line spacing.

Justification

WordPerfect is preset with justification turned on. This means that your printed document has even right margins because WordPerfect adjusts the spacing between words and, if necessary, between characters. The alternative is to turn justification off, making the right margin of your document ragged. No extra spaces between words are added. The difference between justification and ragged right margins is illustrated in Figure 8-10.

You can change the justification setting for all or part of a document by following this procedure:

1. Position the cursor on the Document Initial Codes screen to change the justification starting at the top of the document. Or position the cursor in

Justification on

xxx xxxxx xxxxx xxxxx xxxx xxxx xxxx xxxxx
xxxxx xx xx xxxx xxxx xxx xxxxxx x xxxx xxx xxxx
x xx xxx xxxxxx xx xxx xxxx xxxx xxxx xxxxxx
xxx xx xxx x xxx xx xx xxxx xxxx x xxxxx xxx x
xxxxx xx xx xxxx xxxx xxx xxxxxx x xxxx xxx xxxx
x xxxx xx.

Justification off

xxx xxxxx xxxxx xxxxx xxxx xxxx xxxx xxxxx
xxxxx xx xx xxxx xxxx xxx xxxxxx x xxxx xxx xxxx
x xx xxx xxxxxx xx xxx xxxx xxxx xxxx xxxxxx
xxx xx xxx x xxx xx xx xxxx xxxx x xxxxx xxx x
xxxxx xx xx xxxx xxxx xxx xxxxxx x xxxx xxx xxxx
x xxxx xx.

Figure 8-10. The effect of justification on the right margin

the document itself at the left margin on the line where you want a justification change to begin.

2. Press the FORMAT (SHIFT + F8) key to display the Format menu.
3. Select Line (1 or L) to display the Line Format menu, shown in Figure 8-7. Notice in Figure 8-7 that WordPerfect indicates the current settings.
4. Select Justification (3 or J).
5. Type **Y** to turn justification on, or type **N** to turn it off.
6. Press EXIT to return to the Document Initial Codes screen or your document, depending on your cursor position in step 1.

A justification code—either **[Just On]** or **[Just Off]**—is inserted in the text. The code takes effect from this point to the end of the document or until another justification code that appears farther forward in the text.

Trap: *WordPerfect does not display justification on the Typing screen.*

WordPerfect displays ragged right margins on the screen, even when justification is on. To determine whether your text will be justified when printed, look for the hidden code. Or follow steps 1 through 3 above (in the procedure for changing the justification setting) to check the setting on the Line Format menu; then press CANCEL (F1) until you return to your document.

Tip: *It is possible to preview how justified text will appear on the printed page.*

The View Document feature allows you to see how your text will appear when printed; if justification is on, your text will be justified on the View Document screen. This is only a preview; you can make no editing changes on this screen (refer to the View Document feature in Chapter 14).

Tip: *You can adjust the justification limits between words.*

By default, WordPerfect assumes that when justification is on, the space between words can be compressed by 60% or expanded by 400% to produce an even right margin. Once these compression and expansion limits are reached, then, and only then, will WordPerfect adjust spacing between characters. However, assuming that your printer supports it, you can change these compression and expansion limits for a document, thereby fine-tuning justification for your printer, as follows:

1. Position the cursor where you want to change the justification limits.
2. Press the FORMAT (SHIFT + F8) key to display the Format menu.
3. Select Other (4 or O) to view the Other Format menu.
4. Select Printer Functions (6 or P). The menu shown in Figure 8-11 appears.
5. Select Word Spacing Justification Limits (4 or J).
6. Enter a number that represents a compression percentage, then enter a number that represents an expansion percentage.
7. Press EXIT to return to the document.

```
Format: Printer Functions

     1 - Kerning                                 No

     2 - Printer Command

     3 - Word Spacing                            Optimal
         Letter Spacing                          Optimal

     4 - Word Spacing Justification Limits
           Compressed to (0% - 100%)             60%
           Expanded to (100% - unlimited)        400%









Selection: 0
```

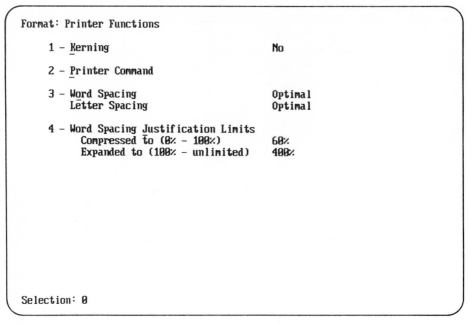

Figure 8-11.   The Printer Functions Format menu

WordPerfect inserts in the text a justification limitation code listing both percentages, such as **[Just Lim:75,700]**. The larger the percentage, the more flexibility WordPerfect has in adjusting spacing between words. An expansion percentage over 999% is considered by WordPerfect to be an unlimited expansion ability. Test this feature on your printer to see if you prefer to change the default justification limits for each document.

Tip: *(When upgrading from 4.2.) You can now set justification limitations.*

Justification is now on the Line Format menu, whereas it was previously on the Print Format menu. In addition, the new Word Spacing Justification Limits feature enables you to control the extent to which WordPerfect handles right justification at the printer.

Hyphenation

End-of-line hyphenation can improve the appearance of your document. For justified text, hyphenation reduces the number of extra spaces inserted between words. For unjustified text, hyphenation can make the right margin less ragged. WordPerfect hyphenates by inserting *soft hyphens*—soft because, like the soft return, the hyphen moves or disappears when text is readjusted and a hyphenated word no longer requires hyphenation.

WordPerfect is preset with hyphenation turned off. As a result, whole words are wrapped onto a new line. No words are hyphenated by the program. In fact, if a word extends from the left margin past the right margin (perhaps in narrow columns) without a space break, WordPerfect inserts a deletable soft return code **[DSRt]** to prevent any need for hyphenation. A space break is not needed in order to have WordPerfect insert a deletable soft return code, unlike the case for a regular soft return code **[SRt]**.

With hyphenation turned on, WordPerfect splits long words that cannot fit at the end of a line. You have two choices when you turn on hyphenation. You can request manual hyphenation, whereby WordPerfect prompts, asking you where to position the hyphen in a word. Or you can request automatic hyphenation, whereby WordPerfect uses an algorithm—which is about 70% accurate—for the correct positioning of the hyphen, and prompts for a hyphen location decision only when a position cannot be determined by the algorithm. To turn on hyphenation:

1. Position the cursor on the Document Initial Codes screen to change the hyphenation setting starting at the top of the document. Or position the cursor in the document itself at the left margin on the line where you want a hyphenation change to begin.
2. Press the FORMAT (SHIFT + F8) key to display the Format menu.
3. Select Line (1 or L) to display the Line Format menu, shown in Figure 8-7. Notice in Figure 8-7 that WordPerfect indicates whether hyphenation is currently on or off.
4. Select Hyphenation (1 or Y). WordPerfect prompts

   1 Off; 2 Manual; 3 Auto: 0

5. To make a selection, type a number or a mnemonic character. The change is now indicated on the Line Format menu.
6. Press EXIT (F7) to return to the Document Initial Codes screen or your document, depending on your cursor position in step 1.

WordPerfect inserts a **[Hyph On]** code in the text if you select manual or automatic hyphenation. If you turn hyphenation off, the code **[Hyph Off]** is inserted.

If you selected manual hyphenation, then each time you come to a word that requires hyphenation, WordPerfect asks for your help in making a hyphenation decision. For example, assume that you turn hyphenation on and later type the word "specification" at the end of a line. If that word needs a hyphen, the following prompt appears

Position hyphen; Press ESC specif-ication

If you approve of the hyphen position, press ESC. Otherwise, reposition the hyphen by pressing LEFT ARROW or RIGHT ARROW before you press ESC. WordPerfect inserts a soft hyphen in the text. On the Reveal Codes screen, this hyphen appears without square brackets, as simply **-**.

If you selected automatic hyphenation, WordPerfect prompts for a hyphen position only when it cannot hyphenate according to its algorithm.

Trap: *You cannot permanently specify automatic versus manual hyphenation in a document.*

WordPerfect allows you to turn hyphenation on or off by inserting a hyphenation code on the Document Initial Codes screen or in the text of the document. When you turn hyphenation on, you specify either manual or automatic hyphenation.

The manual versus automatic hyphenation selection, however, takes effect only during your current working session. If you save the document, use EXIT (F7) to clear the screen, and later retrieve the document, WordPerfect knows that hyphenation is on due to the **[Hyph On]** code on the Document Initial Codes screen or in the text. But WordPerfect assumes *manual* hyphenation—even if you selected the option for automatic hyphenation when you first inserted the code. Thus, if you again desire automatic hyphenation for a new working session, then delete the **[Hyph On]** code and insert a new one, specifying automatic hyphenation.

Tip: *WordPerfect determines which words need hyphenation and where that hyphenation can occur based on hyphenation zone settings.*

WordPerfect determines which words need to be hyphenated depending on what is called the hyphenation zone (H-Zone). An H-Zone extends from a certain measurement before the right margin to a certain measurement after the right margin. This measurement is expressed as a percentage of the line length, and is preset with a left H-Zone setting of 10% and a right H-Zone setting of 4%. Line length depends on your paper size and margin settings. As an example, suppose that a line is 6.5″ long (which is the standard line length for the default settings of paper 8.5 inches wide and 1-inch margins). In that case, the left H-Zone would start 0.65 inch (10% of 6.5 inches) from the right margin, and the right H-Zone would extend 0.26 inch (4% of 6.5 inches) past the right margin. The precise number of characters that these measurements correspond to are dependent upon your printer and font selection. (The right H-Zone setting means that text can extend a bit beyond the right margin, which allows for a more reliable average right margin, especially when using a proportionally spaced font. A right H-Zone of 4% usually means that two to five extra characters are allowed beyond the right margin during hyphenation.)

The hyphenation zone also determines how far you can move the hyphen when WordPerfect prompts for a hyphen location in a word. For a long word, WordPerfect allows you to insert a hyphen only within the confines of the H-Zone.

Figure 8-12 shows an example of four words in the hyphenation zone. "Paraphernalia" and "Specification" both start before the left H-Zone and extend beyond the right H-Zone. Both are therefore candidates for hyphenation. "Historical" will be wrapped to the next line because it begins after the left H-Zone. "Practice" does not extend beyond the right margin, so it will remain at the end of the line.

A word has to be at least as wide as the H-Zone to qualify for hyphenation. You narrow the H-Zone by reducing the left or right H-Zone percent settings, and widen the H-Zone by increasing the H-Zone percent settings. A narrower H-Zone means more hyphenated words, while a wider H-Zone results in fewer hyphenated words. If you don't want characters to extend beyond the right margin during hyphenation, reset your right H-Zone from 4% to 0%.

To change the H-Zone, follow steps 1 through 3 for turning hyphenation on, as described earlier in this section. Then follow these additional steps:

4. Select Hyphenation Zone (2 or Z).
5. Enter the left and right hyphenation zone settings. WordPerfect assumes that you wish to enter the left and right H-Zone settings in percentages.
6. Press EXIT (F7) to return to the document.

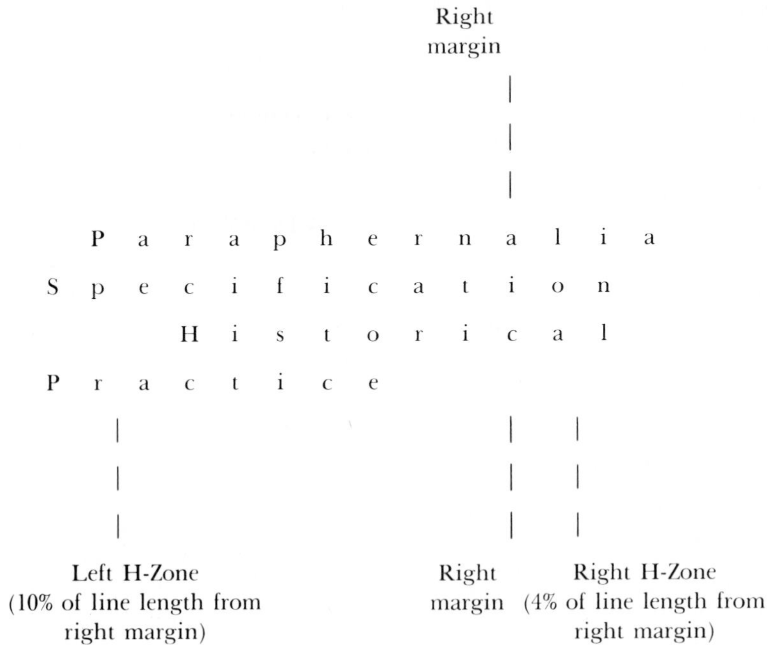

Figure 8-12. The hyphenation zone, which determines when words are hyphenated

WordPerfect inserts a hyphenation zone code into the text, such as **[HZone:0.5%, 0%]**. Only text located after the code is affected by the new H-Zone. Experiment with H-Zones and your printer and fonts, to see which H-Zone settings you prefer for your printed text.

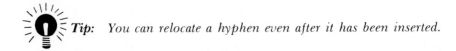

Tip: *You can relocate a hyphen even after it has been inserted.*

Suppose at a hyphenation prompt you move the cursor to hyphenate as follows: "specific-ation." Then you press ESC. But several minutes later you realize that the hyphen is in the wrong place; you really want to hyphenate like this: "specifica-tion." Delete the hyphen as you would delete any other character—

by positioning the cursor after the hyphen and pressing BACKSPACE, or by positioning the cursor on the hyphen and pressing DEL; this forces WordPerfect to again ask for a hyphen location. Now relocate the cursor and press ESC.

Tip: *You don't have to hyphenate a word just because WordPerfect determines it is a candidate for hyphenation.*

When you see the **Position hyphen; Press ESC** prompt, you can cancel hyphenation for that word if you press CANCEL (F1). The entire word is then wrapped to the next line. WordPerfect inserts a hidden code in front of the word—a slash (/)—to cancel hyphenation for that word and to wrap the word to the next line.

Tip: *When a word is automatically selected for hyphenation, you can insert a space instead of a hyphen.*

Suppose you forget to press the SPACEBAR to separate two words you have typed. If WordPerfect requests hyphenation on that word—which, in reality, is two words—move the hyphen between the words. Then press HOME + SPACEBAR. WordPerfect inserts a hard space instead of a hyphen.

Tip: *If WordPerfect prompts for hyphenation while you're performing a command, you can turn hyphenation off temporarily.*

Once you turn hyphenation on, WordPerfect can prompt for hyphen positioning at any time, even if you're doing a spelling check on a document, using the Search feature, using the Replace feature, or moving the cursor. Assume that you're using the Replace feature and WordPerfect prompts for hyphenation. To temporarily turn hyphenation off, press EXIT (F7) when prompted for the first hyphenation request. When the Replace feature is complete, hyphenation is turned on again.

Tip: *There are different types of hyphens you can insert in your text, and one of them allows you to perform hyphenation on your own.*

Because you are able to insert a soft hyphen on your own, you have the option of leaving hyphenation turned off for an entire document and hyphenating an occasional word yourself. Assume that you're at the end of a line and you want to hyphenate on your own. Hold the CTRL key down and type a hyphen (CTRL + HYPHEN). A soft hyphen appears (called soft because it readjusts or disappears if you edit text later and the hyphen is no longer needed). The hyphen you type is identical to the one that WordPerfect inserts when hyphenation is turned on. The code on the Reveal Codes screen is simply **-**. Use a soft hyphen when a word is to be hyphenated only because it falls within the hyphenation zone.

On the other hand, a *hard hyphen* is your choice when you want the hyphen to remain no matter where the word you are hyphenating falls on a line. You create a hard hyphen by pressing the hyphen key alone. This creates the hard hyphen code **[-]**. Remember not to employ the hard hyphen to hyphenate all your words, or as you edit your text you can wind up with a hyphenated word in the "mid-dle" of a line. Use a hard hyphen when a word is to stay hyphenated no matter where it is positioned in the text, as with "error-free," "double-sided," or "letter-writing."

A third possibility is the *hyphen character,* which prevents word wrap from separating a hyphenated word onto two lines. An example is the hyphen you type to represent a minus sign in a formula; such as 550-50=500. Position the cursor where the hyphen is to be placed. Press HOME and then the hyphen (HOME, HYPHEN). This inserts a hyphen character that "glues" together the words on both sides of the hyphen. The hyphen remains, no matter what, and the words are never broken onto two separate lines. (To type a dash, type a hyphen character and then type a hard hyphen. In other words, press HOME, HYPHEN, HYPHEN. The two hyphens that form the dash are kept together on a line.)

A final option is the *invisible soft return.* When a word starts at the left margin and extends beyond the right margin, and hyphenation is off, WordPerfect automatically inserts a deletable soft return code **[DSRt]** in the text to wrap part of a word without hyphenation. You can yourself insert an invisible soft return code **[ISRt]** which has the same effect, by pressing HOME, ENTER.

Tip: *It may be more efficient to turn on manual hyphenation only after typing, or automatic hyphenation only while typing.*

If you select manual hyphenation, WordPerfect pauses whenever a hyphen decision is required, whether you're typing a table or editing a paragraph. These interruptions can be disconcerting, so you might want to move to the top of the document, switch hyphenation on and move the cursor through the text to have WordPerfect check for hyphenation *just before you print*. That way you can hyphenate all words at one time, when hyphenation questions aren't bothersome.

If you select automatic hyphenation, then consider turning it on *while you're typing*. That way you can immediately modify the position of hyphens that WordPerfect places in awkward spots. To do so, position the cursor where you want the hyphen and press CTRL + HYPHEN. Then erase the hyphen that WordPerfect has inserted.

Trap: *Turning hyphenation off does not cancel its effect on words that are already hyphenated.*

Assume that you turn hyphenation on and four words are hyphenated. Later you choose to turn hyphenation off. No new words will be hyphenated, but those four words will retain their hyphens (if they are still positioned in the hyphenation zone). To delete the hyphens, do so manually by pressing BACKSPACE or DEL. Or use the Replace feature to search for a soft hyphen and replace it with nothing. In the search string, type CTRL + HYPHEN; leave the replace string empty.

Tip: *You can decide whether or not WordPerfect should sound a beep each time a prompt for hyphenation appears.*

A WordPerfect default setting is the sounding of a beep during hyphenation, when you are prompted for a hyphenation location. But by selecting the Initial Settings option from the Setup menu, you can turn off the sound of the beep during hyphenation (see Appendix B for details).

Tip: *Purchase hyphenation dictionary modules if you prefer them to the use of an algorithm.*

If you frequently use hyphenation, consider purchasing an optional hyphenation dictionary from WordPerfect Corporation. Two disks are included, which comprise the following files:

- **WP{WP}EN.HYC** The English language module. (Alternatively, you can purchase a foreign-language module—in British English, Canadian French, Danish, Dutch, Finnish, French, German, Icelandic, Italian, Norwegian, Portuguese, Spanish, and Swedish.)
- **WP{WP}EN.HYL** The English language hyphenation dictionary. (Alternatively, you can purchase a British English hyphenation dictionary. Other foreign-language dictionaries will also be available soon.)
- **HYPHEN.EXE** A program that allows you to create an exception dictionary named WP{WP}EN.HYD or given a filename of your choice. You can thus specify how you want certain words, which are not found in the hyphenation module, to be hyphenated. This program also allows you to add or delete words in the exception dictionary, and to test the hyphenation of words in that dictionary.
- **HYPH.DOC** A document containing text that explains the three preceding files and tells how to use them.

When you request automatic hyphenation and have purchased the hyphenation dictionary modules, WordPerfect checks the hyphenation module. If a word is not found in that module, the hyphenation dictionary is used (English or British English) or an algorithm is used (foreign language).

If you purchase a hyphenation module, then you must indicate to WordPerfect where the hyphenation files are located by using the Setup menu (described in Appendix B).

Moreover, if you purchase a foreign-language hyphenation module and you wish to hyphenate by using that module, you must indicate that you wish to do so for a particular document by placing a language code in the text:

1. Move the cursor to the location in your document where you want to change the language code.
2. Press the FORMAT (SHIFT + F8) key to display the Format menu.
3. Select Other (4 or O) to display the Other Format menu.
4. Select Language (4 or L). The cursor moves under the default setting **EN**, which represents the English language dictionary.
5. Type in the two letters that represent the language code for the foreign dictionary you wish to employ, and press ENTER. The language codes are as follows:

CA	Canadian French
DA	Danish
DE	German
EN	English
ES	Spanish
FR	French
IC	Icelandic
IT	Italian
NE	Dutch
NO	Norwegian
PO	Portuguese
SU	Finnish
SV	Swedish
UK	British English

6. Press EXIT (F7) to return to the document.

WordPerfect inserts a language code in the document which takes effect from that point forward to the end of the document (or until the next language code appears). For instance, if you selected the French hyphenation module, then the code inserted is **[Lang:FR]**. (The language code also affects the Speller and Thesaurus features, as described in Chapter 16.)

Tip: *(When upgrading from 4.2.) A new level of sophistication has been added to the Hyphenation feature.*

In version 5, you continue to have options for manual hyphenation (called "aided" hyphenation in version 4.2) and automatic hyphenation. But now, no hyphenation whatsoever will occur when hyphenation is off; WordPerfect inserts deletable soft return codes **[DSRt]** to split lines that are longer than the current margins. In version 4.2, even if hypenation was off, you were forced into hyphenation decisions if a word extended from the left margin to the right margin (in columns, for example).

The hyphenation zone, which determines whether a word is hyphenated, is now set from the right margin as a percentage of the line length, rather than as a fixed distance. Thus, the version 5 H-Zone will adjust accordingly if you make a font change.

Another enhancement in version 5 is the option to purchase a hyphenation module, which offers hyphenation that is based on the module rather than on an algorithm.

Date and Time Format

Typically, placing today's date or the current time in a document is a matter of typing. But WordPerfect has a feature that automatically types the date for you—and does more. The Date/Time feature is controlled by the DATE/OUTLINE (SHIFT + F5) key.

WordPerfect starts with the format assumption that you want to display the date and not the time. The date displays as "Month #, 19##"—May 5, 1989. If you like WordPerfect's default setting for how the date is displayed, then whenever you want today's date to appear—in a report, a letter, or whatever—you have two choices. First, you can insert the date as text (as if you typed it yourself). Second, you can insert the date with an underlying date code, which will automatically update to reflect the current date whenever you retrieve or print that document. For example, assume you insert a date code in your text on May 5, 1989. Two weeks later, you wish to use the document again. When you retrieve the document, the date reads May 19, 1989. Two days later, you print the document. On the printed version the date reads May 21, 1989.

To insert the date, proceed as follows:

1. Position the cursor where you want the date to be inserted.
2. Press the DATE/OUTLINE (SHIFT + F5) key. The following menu appears

   1 Date Text; **2** Date Code; **3** Date Format; **4** Outline; **5** Para Num; **6** Define: **0**

3. Select Date Text (1 or T) to insert the date as if you typed it yourself.

   Or select Date Code (2 or C) to insert the date as a code in the text. WordPerfect inserts the code [**Date: 3 1, 4**], which is visible on the Reveal Codes screen.

You can also customize the way in which the date is inserted in the text. For example, rather than insert "May 5, 1989," you can choose "5/5/89." Or you can add the day of the week and insert "Tuesday—May 5, 1989." Or you can just insert the time of day, such as "9:30 A.M." Or even insert both—"May 5, 1989 at

9:30 A.M." To do so, you must change the date format. Once you do, then you can insert the date; WordPerfect abides by that new format.

To change the date format, follow steps 1 and 2 above, for inserting a date. Then follow these additional steps:

3. Select Date Format (3 or F). WordPerfect displays the Date Format menu, as shown in Figure 8-13. At the very bottom of the menu WordPerfect shows the current date format:

   Date Format: 3 1, 4

   This is the default date format setting, the pattern assumed unless you specify otherwise. The menu lists these numbers and their meaning: 3

```
Date Format

     Character   Meaning
        1        Day of the Month
        2        Month (number)
        3        Month (word)
        4        Year (all four digits)
        5        Year (last two digits)
        6        Day of the Week (word)
        7        Hour (24-hour clock)
        8        Hour (12-hour clock)
        9        Minute
        0        am / pm
        %        Used before a number, will:
                   Pad numbers less than 10 with a leading zero
                   Output only 3 letters for the month or day of the week

     Examples:  3 1, 4        = December 25, 1984
                %6 %3 1, 4    = Tue Dec 25, 1984
                %2/%1/5 (6)   = 01/01/85 (Tuesday)
                8:90          = 10:55am

Date format: 3 1, 4
```

Figure 8-13. The Date Format menu

represents the month spelled out in a word, **1** represents the day, **4** represents all four digits of the year. Therefore, **3 1, 4** translates into "Month #, 19##."

4. Enter a new date format. For instance, suppose that you want the date to display as "5/5/89." Then you must type **2/1/5** and press ENTER. WordPerfect returns you to the Date menu.

Now you can choose Date Text (1 or T), or Date Code (2 or C); the date appears in the format you requested. This new format remains in operation until you turn off the computer or until you change to another date format. You can place punctuation marks or additional words into the format you choose as long as the pattern does not exceed 29 characters. Table 8-1 illustrates various format patterns and examples of what results.

Trap: *The Date function will not work properly unless you enter the current date and time at the start of each computer session.*

Table 8-1. Formatting the Date for Different Results

Date Format Pattern	**Result in Document**
2-1-5	3-18-89
DATE: 2/1/5 (6)	DATE: 3/18/89 (Saturday)
3 1, 4	March 18, 1989
(6) 3 1, 4	(Saturday) March 18, 1989
Notified on 3 1, 4	Notified on March 18, 1989
6, 3 1, 4 at 8:9 0	Saturday, March 18, 1989 at 1:51 pm
TIME: 8:9 0	TIME: 1:51 pm
7:9	13:51
Submitted at 7:9	Submitted at 13:51

How does WordPerfect know the correct date and time? In one of two ways: either your computer has an internal clock, or, if not, when you turned on the computer, you responded to a prompt such as:

Current date is Tues 1-01-1980
Enter new date:_

You entered the current date. Then the computer displayed

Current time is 0:00:55.90
Enter new time:

You entered the current time (this procedure is described in Chapter 1).

If, however, you have no internal clock and you bypassed these prompts, WordPerfect does not know the correct date or time; therefore, the Date function always provides the wrong date and time. You can correct this situation by returning to the DOS prompt (A>, B>, or C>). You can return to DOS temporarily (see Chapter 13), or you can return to DOS by exiting WordPerfect. Once you're in DOS, type **date**. The screen will display, for example,

A>date

Press ENTER. Type the correct date and press ENTER. Type **time**. The screen will display, for example:

A>time

Press ENTER. Type the correct time and press ENTER. Return to or reload WordPerfect. The computer will keep track of the correct date and time until you turn it off. Now you can take advantage of the Date feature.

Tip: *When changing the date format, use the percent sign to insert a leading zero in the date format or to abbreviate months and days.*

You can generate a leading zero in a date when a number is less than ten. To do so, type a percent sign (**%**) in front of the appropriate format number. For example, on May 5, 1989, at 9:30 A.M.:

Format 2/1/5	displays as	5/5/89
Format %2/%1/5	displays as	05/05/89
Format 8:9 0	displays as	9:30 am
Format %8:9 0	displays as	09:30 am

For minutes under ten, a leading zero is automatically included, without the insertion of a percent sign.

You can also abbreviate month and day names to three letters when you are displaying the month and day as text. To do this, type a percent sign (**%**) in front of the appropriate format number. For example, on Thursday, December 15, 1988:

Format (6) 3 1, 4	displays as	(Thursday) December 15, 1988
Format (%6) %3 1, 4	displays as	(Thu) Dec 15, 1988

Trap: *Date codes don't update if you change the date format.*

When you insert a date code, the current date format is saved as part of that code, such as for the date code **[Date: 3 1, 4]**. Thus, if you then change the date format from **3 1, 4** to something else, the new date format will not display unless you delete the old date code and insert a new one.

Trap: *Date codes can cause hyphenation in an awkward spot.*

If a date code is at the end of a line when hyphenation is on, you may find WordPerfect attempting to hyphenate that code with other text on screen. To avoid this hyphenation problem, make sure that the date code is near the beginning of a line or on a line that ends with a hard return.

Tip: *The date code is especially handy in headers and footers.*

You can insert a date code in a header or footer, a handy procedure because you will have the current date and/or time on each page whenever you print out a document. (Chapter 9 tells how to create headers and footers.)

Tip: *The current date can also be inserted by using the* ^D character.

The Merge feature is described in Chapters 24 and 25. If you're performing a merge and you want the current date inserted during the merge, you can use ^D rather than the DATE/OUTLINE key to do so (see Chapters 24 and 25 for details).

Tip: *You can permanently change the default setting for the date format.*

If you find yourself changing the default date format for every document you create, consider changing the default. For example, suppose you prefer that all your documents display the date this pattern: 5/5/89. Instead of changing the date format each time you use WordPerfect, alter the date format initial setting on the Setup menu; that becomes the new default format (see Appendix B for details).

Tip: *(When upgrading from 4.2.) The Date feature has remained basically the same.*

The Date feature has remained basically unchanged, although the Date Code option on the Date menu was referred to in version 4.2 as the Insert Function while the Date Text option was referred to in version 4.2 as the Insert Text option.

One minor enhancement is that you can now abbreviate the month or the day of the week, such as "Mon" for Monday, by using the percent sign.

Tips and Traps Summary

Initial Document Settings

Tip: Place codes on the Document Initial Codes screen to reduce the clutter at the top of a document.

Tips and Traps Summary (*continued*)

Trap: Don't insert characters or certain codes on the Document Initial Codes screen.

Trap: Codes inserted on the Document Initial Codes screen are not visible when you reveal codes.

Tip: Erase codes from the Document Initial Codes screen as you would on the Reveal Codes screen.

Tip: A change on the Document Initial Codes screen affects not only the body of the text, but headers, footers, footnotes, and endnotes as well.

Tip: You can move codes between the Document Initial Codes screen and the body of the document.

Tip: When you insert codes on the Document Initial Codes screen, WordPerfect saves them as part of a document prefix.

Trap: Codes on the Document Initial Codes screen are in effect *only* if you retrieve a document onto a blank screen.

Tip: Consider using the Styles feature if you're making consistent format changes for similar documents.

Tip: Change the default settings permanently by using the Setup menu.

Tip: (When upgrading from 4.2.) The Document Initial Codes screen is a new feature.

Paper Size and Type

Tip: When you change your paper size, text on screen and at the printer is readjusted to maintain current margins.

Tip: Laser printer owners can switch from portrait to landscape printing by changing the paper size.

Tips and Traps Summary (*continued*)

Tip: A change in paper type has an effect only at the printer.

Trap: A specific paper size or type may be unavailable on your printer.

Tip: Change other format settings in addition to paper/size type to print out special documents, such as envelopes or mailing labels.

Tip: (When upgrading from 4.2.) Paper Size/Type is a brand-new feature in version 5.

Margins

Tip: WordPerfect will assume default margins if you try to select invalid margins.

Trap: Don't reset left/right margins when the cursor is within a line of text.

Tip: Make two left/right margin changes when a portion of a document should have margins different from the rest of the text.

Trap: Don't reset top/bottom margins when the cursor is in the middle of a page.

Tip: WordPerfect gives you the ability to center a short page from top to bottom.

Tip: You can check current margin settings at any time.

Tip: You can establish a ruler line to display left/right margin settings continuously on the screen.

Trap: It may appear that margins are changing when you alter your paper size or font.

Trap: A full line of text may not be displayed at one time.

Tip: Left/right margin settings require no special considerations if you plan to bind your document.

Tip: You can set your margins in units other than inches.

Tips and Traps Summary (*continued*)

Tip: It is possible to preview exactly how margins will appear on the printed page.

Tip: (When upgrading from 4.2.) Margins are set differently in version 5.

Tabs

Trap: Don't set tabs wider than the margins.

Trap: Remember to erase old tab stops before setting new ones.

Tip: You can keep track of tab settings in two ways.

Trap: When you set evenly spaced tabs, WordPerfect assumes the left-aligned style unless you specify otherwise.

Trap: Be careful when the position of the tab begins with a decimal point.

Tip: You can set tab stops with dot leaders.

Tip: Although it does not do so for other tab styles, WordPerfect prompts you at a decimal tab stop.

Tip: You can modify the Decimal/Align Character.

Tip: Even after you set tabs, you can create different tab styles with keys other than TAB.

Tip: You can set your tabs in units other than inches.

Tip: (When upgrading from 4.2.) The procedure for setting tabs is similar to what it was previously.

Line Height

Trap: A change in line height is not reflected on the screen, although the number of lines on a page will adjust.

Trap: Be cautious when switching to a fixed line height.

Trap: Not all printers can support the Line Height feature.

Tips and Traps Summary (*continued*)

Tip: You can set your line height in units other than inches.

Tip: (When upgrading from 4.2.) The Line Height feature takes the place of the lines-per-inch setting.

Line Spacing

Trap: WordPerfect may be unable to display line spacing on screen to reflect your setting.

Trap: Not all printers can support fractional line spacing.

Tip: A line-spacing change won't affect text in footnotes and endnotes.

Tip: (When upgrading from 4.2.) Line spacing can now be set more specifically.

Justification

Trap: WordPerfect does not display justification on the Typing screen.

Tip: It is possible to preview how justified text will appear on the printed page.

Tip: You can adjust the justification limits between words.

Tip: (When upgrading from 4.2.) You can now set justification limitations.

Hyphenation

Trap: You cannot permanently specify automatic versus manual hyphenation in a document.

Tip: WordPerfect determines which words need hyphenation and where that hyphenation can occur based on hyphenation zone settings.

Tip: You can relocate a hyphen even after it has been inserted.

Tip: You don't have to hyphenate a word just because WordPerfect determines it is a candidate for hyphenation.

Tips and Traps Summary (*continued*)

Tip: When a word is automatically selected for hyphenation, you can insert a space instead of a hyphen.

Tip: If WordPerfect prompts for hyphenation while you're performing a command, you can turn hyphenation off temporarily.

Tip: There are different types of hyphens you can insert in your text, and one of them allows you to perform hyphenation on your own.

Tip: It may be more efficient to turn on manual hyphenation only after typing, or automatic hyphenation only while typing.

Trap: Turning hyphenation off does not cancel its effect on words that are already hyphenated.

Tip: You can decide whether or not WordPerfect should sound a beep each time a prompt for hyphenation appears.

Tip: Purchase hyphenation dictionary modules if you prefer them to the use of an algorithm.

Tip: (When upgrading from 4.2.) A new level of sophistication has been added to the Hyphenation feature.

Date and Time Format

Trap: The Date function will not work properly unless you enter the current date and time at the start of each computer session.

Tip: When changing the date format, use the percent sign to insert a leading zero in the date format or to abbreviate months and days.

Trap: Date codes don't update if you change the date format.

Trap: Date codes can cause hyphenation in an awkward spot.

Tip: The date code is especially handy in headers and footers.

Tip: The current date can also be inserted by using the ^D character.

Tip: You can permanently change the default setting for the date format.

Tip: (When upgrading from 4.2.) The Date feature has remained basically the same.

9

Controlling Page Breaks, Headers/Footers, and Page Numbering

Think back to the days when you used a typewriter. You'll remember how questions came to mind as your words approached the bottom of a page: "How close am I to the bottom?" "Can I squeeze in one more line?" "Did I leave enough room for a page number?" You probably counted the number of lines already typed so that you would know for sure whether to start a new page. With WordPerfect, there's no need to ask yourself those questions, no need to count the lines on every page. The program inserts page breaks for you automatically.

This chapter explains page breaks and how to regulate them with the FORMAT key. Also addressed is how to create headers and footers, so that, for example, you can place your company name at the top of each page. And you'll learn how WordPerfect can number pages when a document is printed.

Automatic Page Breaks

WordPerfect determines when to break to a new page in your document based on your selection for four of the format settings discussed in Chapter 8:

- **Paper size** The dimensions of the paper on which the document will print. The default setting is for Standard size (8 1/2 by 11 inches), so that the page is 11 inches in length.
- **Top margin** The quantity of white space at the top of a page when printed. The default setting for the top margin is 1 inch.
- **Bottom margin** The quantity of white space at the bottom of a page when printed. The default setting for the bottom margin is 1 inch.
- **Line height** The amount of vertical space allotted for each line when printed. If set to Auto, line height depends on your printer and the font (or attribute) you've selected. For example, if you select the LaserJet Series II printer and a 10-point font, then the line height in your documents automatically changes to six lines of text per vertical inch (approximately 0.16 inch). If set to Fixed, line height can be set to a constant measurement of your choosing.

Assuming the default form and margin settings, WordPerfect will break to a new page after 9 inches of text have been typed. This means that the last line on a page will be located approximately 9.8 inches from the top of the page (and varies depending on line height). Just below that last line, WordPerfect displays a page bar—a row of dashes across the screen. The line below the bar begins a new page, which is reflected by the page indicator "Pg" in the status line.

Accompanying each page bar is a **[SPg]** code, referred to as a soft page break code. The code is "soft" because it adjusts automatically if you insert or delete lines. For example, suppose you add six lines to a paragraph on the first page of a document. The soft page break code, and thus the page bar, will respond by moving up 6 lines to ensure that only 9 inches of text are printed on the page.

If you wish, you can calculate approximately how many actual *lines* of text can fit on a page, as follows:

(Page length − top margin − bottom margin) / line height = number of lines

For instance, assuming the default form and margin settings, and assuming a consistent line height of 1/6 inch, the number of text lines (including blank lines) that can fit on a page is

(11 inches — 1 inch — 1 inch) / 0.1666 inch per line = 54 lines

In this case, WordPerfect will automatically insert a page break after you type 54 lines of text. Remember, however, that based on your printer and font selection, the number of lines that will fit on a page may not equal 54, but perhaps 52 or 56.

What if you wish to change WordPerfect's choice for the page break location for each page in your document? Change one of the settings on which the page end depends—either the size of the form you're printing on, the line height, the font you're using (which automatically alters your line height if the line height is set to Auto), the top margin setting, or the bottom margin setting.

Trap: *A font with a larger type size results in less text on a page, while a smaller type size has the opposite effect—but not always.*

The type size of a font is measured in points, where 72 points equal approximately one inch. If your line height is set to Auto, then the larger the type size (meaning the taller and/or wider the character), the smaller the amount of text that will fit on a page. For instance, more lines of text can fit on a page with 10-point type than with 12-point type.

However, some printers can print only six lines per inch, regardless of the font and its accompanying type size. The line height will always remain at 0.1666 inch. Thus, on some printers, changing the font has no effect on the number of text lines that will print on a page.

Tip: *The Widow/Orphan feature protects against stranded lines at the top or bottom of a page.*

WordPerfect inserts a **[SPg]** code at the end of a page even if that means one line of a paragraph is separated from the rest. When a paragraph's first line is isolated at the bottom of the preceding page, it is called a *widow.* When a paragraph's last line appears at the top of the following page, it is called an orphan. Many people find widows and orphans unsightly.

You can protect against widows and orphans throughout a document by turning on the Widow/Orphan feature. This gives WordPerfect the flexibility to break one line earlier so that potential widows have company, or to break one line later to prevent orphans. For instance, if WordPerfect would normally insert a page break after 54 lines and you turn on Widow/Orphan protection, WordPerfect has the discretion to break pages after line 53, 54, or 55.

Activate the Widow/Orphan feature as follows:

1. Position the cursor at the top of the page where you want the feature turned on. If it is to be turned on for a whole document, move up to the top of page 1.
2. Press the FORMAT (SHIFT + F8) key. The Format menu appears.
3. Select Display (1 or L) to get the Line Format menu. Item 9 on that menu indicates whether Widow/Orphan protection is active with either Yes or No. The default setting is No.
4. Select Widow/Orphan Protection (9 or W).
5. Type **Y**. The menu changes to reflect your choice.
6. Press ENTER to return to the Format menu or press EXIT (F7) to return to the document.

WordPerfect inserts a **[W/O On]** code in the text at the current cursor position, turning on the feature for all pages that follow to the end of the document or until another code to turn it off is encountered. If you wish to turn off Widow/Orphan protection later in the text, reposition the cursor on a later page, and follow steps 1 through 6 above, but this time type **N** for no Widow/Orphan protection. WordPerfect inserts in the text a second code **[W/O Off]** that turns off protection from that point forward.

When Widow/Orphan is on, you may find that certain page bars dance one line up or down as the cursor moves. That's because WordPerfect doesn't recognize a widow or an orphan until the cursor passes through it. There's no need for concern; the feature is operating correctly.

Be warned that for paragraphs of two or three lines, the Widow/Orphan feature is ineffective; if that paragraph falls at the end of a page, there will still be either a widow on one page or an orphan on the next no matter what WordPerfect attempts to do. Thus, for paragraphs of three lines, use the Conditional EOP feature, described in the next section of this chapter, "Controlling Page Breaks."

Trap: *Headers/footers and page numbers reduce the amount of body text on a page.*

When you insert a header, a footer, or page numbering, WordPerfect reduces the number of lines of body text that can fit on a page, depending on the lines occupied by the header/footer (which is explained thoroughly in the last two sections of this chapter, "Headers and Footers" and "Page Numbering").

Trap: *The Advance feature can create a page break in advance of what the text on screen would indicate.*

The Advance feature, described in Chapter 7, directs your printer to place text at a specific distance above, below, to the left of, or to the right of the current position. It can also instruct your printer to print text on a specific line or in a specific column position. It thus enables you to avoid inserting numerous hard returns or spaces when you want text printed at a certain spot on the page.

But the Advance feature can be deceptive. While the status line reflects the change, the position of the text on screen does not. For instance, you may have inserted an advance code on the first line of the page to position the text down 7 inches. In that case, WordPerfect will insert an automatic page break soon after, even though the screen indicates fewer than 20 actual lines of text on that page. If it appears that WordPerfect is inserting an automatic page break in advance of what you would expect, check the Reveal Codes screen for an advance code.

Tip: *(When upgrading from 4.2.) WordPerfect now determines automatic page breaks in a more detailed way.*

In version 5, if line height is set to Auto, then WordPerfect adjusts the line height on a page based on the font you've selected. Because of this new sophistication,

WordPerfect will not always break (assuming the default settings) after line 54, which was the case in version 4.2. Where WordPerfect inserts a page break depends on your printer and font selection. You may find that thinking in terms of inches makes this less confusing.

You'll also notice in version 5 that the Widow/Orphan feature is on the Line Format menu, rather than the Page Format menu.

Controlling Page Breaks

There will be instances in which you know exactly where a page break must occur in your document. For example, you've just typed the title page and you want to insert a page break before you start typing the text of your report. Or you've completed a short letter, and you wish to insert a page break in order to type the address for an envelope on another page. You can insert a page break manually. Just as you force the end of a short line of text by pressing ENTER, you can force the end of a short page of text by pressing HARD PAGE (CTRL + ENTER). In doing so, you insert a page bar in the text, which appears as a row of equal signs =, accompanied by a **[HPg]** code. This code is called a *hard page break.* It is "hard" because, like a hard return, it stays fixed in your text unless you delete it.

In other instances, it does not matter where a page break occurs, as long as WordPerfect's automatic page breaks aren't awkward looking. However, perhaps you've typed a list of items, but the list looks awkward because it is split up at a page boundary. Or a subject heading sits alone at the bottom of a page rather than above the first paragraph on the next page, where it belongs. These inappropriate page breaks can be prevented.

One solution is the Block Protect feature, whereby you can guard against a specific block of text being split by a soft page break. To use this feature:

1. Mark the text you want protected with the BLOCK (ALT + F4) key.
2. With **Block on** flashing, press the FORMAT (SHIFT + F8) key. WordPerfect prompts

   Protect block? (Y/N) No

3. Type **Y** for Yes.

WordPerfect inserts a pair of block protect codes **[BlockPro:On][BlockPro:Off]** that mark off the beginning and the end of the block, thereby safeguarding that area from page breaks.

The other safeguard against a soft page break in an awkward place is the Conditional End of Page (EOP) feature, which keeps lines together so they won't be split between pages. The command tells WordPerfect to break a page when necessary, but only on the condition that WordPerfect not split up a certain number of lines that you specify.

You insert a conditional EOP code just above the lines you want kept together. For instance, to ensure that a heading and two subsequent lines of text are not interrupted by a page break:

1. Count the number of lines that must be kept together. For a heading, one blank line, and two lines of text, the correct number is four.
2. Move the cursor to the line just above the heading (even if there's text on that line).
3. Press FORMAT (SHIFT + F8). WordPerfect displays the Format menu.
4. Select Other (4 or O) to display the Other Format menu, as shown in Figure 9-1.

```
Format: Other

     1 - Advance

     2 - Conditional End of Page

     3 - Decimal Character          .
         Thousands' Separator       ,

     4 - Language                   EN

     5 - Overstrike

     6 - Printer Functions

     7 - Underline - Spaces         Yes
                     Tabs           No




Selection: 0
```

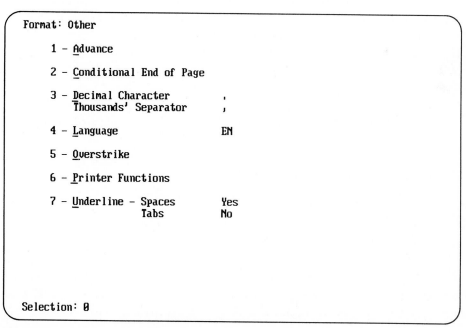

Figure 9-1. The Other Format menu

5. Select Conditional End of Page (2 or C). WordPerfect prompts with:

    Number of Lines to Keep Together:

6. Type the number you figured in step 1 and press ENTER.
7. Press EXIT (F7) to return to the document.

WordPerfect places a code at that position. For example, if you are keeping four lines together, the hidden code is **[CondEOP:4]**. If the heading and the two lines that follow it are positioned so that they fall in the domain of a page break, WordPerfect will now break to a new page just before the heading.

Trap: *Refrain from inserting hard returns to trigger an early page break.*

It is possible to force a page break by pressing ENTER down a page until WordPerfect inserts a soft page code. At first this method seems to work fine. A problem occurs, however, when you attempt to edit your text, thereby adding or removing lines; you will create odd gaps in the middle of pages or pages that consist of only one or two lines. Use the Block Protect, Conditional EOP, or Hard Page feature instead, and you won't have to readjust every line when you edit the document.

Trap: *Don't insert a hard page break in the middle of a line.*

If you press CTRL + ENTER in the middle of a line, WordPerfect places the first half of the line on one page and the second half on the next page—an awkward result. Therefore, position the cursor at the end of the last line you want on a page before inserting a hard page break.

Tip: *Use BACKSPACE to erase a hard page break.*

If you decide to cancel a hard page break, you must delete the **[HPg]** code you inserted. Do this in the same way that you erase a **[HRt]**. That is, position the cursor on the line below the **[HPg]** code, which means just below the page bar, and press BACKSPACE. Or, if you're on the Reveal Codes screen, you can locate the code. Just position the cursor on the **[HPg]** code and press DEL. You have erased the hard page break code; the page bar disappears.

Tip: *Surround text with two hard page break codes to keep that text on its own page.*

Suppose in the middle of a long document that you have a chart that you want to keep on a separate page. Move the cursor just above the chart and insert a hard page break code. Then move past the chart and insert a second hard page break code. This isolates the chart on its own page.

Trap: *Entering hard page breaks on a regular basis causes odd page endings.*

If you succumb to breaking *all* your pages manually by using the Hard Page feature, WordPerfect is unable to automatically readjust the text later on when you insert or delete lines. You will have to readjust text yourself, which can be a time-consuming process. Instead, use a hard page break only in limited circumstances, mainly when you want a page broken at a specific spot no matter how you edit the document later on.

Tip: *You can distinguish between a soft and a hard page break without revealing codes.*

A soft page break is represented by a row of dashes, while a hard page break is denoted by a row of equal signs. You can thus recognize whether WordPerfect chose the page break, which will then be indicated by dashes, or whether you forced the page break, which will be indicated by equal signs.

Tip: *WordPerfect can center a short page, top to bottom.*

You can center a short page of text from top to bottom. For instance, you may wish to center the text of a cover page of a report, as shown in Figure 9-2. Or you may wish to center a two-paragraph letter that you just completed. Instead of changing your top margin setting or inserting a string of hard returns above the text, use the Center Page feature, as follows:

1. Move the cursor to the very top left-hand corner of the page to be centered (before all existing codes).
2. Press the FORMAT (SHIFT + F8) key to display the Format menu.
3. Select Page (2 or P). The Page Format menu appears, as shown in Figure 9-3.

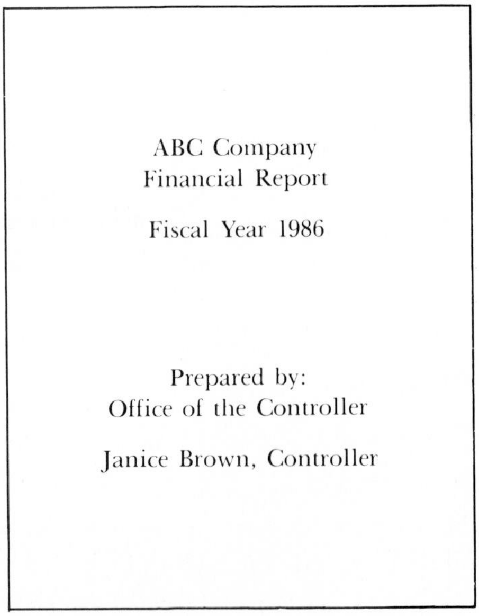
ABC Company
Financial Report

Fiscal Year 1986

Prepared by:
Office of the Controller

Janice Brown, Controller

Figure 9-2. A title page centered top to bottom

```
Format: Page

     1 - Center Page (top to bottom)    No

     2 - Force Odd/Even Page

     3 - Headers

     4 - Footers

     5 - Margins - Top                  1"
                   Bottom               1"

     6 - New Page Number                1
           (example: 3 or iii)

     7 - Page Numbering                 No page numbering

     8 - Paper Size                     8.5" x 11"
                 Type                   Standard

     9 - Suppress (this page only)

Selection: 0
```

Figure 9-3. The Page Format menu

4. Select Center Page (top to bottom) (1 or C). The word "Yes" now appears on the same line as the Center Page option, to indicate that the feature has been activated.
5. Press EXIT (F7) to return to your document.

WordPerfect inserts at that spot a center page code **[Center Pg]**. Make sure this code remains at the very top of the page before other codes or any text; otherwise, it will be ignored at the printer. The status line will not reflect the page centering, since the result happens at the printer.

Also, keep in mind that WordPerfect considers the page to include all characters on the page, including **[HRt]** codes. Thus, if you type a title page, press ENTER ten times, and then insert a hard page break, the ten **[HRt]** codes are part of the page so the text won't be truly centered when the document prints. Delete the ten **[HRt]** codes, and the page will be centered properly.

Tip: *Include blank lines in the Conditional EOP count.*

WordPerfect treats both blank lines and text lines the same way in a Conditional EOP. Therefore, count all blank lines when calculating how many lines must be kept together. For example, if you use double spacing, five lines of text equal ten lines to be kept together.

Tip: *Block Protect and Conditional EOP are each best used in particular instances.*

The Block Protect feature is the most appropriate when you wish to add or delete lines within that block at a later date and still keep the entire block protected. For instance, protect a table with Block Protect; if you edit the table later on, WordPerfect will still guard the entire table against a page break as long as the **[Block-Pro:]** codes surround it.

The Conditional EOP feature is the most appropriate when you wish to protect a title or a heading and a specific number of lines that follow. For instance, you may decide to keep together a heading and the first two lines of the paragraph that follows it. If you later edit the paragraph so that those two lines expand to five lines, Conditional EOP will still keep only the heading and the first *two* lines together.

Tip: *(When upgrading from 4.2.) Control page breaks in version 5 as you did previously.*

The method used to control page breaks has not been altered. You'll notice, however, that the keystrokes to access Conditional EOP are now quite different; this option is now on the Other Format menu, rather than on the Page Format menu.

Headers and Footers

A *header* is one or more lines of information printed at the top of pages, while a *footer* prints at the bottom of pages. You can define one or two headers and one or two headers and one or two footers; a second header or footer is useful if you plan one set of information on even-numbered pages and another set on odd-numbered pages. For example, many books place the book title on even-numbered pages and the chapter name on odd-numbered pages. The first is called header (or footer) A, while the second is called header (or footer) B.

The procedure is similar for creating either a header or a footer:

1. Move to the beginning of the first page where you want a header or footer to appear when printed. For instance, position the cursor at the beginning of the document if you want to print a header/footer on every page in the document.
2. Press FORMAT (SHIFT + F8) to view the Format menu.
3. Select Page (2 or P) to display the Page Format menu.
4. Select Headers (3 or H). Or select Footers (4 or F). WordPerfect prompts, asking whether you wish to choose a header/footer A or B. For instance, if you choose item 3, Headers, then WordPerfect prompts

   1 Header A; **2** Header B: **0**

5. Type a number to select the kind of header or footer you desire. For example, to create a first header, type **1** or **A**. WordPerfect responds with:

   1 Discontinue; **2** Every Page; **3** Odd Pages; **4** Even Pages; **5** Edit: **0**

6. Type a number from 2 to 4 to choose the pages on which you want the header or footer to appear. For example, to print on every page, type **2** or **P**. WordPerfect next displays a clear screen, which is the Header/Footer screen.
7. Type the header or footer information exactly as you would like it to appear (there is a one-page limit to how many lines a header or footer can contain, which in practical terms is no limit at all). For example, assume you want the header "ABC Company" situated at the top left corner of every page. Simply type **ABC Company**.
8. Press EXIT (F7) to save the header or footer and return to the Page Format menu. The menu now indicates the frequency of occurrence for any headers or footers that have been created. For example, if you created a Header A on every page, then next to item Headers, in Figure 9-3, you would now find the message **HA Every Page**.
9. If you wish to create another header or footer, then repeat this process, beginning at step 3 above.

   Or press EXIT (F7) to return to the document.

At the current cursor position, WordPerfect places a header/footer code that inserts a header or footer on every page from that point on. The code indicates the type of header/footer inserted as well as up to the first 50 characters contained in the text. An example is **[Header A:2;**ABC Company]. This indicates that a Header A, containing the text "ABC Company", will be placed on every page. **[Header A:3;**ABC Company] means the header will print only on odd pages, while **[Header A:4;** ABC Company] indicates even pages.

A header prints starting at the top margin of a page. WordPerfect adds one line of white space below the header to separate it from the document text. Similarly, a footer's last line prints at the bottom margin and WordPerfect adds one blank line above the footer. Top and bottom margins are thus preserved.

Trap: *Headers and footers are not visible on the Typing screen.*

A header or footer does not appear in a document. It appears instead on the printed page. Before you print, you can verify that the header or footer has been created and see its first 50 characters by checking the Reveal Codes screen.

Tip: *It is possible to preview exactly how headers and footers will appear on the printed page.*

A feature on the PRINT (SHIFT + F7) key, referred to as View Document, can show you how headers and footers will be positioned on the page when printed. This serves only as a preview; you cannot make editing changes on this preview screen (Chapter 14 describes the View Document feature in detail).

Tip: *Headers and footers can be typed using fancy features.*

The headers and footers you type can employ most of the same enhancements that are available for the document text (as discussed in Chapter 7). Center a header on the page, for example, by pressing CENTER (SHIFT + F6) before typing the header text. Underline a footer by pressing UNDERLINE (F8) before you start typing the text. Print a footer in italics by selecting the appropriate font change. Figure 9-4 shows some examples of fancy footers.

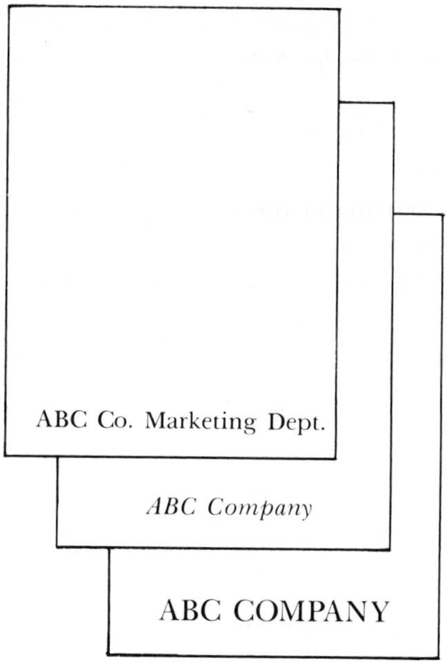

Figure 9-4. Footers with enhancements

You can reveal codes to edit header/footer text enhancements (like underline or a font change) just as you do for regular text—by pressing the REVEAL CODES (ALT + F3) key while viewing the Header/Footer screen.

You can also number pages via headers and footers. Refer to the next section in this chapter, "Page Numbering," for information on this procedure.

Trap: *Header and footer codes should not be preceded by any text at the top of a page.*

When you create a header or footer, make sure that the cursor is at the very top of the page, before any text. If you insert a header code in the middle of a page, for example, the header will not print until the *following* page.

To protect against a header or footer code moving as you add or delete text in your document, place a hard page break in front of the code. However, if the header or footer code resides at the very top of a document, then the hard page break is unnecessary.

Note: Headers and footers cannot be inserted on the Document Initial Codes screen.

The header/footer code can, however, follow other *codes* at the top of the page. In some cases, in fact, it is important that it follow other codes. For example, the header/footer code must follow a left/right margin set code if you want the header/footer to reflect the margin change. (See the following Tip for related information.)

Tip: *The formatting of headers/footers can be the same as or different from the formatting of the body of the text.*

You learned in Chapter 8 that, unless you specify otherwise, a document will be printed using the default format settings (such as left/right margins of 1″). WordPerfect will use these same format settings when printing out headers and footers.

You can, however, alter the format used to print out your headers and footers. You may want the format for printing headers and footers to be the same as for the body of the text. Other times, you may want to use a different format for headers and footers than for the body of the text. As an example, perhaps you want a header to have wider margins than the rest of the text. Follow these guidelines when considering a format change in a document containing headers and/or footers:

- **To Print out a header or footer using the same format as that of the body of the document** Change the format using the Document Initial Codes feature, accessed via the FORMAT (SHIFT + F8) key. When you insert a format code on the Document Initial Codes screen, this code alters the entire document, including headers and footers.
- **To print out a header or footer using the same format as for a certain group of pages** Position the cursor at the top of the page where you want to alter the format. Next, insert a code that changes the format. (For instance, insert a left/right margin code.) Then, insert a header or footer code to the

right of or below the format change code. When you change a document's format within the document itself, this affects all text following the code, including the text of a header or footer when the header or footer code follows the format code.

Note: The exception here is Line Spacing. A header or footer code will ignore a line-spacing code that precedes it in the text unless inserted on the Document Initial Codes screen.

- **To print out a header or footer with a format setting different from the body of the text** Make sure that the cursor is in the Header/Footer screen, positioned before the actual text of the header or footer. Then, change the format for that header or footer. When you insert a format code on the Header/Footer screen, only the header or footer you created will abide by the format change.

Tip: *The font used to print headers/footers can be the same as or different from the font used in the body of the text.*

You learned in Chapter 7 that, unless you specify otherwise, a document will be printed with the default font you designated for your printer (as described in the section entitled "Selecting Your Printer" in Appendix A). WordPerfect will use this same font when printing out headers and footers.

You can, however, alter the font or attribute used to print out your headers and footers. You may want the font for printing headers and footers to be the same one as for the body of the text. At other times, you may want to use one font for a specific header and/or footer, and another for the body of the text. Follow these guidelines when considering a font change in a document containing headers and/or footers.

- **To print out a header or footer with the same font as for the body of the document** Change the font by using the Document Initial Font feature, accessed via the FORMAT (SHIFT + F8) key. Using the FORMAT key to change the initial font of a document alters the entire document, including the font used to print headers and footers.
- **To print out a header or footer using the same font as for a certain group of pages** Position the cursor at the top of the page where you want to alter

the font. Next, insert a font change code by using the Base Font option, accessed via the FONT (CTRL + F8) key. Then, insert a header or footer code to the right of or below the font change code. Using the FONT key to change the font of a document affects all text following the base font code, including header/footer text when a header or footer code follows the font change code.

- **To print out a header or footer with a font or attribute different than for the body of the text** Make sure that the cursor is in the header/footer screen. Then, position the cursor before the text of the header or footer and use the FONT key to change the base font. Or use the BLOCK key to highlight the text and then use the FONT key to change the font attribute (size or appearance). When you insert font or font attribute codes on the Header/Footer screen, only the text of the header or footer will be governed by the font or attribute changes.

Tip: *Existing headers or footers can be edited or discontinued.*

When you need to alter the text of an already existing header or footer, there's no need to start from scratch. Edit the header or footer by first positioning the cursor after the header/footer code. Next, follow steps 1 through 5 for creating a header or footer, as discussed at the beginning of this section. Then, select Edit (5 or E) from the Header/Footer menu. Edit the header or footer as you would edit text in your document. Press EXIT twice to return to the document.

However, if you wish to change the occurrence of that header/footer, then you must start from the beginning. For instance, if you create a header on every page and later decide to print it only on even pages, then you should erase the header code and create a new one.

You can also discontinue a header or footer at any point in a document. The header or footer is canceled for the rest of the document, a convenient option if, for example, you plan on creating a different header or footer for each section of a long document. Position the cursor at the top of the page where you want the header or footer to be discontinued. Next, follow steps 1 through 5 as mentioned above. Then, select Discontinue (1 or D). A header/footer code is inserted, wherein "0" represents the Discontinue option. For instance, if you canceled header A, the code reads

[Header A:1;]

Tip: *The Suppress feature is especially handy when you want to print a header or footer on all but the first page of a document.*

WordPerfect offers the ability to suppress any header or footer on a *single* page. This is useful when you want a header/footer to appear on all but the first page of your correspondence or report—which is often the case. It also comes in handy when one page of a document contains a table or a special figure and a header/footer on that one page would look awkward. To activate the Suppress feature:

1. Position the cursor at the very top of the page (before other codes) where the header or footer should be suppressed.
2. Press FORMAT (SHIFT + F8) to display the Format menu.
3. Select Page (2 or P) to view the Page Format menu.
4. Select Suppress (9 or U). The menu shown in Figure 9-5 appears. Here you have the option of suppressing all headers and footers, or just selected

```
Format: Suppress (this page only)

     1 - Suppress All Page Numbering, Headers and Footers

     2 - Suppress Headers and Footers

     3 - Print Page Number at Bottom Center  No

     4 - Suppress Page Numbering             No

     5 - Suppress Header A                   No

     6 - Suppress Header B                   No

     7 - Suppress Footer A                   No

     8 - Suppress Footer B                   No





Selection: 0
```

Figure 9-5. The Suppress Format menu

ones. (Options are also presented for suppressing page numbers, which are explained in the next section of this chapter, "Page Numbering.")

5. Select an option. If you select options 1 or 2, WordPerfect automatically changes No to Yes where appropriate for options 4 through 8. If you select options 3 through 8, you must type **N** or **Y** to indicate your choice.

   For instance, suppose your document contains a header A with your company name and a footer A containing today's date. You can suppress just the header by changing option 5 to Yes, just the footer by changing option 7 to Yes, or both by setting both to Yes. Alternatively, you can suppress both by choosing option 2, although you will also cancel a header B or footer B on that page, if there is one.

6. Press EXIT (F7) twice to return to your document.

WordPerfect inserts a suppress code in the text, affecting *only that one page.* As an example, if you suppress headers A and B, the code is **[Suppress:HA,HB]**. The code operates for only that one page.

A good strategy when you wish to suppress specific headers or footers on only the first page of your document is to place both the header/footer code and the suppress code, one right after the other, at the top of your document. In that way, the header/footer code is protected from being moved accidentally. At the same time, the header or footer won't print on page 1 of the document.

Trap: *It is all too easy to accidentally insert a header or footer containing no text, which could invalidate a previous header or footer.*

Suppose that in order to create a Header A on every page, you follow steps 1 through 6 as mentioned at the beginning of this section. Then, when you are viewing a blank Header/Footer screen, ready to type the text of the header, suppose that you decide to cancel the header (perhaps because you now realize that you already created a Header A and really meant to select the option for editing it rather than for creating a new Header A). The only way to exit this screen is with the EXIT (F7) key; you cannot use the CANCEL (F1) key to back out of the Header/Footer screen. As a result, when you press EXIT (F7) to return to your document, you will insert a header code into the text, even though you typed no text for the header. The code will appear as follows: **[Header A:2;]**. To completely abort the header, you should then erase the header/footer code you inserted. You can press BACKSPACE to do so. (If you're viewing the Typing screen, WordPerfect will prompt, asking for confirmation that you wish to delete the code; type **Y** to confirm the deletion.)

It is important to remember to erase a header or footer code that you inserted inadvertently; otherwise, you could unwittingly cancel another code of the same type that is nearer to the top of the document. For instance, if the code **[Header A:2;**ABC Company**]** is at the top of the document and the code **[Header A:2;]** is located farther forward in the text, the second code overrides the first, and so the header "ABC Company" won't print on every page; a blank header will print instead. Erase the **[Header A:2;]** code, and then the header "ABC Company" will print on every page.

Trap: *Headers and footers cause page breaks to occur earlier than you might expect.*

Top and bottom margins are preserved when you create headers or footers in a document. What is altered is the amount of document text that can fit on a page. As a result, soft page breaks appear sooner in a document if you include a header and footer than if you don't.

For example, assume you have established a two-line header and a one-line footer. The header counts for three lines (the two first lines of text plus a one-line separator) and the footer counts for two lines (the last text line plus a one-line separator). This reduces the document text on each page by five lines. The document will occupy more pages than it would without headers and footers. The "Ln" indicator on the status line will reflect the change. For instance, assuming the current example, the top line of each page on screen will read **Ln 1.5″** (or something comparable, depending on your printer, font selection, and line-height settings) rather than **Ln 1″**, because the header occupies the first three lines.

The location of all soft page breaks readjusts when you create headers or footers after you've completed a document. If you plan to include headers or footers in your text, create the headers and footers *before* you type the body of your document. That way, as you type you will know where page breaks will occur.

Tip: *Hard returns can widen the white space between headers or footers and the document text.*

You may find that one blank line isn't sufficient to separate a header or footer from the text of your document. Sometimes a document is more visually pleasing with additional white space.

If you want more than one blank line separating a header from the text, include blank lines at the bottom of a header—after you've typed the header text. If you want more than one blank line separating a footer from the text, place blank lines above the footer text. The **[HRt]** codes become part of the header or footer, so that blank lines are inserted as part of the header or footer.

Tip: *The HOME key extends a Search or Replace command to headers and footers.*

In Chapter 4 you learned about the Search feature, which finds phrases in your text. Similarly, the Replace feature (discussed in Chapter 6) finds a character string and substitutes another in a document's text. When you wish to broaden the use of these features to include headers and footers (and footnotes and endnotes), in addition to the document text, perform an extended search. Press HOME before pressing the →SEARCH, ←SEARCH, or REPLACE keys. That way, you can locate and/or replace a string, should it occur in a header or footer.

Tip: *(When upgrading from 4.2.) Header and footer difficulties have been eliminated in version 5.*

If you create a header in version 5, then you'll notice that the "Ln" number on the status line changes to take account of the header. For instance, if you have a two-line header (with one line separating the header from the body of the text), then the status line could read **Ln 1.5"** (approximately, depending on your printer, font selection, and line-height setting) rather than **Ln 1"**. In version 4.2, the status line did not change to indicate the presence of a header.

Moreover, the bottom margin is always preserved in version 5. In version 4.2, footers that extended beyond one line reduced the bottom margin.

You'll have less trouble with headers and footers in version 5. For one thing, it is no longer necessary to update headers and footers if you altered margins *after* inserting a header/footer code (which was the case in version 4.2). Further, you can now insert a **[TAB]** code in a header or footer and have that code remain, rather than being converted into spaces. This eliminates any potential spacing problems when the header or footer is printed. There are also various methods for altering the font used to print a header or footer.

A nice touch is that you can check to see whether a header or footer has been created for the part of the document where your cursor is positioned by checking the Page Format menu, rather than having to hunt for the header/footer code in the text.

Page Numbering

You have two alternatives for producing numbered pages in a printed document. First, you can incorporate a page number into the text of a header or footer. Just place the symbol ^B into the header/footer text. The symbol is produced by pressing CTRL + B. (Don't type a caret ^ and then a B to create the symbol; they're not the same.) An alternative is to insert ^N (also created with the CTRL key). Both ^B and ^N operate the same in a header or footer to produce a page number.

Assume that you want the top of the first page of a memo to read "ABC COMPANY -- Page 1," and that you want each succeeding page to have its correct page number in the same header. At the top of the document, press the FORMAT key and select options until the Header/Footer screen appears for you to type in the text of the header or footer (the specific keystrokes for this are listed at the beginning of the previous section of this chapter, "Headers and Footers"). On the Header/Footer screen, (1) type **ABCCOMPANY -- Page**, (2) press the SPACEBAR once to insert a space, and (3) hold down CTRL and type **B**. The header reads

ABC COMPANY -- Page ^B

When printed, all pages of the document will contain a header with the correct page number.

The second way to number pages avoids the Header/Footer menu entirely. If all you want at the top or bottom of the page is a simple number—without any additional text or symbols—then the Page Numbering feature is quicker to use. You can choose to print numbers at any of eight locations on a page, including

Top:	left corner
	center
	right corner
	left corner on even pages and right corner on odd pages
Bottom:	left corner
	center
	right corner
	left corner on even pages and right corner on odd pages

Or, if you've previously chosen a page number, then you can select a ninth option for no page numbering. This selection discontinues page numbering for the rest of the document (unless you make another numbering selection farther forward in the text). To use the Page Numbering feature, proceed as follows:

1. Position the cursor at the top of the page where you wish to start page numbering. For example, position the cursor at the beginning of a document to insert a number on every page.
2. Press FORMAT (SHIFT + F8) to view the Format menu.
3. Select Page (2 or P) to display the Page Format menu.
4. Select Page Numbering (7 or P). The menu in Figure 9-6 appears.
5. Choose the location where you wish each page number to appear. For instance, select item 6 to center page numbers at the bottom of each page.
6. Press EXIT (F7) until you return to the document.

WordPerfect inserts a hidden code at the current cursor position. If you choose to place page numbers in the bottom center of each page, for example, the code is **[Pg Numbering: Bottom Center]**. Every page from that point on will be numbered at the location you specify.

A page number at the top of the document, like a one-line header, prints just below the top margin. A page number at the bottom, like a footer, prints just above the bottom margin. The page number feature also appropriates one line of white space to separate it from the document text.

Trap: *Page numbering is not visible on the Typing screen.*

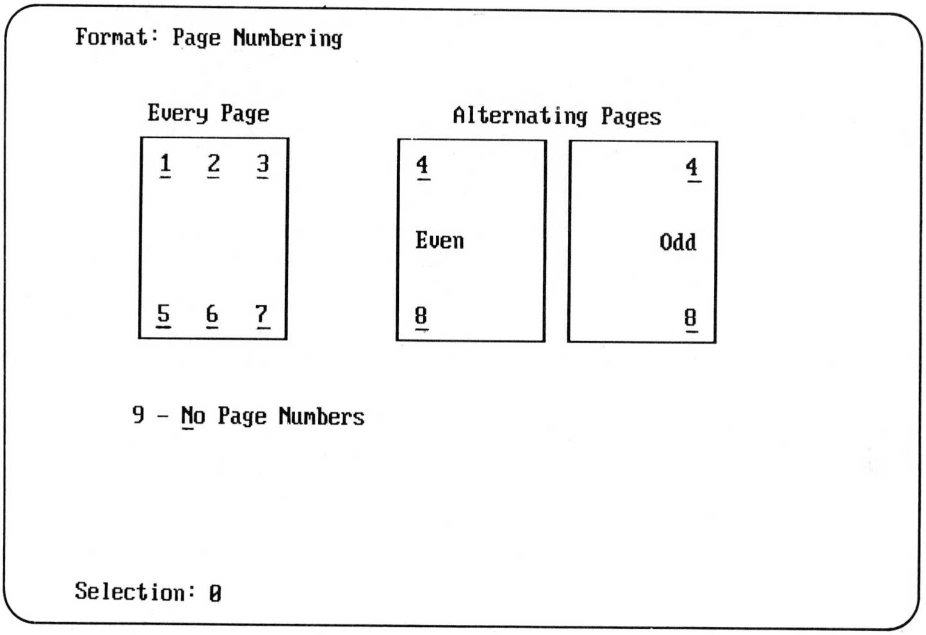

Figure 9-6. *The Page Numbering menu*

Like headers and footers, page numbers don't appear on screen. But you can verify your page numbering selection by revealing codes. In addition, it is possible to preview how a page will look with page numbers, when printed, by using the View Document feature on the PRINT (SHIFT + F7) key (Chapter 14 describes the View Document feature).

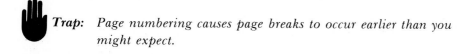

Trap: *Page numbering causes page breaks to occur earlier than you might expect.*

Top and bottom margins are preserved when you use the Page Numbering feature, just as they are when you insert headers or footers in a document. What is altered is the amount of document text that can fit on a page. As a result, soft page breaks appear sooner in a document if you include page numbering than if you don't.

For example, assume you have decided on page numbering at the top left-hand corner of every page. The page number counts for approximately two lines (one line containing the number plus a one-line separator). The document will occupy more pages than it would without page numbering. The "Ln" indicator on the status line will reflect the change. For example, assuming page numbering at the top of every page, the status line will read **Ln 1.33"** (or something comparable depending on your printer, font selection, and line-height settings) rather than **Ln 1"**, when the cursor is on the top line of the document.

Trap: *Don't insert a numeral in a header or footer to represent a page number.*

If you type a header with a specific page number, that number will appear on every page. If the header text reads "ABC Company -- Page 3", then the header on every page will print as page 3. Use ^B or ^N instead.

Trap: *You can select headers/footers and also utilize the Page Numbering feature—but make sure they don't conflict.*

You can include both page numbering and a header or footer in one document; however, you must make sure that they will not conflict. For example, if you include a page number (using ^B) in a header or footer, then make sure that the Page Numbering feature is set for no page numbering; otherwise, the page number prints twice.

Also, if you use both features, make sure that page numbers and headers or footers don't print in the same spot on each page. If you are printing a footer in the bottom center of a page, for example, then make sure that the Page Numbering feature is set for something other than the bottom center; otherwise, the two will print on top of one another.

Tip: *A page numbering code can be inserted on the Document Initial Codes screen.*

You learned in Chapter 8 that you can insert a format code in the document itself or on the Document Initial Codes screen. A code on the Document Initial Codes screen takes effect starting at the top of the document. Like a format code, a page numbering code can also be inserted either in the document itself or on the Document Initial Codes screen. When you wish to number each page of a document with the page numbering feature, inserting the page numbering code on the Document Initial Codes screen protects the code from being accidentally erased or moved when you later edit the document.

Note: If you are numbering pages by creating a header or footer, then you must insert the header or footer code within the document itself; headers and footers are not allowed on the Document Initial Codes screen.

Tip: *If you want symbols or words with your page numbers, you must include the page number in a header or footer.*

The Page Numbering feature inserts only a number, nothing more. If you want the page number to be enhanced with symbols or words—such as "-2-", "Page 2", or "Page 4-2"—then you must create a header or footer and use the ^B symbol to designate page numbers. For instance, a footer might read "-^B-", "Page ^B", or "Page 4-^B".

Tip: *The ^B symbol works anywhere in a document.*

The code ^B transforms itself into a page number not only in a footer or header, but *anywhere* on a page, including in the body of a document. Therefore, if you wish to refer to the current page number in the document text, use ^B. (However, ^N does not work in the document text.)

Tip: *You can reset page numbers and choose between Arabic and Roman numerals.*

WordPerfect numbers pages sequentially beginning at page 1, and prints out whatever page number is indicated after "Pg" on the status line. You can instead use the New Page Number feature, which enables you to start page numbering with any number on any page. Once you assign a new number, WordPerfect continues the sequence. Renumber the first page of the document as page 16, for example, and the following pages are numbered 17, 18, and so on. You may wish to change a page number if you're splitting a long document into two separate files and want the second file to start numbering where the first file stopped. Or, change page numbering if you're typing several letters that are in the same document file, each of which should be numbered starting at page 1.

While selecting a new page number, you can also choose between two types of page numbering styles — either Arabic (1, 2, 3, and so on) or lowercase Roman numeral (i, ii, iii, and so on). Thus, you can number a table of contents in Roman numerals and the body of your document in Arabic numbers. (Arabic is the default setting.)

To renumber a page:

1. Move the cursor to the page you want to renumber.
2. Press FORMAT (SHIFT + F8) to view the Format menu.
3. Select Page (2 or P) to display the Page Format menu.
4. Select New Page Number (6 or N). The cursor moves up to indicate the current page number, ready for you to enter a new page number. WordPerfect reminds you that you can insert the number in either the Arabic or Roman numeral style with the prompt **(example: 3 or iii)**.
5. Type a new page number in either Arabic style or as a Roman numeral and press ENTER.
6. Press EXIT (F7) to return to your document.

A **[Pg Num:]** code is inserted to renumber that page. For example, **[Pg Num:10]** indicates page 10 in Arabic style, while **[Pg Num:i]** indicates page 1 in Roman numeral style. The new page number, *but not the numbering style,* is reflected in the status line.

The GOTO (CTRL + HOME) key, described in Chapter 4 as a method to move to specific pages, abides by the new page numbering, although you must type a number even if the numbering is in Roman numerals. For instance, if you wish to move to page ii, press CTRL + HOME, and type **2** rather than ii.

Because you can renumber pages, it is possible to have the same document containing two or more pages with the same page number. In this case, WordPerfect considers the document separated into sections. For example, suppose you produce a document with the first four pages numbered i through iv, and the next pages renumbered starting at page 1. Pages i through iv become section 1; the next page starts section 2.

When two or more pages have the same number, then employing GOTO can, at first, seem like a confusing method for moving the cursor. Just remember that the cursor moves to a page number based on its original location when you press GOTO. Take the situation with two sections of text: pages i through iv, and pages 1 through 10. When you press CTRL + HOME, type **3**, and press ENTER, WordPerfect will move to page iii if the cursor is located in the first section. WordPerfect will move to page 3 if the cursor is located in the second section. And, if you press CTRL + HOME, type **8**, and press ENTER, WordPerfect will move to page 8 no matter where the cursor is located, since the first section contains no page viii.

Tip: *You can force odd/even numbers on particular pages.*

The Force Odd/Even Page feature makes certain that page numbering on the current page begins with an odd or an even number. This is useful, for example, to ensure that the first page of a report, book chapter, or other document is an odd-numbered page. To force an odd/even page number:

1. Move the cursor to the top of the page where you want the force to take effect.
2. Press FORMAT (SHIFT + F8) to view the Format menu.
3. Select Page (2 or **P**) to display the Page Format menu.
4. Select Force Odd/Even Page (2 or O). WordPerfect responds with:

   1 Odd; **2** Even: **0**

5. Select Odd (1 or O). Or select Even (2 or E).

WordPerfect inserts a code in the text **[Force:Odd]** or **[Force:Even]**. If the page was already going to be as specified, the page retains its number. If not, numbering begins with the next number. For instance, if at the top of page 2 you insert a **[Force:Odd]** code, then the page is renumbered to page 3, and a blank page is inserted as page 2. The change in page number is reflected in the status line.

Tip: *The Suppress feature enables you to cancel page numbering or print a page number on a single page.*

As with headers and footers, page numbering can be suppressed on a single page by using the Suppress feature. You can cancel headers/footers and page numbering separately. To access this feature:

1. Position the cursor at the very top of the page (before existing codes) where the Header/Footer or Page Numbering feature should be suppressed.
2. Press FORMAT (SHIFT + F8) to display the Format menu.
3. Select Page (2 or P) to view the Page Format menu.
4. Select Suppress (9 or U). The menu shown in Figure 9-5 appears.
5. Select an option. If you select option 1 or 2, WordPerfect changes No to Yes where appropriate for options 4 through 8. If you select options 3 through 8, you must type N or Y to indicate your choice.

   For instance, suppose your document contains a header A with your company name and you've selected page numbering in the top center of every page with the Page Numbering feature. You can suppress just the header by changing option 5 to Yes, just the page numbering by changing option 4 to Yes, or both by setting each to Yes. Alternatively, you can suppress both by choosing option 1, though here you will also cancel any other headers or footers on that page.

   Notice in Figure 9-5 that you can also choose to insert a page number in the bottom center of a single page (option 3), but only if you did not select options 1 or 4, which suppress all page numbering.
6. Press EXIT (F7) twice to return to your document.

WordPerfect inserts a suppress code in the text, affecting *only that one page.* As an example, if you suppress only the Page Numbering feature, the code is **[Suppress:PgNum]**. The code operates only for that one page.

Tip: *(When upgrading from 4.2.) WordPerfect now adjusts the position of page numbers on a page.*

In version 4.2, it was necessary to change the column position of page numbers if you modified your document margins. This is no longer the case; the position of numbers will adjust automatically so that they appear at the left margin, in the center, or at the right margin, depending on your selection.

An added feature in version 5 is the ability to force odd/even numbers on particular pages, as described in a previous Tip in this section of the chapter.

Tips and Traps Summary

Automatic Page Breaks

Trap: A font with a larger type size results in less text on a page, while a smaller type size has the opposite effect—but not always.

Tip: The Widow/Orphan feature protects against stranded lines at the top or bottom of a page.

Trap: Headers/footers and page numbers reduce the amount of body text on a page.

Trap: The Advance feature can create a page break in advance of what the text on screen would indicate.

Tip: (When upgrading from 4.2.) WordPerfect now determines automatic page breaks in a more detailed way.

Controlling Page Breaks

Trap: Refrain from inserting hard returns to trigger an early page break.

Trap: Don't insert a hard page break in the middle of a line.

Tip: Use BACKSPACE to erase a hard page break.

Tip: Surround text with two hard page break codes to keep that text on its own page.

Tips and Traps Summary (*continued*)

Trap: Entering hard page breaks on a regular basis causes odd page endings.

Tip: You can distinguish between a soft and a hard page break without revealing codes.

Tip: WordPerfect can center a short page, top to bottom.

Tip: Include blank lines in the Conditional EOP count.

Tip: Block Protect and Conditional EOP are each best used in particular instances.

Tip: (When upgrading from 4.2.) Control page breaks in version 5 as you did previously.

Headers and Footers

Trap: Headers and footers are not visible on the Typing screen.

Tip: It is possible to preview exactly how headers and footers will appear on the printed page.

Tip: Headers and footers can be typed using fancy features.

Trap: Header and footer codes should not be preceded by any text at the top of a page.

Tip: The formatting of headers/footers can be the same as or different from the formatting of the body of the text.

Tip: The font used to print headers/footers can be the same as or different from the font used in the body of the text.

Tip: Existing headers or footers can be edited or discontinued.

Tip: The Suppress feature is especially handy when you want to print a header or footer on all but the first page of a document.

Trap: It is all too easy to accidentally insert a header or footer containing no text, which could invalidate a previous header or footer.

Tips and Traps Summary (*continued*)

Trap: Headers and footers cause page breaks to occur earlier than you might expect.

Tip: Hard returns can widen the white space between headers or footers and the document text.

Tip: The HOME key extends a Search or Replace command to headers and footers.

Tip: (When upgrading from 4.2.) Header and footer difficulties have been eliminated in version 5.

Page Numbering

Trap: Page numbering is not visible on the Typing screen.

Trap: Page numbering causes page breaks to occur earlier than you might expect.

Trap: Don't insert a numeral in a header or footer to represent a page number.

Trap: You can select headers/footers and also utilize the Page Numbering feature—but make sure they don't conflict.

Tip: A page numbering code can be inserted on the Document Initial Codes screen.

Tip: If you want symbols or words with your page numbers, you must include the page number in a header or footer.

Tip: The ^B symbol works anywhere in a document.

Tip: You can reset page numbers and choose between Arabic and Roman numerals.

Tip: You can force odd/even numbers on particular pages.

Tip: The Suppress feature enables you to cancel page numbering or print a page number on a single page.

Tip: (When upgrading from 4.2.) WordPerfect now adjusts the position of page numbers on a page.

10

Working with Styles

Each time you create a document, you determine that document's overall appearance based on the enhancements and formatting possibilities available to you in WordPerfect. For example, perhaps you decide that for an entire document you will set wider-than-usual margins, use double spacing, and turn off right justification (features described in Chapter 8). You also choose to center and boldface all headings and to left-justify and boldface all subheadings (enhancements described in Chapter 7). You have thus designed a style for several elements in your document.

Using WordPerfect's Styles feature, you can define each element in a document, and then have WordPerfect do the work of formatting or enhancing the text for you. Why rely on the Styles feature instead of formatting the document directly?

One reason is that the Styles feature creates dynamic links to elements in your document. If you decide to change the appearance of a certain element, WordPerfect can make the modifications in the entire document. For example, rather than center and *boldface* all headings, suppose that you decide to center and *underline* them. Simply alter the style you established for headings, and all the headings in your document will be updated automatically by WordPerfect to reflect the newly defined style.

Another reason to use the Styles feature is so that you can make intricate formatting or font changes throughout a document very quickly. For instance, you can change the attributes of your text so that it appears with double underline, in italic, and in large print—by using only a few keystrokes.

A third reason to use the Styles feature is because it provides a convenient means by which you can use the same style in more than one document. For example, you might use one previously defined style that contains the text and graphics for a masthead every time you produce a newsletter. Or use another that contains a header and formatting codes when preparing a letter. Activate three other styles for the market share reports you produce every week. Use six other styles to create each chapter in a book that you're authoring. Thus, using the Styles feature saves you time and makes the job of producing standardized documents simple.

Read on to learn how to create, use, and modify styles. You'll also discover how to establish a style library, which can contain a complete list of styles for all your documents.

Creating a Style

A style can consist of any number of WordPerfect codes and/or any amount of standard text. Create a style whenever the way you format and enhance sections of documents is repetitive. Assume, for instance, that you plan to produce monthly sales reports and that you have specific ideas for how you wish to present the material. Here are examples of four separate styles that you would create to make the job easier:

- **Style Example 1: Formatting codes and boilerplate text to begin a document** Create a style that contains a left/right margin code, a justification-on code, and three paragraphs of text that always appear as the opening of the report. This style would be inserted at the beginning of the sales report.

- **Style Example 2: Text enhancement codes for headings** Create a style that centers and boldfaces a block of text. This style would be used to enhance each heading in the sales report.
- **Style Example 3: Formatting codes for paragraphs** Create a style that inserts a tab before a section of text and inserts two hard return codes after that section of text. This style would be used to format basic paragraphs in the report.
- **Style Example 4: Formatting codes for numbered paragraphs** Create a style that inserts a paragraph number and an indent before a section of text and inserts two hard return codes after that section of text. This style would be used to format paragraphs in a numbered list in the report.

When you've decided on a document's design elements and you wish to create various styles, proceed as follows:

1. The cursor can be positioned anywhere on screen in the document for which you wish to create a style. Or, the cursor can be on a clear screen, where you intend to begin typing your document.
2. Press the STYLE (ALT + F8) key. A Styles screen appears, as shown in Figure 10-1. The middle of the screen is blank if you have yet to define a style for that document. Notice the menu of eight items at the bottom of the Styles screen.
3. Select Create (3 or C). (Or you can press the INS key.) The Edit Styles screen appears, as shown in Figure 10-2.
4. Select an item and enter the corresponding information to create a style definition:

   Select Name (1 or N). Then type in a style name and press ENTER. For instance, the name entered for the Style Example 1, described above, might be SRBEGIN, standing for Sales Report, BEGINning of document. Or the name for Style Example 2 might be SR1HEADS, standing for Sales Report, level 1 HEADingS.

   Select Type (2 or T) to choose the style type. WordPerfect displays the menu showing the two style options:

   Type: 1 Paired; 2 Open: 0

   To select a *paired* style type, choose Paired (1 or P). This is the default

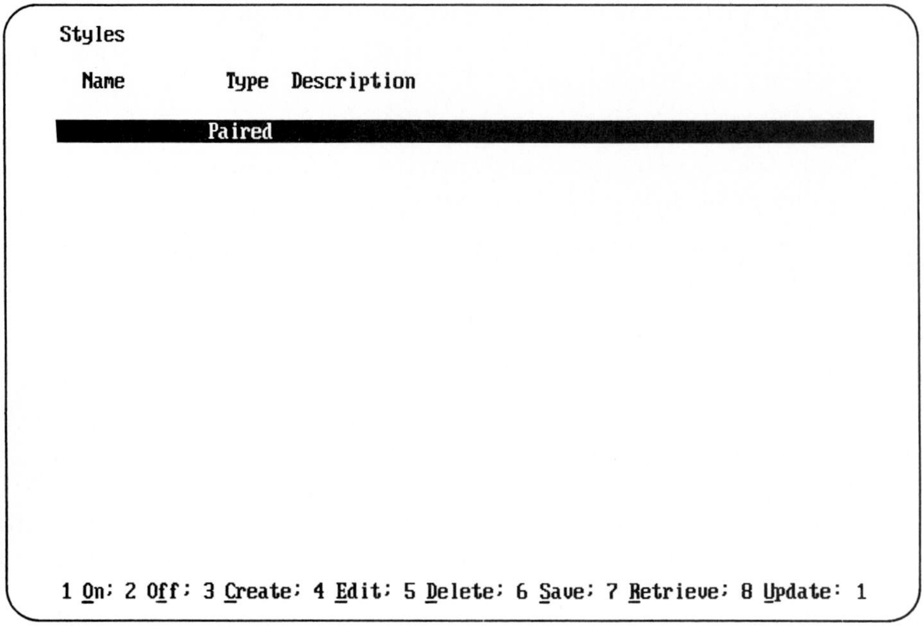

Figure 10-1. *The Styles screen indicating that no styles have yet been created*

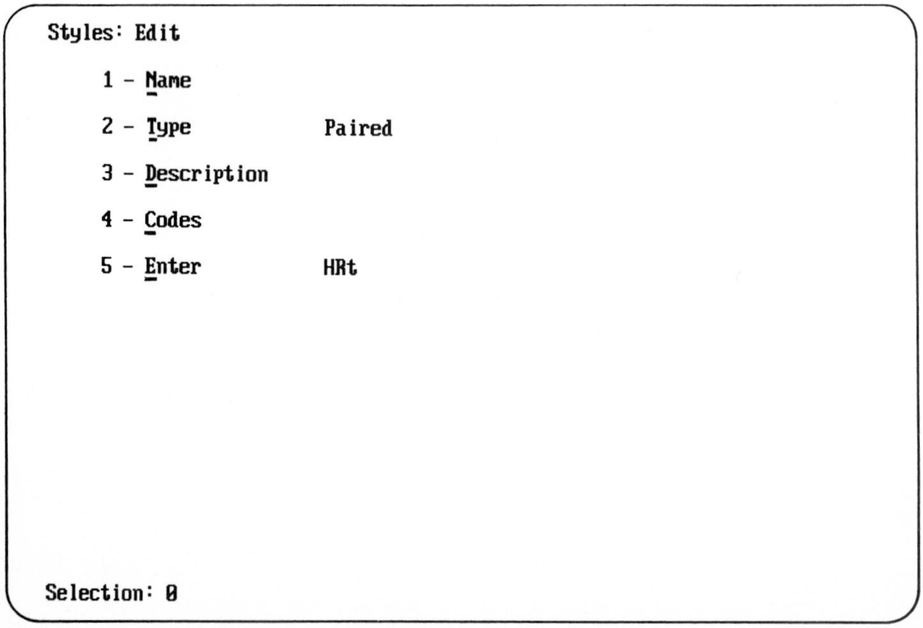

Figure 10-2. *The Edit Styles screen*

setting, as shown in Figure 10-2. It is for styles that must have a beginning and an end, and thus it affects only a specific block of text. For instance, Style Example 2 would be defined as paired, in that it could be turned on before a heading and turned off following that heading. Style Examples 3 and 4 would also be defined as paired.

Or, to select an *open* style type, choose Open (2 or O). This type has only a beginning and is not turned off. For instance, Style Example 1 would be defined as open because the margin and justification codes would affect the entire document (or they would affect the document until another margin or justification code appeared later in the text).

Select Description (3 or D). Then type in a description, up to 54 characters in length, to remind you of what the style does.

Select Codes (4 or C). A Reveal Codes screen appears. If you selected an open style type, then the Reveal Codes screen is completely clear. Type in text and codes as you desire. To include a code, use the same keystrokes that you would use to select that feature during normal typing. For example, to insert **[BOLD]**, press the BOLD (F6) key. To insert **[ITALC]**, press FONT (CTRL + F8), select Appearance (2 or A), and select Italc (4 or I). To insert a **[HPg]** code, press CTRL + ENTER.

If you selected a paired style type, then the screen is clear, except for a **[Comment]** code, as shown in Figure 10-3 (Chapter 3 describes the Document Comment feature). As the text of the Comment box indicates, you should place text and codes that begin the style *before* the comment; place text and codes that end the style *after* the comment.

After inserting text and codes press EXIT to return to the Edit Styles menu.

Select Enter (5 or E), a step that is necessary *only* if you are defining a paired style. This allows you to determine what the function of the ENTER key will be once you use the paired style that you are defining. WordPerfect prompts with the following menu:

Enter: 1 HRt; 2 Off; 3 Off/On: 0

Select HRt (1 or H), if you wish to insert a **[HRt]** code when the style is active, which is the ENTER key's normal function. This is the default setting.

Or choose Off (2 or F), if you want the ENTER key to turn off the style after the style has been turned on.

Or, choose Off/On (3 or O), if you want the ENTER key to turn off the style and then immediately turn it on again for the next block of text.

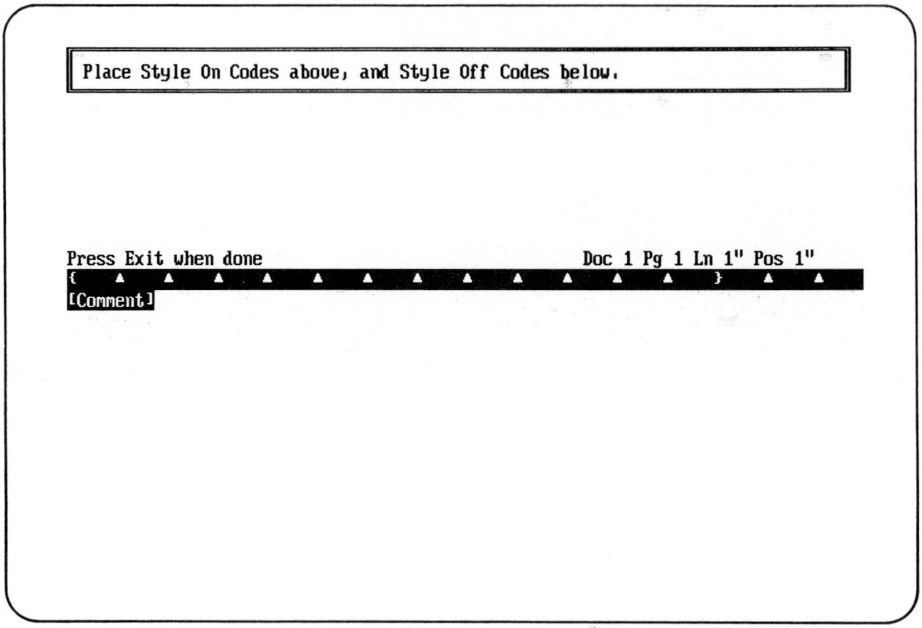

Figure 10-3. The Reveal Codes screen before inserting codes and text for a paired style type

5. Press EXIT (F7) once to return to the Styles menu.
6. Repeat steps 3 through 5 above to create another style. Or press EXIT (F7) to return to your document.

When you create a style, it is saved along with the document on which it was created. From that point on, whenever you press the STYLE key with that document on screen, the list of available styles is displayed on the Styles screen. An example is shown in Figure 10-4, which contains four style definitions. The cursor on the Styles screen occupies almost the full width of the screen, highlighting the name, type, and description of one style at a time.

Tip: *The Styles screen may already contain style definitions the first time you decide to create a style.*

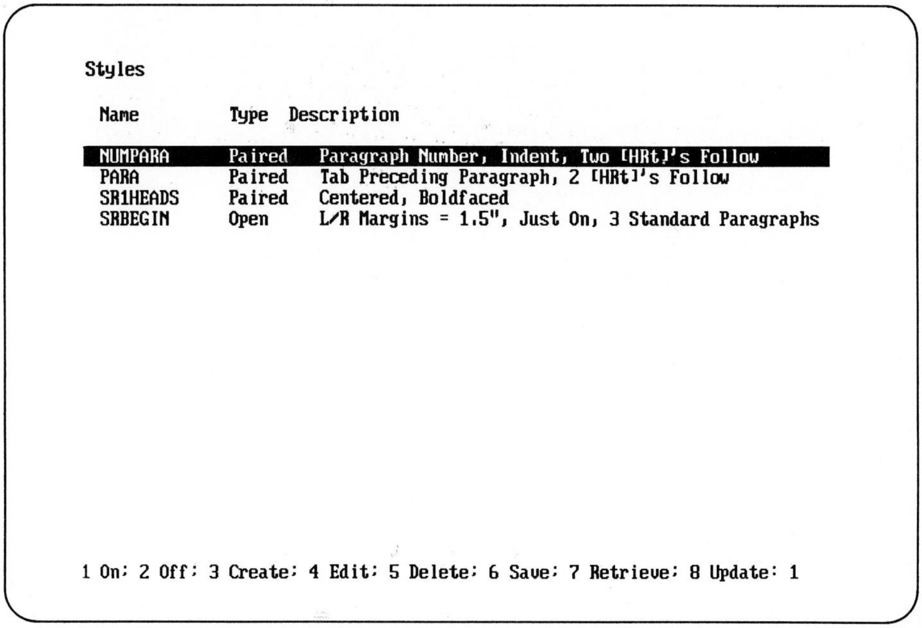

Styles
Name Type Description
NUMPARA Paired Paragraph Number, Indent, Two [HRt]'s Follow
PARA Paired Tab Preceding Paragraph, 2 [HRt]'s Follow
SR1HEADS Paired Centered, Boldfaced
SRBEGIN Open L/R Margins = 1.5", Just On, 3 Standard Paragraphs
1 On; 2 Off; 3 Create; 4 Edit; 5 Delete; 6 Save; 7 Retrieve; 8 Update: 1

Figure 10-4. The Styles screen showing a list of styles

WordPerfect gives you the ability to create a style library, which is a default list of commonly used styles. If you or someone in your office has established a library, then that library will appear the first time that you press STYLE (ALT + F8) to create a style for a specific document (for more on the Style Library feature, see the last section in this chapter, "Managing Styles Between Documents and from a Style Library").

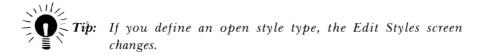

Tip: *If you define an open style type, the Edit Styles screen changes.*

When defining an open style, as described above, it is unnecessary to define how you wish to employ the ENTER key. This is because an open style has only a beginning. Thus, if you choose an open style, then the Edit Styles screen changes; option five, the Enter option, disappears from the Edit Styles screen.

Tip: *Your selection for the ENTER key function depends on the function of the paired style you create.*

When creating a paired style, how do you decide which function is appropriate for the ENTER key? It depends on the nature of the style that you are creating. The rules of thumb are

- Have the ENTER key retain its normal function—that of inserting **[HRt]** codes—if you plan to keep a style active until you've typed many lines of text in which you will need to use the ENTER key frequently to insert **[HRt]** codes. For example, perhaps you'll be typing a table that will be governed entirely by the same pair of style codes. In that case, you'll want to be able to use the ENTER key to end each line of text with a **[HRt]** code.
- Have the ENTER key turn the style off for you if you plan to keep a style active until after you've typed one section of text in which you won't need to insert **[HRt]** codes. For example, perhaps you'll be typing headings periodically in a document. In that case, the ENTER key can quickly turn the style off after you type a heading; you won't turn the style on again until you're ready to type the next heading.
- Have the ENTER key turn the style off and then on again if you plan to type consecutive sections of text that all use the same style. For example, perhaps you'll be typing a list consisting of numbered paragraphs. In that case, the ENTER key can quickly turn the style off for one paragraph and then on again, with the cursor at the proper place (depending on how you defined the style) for the next paragraph.

Refer to the following section of this chapter, "Using Styles," to learn the various methods you can use to turn a style on and off. Then the significance of assigning a specific function to the ENTER key will become clearer.

Trap: *Once you begin to define a style, the CANCEL key won't completely abort your attempt.*

As soon as you select Create (3 or C) from the Styles menu, WordPerfect reserves a place on the Styles screen for a new style. If you then press CANCEL to back out of defining a new style, a new style will nevertheless appear on the Styles screen, although that style will have no name and no description. You should then delete that style from the Styles screen, a procedure that is described in the following Tip.

Tip: *Edit a style that you wish to modify, or delete a style that is obsolete.*

It is quite easy to edit or delete a style that you've created. On the Styles screen, simply position the cursor on the style you wish to edit or delete. Then, from the menu at the bottom of the screen, select Edit (4 or E), to alter the style. The Edit Styles screen appears; here you can edit any part of the style's definition. Press EXIT (F7) twice to return to your document.

Or, from the menu at the bottom of the Styles screen, select Delete (5 or D) to erase the style. (Or you can simply press the DEL key.) WordPerfect prompts for verification:

Delete Style? (Y/N) No

Type **Y** to delete the style. Or type **N** or press ENTER to abort the Delete command. Now press EXIT (F7) to return to your document.

Tip: *A style can be used in more than just the document in which you created it.*

Although a style is saved along with a file, there are several methods for using that style in other documents as well (see the next section of this chapter, "Using Styles," for details).

Tip: *Make style names and descriptions more specific if you plan to use those styles in more than one document.*

Because you can use a style in more than one document, it is a good idea to provide each style with a unique name (even when naming styles that are created in *different* documents), and to clearly specify the exact purpose of each style. For example, you might have one style for headings in business reports and another style for headings in book chapters. You can name the first style BR1HEAD (Business Report, level 1 HEAD), and the other style C1HEAD (Chapters, level 1 HEAD). Then write a description that specifies the exact effect that each style will have on a heading. That way you'll know the type of document for which each style is appropriate, and you'll be able to distinguish between styles that are similar but not quite the same.

Tip: *A certain style may be useful not only for similar documents, but for different documents to be printed on the same printer.*

If you use two or more printers with WordPerfect, each requiring unique format settings, you'll find that the Styles feature can come in handy. Create a separate open style for the formatting you desire with each printer. For instance, perhaps you use your dot matrix printer to print out drafts of your documents. You could create a style that sets wide left/right margins (so that you have room to jot down notes in the margins), sets line spacing to double spaced, and turns on the Line Numbering feature (so that you can refer to each line by a specific number). (Line numbering is described in Chapter 21.) And perhaps you use your daisy wheel printer to print out your final document. You could create another style that sets different margins and line spacing, turns on justification, turns on hyphenation, and prints page numbers. That way, depending on which printer you planned to use to print out your document, you could insert a style code at the top of the document and it would be swiftly formatted for that printer.

Trap: *If Display Document Comments is set to "off," you'll be unable to view the Style Comment box on screen.*

Chapter 3 describes how you can insert comments in your text that are displayed only on screen, but are not printed. The Style Comment box is a related feature.

As a default setting, WordPerfect assumes that you want all comments displayed on the screen. Thus, a Style Comment box, like the one shown in Figure 10-3, will be displayed when you are defining a paired style type.

However, comments can be hidden from view by using the Display option on the SETUP (SHIFT + F1) key. If the Display Document Comments option is set to "off," then the style comment box will be hidden from view as well. Then you should rely on the bottom window on the screen to see the location of the **[Comment]** code. All codes and text that should be inserted when the style is turned off must be inserted after this **[Comment]** code. (See Appendix B for the procedure to change the default settings, with which you can choose whether comments are displayed on screen.)

Tip: *Think of the Comment box as the section of text that will be affected by the style you create.*

When you create a paired style type, the comment is provided to separate the codes and text that make up the on (beginning) style code from those that constitute the off (end) style code. Just imagine that the comment is the section of text that you want the pair of style codes to affect, and design the style accordingly. For example, pretend that the comment is a heading when you're creating a style for headings in your document; insert the on (beginning) style code before the comment and the off (end) style code after it.

Note: When the cursor is *on* the comment code, text or codes that you type will be inserted *before* the comment.

Tip: *When creating a paired style, you need only insert bold, underline, font, and other enhancement codes before the comment.*

As described in Chapter 3, there are two types of codes: single codes, such as margin codes or line-spacing codes, which affect all text from that point to the end of the document (or until the next code of its type further forward in the document), and code pairs, such as bold or underline codes, which bracket the beginning and end points of the text they enhance. When you wish to insert a code pair as part of a paired type of style, it is necessary to insert only the begin (on) code; the end (off) code is assumed. For instance, suppose you are creating a style that changes headings to boldface and small caps. In that case, insert the **[BOLD]** and **[SM CAP]** codes before the comment. Don't bother to insert the **[bold]** and **[sm cap]** codes after the comment (although you can do so, if you so desire); when you use that style (as described in the next section), WordPerfect inserts them for you when the style is turned off.

Even though base font changes insert single codes, these, like paired codes, are also turned off automatically for you when the style is turned off. For example, suppose that your current font is Courier, 10-point. You wish to create a style that changes certain headings to Helvetica, 14-point. Insert the **[Font:Helv 14pt]** code before the comment, and don't bother to insert a code to change the font back to Courier, 10-point, after the comment; when you use that style, WordPerfect inserts a font change code to return to the original font when the style is turned off. Thus, the Style feature is very convenient when you are changing your base font for only a specific section of text.

Tip: *You can quickly create a style by using existing codes in your text.*

You can use codes that are already present in your document as a convenient shortcut when creating a style. Suppose that you've already typed a heading and formatted that heading (such as boldfacing and underlining it). Now you decide to create a paired style type to help you do for all headings what you've just done manually for one. To do so, use the BLOCK (ALT + F4) key to highlight the heading and the codes that surround that heading. Next, press STYLE (ALT + F8), and select Create (3 or C). When you select Codes (4 or C) from the Edit Styles menu, the codes that were in the block will be automatically inserted for you. The on (beginning) codes—such as **[BOLD]**—will be placed before the comment and the off (end) codes—such as **[bold]**—will be placed after the comment.

Use the same procedure if you wish to create an open style type and you've already inserted certain codes (such as margin and tab codes) in your document. When you are defining the style, just remember to change it to the open type.

Trap: *You can't include features on the MARK TEXT key in a style without first blocking the comment.*

The MARK TEXT (ALT + F5) key offers features that enable WordPerfect to automatically generate tables, lists, and indexes for you (as described in Chapter 22). If you plan to create a style to *mark text* for inclusion in a table, a list, or an index that WordPerfect will later generate, then the process is a bit different when performing the Select Codes part of step 4 for creating a style (as described at the beginning of this chapter). Once you've selected Codes (4 or C) from the Edit Styles screen and are ready to insert your mark text codes, you must first position the cursor to the left of or on the **[Comment]** code and press the BLOCK (ALT + F4) key. Next, press the RIGHT ARROW key until the cursor is to the right of the **[Comment]** code. Now you are ready to press the MARK TEXT (ALT + F5) key and insert the code(s) you desire. A **[Mark]** code is placed before the comment, and an **[End Mark:]** code is placed after the comment.

Be aware that other codes that you normally insert in a document by using the MARK TEXT key—such as codes to *define* tables, lists, and indexes—cannot be included in a style.

Trap: *You might not be able to see all the styles on one Styles screen.*

If you've accumulated more than 19 styles, you'll be unable to see all their names on one screen. Just move the cursor down and other styles will come into view. On the Styles screen, the cursor movement keys operate the same way they do on the List Files screen. That is, PGDN or PLUS (on the numeric keypad) moves the cursor to the bottom of the screen, and then to the next screen. PGUP or MINUS (on the numeric keypad) moves the cursor up a screen. Moreover, HOME, HOME, DOWN ARROW positions the cursor on the last style, while HOME, HOME, UP ARROW positions the cursor on the first style.

Trap: *If you don't save a document after creating a new style, that style won't be stored.*

A style is saved with a document only if that document is resaved *after* the style has been created. Therefore, if you create a style, be sure to resave your document so that the style is stored on disk along with the document.

Tip: *Each document you create can contain its own unique list of styles.*

You will learn in Chapter 11 that every time you create a document, WordPerfect earmarks that document with an invisible packet of information about that document's attributes—such as the printer you selected (Chapter 14), Document initial code settings (Chapter 8), and the like. When you save the file, this packet of information is attached to the document.

The list of styles is another document attribute that is stored in that packet of information. Therefore, each document, independent of every other document, can contain its own list of styles.

Tip: *(When upgrading from 4.2.) Styles is a brand-new WordPerfect feature.*

Once you begin working with the Styles feature, you'll wish that version 4.2 had offered it. You are now able to tell WordPerfect how to format recurring elements of your document; no longer must you format similar elements manually, or rely on a macro to help you. In most cases, Styles works more effectively than macros for formatting sections of text because—as you'll learn in the following sections of this chapter—you can change a style and the entire document will be reformatted accordingly.

Using Styles

After creating a style, you can use it in your document as many times as you wish. For example, if a report is to contain 16 headings, then you can use a style that formats headings 16 times. To use a style:

1. Position the cursor on screen where you wish to insert the style.
2. Press the STYLE (ALT + F8) key to display the Styles screen, like the screen shown in Figure 10-4.
3. Move the cursor to the style that you wish to use.

4. From the menu at the bottom of the screen, select On (1 or O). WordPerfect then returns you to your document.

5. Type the text that is to be affected by the style that you just turned on.

6. When an open style type is being used, the code stays on, since it has only a beginning.

   When a paired style type is being used, turn off the style by pressing RIGHT ARROW, which positions the cursor to the right of the style off code, or by pressing STYLE (ALT + F8) and selecting Off (2 or F).

   Or, if you are using a paired style type for which the function assigned to the ENTER key is "Off," then as another method for turning off the style, press ENTER.

   Or, if you are using a paired style type for which the function assigned to the ENTER key is "Off/On," then to turn the style off and, to immediately turn it on again, press ENTER.

When you use an open style type, WordPerfect inserts one code in the text at the current cursor position, which indicates the style name. For instance, suppose that you turn on the style named SRBEGIN. The code inserted is **[Open Style: SRBEGIN]**. This code affects all text from that point forward.

When you use a paired style type, WordPerfect encloses the text that is affected by the style within two codes. For example, suppose that the word "Introduction" is a heading that is governed by SR1HEADS. The codes inserted are

[Style On:SR1HEADS]Introduction**[Style Off:SR1HEADS]**

If you later decide to cancel the effect of a style, you must delete the style code or codes that surround the text. For a style pair, you need to remove only one code in the pair of codes; the other is erased automatically by WordPerfect. On the Reveal Codes screen, position the cursor on the code and press DEL (or position the cursor just to the right of the code and press BACKSPACE). If you're viewing the Typing screen and you press DEL or BACKSPACE to erase a style code, WordPerfect prompts for verification, with a message such as:

Delete [Style On:SR1HEADS]? (Y/N) No

Type **Y** to delete the code. Or type **N** to leave the style code in your document.

Tip: *Moving the cursor through text turns off a paired style type.*

If you press STYLE and select On (1 or O) from the Styles menu to turn on a paired style type, you actually insert—at the same time—both the on (beginning) and the off (ending) code, such as **[Style On:][Style Off:]**. When you later press STYLE and select Off (2 or F), to turn that style off, the cursor actually jumps just to the right of the already present **[Style Off:]** code. This feature also can be switched off automatically when you stop typing by pressing a directional arrow key or another key combination to move the cursor past the style off code. For example, turn on a style, type text, and then press RIGHT ARROW to end the style's effect at the point at which you stopped typing.

Tip: *A style code can be inserted into already existing text.*

If you wish to insert an open style code in a document that you've already typed, position the cursor just before the point at which you want the style to begin taking effect. Then follow steps 2 through 4 for using a style, as outlined at the beginning of this section of the chapter.

If you wish to insert a paired style code around already existing text, then the BLOCK key comes into play. Suppose that you've already typed some words and, as an afterthought, you realize that you would like them to be governed by a certain paired style. Simply use the BLOCK (ALT + F4) key and highlight those words. Now follow steps 2 through 4 for using a style, as described at the beginning of this section. When you use the BLOCK key, it is not necessary to turn off a style; WordPerfect automatically starts the style at the beginning of the block and ends the style after the last highlighted character by inserting the appropriate codes. (This is analogous to the method you use to underline or boldface already existing text by using the BLOCK key.)

Tip: *The style code expands to show more information when the cursor is highlighting the code.*

As you know, WordPerfect codes are shown only after you press REVEAL CODES (ALT + F3) to display the Reveal Codes screen. On this screen, style codes operate a bit differently from other codes. If the cursor is located anywhere but on the style code, then the code offers information only about the type of code it is (whether it is an open, on, or off code), along with the name of the style. However, once you position the cursor on the code itself, the code expands to reveal exactly what the style does—showing both the codes and text that make up that style.

For instance, assume that you've created a style named SR1HEADS to center and boldface headings. When the cursor is not on the style code, the code reads **[Style On:SR1HEADS]**. But if you position the cursor on that code, it will read **[Style On:SR1HEADS;[Cntr][BOLD]]**.

The expanding style code may seem distracting at first. But once you are accustomed to this characteristic, it can assist you whenever you wish to see exactly what a certain style code accomplishes.

Trap: *Text and codes within a style can only be edited on the Edit Styles screen and cannot be searched for independently.*

Remember that while you can insert codes and text into a document by turning on a style, the codes and text are part of the style code; they are not treated as separate entities. You cannot, therefore, edit from the Typing or Reveal Codes screen codes or text contained within a style code. You can delete a style by erasing the style code, but the only way to change the style is on the Edit Styles screen, accessed via the STYLE (ALT + F8) key (and discussed in the first section of this chapter).

Similarly, while you can use the Search or Replace feature to locate a style code in the text, you cannot use these features to locate text or codes contained *within* a style code. (Moreover, you cannot search for a specific style by its name or contents, although you can specify whether you're looking for a Style On code, Style Off code, or Open Style code in the search string.)

Tip: *If you edit a style after using it in your document, the document will update automatically.*

One of the strengths of the Styles feature is that if you use a style throughout your document and then you edit that style, the element affected by that style reformats throughout the document to match the editing change. Suppose, for example, that you type a document in which all the headings are centered and boldfaced according to the style named SR1HEADS. You then decide that you prefer to have all headings centered and changed to italic. Simply edit SR1HEADS, a procedure discussed in the previous section of this chapter, "Creating a Style." As soon as you exit the Styles menu and return to your document, all the headings will be instantly changed from boldface to italic. In fact, this flexibility enables you to continue to change a style until you are satisfied with the result.

Managing Styles Between Documents and from a Style Library

Styles are saved with the document in which they were created. However, you can use styles that originated in one document with any other document—which makes the Styles feature quite powerful. You first save a list of style definitions to disk in its own individual file, independent of the document in which you created those styles. Then you can retrieve that list into a new document, or have WordPerfect do so automatically, at any time.

For example, suppose that you produced a January sales report and you created four styles to use in it. You also wish to use those four styles in future documents. Save the list of four style definitions, independent of the January report, as follows:

1. The cursor can be positioned anywhere on screen in the document for which you created the styles.
2. Press the STYLE (ALT + F8) key to display the Styles screen, like the screen shown in Figure 10-4.
3. From the menu at the bottom of the screen, select Save (6 or S). WordPerfect prompts

   Filename:

4. Enter a filename, abiding by the same rules you use when naming a document file (see Chapter 11 for details on filename conventions), but make sure to enter a name to remind you that this file will contain styles and not a standard document. As an example, if the file is to be named SRSTYLES (standing for Sales Report, STYLES), type **SRSTYLES** and press ENTER. The file will be stored in the default drive/directory. (Be sure

to precede the filename with the drive/directory in which you wish to store the styles, if it is different from the default drive/directory. For instance, if you wish to store the file in C:\WPER\SUE, then type **C:\WPER\SUE\SRSTYLES** and press ENTER.)

The list of four styles has now been stored in its own individual style file.

Whenever you're working on a document and wish to use one or more styles from a list saved into its own file, proceed as follows:

1. Position the cursor anywhere in the document on screen.
2. Press the STYLE (ALT + F8) key to display the Styles screen. The screen may contain no styles or may contain any number of styles that you've already created for that document.
3. Select Retrieve (7 or **R**) from the Styles menu located at the bottom of the screen. WordPerfect prompts

   Filename:

4. Type in the name of the file (preceded by the drive/directory if different from the default) that contains the list of styles you wish to use, and press ENTER.

   If the list of styles you are retrieving contains different names from those that already exist on the Styles screen (or if no files are on the Styles screen), then the list is inserted onto the Styles screen, along with any pre-existing styles.

   If you are retrieving a list that contains style names already contained on the Styles screen, WordPerfect prompts as follows:

   Styles(s) already exist. Replace? (Y/N) No

   Type **N** to retrieve only the styles with a different name, or type **Y** to retrieve every style onto the Styles screen, overwriting pre-existing styles that have the same name.

You can even indicate that a certain list of styles act as your *style library* in WordPerfect. A style library is your default style file—the collection of styles that you want to have attached to *every* document you create when you activate the Styles feature unless you specify otherwise.

You can establish a style library by first saving a list of styles into its own file in the same manner that you save any other list of styles. Then you must perform one additional task to inform WordPerfect that this particular style file will serve as the style library. The SETUP (SHIFT + F1) key is used. Suppose that you stored on disk a list of styles under the filename STYLE.LIB (which stands for STYLE LIBrary). You wish to establish STYLE.LIB as your actual style library. It makes no difference which document is on screen or where your cursor is located. Proceed as follows:

1. Press the SETUP (SHIFT + F1) key. The Setup menu is displayed.
2. Select Location of Auxiliary Files (7 or L). The Location of Auxiliary Files Setup menu is displayed.
3. Select Style Library Filename (6 or L).
4. Enter the pathname of your style library, which means that you enter the drive/directory and then the filename. For example, suppose that the file STYLE.LIB is stored on the hard disk in a directory named C:\WPER. Type **C:\WPER\STYLE.LIB** and press ENTER. Or suppose that the file is stored on drive B. Then type **B:STYLE.LIB** and press ENTER.
5. Press EXIT (F7) to return to your document.

The style library has now been established for every WordPerfect session, or until you again change the style library location on the Setup menu. (For more on the Setup menu, which changes your default settings for a variety of functions and features, refer to Appendix B.)

Once you've established a style library and begin to create a new document, the list of styles that it contains is automatically inserted onto the Styles screen when you press the STYLE (ALT + F8) key. On the other hand, for an existing document (created *before* you established the style library), you have to update your styles for that document if you wish also to have access to the style library. For an existing document, you would

1. Retrieve the existing document on screen, and position the cursor anywhere in that document.
2. Press the STYLE (ALT + F8) key to display the Styles screen. The screen may contain no styles or may contain any number of styles that you've already created for that document.
3. Select Update (8 or U) from the Styles menu located at the bottom of the screen. The style library is inserted onto the Styles screen, along with any

pre-existing styles. Any pre-existing styles that have the same name as a style in the style library will be replaced by the library's style.

> **Note:** You could also select Retrieve (7 or R), as described previously, and enter the filename of the style library. In this case, if the style library contains style names already contained on the Styles screen WordPerfect will prompt, asking if you wish to retrieve only the styles with a different name or every style from the style library, thereby overwriting any pre-existing styles with the same name.

You can now use any of the styles on the list that is displayed in connection with the document on screen.

Tip: *Reserve the style library for styles that you want to have available for all your documents.*

Once you create a style library, the styles listed in the library will automatically be made available to you for every document you create. If you save all of your styles to the style library file, then all of them will always be available to you.

However, if you create a great number of styles, some of which you want to have available only for a specific type of document, then consider placing in the style library file only those styles that you use frequently in most of your documents. Place in separate style files those styles that relate only to specific types of document. For example, if there are certain styles that you use only when you type a sales report, save those styles in a separate file. If there are certain styles that you use only when you type a company newsletter, save those styles in a different file.

Tip: *Make filenames for files containing your style lists descriptive and distinctive, and store those files in a drive/directory where they can be accessed easily.*

Sooner than you realize, you may accumulate a variety of style lists on disk—one list that serves as the style library, another for book chapters, a third for sales reports, and so on. It is a good idea to provide a filename that (1) indicates the type of document for which the list of files is appropriate, and (2) indicates that the file is a collection of styles and not a standard document. For example, describe the type of document in the filename, and indicate in the filename extension that it is a list of styles; name the list of styles for the library LIB.STY, the list for book chapters CHAPS.STY, and the list for sales reports SALESR.STY. Or reverse the method and name the library STYLE.LIB, the list for book chapters STYLE.CH, and the list for sales reports STYLE.SR. Whatever method you choose, be consistent, so that you can quickly identify the files that contain styles, as well as the style types.

You might also establish a logical method for choosing a location to store your styles on disk. The styles for newsletters could be stored alongside the files that contain the text of the newsletters. Or all the files that contain styles could be segregated onto a separate disk or in a separate directory on your hard disk. Floppy disk users should consider storing styles on the disk in drive A (which may be the WordPerfect 2 disk, or another disk, depending on whether you employed the /D option described in Chapter 1), provided that the disk in drive A has sufficient room to store the styles you created. That way, the styles are accessible regardless of which data disk is in drive B.

Trap: *There's no way to view a style file without retrieving it to the Styles screen.*

If you create a style file for a specific type of document, you must know the filename for the style file when you wish to retrieve it. WordPerfect does not offer a list of style files at your request. You can use the LIST FILES (F5) key to view a list of all files in a certain drive or directory, including document files, program files, and style files. But you must be able to recognize on sight those files that contain a list of styles. And you must be ready to type in a style filename when you're viewing the Styles screen and you select the Retrieve option. Thus, it is of critical importance that style filenames be descriptive and distinctive (as suggested in the previous Tip).

Tip: *To add to an existing list of files, use the Retrieve option.*

Suppose that for a certain document you've created two styles, which are both displayed on the Styles screen. Now you wish to retrieve five additional styles that are stored in a separate file. When you use the Retrieve option on the Styles menu, the file you retrieve is added to the two styles already on screen. Now seven styles will be displayed on the Styles screen.

Tip: *You can transfer a previously defined style from one style list to another.*

You may create a style that you want to add to other style lists. For instance, perhaps you previously created a style for headings that you use when typing sales reports. If you also want that style on the style list for newsletters, don't create that style from scratch. Instead, when you're typing a newsletter, retrieve the list of styles for sales reports. Erase all the styles on that list except the style for headings. When you save the style list for newsletters, the headings style will be included.

Trap: *A file containing a list of styles won't be revised automatically when you edit a list on screen.*

You must remember that if you add to, edit, or delete a style and you want the revised style to be reflected in your list, you must again save your style file to disk. Save it under the same filename, and WordPerfect will prompt, asking whether you wish to replace. Type **Y** to replace the file; otherwise, the *document* on which you edited the style will be revised, but not the *file* containing your list of styles.

You may also wish to add to, edit, or delete a style from the style library. To do so, position the cursor on a clear screen and press STYLE (ALT + F8). The style library appears. Make your editing changes, then remember to resave the file by using the same path and filename that you used previously for your style library (the same path and filename indicated in the Setup menu). Type **Y** to replace the file, and it will be revised.

Tip: *WordPerfect is packaged with a list of sample styles.*

The WordPerfect Conversion disk contains a file named LIBRARY.STY that contains examples of possible styles. By examining this file, you may attain a better understanding of ways to take advantage of the Style feature. Here's one way to peruse this file:

1. Floppy disk users should insert the Conversion disk into drive B; hard disk users may already have stored LIBRARY.STY on the hard disk, or, if not, can insert the Conversion disk into drive A or B.
2. On a clear Typing screen, press the STYLE (ALT + F8) key.
3. Select Retrieve (7 or R).
4. Type in **LIBRARY.STY**, preceded by the drive/directory where that file is located. For instance, floppy disk users would type **B:LIBRARY.STY**.
5. Press ENTER to retrieve the list of styles to the Styles screen. Now you can use the Edit option on the Styles menu to examine each style. You can also select to turn on a style and see how text you type is affected by the style.

Tips and Traps Summary

Creating a Style

Tip: The Styles screen may already contain style definitions the first time you decide to create a style.

Tip: If you define an open style type, the Edit Styles screen changes.

Tip: Your selection for the ENTER key function depends on the function of the paired style you create.

Trap: Once you begin to define a style, the CANCEL key won't completely abort your attempt.

Tip: Edit a style that you wish to modify, or delete a style that is obsolete.

Tip: A style can be used in more than just the document in which you created it.

Tips and Traps Summary (*continued*)

Tip: A certain style may be useful not only for similar documents, but for different documents to be printed on the same printer.

Trap: If Display Document Comments is set to "off," you'll be unable to view the Style Comment box on screen.

Tip: Think of the Comment box as the section of text that will be affected by the style you create.

Tip: When creating a paired style, you need only insert bold, underline, font, and other enhancement codes before the comment.

Tip: You can quickly create a style by using existing codes in your text.

Tip: You can quickly create a style by using existing codes in your text.

Trap: You can't include features on the MARK TEXT key in a style without first blocking the comment.

Trap: You might not be able to see all the styles on one Styles screen.

Trap: If you don't save a document after creating a new style, that style won't be stored.

Tip: Each document you create can contain its own unique list of styles.

Tip: (When upgrading from 4.2.) Styles is a brand-new WordPerfect feature.

Using Styles

Tip: Moving the cursor through text turns off a paired style type.

Tip: A style code can be inserted into already existing text.

Tip: The style code expands to show more information when the cursor is highlighting the code.

Trap: Text and codes within a style can only be edited on the Edit Styles screen and cannot be searched for independently.

Tips and Traps Summary (*continued*)

Tip: If you edit a style after using it in your document, the document will update automatically.

Managing Styles Between Documents and from a Style Library

Tip: Reserve the style library for styles that you want to have available for all your documents.

Tip: Make filenames for files containing your style lists descriptive and distinctive, and store those files in a drive/directory where they can be accessed easily.

Trap: There's no way to view a style file without retrieving it to the Styles screen.

Tip: To add to an existing list of files, use the Retrieve option.

Tip: You can transfer a previously defined style from one style list to another.

Trap: A file containing a list of styles won't be revised automatically when you edit a list on screen.

Tip: WordPerfect is packaged with a list of sample styles.

11

Saving, Retrieving, and Document Summaries

Every word you type onto the computer screen is placed in RAM (random access memory), the computer's electronic work space. This allows lightning-speed editing of your text. But all information in RAM is stored only temporarily. Your text disappears from the screen (and thus from RAM) as soon as electricity stops flowing into your computer—whether you turn off the power switch or you experience a power failure.

Before the power goes off, you must store documents on a disk if you ever want to read, edit, or print them again. A disk acts like a filing cabinet; it stores information in separate files, under different filenames, with no dependence on electricity. When the computer is turned off, your text remains intact on disk. The next time you wish to use a particular document that is stored on disk, you can retrieve a copy of that document to the screen. You can read, edit, or print it.

This chapter explains how to save a document on disk and how to retrieve a document from disk when you wish to work with it again. You'll also learn how the Document Summary feature enables you to keep track of a document's author, typist, and subject.

Saving Documents

You can save a document to disk, just as the document appears on the screen, at any time. Each document that you save to the same disk or directory must have a unique filename, which helps your computer keep track of that document and distinguish it from other files. A filename can have a maximum of eight characters. In addition, you can include an optional extension to the filename. An extension is separated from the filename by a period (.) and can contain up to three characters. The only characters allowed in a filename or an extension are letters (uppercase or lowercase are both acceptable), numbers, and any of the following symbols:

! @ # $ % & ( ) - { } ` ' ^ ~

Any other characters and spaces are not allowed in a filename. Here are some examples of valid filenames:

MEMO	MEMO001	MEMO.IHM
ACCOUNT	ACCOUNT#	ACCOUNT#.8
RPT	(88)RPT	(88)RPT.SHW
CINDY	CINDY28	CINDY.LTR

Here are some examples of invalid filenames:

ACCOUNT#1234	(Too many characters in filename)
RPT.JONES	(Too many characters in extension)
MEMO 001	(Contains a blank space)
CINDY*28	(* is an unacceptable character in a filename)

In addition to a filename, each document you wish to store on disk must have a destination—a place on disk where it is saved. The destination, referred to as a *path,* is the drive or directory where the file later can be found on disk. WordPerfect assumes that you want the document saved to the default drive or directory, which initially is set according to how you load WordPerfect. If you are a floppy disk user and you load WordPerfect as suggested in Chapter 1, then the default is drive B, denoted as B: or B:\. If you are a hard disk user and you followed the instructions in Chapter 1 (assuming you created a batch file), then the default when you first load WordPerfect is the directory called WPER\DATA located on the hard disk, which is denoted as C:\WPER\DATA. DATA is a subdirectory of the WPER directory.

When you wish to save a file to disk, you can employ the SAVE key, as follows:

1. Position the cursor anywhere in the document.
2. Press the SAVE (F10) key. WordPerfect responds

   Document to be saved:

3. Type a filename (uppercase or lowercase letters are both acceptable) and press ENTER. A message at the bottom of the screen indicates that WordPerfect is storing the file on the default drive. If the filename is MEMO, for example, floppy disk users see

   Saving B: \MEMO

   Hard disk users see

   Saving C:\WPER\DATA\MEMO

   All prompts clear. Your document remains on screen and the cursor returns to the same location it was at before you pressed SAVE.

An alternative for saving a file to disk is the EXIT key. When you press the EXIT key, there are additional prompts to respond to:

1. Position the cursor anywhere in the document.
2. Press the EXIT (F7) key. WordPerfect responds

   Save document (Y/N)? Yes

3. Type **Y** or any key other than N, or press ENTER. (Type **N** only if you don't wish to save the document.) WordPerfect responds

   Document to be saved:

4. Type a filename (uppercase or lowercase letters are both acceptable) and press ENTER. A message at the bottom of the screen indicates that WordPerfect is storing the file on the default drive. Then WordPerfect prompts

   Exit WP (Y/N)? No (Cancel to return to document)

5. Press the CANCEL (F1) key to keep the document on screen. Or type **Y** to exit WordPerfect. Or type **N** or press ENTER to clear the screen but remain in WordPerfect.

You will find that once a document is stored on disk, the file's path and filename appear at the left-hand corner of the status line. For example, if you are working on a hard disk, the left side of the status line reads

C:\WPER\DATA\MEMO

This means that the filename is MEMO and that the file has been stored to the destination C:\WPER\DATA.

After a document is saved for the first time, WordPerfect remembers its path and filename. Thereafter, whenever you save the document to disk, WordPerfect will suggest the same path and filename. For instance, if you edit your document and then wish to use the SAVE key a second time:

1. Position the cursor anywhere in the document.

2. Press the SAVE (F10) key. WordPerfect responds with the file destination and the filename. For example, on a hard disk the prompt might read

   Document to be saved: C:\WPER\DATA\MEMO

3. Press ENTER to accept the suggestion. WordPerfect checks the data disk and, realizing that a file by that name already exists, prompts you to verify that the document named MEMO should be overwritten with the new version on screen:

   Replace C:\WPER\DATA\MEMO? (Y/N) No

4. Type **Y** to update the previous version of MEMO with the new version. WordPerfect responds

   Saving C:\WPER\DATA\MEMO

   Or type **N** or any key other than Y, or press ENTER, to indicate that you do not wish the version of the file on disk to be overwritten. In that case, WordPerfect again responds

Document to be saved: C:\WPER\DATA\MEMO

You now have the opportunity to type in a new path and/or filename, so that the old version on disk is preserved and a new version of the document is stored to a different destination or under a different name.

Tip: *SAVE is most useful for retaining a document on screen, while EXIT is most effective for clearing the document from the screen.*

The SAVE key will always keep a document on screen after the document has been saved. The EXIT key, on the other hand, enables you to save a document and then offers three options: keep the document on screen, clear the screen, or end your WordPerfect session. The tradeoff for more choices is that the EXIT key requires your response to more prompts than does the SAVE key. Thus, the SAVE key is quicker when you wish to save and then continue in the document; the EXIT key is quicker when you wish to save and then either clear the screen or end the WordPerfect session.

You may wish to always use the SAVE key to store text, and to reserve the EXIT key for clearing the screen or exiting WordPerfect. That way the EXIT key serves as a fail-safe mechanism—just in case you forgot to save that file by pressing SAVE. If you know that you just saved the file with the SAVE key, you can request that WordPerfect not bother saving the file again when you then press the EXIT key.

Trap: *You can't save files to a floppy disk drive that does not contain a formatted disk.*

Assuming that you plan to store documents on a floppy disk, you should have a formatted disk in the disk drive and the disk drive door must be closed before you press the SAVE key. If no disk is in the disk drive or if the drive door is open, then when you press SAVE, WordPerfect responds

Disk drive door may be open—Drive not ready reading drive B
1 Retry **2** Cancel and return to document **1**

Insert a disk, close the drive door, and select 1.

If the disk has not been formatted, WordPerfect prompts

DISK ERROR 27 reading drive B
1 Retry 2 Cancel and return to document **1**

or

ERROR: File Creation Error

In this case, turn to Appendix A for the procedure to format a disk.

Note: You can format a disk without actually exiting WordPerfect; to do so, see the section "Accessing the Disk Operating System" in Chapter 13.

Trap: *If you do not have sufficient space available on disk, you cannot store a document.*

A disk has a limited amount of space and can fill to capacity. If a disk has no space available when you try to save, WordPerfect responds with a "disk full" message. Floppy disk users should always have another formatted disk ready to slip into the disk drive in case the "disk full" message appears. Chapter 13 describes how to monitor the available space on a disk and how to erase files you no longer need, which makes space available for new files.

Tip: *Press LIST FILES to discover the default drive/directory.*

You can check at any time which drive or directory WordPerfect is assuming to be the default for a computer session. Press the LIST FILES (F5) key and WordPerfect prompts with the current default directory. Suppose the default is disk drive B. Then the prompt reads

Dir B: *.*

The symbols *.* mean that WordPerfect is referring to all the files in that drive, whatever the filename or extension. Or, if the default is \WPER\DATA on the hard disk, the prompt reads

Dir C:\WPER\DATA*.*

Press CANCEL (F1) to clear the prompt. (Alternatively, you can press ENTER to see a list of files in that drive/directory, as discussed in Chapter 13.)

See the next Tip for ways to change the default drive/directory.

Tip: *Several options enable you to change the default drive/directory.*

You may wish to save documents to different destinations. Floppy disk users may wish to switch to another drive. Hard disk users may wish to switch to another drive or to another directory on the hard disk. You can direct WordPerfect to save to other drives or directories in several ways. The alternative you choose depends on how often you save to a drive other than the default drive.

If you never save to the default drive, then you may want to permanently alter the default. To do so, you must change the way that you load WordPerfect (Appendix A explains this procedure).

If the drive to which you want to save files varies, based on the day or the person sitting at the computer, then you may want to change the default for one particular computer session (or until you change the default again). To do so:

1. Press the LIST FILES (F5) key. WordPerfect prompts with the current default directory. Assume the default is \WPER\DATA. The prompt reads

   Dir C:\WPER\DATA*.* **(Type = to change default Dir)**

2. As WordPerfect indicates, press the EQUAL (=) key. WordPerfect responds

   New directory = Dir C:\WPER\DATA

   The cursor is positioned on the drive letter.

3. Type in the new drive and directory, or simply edit the directory indicated. The drive letter must be followed by a colon. For example, to change to drive A, type **A:**. To change to drive B, type **B:**. To change to the

\WPER\SUE subdirectory on drive C, type **C:\WPER\SUE**.

4. Press ENTER. WordPerfect responds by indicating the new drive and subdirectory, such as

   Dir A:*.*

   or

   Dir C:\WPER\SUE*.*

5. Press the CANCEL (F1) key to erase the directory prompt from the screen. (Alternatively, you can press ENTER to see a list of files in that drive/directory. See Chapter 13 for further discussion of the LIST FILES key.)

You now have set a new default directory—but only until you turn off the computer. When you next reload WordPerfect, WordPerfect assumes the original default drive.

If you want to direct WordPerfect to another disk drive one time only, perhaps for just one document, then there's a temporary alternative. Press SAVE (F10) or EXIT (F7), and when WordPerfect prompts

Document to be saved:

type the filename preceded by a specific destination (path). If you are referring to a drive with subdirectories, always include a backslash (\) before the filename, just as you do before a subdirectory name. For example, C:\WPER\SUE\MEMO is correct; C:\WPER\SUEMEMO is not. On the other hand, if the destination is a drive with no subdirectories, such as A or B, you can type a backslash before the filename, although this is unnecessary— A:\MEMO or A:MEMO are both acceptable. By typing a path and a filename, you direct WordPerfect to save that one particular file to the drive and directory specified. The default drive remains unchanged.

Tip: *Store related files together on the same disk or in the same directory.*

If you store files on floppy disks, it is efficient to designate certain disks for certain types of files. For example, reserve one disk for files related to the budget, and another for files related to administrative issues. Or, each disk can store files related to a specific client. Or, each disk can store files authored by a certain person. When you're ready to save a file to disk, place the appropriate disk in drive B before pressing the SAVE or the EXIT key.

If you store files on a hard disk, it is efficient to designate certain directories for certain types of files. For instance, use the directory C:\WPER\DATA for general documents. Create a directory named C:\WPER\BUD to contain documents related to the budget. Another directory, named C:\WPER\ADMIN, can contain documents related to administrative matters. And, C:\WPER\SUE can contain Sue's personal files. When you're ready to save a file to a specific directory, change the default, as described in the preceding Tip (Chapter 13 describes how to create new directories using WordPerfect).

By storing related files together, you'll have a much easier time finding a specific file later on.

See the next Tip, which addresses a related issue—choosing descriptive filenames for each document.

Tip: *Choose descriptive, meaningful filenames.*

Save each document under a filename that helps you to identify that file; otherwise, you'll spend hours searching for the file you want. For example, don't name your first file STEVEN1, your second file STEVEN2, your third file STEVEN3, and so on. Instead, develop an effective filing scheme.

Your choice of a filing scheme will depend on how you organize your hard or floppy disk (see the preceding Tip), how many people share a disk, and the kinds of documents you type. If a number of people share the same disk, then perhaps each person's initials can be the first two letters of a filename: MMBUDGET, MMLTR1, JBREPORT, or JBDOC. Or, initials can be indicated in the extension: BUDGET.MM, LTR1.MM, REPORT.JB, or DOC.JB. Another option is to indicate the document's contents in the extension. All reports can end with .RPT, all letters with .LTR, all memos with .MMO, and all temporary files with .TMP.

If you maintain numerous documents on the same client or legal case, then perhaps you will want to develop a filing scheme around client names. All files relating to Mr. Jones can have the extension .JON, and those relating to Ms. Smith can have the extension .SMI. Or, one client can be assigned the extension .001, and another the extension .002, with all extensions and the name of the person they refer to documented in a log book kept by your computer.

However you decide to set up your files, select a filing scheme as early as possible. It's much more difficult to organize after you've accumulated 100 files than when you're starting with a brand-new disk (Chapter 13 describes other ways to manage files once they're on disk).

Trap: *Don't forget to resave a file if you make changes on the screen.*

When you store a document and later edit that file on the screen, your revisions are not automatically reflected on disk. You must remember to save the document again before you clear the screen or before you exit WordPerfect. Otherwise, you'll lose the revisions.

Trap: *Don't make files too large.*

Avoid creating a document so large that it becomes cumbersome to maneuver in. How large is too large? The maximum size of a file depends on the disk space available to you and on the size of your computer's RAM. Obviously, computers equipped with hard disks and expanded memory (more than 640K) can handle larger documents more comfortably. If you don't have a hard disk or expanded memory, then a good rule of thumb is to keep your files smaller than 50,000 bytes (about 22 single-spaced pages). Even with a hard disk, keep your files at 20 to 70 pages in length to maximize speed in editing your document.

A good strategy when creating a massive report or book is to store sections of it in separate files so you can manage it more easily. You can also employ the Master Document feature to avoid creating a large, difficult-to-edit document. For instance, a master document for a book could contain a table of contents and subdocuments for each chapter (see Chapter 12 for more on the Master Document feature).

Tip: *Save a document to disk at regular intervals.*

To guard against losing text to a power failure, you should save your work frequently to disk. Many computer users have learned to do so the hard way — either because they turned off the computer without saving their work or because there was an untimely power failure. If you save a document to disk every 20 minutes, then a power failure can put you only 20 minutes behind. Work for six hours straight without saving, however, and an unfortunate power failure will teach you to save your work often.

With WordPerfect it takes only seconds to save your work; the SAVE key is perfect for doing this. Save every 15 to 30 minutes, continually replacing the old version with the new. You'll be thankful you did on that day when, with just a bit more work to do, the power fails in your building and your document vanishes from the screen.

Tip: *Get extra protection against power failures with the Timed Backup feature.*

If you often become so engrossed in your work that you forget to save to disk at regular intervals, then get WordPerfect to do it for you. Appendix B describes the Timed Backup feature, an option on the Setup menu that directs WordPerfect to periodically save a document in a temporary backup file. If you decide to back up your work at ten-minute intervals, for example, the computer pauses every ten minutes, and this prompt appears at the bottom of the screen:

*** Please Wait ***

This means that WordPerfect is updating the backup file.

Consider using the Timed Backup option if you have trouble remembering to save frequently as a precaution against a power failure. the backup file is temporary; it will disappear as soon as you exit WordPerfect. *Therefore, backup is no replacement for storing a file on disk by using the SAVE or EXIT key* at the end of a WordPerfect session. You can activate the Timed Backup option as a permanent feature by using the Setup menu (see Appendix B).

Trap: *Because a disk can become damaged, you must take precautions.*

Although a disk stores information independent of electricity, a disk—whether a hard disk or a floppy—can become damaged, or it can wear out without warning. One day it may simply refuse to operate. It is vital that you take precautions against this unfortunate event.

To protect yourself in the event that a disk fails, you must, in one way or another, make a copy of each new or revised file on a separate disk. Floppy disk users store backup copies on a second floppy disk. Hard disk users store backups on floppy disks (or on tape backup systems). Some users have a standard backup procedure; perhaps they use the DOS BACKUP command, for example. But some system must be used. (Chapter 13 describes how you can copy files to other destinations from within WordPerfect.)

Tip: *You can retain both the old and the new version of a document on disk.*

There may be times when you want to save two versions of the same document. In that case, each version must be given a unique name; otherwise, WordPerfect overwrites one of the files.

Suppose you save a report, which is intended for your company's marketing department, on a floppy disk under the name MARKET.RPT. Later you revise the document slightly to stress different items for the chief executive officer. Press SAVE and WordPerfect responds

Document to be saved: B:\MARKET.RPT

Type in a separate filename, such as CEO.RPT, right on top of the old filename. Press ENTER. You have now saved two similar documents in separate files.

Tip: *Protect against accidentally overwriting a file by using the Original Backup feature.*

You can set up a system wherein an old file is renamed automatically with the extension .BK! when you replace that file with a new one. In this way, you can safeguard against inadvertently overwriting an important document. This feature is activated from the WordPerfect Setup menu (described in Appendix B). If you activate this feature, make sure you give each document a unique filename and not just a different file extension. If one file is JONES.1 and another is JONES.2, then there's only one backup for two documents—JONES.BK!—and WordPerfect will be unable to back up both of them.

Tip: *You can save just part of a document to disk—either by creating a new file or by appending to an existing file.*

At times you might want to save to disk only part of what's on the screen. Perhaps page 1 of a document is an outline that you want to save in a separate file. Perhaps one paragraph is a standard item that you want to use frequently, and thus you wish to store it in its own separate file. Or, maybe there's a paragraph that seems more appropriate in another file that is already stored on disk.

Use the BLOCK (ALT + F4) key to block the text that you want to store in another file. What you do next depends on whether you want the block saved to its own file or attached to the end of an existing file. To store the block in a new file of its own:

1. With **Block on** flashing, press SAVE (F10). WordPerfect responds

   Block Name:

2. Type an original filename and press ENTER. WordPerfect saves that block to disk. (If a file by that name is currently stored, WordPerfect will prompt, asking if you wish to replace the file on disk with the highlighted block.)

To store the block at the end of an existing file:

1. With **Block on** flashing, press MOVE (CTRL + F4). WordPerfect responds with the Move menu:

Move: 1 Block; 2 Tabular Column; 3 Rectangle: 0

2. Select Block (1 or B). Now WordPerfect responds

   1 Move; 2 Copy; 3 Delete; 4 Append: 0

3. Select Append (4 or A). WordPerfect asks

   Append to:

4. Type the name of a file currently existing on disk (preceded by a path if different from the default) and press ENTER. WordPerfect saves that block to the end of the existing file.

   Or, if a file by that name does not exist, WordPerfect will create the document for you.

Chapter 12 describes a variety of other ways to work between documents.

Tip: *A document's filename can be suppressed on the status line once you store the document.*

After you store a copy of your document on disk for the first time, the filename you chose appears to the left on the status line. For example, if you name a document MEMO and store that document on drive B, the status line for that document will read

B:\MEMO

Or, if you have a hard disk and you store the document in a subdirectory called WPER\DATA, the status line will read

C:\WPER\DATA\MEMO

Using the Setup menu (discussed in Appendix B), you can permanently suppress the filename displayed on the status line.

Tip: *The Locked Document feature gives you the ability to use a password when saving a document.*

Office mates can be excluded from retrieving or printing your confidential WordPerfect files. By using the Locked Document feature, you can save to disk with a password. Only those who know the password can use the file again—whether to read it, edit it, or print it. This is like placing a manila file folder in a locked desk drawer or in a filing cabinet and keeping guard over the key.

A document password can contain up to 25 characters—numbers, letters, symbols, or spaces. It is critical that you remember exactly how you spelled the password; otherwise, even you will be locked out. To "lock" a document:

1. Position the cursor anywhere in the document.
2. Press the TEXT IN/OUT (CTRL + F5) key. WordPerfect displays the following menu:

   1 DOS Text; **2** Password; **3** Save Generic; **4** Save WP 4.2;
   5 Comment: **0**

3. Select Password (2 or P). WordPerfect prompts

   Password: 1 Add/change; **2** Remove: **0**

4. Select Add (1 or A). WordPerfect responds

   Enter Password:

5. Type in a password and press ENTER. For security, WordPerfect does not display what you just typed. Instead, to verify the password, WordPerfect prompts

   Re-Enter Password:

6. Retype the password, exactly as you did the time before. If the two passwords differ, WordPerfect displays an error message and starts over again with the **Enter Password:** prompt. If the two passwords are identical, all prompts clear.
7. Now save the document, using either the SAVE or the EXIT key. When you save the document, the password is attached to that file. From then on, every time you save the file the same password is automatically saved with it.

You can change the password at any time by repeating steps 1 through 6 above. But be sure to remember your password. If you don't remember it, you've locked yourself out! You can guard against forgetting a password by using letters or numbers that you are unlikely to forget. For example, use your birthdate, your middle name, your social security number, or your license plate number (but choose something that isn't obvious to your colleagues). Or, hide a copy of the password in your desk. It is important to take precautions against being locked out of your own file.

To "unlock" a document, follow steps 1 through 3 above, and then select Remove (2 or R). Remember to then resave the document, so that the password is removed permanently from the file.

Tip: *WordPerfect offers the Fast Save feature so you can save files quickly.*

Whenever you press SAVE (F10) or EXIT (F7) and store a document on disk, WordPerfect saves the document with all its formatting intact. However, if you prefer speed over form, WordPerfect offers the Fast Save feature. When the Fast Save feature is turned on, documents are saved unformatted and are therefore saved to disk more quickly. (You can cancel Fast Save for a specific document even when Fast Save is on by pressing HOME, HOME, DOWN ARROW to move the cursor to the bottom of the document just before saving; for that document, the Fast Save feature is ignored, and the document is saved formatted.)

But there is a trade-off for the added speed that comes with the Fast Save feature, which becomes apparent when you want to print out a document. As described in Chapter 14, there are two basic ways to print a document: directly from screen or from disk. With the Fast Save feature off (the default setting), you can print using either method. With Fast Save turned on, you can print only from screen (unless you pressed HOME, HOME, DOWN ARROW just before you saved that document to disk).

If you often print documents from disk, then consider leaving WordPerfect with Fast Save turned off. It takes a few more seconds to save your file, but you'll be able to print both from screen and from disk. Conversely, if you rarely print from disk, then perhaps you'll want to turn on Fast Save. The Fast Save feature is turned on by using the Setup menu (see Appendix B for details on the Setup menu).

Tip: *Use the Setup menu to ensure that you complete a document summary before you save to disk.*

In the last section of this chapter, "Document Summaries," you will learn about the Document Summary feature, which enables you to store basic information about each document you create. The summary is a quick way to identify who wrote a document and who typed it, and it can provide helpful descriptive comments. If you plan to create a summary for each document, you can have WordPerfect remind you to do so as you save a newly created document. When you press SAVE or EXIT to store a new document, a document summary form appears automatically. This is controlled by the Setup menu (see Appendix B).

Tip: *When you save a document on disk, WordPerfect tags that file with a packet of related information.*

Every time you create a document, WordPerfect earmarks the document with a prefix of information about that document's attributes, such as the printer you selected, the initial font you selected, the initial format settings, and the like. When you save the file, this prefix is attached to the document. Therefore, even if you make a different selection for another document that you work on later, files already on disk will be unaffected by the change, even when retrieved to the screen. For example, if you select a new printer and later retrieve a file, whatever printer was selected when you last saved the file will be the active printer definition.

Tip: *(When upgrading from 4.2.) Some procedures for saving a document have changed and others have been added.*

Although the basic process to save documents remains the same as in version 4.2, you'll notice that the method for locking documents has become much more straightforward in version 5. You can now add a password simply by using the TEXT IN/OUT key before you save the document to disk. Also, you can use the Append feature to add a block of text to the end of a locked file; this was impossible before.

A brand-new feature is Fast Save, which enables you to store a document on disk with lightning speed, if you don't mind the fact that the document is unformatted on disk (refer to an earlier Tip in this section for details).

Another new feature is WordPerfect's ability to store a prefix along with a document. This prefix contains the document's attributes—such as initial settings, printer, and fonts. This enables each document to be governed only by its own settings.

Retrieving Documents

When you want to retrieve a document stored on disk, you must tell WordPerfect the document's path and filename. WordPerfect assumes that the file's path (the drive/directory where it is stored) is the default drive/directory, unless you specify differently. To retrieve a file:

1. Make sure that the screen is clear.
2. Press the RETRIEVE (SHIFT + F10) key. WordPerfect prompts

   Document to be retrieved:

3. Type the filename and press ENTER. You must type the name exactly as you did when the file was saved (except that using uppercase or lowercase letters makes no difference). If you included an extension, you must type that as well. For example, if the file is called JONES.LTR, you cannot simply type JONES to retrieve the file.

   If WordPerfect cannot locate a file, it responds

   ERROR: File not found

   and prompts you to type in a new filename or edit what you typed.

Tip: *Whenever you retrieve a file, the original file still remains on disk.*

When you retrieve a file, WordPerfect places only a copy of the file on screen; the original still remains on disk. Thus, if you retrieve a file but make no changes in it, there's no need to resave the file—an exact copy is already housed on the disk. Simply clear the screen when you're done reviewing it.

Tip: *Make sure WordPerfect is retrieving from the correct drive or directory.*

If WordPerfect cannot locate a file even though you spelled the filename correctly, perhaps it is looking in the wrong place. WordPerfect checks the default drive unless you specify otherwise. If you wish to retrieve a file called MEMO located on drive A, and the default is another drive or directory, then, when WordPerfect prompts for a filename, you must type **A:\MEMO**. If MEMO is in the \WPER\SUE subdirectory on the hard disk, then type **C:\WPER\SUE\MEMO**.

Only if a file is in the default drive or subdirectory can you simply type in the filename. (Refer to the previous section of this chapter, "Saving Documents," for ways to alter the default drive or directory.)

Trap: *Don't retrieve a non-WordPerfect document.*

Don't retrieve any file created by using another software package. If you do, WordPerfect might offer a message about an "incompatible file format." In odd circumstances, the computer system may lock up, meaning that it won't respond no matter which key you press. Files that you should *not* retrieve include the following:

- **WordPerfect system files** These include files supplied on your WordPerfect disk with names that start with WP or {WP} or files with the extension .EXE. (In general, WordPerfect will not allow you to retrieve such files.)
- **Documents created by other programs** If you wish to use a WordStar file in WordPerfect, for example, you must first convert that file into WordPerfect format (described in Chapter 28) before you retrieve it.
- **Version 5 documents if you use version 4.2 or an earlier version** If you created a file using version 5 of WordPerfect, don't try to use that file in version 4.2. (The reverse is not true; you *can* retrieve a 4.2 document into version 5. Refer to Chapter 28 for ways to work between different versions of WordPerfect.)

If you inadvertently retrieve a non-WordPerfect file and the computer system locks up, then you must clear RAM—either by turning the computer off or by pressing CTRL + ALT + DEL, the system reset key combination—and reload WordPerfect in order to continue. You will lose any information on screen that hasn't been saved to disk (another example of why it is critical to save frequently to disk).

Trap: *You must remember to clear the screen before retrieving a document; WordPerfect does not clear it for you.*

When you retrieve a file, WordPerfect retains whatever text is already on screen. If you type a memo and then retrieve a report, for example, the memo and the report are both on the screen. Unless you want to combine new text with a document on disk (a process that is described in Chapter 12), clear the screen by pressing the EXIT key before you retrieve a document.

The concept of clearing the screen before retrieving is critical, and must be kept in mind. Countless WordPerfect users have, at one time or another, typed and stored a document and then retrieved it, only to find two copies of that document on screen. That's because the user didn't clear the screen before retrieving the document.

It is also important to clear the Typing screen so that any formatting changes you made on a Document Initial Codes screen (accessed from the Format menu, as discussed in Chapter 8) and other document attributes take effect when you retrieve that document. If the Typing screen contains even one character, the document's initial codes are lost and other information stored in the document's prefix of information is lost, when you retrieve the document.

Tip: *If you forget a filename, you can list all the files on disk to refresh your memory.*

What if you're ready to retrieve a certain document but you can't remember its filename or the disk on which it resides? You can view a list of files in any drive/directory that you specify by pressing the LIST FILES (F5) key. The List Files menu then allows you to retrieve any file listed (refer to Chapter 13 for details).

Trap: *If a document is too large, WordPerfect may be unable to retrieve it.*

As you retrieve a file, WordPerfect places as much of it as possible into RAM. Any spillover is stored in overflow files on disk. If the WordPerfect disk has insufficient room (a situation that is mainly restricted to computers without hard disks or with limited RAM), then WordPerfect will prompt, with a message such as **Not enough room on WP disk to retrieve text.** In this case, you must erase any unnecessary files from the WordPerfect disk (perhaps a printer definition—which ends with the extension .PRS—that you rarely use). Another alternative is to redirect your overflow files to the data disk in drive B by using the \D option (described in Chapter 1). Or, if you have information in both of WordPerfect's document screens, clear both screens. (Chapter 12 describes how you can work with two WordPerfect documents on two separate screens.) Or, you might consider purchasing additional memory for your computer.

Trap: *You must know the correct password to retrieve a locked file.*

The Locked Document feature (described in the first section of this chapter, "Saving Documents") enables you to attach a password to a document. If you attempt to retrieve a file that has a password, WordPerfect will prompt with the following:

Enter Password:

Type in the password exactly as spelled when you created it (although it makes no difference whether you use upper- or lowercase letters), and press ENTER. If the password is correct, the file will be retrieved. If the password is incorrect, WordPerfect will respond with an error message. For instance, if the filename is MEMO, WordPerfect displays

ERROR: File is locked -- MEMO

WordPerfect will then ask for the name of the file to be retrieved. Press ENTER and retype the password if you wish to try again.

Note that there is no way to retrieve a document if you don't know the correct password.

Tip: *(When upgrading from 4.2.) Retrieve documents as you did before.*

The RETRIEVE key has not been altered in version 5, except for a minor change: locked documents are more securely password-protected in version 5. Every time you retrieve a locked document, all files associated with the editing of that document—such as backup files, undelete files, move files, and the like—are now also locked.

Document Summaries

WordPerfect provides the opportunity to create a document summary, which will remain attached to a file once you save that file to disk. A document summary offers a quick way to find out who wrote a document and who typed it, and it provides helpful descriptive comments about the contents of that document. A document summary is made on a predesigned form. WordPerfect automatically enters the current date onto the form. It also enters the document's *system filename,* which is how the summary refers to the eight-character name with the optional three-character extension that you use when storing or retrieving that document. You have the option to insert on the form the following items, which can each contain up to 39 characters:

- Descriptive Filename
- Subject/Account
- Author
- Typist

In addition, you can insert any comments about the document, up to 780 characters in length. The comments are stored in a double-line box at the bottom of the document summary form.

A summary can be created before you type a single word, or after you've typed ten pages. However, remember to create the summary on the same day that you *start* the document, so that the correct date is inserted on the form by WordPerfect. You can complete only one summary per document. To create a summary:

1. Position the cursor anywhere in the document.
2. Press the FORMAT (SHIFT + F8) key. The Format menu appears.
3. Select Document (3 or D). The Document Format menu appears.
4. Select Summary (5 or S). The predesigned form for a document, assuming that you haven't yet typed the document, appears on screen as shown in Figure 11-1. The form for a document that you've already typed and saved

```
Document Summary

          System Filename                     (Not named yet)

          Date of Creation                    July 22, 1988

     1 - Descriptive Filename

     2 - Subject/Account

     3 - Author

     4 - Typist

     5 - Comments

Selection: 0
```

Figure 11-1. Document Summary screen for a document not yet typed or named

to disk at least once is shown in Figure 11-2. Notice in Figure 11-2 that WordPerfect inserts the system filename for you. In addition, WordPerfect inserts in the Comment box the first 400 characters of the document.

5. Select an item by pressing the corresponding number and then type the information. For instance, to insert the author's name, type **3** or **A** and then type the name.
6. Press ENTER to end that entry.
7. Repeat steps 5 and 6 until all the items on the form have been completed (you can leave any item blank by not selecting the corresponding number).
8. Press EXIT (F7) to save the summary and return to the document.

```
Document Summary

         System Filename                  C:\WPER\DATA\JONES1.MMO

         Date of Creation                 July 22, 1988

     1 - Descriptive Filename

     2 - Subject/Account

     3 - Author

     4 - Typist

     5 - Comments
 ┌──────────────────────────────────────────────────────────────────────────┐
 │TO:  Donna Wong, Legal Department:  I met with Mr. Jacob Jones last       │
 │Friday.  As you know, Mr. Jones is a partner in the law firm of Barnes,   │
 │Jacoby and Jones. He has numerous years of experience with insurance cases│
 │such as the one we find ourselves immersed in.  Mr. Jones posed several   │
 │questions which must be answered before he can provide us with any advice │
 └──────────────────────────────────────────────────────────────────────────┘

Selection: 0
```

Figure 11-2. Document Summary screen for a document saved to disk at least once

When you reveal codes, you will not see a code indicating that a document summary has been created. Rather, the document summary is stored as part of an invisible packet of information (prefix), which is attached to the document.

If you wish to review and/or edit a document summary, repeat steps 1 through 8 above.

Tip: *WordPerfect attempts to name your file if you indicate a descriptive filename when filling out the document summary form.*

If you create a summary before saving the document at least once on disk, WordPerfect indicates that the system filename is **(Not named yet)**, as shown in Figure 11-1. The system filename is what you use when saving or retrieving a document—and is restricted to an eight-character name and a three-character extension.

On the other hand, a descriptive filename can be up to 39 characters in length. It provides a further explanation of what the abbreviated, 11-character system filename represents.

If you fill out a descriptive filename, then WordPerfect will automatically truncate that name to suggest a system filename for you. For example, suppose that from the screen in Figure 11-1 you select item 1 and type **Memo to Donna**. Once you press ENTER, WordPerfect will insert **MEMOTODO.N** as the system filename. Or, if you type **Met with Jones**, WordPerfect will insert **METWITHJ.ON** as the system filename. Then, when you exit the Document Summary screen and return to your document, the lower left-hand corner of the status line contains that "suggested" system filename.

WordPerfect provides the opportunity to save the document under that suggested name. As you save that document for the first time, you can accept that suggestion. Or you can simply type your own filename, in which case the status line and the document summary will be updated to reflect the name that you assigned to the document.

Tip: *WordPerfect attempts to fill out the Subject/Account entry for you.*

When you create a summary for text that has already been typed, WordPerfect automatically reads the first 400 bytes (approximately 400 characters) of the document to find the document's subject. It searches for what is referred to as a *subject search string,* which is a group of characters that marks the document's subject.

The default subject search string is "RE:". Therefore, should your document contain "RE:" in the first 400 characters, any phrases that follow, up to the first 39 characters or up to the first hard return, will be inserted in the Subject/Account entry. For instance, suppose that the following is near the top of a document:

RE: Meeting with Jacob Jones

Figure 11-3 shows how WordPerfect automatically inserts that phrase as the Subject/Account.

The subject search string can be changed from the default of "RE:" to another short phrase of 39 characters or fewer. For example, if you commonly type memorandums in which the subject is listed after "TOPIC—", then change the subject search string accordingly. This can be accomplished through the Initial Settings option on the Setup menu (see Appendix B for more on the Setup menu).

Tip: *WordPerfect remembers the Author and Typist information during the same working session.*

Once you complete one document summary, WordPerfect keeps track of your Author and Typist responses. Thereafter, and until you either change your responses or exit WordPerfect, these items will be filled out for you, with your original information, each time you create a new summary for a different document. Of course, you can edit either item.

Tip: *The Comment box is like a five-line document window.*

If you've typed your document and then create a summary, the Comment box contains the first 400 characters from that document. You can view only five lines of text at a time; to see additional text, select 5, Comments, and then move the

```
Document Summary

        System Filename              C:\WPER\DATA\JONES1.MMO

        Date of Creation             July 22, 1988

    1 - Descriptive Filename

    2 - Subject/Account              Meeting with Jacob Jones

    3 - Author

    4 - Typist

    5 - Comments
 TO:  Donna Wong, Legal Department; RE:  Meeting with Jacob Jones;  I met
 with Mr. Jacob Jones last Friday.  As you know, Mr. Jones is a partner in
 the law firm of Barnes, Jacoby and Jones. He has numerous years of
 experience with insurance cases such as the one we find ourselves immersed
 in.  Mr. Jones posed several questions which must be answered before he

Selection: 0
```

Figure 11-3. Document Summary screen on which WordPerfect has inserted the Subject/Account information

cursor down through the text just like on the Typing screen. Thus, the Comment box is initially just a window on your first lines of text.

You can quickly erase those characters if you prefer to create a comment of your own. Move the cursor to the top of the Comment box and press CTRL + PGDN, which on the Typing screen deletes to the end of a page. In this case, the box is cleared. Type and edit your comment as you would regular text (except that advanced editing features such as Block and Move are inoperative). You can boldface or underline text in a comment. And remember that the maximum number of characters you can type in a comment box is 780.

Trap: *The summary's date of creation cannot be altered.*

It is WordPerfect that fills out the document's date of creation. That date cannot be changed by you. Editing changes to that document on another day do not affect this date of creation.

If you plan to use the Document Summary feature, be sure to create the summary on the same day that you first create the document. If you don't, the summary will not truly indicate the day the document was first typed and stored on disk (see the second Tip below for a method to remind yourself to create document summaries).

Tip: *Remember to update the document summary if you use an existing document to create a new document.*

You learned in the first section of this chapter, "Saving Documents," that you can save both the old and the new versions of a document on disk; simply retrieve a file from disk, edit it as you wish, and resave under a new filename. If you do resave a file under a new name, and a document summary has already been created for the original file, remember to revise the document summary to reflect the contents of the new file before resaving the file under a new filename (the date of creation will not change, however).

Tip: *WordPerfect can force you to fill out a summary for each new document you create.*

You may decide to institute the use of the Document Summary feature as a standard procedure in your office. That is, each new document created by someone in your office must have a document summary. If you decide to institute this procedure, WordPerfect can be set so that a document summary form is automatically displayed when the user presses SAVE or EXIT to store a new document for the very first time. This setting can be chosen through the Initial Settings option on the Setup menu (see Appendix B).

Tip: *Document summaries help you find the file you're looking for quickly and easily.*

A document summary can come in handy when you are trying to find a specific document whose filename you can't remember. Chapter 13 describes the Look feature, whereby you can view the contents of a file without having to retrieve that file to the screen. Using this feature, you can quickly peruse many files. When a summary has been created for a document, it is the summary that is first displayed on the Look screen.

Chapter 13 also describes the Word Search feature, whereby you can ask WordPerfect to find those files that contain a specific word pattern. You can request that WordPerfect check the document summary for that word pattern. For instance, WordPerfect can find only those files in which the entry for Author contains a specific name or only those files in which the Subject/Account contains the word "Finance". You may find, then, that by filling out a document summary for each document, you can track down a file much more easily.

Tip: *(When upgrading from 4.2.) The Document Summary feature has been modified.*

In version 5, the Document Summary feature works quite differently. It is no longer accessed through the TEXT IN/OUT key, but rather via the FORMAT key. Also, you can now insert additional information on the predesigned form. And, when you create a summary, no code is inserted in the text: instead, the summary is stored as part of an invisible prefix that is attached to the file.

Tips and Traps Summary

Saving Documents

Tip: SAVE is most useful for retaining a document on screen, while EXIT is most effective for clearing the document from the screen.

Trap: You can't save files to a floppy disk drive that does not contain a formatted disk.

Trap: If you do not have sufficient space available on disk, you cannot store a document.

Tip: Press LIST FILES to discover the default drive/directory.

Tip: Several options enable you to change the default drive/directory.

Tip: Store related files together on the same disk or in the same directory.

Tip: Choose descriptive, meaningful filenames.

Trap: Don't forget to resave a file if you make changes on the screen.

Trap: Don't make files too large.

Tip: Save a document to disk at regular intervals.

Tip: Get extra protection against power failures with the Timed Backup feature.

Trap: Because a disk can become damaged, you must take precautions.

Tip: You can retain both the old and the new version of a document on disk.

Tip: Protect against accidentally overwriting a file by using the Original Backup feature.

Tip: You can save just part of a document to disk—either by creating a new file or by appending to an existing file.

Tips and Traps Summary (*continued*)

Tip: A document's filename can be suppressed on the status line once you store the document.

Tip: The Locked Document feature gives you the ability to use a password when saving a document.

Tip: WordPerfect offers the Fast Save feature so you can save files quickly.

Tip: Use the Setup menu to ensure that you complete a document summary before you save to disk.

Tip: When you save a document on disk, WordPerfect tags that file with a packet of related information.

Tip: (When upgrading from 4.2.) Some procedures for saving a document have changed and others have been added.

Retrieving Documents

Tip: Whenever you retrieve a file, the original file still remains on disk.

Tip: Make sure WordPerfect is retrieving from the correct drive or directory.

Trap: Don't retrieve a non-WordPerfect document.

Trap: You must remember to clear the screen before retrieving a document; WordPerfect does not clear it for you.

Tip: If you forget a filename, you can list all the files on disk to refresh your memory.

Trap: If a document is too large, WordPerfect may be unable to retrieve it.

Trap: You must know the correct password to retrieve a locked file.

Tip: (When upgrading from 4.2.) Retrieve documents as you did before.

Tips and Traps Summary (*continued*)

Document Summaries

Tip: WordPerfect attempts to name your file if you indicate a descriptive filename when filling out the document summary form.

Tip: WordPerfect attempts to fill out the Subject/Account entry for you.

Tip: WordPerfect remembers the Author and Typist information during the same working session.

Tip: The Comment box is like a five-line document window.

Trap: The summary's date of creation cannot be altered.

Tip: Remember to update the document summary if you use an existing document to create a new document.

Tip: WordPerfect can force you to fill out a summary for each new document you create.

Tip: Document summaries help you find the file you're looking for quickly and easily.

Tip: (When upgrading from 4.2.) The Document Summary feature has been modified.

12

Working Between Documents

Documents are rarely islands unto themselves. There may be times when you want to work with two documents simultaneously. Other times you may want to exchange information between documents. Perhaps there's a standard paragraph that you want to insert into many of the letters you type, or sections of a report that you wish to combine into one master document.

This chapter first describes how to work with two documents simultaneously on screen—either by switching back and forth between two separate Typing screens or by splitting the screen into two windows in order to view two documents at once. Then you'll discover how WordPerfect can compare the content of two documents by using its Document Compare feature. And you will learn how to combine documents by transferring document sections from one file to another or by using the Master Document feature.

Two Documents on Two Screens

WordPerfect can manage two documents in RAM at the same time, a capability that is extremely convenient. You can switch back and forth between two reports that you must complete today, compare the information contained in two separate memos, or keep an outline on one screen to refer to as you write text on the other screen.

You can create a second document screen at any time. Simply press the SWITCH (SHIFT + F3) key. You'll know that you're in the second screen because after a few seconds a clear Typing screen appears with a status line that reads **Doc 2**. Press SWITCH a second time and WordPerfect transfers you back to the first screen; the status line now reads **Doc 1**.

The Doc 2 screen remains independent and offers all the same WordPerfect features as the Doc 1 screen. If you type text or retrieve a document onto one screen, you will not alter the document on the other screen. In fact, it is easy to forget that a second document resides in the computer's memory if you don't switch back to view it periodically.

Tip: *You can use the Copy or the Move command to transfer information between the two documents on two screens.*

Move or copy text between separate documents on two screens just as you move or copy text on one screen. For example, suppose you want to copy a sentence from the second document screen to the first. While in document 2, copy that sentence using the MOVE key (described in Chapter 6). Next, press SWITCH to transfer to document 1. Position the cursor where you want the sentence relocated and press ENTER to move the sentence into document 1.

Tip: *WordPerfect reminds you about a second document on screen.*

When you work with two screens, WordPerfect won't let you exit the program without deciding on the fate of both. Suppose two screens are active and you're currently viewing document 1. When you press EXIT, WordPerfect prompts you to indicate whether you wish to save that document. Next, instead of allowing you to exit WordPerfect, the program prompts

Exit Doc 1? (Y/N) N

Type **Y** and WordPerfect clears document 1, switching you to the document 2 screen. Type **N** and WordPerfect clears the text, but the cursor remains in document 1. Once you clear either document 1 or document 2, pressing EXIT then enables you to leave WordPerfect.

Tip: *Timed Backup works with both document screens.*

Appendix B describes the Timed Backup feature, which directs WordPerfect to periodically save a document in a temporary backup file called **WP{WP}.BK**1. If you're working on the Doc 2 screen rather than the Doc 1 screen, then WordPerfect saves the second document in a temporary backup file called **WP{WP}.BK**2.

Tip: *You can have access to more than two document screens if you have sufficient memory and the appropriate software.*

If your computer is equipped with a large amount of expanded memory, then you have the ability to load additional copies of WordPerfect into memory and in that way open as many WordPerfect documents as you have available memory for. You will need not only expanded memory, but also a software package that enables you to load and run more than one software package into memory at the same time—such as WordPerfect Library (a companion package to WordPerfect) or a windowing package such as DESQview from Quarterdeck Office Systems.

If you have the capability and do decide to load more than one copy of WordPerfect at the same time, keep in mind that each copy of WordPerfect must use a unique drive or directory for its overflow files, which are created as you work on documents. When you load a second copy of WordPerfect, the program will prompt

Are other copies of WordPerfect currently running? (Y/N)

(This is the same message you get when reloading WordPerfect after experiencing a machine or power failure, as described in Chapter 1.) Type **Y** and then, when prompted, type in a different drive/directory to store the overflow files for the second copy of WordPerfect. Now you can run two copies side by side and have access to four document screens.

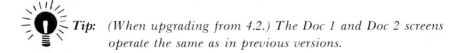

Tip: *(When upgrading from 4.2.) The Doc 1 and Doc 2 screens operate the same as in previous versions.*

Use two document screens and switch back and forth between them just as you did when using version 4.2.

Two Documents on One Split Screen

Not only can two documents be displayed on two separate screens, but they also can be displayed on one screen that is split into two windows. It is easy to use a split screen to compare documents or to quickly transfer information from one document to another. To create two windows:

1. Position the cursor anywhere on the screen displaying document 1 or document 2.
2. Press the SCREEN (CTRL + F3) key. The Screen menu appears.

   0 Rewrite; **1** Window; **2** Line Draw: **0**

3. Choose Window (1 or W). WordPerfect indicates the number of lines in the current window. If your monitor is of standard size, for example, the message is

   Number of Lines in this window: 24

4. Type a number that represents the number of lines you wish to view in the window for the document you're currently viewing. Press ENTER.

Document 1 is always displayed in the top window; document 2 is displayed in the bottom window in whatever screen space is left over.

After you create two windows, a status line appears at the bottom of each— one indicating **Doc 1**, and the other indicating **Doc 2.** In addition, the two windows are separated by a ruler line (also called a tab ruler)—the same ruler line that appears when you use the Reveal Codes screen. Remember that the ruler line is a solid bar, on which triangles represent tab stops, square brackets [ ] represent the left and right margins, and curved braces { } represent the left and right margins where a tab also is located. Figure 12-1 shows a screen split into two windows with a different document in each.

To switch between the two windows press SWITCH, just as you do when switching between two screens. You can tell which window is active because the cursor is located in the active one, and also because the triangles (tab stop markers) on the ruler line point toward the active window1. In Figure 12-1, for example, notice that the tab stop markers are pointing up, meaning that the cursor is currently working in the Doc 1 window. Type or edit text in a window just as you would on the full-size Typing screen.

When you split the screen in half and then press a function key, the resulting prompt or menu is displayed at the bottom of the active window, not at the bottom of the screen. For instance, if you're viewing a split screen with the cursor in the top window, when you press EXIT the prompt **Save document? (Y/N) Yes** will appear in the top window, just above the tab ruler that splits the screen in half. This may be confusing at first, since it becomes habit to check the bottom of the screen for any prompts or messages.

Tip: *The Window feature lets you establish a ruler line on the Typing screen without splitting the screen.*

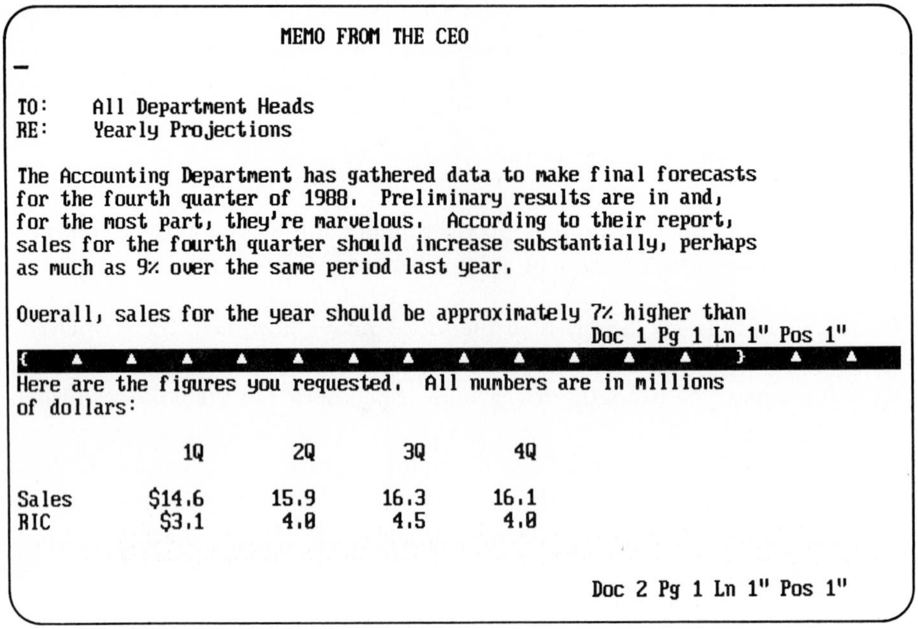

```
                         MEMO FROM THE CEO
_

TO:     All Department Heads
RE:     Yearly Projections

The Accounting Department has gathered data to make final forecasts
for the fourth quarter of 1988. Preliminary results are in and,
for the most part, they're marvelous. According to their report,
sales for the fourth quarter should increase substantially, perhaps
as much as 9% over the same period last year.

Overall, sales for the year should be approximately 7% higher than
                                            Doc 1 Pg 1 Ln 1" Pos 1"
{ ▲  ▲  ▲  ▲  ▲  ▲  ▲  ▲  ▲  ▲  ▲  ▲  ▲  }  ▲  ▲
Here are the figures you requested. All numbers are in millions
of dollars:

              1Q         2Q         3Q         4Q

Sales       $14.6       15.9       16.3       16.1
RIC          $3.1        4.0        4.5        4.0

                                            Doc 2 Pg 1 Ln 1" Pos 1"
```

Figure 12-1. A split screen showing two documents

In addition to splitting the screen in two, the Window feature also permits you to shrink the screen by one line so you can view a ruler line (tab ruler) at the bottom of the screen. With this feature, you can keep track of your current margin and tab settings—a convenience if you are typing a table aligned on tab stops.

To display a ruler line, simply choose a window size that is one line less than the size of a full screen. For example, on a standard-size screen, choose a window with 23 lines and you'll view a screen as illustrated in Figure 12-2.

Tip: *On a split screen, each window can range from 2 to 20 lines in size.*

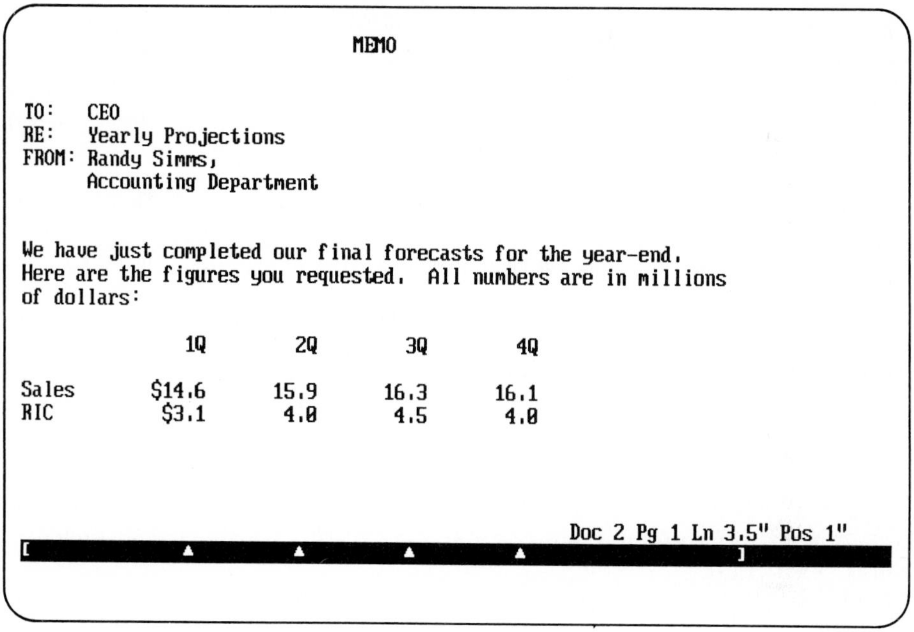

Figure 12-2. A screen with a ruler line for one document

On a standard, 25-line screen display, the Typing screen contains 24 lines, with one line taken up by the status line information. When you split the screen into windows, *three* lines are occupied with document information—two status lines (one for each of the two windows) and one ruler line splitting the windows. Therefore, on a split screen, 22 lines remain available for text, to be shared by the windows.

A window cannot be smaller than two lines, so that on a standard-size monitor a window can range from two to 20 lines in size. The other window takes whatever number of lines is left over. In other words, if you decide to shrink the Doc 1 window to 15 lines, then the Doc 2 window will occupy seven lines (22 lines minus 15 lines). If the screen is split evenly, each window will display 11 lines of text.

If you attempt to enter a window size as 21 or 22 lines, WordPerfect will assume that you meant 23 lines, and it will display a ruler line (as discussed in an earlier Tip).

Of course, if the size of your screen display does not equal 25 lines, then the size of each window will differ from the range of two to 20 lines.

Tip: *You can use the directional arrow keys to size the Doc 1 and Doc 2 windows.*

When WordPerfect prompts for the number of lines in a window, you can use the directional arrow keys as an alternative to typing in a number. If the cursor is in the Doc 1 window, then press UP ARROW to shrink the window, or press DOWN ARROW to expand it. If the cursor is in the Doc 2 window, then the arrow keys function in the opposite manner: press UP ARROW to expand the window, or press DOWN ARROW to shrink it.

Be warned, however, that using the arrow keys can be confusing at first, since a window cannot be sized for 21 or 22 lines (see the preceding Tip). For instance, if the Doc 1 window is 24 lines in size, when you press UP ARROW WordPerfect will size the window at 23 lines. Press UP ARROW again and now the window is sized at 20 lines.

Trap: *If you view the same document in both windows, an update in one causes no change in the other.*

You can choose to see two parts of the same document by creating two windows, retrieving the same file into both, and positioning the cursor at different locations in the text in each window. But don't forget that the two windows are independent. If you make revisions in one window, the text in the other is not automatically updated.

Tip: *Clear the windows in the same way that you create them.*

When you wish to return to a full-size display, press SCREEN and again choose Window (1 or W). At the prompt

Number of Lines in this window:

type **0** or a number that is one less than the capacity of your display, or any larger number. On a standard monitor, for example, type **0** or any number equal to or greater than 24. When you press ENTER, the screen will return to showing one document at a time.

Tip: *Text remains in RAM even after you clear a window.*

Once you clear windows, the text in the second window disappears from view, but the document is still in RAM. Press SWITCH (SHIFT + F3) and you'll have a full-screen view of that second document.

Tip: *The second window disappears temporarily when on the Reveal Codes screen.*

If you're viewing a split screen and you press REVEAL CODES (ALT + F3), the screen responds in the usual way. Suppose your cursor is in the Doc 1 window. When you reveal codes, the text of Doc 1 remains in the top window, and the same text with codes revealed is displayed in the bottom window in place of the Doc 2 text. Return to the Typing screen by pressing REVEAL CODES and the split screen showing Doc 1 and Doc 2 returns.

Tip: *(When upgrading from 4.2.) The Split Screen feature operates the same as in previous versions.*

Use a split screen just as you did in version 4.2.

Comparing Documents

With the Document Compare feature, WordPerfect can automatically compare a document on screen to a file on disk. The documents are compared phrase by phrase, with a phrase defined as the text between punctuation marks, which include the period, the question mark, the exclamation point, and the comma. The result is marked with redline or strikeout codes that indicate where the text in the two documents differs (for a full discussion of the redline and strikeout features, refer to Chapter 5).

The Document Compare feature is helpful when you retrieve a document to screen, edit that document, and then wish to compare the revised, on-screen text with the original version on disk. It is also useful in law offices for detecting modifications on legal contracts.

To compare two documents:

1. Make sure that one document is stored on disk. The second document should be on screen; retrieve that second file if necessary.
2. Press the MARK TEXT (ALT + F5) key to display the following menu:

   1 Auto Ref; **2** Subdoc; **3** Index; **4** ToA Short Form; **5** Define; **6** Generate: **0**

3. Select Generate (6 or G). The Generate Mark Text menu appears, as shown in Figure 12-3.
4. Select Compare Screen and Disk Documents and Add Redline and Strikeout (2 or C). WordPerfect prompts for a filename, suggesting the name of the file you retrieved to the screen before activating the Document Compare feature:

   Other Document:

5. Press ENTER to accept the suggested filename, or type a filename and then press ENTER.

In moments, WordPerfect marks the on-screen document. On-screen text that does not exist in the file on disk is redlined. Text in the file on disk that does not exist

```
Mark Text: Generate

     1 - Remove Redline Markings and Strikeout Text from Document

     2 - Compare Screen and Disk Documents and Add Redline and Strikeout

     3 - Expand Master Document

     4 - Condense Master Document

     5 - Generate Tables, Indexes, Automatic References, etc.

Selection: 0
```

Figure 12-3. The Generate Mark Text menu

in the document on screen is copied to the on-screen document with strikeout codes inserted.

Figure 12-4 shows an example of the result when, after two documents are compared, the on-screen text is printed. (The printed version, rather than the screen version, is illustrated so that you can clearly see the redline and strikeout marks.) The redline appears in Figure 12-4 with a shadowed background, while strikeout appears as a solid line through the middle of the characters. Notice, for example, that the results indicate that the text on screen is addressed to "All Sales Managers," while the file on disk is addressed to "All Department Heads."

If a section of text is in a different location in the on-screen version than on disk, then WordPerfect borders that text with two messages: ~~**THE FOLLOWING TEXT WAS MOVED**~~ and ~~**THE PRECEDING TEXT WAS MOVED.**~~ Figure 12-4

MEMO FROM THE CEO

TO: All Sales Managers
~~All Department Heads~~
RE: Yearly Projections

The Accounting Department has gathered data to make final forecasts for the fourth quarter of 1988. Preliminary results are in and, for the most part, they're terrific. ~~they're marvelous.~~ According to their report, sales for the fourth quarter should increase substantially, perhaps as much as 10% over the same period last year. ~~perhaps as much as 9% over the same period last year.~~
~~THE FOLLOWING TEXT WAS MOVED~~

We'll be working on developing goals for next year and will send a questionnaire for your own estimates in a few weeks. ~~Thank you.~~
~~THE PRECEDING TEXT WAS MOVED~~

Overall, sales for the year should be approximately 7% higher than last year. The most striking increase is in the southern region. Florida showed an increase of 23% over last year. Congratulations to Sales Manager Bob Carleston! ~~Congratulations to Bob Carleston; he has officially won the trip to Hawaii!~~

Figure 12-4. The printed result after activating the Document Compare feature

indicates that the second paragraph of text on screen is in a different location than it is on disk.

Tip: *Document Compare examines not only the basic text of the two documents, but also headers, footers, footnotes, and endnotes.*

The Document Compare feature checks the entire contents of the documents in question — even the text of headers, footers, footnotes, and endnotes. If a header or footer differs from one document to the other, then the on-screen header/footer code is redlined, and the header/footer code contained in the document on disk is copied on screen and marked with strikeout codes. You can reveal codes to see the extra header/footer code that WordPerfect inserted into the text. Or, when you print out the document, and assuming that the header/footer codes were located at the top of each document, the on-screen header/footer will print on the first page, and the header/footer for the document on disk will print on succeeding pages.

If a footnote or endnote differs between documents, then the text is marked within the note itself. You can review the differences by proceeding as if you plan to edit the note, so that the Footnote or Endnote Typing Screen appears. The on-screen footnote or endnote text will appear redlined, and the text of the footnote or endnote contained in the document on disk will be marked with strikeout codes.

Tip: *After WordPerfect has compared the two documents, you have a variety of options.*

Once two documents are compared, the rest is up to you. You have a variety of choices. First, you can move the cursor phrase by phrase to each redline or strikeout code in the text and decide which version of that phrase you prefer. Delete the rejected text, along with the accompanying redline or strikeout code.

Or, you can simply print out the result, as was done in Figure 12-4. That way you can see the changes quite clearly, and if you wish, you can solicit suggestions for the final version of your document by distributing the printed text.

Or, you can remove all the redline codes and strikeout text with its accompanying codes from the on-screen document. In this way, you are returning the on-screen text to the form in which it appeared *before* WordPerfect performed a document compare for you — meaning that you prefer the on-screen version to the disk version of the document. To remove all the redline codes and strikeout text with codes, follow steps 1 through 3 as shown at the beginning of this section, so that the Generate Mark Text menu is on screen. Then, select Remove Redline

Markings and Strikeout Text from Document (1 or R). To verify, WordPerfect prompts with the following:

Delete redline markings and strikeout text? (Y/N) No

Type **Y**, and very shortly all redline marks will disappear and all strikeout text will be deleted.

Tip: *Use the Search feature to move quickly to the redline or strikeout codes after comparing two documents.*

With the result of a document compare on screen, you can quickly hop to each place where the two documents differ. Use the Search feature to do this.

For example, to move to each redline code:

1. Position the cursor at the top of the document and press the →SEARCH (F2) key.
2. Now follow the procedure you would normally use to insert the **[REDLN]** code: press the FONT (CTRL + F8) key, select Appearance (2 or A), and select Redline (8 or R). The search prompt now reads

   → Srch: [REDLN]

3. Press the →SEARCH or ESC key to move the cursor to the first redline code in the text. Continue searching until all the text marked for redline has been found and acted upon.

See Chapter 4 for further information on the Search feature.

Tip: *The Document Compare feature operates correctly even if the two documents are formatted differently.*

Don't worry if the text on screen and the document on disk are different in how they are formatted. Even with differing margin and line-spacing settings, for example, the comparison will operate effectively.

Tip: *You can change the way text marked for redline or strikeout appears on screen or when printed.*

Redline and strikeout can appear on screen in various ways, depending on your computer monitor and its graphics capabilities. Color monitor users can see redlined text and text marked with strikeout in different colors or fonts. Monochrome monitor users have choices such as boldface or blinking text. These are accomplished with option 3, Display, on the Setup menu (for more on the Setup menu, refer to Appendix B).

Similarly, redlined text and text marked with strikeout can be printed in various ways, depending on your printer's capabilities (Chapter 5 addresses this in more detail).

Tip: *(When upgrading from 4.2.) Document Compare is a brand-new feature in version 5.*

Redline and strikeout were available in previous versions of WordPerfect; however, the codes had to be inserted manually when comparing two documents. In version 5, you can let WordPerfect do the work for you with the Document Compare feature.

Combining Files

Because WordPerfect retains whatever is on the screen when another document is retrieved, you can combine files easily. For instance, suppose that you store a commonly used paragraph in its own file on disk. If you wish to insert that paragraph in a document on screen, position the cursor where you want the paragraph to appear, press RETRIEVE (SHIFT + F10), type in the paragraph's filename, and press ENTER. (A second method for retrieving text is on the List Files menu, as discussed in Chapter 13.)

Because it is so easy to combine text, you can set up a library of commonly used paragraphs, each stored in its own separate file. In this way you create a system of "boilerplate" files. (One naming scheme is to call the files P1, P2, and so on; but make sure to keep track of the contents of each file. Or, use longer filenames, such as OPENING for an opening paragraph in a letter, CLOSE for the closing paragraph, and so on.) Retrieve separate files into one document on screen and you can create a new document with little actual typing. Then save that new document under its own filename.

Trap: *Watch out for formatting codes when you combine files.*

How you format a document when you combine files depends on how you inserted the formatting codes. As you learned in Chapter 8, there are several ways to insert formatting codes in order to change features, such as line spacing or margin setting, in a document. First, you can change the initial settings for a document by inserting format codes on the Document Initial Codes screen. In this case, the format codes are stored in the invisible prefix (or packet of information) that gets saved along with the file. Second, you can insert codes directly into the text of the document. In this case, the format codes are shown when you view the Reveal Codes screen.

Suppose you begin a document by typing several sentences, positioning the cursor below those sentences, and then retrieving from disk a file named P1. If the file named P1 contains formatting codes in the invisible prefix, those codes are not combined with the document on screen; instead, they are ignored. It is the initial settings of the document on screen that take precedence. The formatting of P1 will be affected by the current document's initial settings and by any other codes in the text above where you retrieved P1.

On the other hand, if P1 contains formatting codes within the body of the text itself, those codes are inserted along with the text when you retrieve the file. The formatting of any text that you type below the point at which you retrieved P1 will be affected by the formatting codes brought into the document along with the text of P1.

Trap: *Watch out when you save after combining files.*

If you've retrieved one or more documents to the screen, then when you save, the filename of the first file retrieved is suggested as the filename to be used. This makes it very easy to overwrite a file that may contain a boilerplate paragraph.

For example, suppose that you have on disk boilerplate paragraphs with filenames like P1, P2, P3, and so on. On screen, you retrieve P1. After typing additional text, you retrieve P2. Then you finish the letter and press SAVE to store the letter on disk. WordPerfect will prompt for a filename and suggest that you store the file under the name P1, since this was the first paragraph you retrieved from disk in order to begin the new document. Don't accept this suggestion; if you do, you'll be replacing the boilerplate paragraph. Instead, save the letter under a unique filename.

Tip: *Add text that is on screen to an existing file on disk by using the Append feature.*

You've learned that you can combine a file on disk with text on screen by using the RETRIEVE key. Conversely, you can add text on screen to a file on disk by using the Append feature. On-screen text that you highlight is placed at the end of the existing file on disk.

Assume that you just typed a page but realize that two paragraphs from that page would also be appropriate in a document that you created earlier. To copy those paragraphs to the already existing file:

1. Use the BLOCK (ALT + F4) key to mark the boundaries of the paragraphs. **Block on** flashes on screen.

2. Press the MOVE (CTRL + F4) key. The following menu appears:

   Move: 1 Block; **2** Tabular Column; **3** Rectangle: **0**

3. Select from this menu the type of text you wish to append. For instance, if you wish to append a standard block (such as the two paragraphs), then choose Block (1 or B). (For information on moving tabular columns or rectangles, refer to Chapter 6.) Then WordPerfect provides another menu:

   1 Move; **2** Copy; **3** Delete; **4** Append: **0**

4. Select Append (4 or A). WordPerfect prompts

   Append to:

5. Type the name of the file on disk and press ENTER. If WordPerfect locates that file, it places a copy of the marked text into the file on disk and clears the Block command. Or, if WordPerfect cannot locate the named file, it creates a new file by that name.

If you wish to append one sentence, paragraph, or page of text, you do not need to block the text before pressing the MOVE key. For example, suppose that you wish to append one full page of text that is currently on screen to a file on disk. To do this, position the cursor on the page you wish to append and press MOVE (CTRL + F4). The following menu appears:

Move: 1 Sentence; 2 Paragraph; 3 Page; 4 Retrieve: 0

Select Page (3 or A), and then continue with steps 4 and 5 as outlined above.

You can use the Append feature even if the file on disk is locked (meaning that you must know the password to retrieve that file).

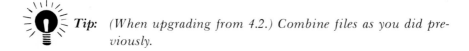

Tip: *(When upgrading from 4.2.) Combine files as you did previously.*

As in version 4.2 combine documents in version 5 by pressing the RETRIEVE key. Differences do exist in the Append feature, however: you can now append a tabular column or rectangle in addition to a block, and append to a locked file, and WordPerfect will create a new file if the file you wish to append to is not found on disk.

Master Documents

WordPerfect gives you the ability to connect smaller files together into a comprehensive document by using the Master Document feature. A master document comprises text and one or more subdocuments. For example, a master document for a book might include a title page, a table of contents, and subdocuments for each chapter. Or, a master document for a standard proposal might include an introduction and subdocuments for each section. Think of the master document as containing the basic skeleton of a large document; the subdocuments are separate files that are slotted into specific locations in that basic skeleton.

A master document frees you from working with a large, cumbersome file. Your text is broken up into manageable pieces that are easy to edit. Of equal importance is the fact that the Master Document feature enables you to print out a document where all global features—such as footnotes and page numbers—are consistent throughout, even though the document is composed of separate subdocuments. Master documents also enable you to generate a table of contents, a reference list or bibliography, or an index, across many subdocuments. For example, if the master document is for a book and is a composite of chapter subdocuments, then you can have WordPerfect create a table of contents for the entire book, chapter by chapter (be sure to check Chapter 22 to learn about generating lists, indexes, and tables).

To create a master document, simply start typing as you would for any document. In the location at which you want a subdocument to be included, you must insert a code into the master document, as follows:

1. Position the cursor where you want to include the subdocument.
2. Press the MARK TEXT (ALT + F5) key to display the following menu:

   1 Auto Ref; **2** Subdoc; **3** Index; **4** ToA Short Form; **5** Define; **6** Generate: **0**

3. Select Subdoc (2 or S). WordPerfect prompts

   Subdoc Filename:

4. Type in the name of the file that you wish to include (preceded by the file's path if that file is stored in a different drive/directory than the default), and press ENTER.

WordPerfect inserts a subdocument code into the text. For example, if the subdocument to be included is named BKGROUND.88, then the code inserted is **[Subdoc:**BKGROUND.88]. Because the code is visible only on the Reveal Codes screen, WordPerfect displays a comment that is visible on the Typing screen to indicate where the subdocument has been included. The comment is in a single-line box and contains the name of the subdocument. An example is shown in Figure 12-5. You can include any number of subdocument codes in a master document.

When you wish to see the master document in its entirety—including all text of all subdocuments—then you must *expand* the master document. To do so:

1. Make sure the master document is on screen.

```
Introduction

     ABC Company is pleased to prepare this proposal for training
members of your staff on the use of microcomputers in the business
setting.  It contains background information on ABC Company's
training experience over the past 10 years, a list of our clients,
and a suggested course curriculum to meet the training needs of
your organization.  The last pages provide a cost estimate for the
training services you require.


Background on ABC Company

 Subdoc: BKGROUND.88




                                    Doc 1 Pg 1 Ln 1" Pos 1"
```

Figure 12-5. A master document with a subdocument Comment box

2. Press the MARK TEXT (ALT + F5) key to display the Mark Text menu.
3. Select Generate (6 or G). The Generate Mark Text menu appears, as shown in Figure 12-3.
4. Select Expand Master Document (3 or E).

Wherever a **[Subdoc:]** code is located in the text, it is deleted and replaced with the following:

- A **[Subdoc Start:]** code. For example, if the subdocument is named BKGROUND.88, then the code inserted is **[Subdoc Start:**BKGROUND.88**]**. The code is visible only on the Reveal Codes screen; WordPerfect displays a comment that is visible on the Typing screen.
- The text of the subdocument.

- A **[Subdoc End:]** code. For example, if the subdocument is named BKGROUND.88, then the code inserted is **[Subdoc End:**BKGROUND.88**]**. The code is visible only on the Reveal Codes screen, so WordPerfect displays a comment that is visible on the Typing screen.

Figure 12-6 shows a portion of a master document that has been expanded. Notice the comments in single-line boxes that mark the boundaries of the subdocument that has been inserted, which, in this case, is only two paragraphs in length.

Once a master document is expanded, you can peruse it, print it, or edit it. You can edit the text of any subdocument, as well as the text of the master document.

You can also *condense* the master document, meaning that you replace the subdocument text with the subdocument codes. In this way you can collapse the master document back to its basic skeleton, making it a smaller, more manageable file. To do so:

1. Make sure the master document is on screen.
2. Press the MARK TEXT (ALT + F5) key to display the Mark Text menu.
3. Select Generate (6 or G). The Generate Mark Text menu appears, as shown in Figure 12-3.
4. Select Condense Master Document (4 or C). WordPerfect responds with the prompt:

   Save Subdocs (Y/N)? Yes

   This prompt appears so that, in case you edited any text in a subdocument, those editing changes will be updated on disk.
5. Type **N** if you have made no editing changes to any of the subdocuments. The master document will collapse into its shorter form (as in Figure 12-5, for example), with subdocuments deleted from the master.

   Or type **Y** or press ENTER if you have made editing changes in any of the subdocuments. Then WordPerfect will prompt, asking whether you wish to replace the version of each subdocument on disk. For example, suppose the first subdocument is named BKGROUND.88. WordPerfect prompts

   Replace BKGROUND.88? 1 Yes; **2** No; **3** Replace All Remaining: **0**

```
setting.  It contains background information on ABC Company's
training experience over the past 10 years, a list of our clients,
and a suggested course curriculum to meet the training needs of
your organization.  The last pages provide a cost estimate for the
training services you require.


Background on ABC Company

 Subdoc Start: BKGROUND.88

     ABC Company has offered microcomputer training services for
the past ten years.  Our programs are the cost effective solution
to educating employees in this fast-changing computer world.   More
than 50,000 people, from large corporations to small businesses,
have taken advantage of our services.

     Our professional instructors have both the product knowledge
and the teaching skills to help employees become more efficient and
productive in their daily tasks.

 Subdoc End: BKGROUND.88
                                          Doc 1 Pg 1 Ln 1" Pos 1"
```

Figure 12-6. Portion of a master document after it has been expanded

Select Yes (1 or Y) to replace the version on disk with the edited version of the subdocument. Select No (2 or N) and WordPerfect will request a new filename to store the subdocument under. Select Replace all remaining (3 or R) and WordPerfect will replace the versions on disk with the edited versions of all the subdocuments. Then the master document will collapse into its shorter form.

Tip: *Expand a master document before you print.*

You can print the master document at any time. If you print the condensed version, then you will print out only the text of the master document. If you print the expanded version, you will print out the text of the master document and of all subdocuments. Thus, remember to expand a master document when you're ready to print it out in its entirety.

Tip: *When you expand a master document, WordPerfect notifies you if no subdocument by the name you specified exists.*

As you expand a master document, WordPerfect finds each subdocument by the name you specified in the **[Subdoc:]** code. If WordPerfect cannot find such a file, it informs you of the situation and prompts for instructions. For instance, if it can't find a file named BKGROUND.88, WordPerfect prompts

Subdoc not found (Press Enter to skip): BKGROUND.88

Press ENTER to continue expanding the master document anyway. The **[Subdoc:** BKGROUND.88] code remains in the text. Or press CANCEL (F1) to stop the expansion procedure.

If the file is not found, perhaps you made a typo when inserting the subdocument code; you'll need to erase the **[Subdoc:]** code and insert a new one with the filename spelled correctly. Another possibility is that the file is located in a drive/directory other than the default. In this case, you must insert a **[Subdoc:]** code with the filename's path identified, such as **[Subdoc:\WPER\SUE\BKGROUND.88]**.

Tip: *Condense a master document before you save it on disk.*

Each subdocument is stored in a separate file. Therefore, if you save a master document that has been expanded, you're storing subdocuments twice—in their own files and as part of the master. This is an inefficient use of disk space. Instead, it is wiser to store a master document that has been condensed.

If you press SAVE or EXIT to store a master document and that document is in expanded form, WordPerfect offers the opportunity to condense it first. WordPerfect prompts

Document is expanded, condense it? (Y/N) Yes

Type **Y** to condense the document. If you do, WordPerfect offers the opportunity to save the subdocuments, and finally saves the master. Or type **N** to leave the document expanded while it is stored.

If a master document is saved in expanded form, then from that point on you will not be prompted to condense it when you subsequently save it. Thus, if you wish to condense the master the next time you save it, you will have to remember to condense the master manually first.

Tip: *Numbering and option codes can be placed anywhere in either the master document or subdocuments.*

When a master document is expanded, numbering and option codes remain consistent with the way they operate in a single WordPerfect document. Suppose, for example, that you use the Paragraph Numbering feature (see Chapter 21) to number paragraphs in the master as well as in several subdocuments. When expanded, the paragraphs will be numbered consecutively, just as if the paragraphs were all numbered in one document. Option codes for graphics boxes, footnotes, endnotes, page numbering, and line numbering will be correct as well.

Therefore, feel free to insert codes in either the master document or in subdocuments. When you insert a code, it takes effect from that point forward in the master document. However, check the following Trap for some special considerations.

Trap: *Remember that any formatting codes in a subdocument will affect the master document.*

Keep in mind that when the text of a subdocument is included in the master, any formatting codes in that subdocument are included as well (unless the codes were inserted in the subdocument's Document Initial Codes screen). If a subdocument contains a margin set code following paragraph two, for example, then after the master is expanded, that margin set code is not restricted to the subdocument; it will affect text to the end of the master document or until the next margin set code appears farther on in the document.

Therefore, if you want one subdocument to have different format settings from the rest, remember to insert a format code not only at the top of the subdocument but also at the bottom, to return the rest of the master to its initial format settings.

If you want to alter the format for an entire document, place the format codes at the top of the master document or on the master document's Document Initial Codes screen.

Trap: *Don't generate tables, lists, and indexes from subdocuments, but rather from the master.*

An advantage to using master documents is that you can generate tables, lists, and indexes for the whole document, including the subdocuments. You can, for example, generate a table of contents for an entire book even though chapters are housed in separate files. To do so, you should insert the define code for the table in the body of the master document in order to generate the table of contents from the master document. (Refer to Chapter 22 for more on generating tables, lists, and indexes.)

Tip: *The Automatic Reference feature can be tapped in connection with master documents.*

Chapter 21 describes how the Automatic Reference feature allows you to include references to other pages, footnotes, endnotes, or figures; a reference will automatically update if the page, note, or figure to which it is tied is relocated. For instance, you may have in your text a sentence that reads "See Footnote number 4 for further details." The number 4 is actually a reference that will update, should you edit the text in such a way that the footnote becomes footnote 3 or 6.

You may find the Automatic Reference feature helpful as you create a master document and its associated subdocuments. The Automatic Reference feature operates correctly even if the reference in one subdocument (or in the master document) is tied to a page, footnote, endnote, or figure contained in a different subdocument.

Tip: *A master document can be used as a subdocument in another master document.*

With the Master Document feature, you can create a complicated web of interlocking documents. For instance, perhaps you decide to create a master document for a long chapter in a book. The subdocuments are the separate sections of that chapter. In turn, the master document for that long chapter can serve as a subdocument in a master document for the entire book.

Tip: *(When upgrading from 4.2.) Master Document is a brand-new feature in version 5.*

With the new, exciting Master Document feature, you can now manage large documents more easily than before and can compile footnotes or generate tables across separate documents. If you have a cumbersome document on disk that you created in version 4.2, consider saving sections in separate files (the Block Save or Append feature, described in this chapter, is convenient for doing so), and then deleting those sections from the main document. The main document becomes the master, and each separate file becomes a subdocument.

Tips and Traps Summary

Two Documents on Two Screens

Tip: You can use the Copy or the Move command to transfer information between the two documents on two screens.

Tips and Traps Summary (*continued*)

Tip: WordPerfect reminds you about a second document on screen.

Tip: Timed Backup works with both document screens.

Tip: You can have access to more than two document screens if you have sufficient memory and the appropriate software.

Tip: (When upgrading from 4.2.) The Doc 1 and Doc 2 screens operate the same as in previous versions.

Two Documents on One Split Screen

Tip: The Window feature lets you establish a ruler line on the Typing screen without splitting the screen.

Tip: On a split screen, each window can range from 2 to 20 lines in size.

Tip: You can use the directional arrow keys to size the Doc 1 and Doc 2 windows.

Trap: If you view the same document in both windows, an update in one causes no change in the other.

Tip: Clear the windows in the same way that you create them.

Tip: Text remains in RAM even after you clear a window.

Tip: The second window disappears temporarily when on the Reveal Codes screen.

Tip: (When upgrading from 4.2.) The Split Screen feature operates the same as in previous versions.

Comparing Documents

Tip: Document Compare examines not only the basic text of the two documents, but also headers, footers, footnotes, and endnotes.

Tips and Traps Summary (*continued*)

Tip: After WordPerfect has compared the two documents, you have a variety of options.

Tip: Use the Search feature to move quickly to the redline or strike-out codes after comparing two documents.

Tip: The Document Compare feature operates correctly even if the two documents are formatted differently.

Tip: You can change the way text marked for redline or strikeout appears on screen or when printed.

Tip: (When upgrading from 4.2.) Document Compare is a brand-new feature in version 5.

Combining Files

Trap: Watch out for formatting codes when you combine files.

Trap: Watch out when you save after combining files.

Tip: Add text that is on screen to an existing file on disk by using the Append feature.

Tip: (When upgrading from 4.2.) Combine files as you did previously.

Master Documents

Tip: Expand a master document before you print.

Tip: When you expand a master document, WordPerfect notifies you if no subdocument by the name you specified exists.

Tip: Condense a master document before you save it on disk.

Tips and Traps Summary (*continued*)

Tip: Numbering and option codes can be placed anywhere in either the master document or subdocuments.

Trap: Remember that any formatting codes in a subdocument will affect the master document.

Trap: Don't generate tables, lists, and indexes from subdocuments, but rather from the master.

Tip: The Automatic Reference feature can be tapped in connection with master documents.

Tip: A master document can be used as a subdocument in another master document.

Tip: (When upgrading from 4.2.) Master Document is a brand-new feature in version 5.

13

Managing Files on Disk

A floppy disk can potentially hold more than 100 documents; hard disks can hold many times more. Sooner than you think, you will accumulate hundreds of memos, reports, contracts, and letters. The challenge is to manage all those files. Luckily, WordPerfect provides a great deal of support. How do you keep track of all those filenames? WordPerfect does this for you. How do you find a document when you've forgotten its filename? WordPerfect provides a list of filenames, lets you browse through the contents of files, and searches through them for you. How do you maintain an organized disk system? WordPerfect gives you the ability to rename, erase, and copy files. If you prefer to use DOS for file management, WordPerfect exits temporarily to DOS, too. This chapter describes how WordPerfect assists you in managing files.

Displaying a List of Files

Once you fill a disk, it is nearly impossible to remember each document's filename. In WordPerfect the LIST FILES (F5) key is your gateway to assistance. The cursor can be anywhere on the Typing screen when you press LIST FILES (F5).

When you press this key, WordPerfect displays the default drive or directory at the bottom of the screen. (Remember that the default is where WordPerfect assumes you wish to store and retrieve documents, unless you specify otherwise.)

If, for example, the default drive is B, this message appears:

Dir B:*.* (Type = to change default Dir)

If the default is the WPER\DATA directory on a hard disk, this message appears:

Dir C:\WPER\DATA*.* (Type = to change default Dir)

The symbols *.* mean WordPerfect is referring to all the files in that drive or directory, regardless of their filenames or extensions.

Press ENTER to view the list of files in the default drive/directory. Or type in the name of another drive or directory for which you wish to display files, and press ENTER. For instance, type **A:** and press ENTER. Or, type **C:\WPER\SUE** and press ENTER.

A List Files screen, such as in Figure 13-1, appears. There are three sections to this screen: the header at the top of the screen, a list of files that takes up the bulk of the screen, and a List Files menu at the bottom.

In the header, the first line provides the following information:

- The current date and time.
- The drive/directory for which files are being listed. For example, Figure 13-1 indicates that the files listed are housed in C:\WPER\DATA.

The second line of the header offers the following items:

- **Document size** The size of the document on the Typing screen when you pressed the LIST FILES key. Size is measured as the number of characters, known as bytes. Approximately 2000 to 3000 bytes occupy one single-spaced page of text. (In addition, approximately 300 bytes are added to a new document as soon as you start typing. This is an invisible document prefix, which contains a packet of information about that document's attributes—such as the document's internal settings and font, the printer selected, graphics, and the document summary, if any. The prefix increases in size as you take advantage of various WordPerfect features, and it can drastically increase file size.) If the Typing screen is clear when you press LIST FILES, then the Document size on the List Files screen will read **0**.

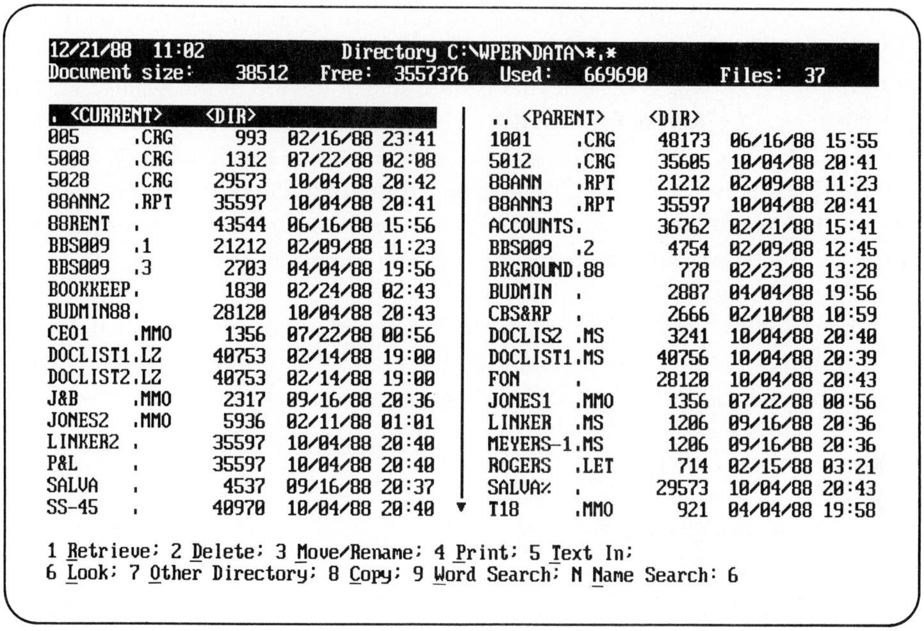

12/21/88 11:02 Directory C:\WPER\DATA*.*
Document size: 38512 Free: 3557376 Used: 669690 Files: 37
. <CURRENT> <DIR>
.. <PARENT> <DIR>
005 .CRG 993 02/16/88 23:41
1001 .CRG 48173 06/16/88 15:55
5008 .CRG 1312 07/22/88 02:08
5012 .CRG 35605 10/04/88 20:41
5028 .CRG 29573 10/04/88 20:42
88ANN .RPT 21212 02/09/88 11:23
88ANN2 .RPT 35597 10/04/88 20:41
88ANN3 .RPT 35597 10/04/88 20:41
88RENT . 43544 06/16/88 15:56
ACCOUNTS. 36762 02/21/88 15:41
BBS009 .1 21212 02/09/88 11:23
BBS009 .2 4754 02/09/88 12:45
BBS009 .3 2703 04/04/88 19:56
BKGROUND.88 778 02/23/88 13:28
BOOKKEEP. 1830 02/24/88 02:43
BUDMIN . 2887 04/04/88 19:56
BUDMIN88. 28120 10/04/88 20:43
CBS&RP . 2666 02/10/88 10:59
CE01 .MMO 1356 07/22/88 00:56
DOCLIS2 .MS 3241 10/04/88 20:40
DOCLIST1.LZ 40753 02/14/88 19:00
DOCLIST1.MS 40756 10/04/88 20:39
DOCLIST2.LZ 40753 02/14/88 19:00
FON . 28120 10/04/88 20:43
J&B .MMO 2317 09/16/88 20:36
JONES1 .MMO 1356 07/22/88 00:56
JONES2 .MMO 5936 02/11/88 01:01
LINKER .MS 1206 09/16/88 20:36
LINKER2 . 35597 10/04/88 20:40
MEYERS-1.MS 1206 09/16/88 20:36
P&L . 35597 10/04/88 20:40
ROGERS .LET 714 02/15/88 03:21
SALVA . 4537 09/16/88 20:37
SALVA% . 29573 10/04/88 20:43
SS-45 . 40970 10/04/88 20:40
T18 .MMO 921 04/04/88 19:58
1 Retrieve; 2 Delete; 3 Move/Rename; 4 Print; 5 Text In;
6 Look; 7 Other Directory; 8 Copy; 9 Word Search; N Name Search: 6

Figure 13-1. The List Files screen

- **Free** The amount of free space still available on that disk to store files, also measured in bytes. Notice in Figure 13-1 that more than 3,500,000 bytes (3.5 megabytes) still are unoccupied on the hard disk, which is drive C.

- **Used** The amount of space on that disk occupied by the current directory, also measured in bytes. (If you're viewing a list of files for a floppy disk that has no directories, then "Used" indicates the total number of bytes occupied on the disk.) Figure 13-1 indicates that the files in C:\WPER\DATA take up 669,690 bytes on the hard disk.

- **Files** The number of files in the current directory. Figure 13-1 indicates that C:\WPER\DATA contains 37 files. (If you're viewing a list of files for a floppy disk that has no directories, then this shows the number of files on the entire disk.)

The screen's middle section lists the directories and files that are in the current drive/directory. The current and parent directories are always listed first. The current directory reflects the one that is indicated at the top of the header. The line item reads **. <CURRENT> <DIR>**. The parent directory is the directory just above the current one in the hierarchical structure. The line item reads **.. <PARENT> <DIR>**. In Figure 13-1, for example, the current directory refers to \WPER\DATA. The parent directory refers to \WPER. Subdirectories that may exist under the current directory are listed next, in two columns and alphabetized row by row; they are identified with the extension <DIR>.

The files are listed last, also alphabetized row by row. Filenames that begin with numbers are positioned before the filenames that begin with letters. WordPerfect provides several pieces of information about each file:

- Filename, including an extension if that file has one
- Size of the file, measured in bytes
- Date and time that file was last saved to disk

The List Files cursor occupies the full width of a column. Notice in Figure 13-1 that the List Files cursor is highlighting **. <CURRENT> <DIR>**. You can move the cursor through the list of files by pressing a directional arrow key, or you can use another cursor movement key, such as PGUP, PGDN, or the PLUS or the MINUS key on the numeric keypad. Pressing HOME, HOME, DOWN ARROW moves the cursor to the last file on the list; pressing HOME, HOME, UP ARROW moves the cursor back to the top of the list.

At the bottom of the List Files screen is a menu with ten options available to you. You can perform tasks such as retrieving, deleting, or copying files. Eight of the ten menu items—the ones that relate to managing files on disk—are discussed in the following sections of this chapter. (For a discussion of the Print option, which enables you to print out a document, see Chapter 14. For a discussion of the Text In option, which enables you to retrieve a DOS text file, refer to Chapter 28.)

You can clear the List Files screen at any time by pressing CANCEL (F1), EXIT (F7), or the SPACEBAR.

Trap: *You might not be able to see all the files on one screen.*

If you've accumulated more than 36 files on one disk or in one directory, you'll be unable to see all their names on one List Files screen. Just move the cursor down with the DOWN ARROW key or another cursor movement key until the other files come into view. You can tell if there are more files than you can see on one screen. If the line separating the two columns contains an arrow at the bottom (as it does in Figure 13-1), then move the cursor down in order to see additional files. Conversely, if the line separating the two columns contains an arrow at the top, then move the cursor up to view additional files.

Tip: *You can move through the list of files by performing a name search.*

In addition to moving from file to file with the cursor movement keys, you can move to a specific file by using the Name Search option on the List Files menu. Type the letter **N** or press the →SEARCH (F2) key. The menu disappears from the bottom of the List Files screen, and the following prompt appears in the lower right-hand corner:

(Name Search: Enter or arrows to Exit)

Then, begin to type the filename. Type the letter **C**, for example, and the cursor moves to the first file that begins with the letter C. Type a second character and the cursor jumps to the first file that begins with those two characters. Stop typing characters as soon as enough have been provided so that WordPerfect highlights the file to which you wish to move the cursor. (If you make a typing error, use the BACKSPACE or DEL key to correct it.) Then press EXIT (F7) or CANCEL (F1) to exit the Name Search option; now you can choose another option on the List Files menu, and that option will focus on the highlighted file. Or press an arrow key to exit Name Search and, at the same time, move the cursor.

Tip: *Refer to the List Files screen to determine when to switch to a new floppy disk.*

A standard, double-sided, double-density disk—used on computers such as the

IBM PC—can store approximately 360,000 bytes, comparable to approximately 120 to 180 single-spaced pages of text. A standard, double-sided, quad-density disk—used in the quad-density drive of the standard IBM AT—can store four times as much. Although the capacity of hard disks varies, the smallest hard disk usually holds at least 29 times as much information as a double-density disk.

Clearly, a double-density disk fills to capacity first (although the others also fill up eventually). To determine how much free space is still available on a disk, check the List Files header, and refer to the item "Free:." As disk space gets low, consider erasing unwanted files (as described in a later section of this chapter, "Managing Files on Disk") or switching to an empty disk.

When does disk space get low? When do you switch to a new disk? That depends on the size of your largest file. When you revise a file and resave it, WordPerfect temporarily saves both the original file and the revision on the disk. If you want the revision to be stored on that disk, then you must have available enough room to accommodate two copies of the file. If your largest file occupies 15,000 bytes, for example, then retain *at least* 15,000 bytes of available disk space.

There's a second capacity consideration as well. If you're a floppy disk user who uses the Timed Backup option (described in Appendix B) to store temporary backup files (such as WP{WP}.BK1) onto drive B, you must also make room for WordPerfect to store those files. For example, save an additional 15,000 bytes if your largest file occupies 15,000 bytes.

Trap: *The date and time on the List Files screen will be incorrect if you bypass the date and time when starting the computer.*

If, as suggested in Chapter 1, you enter the correct date and time at the beginning of a WordPerfect session (or if you have an internal clock that records the time even when the computer is off), WordPerfect can keep track of the time for the rest of that session. When you save the document, WordPerfect then stamps the current date and time onto that file. If you bypass the date and time at the beginning of a WordPerfect session, however, then WordPerfect will not display the correct date and time on your file when you save it. (To correct the date and time, you can go temporarily to DOS, a procedure described in the last section of this chapter, "Accessing the Disk Operating System.")

Tip: *You can change the default drive before or after you view the List Files screen.*

In Chapter 11, you learned how to alter the default drive without using the List Files menu, as follows: (1) press the LIST FILES (F5) key, (2) press the EQUAL key (=), and (3) type in the new default drive or directory (such as A:, C:\WPER\SUE, and so on), and (4) press ENTER. If you press ENTER a second time, you will view the List Files screen for the new default drive/directory.

You can also change the default directly from the List Files screen: (1) from the List Files menu, select Other Directory (7 or O), (2) type in the new default drive or directory, and (3) press ENTER. If you press ENTER again, you can view a list of files in that drive or directory.

Using either of these methods, you modify the default drive for an entire working session (or until you change it again).

Tip: *You can display a list of files in drives or directories other than the default drive/directory.*

To *temporarily* display files in another drive or directory from within the List Files screen:

1. Position the cursor at the upper left-hand corner of the list, on the item **. <CURRENT> <DIR>**, as shown in Figure 13-1.
2. Press ENTER or select Look (6 or L).
3. Type in another drive or directory (such as A:, C:\WPER\SUE, and so on).
4. Press ENTER.

In addition, if you remain in the same disk drive (typically on a hard disk) but wish to take a look at files in a different directory, you have a second option. As you know, directories are structured like family trees: a subdirectory might have a parent above it or a subdirectory below it. If you wish to view files in the parent of the current directory: (1) move the cursor to the item on the List Files screen that reads **.. <PARENT> <DIR>**, (2) press ENTER or select Look (6 or L), and (3) press ENTER again.

If the directory you wish to see is a subdirectory of the one currently on screen: (1) move the cursor to that subdirectory name, (2) press ENTER or select Look (6 or L), and (3) press ENTER again. Continue with these steps and you can view files anywhere in the directory structure.

Using either method, you are getting a temporary look at the contents of another drive/directory, but you are *not* changing the default. When you exit the List Files screen and later press LIST FILES (F5) and ENTER, WordPerfect again displays the files for the default drive/directory.

There is also a method to view the List Files screen for the directory on your hard disk that you last looked at, whether or not it is the default: press LIST FILES (F5) *twice* in a row, instead of pressing LIST FILES (F5) and ENTER. For instance, suppose that the default directory is C:\WPER\DATA and that you temporarily display a list of files in C:\WPER\SUE. Then you press CANCEL (F1) to exit the List Files screen. If you then press LIST FILES (F5) twice in a row, you will be returned automatically to the list of files in the directory you last displayed, which is C:\WPER\SUE (in fact, the cursor will be located on the last file you highlighted before exiting List Files). Conversely, if you press LIST FILES (F5) and ENTER, you will be shown a list of files in C:\WPER\DATA, the default. Pressing LIST FILES twice is convenient to quickly return to a list of files in a certain directory that you last displayed and that is not the default.

Trap: *Don't forget to type a colon (:) after specifying a disk drive.*

WordPerfect recognizes a drive only when a letter is followed by a colon. If, when prompted for a new directory, you type **A:**, WordPerfect understands that you're referring to a disk drive. If you type just **A**, WordPerfect assumes that you're referring to a document on the default drive with the filename A. When referring to a drive, therefore, always follow the drive letter with a colon, such as A: or B:. You can insert a backslash (\ ) (as in A:\ or B:\), although this is unnecessary if you're referring to a drive that has not been subdivided into directories.

Tip: *The question mark (?) and the asterisk (*) are wild cards, available when you wish to restrict the List Files screen to specific files.*

You probably follow a pattern when naming your files (a procedure that is recommended in Chapter 11 because it enables you to identify the contents of your files by a glance at their filenames). For example, you might give all letters the extension .LTR, or you might have all files written by Betty Brown start with the letters BB. Then you can request that WordPerfect provide a list of only those files.

Two wild cards can be used when you request a restricted list of files in a drive/directory: the question mark (?), which represents one single character, and the asterisk (*), which represents any number of characters.

Press the LIST FILES key, and when WordPerfect prompts

Dir B: *.*

or

Dir C: \WPER \DATA *.*

the two asterisks mean that WordPerfect will display a list of all files, regardless of filename or extension. To indicate a list of specific files, you must edit this prompt.

If you wish to view only those files with the extension .LTR in drive B, for example, then edit the prompt to read

Dir B: *.LTR

To view files with an extension that starts with L, ends with R, and has any letter in the middle, and are in drive B, change the prompt to

Dir B: *.L?R

If you wish to view only those files that begin with the letters BB in the \WPER \DATA directory, then change the prompt to read

Dir C: \WPER \DATA \BB*.*

Note: The end of the prompt must read BB*.*, and not BB.*. The BB*.* tells WordPerfect to list those files that have a filename *starting* with BB, followed by any additional characters and having any extension. On the other hand, BB.* indicates files named simply BB and having any extension.

Now press ENTER. Only the files with the filename pattern that you specified will be displayed.

Trap: *Don't use wild cards when specifying a drive or directory.*

Use wild cards only when referring to filenames, and not when specifying a drive or directory. For example, if you type in a drive as *:\, WordPerfect responds

ERROR: Invalid drive/path specification

Tip: *Use the PRINT key to produce a list of files on paper.*

You can print out a copy of the files contained in a specific drive/directory. With the List Files screen displayed, simply press the PRINT (SHIFT + F7) key. A sample of the printed result is shown in Figure 13-2. WordPerfect indicates the current date, the time, and available disk space, and then lists the files on that drive or directory.

Tip: *(When upgrading from 4.2.) In version 5, the List Files screen has changed slightly.*

The most visible change on the List Files screen is in the header, which now contains two more pieces of information than it did previously—the amount of space used and the number of files in the current drive/directory. Moreover, an arrow now indicates if there are more files in the drive/directory than can be displayed on one screen.

If, in version 5 (as in version 4.2), you press LIST FILES (F5) and ENTER, WordPerfect displays the List Files screen for the default drive/directory. But a new feature in version 5 allows you to return to the List Files screen for the directory you just looked at; to do this, press LIST FILES (F5) twice in a row.

```
12/21/88  11:07                  Directory C:\WPER\DATA\*.*
Free:  3557376

. <CURRENT>     <DIR>                       .. <PARENT>     <DIR>
005       .CRG     993  02/16/88 23:41      1001      .CRG   48173  06/16/88 15:55
5008      .CRG    1312  07/22/88 02:08      5012      .CRG   35605  10/04/88 20:41
5028      .CRG   29573  10/04/88 20:42      88ANN     .RPT   21212  02/09/88 11:23
88ANN2    .RPT   35597  10/04/88 20:41      88ANN3    .RPT   35597  10/04/88 20:41
88RENT    .      43544  06/16/88 15:56      ACCOUNTS.        36762  02/21/88 15:41
BBS009    .1     21212  02/09/88 11:23      BBS009    .2      4754  02/09/88 12:45
BBS009    .3      2703  04/04/88 19:56      BKGROUND.88        778  02/23/88 13:28
BOOKKEEP.         1830  02/24/88 02:43      BUDMIN    .       2887  04/04/88 19:56
BUDMIN88.        28120  10/04/88 20:43      CBS&RP    .       2666  02/10/88 10:59
CEO1      .MMO    1356  07/22/88 00:56      DOCLIS2   .MS     3241  10/04/88 20:40
DOCLIST1.LZ      40753  02/14/88 19:00      DOCLIST1.MS      40756  10/04/88 20:39
DOCLIST2.LZ      40753  02/14/88 19:00      FON       .      28120  10/04/88 20:43
J&B       .MMO    2317  09/16/88 20:36      JONES1    .MMO    1356  07/22/88 00:56
JONES2    .MMO    5936  02/11/88 01:01      LINKER    .MS     1206  09/16/88 20:36
LINKER2   .      35597  10/04/88 20:40      MEYERS-1.MS       1206  09/16/88 20:36
P&L       .      35597  10/04/88 20:40      ROGERS    .LET     714  02/15/88 03:21
SALVA     .       4537  09/16/88 20:37      SALVA%    .      29573  10/04/88 20:43
SS-45     .      40970  10/04/88 20:40      T18       .MMO     921  04/04/88 19:58
T6        .MMO    1463  02/22/88 11:31
```

Figure 13-2. A printout of a List Files screen

The Name Search option has also been altered. You cannot simply start typing a letter of the alphabet and have the cursor move to a filename that begins with that letter; you must type the letter **N** or press the →SEARCH (F2) key first, and then start typing characters. (The extra keystroke is required because of the mnemonics added on the List Files menu.)

Retrieving and Looking at Files

You can use the LIST FILES key to retrieve a file, as an alternative to using the RETRIEVE (SHIFT + F10) key (discussed in Chapter 11). This is often a quicker method of retrieving a file if you're a slow typist, or if you can't remember the precise spelling of a filename unless you can see it on the screen. To retrieve a file by this method,

1. Press LIST FILES (F5) and then press ENTER to view a list of files in the default drive/directory. Or type in a new drive/directory and press ENTER.
2. Move the cursor to highlight the file you wish to retrieve.
3. Select Retrieve (1 or R) from the List Files menu.

If text is currently on the Typing screen, WordPerfect prompts, asking you to verify that you wish to retrieve the highlighted file into the current document. This is a valuable prompt since, if you do not view the Typing Screen, you might forget about a document on that screen and inadvertently combine two documents. Type **Y** to retrieve the file; the List Files screen disappears as WordPerfect retrieves the document to the screen at the current cursor position. Or type **N** or press ENTER to abort the command; the List Files screen remains.

Sometimes you may not know which file it is that you wish to retrieve. Or, you may wish to peek at the contents of a file without actually retrieving that file to screen. In such cases, the Look feature comes in handy.

The Look feature lets you quickly check a document's contents without actually retrieving that file. It doesn't disrupt text that is currently on the Typing screen, but it gives you a sneak preview of another document. This enables you to peruse text or to verify that a certain file contains the information you desire, before you retrieve that file. To look at a document:

1. On the List Files screen, move the cursor to highlight a file that you wish to display.
2. Select Look (6 or L), or simply press ENTER. (The reason you can press ENTER is that the List Files menu assumes your selection is Look. Notice that at the bottom of Figure 13-1 the preselected choice—the number at the end of the menu—is 6.)

   WordPerfect displays the file, with a header indicating that file's name and size. An example is shown in Figure 13-3.
3. Press any of the cursor movement keys that move the cursor up or down to peruse the contents of that file. Press EXIT (F7) or CANCEL (F1) to return to the List Files screen.

You can repeat steps 1 through 3 as often as necessary until you've located the file you are seeking. Then retrieve it as usual.

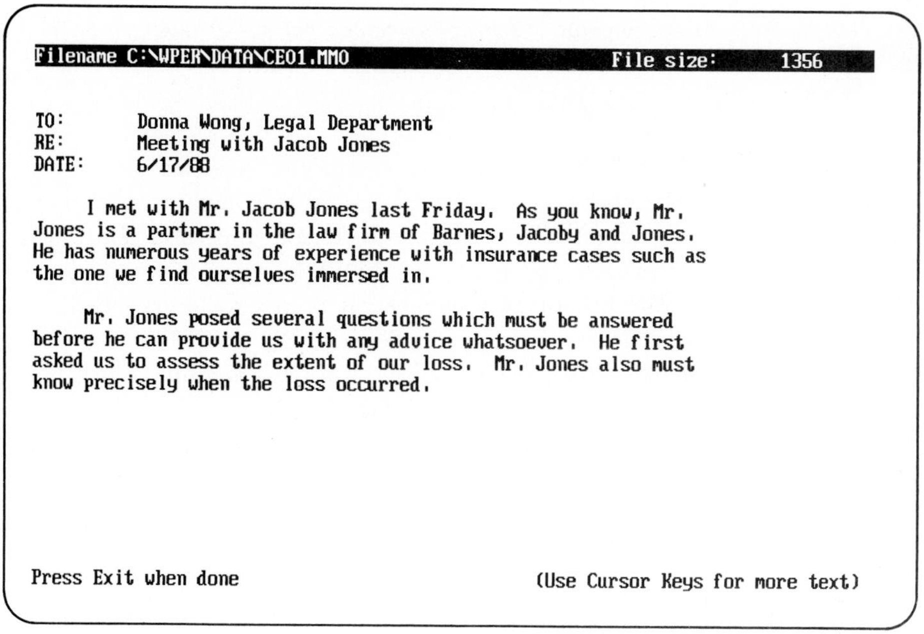

Filename C:\WPER\DATA\CE01.MMO
File size: 1356
TO: Donna Wong, Legal Department
RE: Meeting with Jacob Jones
DATE: 6/17/88
I met with Mr. Jacob Jones last Friday. As you know, Mr. Jones is a partner in the law firm of Barnes, Jacoby and Jones. He has numerous years of experience with insurance cases such as the one we find ourselves immersed in.
Mr. Jones posed several questions which must be answered before he can provide us with any advice whatsoever. He first asked us to assess the extent of our loss. Mr. Jones also must know precisely when the loss occurred.
Press Exit when done
(Use Cursor Keys for more text)

Figure 13-3. A document on the Look screen

Note: As described in the previous section of this chapter, "Displaying a List of Files," the Look feature enables you to view not only the contents of certain files, but also the contents of specified directories.

Trap: *Pressing the ENTER key won't retrieve a file.*

After you have displayed a list of files, it seems to be almost a reflex to attempt a file retrieval by highlighting a filename with the cursor and pressing ENTER. Suppress that urge. If you highlight a file and press ENTER, you will activate the Look feature, but you won't actually retrieve the file. You must select option 1, Retrieve, on the List Files menu to retrieve a file to the screen.

Trap: *You must remember to clear the screen before retrieving a document; WordPerfect does not clear it for you.*

You learned in Chapter 11 that you must remember to clear the screen before retrieving a file with the RETRIEVE key; otherwise, you may inadvertently combine documents or produce duplicates of the same text. You must also remember to clear the screen before retrieving a file from the List Files screen. On the List Files screen, this can be more difficult to remember; it is easy to forget whether the Typing screen has been cleared, since you can't see it. But check the item "Document size:" in the header on the List Files screen. If it reads anything other than 0, don't retrieve a file (unless you *want* to combine files).

One safeguard against accidentally combining files is that if you select to retrieve a document on a screen that currently contains text, WordPerfect prompts

Retrieve into current document? (Y/N) No

If you see this prompt and wish to combine files, type **Y**. But if you don't wish to combine files, then type **N** or press ENTER to abort the retrieve command. Next, return to the Typing screen and press the EXIT key to clear the screen. Now you are ready to return to the List Files screen and retrieve your document.

Tip: *If a document summary has been created for a file, it will be displayed when you use the Look feature.*

Chapter 11 describes how you can create a document summary that contains background information on a document. When you use the Look feature to glimpse at a file's contents, the document summary—if one was created for that document—is the first text displayed. An example of how a document summary appears on the Look screen is shown in Figure 13-4. You can press the DOWN ARROW key to display the text of the document.

Trap: *You can't view the contents of a locked document with the Look feature without a password.*

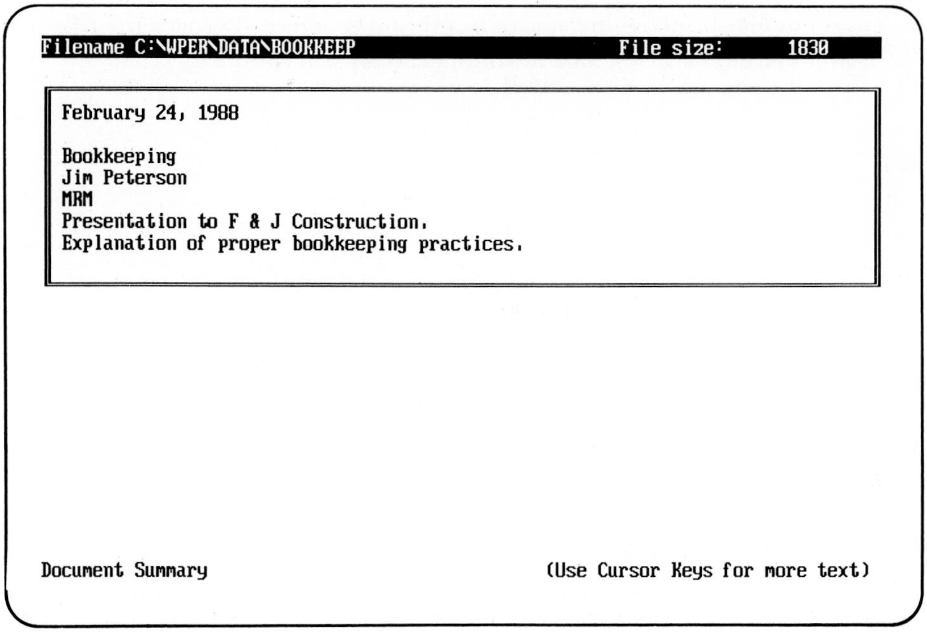

Figure 13-4. A document summary on the Look screen

When you attempt to glimpse at a locked file by using the Look feature, WordPerfect will prompt you for a password. If you don't know the password, you're out of luck; you can't view the file's contents. (See Chapter 11 for more on locking files with a password.)

Trap: *Not all of a document's format is displayed on the Look screen.*

Technically, when you use the Look feature to view a document, the document has not yet been retrieved into WordPerfect. Certain formatting specifications—

such as double spacing—are not reflected on the screen. Retrieve the file, however, and the format of the document appears as you specified.

Tip: *You can move quickly through a document on the Look screen.*

When you are viewing a document on the Look screen, several keys enable you to move quickly through the document to a specific section that you wish to review. If you press CTRL + S (or, more simply, if you type the letter **S**), the text will scroll by quickly—a convenience when you wish to check some text in the middle or at the end of a long document. Type any character to stop the scrolling.

Also, you can use the →SEARCH (F2) or ←SEARCH (SHIFT + F2) keys to move to a specific string of characters (the Search feature is described in detail in Chapter 4). The cursor moves to the left margin of the line in which the search string is located, highlighting the search string in that line of text. One limitation of this feature is that you are unable to include codes in the search string on the Look screen.

Tip: *(When upgrading from 4.2.) The Retrieve and Look features have been enhanced.*

When the Typing screen contains text and you attempt to retrieve a file using the List Files menu, WordPerfect will now prompt you, asking for verification. This is a precaution against your unintentionally retrieving the text of a file into a document already on screen. In version 4.2, it was all too easy to combine two documents without realizing it.

You can now scroll backward as well as forward in Look. Moreover, you can simply press CTRL + S, or just type **S**, to scroll quickly through a document, or you can use the Search feature to move the cursor to the line on which a specific word or phrase is located. With these enhancements, you may find yourself using the Look feature more than ever.

Searching for Files

A sophisticated feature for seeking out a file or a group of files is Word Search, which narrows the document hunt for you. WordPerfect can mark files on the List Files screen that have in common a *word pattern,* which is a word or phrase of up to 39 characters in length. That word pattern can be searched for in a document summary (for files that have one), in the first page or the first 4000 characters of a document (whichever comes first), or in the text of the entire document. To initiate a word search from the List Files screen:

1. Select Word Search (9 or W) from the List Files menu. WordPerfect displays the Search menu:

   Search: 1 Doc Summary; **2** First Page; **3** Entire Doc; **4** Conditions: **0**

2. Select from options 1, 2, or 3 to search for a word pattern. For example, select 1 or D to search for a word pattern in a file's document summary. WordPerfect prompts with:

   Word pattern:

3. Type in a word pattern up to 39 characters in length (upper- or lowercase letters are both acceptable). For example, type **ABC Corporation** to search for all files that mention that company name.

4. Press ENTER to initiate the search. WordPerfect prompts as it searches each file on the List Files screen. Or press CANCEL (F1) or EXIT (F7) to abort the search and return to the List Files screen.

After a search is performed, WordPerfect rewrites the List Files screen as in the example shown in Figure 13-5, and marks with an asterisk those files that meet the search conditions. The asterisk is located just to the right of the file size. Also, the number of marked files (and the amount of disk space occupied by those marked files) is listed next to "Marked:" and "Used:" headings provided at the top of the List Files screen. If no files are found in the current drive/directory that meet the search conditions, then no files are marked, and WordPerfect responds with:

*** Not found ***

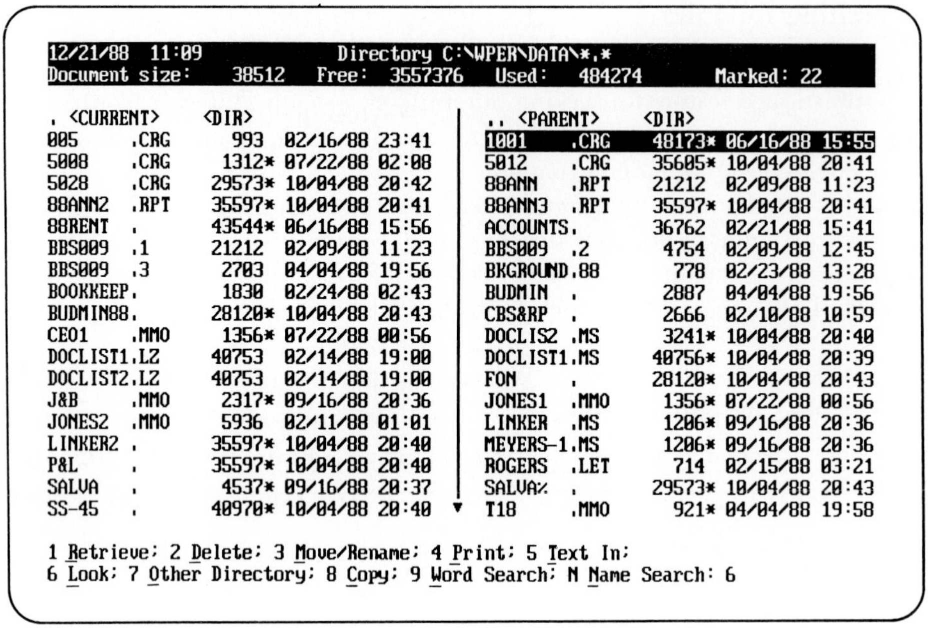

12/21/88 11:09 Directory C:\WPER\DATA*.*
Document size: 38512 Free: 3557376 Used: 484274 Marked: 22
. <CURRENT> <DIR>
005 .CRG 993 02/16/88 23:41
5008 .CRG 1312* 07/22/88 02:08
5028 .CRG 29573* 10/04/88 20:42
88ANN2 .RPT 35597* 10/04/88 20:41
88RENT . 43544* 06/16/88 15:56
BBS009 .1 21212 02/09/88 11:23
BBS009 .3 2703 04/04/88 19:56
BOOKKEEP. 1830 02/24/88 02:43
BUDMIN88. 28120* 10/04/88 20:43
CE01 .MMO 1356* 07/22/88 00:56
DOCLIST1.LZ 40753 02/14/88 19:00
DOCLIST2.LZ 40753 02/14/88 19:00
J&B .MMO 2317* 09/16/88 20:36
JONES2 .MMO 5936 02/11/88 01:01
LINKER2 . 35597* 10/04/88 20:40
P&L . 35597* 10/04/88 20:40
SALVA . 4537* 09/16/88 20:37
SS-45 . 40970* 10/04/88 20:40
.. <PARENT> <DIR>
1001 .CRG 40173* 06/16/88 15:55
5012 .CRG 35605* 10/04/88 20:41
88ANN .RPT 21212 02/09/88 11:23
88ANN3 .RPT 35597* 10/04/88 20:41
ACCOUNTS. 36762 02/21/88 15:41
BBS009 .2 4754 02/09/88 12:45
BKGROUND.88 778 02/23/88 13:28
BUDMIN . 2887 04/04/88 19:56
CBS&RP . 2666 02/10/88 10:59
DOCLIS2 .MS 3241* 10/04/88 20:40
DOCLIST1.MS 40756* 10/04/88 20:39
FON . 28120* 10/04/88 20:43
JONES1 .MMO 1356* 07/22/88 00:56
LINKER .MS 1206* 09/16/88 20:36
MEYERS-1.MS 1206* 09/16/88 20:36
ROGERS .LET 714 02/15/88 03:21
SALVA% . 29573* 10/04/88 20:43
T18 .MMO 921* 04/04/88 19:58
1 Retrieve; 2 Delete; 3 Move/Rename; 4 Print; 5 Text In;
6 Look; 7 Other Directory; 8 Copy; 9 Word Search; N Name Search: 6

Figure 13-5. The List Files screen with files marked after a word search

If the List Files screen does contain marked files, you can move the cursor in the List Files screen from one marked file to another. A quick way to move forward from one marked file to another is to press TAB. Move backward by pressing SHIFT + TAB. You can use the Look feature (as described in the previous section of this chapter, "Retrieving and Looking at Files,") to check the contents of each of the marked files, or retrieve a specific file.

You can also initiate a complicated word search in which you specify more than one search condition by using the Conditions option on the Search menu. This option enables you to find a word pattern in a document summary or in the document itself, and also to find files that have a certain file date, which is the last date the file was saved to disk (as shown on the List Files screen). You can specify a range of dates, and the file(s) that you seek must have a date that falls within that time frame. For example, you can look for files with three conditions: when the document summary lists "Joan Smith" as the typist; when the first page of the document mentions "ABC Corporation"; and when the file was last saved sometime on or after March 4, 1988. To use the Conditions option:

1. Select Word Search (9 or W) from the List Files menu. WordPerfect displays the Search menu:

   Search: 1 Doc Summary; **2** First Page; **3** Entire Doc; **4** Conditions: **0**

2. Select Conditions (4 or C). The Word Search menu, shown in Figure 13-6, is displayed. Notice that option 1 on this menu, "Perform Search on," indicates how many files will be included in the word search.

3. Select an item corresponding to the search condition, and enter the search condition. You can do one of the following:

   - Select File Date (4 or D). WordPerfect assumes that you wish your search to be based on a date, and changes the "No" to "Yes" next to the heading "File Date" in Figure 13-6. Press ENTER. Then, enter in a "From" date and a "To" date in either of the following formats—mm/dd/yy or m/d/yy. For instance, if the start of the date range is March 4, 1988, then next to the heading "From," type in **03/04/88** or **3/4/88**.

   - Select First Page (5 or F), type in a word pattern, and press ENTER. For example, type **ABC Corporation** and press ENTER.

   - Select Entire Doc (6 or E), type in a word pattern, and press ENTER.

   - Select Document Summary (7 or S) press UP ARROW or DOWN ARROW to move to the appropriate heading, type in a word pattern, and press ENTER until your cursor exits this section of the menu or press EXIT (F7) to leave this section immediately. For example, press DOWN ARROW until the cursor is next to the heading "Typist," type **Joan Smith**, and press ENTER twice.

4. Repeat step 3 if you wish to specify more than one search condition.

5. Select Perform Search on (1 or P), or press ENTER. WordPerfect prompts as it searches each file.

```
Word Search

   1 - Perform Search on                     All 37 File(s)

   2 - Undo Last Search

   3 - Reset Search Conditions

   4 - File Date                             No
         From (MM/DD/YY):                    (All)
         To   (MM/DD/YY):                    (All)

                 Word Pattern(s)

   5 - First Page
   6 - Entire Doc
   7 - Document Summary
         Creation Date (e.g. Nov)
         Descriptive Name
         Subject/Account
         Author
         Typist
         Comments

Selection: 1
```

Figure 13-6. The Word Search menu

Once the search is complete, WordPerfect rewrites the List Files screen and marks with an asterisk those files that meet *all* the search conditions. The asterisk is located just to the right of the file size. If no files are found in the current drive/directory that meet the search conditions, no files are marked, and WordPerfect returns the prompt

*** Not found ***

Tip: *It is possible to limit the files displayed on the List Files screen to a filename pattern before initiating a search.*

You learned previously that you can restrict the List Files screen to certain files that have in common a filename pattern— such as filenames that begin with the letters BB or have extensions of .LTR. This is helpful for narrowing down a list of files before initiating a search.

Suppose you wish to search through a directory that contains 80 files, but you know that all the file(s) you are seeking have a filename extension of .RPT. In this case, press LIST FILES (F5), and when WordPerfect prompts

Dir C:\WPER\DATA*.*

edit that prompt to read

Dir C:\WPER\DATA*.RPT

Press the ENTER key and WordPerfect lists only those files with the extension .RPT. Now you're ready to perform a search on only that limited list of files.

Tip: *You can specify that during a word search WordPerfect inspect only specific, marked files.*

In addition to narrowing down a search according to a filename pattern (as described in the previous Tip), you can narrow down a word search to only certain documents that you select individually. On the List Files screen, highlight a file that you wish to search through and type an asterisk (*). An asterisk then appears next to the file size number, indicating that the file is marked. (The asterisk works like a toggle switch—press the asterisk key again and that unmarks the file.) Place an asterisk next to all the files that you wish to include in the search. The upper right-hand corner of the List Files header keeps track of how many files you have marked ("Marked:") and how much disk space those marked files occupy ("Used:").

If you wish to mark the majority of files on the List Files screen, there's a quick way to do so. Instead of inserting the asterisk file by file, simply press the MARK TEXT (ALT + F5) key, or press HOME and type *. All files are marked. Now move the cursor and individually unmark the files that you don't want to include in the search.

Once the appropriate files are marked, select Word Search (9 or W). Now enter your search conditions and begin the search. If you choose to search for

Conditions (option 4 on the Search menu), you will then view the Word Search menu as shown in Figure 13-6, where WordPerfect will tell you how many files you have marked to be included in the search. When no files have been marked, then the information next to option 1, which reads "Perform Search on," indicates the total number of files that are on the List Files screen, such as "All 37 File(s)," as shown in Figure 13-5. However, suppose you marked eight files. Then that item will read "8 Marked Files." The search will be limited to the marked files only; from that list of eight, after a search, you may be left with anywhere from no marked files to eight marked files.

After the word search, you may wish to conduct another search using those newly marked files. Select Word Search (9 or W) from the List Files menu to begin another word search. Alternatively, you may wish to conduct another search on the original marked files. But because of the most recent search, you may have fewer files marked. To move back one search level, select Undo Last Search (2 or U) from the Word Search menu. For instance, if you had marked eight files and after a search you were left with two marked files, then from the Word Search menu, shown in Figure 13-6, select 2 or U; the original eight files are again marked. Now you're ready for another search.

If you clear the List Files screen by pressing EXIT (F7) or CANCEL (F1) and you wish to return to that screen with the same files marked, then press LIST FILES (F5) twice in a row rather than pressing LIST FILES (F5) and the ENTER key.

There's a quick way to move the cursor to each marked file on the List Files screen. Press TAB to jump forward to the next marked file, or press SHIFT + TAB to move backward to the previous marked file.

Trap: *Don't forget to check all items on the Word Search menu before performing a new search.*

If you've already performed a word search from the Word Search menu (which is shown in Figure 13-6), WordPerfect retains in memory the most recently used search conditions when you perform another search. Remember that if you are about to perform another search on the Word Search menu (meaning that you selected option 4, Conditions, from the Search menu), a file must meet *all* the conditions in order to be marked. Thus, be sure to check all the items on the Word Search menu, and change them appropriately, before performing a new search.

Tip: *You have flexibility in specifying file dates.*

When you wish to perform a word search for files last saved on specific dates, or during a certain range of time, you have a variety of options. You can leave an item blank when entering a date to indicate a range. For example, to enter July 1988, type **7//88**. Here are some additional examples:

- To specify only those files last saved on February 15, 1988, type information next to both the "From" and "To" headings as **2/15/88**.
- To specify those files last saved before February 15, 1988, leave the "From" blank (in which case WordPerfect assumes "All"). Type the "To" date as **2/15/88**.
- To specify those files last saved since September 1988, type the "From" date to read **9//88**, and leave the "To" date blank.

Tip: *Follow certain rules when you indicate a word pattern of two or more words.*

You can search for a word pattern either within a document summary or within the text of the document itself. When your word pattern contains two or more words, WordPerfect abides by certain rules. If you type words separated by a space or a semicolon (;), the program searches for documents that contain both words, in any order. For example,

FURNITURE SALE

refers to files that contain *both* "furniture" *and* "sale". The same applies to

FURNITURE;SALE

If you type words separated by a comma, WordPerfect searches for documents that contain *either* word. For example, typing

FURNITURE,SALE

finds files that contain "furniture" *or* "sale".

If you type words with a space between them and enclosed in quotation marks, WordPerfect searches for documents that contain that phrase with the words in that exact order. For example, typing

"FURNITURE SALE"

finds files containing the phrase "furniture sale".

You can combine spaces, semicolons, quotation marks, and commas in a word pattern. WordPerfect performs the operation from left to right. For example, typing

"FURNITURE SALE",TABLES LAMPS

finds documents that contain the phrase "furniture sale" *or* that mention both tables *and* lamps.

Uppercase and lowercase letters make no difference when typing a word pattern.

Tip: *Wild cards are acceptable in a word pattern.*

You learned in the first section of this chapter, "Displaying a List of Files," about using the wild cards (?) and (*) when specifying files in a filename pattern. You can use the same two wild cards in a word pattern. The question mark (?) stands for one character, while the asterisk (*) represents any number of characters.

Suppose you want to search for documents that mention employee identification numbers, where those employee numbers all start with the characters MD1 and end with the number 5. As a word pattern you can type

MD1*5

WordPerfect then matches numbers such as MD15, MD1225, MD19755, MD19933a5, or MD145593m5.

Or, if you want to search for only those documents mentioning employee identification numbers with two characters after the MD1 and ending with the number 5, type the following as your word pattern:

MD1??5

WordPerfect then matches numbers such as MD1225 and MD1285.

Tip: *(When upgrading from 4.2.) Word Search is now a powerful feature.*

The Word Search feature has been completely revamped in version 5, offering you some sophisticated search capabilities—such as searching by date, by specific items in a document summary, by a word pattern in the document itself, or by a combination of these. Also, the ability to reset search conditions to address previously marked files is available.

Managing Files

The LIST FILES key assists you in maintaining an orderly filing system of documents, which includes the ability to rename files, move files, delete files, and copy files.

Renaming files is convenient if a filename you chose previously turns out to be cryptic or if you decide to change your filing system. To rename a file:

1. Highlight a document on the List Files screen.
2. Select Move/Rename (3 or M). WordPerfect responds

   New name:

   and suggests the current filename. For example, if the cursor is on the file named ROGERS.LET, which is in the directory \WPER\DATA on the hard disk, then WordPerfect prompts

New name: C:\WPER\DATA\ROGERS.LET

3. Edit the prompt to type in a new filename and press ENTER. The change is reflected in moments on the List Files menu. For example, edit the prompt to read

    New name: C:\WPER \DATA\SMITH.LET

    if you wish to rename the file SMITH.LET. Press ENTER.

Moving files is useful when you realize that a file you saved is more appropriately housed on a different disk or in another directory. WordPerfect copies the file to the new drive or directory indicated and deletes the file from the original drive or directory where it had been stored. To move a file, follow steps 1 and 2 above as if you were about to rename a file. But step 3 is different, in that you would edit the prompt to type in a new *path* and press ENTER. For example, edit the prompt to read

New name: C:\WPER\SUE\ROGERS.LET

if you wish to move the file to the subdirectory named \WPER \SUE on the hard disk. Or edit the prompt to read

New name: C:\WPER\SUE\SMITH.LET

if you wish to move the file to the subdirectory named \WPER \SUE *and* you wish to rename the file SMITH.LET, both in the same command.

When you delete old files, you reduce unnecessary clutter and you create space for new files. Suppose you wish to delete from drive B an outdated file called HARDY.LTR. To delete this file:

1. Highlight that filename on the List Files screen.
2. Select Delete (2 or D). WordPerfect responds

    Delete B:\HARDY.LTR? (Y/N) No

    WordPerfect prompts you to verify the command before it permanently erases the file from disk.

3. Type **Y** to erase the file permanently, or type **N** or press ENTER to abort the command.

Be careful when you delete a file because it will disappear for good (unless you have a separate software package, such as The Norton Utilities or Mace Utilities, which can recover a deleted file from your disk).

Copying files allows you to create an exact duplicate of a file and store it on a separate disk or in another directory. Typically, floppy disk users store an original file on one floppy disk and a copy on another. Hard disk users save the original file on the hard disk and a copy on a floppy.

Making backup copies of files is imperative. If you accidentally delete a file tomorrow, for example, you'll have a backup on another disk if you created it today. Another reason is equipment failure. Whether it is the disk itself or the disk drive that fails, one day you might be unable to retrieve a document from disk. Disks provide no warning when they fail. Precautions must be taken, whether you store documents on hard or floppy disks (hard disks can fail, too).

It is also handy to copy a file to another disk so a document can be in two places at once. Perhaps, for example, a document that you wish to work on at home is stored on the hard disk at work. You can make a copy onto a floppy disk, slip the floppy into your briefcase, and head for your home computer. To copy a file:

1. On the List Files screen, highlight the file to be copied.
2. Select Copy (8 or C). WordPerfect responds

   Copy this file to:

3. Type in the drive and directory where you will place a copy of the original file. For example, to place a copy on the disk in drive A, type **A:**. The prompt now reads

   Copy this file to: A:

4. Press ENTER. WordPerfect places a copy of that file on the disk in drive A, using the same filename.

Tip: *A well-managed, well-organized filing system saves you time.*

Why not let files accumulate in a haphazard manner and rely on WordPerfect to locate a specific one for you? Because organizing your filing system saves time, for the following reasons:

- Frequently relying on the Look or the Word Search feature because you can't remember a filename is more time-consuming than recognizing a filename on sight.
- Placing files anywhere soon entails the need to look through numerous disks or directories to find out where a specific file is stored.
- When you clutter a disk with outdated files, you occupy needed storage space and you'll run out of capacity faster than you realize.
- Chances are that an unorganized filing system is also one that hasn't been backed up onto another disk—which could be disastrous if your disk fails.

A well-managed filing system enables you to function faster, with fewer distractions. You'll be more productive, which is the goal of using a personal computer. It is wise, therefore, to take full advantage of the file management capabilities offered on the List Files menu which can help keep a well-organized set of documents on disk.

Hard disk users note that it is imperative to take full advantage of your ability to separate the hard disk into separate directories. Storing hundreds (or even thousands!) of files in the same directory quickly causes chaos: you'll have problems locating the file you want, and WordPerfect operates sluggishly on the List Files screen because of the great volume of files it must deal with. On the other hand, storing a maximum of 200 files or so in each directory creates an organized, efficient filing system. Thus, make sure to segregate your hard disk into directories that are organized by topic or person, and then store your files in the appropriate directories. If you haven't done so yet, use the Other Directory feature on the List Files menu to subdivide your hard disk now (see the Tips below for the method to do so). Then, use the Rename/Move feature on the List Files menu to reorganize the location of your files.

Tip: *You can delete, move, or copy many files at once by marking them with an asterisk.*

In a previous section of this chapter, "Searching for Files," you learned that you can mark specific files before requesting a word search. Then WordPerfect searches only the marked files. Similarly, you can mark files that you want to delete, move, or copy. WordPerfect prompts for verification that you wish to address the marked files and then deletes, moves, or copies those marked files with one command.

For example, suppose that today you created four files. You now wish to make a backup copy of each file on another disk to protect against a disk failure. Press the LIST FILES (F5) key to display the List Files screen. Move the cursor to highlight the first file and type an asterisk (*). Continue until all four files are marked. Select Copy (8 or C). WordPerfect prompts

Copy Marked Files? (Y/N) No

Type **Y** to verify. Now, in response to a second prompt, type the drive or directory to which you want the files copied. WordPerfect copies all four files at once. (To abort, type **N**, in which case WordPerfect reverts to proceeding as though you want to copy just the file highlighted by the cursor.)

You can quickly mark every file on a list for deleting, moving, or copying just as you can mark all files in a wofd search. Display the List Files screen. Then, press the MARK TEXT (ALT + F5) key, or press HOME and type *, so that an asterisk appears beside each filename. If you desire, you can then unmark individual files by highlighting the filename and typing an asterisk. Now you can delete, move, or copy all the files on the List Files screen that are marked by using one command.

When the List Files screen contains marked files, move the cursor to the next marked file quickly by pressing TAB, and move to the previous marked file by pressing SHIFT + TAB.

If you clear the List Files screen by pressing EXIT (F7) or CANCEL (F1) and wish to return to that screen with the same files marked, then press LIST FILES (F5) twice in a row rather than pressing LIST FILES and ENTER.

Tip: *Hard disk users who maintain small directories can save time and avoid the DOS BACKUP command.*

A hard disk holds much more information than the approximately 360,000 bytes (120 to 180 pages) that can fit on one 5 1/4-inch, double-density floppy disk. That's why it is common practice to segment a hard disk into directories so that order is maintained on disk.

Don't keep too many files in one directory or you'll find that the List Files screen is quite slow to work with. How much the screen slows down depends on your computer and on the amount of memory it is equipped with; if, when you press LIST FILES, it takes five seconds or so for the List Files screen to appear, then consider moving some files to another directory.

Another reason to maintain small directories is to avoid the use of the BACKUP command. You've learned about the importance of making a second copy of files so that if a disk is damaged, you have a backup of your files. BACKUP is a DOS command used to make a backup copy of all files from a hard disk onto floppies. It prompts you when a floppy disk is full, so that you know when a new one needs to be inserted in order to continue the backup procedure. Many users find this command to be cumbersome. If you maintain fewer than 360,000 bytes in each directory on a hard disk, you can bypass DOS and the BACKUP command entirely when backing up files onto a 5 1/4-inch, double-density disk. (Or, maintain less than 1.2 MB if you use quad-density disks.) Instead, you can use WordPerfect's Copy option on the List Files menu to copy an entire subdirectory onto a floppy. All the files in each directory will fit onto one floppy.

Trap: *Don't delete any WordPerfect system files.*

The WordPerfect program is stored in files on your WordPerfect diskettes. (If you're a hard disk user, these files reside on your hard disk, most likely in a separate directory from where you store your data.) Do not erase any of these files or the program will not work properly. In general, do not erase any file with a filename that starts with WP or {WPI or that has an extension of .FIL, .EXE, .WP, or .TST. Examples of WordPerfect files that must not be erased include WP.EXE, WP.DRS, WP.FIL, WP.MRS., and WP{WP}.SET. In most cases, WordPerfect's Delete feature will not even allow you to erase these files (and thus you would be forced to use a DOS command if you did want to erase a WordPerfect file from disk). Refer to Appendix A for a complete list of WordPerfect files.

Tip: *You can create or delete a subdirectory by using the LIST FILES (F5) key.*

If you've already set up directories to partition your hard disk into manageable sections, you've probably used the MKDIR (MD) command in DOS to make a directory. You've also probably used the RMDIR (RD) command to remove one. With WordPerfect, you can use the LIST FILES key instead.

You can create a directory in the same way that you change the default for a working session. For example, to create a directory called WPER \BUD:

1. Press the LIST FILES (F5) key.
2. Press the EQUAL (=) key.
3. Instead of the directory that WordPerfect suggests, type **C: \WPER \BUD**.
4. Press ENTER. WordPerfect prompts

    Create C: \WPER \BUD? (Y/N) No

5. Type **Y** to create that new directory.

You can also create a directory when viewing the List Files screen. Select option 7, Other Directory, and follow steps 3 through 5 above.

If you wish to delete a subdirectory, display the List Files screen for the parent directory of the subdirectory you wish to delete. Now, highlight the subdirectory you wish to delete and select Delete (2 or D). When WordPerfect prompts you for a verification, type **Y**. Keep in mind that you can only delete a directory that contains no files. If a directory contains files, WordPerfect prompts

ERROR: Directory not empty

You must then erase all the files from that subdirectory before you can erase the subdirectory itself.

Tip: *(When upgrading from 4.2.) WordPerfect now makes it easy to move files between disks and/or directories.*

The Copy and Delete options on the List Files menu operate as they did in version 4.2. The Other Directory option is identical to what used to be called the Change Directory option.

The major enhancement in enabling you to manage files is WordPerfect's new Rename/Move option. Not only can you rename files as you could before, but in version 5 you can quickly move files to a new location. In version 4.2, you moved files in several steps—by copying those files to their new location and then deleting them from their old location.

Another enhancement on the List Files screen is that if you use an asterisk to mark specific files for deleting, moving, or copying, you can move the cursor quickly between those files—forward with the TAB key and backward with the SHIFT + TAB key.

Accessing the Disk Operating System (DOS)

Those of you who are familiar with DOS have undoubtedly observed that by using the LIST FILES key you can do a good part of what you would otherwise rely on DOS to accomplish. If you're more comfortable with the DOS commands or wish to complete certain tasks not possible from within WordPerfect, then DOS is easily available. You can go to DOS temporarily from within WordPerfect.

To go to DOS, press the SHELL (CTRL + F1) key. WordPerfect displays the following:

1 Go to DOS: **0**

Select Go to DOS (1 or G). The WordPerfect Typing screen temporarily disappears, and a DOS prompt appears—such as C:\WPER\DATA> or C> or A:\>. A message above the DOS prompt indicates that to return to WordPerfect, you must type the word **exit** at the DOS prompt and press the ENTER key.

Trap: *You can't access DOS unless the COMMAND.COM file is available.*

When you access DOS, the computer looks for a DOS file called COMMAND.COM. If you are a floppy disk user, that file is on the disk you used to load DOS and WordPerfect. Make sure that disk is in drive A or you'll be unable to exit to DOS temporarily.

Trap: *If there's insufficient memory, you can't access DOS temporarily.*

In order to access DOS temporarily, your computer must have sufficient memory available to load a copy of the command processor. If it doesn't, WordPerfect won't exit temporarily. Your alternatives, then, are either to wait until you exit WordPerfect before using DOS, or to purchase more RAM (which is possible for most, but not all, computers).

Tip: *Exit to DOS differently if you use the WordPerfect Library.*

The SHELL key can manage the integration of many WordPerfect Corporation products. If you use WordPerfect along with the WordPerfect Library, then pressing the SHELL key brings up a different menu than when you use WordPerfect alone. You must first choose the option called Go to Shell. From there you can exit to DOS.

Tip: *Review your DOS manual if you're unfamiliar with the DOS commands.*

Certain tasks can be performed only in DOS. One of these is using the FORMAT command, for example, which prepares a disk to store information. In addition, floppy disk users can use the DISKCOPY command to make an exact duplicate of an entire disk. Hard disk users can use the BACKUP command to make copies of files from the hard disk to many floppies. The DOS manual provides details about these and other commands (see Appendix A for a review of the FORMAT command).

Trap: *Certain tasks should not be performed when you exit to DOS temporarily.*

When exiting to DOS temporarily, avoid using the CHKDSK/F and DELETE commands with files on the WordPerfect disk. In addition, although you can run another program while in DOS temporarily, do not *load* any TSR programs at this point. TSR, which stands for "Terminate and Stay Resident," refers to software programs such as SideKick, which remain in memory and out of the way until you call upon them. Always load TSR programs at the beginning of a working session—when you first turn on your computer but before loading WordPerfect.

Tip: *WordPerfect can work with DOS text files.*

Chapter 1 mentions that a batch file, written in DOS, can be a useful tool for loading WordPerfect automatically (Appendix A describes the procedure for creating a batch file). Using the LIST FILES key, you can retrieve a DOS text file, such as a batch file, and edit the file with the WordPerfect editing keys. Those of you who have modified a batch file in DOS will appreciate the advantages of this right away. Similarly, you can export WordPerfect files into DOS format (refer to Chapter 28 for details).

Trap: *Don't forget to return to WordPerfect and exit before turning off the computer.*

Chapter 1 implores you not to turn off the computer until you exit WordPerfect properly and see the DOS prompt on the screen. When you go to DOS temporarily, the DOS prompt is in full view, but you have not left WordPerfect properly. Don't forget to return to WordPerfect and press EXIT (F7) to quit WordPerfect before you touch the power switch.

Tip: *(When upgrading from 4.2.) The ability to go temporarily to DOS operates just as it did previously.*

Go to DOS by using the SHELL (CTRL + F1) key, just as you did in version 4.2.

Tips and Traps Summary

Displaying a List of Files

Trap: You might not be able to see all the files on one screen.

Tip: You can move through the list of files by performing a name search.

Tip: Refer to the List Files screen to determine when to switch to a new floppy disk.

Trap: The date and time on the List Files screen will be incorrect if you bypass the date and time when starting the computer.

Tip: You can change the default drive before or after you view the List Files screen.

Tip: You can display a list of files in drives or directories other than the default drive/directory.

Trap: Don't forget to type a colon (:) after specifying a disk drive.

Tip: The question mark (?) and the asterisk (*) are wild cards, available when you wish to restrict the List Files screen to specific files.

Trap: Don't use wild cards when specifying a drive or directory.

Tip: Use the PRINT key to produce a list of files on paper.

Tip: (When upgrading from 4.2.) In version 5, the List Files screen has changed slightly.

Retrieving and Looking at Files

Trap: Pressing the ENTER key won't retrieve a file.

Trap: You must remember to clear the screen before retrieving a document; WordPerfect does not clear it for you.

Tips and Traps Summary (*continued*)

Tip: If a document summary has been created for a file, it will be displayed when you use the Look feature.

Trap: You can't view the contents of a locked document with the Look feature without a password.

Trap: Not all of a document's format is displayed on the Look screen.

Tip: You can move quickly through a document on the Look screen.

Tip: (When upgrading from 4.2.) The Retrieve and Look features have been enhanced.

Searching for Files

Tip: It is possible to limit the files displayed on the List Files screen to a filename pattern before initiating a search.

Tip: You can specify that during a word search WordPerfect inspect only specific, marked files.

Trap: Don't forget to check all items on the Word Search menu before performing a new search.

Tip: You have flexibility in specifying file dates.

Tip: Follow certain rules when you indicate a word pattern of two or more words.

Tip: Wild cards are acceptable in a word pattern.

Tip: (When upgrading from 4.2.) Word Search is now a powerful feature.

Managing Files on Disk

Tip: A well-managed, well-organized filing system saves you time.

Tips and Traps Summary (*continued*)

Tip: You can delete, move, or copy many files at once by marking them with an asterisk.

Tip: Hard disk users who maintain small directories can save time and avoid the DOS BACKUP command.

Trap: Don't delete any WordPerfect system files.

Tip: You can create or delete a subdirectory by using the LIST FILES (F5) key.

Tip: (When upgrading from 4.2.) WordPerfect now makes it easy to move files between disks and/or directories.

Accessing the Disk Operating System (DOS)

Trap: You can't access DOS unless the COMMAND.COM file is available.

Trap: If there's insufficient memory, you can't access DOS temporarily.

Tip: Exit to DOS differently if you use the WordPerfect Library.

Tip: Review your DOS manual if you're unfamiliar with the DOS commands.

Trap: Certain tasks should not be performed when you exit to DOS temporarily.

Tip: WordPerfect can work with DOS text files.

Trap: Don't forget to return to WordPerfect and exit before turning off the computer.

Tip: (When upgrading from 4.2.) The ability to go temporarily to DOS operates just as it did previously.

14

Printing a Document

The prediction that computers would mean the end of our paper-oriented society has yet to come true. While it is true that more and more people are exchanging information directly via computers, for the most part, the final product is still, ultimately, a piece of paper. People are more accustomed to sending and receiving communications on paper.

WordPerfect can help you with your printed communications, taking full advantage of your printer's capabilities. You can print a WordPerfect document quickly, easily, and as many times as you wish. If you print a document and then discover a typing error, you can edit the document on screen and simply print it out again — either the entire document or just the corrected pages. Each time you tell WordPerfect to print all or part of a document, you create a *print job.* Each print job is added to a *job list,* and is printed in the order requested; it must wait its turn on the list, just like we must wait in line for our turn at the bank. This chapter describes the alternatives for routing documents to the printer, that is, printing from screen or printing from disk. You'll also learn how to control print jobs once they are in the job list (such as how to cancel a print job), and about print options and special print features. Make sure that you have selected a printer, as described in Appendix A, before you read on.

Note that the next chapter offers methods for uncovering the capabilities of your printer and for troubleshooting if your printer isn't printing properly or if it refuses to print.

Printing from the Screen

One of WordPerfect's finest features is its ability to print any document currently on screen. This is pure convenience; you can print a document within seconds of editing it. Print an entire document, or just one page, as follows:

1. Turn on your printer and, if necessary for your printer, position your paper so that the print head (the mechanism that prints the actual characters) is at the top of a page.
2. If you plan to print a whole document, position the cursor anywhere within that document. Or, if you plan to print one page, locate the cursor anywhere on that page.
3. Press the PRINT (SHIFT + F7) key. WordPerfect displays the Print screen, as shown in Figure 14-1 (which assumes the HP LaserJet Series II as the selected printer).
4. If you want to print the entire document, select Full Document (1 or F). Or, if you want to print only the page on which the cursor is currently located, select Page (2 or P).

The Print menu clears from the screen, you are returned to your document, and in moments the printer starts operating. After the text is printed, the final page of the job feeds completely through the printer so that the printer is ready for the next print job.

It is handy to print from the screen if a document is already on screen. In fact, there's no need to save a document to disk if you never plan to edit, print, or refer to that document again. Just type the text, print it, and clear the screen; the text hasn't occupied any space on the disk. However, do remember to save your document (see Chapter 11) if you wish to edit or print that document in the future.

Trap: *Sometimes it takes a few moments before printing begins.*

```
Print

     1 - Full Document
     2 - Page
     3 - Document on Disk
     4 - Control Printer
     5 - Type Through
     6 - View Document
     7 - Initialize Printer

Options

     S - Select Printer                  HP LaserJet Series II
     B - Binding                         0"
     N - Number of Copies                1
     G - Graphics Quality                Medium
     T - Text Quality                    High


Selection: 0
```

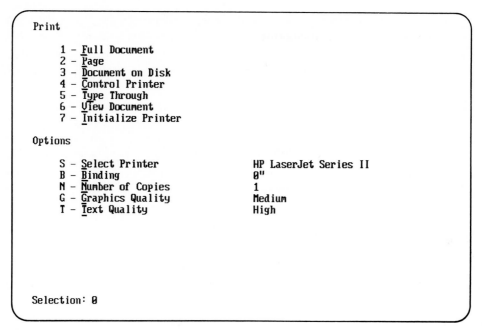

Figure 14-1. The Print screen

When you print a document from screen, WordPerfect places a temporary copy of that document on disk (with a name such as WP}WP{1 if the print job is number 1) and prints the document. Thus, it may take a few seconds before printing begins. After the printing is complete, that temporary copy is erased automatically.

If you select to print just a page, and that page is not page 1 of your document, WordPerfect proceeds through the document placed in memory—starting at page 1—until it reaches the page you wish to print. Again, it may take a few seconds before printing begins.

Trap: *If you manually feed paper into the printer or the document requires a cartridge change, printing from the screen won't start automatically.*

When you initially defined your printer(s) to work with WordPerfect (as described in Appendix A), you specified various forms (such as standard, envelopes, labels, and so on) and their locations: continuous feed, sheet feed from a specific bin number, or manual feed. You also specified whether each form is initially present in your printer. For continuous or sheet-fed paper with the form defined as initially present, the paper is fed into the printer for you, and printing can begin immediately.

However, if you select a paper size/type such that paper must be placed in the printer manually or if the form is defined as not initially preset, then WordPerfect pauses before it prints and sounds a beep to signal you to insert the proper paper in the printer. Make sure the paper is inserted correctly. Then you must signal WordPerfect that it can begin to print the page. To tell WordPerfect to start printing from screen:

1. Press the PRINT (SHIFT + F7) key.
2. Select Control Printer (4 or C). The Control Printer menu appears, as shown in Figure 14-2. Notice in Figure 14-2 that next to the heading "Action," the remark reads, **Insert paper; Press "G"** to continue. At the bottom of the screen is the Control Printer menu, which lists five options.
3. Select Go (start printer) (4 or G). The printer begins to print.
4. If you are printing only one page, press EXIT (F7) to return to your document, or press CANCEL (F1) to return to the Print screen.

   Or, if you are printing more than one page, wait until one page has been printed. Then insert a new sheet of paper and again select Go (start printer) (4 or G). Continue to insert paper and select option 4 until all pages have been printed. Then press EXIT (F7) to return to your document, or press CANCEL (F1) to return to the Print screen.

Remember to select the correct paper type for the job. For instance, you would select the envelope paper type to print out a page containing an address to be printed on an envelope, for example, and you would select the standard landscape paper type to print text sideways on the page (if your printer supports landscape mode). For more on inserting paper size/type codes into your text to dictate the form in which a document or certain pages of a document will print, refer to Chapter 8.

For more information on the Control Printer menu, refer to a later section in this chapter, "Controlling Print Jobs."

You may also need to signal WordPerfect with the Go command if you inserted a font change code into your document that requires you to insert a dif-

```
Print: Control Printer

Current Job

Job Number: 2                                   Page Number:  1
Status:     Printing                            Current Copy: 1 of 1
Message:    None
Paper:      Standard 8.5" x 11"
Location:   Continuous feed
Action:     Insert paper
            Press "G" to continue

Job List

Job  Document            Destination           Print Options
 2   (Screen)            LPT 1


Additional Jobs Not Shown: 0



1 Cancel Job(s); 2 Rush Job; 3 Display Jobs; 4 Go (start printer); 5 Stop: 0
```

Figure 14-2. The Control Printer screen when waiting for a "Go" signal

ferent cartridge into your printer in order for your printer to use the font you selected.

Trap: *You may be unable to print a large document from the screen.*

WordPerfect prints from the screen by creating a temporary file. This method works well as long as there's enough room on the disk. Floppy disk users, however, might encounter a "disk full" message when printing a long document; if that happens, there are several options. First, insert a disk in drive B that has more space available. Or print that file from disk (as described in the next section of this chapter).

Tip: *Use the BLOCK key to print a portion of a page or to print consecutive pages from the screen.*

WordPerfect provides only two choices on the Print menu when you print a document directly from the screen: the full document, or just one page of that document. What if you wish to print only one paragraph? Or one and one-half pages? Or four pages? You can do this by using the BLOCK key:

1. Press the BLOCK (ALT + F4) key to mark the text that you wish to print—whether it is one paragraph or four pages. **Block on** flashes on the screen.
2. Press the PRINT (SHIFT + F7) key. Instead of the Print screen appearing, WordPerfect responds

   Print block? (Y/N) No

3. Type **Y** to print the highlighted text. The printer starts printing. Or type **N** or press any key other than **Y** to cancel the command.

If you type **Y**, the block will begin printing, starting at the top of the paper in the printer (abiding by top margin settings), even if that block is located near the bottom of the page on screen.

Tip: *Continue to perform other word processing tasks while your document is printing from screen.*

There's no need to wait until a job is printed to perform other word processing tasks. WordPerfect offers a built-in print buffer so that, after you've sent a print job to the job list, you can go on to another task—whether that task is to clear the screen and begin a new document, to edit the document on screen, or to send another job to the printer. WordPerfect is able to print a job and carry out other tasks at the same time. Be aware that WordPerfect's response time might be slower because the program is splitting its time between two different functions—printing and the other task you are performing.

Trap: *Once you send a print job to the printer, editing changes you make on that document won't be reflected in that print job.*

Because you can have WordPerfect print a document at the same time it is performing another task (see the preceding Tip), it is possible to edit the very document that you have just sent to the printer. Suppose that you've just sent a ten-page document to the printer and you then notice and correct a typographical error on page 6. Because you corrected the mistake after sending the print job, WordPerfect won't know about the correction; the original version of the document is the version that will be printed. Thus, after you correct the typo, you will have to print page 6 again.

Tip: *You may wish to select specific print options or access other print features before you print from screen.*

WordPerfect is preset with certain default settings that determine how a job is printed. For example, the middle portion of Figure 14-1 indicates that this print job will be sent to an HP LaserJet Series II printer, and that only one copy will be printed. However, you can change these settings before you print.

You may also wish to take advantage of other print features before printing. For instance, you might want to download soft fonts for a particular document. Or you may wish to view the document on screen to check its current formatting before you send it to the printer. (Refer to a later section of this chapter, "Print Options," for more information.)

Tip: *(When upgrading from 4.2.) The Print menu has been modified.*

You'll notice when you press the PRINT (SHIFT + F7) key that you no longer get a line menu at the bottom of the screen, as you did in version 4.2. Instead, a full-screen menu appears. However, the keystrokes you use to print out a full document (previously referred to as "full text"), or to print out a single page have not changed.

Printing from Disk

The alternative to printing directly from the screen is to print a document that is already stored on disk. If you print from disk, it doesn't matter what is currently on the WordPerfect Typing screen (whether it's the document you wish to print, another document, or no text at all) or where the cursor is located. And you can print in one of two ways: by using the Print menu or by using the List Files menu.

Use the Print menu when you know the filename of the document you wish to print:

1. Turn on your printer and, if necessary for your printer, position your paper so that the print head (the mechanism that prints the actual characters) is at the top of a page.
2. Press the PRINT (SHIFT + F7) key. Wordperfect displays the Print screen, as shown in Figure 14-1.
3. Select Document on Disk (3 or D). At the bottom of the Print screen, WordPerfect prompts

   Document name:

4. Type in the name of the document you wish to print (preceded by that file's drive or directory if the file is not in the default drive/directory), and press ENTER. WordPerfect prompts

   Page(s): (All)

5. Press ENTER to print all pages of the document. Or type in the page numbers you wish to print, and press ENTER (see the Tips later in this chapter section for directions on how to specify page numbers). Or press CANCEL (F1) to abort the print job.

The Print menu remains on screen after you send a print job to the printer. Now you can add other documents to the job list, or press CANCEL (F1) or EXIT (F7) to return to the Typing screen.

When you wish to print a document from disk but cannot remember its filename, you can turn to the List Files menu:

1. Turn on your printer and, if necessary for your printer, position your paper so that the print head (the mechanism that prints the actual characters) is at the top of a page.
2. Press the LIST FILES (F5) key. WordPerfect responds by prompting you with the default drive and directory.
3. If you wish to print a file stored on the default drive and directory, press ENTER.

   Or, if you wish to print a file stored elsewhere, type in a different drive and directory and press ENTER.

   WordPerfect displays the List Files screen for the drive/directory that you specified (for a full description of the options on the List Files screen, refer to Chapter 13).
4. Move the cursor to highlight the file that you wish to print.
5. Select Print (4 or P). WordPerfect prompts

   Page(s): (All)
6. Press ENTER to print all pages of the document. Or type in the page numbers for the pages you wish to print and press ENTER (see the Tips later in this chapter section for directions on how to specify page numbers). Or press CANCEL (F1) to abort the print job.

The List Files menu remains on screen after you send a print job to the printer. Continue to send other print jobs to the printer, or press CANCEL (F1) or EXIT (F7) to return to the Typing screen.

It is convenient to print from disk if the document you wish to print is very long, or if it is not currently displayed on screen. Printing from disk is also advantageous if you wish to print many documents in a row. While one document is printing, continue to follow the steps outlined above—using either the Print menu or the List Files menu—to send additional print jobs to the printer, where they will wait their turn in line to be printed.

Trap: *To print from disk, a document must be stored exactly as you wish it to be printed.*

You must store a document on disk in the same form that you want it to have when it is printed. In other words, if you have just edited a document on screen, save it to disk before you print it. If you don't, you'll print out the old version of the document rather than the recently edited version.

Trap: *WordPerfect cannot find a document to print if the filename, disk drive, or directory you specified is incorrect.*

If you wish to print a document by using the Print menu but WordPerfect cannot find that file, the following prompt appears:

ERROR: File not found

and WordPerfect prompts you to type in another document name, in order to try again.

You must type a correctly spelled filename for WordPerfect and you must include an extension if that file has one. For instance, if you originally named a file MEMO1.LJB, then you cannot type MEMO.LJB, MEMO1, or MEMO1.LB. You must type in the full name exactly as it was originally entered.

You must also indicate the drive and directory where the file is stored if it is not in the default drive/directory. For example, suppose you wish to print out a file named MEMO1.LJB. If the default directory is WPER\DATA on a hard disk, for example, but the document is stored on WPER\SUE, then when you indicate the document to be printed, type **C:\WPER\SUE\MEMO1.LJB**. (See Chapter 11 for more information on determining and changing the default drive and directory.)

Trap: *If you manually feed paper into the printer or the document requires a cartridge change, printing from disk won't start automatically.*

Just like when you print from screen, when you print from disk and your printer is defined for manual-feeding or you are using a form defined as not initially present, WordPerfect pauses before it prints each page—including the first page—and sounds a beep to signal you to insert a piece of paper in the printer.

Make sure the paper is inserted correctly. Then you must signal WordPerfect that it can begin to print each page. To tell WordPerfect to start printing from disk:

1. From the Print menu, select Control Printer (4 or C). The Control Printer menu appears, as shown in Figure 14-2. Notice in Figure 14-2 that next to the heading "Action," the remark reads, **Insert paper; Press "G"** to continue. At the bottom of the screen is the Control Printer menu, which lists five options.
2. Select Go (start printer) (4 or G). The printer begins to print.
3. Wait until one page has been printed. Then insert a new sheet of paper and again select Go (start printer) (4 or G). Continue to insert paper and select option 4 until all pages have been printed. Then press EXIT (F7) to return to your document, or press CANCEL (F1) to return to the Print screen.

For more on inserting paper size/type codes into your text to dictate the form in which a document or certain pages of a document will print, refer to Chapter 8.

For more information on the Control Printer menu, refer to a later section in the chapter, "Controlling Print Jobs."

You may also need to signal WordPerfect with the Go command if you inserted a font change code into your document that requires you to insert a different cartridge into your printer in order for your printer to use the font you selected.

Trap: *You may be unable to print from disk if you use the Fast Save option.*

WordPerfect offers the Fast Save option, whereby you can save a document to disk without formatting the document. This reduces the time it takes to save the document. As a default, Fast Save is set to "Off," but can be turned on using the Setup menu (as described in Appendix B.)

But documents stored on disk when Fast Save is *on* cannot be printed from disk unless you override Fast Save by pressing HOME, HOME, DOWN ARROW to move the cursor to the bottom of the document, just before you press SAVE (F10) or EXIT (F7) to save the document. HOME, HOME, DOWN ARROW formats the document while saving it, even if Fast Save is on.

If Fast Save is on and you do not format the document before saving it, that document can be printed only from screen, and not from disk. When you attempt to print from disk, WordPerfect displays an error message and ignores your Print command.

The Fast Save option is advantageous if you rarely print from disk, instead performing the majority of your printing tasks directly from screen.

Tip: *If you are printing a locked file from disk, WordPerfect will prompt for the correct password.*

Chapter 11 describes the Locked Document feature, whereby you can save a document to disk with a password. A locked document can be retrieved to the screen only if the user indicates the proper password. Similarly, when you attempt to print a locked document, WordPerfect prompts for its password. If the correct password is entered, WordPerfect will print the document; otherwise, WordPerfect will display the message **ERROR: Incompatible file format** and will ignore your print request.

Tip: *You can specify any range of consecutive or nonconsecutive pages that you wish to print.*

When printing from disk, whether using the Print or the List Files menu, you can print just one page, a range of consecutive pages (such as pages 4 through 8), or a range of nonconsecutive pages (such as pages 5, 9, and 16) in one print job. When WordPerfect prompts with

Page(s): (All)

proceed as follows:

- To print one page, simply type in the page number. For example, suppose you wish to print only page 4 of a document. Type **4** and press ENTER.
- To print any number of consecutive pages, type the beginning and the ending numbers of the consecutive pages, separated by a hyphen. For instance, if you wish to print pages 14 through 22, type **14-22** and press ENTER.

However, if you wish to print starting at the first page of a document, you need not specify page 1. For example, to print pages 1 through 6, you can simply type **-6** and press ENTER.

Similarly, if you wish to print ending at the last page of a document, you need not specify the last page. For example, suppose that you wish to print pages 16 through 25, where page 25 is the last page. Simply type **16-** and press ENTER.

- To print any number of nonconsecutive pages, type each page number, separated by a comma. For example, to print pages pages 3, 15, and 20, type **3,15,20** and press ENTER.

You can specify both consecutive and nonconsecutive pages in a print job. For instance, if you wish to print pages 3, 4, and 15 through 20, then type **3,4,15-20** and press ENTER.

Be sure *not* to press the SPACEBAR at any time while specifying a range of consecutive or nonconsecutive numbers, unless you use a space in place of a comma to separate distinct ranges. For example, typing **10 - 12** is incorrect. So is typing **3, 7, 9**. However, typing **3-6 10-22** is acceptable (and is identical to typing **3-6,10-22**).

(See the following Tip if you've renumbered pages in your document.)

Tip: *If you've renumbered pages in a document, use the new numbers to print selected pages.*

Chapter 9 describes how you can use the New Page Number option to renumber pages with either Roman (i, ii,. . .) or Arabic (1, 2,. . .) numerals. If you renumbered pages, then use the new numbers when specifying pages to print. For example, if you renumber an entire document to start at page 50, then, when you wish to print the second page of the document, specify page 51, not page 2. Or, if you renumber a document to start at page i, then, when you wish to print the second page, specify page ii, not page 2.

Further, you may have renumbered pages several times in the same document, alternating between Roman and Arabic numerals. You can specify sections by typing the section number followed by a colon and then the page numbers for the pages in the section that you wish to print. WordPerfect considers sections for Roman and Arabic numerals separately. If no section number is indicated, then the first page of the document that matches the entered page number is printed.

For example, suppose your document is a 20-page annual report that you divided into four sections, each numbered independently, as follows:

Pages i through iii — Introduction
Pages 1 through 5 — 1988 Profitability
Pages 1 through 10 — Projections
Pages i through ii — Index

When printing the annual report from disk, whether using the Print or the List Files menu, when WordPerfect prompts with

Page(s): (All)

proceed as follows:

- To print all of the Introduction, type either **1:i-iii** or **i-iii** and press ENTER.
- To print page 3 of the 1988 Profitability section, type either **1:3** or **3** and press ENTER.
- To print all of the Projections section, type **2:1-10** and press ENTER.
- To print page ii of the Index, type **2:ii** and press ENTER.
- To print the first page of both the 1988 Profitability section and the Projections section, type **1:1,2:1** and press ENTER.
- To print all of the 1988 Profitability section and all of the Projections section, type **1:1-2:10** and press ENTER.

Be sure *not* to press the SPACEBAR at any point before or after the colon, unless you use a space in place of a comma to separate distinct ranges. For instance, typing **2: 1-4** is incorrect. So is typing **2: 1 - 4**. However, it is acceptable to type **1:3-5 2:2-10** (which is identical to typing **1:3-5,2:2-10**).

Tip: *An advantage to printing with the List Files menu is that you can request that two or more documents be printed in one Print command.*

When printing from the List Files screen, you can mark files with an asterisk before printing; in that way, you can request that a number of documents be sent to the job list at once. WordPerfect assumes that you wish to print the full text of each document.

To print more than one document from the List Files screen, press the LIST FILES (F5) key to display a list of files for a specific drive/directory. Then move the cursor to highlight the first file you wish to print and type an asterisk (*); you have now marked that file. Continue until you've marked all files that you wish to print. (The asterisk works like a toggle switch, so to unmark a file, move the cursor back to that file and type an asterisk; the mark disappears.) Now, when you select Print (4 or P), WordPerfect prompts

Print marked files? (Y/N) No

Type **Y** to place the marked files in the job list to be printed; they will be printed in alphabetical order. Type **N** to abort the Print command.

Remember that if you print files that are marked, WordPerfect assumes that you wish to print every page in each document.

Tip: *Continue to perform other word processing tasks while your document is printing from disk.*

Just like when you print from screen, when you print from disk there's no need to wait until a job is printed to perform other word processing tasks. WordPerfect is able to print a job and carry out other tasks at the same time. Be aware that WordPerfect's response time might be slower because the program is splitting its time between two different functions—printing and another task.

Tip: *You may wish to select specific print options or access other print features before you print from disk.*

WordPerfect is preset with certain default settings that determine how a job is printed. For example, the center portion of Figure 14-1 indicates that this print job will be sent to an HP LaserJet Series II printer, and that only one copy will be printed. However, you can change these settings before you print.

You may also wish to take advantage of other print features before printing. For instance, you might want to download soft fonts for a particular document. Or you may wish to view the document on screen to check its current formatting before you send it to the printer. (Refer to a later section of this chapter, "Print Options," for more information.)

Tip: *(When upgrading from 4.2.) The ability to print from disk has been enhanced.*

In version 4.2, you printed from disk where you entered a filename via the Control Printer menu. This is no longer the case in version 5; print by selecting the Document on Disk option directly from the Print menu.

In version 5, you now have the ability to specify a range of pages when printing from the List Files menu; previously, your only choice was to print out the entire document.

Fast Save is a new feature in version 5. If you turn Fast Save on so that your documents are stored on disk more quickly, then you will be unable to print your documents from disk unless you position the cursor at the bottom of a document before saving it. (See the earlier Tips in this chapter section for details on these enhancements.)

Also, in version 5, you have the ability to print a locked file from disk; WordPerfect will prompt for the correct password. In version 4.2, you could print a locked document only from screen.

Controlling Print Jobs

As soon as you create a print job, WordPerfect assigns that job the next consecutive print number and stores the job by that number in the WordPerfect job list. As one job is printing, you can continue to request additional print jobs; each is placed on the list, waiting for its turn at the printer.

At any time you can check the status of your print jobs, cancel jobs, or change the order in the job list. To do so, press PRINT (SHIFT + F7) and select Control Printer (4 or C). You'll view the Control Printer screen. Figure 14-3 shows this screen with no jobs in the print queue, while Figure 14-4 shows the same screen after two jobs have been sent to the printer.

There are three main sections on the Control Printer screen. At the top, under the heading "Current Job," WordPerfect offers information about the job that is currently printing, as shown in Figures 14-3 and 14-4. Figure 14-3 indicates that there are no print jobs. Figure 14-4, on the other hand, indicates the current job number (5), gives the job status (printing), lists any relevant messages (none), and provides information about the paper size the job is printing on (Standard 8.5″ X 11″), the form location (continuous feed), any action required to print (none), the page number that is being sent to the printer (page 1) and what copy of the job is printing (1 of 1).

The second section offers information about all the print jobs in the job list. Under the heading "Job List," WordPerfect displays up to the next three jobs to be printed. The print job currently at the printer is listed first, followed by the two that may be waiting their turn. You can tell from this job list which document is to be printed, the printer destination (the port at the back of the computer that the printer is attached to) and whether you've chosen any special print options (which are described in the next section of this chapter, "Print Options"). Also indicated are any additional jobs not shown on the Control Printer screen

```
Print: Control Printer

Current Job

Job Number: None                                Page Number:  None
Status:     No print jobs                       Current Copy: None
Message:    None
Paper:      None
Location:   None
Action:     None


Job List

Job  Document              Destination          Print Options



Additional Jobs Not Shown: 0



1 Cancel Job(s); 2 Rush Job; 3 Display Jobs; 4 Go (start printer); 5 Stop: 0
```

Figure 14-3. The Control Printer screen with no print jobs

```
Print: Control Printer

Current Job

Job Number: 5                                   Page Number:  1
Status:     Printing                            Current Copy: 1 of 1
Message:    None
Paper:      Standard 8.5" x 11"
Location:   Continuous feed
Action:     None


Job List

Job  Document              Destination          Print Options
 5   (Screen)              LPT 1
 6   C:\WPER\DATA\BUDMIN   LPT 1


Additional Jobs Not Shown: 0



1 Cancel Job(s); 2 Rush Job; 3 Display Jobs; 4 Go (start printer); 5 Stop: 0
```

Figure 14-4. The Control Printer screen showing print jobs

(since there's only enough room to display three jobs at one time). You can see in Figure 14-4 that two jobs are listed: job 5, which is a document sent to the printer from screen; and job 6, which is a document printed from disk, whose path and filename are C:\WPER\DATA\BUDMIN.

At the very bottom of the screen is the Control Printer menu. Five options are offered, enabling you to do the following:

- **To Cancel one or more print jobs from the job list** Select Cancel Job(s) (1 or C). Then, simply press ENTER to cancel the job currently printing; or type the number of another print job you wish to cancel and press ENTER to cancel that job; or type an asterisk and, when prompted, type **Y** to confirm that you wish to cancel all the print jobs in the job list.

  For example, if job 3 is currently printing and you wish to cancel job 4, then when you select Cancel Job(s), WordPerfect prompts

  Cancel which job? (*=All Jobs) 3

  Type **4** and press ENTER; print job 4 is erased from the job list.

If you type * and type **Y** to cancel *all* jobs, WordPerfect may request additional confirmation. Type **Y** to cancel all jobs, or type **N** to abort the command.

- **To rush a print job to the top of the job list** Select Rush Job (2 or R). WordPerfect assumes that you wish to move the print job at the bottom of the job list to be the next one printed, so just press ENTER to have this done, or type in the number of another job you wish to rush and press ENTER.

  WordPerfect will prompt, asking whether you wish to interrupt the current job. Type **Y** to have the current job interrupted in order to print the rushed job (in which case the current job will continue printing *after the rushed job* is printed), or **N** to print the rushed job *after the current job* is completed. Also, if you do type **Y** to interrupt the current job, WordPerfect will assume that you wish to complete the page of the current job now printing before starting the rushed job; type **R** (as will be indicated next to the heading "Action") to stop printing even the page now printing, in order to print the rushed job immediately.
- **To display all print jobs that are currently not shown** Select Display Jobs (3 or D). The Control Printer screen disappears as WordPerfect displays a complete list of jobs waiting to be printed. As many as the last 24 jobs in the list are shown. Press any key to return to the Control Printer screen.
- **To restart the printer** Select Go (start printer) (4 or G). This command resumes the printing process after the printer has stopped automatically so you can manually insert another form or a new font cartridge (if you changed the font within a document). It also resumes the printing process after you request that the printer stop (as described in the next item in this list).
- **To stop the printer without canceling the print job** Select Stop (5 or S) and then type **Y** to confirm or **N** to abort the Stop command. This command is useful when you wish to correct a printer problem, such as a paper jam or a ribbon that runs out. After resolving the problem, be sure to reset the printer and/or advance the paper to the top of the next page and select Go (start printer) (4 or G), to restart the printing. If at least one page of a multi-page document was already printed before you selected Stop, then you are prompted to enter the page number for which printing should resume.

Tip: *After you stop or cancel a job, you may need to clear out the job list.*

Depending on your printer, after you cancel a print job you may need to select Go (start printer) (4 or G) to complete the Cancel command. WordPerfect will inform you if this is the case with a message next to the heading "Action" on the Control Printer screen.

Moreover, once you stop and then cancel a print job, you may also need to select Go (start printer) (4 or G) to complete the Cancel command. Again, WordPerfect informs you of this on the Control Printer screen. Simply select Go (start printer) to complete the command.

Trap: *Many printers won't stop immediately after you stop the printer or cancel a job.*

Many printers have a *buffer,* a storage area that holds text until the text is actually printed. Depending on the size of your printer's buffer, it may hold one page of text, more than one page, or more than one print job. When you stop or cancel the job that is currently printing, WordPerfect immediately stops sending text to the printer. However, the printer won't stop until its buffer is empty. Thus, if you wish to stop the printing immediately, turn off the printer and then turn it on again (or press the reset button on your printer, if your printer has one). This clears out the buffer.

In fact, if you want to cancel a print job immediately, you can reach over and turn off the printer before you select Cancel (1 or C) to cancel the current print job. But don't forget to select Cancel to cancel the job or the printer will start printing again as soon as you turn it back on.

Be aware that once WordPerfect sends a complete print job to the printer, that job is deleted from the job list. Therefore, if the print buffer is large enough to contain more than one print job, when you turn off the printer, all the print jobs that have already been sent to the printer are lost.

Tip: *(When upgrading from 4.2.) The options for controlling print jobs remain the same.*

The Control Printer screen now contains more information on the current job than in version 4.2. But the same options are available to control print jobs in version 5 as were available in version 4.2.

Print Options

Just as WordPerfect makes margin, tab, and other formatting assumptions, it also makes initial assumptions about five aspects of the printing process. It displays these settings on the lower half of the Print screen, as shown in Figure 14-1, under the heading "Options." These settings can be changed before you send a job to the printer.

The first setting relates to the *printer selected* for printing your document. Each time you begin a new document, WordPerfect records whatever printer is currently listed on the Print screen as the one you wish to use. Once the document is saved, that printer selection is stored with the document in a "prefix," an invisible packet of information about that document. When you retrieve that document to screen, the Print screen indicates which printer was selected for that document when you last saved it to disk. If you use only one printer, then it will be unnecessary to select a different printer once WordPerfect has been set up to work with your printer (as described in Appendix A).

If you have more than one printer, however, you can change the printer selection before printing out a job. To do this, the document for which you wish to select a new printer should be on screen. (Or the screen may be clear because you are about to type a new document.) Then follow this procedure to change your printer selection:

1. Press PRINT (SHIFT + F7) to display the Print screen, as shown in Figure 14-1.
2. Choose S, Select Printer, to view a list of currently defined printers. Figure 14-5 shows an example in which three printers have been defined (see Appendix A for the method to define printers). An asterisk appears next to the currently selected printer—the HP LaserJet Series II.
3. Move the cursor to the name of the new printer you wish to use to print out your document.
4. Choose Select (1 or S). The asterisk now moves to the printer where your cursor is located, and you are returned to the Print screen.
5. If you wish to print the document from screen, you are now ready to print a document using the currently defined printer. Select Full Document (1 or F) or Page (2 or P) from the Print screen when you're ready to print.

   If you wish to print the document from disk, you must save the document after having selected a new printer. Then you are ready to print the document from disk with the new printer selected for it.

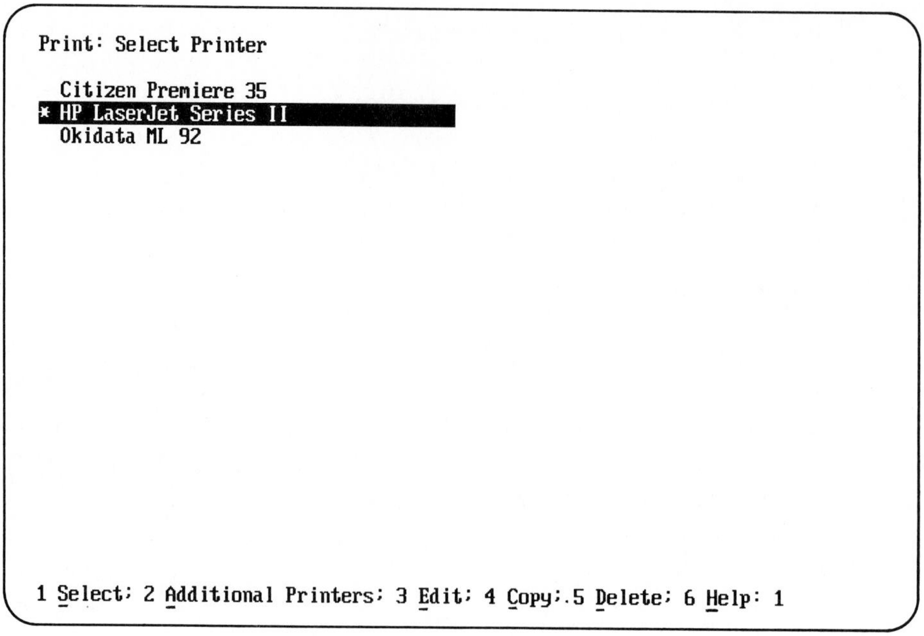

Figure 14-5. The Select Printer menu

The new printer you selected will remain in effect for all new documents you create until you again change your printer selection.

A second WordPerfect setting relates to *binding width.* WordPerfect is initially set with a binding width of zero. If you plan to bind your printed document like a book, with text on both sides of the page, then you will want to change the binding width so that text shifts by the amount you specify—to the right on odd-numbered pages and to the left on even-numbered pages—allowing space for holes or bindings. The binding width does not override your left margin, but just adds to it. To establish a binding width:

1. Press PRINT (SHIFT + F7) to display the Print screen, as shown in Figure 14-1.
2. Select B, Binding, and enter the binding-width setting. For instance, type **.5** and press ENTER to establish a one-half-inch binding width.
3. Now send your print job to the job list.

The new binding width takes effect for an entire working session, or until you change it again.

A third option concerns the *number of copies.* WordPerfect assumes that you wish to print out only one copy of each print job. If you wish to print multiple copies of a print job, modify this setting, as follows:

1. Press PRINT (SHIFT + F7) to display the Print screen.
2. Select N, Number of Copies, and enter the number of copies you wish to produce for the next print job.
3. Now send your print job to the job list.

The number-of-copies setting stays in effect for an entire working session, or until you change it again.

WordPerfect's last two settings concern the *quality level* with which your *text and/or graphics* will be printed. WordPerfect assumes that if your document contains graphics (refer to Chapter 18), then you wish to print out the graphics in medium quality, and that the text should be printed in high quality. A better quality means a better resolution on the printed page. You can use the Quality options to print only the graphics, only the text, or to print both. To change the quality:

1. Press PRINT (SHIFT + F7) to display the Print screen.
2. Select G, Graphics Quality, or T, Text Quality. WordPerfect provides a menu with four options. For example, if you selected G, the menu that displays is:

   Graphics Quality: 1 Do Not Print; **2** Draft; **3** Medium; **4** High: **3**

   The same options are available for text quality.
3. Select an option from the menu provided. The higher the quality you choose, the more time required to print the job.
4. Now send your print job to the job list.

The new graphics and text quality settings take effect for an entire working session, or until you change them again.

Trap: *Before you can select a specific printer, you must add it to the list of printers you plan to use.*

When you first purchase WordPerfect, the program is set up with no printer selected. It is your job to inform WordPerfect as to which printers you will be using to print out your documents. If you don't define a printer first, you can't select it for printing out documents. (Refer to Appendix A for the procedure to inform WordPerfect of the printers you plan to use or to edit the list of defined printers.)

Tip: *If you exit WordPerfect and then return, the printer you last selected stays in effect.*

Once you select a different printer, that printer is selected permanently until you change it again. For example, suppose you select a certain printer, type and print out several documents, and exit WordPerfect at the end of the day. The next day, upon loading WordPerfect, the last printer you selected the previous day will be in effect.

However, when you retrieve a document to screen that was saved with a *different* printer selected, the Print menu for that document will reflect the change. For instance, suppose that you have selected the HP LaserJet Series II as your printer. Later, you retrieve a memo to screen that you stored several days ago when you had the Okidata ML 192 selected; the Okidata was stored as part of that memo's invisible packet of information, so that now the Print menu for that memo will show the Okidata as the selected printer. But if you clear your screen, the Print menu will revert to the HP LaserJet as your selected printer.

All other print options work differently, reverting to the default setting. For example, if you choose to print three copies of several documents and then exit WordPerfect, the next time you load WordPerfect the number of copies will be reset to one.

Note: When you retrieve a document with a different printer selected, and if that different printer is not found on the list of printers defined on your computer, then WordPerfect prompts with the message **Document formatted for default printer**. WordPerfect reformats the document for the currently selected printer.

Trap: *If you print from disk, the printer listed on the Print screen may be different from the one selected for the document on disk that you wish to print.*

You may have selected a certain printer yesterday, when you saved a document to disk, and a different printer today. If you then attempt to print that document from disk, WordPerfect detects that the two printer selections are different, and prompts

Document not formatted for current printer. Continue? (Y/N) No

If you type **N** or press ENTER, you will abort the Print command. If you type **Y**, the printing begins with the currently selected printer, even though the document was not formatted for it. Because of this, the print job may not take into consideration the special capabilities of your printer (such as certain font changes), and the printed page may look different than you intended. You can print from screen instead, to take full advantage of the printer you have currently selected (see the next Tip).

Tip: *When you select a new printer for a document on screen, corresponding fonts are selected.*

Occasionally, you may want to print a document that you originally selected for one printer on another printer. The printers will likely have completely different initial fonts, so that printing with another printer would, typically, result in odd font and other printer-specific characteristics on the printed page. Instead, WordPerfect offers an intelligent printing feature, so that fonts and other characteristics that most closely match the old printer are automatically selected.

For example, suppose you create a document in italics, in a large font and with proportional spacing, where the printer selected is a specific laser printer. You can then choose that the document print on a dot matrix printer, without altering the document. Just retrieve the document to screen, select the dot matrix printer, and print. The intelligent printing feature will try its best (given the selected printer's limitations) to print using fonts and features similar to those established for the laser printer.

Tip: *You can print a document to disk and send it to a printer at a future time.*

You can print a WordPerfect file not to a printer, but to a disk and in this way create a DOS text file. The document is saved on disk, along with those characters and codes that ordinarily are sent to the selected printer to tell the printer how to print out the document properly. You print to disk by defining a printer such that the document is sent to a particular file, rather than to a certain printer port; see Chapter 28 for further details on creating a DOS text file by printing to disk.

Once you print to disk, you can then send that file to a printer at any time without loading WordPerfect, directly from DOS, using the DOS PRINT command. Since all the printer codes are stored in the file, the document will print out properly for the printer you selected when you saved the file. Printing to disk is advantageous when you plan to print out that file later, at a work station that doesn't have the WordPerfect program.

Tip: *For one-sided copies, don't bother with the Binding feature.*

The Binding feature is generally used only for double-sided copies, so that the text that will appear on the front shifts to the right and the text that will appear on the back of a two-sided page shifts to the left.

If you plan to print and bind one-sided copies instead of two-sided copies, then don't use the Binding feature. Instead, simply increase the left margin for holes or bindings.

Tip: *You can set your binding width in units other than inches.*

When you first start up WordPerfect, the program assumes that you wish to enter binding, and all other settings, in inches. Thus, if you enter a binding of **1.5**, WordPerfect assumes you mean 1.5 inches. However, you can also enter your binding width in three other units of measure: centimeters, points, or version 4.2 units (horizontal or vertical). Type in the setting, followed by a letter to represent the unit of measure you desire. To enter a binding width of centimeters, for example, type **5c**. To enter a width setting of 50 points, for example, type **50p**. To enter a width setting of horizontal position 5 (the version 4.2 unit of measure), type **5h**. WordPerfect converts your entry into inches.

Tip: *You can print a page twice if your printer can't print both text and graphics in the same print job.*

Certain printers can print text or graphics, but not in the same printing. If this is the case, use the Do Not Print option on the Graphics Quality menu to suppress printing of graphics and to print out your text only. Next, reinsert your paper in the printer. Then, use the Do Not Print option on the Text Quality menu to suppress printing of text and to print out your graphics only. In this way, you can circumvent that printer limitation.

Trap: *Print quality might not change, depending on your printer.*

Dot matrix printers can print in varying qualities. For instance, if you select draft quality, the print head makes only one pass to print each character. But if you choose high quality (often referred to as Near Letter Quality), then the print head makes several passes, so that the letters are crisper, with higher resolution.

Certain printers are able to print in only one resolution—that is, they print the same regardless of whether you choose the high, medium, or draft option on the Text Quality and Graphics Quality menus.

Tip: *(When upgrading from 4.2.) Various print options have been added.*

The option to select a printer before you print is available, as in version 4.2. However, you no longer select a printer number (where you had to know what printer that number corresponded to). Rather, you choose your printer from a list that offers descriptive printer names; the process is easier and more versatile.

Another difference in version 5 is that the printer you select for a document is "attached" to the document (by means of an invisible packet of information) when you save it. Thus, various documents, formatted for different printers, can be stored on disk. When you print, the printer you selected for a document is the one used. And, you can later change the printer for any given document by retrieving it to screen and then selecting a new printer; WordPerfect's intelligent printing feature translates any font changes to correspond to those available for the newly selected printer.

The options for binding and number of copies are still available. However, there is no longer a simple method for changing these options for a single print job. You must change the Binding and Number of Copies options before the single job and again after the job because, unless changed, these option settings are now in effect for an entire working session.

Additional print options have been included in version 5, so that you can select the quality with which your text and graphics print out. Previously, the text quality was determined by the font you selected.

Special Print Features

There are three print features that enhance your ability to print: the View Document feature, the Type Through feature, and the Initialize Printer feature.

View Document enables you to preview how a printed page will appear. It shows a variety of features that are not displayed on the Typing screen, such as right justification, headers, footers, page numbering, top and bottom margins, footnotes, endnotes, double underlining, a change in point size for a certain font you selected, redline, strikeout, and graphics you inserted in a document. It is a useful way of checking to make sure that you approve of how you've formatted the document before printing, and to see if you inadvertently inserted or left out a format setting. By viewing before printing, you can save on the cost of printer ribbons and paper. To view a document:

1. The document you wish to view must be on screen. Position the cursor on the first page that you wish to preview.
2. Press PRINT (SHIFT + F7). WordPerfect displays the Print screen.
3. Select View Document (6 or V). In moments, WordPerfect rewrites the screen, showing the full page on which your cursor is located. An example is shown in Figure 14-6.
4. To change what you are viewing:

   Use the cursor movement keys to move through the text from page to page. PGUP and PGDN will show the previous page or the next page. In addition, press HOME, HOME, UP ARROW to view the first page of your document, or HOME, HOME, DOWN ARROW to view the last page.

   Use the View Document menu at the bottom of the screen to change the proportions of your view. Type **1** to select 100%, which shows a portion of the page at its actual size. Type **2** to select 200%, which shows a

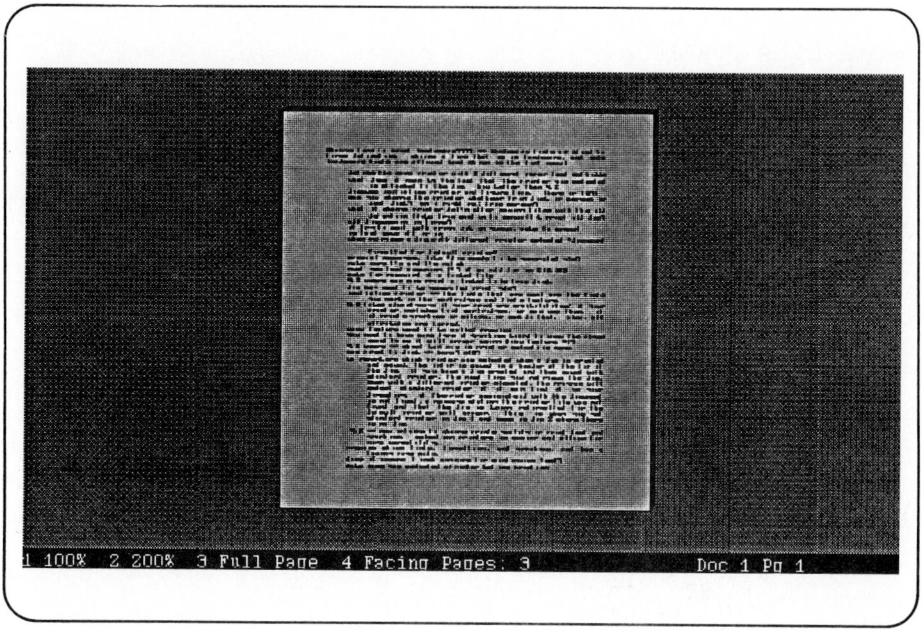

Figure 14-6. The View Document screen showing a full page

portion of the page at twice its actual size, affording a "close-up" view. Type 3 to select Full Page, whereby you see the entire page (which WordPerfect assumes when you first enter the View Document screen). Or type 4 to select Facing Pages, so that an odd-numbered page is displayed to the right and an even-numbered page to the left.

5. Press EXIT (F7) to return to your document, or press CANCEL (F1) to return to the Print screen.

You cannot edit a document or use any of the function key commands while using the View Document feature. You must exit the View Document screen, make any necessary editing changes, and then you can view the document again.

Another unique feature in WordPerfect allows you to control the printer directly from the keyboard, as if you were using a typewriter. This feature, called *Type Through*, is handy when you need to fill out a predesigned form or address one envelope. You can type line by line or character by character.

When you access Type Through, you won't affect any text already on the screen. To use this feature:

1. Turn on your printer and insert the paper on which you wish to print.
2. Press the PRINT (SHIFT + F7) key.
3. Select Type Through (5 or Y). WordPerfect responds

   Type Through by 1 Line; 2 Character

4. Select Line (1 or L), and WordPerfect displays the screen shown in Figure 14-7. Or select Character (2 or C), and WordPerfect displays an almost identical screen, except that the main heading indicates that it is for *character* rather than *line* Type Through. You are now ready to type.

Using Type Through by line, you can type up to 250 characters on one line. But word wrap is unavailable in Type Through; if you print more characters than

```
Line Type Through printing

Function Key          Action

Move                  Retrieve the previous line for editing
Format                Do a printer command
Enter                 Print the line
Exit/Cancel           Exit without printing












                                                         Pos 1
```

Figure 14-7. The Type Through by Line menu

the screen can display, characters are pushed off the screen to the left, and only those characters that fit on a line will print. Also, you lose your left margin. To control type when you print line by line:

- Position the print head horizontally on the page by pressing the SPACEBAR before you type letters or numbers.
- Move the cursor between characters by using LEFT ARROW and RIGHT ARROW.
- Edit characters using BACKSPACE, DEL, and DELETE EOL (CTRL + END).
- Insert any special printer commands (described in Chapter 15) by using the FORMAT (SHIFT + F8) key.
- Print a line by pressing ENTER. If you press ENTER when on a blank line, the paper in your printer will move up one line, so that you can position the print head vertically. (On some printers, UP ARROW moves the paper up one line, while DOWN ARROW moves the paper down one line.)
- Recall and edit the line you just printed by pressing MOVE (CTRL + F4).

Using Type Through by character, you have no opportunity to edit; characters are printed as you press them. To clear a line of text from the screen, move the cursor back to the first character and press DELETE EOL (CTRL + END).

Whether using Type Through by line or character, to exit without printing or after having completed Type Through, press EXIT (F7) or CANCEL (F1).

The *Initialize Printer* feature is used when you work with *soft fonts,* which are fonts stored on disks rather than in the cartridges that you insert in your printer. Soft fonts are available for a variety of printers. To use soft fonts, you must *download* them, meaning that you transfer instructions on how to print using those fonts from disk into the printer's memory.

You indicate to WordPerfect which soft fonts you have available when you define your printers (Appendix A). You can designate certain soft fonts as *always present* when a print job begins, and other soft fonts as *available to be loaded* for a particular print job. Then, when you select Initialize Printer (7 or I), from the Print menu, WordPerfect initiates a special print job that downloads all the fonts marked "always present"; other fonts that were previously loaded into the printer's memory are erased. Now these fonts are available to you for print jobs until you exit WordPerfect or turn off your printer. (Fonts marked "available to be loaded" are downloaded as part of a specific print job, and then cleared from the printer's memory after the print job is complete.) Refer to Appendix A for more on marking specific soft fonts.

Tip: *You can move to specific pages when displaying the View Document screen.*

As you use the View Document feature, you can use the GOTO (CTRL + HOME) key combination to quickly move to a certain page number. Figure 14-6, for example, indicates in the lower right-hand corner that currently, page 1 of the document in the Doc 1 screen is in view. Suppose you wish to move to page 12. Press CTRL + HOME, and WordPerfect prompts at the bottom of the View Document screen:

Go To

Type **12** and press ENTER. In moments, the View Document screen is rewritten, displaying page 12.

Tip: *To use the View Document feature more effectively, consider purchasing a graphics card if your computer isn't currently equipped with one.*

The View Document feature can be used without a graphics display card. However, if you wish to view graphics images and fonts in detail, then consider purchasing and installing a graphics card.

Trap: *Some printers cannot support the Type Through feature.*

Some printers cannot support character-by-character printing; others cannot support Type Through at all. WordPerfect indicates this. For instance, if you attempt to select Type Through on an HP LaserJet Series II, a printer that does not support Type Through at all, then WordPerfect responds

Feature not available on this printer

You are then returned to your document. Test this feature on your printer to see if it is available to you.

In general, most daisy wheel printers support Type Through both by line and by character; dot matrix printers support Type Through only by lines; and laser printers don't support Type Through.

Should your printer not support Type Through and you wish to print on preprinted forms, then refer to the Advance feature for assistance, as described in Chapter 7.

Trap: *You may be unable to initialize your printer properly.*

If you attempt to initialize your printer and you get an error message, the problem may be that you haven't indicated to WordPerfect where on disk the files containing the soft fonts are stored. You do this when specifying cartridges and fonts as you define your printer (see Appendix A for details).

Another explanation is that WordPerfect doesn't recognize the soft fonts because of their filenames or other characteristics. In that case, you will need to employ a program named PTR.EXE, a WordPerfect program that allows you to alter your printer's definition (Chapter 15 explains PTR.EXE).

Also keep in mind that you need only initialize your printer for fonts marked "always present." Other soft fonts are loaded into the printer as they are needed, and you should not initialize your printer for these. Depending on the fonts that you wish to download, you may need to purchase additional memory for your printer (1 MB of memory is usually sufficient).

Tip: *(When upgrading from 4.2.) View Document has been significantly enhanced, and now there is a simple way to download fonts.*

The View Document feature (previously called Preview) enables you to preview more than you could in version 4.2. Not only can you see right justification, headers, footers, page numbering, top and bottom margins, footnotes, and endnotes, but you can now view different font styles, proportional spacing, or superscript and subscript. Moreover, you can request a view in different proportions, or you can view facing pages.

The Type Through feature remains basically the same as in version 4.2.

In version 5, you can now download fonts easily, which will be a welcome enhancement for laser printer owners.

Tips and Traps Summary

Printing from the Screen

Trap: Sometimes it takes a few moments before printing begins.

Trap: If you manually feed paper into the printer or the document requires a cartridge change, printing from the screen won't start automatically.

Trap: You may be unable to print a large document from the screen.

Tip: Use the BLOCK key to print a portion of a page or to print consecutive pages from the screen.

Tip: Continue to perform other word processing tasks while your document is printing from screen.

Trap: Once you send a print job to the printer, editing changes you make on that document won't be reflected in that print job.

Tip: You may wish to select specific print options or access other print features before you print from screen.

Tip: (When upgrading from 4.2.) The Print menu has been modified.

Printing from Disk

Trap: To print from disk, a document must be stored exactly as you wish it to be printed.

Trap: WordPerfect cannot find a document to print if the filename, disk drive, or directory you specified is incorrect.

Tips and Traps Summary (*continued*)

Trap: If you manually feed paper into the printer or the document requires a cartridge change, printing from disk won't start automatically.

Trap: You may be unable to print from disk if you use the Fast Save option.

Tip: If you are printing a locked file from disk, WordPerfect will prompt for the correct password.

Tip: You can specify any range of consecutive or nonconsecutive pages that you wish to print.

Tip: If you've renumbered pages in a document, use the new numbers to print selected pages.

Tip: An advantage to printing with the List Files menu is that you can request that two or more documents be printed in one Print command.

Tip: Continue to perform other word processing tasks while your document is printing from disk.

Tip: You may wish to select specific print options or access other print features before you print from disk.

Tip: (When upgrading from 4.2.) The ability to print from disk has been enhanced.

Controlling Print Jobs

Tip: After you stop or cancel a job, you may need to clear out the job list.

Trap: Many printers won't stop immediately after you stop the printer or cancel a job.

Tip: (When upgrading from 4.2.) The options for controlling print jobs remain the same.

Tips and Traps Summary (*continued*)

Print Options

Trap: Before you can select a specific printer, you must add it to the list of printers you plan to use.

Tip: If you exit WordPerfect and then return, the printer you last selected stays in effect.

Trap: If you print from disk, the printer listed on the Print screen may be different from the one selected for the document on disk that you wish to print.

Tip: When you select a new printer for a document on screen, corresponding fonts are selected.

Tip: You can print a document to disk and send it to the printer at a future time.

Tip: For one-sided copies, don't bother with the Binding feature.

Tip: You can set your binding width in units other than inches.

Tip: You can print a page twice if your printer can't print both text and graphics in the same print job.

Trap: Print quality might not change, depending on your printer.

Tip: (When upgrading from 4.2.) Various print options have been added.

Special Print Features

Tip: You can move to specific pages when displaying the View Document screen.

Tip: To use the View Document feature more effectively, consider purchasing a graphics card if your computer isn't currently equipped with one.

Tips and Traps Summary (*continued*)

Trap: Some printers cannot support the Type Through feature.

Trap: You may be unable to initialize your printer properly.

Tip: (When upgrading from 4.2.) View Document has been significantly enhanced, and now there is a simple way to download fonts.

15

Solving Printer Mysteries

There are three basic categories of printers: dot matrix printers, which use pins to create characters; daisy wheel printers, which use wheels or thimbles, whereby a raised symbol hits the page to create fully formed characters; and laser printers which focus light on a page to draw characters. Within each category there are numerous brands. Each printer has its own set of characteristics, as well as its own idiosyncratic ways of operating.

Unfortunately, you may encounter a glitch when getting your printer to operate correctly. The WordPerfect software reduces printer problems, but so many types of printers are manufactured and the connection between the printer, the computer, and the software is so complex that even WordPerfect users face an occasional frustration. The first two sections of this chapter suggest ways to troubleshoot if your printer isn't printing at all, or if it isn't printing properly.

Most people want to use a printer to its maximum. The WordPerfect software has been set up to tap many of your printer's features, so all you need to do is discover exactly how your printer and WordPerfect work together. The last section of this chapter describes how to uncover your printer's special talents and shortcomings when working in conjunction with WordPerfect. You also learn about a special printer program named PTR.EXE, which enables you to alter how WordPerfect and your printer have been defined to work together. Using PTR.EXE, you can customize your printer specifications for your own special needs.

Determining the Cause When the Printer Does Not Print

It is aggravating to try to print a document that you need in five minutes only to find that the printer doesn't so much as sputter or cough—it totally ignores your command to print. If this happens, don't try again to print. Instead, check the message on WordPerfect's Control Printer menu, which often indicates the problem, or at least provides a hint. (The Control Printer menu also manages print jobs, as described in Chapter 14.)

To display the Control Printer menu, press PRINT (SHIFT + F7) and select Control Printer (4 or C). Figure 15-1 shows an example of the Control Printer menu. When a job is printing, at the top of the screen, where information on the

```
Print: Control Printer

Current Job

Job Number: 5                                    Page Number:  None
Status:     Initializing                         Current Copy: None
Message:    Printer not accepting characters
Paper:      None
Location:   None
Action:     Check cable, make sure printer is turned ON


Job List

Job  Document              Destination           Print Options
 5   (Screen)              LPT 1
 6   C:\WPER\DATA\BUDMIN   LPT 1


Additional Jobs Not Shown: 0



1 Cancel Job(s); 2 Rush Job; 3 Display Jobs; 4 Go (start printer); 5 Stop: 0
```

Figure 15-1. Control Printer menu with error message

current job is offered, a message next to the heading "Status" reads "Printing," and the remark next to the heading "Action" reads "None"; all is well, and the print job is proceeding.

When there are no jobs in the job list, the remark next to the heading "Status" reads "No print jobs." If you try to print and you check the Control Printer screen only to find the "No print jobs" message, then WordPerfect did not register your Print command; perhaps you inadvertently pressed the wrong key to begin the print job, so you should try again.

But if there is another problem, this message area near the top of the screen often tells you why. For example, Figure 15-1 shows the message that occurs when you try to print but your printer is turned off. After the heading "Job Status," WordPerfect indicates "Initializing," meaning that WordPerfect is attempting to send the job to the printer. After the heading "Message," a remark reads "Printer not accepting characters." And the remark next to "Action" indicates what you should attempt to do to rectify the printing problem: "Check cable, make sure printer is turned ON." The Control Printer menu might not indicate the exact problem, but it can certainly narrow down the possibilities, so check this menu when your printer isn't operating at all.

Trap: *The message "ERROR: File not found" may indicate that the file you wish to print does not exist or that there is a problem with the WordPerfect program.*

When you are printing a file from disk using the Control Printer menu, WordPerfect must be able to locate that file on disk. If it can't, and the message "ERROR: File not found" displays at the bottom of the screen, then the possible explanations for this message include the following:

- You typed the filename incorrectly.
- You forgot to type the filename's extension. For example, if a document's filename is JONES.LTR, you cannot type the filename as just JONES.
- You didn't specify the correct drive or directory. WordPerfect assumes the default drive and directory unless you specify otherwise by preceding the filename with another drive or directory. For example, if the file is in drive A and the default is drive C (the hard disk), then the filename must be preceded by A:, such as in A:JONES.LTR.

- The file was accidentally erased from the disk.
- The file is on screen but you haven't yet saved it onto disk.

Use the List Files menu (described in Chapter 13) to view a list of files on disk. That way, you can see exactly how the filename is spelled and in which subdirectory it is located—or if it's on disk at all.

Moreover, WordPerfect cannot print without access to certain printer files on the WordPerfect disk (or in the WordPerfect subdirectory of the hard disk). These files are created on disk when you define your printers (as described in Appendix A), and end with the filename extension .PRS. For example, the printer file to print with an HP LaserJet Series II is named HPLASEII.PRS (unless you change the name). If, when you try to print, the Control Printer menu displays the message "ERROR: File not found," then other possible reasons and solutions include the following:

- Floppy disk users have removed from drive A the WordPerfect disk where the printer files are stored. Replace the WordPerfect disk, cancel the current job, and try again.
- Hard disk users have placed the printer files in a subdirectory where WordPerfect can't find them. WordPerfect assumes that the printer files are in the same subdirectory where its main program file, named WP.EXE, is found. Either move the printer files to this subdirectory or use the Setup menu to indicate to WordPerfect that the printer files are in another subdirectory (by using the Location of Files option on the Setup menu, as described in Appendix B).
- You haven't defined your printer or sheet feeder properly— or at all. Turn to Appendix A for instructions.
- You've accidentally deleted or damaged those printer files. Turn to Appendix A, since you need to redefine your printers to create those files again, with the extension .PRS.

Trap: *The message "Printer not accepting characters" often indicates a printer definition or cable problem.*

The link between the computer and a printer must be correct in order for the printer to transform electronic impulses into marks on paper. If it is not, you will often see the following message on the Control Printer menu: "Printer not accepting characters." This may indicate any of the following problems:

- Your printer is not set up to print. It could be turned off or be off-line (meaning that the link between the printer and the computer is turned off). The printer ribbon could be positioned incorrectly in the printer. Or switches inside the printer could have been set incorrectly. For example, for serial printers, the switches on your printer must match the baud, parity, and stop-bit settings that you indicated when defining your printer (as described in Appendix A).

  Make sure that the printer is on, that the printer is on-line (there's usually a light that illuminates on the printer when it is on-line, as described in the printer manual), that the ribbon is inserted correctly, and that printer settings are correct. Check your printer manual for switch settings.

- The cable connecting the printer to the computer is cracked, loose, plugged into the wrong spot at the back of your computer, or it is the wrong type for your printer. Inspect the cable; if it looks worn, replace it. If you have other ports in which to plug the cable into the back of the computer, try one of those. Check with a dealer to see whether you have the proper cable.

- Your printer connection was defined incorrectly. When you define your printer during installation, WordPerfect needs to know the name of the plug (port) you're using—parallel or serial. A parallel port is labeled as LPT, whereas a serial port is labeled as COM. Which you use depends on your printer. Also, if your printer requires a serial port, WordPerfect needs to know certain other specifics, such as baud rate, parity, and stop bit. You should check your printer manual to see which type of port your printer requires and what the baud, parity, and stop bit should be set for. WordPerfect also needs to know the plug number. If you have two parallel plugs, for example, then you must indicate whether the printer is in LPT 1 or LPT 2.

  If you chose the wrong type of port, the wrong specifics for a serial port (such as the baud rate), or the wrong printer port number, then you must redefine your printer for WordPerfect before you can print. If you need to redefine your printer port, see Appendix A.

Trap: *The message "Press "G" to continue" indicates that WordPerfect is waiting for a signal.*

At certain times, WordPerfect will not print until you signal that you are ready. When you see on the Control Printer menu, the message "Fix printer -- Press "G" to continue," one of the following problems might exist:

- You defined your printer for manually fed paper or you are using a form defined as not initially present in your printer. (Appendix A describes how to define your printer and printer forms.) WordPerfect is waiting for a signal that the paper has been inserted. Insert the paper and type **G,** Go (start printer) (4 or G).
- During the course of typing the document you wish to print, you embedded a Font Change code in the document. Some printers require that you change a print wheel or cartridge before a certain font can be produced. (When you define printers, you can indicate whether a certain cartridge is always available or if it must be inserted during a print job in order to be used.) If you don't have the appropriate print wheel or cartridge, you can select Go (4 or G) to continue anyway. If you have the print wheel or the cartridge you need, replace it and type **G** to continue.
- You previously stopped a print job but haven't yet typed **G** to restart the printing. Type **G**.
- You previously canceled a print job but haven't yet typed **G** to clear the job list. Type **G**.

Trap: *The message "ERROR: Incompatible file format" means that a problem exists with the file you wish to print.*

When the message "ERROR: Incompatible file format" is displayed at the bottom of the screen, this could mean that you are attempting to print out a document that has been formatted for another software package; WordPerfect is unable to print it. A solution may be to convert your document to WordPerfect format; see Chapter 28 for details.

Another cause for this message is that the file you are attempting to print has been locked with a password, and you have typed the incorrect password. You must know the correct password in order to print a locked file. (See Chapter 11 for more on locking documents with a password.)

Tip: *Try printing from disk if you get a "disk full" message.*

As described in Chapter 14, a temporary print file is created when you print from the screen. If a document is so large that WordPerfect has no room for the temporary file on a disk, you'll get a "disk full" message. In that case, print from disk—using either the Control Printer or the List Files menu.

Tip: *As a last resort before you call for printing help, try starting all over again.*

When you encounter a printer problem, be sure to follow the instructions next to the heading "Action" for possible solutions. But if you've verified that the printer has been defined correctly, if you've jostled the cable and it's snug in its port, if you've typed **G**—if you've done it all and you're still stumped—try one more approach. Cancel all the jobs in the job list (see Chapter 14), turn off the printer, turn it on again, and try one more time to print. If even that fails, your next option is to confer with an office mate, call your computer dealer, or call WordPerfect Corporation (see Appendix C for WordPerfect Corporation's telephone number).

Tip: *(When upgrading from 4.2.) Most error messages remain the same in version 5.*

In general, the error messages you may have encountered in version 4.2 will be the same in version 5. One new error message, however, informs you of an incompatible file format if you're attempting to print a file created by using another software package; previously, WordPerfect didn't warn you if this was the case. Also, the new "Action" heading on the Printer Control screen indicates what tasks to perform should you encounter a printing problem.

Determining the Cause When the Printer Does Not Print Correctly

Almost as frustrating as not being able to print is producing a document with odd margins, extra characters, or jibberish instead of letters, or without the features and enhancements that you inserted in the text.

If the fonts, margins, spacing, or other formats are incorrect, then the problem, and therefore the solution, is often in finding the format codes hidden in your document. Retrieve your document to the screen, move the cursor to the spot where the problem occurred, and reveal codes. As you move your cursor through the text, look for a code that was added accidentally. One extra code is enough to throw an entire document out of whack. If you find one, delete it. If a code is missing, insert it. If the code is in the wrong place, move it; remember that a code takes effect only from the point at which it is embedded in the document. Then resave the document and try printing again.

If the problem is that the letters are unintelligible or that there are extra characters, there could be an equipment problem or a printer definition problem. Refer to the Tips in the previous section of this chapter, "Determining the Cause When the Printer Does Not Print"; for the same reasons that a printer might not print at all, it also might print improperly. For instance, the cable connecting the printer and the computer may be loose or cracked, or the baud, parity, and stop-bit switches in the printer do not match those you indicated to WordPerfect when defining your printer. Refer also to the Tips and Traps below.

Tip: *When you suspect the printer problem is caused by misplaced codes, you can locate codes quickly by using the Search feature.*

When searching for specific hidden codes, try using the Search feature (see Chapter 4) to locate hidden codes in a document. For example, suppose that a document produces correct margins, but then the margins change drastically several times in the middle of the document. Use the Search feature to quickly find a misplaced or incorrect margin code.

Trap: *A format problem or unrecognizable characters in a document could indicate incorrect switch settings.*

Sometimes you must change a switch at the printer in order for a document to print correctly. Perhaps the auto line-feed, form-feed, or return switch at the printer is on and is thus causing double spacing; it should be turned off. The NEC 3550 won't print features such as superscript and subscript properly unless the switch labeled SW2-5 is put in the "On" position. Switches must also be changed if you try to print with wide margins but the text does not print past column 80; this occurs with the IBM QuietWriter. Check your printer manual for possible switch setting changes, or call your dealer or WordPerfect Corporation for assistance.

Tip: *To use certain fonts, you may need to insert a new print wheel or initialize your printer.*

If your printer is printing in the wrong font and you've checked your Document Initial Font and font change codes to find that they're correct, remember that on some printers you must insert a new print wheel or cartridge to have access to certain fonts.

Also, if you use soft fonts on a laser printer, you indicate to WordPerfect which soft fonts you have available when you define your printers (Appendix A). You can designate certain soft fonts as *always present* when a print job begins, and other soft fonts as *available to be loaded* for a particular print job. You must remember to initialize your printer at the beginning of a working session with WordPerfect if you wish to use those fonts marked as "always present." You would press the PRINT (SHIFT + F7) key, and select Initialize Printer (7 or I). WordPerfect initiates a special print job that downloads all the fonts marked as "always present"; any other fonts that were previously loaded into the printer's memory are erased. Now these fonts are available to you for print jobs until you exit WordPerfect or turn off your printer.

Tip: *Try using a different cable if your serial printer prints unintelligible characters or loses characters.*

If you use a serial printer and find that a document prints out with odd characters or stops printing at the same place each time you try printing, then the problem may be an improper serial cable; check the cable and ask your computer dealer.

Trap: *Not all printers can access all the features available in WordPerfect.*

In order to use the more advanced features, such as Redline, Strikeout, Superscript, Subscript, or Type Through, your printer must be able to support them. Some of these features can be tested by printing out the WordPerfect file named PRINTER.TST, as described in the following section of this chapter, "Uncovering/Altering Printer Capabilities." You must test other features by attempting to use them. If the feature you want to use doesn't work properly, check your printer manual to see if that feature can be supported. If it can, you may need to change your printer definition to access it, by using the Printer program (also described in the last section of this chapter). If it cannot be supported, you must do without this feature when using this particular printer.

Tip: *You may be able to change how WordPerfect and your printer work together if you dislike how a certain feature prints out on your printer.*

If you dislike the printed result when using certain features, or if your printer has capabilities not being tapped by WordPerfect, then a Printer program provided by WordPerfect is available, so that you can create your own printer definition. This program is also useful if you own a printer that is not listed on the WordPerfect printer disks, meaning that it has not already been defined by WordPerfect. For details, refer to the last section of this chapter.

Tip: *Check the sheet feeder definition or top margin codes if your text starts too low on the page or prints within the top or bottom margin.*

If you use a sheet feeder but your paper rolls up too far before it starts to print, check the top margin code you set for your document. Then try adjusting the top margin to zero. Or, if unintelligible text prints at the top or bottom of a page, the problem could be in your printer definition. When you define printers for WordPerfect, you must also define a sheet feeder, if you use one. You may have selected a sheet feeder when you have none, or you may have selected the wrong sheet feeder, and must therefore redefine your printer (as described in Appendix A).

Tip: *(When upgrading from 4.2.) Version 5 has been designed to tap more of your printer's capabilities.*

A major emphasis in the design of version 5 was to ensure that the full range of your printer's abilities would be accessed by WordPerfect. As a result, you will, no doubt, be more satisfied with how WordPerfect and your printer work together. If not, refer to the suggestions in the following section of the chapter.

In version 4.2, you may have used a separate program named XON-XOFF.COM, which was provided with the WordPerfect package, to activate the XON/XOFF protocol for your particular computer and printer setup. Using this program is not necessary in WordPerfect version 5 because the XON/XOFF protocol is now part of the WP.EXE program.

Uncovering/Altering Printer Capabilities

To get the maximum from your printer, you must understand how it works with WordPerfect. One way to do this is to print out a file housed on the WordPerfect Conversion disk named PRINTER.TST. This file helps you determine which features your printer is capable of producing on the printed page.

PRINTER.TST shows how your printer handles features such as Bold, Italic, Shadow, Small Caps, Double Underlining, Superscript, Subscript, Redline, Strikeout, and Graphics. Print out this file on your printer to help test your printer features and font definitions. It is a standard WordPerfect file, so you should print it as you would any of your own documents. Floppy disk users should place the Conversion disk in drive B; hard disk users should have this file on the hard disk in the subdirectory where the majority of the WordPerfect program files are stored. Next, turn on your printer, retrieve PRINTER.TST to the screen, and print from the screen (see Chapter 14 for a review of printing).

The PRINTER.TST document is two pages in length. Figure 15-2 shows the result of printing the first page of PRINTER.TST on an HP LaserJet Series II, while Figure 15-3 shows page 2 printed on the same printer. (When you print out your PRINTER.TST file, it might have slightly different information; the exact wording of each file depends on the version of WordPerfect you have and its release date.) Notice how you can see which features and fonts each printer is

WordPerfect 5.0
Printer Test Document

In this paragraph, each word associated with a feature is printed with that feature (e.g., **bold**, ^{super}script, $_{sub}$script, and ~~strikeout~~). Print attributes have been expanded in WP 5.0 to include fine, small, normal, large, very large, and extra large sizes of print. Some further additions to the list are italics, **shadow**, outline, and SMALL CAPS. The default redline method should have a shaded background or a dotted line under the characters.

If a feature described does not appear on your printout, your printer may not have that capability.

Continuous	Double underlining	Text
Non-Continuous	Double underlining	can be
Continuous	Single underlining	flush
Non-Continuous	Single underlining	right
You may also choose to not underline spaces		

Left	Decim.al	Center	Right
Tabs	T.abs	Tabs	Tabs

This text is left/right indented. Notice that the text is indented from both margins according to the tab settings. The indenting will continue until the "Enter" key is pressed.

(Double spacing) WordPerfect 5.0 integrates text and graphics. A graphic image can be placed anywhere on the page. The image can easily be scaled, moved, and rotated.

(1.5 spacing) Fonts may be mixed and changed randomly without affecting margins, tabs or column definitions. Normal text. Advanced up .08". Normal text. Advanced down .08". Normal.
Advance can be used to S P R E A D characters out, or change how they APPEAR. Back to the normal baseline.

Figure 15-2. PRINTER.TST page 1 printout on an HP LaserJet Series II

IMPROVED PARALLEL COLUMNS — Parallel columns now extend past a page break. Script writers and others will find this feature to be especially convenient.

MASTER DOCUMENTS — The master document feature combines files (e.g., chapters in a book, files on a network) for generating tables of contents, etc.

This paragraph is printed in 8 LPI. We can place this in eight lines per inch by going into Shift F8 and using fixed line height. The rest of the document's line height is fixed at 6 LPI. Already the world's most powerful word processor[1], WordPerfect continues its tradition of excellence by adding several new features.

INTEGRATED TEXT AND GRAPHICS

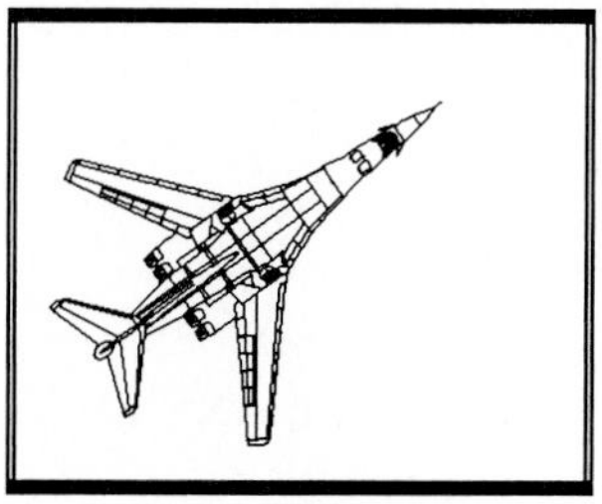

5.0 TAKES OFF!

The smooth integration of text and graphics in WordPerfect 5.0 makes designing newsletters, reports, and professional documents much easier. A graphic image can be scaled, moved, and rotated. Sizing and cropping are quick and easy. You can also indicate the style and thickness of the border, and include a caption. The graphic image can be placed anywhere on the page, inserted in a line, tied to a paragraph, or included in a header or footer. The program also is shipped with a utility that allows you to capture the screen from any graphics program, converting it to a WordPerfect Graphics image file. You can then use the image within WordPerfect. This facilitates the use of various graphics programs to create graphics to be used within WordPerfect. 5.0 is designed to work with many of the most popular graphics programs available on the market. The preview feature now lets you display an entire page of text and graphics at once, zoom in for a detailed look, or view facing pages together.

[1] WordPerfect is the number 1 selling word processor in the U.S., in Canada, and in six European countries. Research estimates now show that WordPerfect sales account for approximately 40% of the market share for word processors.

Here is a test of line draw, single, double and mixed:

WordPerfect 5.0 Printer Test Document — Page 2

Figure 15-3. PRINTER.TST page 2 printout on an HP LaserJet Series II

capable of. With this text, you can see how your printer will react to many WordPerfect commands—and thus learn a great deal about your printer.

A second way to uncover printer capabilities is through the help available when you select printers. Press PRINT (SHIFT + F7) and choose S, Select Printer. WordPerfect shows a list of printers you have defined to work with WordPerfect (a procedure described in Appendix A). Move the cursor to highlight the printer for which you desire background information, and then select Help (6 or H). For some printers (but not all), a screen appears with background information on your printer. For instance, that screen might indicate that your printer doesn't support the Type Through feature or graphics or proportional spacing. Or it may indicate how many fonts are allowed per printed page. Use the cursor keys to view more text, press the SWITCH (SHIFT + F3) key for information on sheet feeders for your printer, or press EXIT (F7) to return to the list of printers you have defined.

A third help is a special Printer program provided by WordPerfect Corporation, named PTR.EXE. With PTR.EXE, you can examine how your printer has been specified by WordPerfect Corporation to operate with WordPerfect. For example, you can view the proportional spacing table, which lists widths for characters that WordPerfect uses to proportionally space each character. Moreover, using PTR.EXE, you can permanently alter or add to these specifications.

Here's a sampling of what PTR.EXE can help you examine or change:

- The character used to denote strikeout
- The resolution for low, medium, and high quality graphics
- The manner in which boldface or underlining is printed
- The character map for a particular font—the list of characters available and the code that the printer expects in order to print each character
- The proportional spacing table, which determines how each character will be spaced, relative to other characters, when you use a proportionally spaced font
- Automatic font changes, which are weight and scaling tables that determine the font that is printed when you select an attribute such as large, italics, or small caps
- How your sheet feeder operates

Basically, by changing a printer's specifications, you are changing the codes that tell the printer how to perform with WordPerfect. Alter printer specifications only if you are comfortable with printer codes and the features of your printer.

Printer specifications for a *collection* of printers are found on the WordPerfect Printer disks in files named WPRINT1.ALL, WPRINT2.ALL, WPRINT3.ALL, and WPRINT4.ALL. Printer specifications for a *single* printer definition are found in files with the extension .PRS (such as HPLASEII.PRS for the HP LaserJet Series II or OKML92.PRS for the Okidata ML 92 dot matrix printer, and are created when you define for WordPerfect the printers that you will be working with, as described in Appendix A). Files with the .ALL extension are used as a resource to create the .PRS files, but cannot be used directly for printing. You can alter a printer specification in either a .PRS or .ALL file.

PTR.EXE is found on its own WordPerfect program disk, which is labeled "PTR program." To access this program:

1. Make sure that you're in DOS, viewing the DOS prompt.
2. Floppy disk users should insert the disk containing the .ALL file (such as Printer 1) or the .PRS file (WordPerfect 2) to be altered into drive A and the PTR program disk into drive B. Then, make sure the default drive is A by typing **A:** and pressing ENTER.

   Hard disk users should change to the directory where the WordPerfect printer files and the Printer program are stored. For example, if they are stored in \WPER, then type **CD \WPER**, and press ENTER. (If you have not copied the file named PTR.EXE onto your hard disk, then insert the Printer program disk in drive A.)
3. Floppy disk users should type **B:PTR** at the A prompt. The screen reads

   A>B:PTR

   Hard disk users should type **PTR** at the C prompt. The screen reads

   C>PTR

   or

   C: \WPER>PTR

   (If you have not copied PTR.EXE onto the hard disk, then with the Printer program disk in drive A, type **A:PTR**.)
4. Press ENTER to start the printer program.

Once the Printer program is loaded, you will want to retrieve a printer definition file for editing. Press RETRIEVE (SHIFT + F10), and then enter in the path and filename of the printer definition file for the printer with which you wish to work. For instance, a floppy disk user might type **A:HPLASEII.PRS**, and press ENTER. Or a hard disk user might type **C: \WPER \HPLASEII.PRS**, and press ENTER. That filename appears on screen. Press ENTER to view a partial list of printer specification categories for that printer; an example for the HP LaserJet Series II is shown in Figure 15-4. (Or, if you retrieved a file with the extension .ALL so that you are viewing a list containing more than one printer, position the cursor on the printer that you wish to modify, and press ENTER.)

To view additional printer specification categories not currently on screen, continue to press DOWN ARROW. You can also use other cursor movement keys, such as PGUP, PGDN, PLUS (on the numeric keypad), MINUS (on the numeric keypad), HOME, HOME, UP ARROW, or HOME, HOME, DOWN ARROW. Or, use the Name Search feature to move the cursor to a specific category by typing the first letter or letters of the name of the category. (For example, type **F**, and the cursor will move to "Fonts.") The category on which the cursor is located will be brighter than the other categories.

```
File: C:\WPER\HPLASEII.PRS

                         Printer: HP LaserJet Series II

  Initialize and Reset
  Horizontal Motion
  Vertical Motion
  Margins and # Fonts/Page
  Type Through
  Miscellaneous Printer Functions
  Movement for Super/Subscript, Advances & Graphics
  Fonts
  Groups
  Resources
  Forms
  Graphics Resolutions
  Bitmap Graphics
  Rules and Shaded Boxes
  Bold
  Underline
  Double Underline
▼ Italics

Press Enter to Look or Edit: A - Z Name Search:
Do all that apply
```

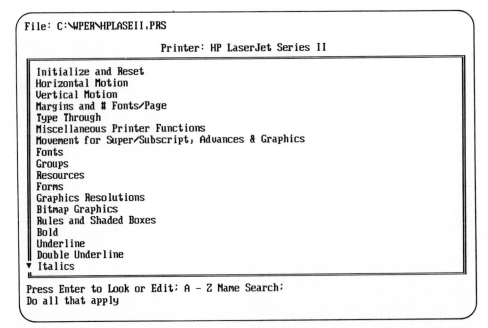

Figure 15-4. Partial list of printer specification categories when in the Printer program

To select a category, position the cursor and press ENTER. Now you are ready to review information about your printer specifications, or to edit the specifications within that particular category.

When in the printer program, always use the ENTER key to view submenus of the menu on screen and use the EXIT (F7) key to back out of a menu (rather than CANCEL (F1), which is the function key used in WordPerfect). Then follow the instructions provided at the bottom of the screen. Press EXIT (F7) when you're back at the main Printer program screen and are ready to save any changes you made to a printer specification and/or wish to exit the Printer program.

From anywhere within the Printer program, you can access a file named PTR.HLP, which provides detailed instructions on how to use the Printer program. Press HELP (F3) to display a function key template for the Printer program, and then press a function key for further information. Or press SCREEN HELP (CTRL + F3) for information on the items currently displayed on screen. Or press ITEM HELP (ALT + F3) for information on the item on which the cursor is currently located. To exit the Help feature, press EXIT (F7) or the SPACEBAR.

Tip: *Print out PRINTER.TST for each font your printer is capable of producing.*

Certain features may operate differently on your printer, depending on the font you've selected for printing. For instance, one font may print in italic, while another font does not. Thus, print out PRINTER.TST for each font available to you, so that you gain an understanding of the connection between a given font and a given feature. (See Chapter 7 for the method to change the font in a document.)

Tip: *Change the print wheel if you hear a beep while printing the PRINTER.TST files.*

Laser and daisy wheel printers often require users to insert a new print wheel or cartridge to produce specific fonts. WordPerfect provides the opportunity by pausing. If you hear a beep and have another print wheel or cartridge, insert it. To continue, whether or not you've inserted a new wheel or cartridge, (1) press PRINT (SHIFT + F7), (2) select Control Printer (4 or C), and (3) select Go (start printer) (4 or G).

Tip: *If a special capability has not been defined for your printer, you can use printer commands rather than PTR.EXE to activate those capabilities.*

If WordPerfect has not been set up to use certain capabilities of your printer, you can insert printer commands directly into your document at a specific location rather than tamper with PTR.EXE. You send printer commands either directly or via a file in which you've already stored the printer commands. Perhaps your printer can produce a font not defined by WordPerfect, and you wish to insert a long string of commands to access that font at a particular point in your document. You must refer to your printer manual to find the specific string of printer commands. Then use the FORMAT (SHIFT + F8) key, as follows:

1. Position the cursor at the point in your document where you want the Printer command to take effect.
2. Press the FORMAT (SHIFT + F8) key to display the Format menu.
3. Select Other (4 or O), to display the Other Format menu.
4. Select Printer Functions (6 or P) to display the Printer Functions menu.
5. Select Printer Command (2 or P). WordPerfect prompts

   1 Command; 2 Filename: **0**

   If you select Command (1 or C), WordPerfect prompts, asking for a command. Enter the commands to be sent to the printer. Any command code less than 32 decimal and greater than 126 decimal must be entered in angle brackets. For example, if the code for condensed (17-pitch) on your printer is ESC 15, enter the command as <27><15>. (27 is the decimal equivalent for ESC). Codes between 32 and 126, which represent printable characters, can be typed or entered in decimal or in angle brackets.

   Or, if you select Filename (2 or F), WordPerfect prompts for a document name. The file should already be on disk and should contain a number of command codes that you entered by using BASIC or a text editor. Enter the filename.
6. Press EXIT (F7) to return to the document.

WordPerfect inserts a code in the text at the current cursor position so that the printer command contained in the code will be downloaded to your printer when the code is encountered during printing. An example of the printer command code, when you enter commands directly, is **[Ptr Cmnd:<27><15>]**. The printer command code, assuming that you entered the filename SPFONT, would be **[Ptr Cmnd:SPFONT]**.

If you plan to download printer command files, be sure to indicate a pathname for where those files will be stored. You do so when you define your printer, by using the Select option on the Print menu (see Appendix A for more information on defining your printer).

Tip: *To change a printer specification using PTR.EXE, you must have a good working knowledge of your printer's codes.*

PTR.EXE is technically oriented, and will be quite difficult to work with if you are a novice user. You should have an understanding of how to read your printer manual and be able to read printer codes in order to work with PTR.EXE to change a printer specification. Luckily, most users will never need to access PTR.EXE because so many printer specifications have been predefined by WordPerfect Corporation.

Trap: *You must know the name of the printer file you wish to examine or edit before loading PTR.EXE.*

As previously mentioned, you can use the Printer program to alter a file with the extension .ALL or a file with the extension .PRS. You must know the name of the file you wish to edit before you enter the Printer program; there is no key comparable to LIST FILES from within the Printer program which allows you to peruse the .PRS and .ALL files. Therefore, check the name of the printer file you wish to examine or edit—either from within WordPerfect, by using the List Files screen, or from DOS, by using the DIR command—before you load the Printer program.

Tip: *(When upgrading from 4.2.) PRINTER.TST has been updated and the Printer program has been completely revamped in version 5.*

In version 4.2, two test files were available to test the features of your printer: PRINTER.TST and PRINTER2.TST. In version 5, these have been combined into one file named PRINTER.TST. PRINTER.TST has naturally been upgraded so that features new to version 5 (such as font attributes and graphics) can also be tested on your printer.

Version 4.2 offered a file named PRHELP.EXE, which provided background information on your printer. This file is not available in version 5. Instead, a Help screen can be displayed when you follow these steps: press PRINT (SHIFT + F7); choose S, Select Printer; position the cursor on the printer for which you want background information; and choose Help (6 or H).

The Printer program in version 5 has been changed. In version 4.2 it was found in a file named PRINTER.EXE, and was used to change a character map or a proportional spacing table in WPFONT.FIL or WPFONT.ALL. In version 5, the Printer program is found in a file named PTR.EXE, and it alters printer specifications in files named with the .PRS extension or the .ALL extension.

Tips and Traps Summary

Determining the Cause When the Printer Does Not Print

Trap: The message "ERROR: File not found" may indicate that the file you wish to print does not exist or that there is a problem with the WordPerfect program.

Trap: The message "Printer not accepting characters" often indicates a printer definition or cable problem.

Trap: The message "Press "G" to continue" indicates that WordPerfect is waiting for a signal.

Trap: The message "ERROR: Incompatible file format" means that a problem exists with the file you wish to print.

Tip: Try printing from disk if you get a "disk full" message.

Tip: As a last resort before you call for printing help, try starting all over again.

Tips and Traps Summary (*continued*)

Tip: (When upgrading from 4.2.) Most error messages remain the same in version 5.

Determining the Cause When the Printer Does Not Print Correctly

Tip: When you suspect the printer problem is caused by misplaced codes, you can locate codes quickly by using the Search feature.

Trap: A format problem or unrecognizable characters in a document could indicate incorrect switch settings.

Tip: To use certain fonts, you may need to insert a new print wheel or initialize your printer.

Tip: Try using a different cable if your serial printer prints unintelligible characters or loses characters.

Trap: Not all printers can access all the features available in WordPerfect.

Tip: You may be able to change how WordPerfect and your printer work together if you dislike how a certain feature prints out on your printer.

Tip: Check the sheet feeder definition or top margin codes if your text starts too low on the page or prints within the top or bottom margin.

Tip: (When upgrading from 4.2.) Version 5 has been designed to tap more of your printer's capabilities.

Uncovering/Altering Printer Capabilities

Tip: Print out PRINTER.TST for each font your printer is capable of producing.

Tips and Traps Summary (*continued*)

Tip: Change the print wheel if you hear a beep while printing the PRINTER.TST files.

Tip: If a special capability has not been defined for your printer, you can use printer commands rather than PTR.EXE to activate those capabilities.

Tip: To change a printer specification using PTR.EXE, you must have a good working knowledge of your printer's codes.

Trap: You must know the name of the printer file you wish to examine or edit before loading PTR.EXE.

Tip: (When upgrading from 4.2.) PRINTER.TST has been updated and the Printer program has been completely revamped in version 5.

II

Complementary Features

16

Using the Speller and Thesaurus

When you're typing or proofreading a document, the last thing you want to do is to leaf through a thick, cumbersome dictionary or thesaurus. It slows you down and interrupts your concentration. WordPerfect offers an alternative. Instead of reaching for the dictionary to check the spelling of a word, press a few keys to access WordPerfect's Speller. Or use the Speller to proofread the entire document. Instead of grabbing the thesaurus to find just the right word, press a few keys to activate WordPerfect's on-disk thesaurus. You will learn in this chapter how the Speller feature and the thesaurus can help you produce error-free documents, with words that reflect precisely the meaning you wish to convey.

The Speller

WordPerfect checks the spelling of your words by comparing them with words in its dictionary, a file on the WordPerfect Speller disk called WP{WP}EN.LEX. The dictionary is composed of two parts: a common word list and a main word list.

The common word list contains only about 2500 key words; WordPerfect checks this shorter list first. The main list contains 115,000 words and is checked only if a word isn't found in the common word list. This sequence speeds WordPerfect's ability to proofread your document.

A word not listed in the dictionary is brought to your attention during a spelling check. If the word is misspelled, you can choose from a list of suggested words or edit the word on your own. If the word is correctly spelled, you can skip over that word or direct WordPerfect to add that word to a supplement to the dictionary, a file called WP{WP}EN.SUP. In this way you can tailor the dictionary to include technical words or proper nouns that you regularly include in your documents.

The dictionary is so comprehensive that you may find yourself adding very few words to the supplement. It contains a variety of medical terms (such as arteriosclerosis and gastrogenic), legal terms (such as deposition and jurisprudence), and even common names (such as Bonnie, David, Jonathan, and Melissa) and last names (such as Cohen, Jones, Letterman, and Wang), to name a few. Unless your documents contain rare or highly technical words, you'll find that the WordPerfect dictionary contains most of the words you use every day. And you can always use the supplement to add words that are unique to your field.

You can check spelling for a whole document, for one page, or for just one word. To begin the spelling check process:

1. Place the text for which you wish to check spelling on the Typing screen.

2. To check spelling for the entire document, you can position the cursor anywhere in the text. Or, to check spelling for a page, move the cursor to that page. Or, to check spelling for a word, position the cursor on any character within that word.

3. Floppy disk users must place a copy of the WordPerfect Speller disk in the default drive (drive B). Hard disk users should have the dictionary files already stored on the hard disk (if not, refer to Appendix A).

4. Press SPELL (CTRL + F2). In a few moments WordPerfect responds

   Check: 1 Word; **2** Page; **3** Document; **4** New Sup. Dictionary;
   5 Look Up; **6** Count: **0**

5. Choose from the first three items on the menu. For example, if you wish to check spelling for an entire document, select Document (3 or D). WordPerfect responds

   * **Please Wait** *

   The Speller feature is now activated.

WordPerfect sorts through its dictionary. Words found in the dictionary are considered correct and thus passed over. If all text is recognized in the dictionary, the spelling check ends.

But if you used a word that is not listed in the dictionary, that word is highlighted in reverse video and the Typing screen splits in two. The top half of the screen displays 11 lines of your document, including the line containing the misspelled word. The bottom half of the screen displays a list of possible replacements (words that are different by a single letter or by two letters typed in reverse sequence), as well as a prompt for further action. For instance, Figure 16-1 shows the Speller paused at "exsiting".

When a misspelled word is highlighted and the spelling you want is in the list provided at the bottom of the screen, simply type the letter that corresponds to the correct word. WordPerfect replaces the misspelled word with the correct word and moves on to the next misspelled word. In Figure 16-1, for example, you would type **A** to have WordPerfect insert the word "exciting" in place of "exsiting". (If the list extends beyond the screen, press ENTER to view more words in the replacement list.)

```
     An exsiting San Francisco clothing store wants a manager for
its $1 million business.  We are expanding our operations, opening
a new store downtown.  We want someone experienced in buying,
merchandising, planning and personnel supervision.
     The new store will open in June, but we want you involved now!
Show us that you have what it takes.  Send resume to:  Anna Jones,
Post Office Box 3445B, San Francisco, CA  94101



==============================================================================

  A. exciting                B. existing                C. exiting





Not Found: 1 Skip Once; 2 Skip; 3 Add Word; 4 Edit; 5 Look Up:  0
```

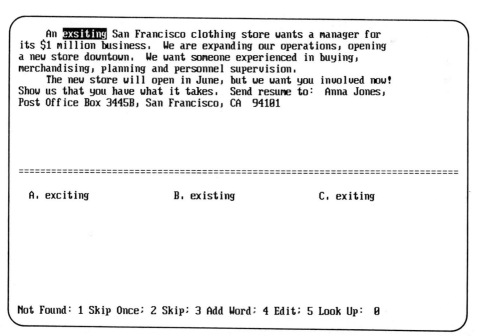

Figure 16-1. The Speller screen with suggestions for "exsiting"

When a word is misspelled and the correct spelling is not on the list provided, you may choose one of two options:

- Edit the word yourself. On the Not Found menu, select 4, Edit, or just press the LEFT ARROW or RIGHT ARROW key. WordPerfect places the cursor on that word in the text. Use the directional arrow keys, typing keys, DEL, and BACKSPACE to edit the word, and then press EXIT (F7) to continue the spelling check.

- View a new list of words from the dictionary based on a word pattern that you type. Select Look Up (5 or L). WordPerfect provides the prompt:

  Word or word pattern:

  Type in a word pattern, using wild cards when you're not sure of the word's spelling—the asterisk (*) to substitute for any number of characters and the question mark (?) to substitute for a single character.

  For example, if at the prompt you type **exc*ing** and press ENTER, WordPerfect offers a long list of words starting with "exc", ending with "ing", and having any number of letters in between, as shown in Figure 16-2. If you type **ex?iting** and press ENTER, WordPerfect provides a shorter list, with one letter substituted for the question mark, and thus offers only the word "exciting".

  When WordPerfect provides a word or a new list of words, you can press a letter to select a word from the new list or press ENTER to try another word pattern. Exit the Look Up option by pressing CANCEL (F1) at the **Word or word pattern:** prompt. You are returned to the Not Found menu.

When the word that is highlighted by WordPerfect is spelled correctly but is not in WordPerfect's dictionary, you have three different options to choose from on the Not Found menu:

- Ignore this one occurrence of the word. Select 1, Skip Once. WordPerfect continues with the spelling check. This is a convenient option when the highlighted word is a technical word or a proper noun that you use infrequently.

- Ignore this word for the rest of the current spelling check. Select 2, Skip. This is a convenient option when the highlighted word is a technical word or a proper noun used repeatedly throughout the document.

```
     An exsiting San Francisco clothing store wants a manager for
its $1 million business.  We are expanding our operations, opening
a new store downtown.  We want someone experienced in buying,
merchandising, planning and personnel supervision.
     The new store will open in June, but we want you involved now!
Show us that you have what it takes.  Send resume to:  Anna Jones,
Post Office Box 3445B, San Francisco, CA  94101




==============================================================================

  A. excavating              B. exceeding               C. excelling
  D. excepting               E. excerpting              F. exchanging
  G. excising                H. exciting                I. exclaiming
  J. excluding               K. excogitating            L. excommunicating
  M. excoriating             N. excreting               O. excruciating
  P. exculpating             Q. excusing


Select Word: 0
```

*Figure 16-2. The Look Up option finding replacements for "exc*ing"*

- Include this word in the dictionary supplement, which serves as an addition to the main dictionary. Select 3, Add Word. WordPerfect will never again highlight the word as misspelled—in the current spelling check or in any checks in the future. This is a convenient option for technical words or proper nouns that occur frequently in the documents that you type.

After you decide on the fate of a highlighted word, the spelling check continues, until the next misspelled word is found (unless you choose only a word check).

After a *word check,* the cursor moves to the next word in the text. The Spell menu remains on the screen. Select a new option to continue, or press CANCEL (F1), EXIT (F7), or the SPACEBAR to end the spelling check.

After a *page check,* WordPerfect lists the total number of words on that page. Press any key to return to the Spell menu. Then select a new option, or press CANCEL (F1), EXIT (F7), or the SPACEBAR to exit.

After a *document check,* WordPerfect lists the total number of words in the document. Press any key to end the spelling check. The Spell menu does not reappear automatically.

After a spelling check is complete, floppy disk users should remove the Speller disk from drive B and replace it with the data disk that was there previously.

Tip: *The CANCEL (F1) key aborts the spelling check.*

You can stop the spelling check process at any time. Simply press CANCEL (F1) until there are no more spelling check messages at the bottom of the Typing screen. The number of times you must press CANCEL depends on where you are in the spelling check. If the Spell menu is on the screen, you need to press CANCEL only once.

Tip: *You can perform a word count without performing a spelling check.*

You can count the number of words in your document without checking the spelling of words within the document. To do this, the document must be on the Typing screen. Press SPELL and select Count (6 or C). WordPerfect provides a word count on the screen. Press CANCEL to exit the Speller feature. This is a useful feature for writers who must submit an article that contains a specific number of words.

Tip: *The Speller can check a block of text.*

If you wish to check spelling for a block of text that isn't a discrete unit, that is, a block of text that is not composed of one word, one page, or one document, you can block text before pressing SPELL. Press BLOCK (ALT + F4) and mark the beginning and the end of the block. Next, press SPELL. WordPerfect begins immediately to check spelling within the block. After you've made any corrections to words not recognized by its dictionary, WordPerfect provides a word count for that block. Press any key to exit the spelling check.

Tip: *The Speller checks headers, footers, footnotes, endnotes, and graphics.*

When you check spelling for a page or a document, WordPerfect also checks spelling for any headers, footers, footnotes, or endnotes located on that page or document. Also, WordPerfect checks the spelling in graphics captions or graphics text boxes. Alternatively, you can check spelling for just a header, footer, footnote, endnote, or in a graphic without checking the body of your text. For example, to check spelling for a header, display the header on the Typing screen by choosing to edit it (as described in Chapter 9). Press SPELL. Then choose 2, Page, or 3, Document, to check spelling for the header.

Trap: *Even after you edit a word, WordPerfect continues to highlight it if it's not in the dictionary.*

If you edit a highlighted word on your own, WordPerfect checks the edited version before moving on. WordPerfect will remain on that word if the edited word is still not in the dictionary. You must then choose to skip the word or to add it to the supplement in order to continue the spelling check.

Trap: *There's no way to move backward during a spelling check.*

If you happen to select the wrong option after WordPerfect highlights a word, you cannot go backward. Either complete the spelling check process and then return to that word, or press CANCEL (F1) until you exit the spelling check and then start the spelling check procedure again.

Tip: *The Speller checks for the occurrence of double words.*

WordPerfect stops at a word that appears twice in a row and highlights both occurrences. A prompt at the bottom of the screen lists possible options, as shown in Figure 16-3. You can choose to skip the double words so that both of them remain in the document, delete the second occurrence, edit the text, or turn off the double word feature until the end of the current spelling check.

Tip: *The Speller highlights words that contain numbers.*

The Speller skips over numbers during a spelling check. For example, if you type an address such as **9000 Main Street**, WordPerfect will ignore the "9000".

But if a word contains a combination of letters and numbers, WordPerfect highlights that word, suggesting alternatives based on the letters in that word. An

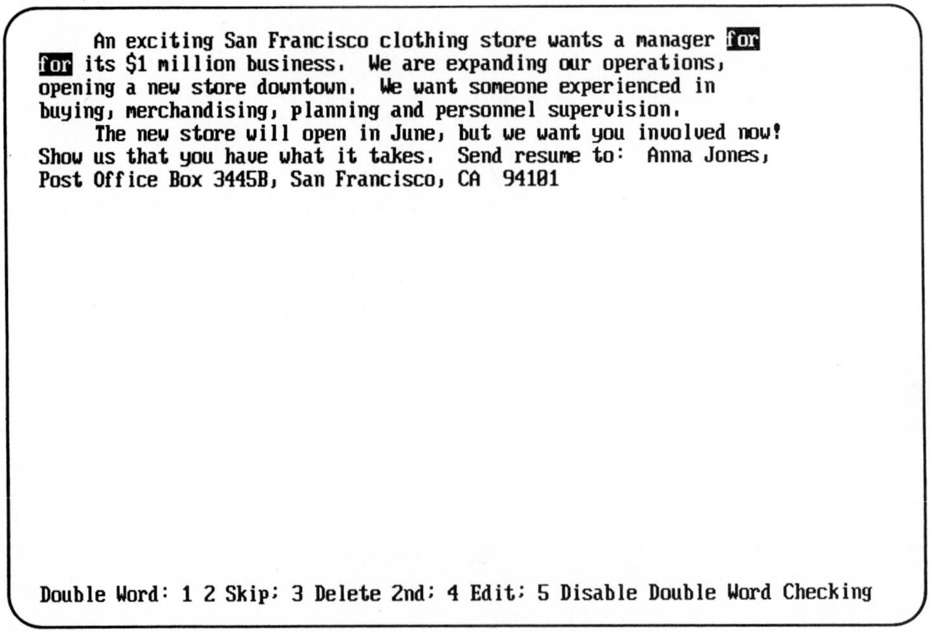

An exciting San Francisco clothing store wants a manager for
for its $1 million business. We are expanding our operations,
opening a new store downtown. We want someone experienced in
buying, merchandising, planning and personnel supervision.
The new store will open in June, but we want you involved now!
Show us that you have what it takes. Send resume to: Anna Jones,
Post Office Box 3445B, San Francisco, CA 94101
Double Word: 1 2 Skip; 3 Delete 2nd; 4 Edit; 5 Disable Double Word Checking

Figure 16-3. Checking for the occurrence of double words

example is shown in Figure 16-4. Select an item from the Not Found menu to continue.

Tip: *WordPerfect assumes that a word you correct once should also be corrected if it occurs again in the document.*

When you select the correct spelling from the word list provided by WordPerfect, that selection is used by WordPerfect throughout the document. For example, suppose you misspelled "receive" as "recieve" throughout a document. If you correct the first occurrence by choosing from the word list, all other occurrences of "recieve" will also be corrected.

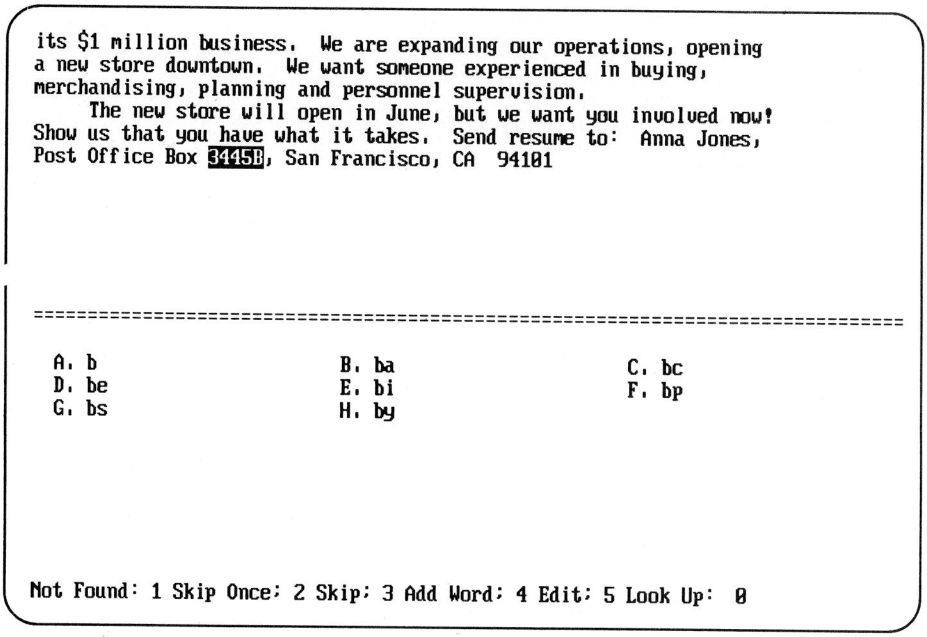
its $1 million business. We are expanding our operations, opening
a new store downtown. We want someone experienced in buying,
merchandising, planning and personnel supervision.
The new store will open in June, but we want you involved now!
Show us that you have what it takes. Send resume to: Anna Jones,
Post Office Box 3445B, San Francisco, CA 94101
A. b
B. ba
C. bc
D. be
E. bi
F. bp
G. bs
H. by
Not Found: 1 Skip Once; 2 Skip; 3 Add Word; 4 Edit; 5 Look Up: 0

Figure 16-4. Checking for words that contain numbers

Tip: *The Speller maintains a word's case.*

WordPerfect maintains the distinction between upper- and lowercase. If, for example, you must substitute another word for "Exsiting", the new word you choose from the list provided will start with a capital letter.

Tip: *You can check spelling for a word not yet on the Typing screen.*

Check the spelling of a word even before you type it by choosing the Look Up option directly from the Spell menu. Press SPELL and choose 5, Look Up. WordPerfect responds

Word or word pattern:

Type in your guess at the spelling of the word and press ENTER. You can use the wild cards (* and ?), as described earlier in this section of the chapter, to fill in where you're not sure of certain letters—such as in "surpri?e", if you're not sure if the word contains an "s" or a "z". If you don't include wild cards, WordPerfect checks the word phonetically, that is, by the way that the word sounds.

WordPerfect responds with a list of possible word choices from its dictionary. Find the spelling of the word you want to type. Press CANCEL (F1) twice to exit the spelling check and you're ready to type in the correct spelling of the word.

Trap: *Avoid using wild cards as the first letter in a word pattern during a Look Up.*

If you specify a word pattern starting with a wild card, such as "*citing", the Look Up process takes a long time. Start the word pattern with a specific letter to narrow down the search for WordPerfect.

Trap: *A spelling check is no substitute for a final proofreading.*

WordPerfect's spelling check frees you from proofreading for misspellings (which is more than half the battle), but its abilities stop there. For one thing, while WordPerfect's dictionary checks for proper spelling, it won't check for the incorrect use of a homonym (such as see/sea, two/too/to, be/bee, and so on). Therefore, WordPerfect won't pause at the sentence

I ordered *too* dozen pens yesterday.

even though the correct spelling is "two" and not "too". Nor can WordPerfect check to see if a sentence makes sense. Since "pins" is in its dictionary, WordPerfect will not stop at the sentence

I placed orders for ball point and fountain *pins.*

even though the correct word is "pens" and not "pins".

Moreover, the Speller doesn't stop to check numbers unless they are contained in a word in combination with letters. You cannot rely on the Speller to check ZIP codes, telephone numbers, social security numbers, and the like.

And, the Speller won't stop if you accidentally include certain symbols in the middle of a word. For instance, the Speller won't pause at "doz~en".

Even after a spell check, peruse a document yourself for grammatical and stylistic content. Also, verify any numbers you typed, and check for possible typos involving symbols.

Trap: *During a spelling check, you cannot add to the supplementary dictionary unless you have room on the Speller disk and in RAM.*

You can add words to the dictionary supplement only if you have enough available RAM and enough free disk space to store those words. The first time you add a word to the supplement (by choosing 3, Add Word, on the Not Found menu), that word is placed in a temporary file in the computer's memory. Once the spelling check is complete, the word is stored on disk in the WP{WP}EN.SUP file, the supplement to the dictionary.

If, when you add words to RAM, the message **Dictionary Full** appears, exit the Speller by pressing CANCEL (F1) to add the words in memory to WP{WP}EN.SUP. Then initiate another spelling check for the rest of the document.

If you try to place a word on disk at the end of the spelling check but there's no room available on the disk, then that word is not stored in the supplement. On a hard disk, that's probably not an issue. If you're a floppy disk user, however, and assuming you use double-density disks, the Speller disk starts out packed with dictionary words, with space available for only about 2000 more words of your choosing (20,000 bytes). Do not use up the available space by placing other files (such as the DOS file COMMAND.COM) on the Speller disk. Reserve the Speller disk for three files only: WP{WP}EN.LEX (the dictionary), WP{WP}EN.SUP (the supplement), and SPELL.EXE (the Speller utility described in the next section of this chapter). That way you'll reserve the space needed to add words permanently to the supplement.

Tip: *Add words to or delete words from the supplementary dictionary by treating it like a standard document.*

The file WP{WP}EN.SUP contains all the words you added by choosing 3, Add Word, from the Not Found menu. Occasionally, however, you might add a word to the supplement by mistake—such as an incorrectly spelled word—that you will want to delete. You might also have in mind certain words that you would like to include in the supplement. Both of these tasks, that is, deleting and inserting words in the supplement, are possible.

Starting with a clear screen, retrieve the supplementary dictionary, which is the file named WP{WP}EN.SUP, in the same way you would retrieve any WordPerfect file. You'll notice that each word is on its own line, followed by a **[HRt]**. You can delete a word and the **[HRt]** that follows it. Or you can move the cursor to a blank line, type in a word, and press ENTER to insert a **[HRt]** code. Now, resave the file.

Do not try this method with the dictionary; use it *only* with the supplement! (See the next section, "The Speller Utility," for ways to add or delete words in the main dictionary.)

Tip: *You can check spelling with an alternative supplementary dictionary.*

It may be appropriate for you to create more than one supplementary dictionary. Perhaps you wish to create one to check legal documents, and another to check personal documents. To create a supplementary dictionary, start with a clear Typing screen. Type each word on a separate line. Then, save this file. (The next section of this chapter, "The Speller Utility," describes a second method for creating a new supplementary dictionary.)

When you're ready to use a supplementary dictionary other than WP{WP}EN. SUP, press the SPELL key and select the option called New Supplementary Dictionary (4 or N). Type in the path (drive/directory) and filename and press ENTER. Now when you initiate a word check, a page check, or a document check, WordPerfect will use the file you specified as the supplement.

Trap: *If you use the dictionary or supplement from other than the default drive or directory, you must notify WordPerfect.*

WordPerfect assumes that the dictionary and the supplementary dictionary reside either on the directory where the main WordPerfect program file (WP.EXE) is housed or on the default drive or directory.

If the dictionary or supplement is not where WordPerfect assumes it should be, when you press SPELL WordPerfect provides a message such as:

> **WP{WP}EN.LEX not found: 1** Enter Path; **2** Skip language; **3** Exit Spell: **3**

To indicate a temporary path where the dictionary or supplement can be found, select Enter Path (1 or P), and then type in the drive/directory. For instance, if the Speller disk is in drive A rather than drive B, type **A:** and press ENTER. (If you view the menu because you forgot to place the Speller in drive B, simply press ENTER to clear the prompt, insert the Speller disk, and press SPELL again to start over.) Or, if the dictionary is in the \WPER \SPELL directory on the hard disk, type **C: \WPER \SPELL** and press ENTER.

Or to simply count the number of words, select Skip language (2 or S). WordPerfect then doesn't bother to check for misspellings.

Or select Exit Spell (3 or E), or press ENTER, to cancel the spelling check.

If you constantly receive this menu, then WordPerfect is always searching the wrong drive or directory for the main dictionary or supplement. In this case, either copy the dictionary or supplement to the directory where WP.EXE is housed, or *permanently* change where WordPerfect looks for the dictionary or supplement by using the Location of Auxiliary Files option on the Setup menu (described in Appendix B).

Tip: *Purchase a foreign-language dictionary if you write documents in foreign languages.*

The dictionary that is included with the American English version of WordPerfect is the English dictionary. That's what the EN stands for in the dictionary's filename, WP{WP}EN.LEX.

However, if you create multilingual documents, consider purchasing additional dictionaries from WordPerfect Corporation. WordPerfect offers spelling dictionaries in 13 other languages: British English, Canadian French, Danish, Dutch, Finnish, French, German, Icelandic, Italian, Norwegian, Portuguese, Spanish, and Swedish.

If you purchase a foreign-language dictionary and wish to check your spelling by using that dictionary, you must indicate to WordPerfect that you wish to use that foreign-language dictionary. You do so by placing a language code in the text:

1. Move the cursor to the location in your document where you want to change the language code. For instance, if you wish to check spelling for an entire document by using a foreign-language dictionary, place the cursor at the top of that document.
2. Press the FORMAT (SHIFT + F8) key to display the Format menu.
3. Select Other (4 or O) to display the Other Format menu.
4. Select Language (4 or L). The cursor moves under the default setting **EN**, which represents the English language dictionary (as well as the English language thesaurus and the hyphenation module).
5. Type in the two letters that represent the language code for the foreign dictionary you wish to employ, and press ENTER. The language codes are as follows:

CA	Canadian French	IT	Italian
DA	Danish	NE	Dutch
DE	German	NO	Norwegian
EN	English	PO	Portuguese
ES	Spanish	SU	Finnish
FR	French	SV	Swedish
IC	Icelandic	UK	British English

6. Press EXIT (F7) to return to the document.

WordPerfect inserts a language code in the document which takes effect from that point forward to the end of the document (or until the next language code appears). For instance, if you selected the French dictionary, then the code inserted is **[Lang:FR]**. As a result, when you press the SPELL (CTRL + F2) key to initiate a spelling check, WordPerfect will use the dictionary file named WP{WP}FR.LEX, rather than WP{WP}EN.LEX.

Note: The language code also affects the thesaurus, as described in the last section of this chapter, "The Thesaurus," as well as the hyphenation module that you use, as described in Chapter 8.

Be sure to store foreign-language dictionaries in the same place that you store your English dictionary so that WordPerfect can find the dictionaries on disk. Otherwise, WordPerfect will prompt, asking for the path where the foreign-language dictionary is found.

Tip: *(When upgrading from 4.2.) The spelling check procedure remains basically the same in version 5.*

Continue to make spelling checks on your document as you did when using version 4.2. You'll notice that the Phonetic option, a feature that was rarely used, has been deleted from the Not Found menu.

Another change is that there is no longer a special menu displayed when, during a spell check, WordPerfect encounters a word containing numbers. Instead, the Not Found menu appears. As a result, you can no longer request that WordPerfect ignore words containing numbers for the rest of the spell check. On the other hand, in version 5 you can add words containing numbers to the supplementary dictionary such as "2d" or "4th" during the spell check, which was not possible in version 4.2. You'll also notice that the filenames for the dictionary and supplementary dictionary have been changed.

You can convert supplementary dictionaries from version 4.2 for use in version 5. Using version 5, retrieve the supplementary dictionary to the screen and then resave it under the name WP{WP}EN.SUP (or under a different filename if you use more than one supplementary dictionary). Or you can convert the supplementary dictionaries using the Speller utility, which is described in the next section. (Also, see Chapter 28 for information on converting other version 4.2 files, including version 4.2 main dictionaries, into version 5 format.)

If you wish to use a foreign-language dictionary, then in version 5 you must insert a language code in your document (see the preceding Tip for more information).

The Speller Utility

The Speller utility helps you manage the words in your dictionary and supplement. Work with this utility if you wish to create a new supplementary dictionary, add a whole list of words to the dictionary or supplement, delete a list of words, or find out which words are in the dictionary. Otherwise, you will never need to use this utility. In fact, there is no reason to use the Speller utility on a casual basis; shuffle words too much and you're liable to hamper the effectiveness of the dictionary or accidentally erase part of it.

The Speller utility is accessed from DOS. To start the Speller utility:

1. Floppy disk users should place the Speller disk in drive A and a data disk in drive B (if it contains supplementary dictionaries or files of words not housed on the Speller disk), and should make sure that the DOS prompt reads **A>**. (If not, then at the DOS prompt, type **A:** and press ENTER.) Hard disk users should change to the directory where the dictionary file (WP{WP}EN.LEX) and the Speller utility file (SPELL.EXE) are both stored. (These two files should be in the same directory.)
2. At the DOS prompt (**A>** or **C>**), type **SPELL** and press ENTER.
3. After a few moments, the Speller Utility menu appears on the screen, as shown in Figure 16-5. In the upper right-hand corner of the menu, **WP{WP}EN.LEX** signifies that you are addressing WordPerfect's main dictionary.

You can now discover which words are housed in the dictionary. You can view all the words in the common word list by choosing 5, Display common word list. The words are displayed alphabetically, one screen at a time. Press any letter

```
Spell -- WordPerfect Speller Utility                              wp{wp}en.lex

0 - Exit
1 - Change/Create dictionary
2 - Add words to dictionary
3 - Delete words from dictionary
4 - Optimize dictionary
5 - Display common word list
6 - Check location of a word
7 - Look up
8 - Phonetic look up
9 - Convert 4.2 Dictionary to 5.0

Selection:
```

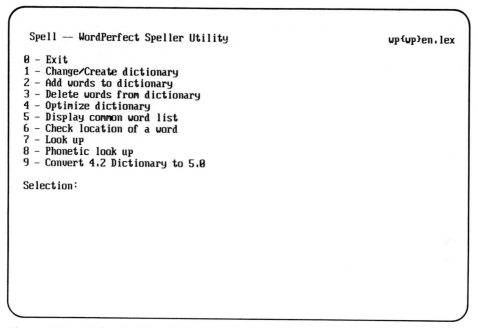

Figure 16-5. *The Speller Utility menu*

or cursor movement key (such as PGDN) to view the words screen by screen. Press CANCEL (F1) or the SPACEBAR to return to the Speller Utility menu.

You can find out whether a specific word is in the common word list or the main word list by selecting 6, Check location of a word. When WordPerfect prompts **Word to check:**, enter the word. WordPerfect indicates whether that word is in one of the lists, or whether it is not found. Press CANCEL (F1) to return to the Speller Utility menu.

You can also view a specific group of words in the dictionary by selecting 7, Look up, and, when WordPerfect prompts **Word Pattern:**, by entering the pattern. This option operates the same as the Look Up option in the spelling check menu. For instance, to find those words that begin with the letters "spe", type **spe*** at the prompt and press ENTER. After the words matching that pattern are displayed, you can press CANCEL (F1) or ENTER to return to the Speller Utility menu.

You also can determine the spelling of a word based on how that word sounds by selecting 8, Phonetic look up, and, when WordPerfect prompts **Word**, by entering the word phonetically. For instance, type **enuf** and press ENTER. WordPerfect will suggest "enough". Press CANCEL (F1) to return to the Speller Utility menu.

Tip: *Use the Speller utility to transfer words from the supplement to the dictionary.*

At some point you may amass so many words in the supplement that the message **Dictionary Full** appears on the screen during a spelling check. You can correct this problem by transferring the words in WP{WP}EN.SUP into the main dictionary and by then deleting the WP{WP}EN.SUP file. Follow this procedure:

1. From the Speller Utility menu, select 2, Add words to dictionary. WordPerfect responds with the menu shown in Figure 16-6.
2. You can add the words to the common word list or to the main word list. In general, since supplementary words appear infrequently, you should add the words to the main word list. Select 4, Add to main word list (from a file). WordPerfect prompts you for a filename.
3. Type **WP{WP}EN.SUP** and press ENTER.

```
 Spell -- Add Words                                         wp{wp}en.lex

0 - Cancel - do not add words
1 - Add to common word list (from keyboard)
2 - Add to common word list (from a file)
3 - Add to main word list (from keyboard)
4 - Add to main word list (from a file)
5 - Exit

Selection:
```

Figure 16-6. The Add Words menu in the Speller utility

4. Select 5, Exit, to begin the addition process. Be patient because the entire dictionary is updated, from A through Z. Even adding a few words can take 20 minutes. (If you're a floppy disk user, there may not be sufficient room on the Speller disk to create the temporary files WordPerfect uses to add to the dictionary. The Speller utility prompts you if that's the case. Place a data disk with available space in drive A and press ENTER to continue.)
5. Exit the Speller utility by choosing 0, Cancel, and then 0, Exit.
6. Erase the WP{WP}EN.SUP file from the Speller disk. (You can do this by using DOS or by loading WordPerfect and using the LIST FILES key, as described in Chapter 13.)

The next time you add a word during a spelling check, WordPerfect creates a new WP{WP}EN.SUP file with space for more words.

Tip: *You can add words to or delete words from the dictionary directly.*

You can add a whole group of words to the dictionary by selecting 2, Add words to dictionary, from the Speller Utility menu. WordPerfect responds with the Add Words menu shown in Figure 16- 6.

You have two choices for *where* you add words and two choices regarding *how* you add them. First, you can place the words in the main word list or you can place them in the common word list. Add them to the main word list unless they appear constantly within your documents. Second, you can add the words by typing them directly on the keyboard or by transferring them from a file. If you choose to type directly from the keyboard, press ENTER after you type each word. The word disappears and you can type in the next one. (You can also separate words by pressing the SPACEBAR.) If you choose to transfer words from a file, you should already have created a document in WordPerfect that contains only those words that you want to add, with each word placed on a separate line.

Suppose you wish to add 30 technical words to the main word list of the dictionary directly from the keyboard.These are the singular and plural forms of various words. From the Speller Utility menu:

1. Select 2, Add words to dictionary.

2. Select 3, Add to main word list (from keyboard). WordPerfect prompts for the first word.
3. Type each of the 30 words, pressing ENTER after typing each one. Make sure each is correctly spelled before pressing ENTER.
4. After you've typed all the words, choose 5, Exit.

If you wish to add words from a file, review the preceding Tip for the procedure (but substitute your supplementary dictionary's filename in place of WP{WP}EN. SUP). The process for adding words to the dictionary is long, requiring 20 minutes or more. Once the Speller Utility menu reappears, the process is complete.

The process for deleting words is similar to the process for adding words. Select 3, Delete words from dictionary, from the Speller Utility menu. The Delete Words menu offers choices comparable to those on the Add Words menu.

Trap: *Don't use the Speller utility to add just a few words.*

The Speller utility is used for making a major change in a dictionary. If you want to add just a few words, don't use the Speller utility. Instead, add these words in the normal spelling check process by selecting 3, Add Word, from the Not Found menu. The process will take only a fraction of the time required to use the Speller utility.

Tip: *You can create and use additional supplementary dictionaries.*

If many of your documents contain technical words, you can create a separate supplementary dictionary of those special words and use it only on certain documents. Using the Speller Utility menu, select 1, Change/Create dictionary. WordPerfect prompts you for the filename; type a name of eight characters or fewer with a three-letter extension, just as you do to name a WordPerfect file. If the filename is unique, you are prompted to verify that you wish to create a new dictionary. Type **Y**.

The Speller Utility menu remains on screen, but the upper right-hand corner displays the new dictionary name rather than **WP{WP}EN.LEX**. All the items on the Speller Utility menu now relate to that new dictionary file. Choose 2, Add words to dictionary. After you've added words to the dictionary (described in a preceding Tip), you should choose option 4, Optimize dictionary. Then you can use this new supplementary dictionary during a spelling check, along with WordPerfect's dictionary.

Tip: *(When upgrading from 4.2.) The Speller utility remains the same in version 5.*

The Speller utility has not changed in version 5, except that there is a new option 9, Convert 4.2 Dictionary to 5.0. WordPerfect will prompt for the name of the 4.2 dictionary (be sure to precede the filename with the proper drive/directory if different from the default) and then for the name of the version 5 dictionary you wish to create. In this way, you can convert all the supplementary dictionaries you established in version 4.2 into version 5 format.

The Thesaurus

WordPerfect can provide a list of synonyms as well as antonyms for a specific word. The list can help you understand the meaning of a certain word, it can provide a word that fits in better with your text, or it can offer an alternative word if you find yourself repeating a certain word too frequently. There are 100,000 words on the Thesaurus disk in a file called WP{WP}EN.THS. Of those, 10,000 are *headwords,* meaning that they can be looked up; the others appear only as synonyms or antonyms. To use the thesaurus:

1. Floppy disk users should place a copy of the WordPerfect Thesaurus disk in the default drive (drive B). Hard disk users should have the thesaurus files already stored on the hard disk (if not, refer to Appendix A).
2. Position the cursor on any character in the word you wish to look up.
3. Press THESAURUS (ALT + F1). The screen splits in two. The top of the screen displays four lines of your text and highlights the word being searched for in the thesaurus. The bottom of the screen lists alternative words, as in Figure 16-7, which shows the thesaurus entries for the word "want".

Notice in Figure 16-7 that nouns (n) and verbs (v) are separated. When a word has synonyms that are adjectives (a), the adjectives also are separated. Words with similar connotations are placed in subgroups, preceded by a number. Antonyms (ant) are included at the end of the list.

4. If the substitute word that you want is in the first column, select 1, Replace Word. WordPerfect responds

   Press letter for word:

   Type the letter corresponding to the word you wish to substitute. WordPerfect replaces the original word with the alternative and automatically exits the thesaurus.

   Or, if the substitute word is in another column, press RIGHT ARROW until the highlighted letters move to the column where the word you want is located. (Whichever column has letters beside it becomes the active column—the one from which you can select a word.) Then select 1, Replace Word, and type the corresponding letter.

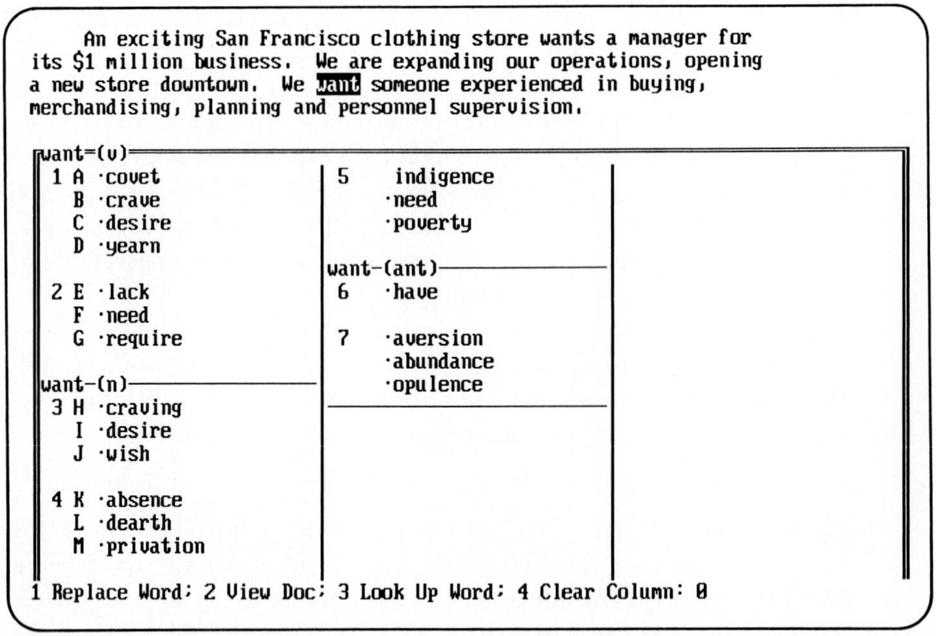

Figure 16-7. The Thesaurus screen with suggestions for "want"

Or, to exit the thesaurus without replacing a word, press CANCEL (F1), EXIT (F7), or the SPACEBAR.

Tip: *You can continue searching the thesaurus for additional words.*

If after viewing a list of synonyms you still don't find the word you need, you can continue asking the thesaurus to look up additional words. Words on the list that are preceded by bullets are headwords and thus can be looked up. In Figure 16-7, for example, the word "indigence" (at the top of the second column) cannot be looked up; all the other words can be. Type **G**, for example, and column 2 is replaced with synonyms and antonyms for the word "require", as shown in Figure 16-8. (Notice that the synonyms for "want" are now confined to the first column because the second column is occupied.)

You can even look up synonyms for a word not listed as a synonym or an antonym. Simply select 3, Look Up Word. WordPerfect responds

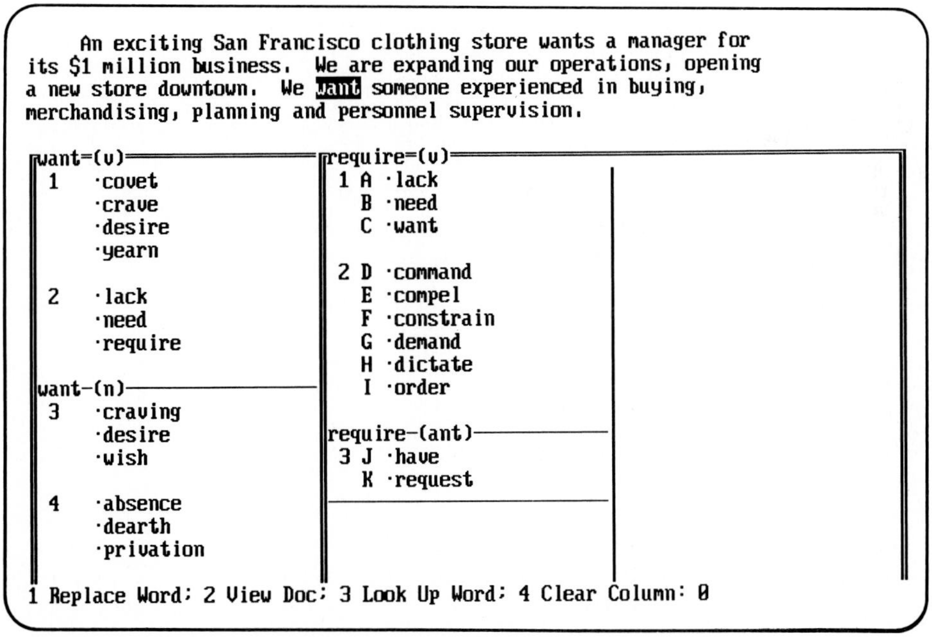

Figure 16-8. The Thesaurus screen with suggestions for "want" and "require"

Word:

Type in a new word and press ENTER. Now the next column contains synonyms/antonyms for that new word.

Up to three words and their references can be displayed side by side in three columns. You can select 4, Clear Column, or press BACKSPACE or DEL to clear the list for the last word requested. To clear the thesaurus from the screen, press CANCEL (F1).

Trap: *Not all words are headwords.*

When a request is made for synonyms for a word that is not a headword, you'll encounter the message **Word not found**. WordPerfect then provides the opportunity to try with another word. Think of a related word. For example, if you look up synonyms for the word "hello", you'll find that it isn't a headword. Instead, try "welcome", and you'll be provided with more than a dozen synonyms and antonyms.

Trap: *Sometimes, not all the synonyms for a word can fit on screen.*

If a headword has a long list of synonyms, perhaps not all of them will fit on the screen at one time. If that word is the only word for which synonyms are displayed, it can occupy all three columns. If you then look up another word, the first word is restricted to the first column. Thus, you won't see all its synonyms (or antonyms) unless you use the cursor movement keys (see the next Tip).

Tip: *You can move within the list of words with the cursor movement keys.*

The column that contains the letters is the one from which you can select a substitute word. It is the active column. Cursor movement keys allow you to move quickly through a list of synonyms to find a particular word:

- The UP ARROW and DOWN ARROW keys move from subgroup to subgroup for one word, while the LEFT ARROW and RIGHT ARROW keys move from column to column.
- The GOTO (CTRL + HOME) key moves a specific subgroup to the top of the currently active column. For example, to view subgroup 6 of the active column, which may not at present appear on screen, press CTRL + HOME, type **6**, and press ENTER.
- The PGUP key (or MINUS key on the numeric keypad) moves up a full screen to reveal additional subgroups, while the PGDN key (or PLUS key on the numeric keypad) moves down a full screen to reveal additional subgroups for a particular word.
- HOME, HOME, UP ARROW moves to the first subgroup, while HOME, HOME, DOWN ARROW moves to the last subgroup for the particular word in the active column.

Tip: *You can look through a document while the thesaurus entries are on the screen.*

You may, at times, wish to read another section of your text before selecting an alternative word. To do so, select 2, View Doc. The cursor jumps up to the four lines of text at the top of the screen. Move the cursor with the directional arrow keys. When you press EXIT (F7), the cursor returns to the thesaurus entries at the bottom of the screen.

Trap: *The thesaurus doesn't take grammar into account.*

Be cautious when you replace a word with a synonym; it might not be grammatically correct. For example, suppose you search for an alternative to the word "buying". Figure 16-9 illustrates that the thesaurus finds synonyms for "buy", not "buying". Therefore, if you choose a substitute from the list provided, be sure to check the sentence and correct the grammar before you move on. If you choose to insert "purchase" in place of "buy", for example, then edit the new word to read "purchasing" after you exit the thesaurus.

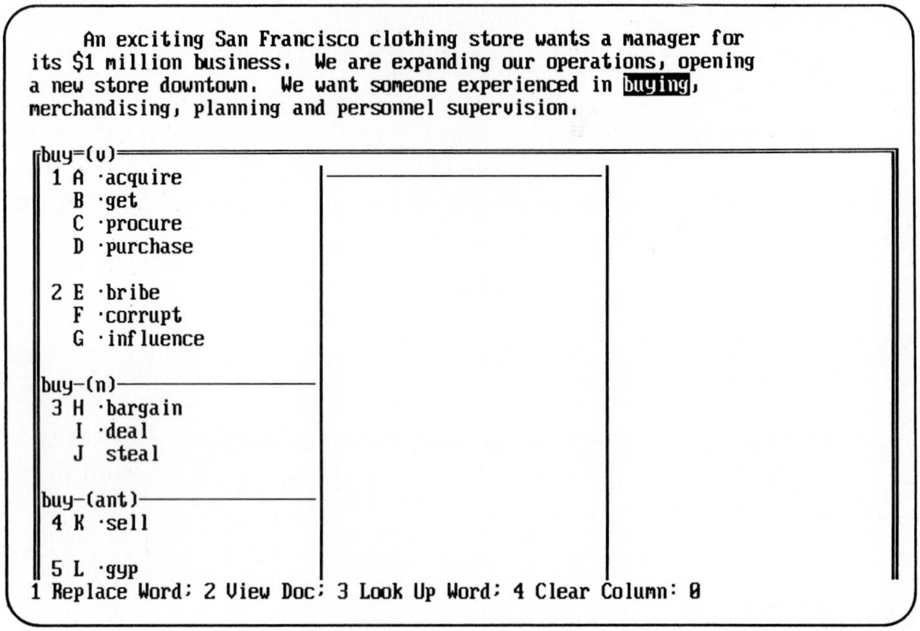

Figure 16-9. Synonyms for "buy" rather than "buying", the word highlighted in the text

Tip: *The thesaurus maintains a word's case.*

WordPerfect recognizes the distinction between upper- and lowercase. If, for example, you replace "Welcome" with another word, that other word will be inserted with its first letter capitalized.

Tip: *You can use the thesaurus to look up a word not yet on the Typing screen.*

If you wish to check alternatives for a word not yet on the Typing screen, simply move the cursor to the empty space where you want to type the next word and press the THESAURUS key. WordPerfect displays a thesaurus screen with no synonyms listed but with a prompt requesting a word. Type in a word and press ENTER. The thesaurus is now active; choose option 1, Replace Word, if you've found the word you want, or select any of the other Thesaurus menu options.

Trap: *If you use the thesaurus from other than the default drive or directory, you must notify WordPerfect.*

WordPerfect assumes that the thesaurus resides either in the directory where the main WordPerfect program file (WP.EXE) is housed, or on the default drive or directory.

If you wish to store the thesaurus file WP{WP}EN.THS on another drive or directory, you must indicate where that file is stored by using the Location of Auxiliary Files option on the Setup menu (described in Appendix B).

Tip: *Purchase a foreign-language thesaurus if you write documents in foreign languages.*

The thesaurus that is included with the American English version of WordPerfect is the English thesaurus. That's what the EN stands for in the thesaurus's filename, WP{WP}EN.THS.

However, if you create multilingual documents, consider purchasing additional thesauruses from WordPerfect Corporation. They are available in 13 other languages: British English, Canadian French, Danish, Dutch, Finnish, French, German, Icelandic, Italian, Norwegian, Portuguese, Spanish, and Swedish.

If you do purchase a foreign-language thesaurus and wish to use it in a document, you must place a language code in the text. To do so:

1. Move the cursor to the location in your document where you want to change the language code. For instance, if you wish to use a foreign-language thesaurus for an entire document, place the cursor at the top of the document.

2. Press the FORMAT (SHIFT + F8) key to display the Format menu.

3. Select Other (4 or O) to display the Other Format menu.
4. Select Language (4 or L). The cursor moves under the default setting **EN**, which represents the English language thesaurus (as well as the English language dictionary and the hyphenation module).
5. Type in the two letters that represent the language code for the foreign thesaurus you wish to employ, and press ENTER. The language codes are as follows:

CA	Canadian French	IT	Italian
DA	Danish	NE	Dutch
DE	German	NO	Norwegian
EN	English	PO	Portuguese
ES	Spanish	SU	Finnish
FR	French	SV	Swedish
IC	Icelandic	UK	British English

6. Press EXIT (F7) to return to the document.

WordPerfect inserts a language code in the document which takes effect from that point forward to the end of the document (or until the next language code appears). For instance, if you selected the French thesaurus, then the code inserted is **[Lang:FR]**. As a result, when you press the THESAURUS (ALT + F1) key to activate the Thesaurus feature, WordPerfect will use the thesaurus file named WP{WP}FR.THS rather than WP{WP}EN.THS.

Note: The language code also affects the dictionary, as described in the first section of this chapter, "The Speller," as well as the hyphenation module that you use, as described in Chapter 8.

Be sure to store foreign-language thesauruses in the same place that you store your English thesaurus so that WordPerfect can find them on disk.

Tip: *(When upgrading from 4.2.) The procedure for using the thesaurus remains the same in version 5.*

Use the THESAURUS key as you did in version 4.2. The filename of the thesaurus has changed. Instead of TH.WP, it is now called WP{WP}EN.THS.

If you wish to use a foreign-language thesaurus, then in version 5 you must insert a language code in your document (as described in an earlier Tip in this chapter section).

Tips and Traps Summary

The Speller

Tip: The CANCEL (F1) key aborts the spelling check.

Tip: You can perform a word count without performing a spelling check.

Tip: The Speller can check a block of text.

Tip: The Speller checks headers, footers, footnotes, endnotes, and graphics.

Trap: Even after you edit a word, WordPerfect continues to highlight it if it's not in the dictionary.

Trap: There's no way to move backward during a spelling check.

Tip: The Speller checks for the occurrence of double words.

Tip: The Speller highlights words that contain numbers.

Tip: WordPerfect assumes that a word you correct once should also be corrected if it occurs again in the document.

Tip: The Speller maintains a word's case.

Tip: You can check spelling for a word not yet on the Typing screen.

Trap: Avoid using wild cards as the first letter in a word pattern during a Look Up.

Trap: A spelling check is no substitute for a final proofreading.

Trap: During a spelling check, you cannot add to the supplementary dictionary unless you have room on the Speller disk and in RAM.

Tips and Traps Summary (*continued*)

Tip: Add words to or delete words from the supplementary dictionary by treating it like a standard document.

Tip: You can check spelling with an alternative supplementary dictionary.

Trap: If you use the dictionary or supplement from other than the default drive or directory, you must notify WordPerfect.

Tip: Purchase a foreign-language dictionary if you write documents in foreign languages.

Tip: (When upgrading from 4.2.) The spelling check procedure remains basically the same in version 5.

The Speller Utility

Tip: Use the Speller utility to transfer words from the supplement to the dictionary.

Tip: You can add words to or delete words from the dictionary directly.

Trap: Don't use the Speller utility to add just a few words.

Tip: You can create and use additional supplementary dictionaries.

Tip: (When upgrading from 4.2.) The Speller utility remains the same in version 5.

The Thesaurus

Tip: You can continue searching the thesaurus for additional words.

Trap: Not all words are headwords.

Trap: Sometimes, not all the synonyms for a word can fit on screen.

Tips and Traps Summary (*continued*)

Tip: You can move within the list of words with the cursor movement keys.

Tip: You can look through a document while the thesaurus entries are on the screen.

Trap: The thesaurus doesn't take grammar into account.

Tip: The thesaurus maintains a word's case.

Tip: You can use the thesaurus to look up a word not yet on the Typing screen.

Trap: If you use the thesaurus from other than the default drive or directory, you must notify WordPerfect.

Tip: Purchase a foreign-language thesaurus if you write documents in foreign languages.

Tip: (When upgrading from 4.2.) The procedure for using the thesaurus remains the same in version 5.

17

Creating Special Characters and Line Drawings

WordPerfect enables you to use more characters in your documents than those that are actually shown on your keyboard. With WordPerfect, you have easy access to special characters. For example, if you're in a law office, you might want to use the paragraph symbol, the section symbol, the copyright symbol, or the trademark symbol. If your document is number-oriented, the one-half and one-quarter symbols are vital. If you send foreign correspondence, various accent marks, such as the umlaut, might be needed. But you must determine whether your screen can display a special character that you wish to insert in a document, and you must also check to see if your printer can print the special characters you need.

In addition, some of you may wish to draw boxes or graphs with solid lines and crisp corners. The Line Draw feature allows you to create line drawings using special box drawing characters. In this chapter you learn how to include special characters and create line drawings in your documents.

Special Characters on the Screen

WordPerfect offers extensive support for over 1500 special characters—such as multinational characters, mathematical/scientific symbols, the Greek and Hebrew alphabets, and typographical symbols.

Which special characters can be displayed on screen depends on your monitor and graphics display card. A file provided on the WordPerfect Conversion disk, CHARACTR.DOC, helps you determine which special characters can be displayed on your computer screen and how to insert them in your documents. CHARACTR.DOC is a standard WordPerfect file, so you can retrieve it as you would any of your own documents. Floppy disk users should place the Conversion disk in drive B; hard disk users should have this file on the hard disk. Retrieve CHARACTR.DOC to the Typing screen.

CHARACTR.DOC is more than 60 pages in length. It is segmented into 13 sections. Each section contains a WordPerfect character set, where a character set represents a related group of characters. Table 17-1 lists the character set names and numbers and describes the special characters housed in each.

WordPerfect has assigned a specific WordPerfect character number to each special character. The WordPerfect character number is composed of the character set number, a comma, and a character number from within the set. For example, Figure 17-1 shows part of the first page of the CHARACTR.DOC file, which contains characters in Character Set 0, the ASCII character set (the standard letters, numbers, and symbols that are on your computer keyboard). Notice that the exclamation point is assigned the WordPerfect character number 0,33. Or, the number 1 is assigned the WordPerfect character number 0,49. All computer monitors are able to display the characters in the ASCII character set. (This is because all the characters in the ASCII character set can be accessed directly from the keyboard, and are therefore not considered to be "special" characters.)

All of the character sets other than the ASCII character set contain special characters, not all of which can be displayed on screen. For instance, Figure 17-2 is a screen showing some of the special characters contained in Character Set 4, the Typographic Symbols character set. On this particular screen, many special characters are displayed—such as the bullet, the section sign, the yen symbol, and the one-half symbol. However, the registered trademark, copyright, and base asterisk symbols cannot be displayed; a shaded square box is displayed instead. Thus, by viewing the CHARACTR.DOC file on your computer display, you can see which symbols will be displayed and which will be shown instead as a shaded

Table 17-1. WordPerfect Character Sets, Which Are Listed in the CHARACTR. DOC file

Character Set	Character Set Number	Contents
ASCII	0	ASCII space through tilde—symbols commonly found on the computer keyboard
Multinational 1	1	Common capitalizable multinational characters, diacritical marks, and noncapitalizable multinational characters
Multinational 2	2	Rarely used noncapitalizable multinational characters and diacritical marks
Box Drawing	3	All 81 double- and single-box-drawing characters
Typographic Symbols	4	Common typographic symbols not found in ASCII
Iconic Symbols	5	Rarely used "picture" (icon) symbols
Math/Scientific	6	Nonextensible, nonoversized math/scientific characters not found in ASCII set
Math/Scientific Extension	7	Extensible and oversized math/scientific characters
Greek	8	Full Greek character set for ancient and modern applications
Hebrew	9	Full Hebrew character set for ancient and modern applications
Cyrillic	10	Full Cyrillic character set for ancient and modern applications
Japanese Kana	11	Characters for Hiragana or Katakana (the type is determined by the typeface)
User-Defined	12	255 user-definable characters

square on screen. Certain special characters cannot be displayed because of the limitations of your computer monitor/display card combination.

What if you wish to type into a document a special character that you cannot access directly from the keyboard (that is, from other than Character Set 0)? The

```
*****************************************************************
ASCII
*****************************************************************
Charset: 0
Contains: ASCII space through tilde.
*****************************************************************
0,32        (Space)
0,33    !   (Exclamation Point)
0,34    "   (Double Quote)
0,35    #   (Number/Pound)
0,36    $   (Dollars)
0,37    %   (Percent)
0,38    &   (Ampersand)
0,39    '   (Single Quote)
0,40    (   (Left Parenthesis)
0,41    )   (Right Parenthesis)
0,42    *   (Asterisk)
0,43    +   (Plus)
0,44    ,   (Comma)
0,45    -   (Hyphen)
0,46    .   (Period)
0,47    /   (Forward Slash)
0,48    0
0,49    1
0,50    2
0,51    3
0,52    4
0,53    5
0,54    6
0,55    7                                   Doc 1 Pg 1 Ln 1" Pos 1"
```

Figure 17-1. A portion of Character Set 0 from CHARACTR.DOC

Compose feature can be used to insert in your document any of the special characters listed in the CHARACTR.DOC file—even if that character will be displayed as a shaded box, rather than as the actual character, on your screen. You must know the character's WordPerfect character number. Then you're ready to use the COMPOSE key:

1. Position the cursor where you want the special character to appear.
2. Press the COMPOSE (CTRL + 2) key. You will *not* see a menu or message on screen.

****
Typographic Symbols
****
Charset: 4
Contains: Common typographic symbols not found in ASCII.
****

4,0	•	Bullet
4,1	○	Hollow Bullet
4,2	■	Square Bullet
4,3	·	Small Bullet
4,4	■	Base Asterisk
4,5	¶	Paragraph Sign
4,6	§	Section Sign
4,7	¡	Inverted Exclamation Point
4,8	¿	Inverted Question Mark
4,9	«	Left Double Guillemet
4,10	»	Right Double Guillemet
4,11	£	Pound/Sterling
4,12	¥	Yen
4,13	₧	Pesetas
4,14	ƒ	Florin/Guilder
4,15	ª	Feminine Spanish Ordinal
4,16	º	Masculine Spanish Ordinal
4,17	½	1/2
4,18	¼	1/4
4,19	¢	Cent
4,20	^{2}	Power of 2
4,21	^{n}	Power of n
4,22	■	Registered Trademark
4,23	■	Copyright

Figure 17-2. A portion of Character Set 4 from CHARACTR.DOC

3. Type the WordPerfect character number.
4. Press ENTER. The results are shown on screen.

For example, the legal section symbol § is found in Character Set 4 of the CHARACTR.DOC file. Its WordPerfect character number is 4,6 (as shown in Figure 17-2). Thus, to insert the section symbol, you would position the cursor, press COMPOSE, type **4,6** and press ENTER.

Remember that not all the special characters can be displayed on screen. Refer to the next section of this chapter, "Special Characters at the Printer," when you wish to print a document that contains special characters—whether they are displayed on screen as an actual character or as a shaded square.

Tip: *The Compose feature produces no on-screen prompt.*

Unlike most WordPerfect features, when you use the Compose feature, no prompt appears on screen. As a result, you might think that the Compose feature is really accessed with another key combination, such as CTRL + *F2*. But CTRL + 2 is, in fact, correct. You will just not see a menu or message on screen when you press COMPOSE. Type the WordPerfect character number and press ENTER, and the special character will be displayed.

Why is there no prompt with the Compose feature? So there won't be a distracting message if you're in the middle of a WordPerfect menu or command (such as using the Search feature) when you wish to insert a special character. (Read the following Tip if you prefer to insert special characters using a method that prompts you.)

Tip: *Use CTRL + V to insert a special character if you prefer to see an on-screen prompt.*

There is an alternative to the COMPOSE key. When you wish to insert a special character in your text and wish to be prompted as you do so, the key combination to use is CTRL + V:

1. Move the cursor to where you want the special character to appear.
2. Press CTRL + V. WordPerfect prompts

   Key =

3. Type in the WordPerfect character number that corresponds to the special character you wish to produce (such as **4,6** for the section sign).
4. Press ENTER. The special character appears on screen.

Tip: *Use a shortcut to insert digraphs and diacritical marks in your documents.*

Digraphs are two vowels or two consonants combined to express one sound—such as æ or Æ. Diacritical marks are a vowel or consonant combined with a symbol to express one sound—such as n or u. Table 17-2 shows additional examples of digraphs and diacritical marks.

Table 17-2. Character Combinations for Digraphs and Diacritical Marks

DIGRAPHS

Characters to be typed	**Result on screen**
AE	Æ
ae	æ
IJ	Ĳ
ij	ĳ
OE	Œ
oe	œ
ss	ß
ox	©
-L	£

DIACRITICAL MARKS

Characters to be typed	**Result on screen**
'a	à
'E	É
'e	é
"o	ö
,c	ç
~n	ñ
^ u	û

Digraphs and diacriticals are part of Character Sets 1 and 2. (Character Set 1 contains the more commonly used digraphs and diacritics.) When inserting a digraph or diacritical mark in your document, you could look up its corresponding WordPerfect character number in CHARACTR.DOC and then press COMPOSE, type in its WordPerfect character number, and press ENTER. A quicker method, however, circumvents the need to discover a digraph's or diacritical mark's corresponding WordPerfect character number. Instead, you can use the Compose feature and type the two characters that make up the digraph or diacritical mark. You can type the characters in either order, but make sure that you type the uppercase or lowercase correctly. Use the Compose feature, as follows:

1. Position the cursor where you want the special character to appear.
2. Press the COMPOSE (CTRL + 2) key. Or, press CTRL + V.
3. Type the first character of the digraph or diacritical mark.
4. Type the second character of the digraph or diacritical mark. The results are shown on screen.

For example, to create the symbol Æ , you would position the cursor, press COMPOSE, type **A**, and type **E**. (Or, position the cursor, press COMPOSE, type **E**, and type **A**.)

When you insert a digraph or diacritical using its WordPerfect character number, you press ENTER as a final step; when using a combination of two keyboard characters as described above, that final step (pressing ENTER) is unnecessary.

You may find that digraphs and diacritical marks are the only type of special character that you need to insert in your documents. If this is the case, then you will not need to use CHARACTR.DOC to find the corresponding WordPerfect character numbers.

Keep in mind that your computer screen may or may not be able to display all the digraphs and diacritical marks that you insert in a document.

Tip: *Once you've inserted a special character on screen, reveal codes to reference its WordPerfect character number.*

When you insert a special character on screen that is contained in any of the Character Sets 1 through 12, WordPerfect inserts a hidden code that indicates the special character and its corresponding WordPerfect character number. Position the cursor on that special character and then, if you're viewing the Typing screen, press the REVEAL CODES (ALT + F3) key to view the Reveal Codes screen. For instance, suppose you insert the section symbol on screen (§). When you position the cursor on the section symbol and reveal codes, you'll see the following: **[§:4,6]**. This code indicates that the special character is the section symbol, whose WordPerfect character number is 4,6. Note that the code appears only when the cursor is *on* the special character and not when the cursor is in another location on the Reveal Codes screen.

Tip: *In addition to CHARACTR.DOC, a file named CHARMAP.TST provides WordPerfect character numbers.*

WordPerfect actually offers two ways to determine a special character's WordPerfect character number. First, you can check its character number in CHARACTR. DOC, as previously described. Second, you can check its character number in CHARMAP.TST, another file contained on the Conversion disk. CHARMAP.TST presents each special character and character number in matrix form, without a written description of each special character. CHARMAP.TST is therefore a much shorter file (seven pages in length) and is convenient when you wish to test whether special characters can be produced by your printer. CHARMAP.TST is described in more detail in the next section, "Special Characters at the Printer."

Tip: *Keep track of the WordPerfect character numbers for special characters you use often.*

If you use just a few special characters—perhaps a few typographical symbols—but you use them time and again in documents, keep handy a list of their corresponding WordPerfect character numbers. That way, you won't need to refer to

CHARACTR.DOC each time you wish to insert a special character in your text. Also, be sure to read the following Tip if you use various types of special characters, and you use them frequently.

Tip: *If you consistently use certain special characters, be sure to create a keyboard definition for them.*

WordPerfect offers the Keyboard Layout feature, whereby you can assign functions to specific keys, thus creating your own keyboard definition. You can then elect to use that definition at any time.

If you frequently use a certain group of special characters, then create a keyboard definition for them. For example, suppose you type legal documents, and therefore need access to certain legal characters. You could create a keyboard definition, using WordPerfect character numbers, wherein you assign the paragraph symbol to the key combination CTRL + P, the section symbol to the key combination CTRL + S, and the trademark symbol to the key combination CTRL + T. Then, when you activate that keyboard definition, you can simply press CTRL + S, for example, to insert the section symbol in your document.

Suppose you also type scientific documents, and therefore need access to certain mathematical symbols. You could create another, separate keyboard definition wherein you assign the summation symbol to CTRL + S, the division symbol to CTRL + D, and the approximately equal symbol to CTRL + A. With this other keyboard definition activated, you would simply press CTRL + S to insert the summation symbol, for example.

Of course, you could assign all your special symbols to the same keyboard definition. And they could be assigned to key combinations other than CTRL and a letter. The flexibility is great. If you use special characters often, refer to Appendix B, which describes how to use the Keyboard Layout feature, housed on the Setup menu.

Tip: *You can use special characters in either the search or the replace string.*

A special character can be used in the search string or the replace string the same way that any number, letter, or punctuation mark can. For example, assume that you wish to replace every occurrence of the dollar sign $ with the section symbol §. Press REPLACE (ALT + F2) and, for the search string, type **$**. Press →SEARCH (F2) and, for the replace string, press COMPOSE (CTRL + 2), type **4,6**, and press ENTER. This produces the section symbol as the replace string, so that when you initiate the Replace command, WordPerfect substitutes the section symbol for all occurrences of the dollar sign.

Tip: *You can type certain special characters in your document using ASCII decimal value conventions.*

WordPerfect assigns special characters using its own numbering system. In this way, you have access to literally hundreds of special characters.

Some of you may be familiar with *ASCII decimal values,* which are numbers assigned to a limited number (256) of characters contained in the IBM extended character set. (The IBM extended character set is used as a standard for printers.) If you wish to insert one of these 256 characters in your document, and you know its ASCII value, then you have an alternative to using the Compose feature:

1. Move the cursor to where you want the special character to appear.
2. If necessary, press NUM LOCK so that your numeric keypad can be used to enter numbers rather than to move the cursor.
3. Hold ALT down and, while holding it down, use the numeric keypad to type in the decimal value.
4. Release ALT. The special character appears on the screen.

If you wish to use this method, refer to Figure 17-3 for a list of ASCII decimal values. The information is presented in matrix form. Find the special character and then add its corresponding horizontal number (ranging from 0 to 19 in increments of 1) to its vertical number (0 to 240 in increments of 20). For example, the heart symbol equates to the ASCII value 3 (3 + 000), while the one-half symbol equates to 171 (11 + 160). (Those of you who have worked with version 4.2 of WordPerfect may recognize that Figure 17-3 is a printout of the version 4.2 file named FONT.TST.)

If you are unfamiliar with ASCII decimal values, there's no need to become familiar with them in order to use WordPerfect; it is wiser to become familiar with WordPerfect's character numbers, because they offer a wider variety of special characters to choose from, and you can use the Compose feature to insert those special characters in your text.

Tip: *Depending on your monitor and graphics card, you may be able to view as many as 512 characters on screen.*

	00	01	02	03	04	05	06	07	08	09	10	11	12	13	14	15	16	17	18	19
000		☺	●	♥	♦	♣	♠	•	◘	○	◙	♂	♀	♪	♫	☼	►	◄	↕	‼
020	¶	§	▬	↨	↑	↓	→	←	∟	↔	▲	▼		!	"	#	$	%	&	'
040	(	)	*	+	,	-	.	/	0	1	2	3	4	5	6	7	8	9	:	;
060	<	=	>	?	@	A	B	C	D	E	F	G	H	I	J	K	L	M	N	O
080	P	Q	R	S	T	U	V	W	X	Y	Z	[	\	]	^	_	`	a	b	c
100	d	e	f	g	h	i	j	k	l	m	n	o	p	q	r	s	t	u	v	w
120	x	y	z	{	ǀ	}	~	⌂	Ç	ü	é	â	ä	à	å	ç	ê	ë	è	ï
140	î	ì	Ä	Å	É	æ	Æ	ô	ö	ò	û	ù	ÿ	Ö	Ü	¢	£	¥	₧	ƒ
160	á	í	ó	ú	ñ	Ñ	ª	º	¿	⌐	¬	½	¼	¡	«	»	░	▒	▓	│
180	┤	╡	╢	╖	╕	╣	║	╗	╝	╜	╛	┐	└	┴	┬	├	─	┼	╞	╟
200	╚	╔	╩	╦	╠	═	╬	╧	╨	╤	╥	╙	╘	╒	╓	╫	╪	┘	┌	█
220	▄	▌	▐	▀	α	β	Γ	π	Σ	σ	µ	τ	Φ	Θ	Ω	δ	∞	φ	ε	∩
240	≡	±	≥	≤	⌠	⌡	÷	≈	°	•	·	√	η	²	▪	(end)				
	00	01	02	03	04	05	06	07	08	09	10	11	12	13	14	15	16	17	18	19

Figure 17-3. ASCII decimal value equivalents for 256 characters

If you have an EGA or a VGA monitor, or if you have a Hercules Graphics Card Plus or a Hercules InColor Card with RamFont, your screen has the capability to increase the displayable characters from 256 to 512. You can do this by using the Display option on the Setup menu (refer to Appendix B, which explains how to do this).

Trap: *Special characters you see on the screen might not be what you get on your printout.*

Whether a special character displays on your computer screen has no relation to whether it can be printed on your printer. Just because you can view a special character on screen doesn't necessarily mean that it will appear on the printed page. Moreover, a special character that appears on screen as a shaded box may appear as the actual character on the printed page. Refer to the next section of this chapter, "Special Characters at the Printer," which discusses printing out documents that contain special characters.

Tip: *You can create a user-definable character set for your printer.*

As shown in Table 17-1, Character Set 12 is reserved as user-defined. This means that, for a particular printer, you can designate certain special characters to be assigned to any WordPerfect character number from 12,0 to 12,255. This is useful if your printer supports the printing of special characters not already defined by WordPerfect.

To define Character Set 12, you must exit WordPerfect and load the Printer program (PTR.EXE) and then retrieve the .PRS file corresponding to the printer for which you wish to define additional characters—as described in Chapter 15. While viewing the printer specification categories for your printer, you would (1) select "Fonts," (2) choose a font for which you wish to map special characters to, (3) select "Character Map," (4) choose a character map, and (5) use the cursor to move down to Character Set 12 and begin entering printer command strings for each WordPerfect character number, such as 12,0 and 12,1 and so on. Then, exit until you are out of the printer program.

Note: You can even use the Printer program to reassign special characters from other character sets to new WordPerfect character numbers of your choosing.

Should you find it necessary to define Character Set 12, be sure that you record what special characters you've linked to each WordPerfect character number. One way to do so is in the file named CHARACTR.DOC. Once you reload WordPerfect, you can retrieve CHARACTR.DOC, position the cursor at the end of the document under the heading "User-definable," and then type in each WordPerfect character number and its corresponding special character. Resave the file, and now you have a record of not only Character Sets 0 to 11, but user-definable Character Set 12 as well.

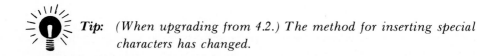

Tip: *(When upgrading from 4.2.) The method for inserting special characters has changed.*

WordPerfect has altered the method you use to place special characters in your text. So that you have access to a wide variety of characters (and not just the IBM extended character set, as in version 4.2), each character has been assigned a WordPerfect character number. You use the COMPOSE key to insert that character in the text.

For those of you who feel you'll miss the CTRL/ALT key mapping that was available in version 4.2, be sure to learn about the Keyboard Layout feature (Appendix B). With this feature, you can map special characters to specific key combinations as you did previously by creating a keyboard definition. And, by creating numerous keyboard definitions, you attain additional flexibility by establishing many different maps of special characters—one map for legal documents, one for foreign-language documents, and so on.

Special Characters at the Printer

How do you determine which special characters will print out on your printer? You must experiment with your printer and WordPerfect, printing out a document containing special characters. One alternative for experimenting with special characters on your printer is to insert special characters into one of your documents using the Compose feature (as described in the previous section of this chapter), and then to print out that document. A second alternative is to print out those pages of CHARACTR.DOC that already contain the special characters that you wish to include in your documents. The third, and probably the quickest, alternative is to print a test file named CHARMAP.TST, which, like CHARACTR.DOC, is housed on the Conversion disk. CHARMAP.TST lists in matrix form all characters in each character set (or character *map,* as each character set is referred to in CHARMAP.TST). Because CHARMAP.TST presents the special characters in matrix form and does not include a written description of each special character, it is only 7 pages long, as opposed to the 62 pages in CHARACTR.DOC. CHARMAP.TST is therefore handier when you wish to test your printer for all 1500 special characters supported by WordPerfect.

Figure 17-4 shows an example of a printout of the first page of CHARMAP.TST on an HP LaserJet Series II printer (using the Courier pitch 10 PC-8 font). For a particular character set, you can decipher each special character's WordPerfect character number using the matrix provided. Find the special character and then add its corresponding horizontal number (ranging from 0 to 19 in increments of 1) to its vertical number (usually 0 to 240 in increments of 20); this determines the character number for the character set. For instance, the AE Digraph (Æ) is number 36 (horizontal number 16 plus vertical number 20) in Character Set 1; thus, its WordPerfect character number is 1,36.

The blank spaces in Figure 17-4 indicate those characters that didn't print. For instance, notice that special characters corresponding to WordPerfect character numbers 1,15 through 1,20 would not print.

Once you print, you'll find that some of the special characters won't print out on your printer. Other special characters *will* print—even some that are not displayed on your monitor. From the printout, you know your printer's specific set of characters. Unfortunately, most printers cannot print *all* of the 1500 special characters available through WordPerfect.

Tip: *Your printer may support more than one set of characters.*

If you have a laser or a daisy wheel printer, different special characters are possible, depending on the print wheel or cartridge installed in your printer, or on the fonts you have downloaded. If you have a dot matrix printer, different characters may be possible, depending on the font you choose. That's because different fonts are often produced by different character sets.

```
This prints all characters in Character Map 0

     0                   1
     0 1 2 3 4 5 6 7 8 9 0 1 2 3 4 5 6 7 8 9 |

030        ! " # $ % & ' ( ) * + , - . / 0 1 |

050  2 3 4 5 6 7 8 9 : ; < = > ? @ A B C D E |

070  F G H I J K L M N O P Q R S T U V W X Y |

090  Z [ \ ] ^ _ ` a b c d e f g h i j k l m |

110  n o p q r s t u v w x y z { | } ~       |

     0 1 2 3 4 5 6 7 8 9 0 1 2 3 4 5 6 7 8 9 |
     0                   1

This prints all characters in Character Map 1

     0                   1
     0 1 2 3 4 5 6 7 8 9 0 1 2 3 4 5 6 7 8 9 |

000  `   ˜ ^ - / ´ ¨ ¯       ,   °           |

020    ¯   β     Á á Â â Ä ä À à Å å Æ æ Ç ç |

040  É é Ê ê Ë ë È è Í í Î î Ï ï Ì ì Ñ ñ Ó ó |

060  Ô ô Ö ö Ò ò Ú ú Û û Ü ü Ù ù Ÿ ÿ Ã ã Đ đ |

080  Ø ø Õ õ Ý ý Đ ð Þ þ     Ā ā     Ć ć     |

100  Ĉ ĉ                 Ē ē     Ǵ ǵ         |

120      Ĝ ĝ     Ĥ ĥ Ħ ħ     Ī       Ĩ       |

140  Ĵ       Ĺ ĺ                 Ń ń         |

160          Ō ō     Ŕ ŕ         Ś ś Š š     |

180  Ŝ ŝ         T t         Ū ū     Û û Ũ ũ |

200  Ŵ ŵ Ŷ ŷ Ź ź             D̄ d̄ L̄ l̄ N̄ n̄ R̀ r̀ |

220  S̄ s̄ T̄ t̄     Ỳ ỳ                         |

     0 1 2 3 4 5 6 7 8 9 0 1 2 3 4 5 6 7 8 9 |
     0                   1
```

Figure 17-4. Printout of the first page of CHARMAP.TST

If you're printing a document that contains a special character that is not available when using the currently selected font, WordPerfect checks other fonts available to it in an attempt to find another font wherein that special character is available. With this highly sophisticated feature, frequent font changes— to get a certain symbol to print— are unnecessary.

However, WordPerfect can check other fonts only if those other fonts are available to WordPerfect at the time of printing. To determine whether your printer has more than one character set, print out the relevant pages of CHARMAP.TST each time you make a new font available to WordPerfect. For example, daisy wheel printer users should be sure to switch print wheels after printing out the file for the first time, and then print those same pages of CHARMAP.TST all over again with another print wheel. Make sure that you insert a font change code in your document before you print.

Tip: *Use the Superscript/Subscript feature to produce certain raised or lowered symbols that your printer might not otherwise produce.*

Chapter 7 describes how to raise letters slightly above or below the standard line of text by using a superscript or a subscript. Using the Superscript/Subscript feature may enable you to produce special characters that are otherwise unavailable to you. For example, suppose you're reporting temperatures and you must type the degree symbol. You've tried to print that symbol using CHARMAP.TST (the degree symbol has a WordPerfect character number of 6,36), but it does not print. Instead, use a superscript to create the degree symbol, as follows: (1) press the FONT (CTRL + F8) key, (2) select Size (1 or S), (3) select Suprscpt (1 or P), (4) type the letter **o**, and (5) press RIGHT ARROW to turn Superscript off. Now try to print and see if you can produce the degree symbol. (See Chapter 7 for more on the Superscript/Subscript feature.)

Tip: *Use the Overstrike feature to produce special characters that your printer might not otherwise produce.*

The Overstrike feature allows you to print two or more characters in the same position. You can use this feature to print digraphs or diacritical marks that your printer might not otherwise produce. To use Overstrike:

1. Position the cursor where you want the special character to appear.
2. Press the FORMAT (SHIFT + F8) key to display the Format menu.
3. Select Other (4 or O), to display the Other Format menu.
4. Select Overstrike (5 or O). WordPerfect prompts

    1 Create; **2** Edit: **0**

5. Select Create (1 or C). WordPerfect prompts

    [Ovrstk]

6. Type in the characters, and then press ENTER. (You can also type in attributes, such as boldface or underline, as part of the special character you wish to create.)
7. Press EXIT (F7) to return to your document.

On the Typing screen, only the last character you typed appears on screen. However, if you reveal codes, you will see that a code is inserted that contains all of the characters you entered. For example, suppose that you created an overstrike typing the combination **a'**. The Typing screen simply shows an apostrophe ('), *but the code inserted is* **[Ovrstk:a']**. Both characters will be printed in the same position.

You also have the ability to edit an overstrike code. When you want to edit an overstrike, WordPerfect searches backward in the text and displays the first overstrike it encounters (or, if it finds no overstrike, then it searches forward). Thus, to edit an overstrike code, you would position the cursor *after* that overstrike. Follow steps 2 through 4 above for using Overstrike, and then follow these additional steps:

5. Select Edit (2 or E). The overstrike characters appear on screen.
6. Edit the overstrike, and then press ENTER.
7. Press EXIT (F7) to return to your document.

Tip: *(When upgrading from 4.2.) The Overstrike feature has been enhanced.*

As you learned in the previous section, "Special Characters on the Screen," CHARMAP.TST is the new file in version 5 which contains a matrix of special characters in each character set available for printing from within WordPerfect. It is this file that you can print in order to test your printer's capabilities.

If you wish to use the Overstrike feature to print a special character, you'll now find this feature on the FORMAT (SHIFT + F8) key. The Overstrike feature has been enhanced, so that you can now print more than two characters in the same position, and even include attributes in the overstrike. Also, the overstrike code can be edited.

Line Drawing

With the Line Draw feature, you can draw straight lines, either alone or combined with words. Draw graphs to visually represent the numbers contained in a report, build organizational charts, or design newsletter headers—all are possible.

You can draw lines before or after you type text. And you can choose a variety of special characters when you draw, as long as those characters can be printed by your printer. To use the Line Draw feature:

1. Move the cursor to the line where you wish to start drawing.
2. Press SCREEN (CTRL + F3) to display the Screen menu.

   0 Rewrite; **1** Window; **2** Line Draw: **0**

3. Select Line Draw (2 or L). The Line Draw menu appears, as shown here:

   1 ¦; **2** ¦¦; **3** ∗; **4** Change; **5** Erase; **6** Move: **1**

   WordPerfect starts with the assumption that you wish to draw using a single line. (Note that the menu suggests selection 1.)

4. Using the directional arrow keys, begin moving the cursor. Tiny arrows appear on screen, pointing your way as you continue to move the cursor. With each cursor movement, a tiny arrow pushes forward, drawing a single solid line behind it, as if that arrow were a pencil. As you change the direction of the cursor, the arrow changes direction as well, and a corner is automatically inserted. If you use all four directional arrow keys, you can draw a box, as shown in Figure 17-5.

Note: Tiny arrows are not shown on screen in Figure 17-5; an arrow disap-

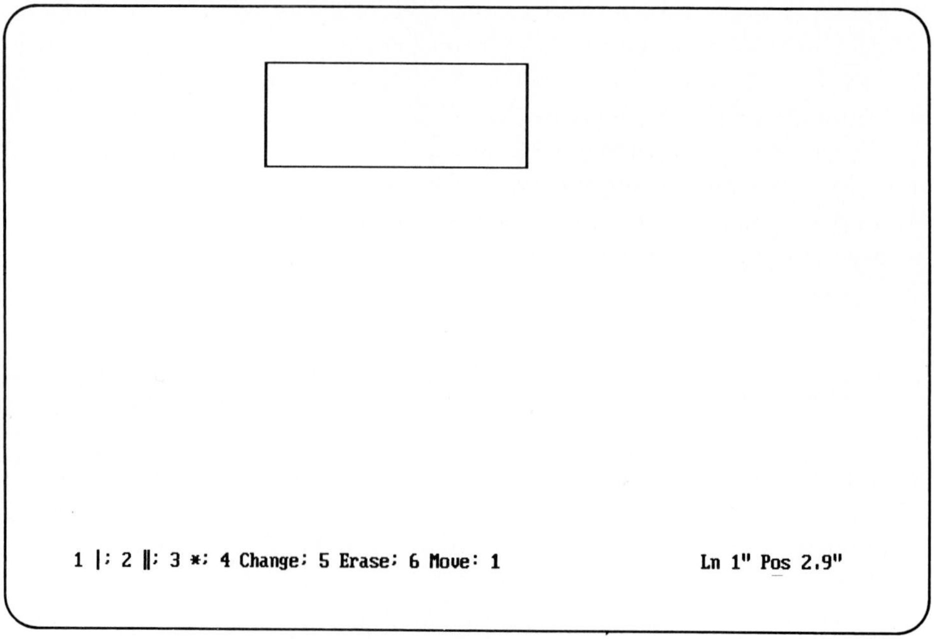

Figure 17-5. A box drawn with Line Draw

pears when it crosses over an existing line, as it does when you complete the final corner of a box.

The Line Draw feature is set up so that it works well with text. Reveal codes and you will see that WordPerfect places a hard return code **[HRt]** at the end of each line. The feature works as if you are in the Typeover mode. As you draw, the cursor overwrites text that is already on the screen with your draw character. If the cursor encounters a hidden code, that code and all that follows it are pushed forward. Line Draw will continue downward, even past a page break, but it won't exceed your right margin setting.

The Line Draw menu remains on the screen as you draw, so that you can change options easily, at any time. If you want to erase what you've just drawn, select 5, Erase, and retrace as if you had an eraser in your hand. If you want to move the cursor to a new spot without drawing or erasing, select 6, Move. Move the cursor as if you were temporarily lifting a pencil from the page. (When you choose Line Draw's Move option and the cursor moves into an area where nothing has been typed, spaces are inserted so that the cursor can move freely wherever you wish to position it.) Then select 1 to begin drawing with the single line again.

You can also change your draw character from a single line to another symbol. Select 2 to draw with a double line, or select 3 to draw with another character. WordPerfect assumes the third character to be an asterisk, but by using option 4, Change, you can modify the third draw character. To do so, select 4, Change, and WordPerfect responds with another menu:

```
1 ░; 2 ▒; 3 ▓; 4 █; 5 ▄; 6 ▌; 7 ▐; 8 ▀; 9 Other: 0
```

You can then choose your third draw character from one of the eight choices provided. Or choose 9, Other, and WordPerfect prompts

Solid Character:

Type in any symbol of your choosing, such as the number sign (#), the minus sign (−), the plus sign (+), or any other special character that your printer will print (inserted by using the Compose feature, as described in the first section of this chapter, "Special Characters on the Screen"). That new symbol now appears on the Line Draw menu as the third possible draw character that you can choose. The symbols you use when drawing can be quite varied. Figure 17-6 shows a graph drawn by using six different symbols.

When you wish to exit the Line Draw feature, press EXIT (F7) or CANCEL (F1), or type **0**.

Trap: *Be cautious as you combine text with a line drawing on screen.*

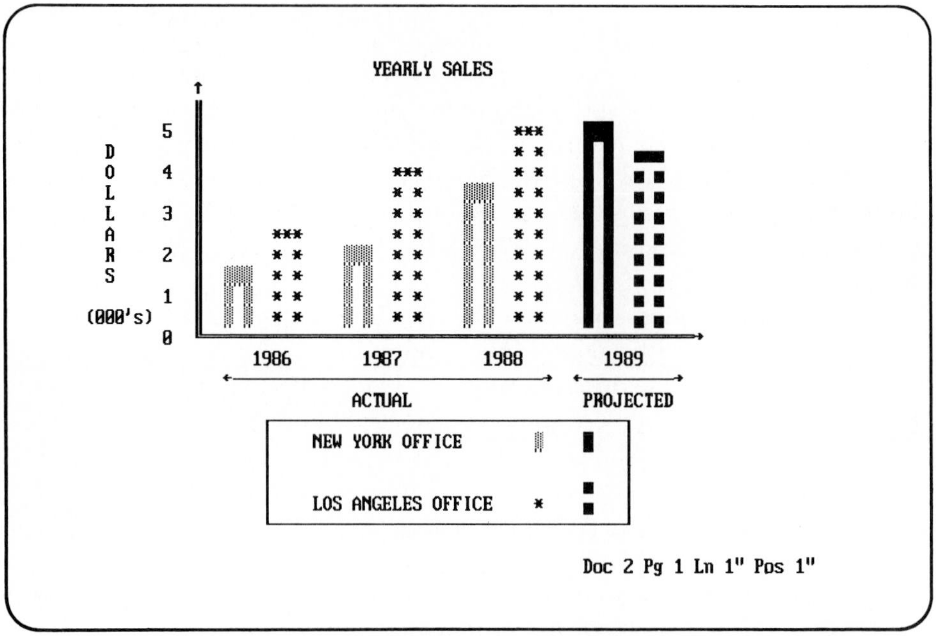

Figure 17-6. A graph drawn with Line Draw using various draw characters

When you want to have text around a line drawing, you can either type first or draw first.

If you prefer to draw first, then you should switch to the Typeover mode (press INS) before you begin typing text. In this way, the lines won't move as you type the text. In addition, don't press ENTER when you are on the same line as a drawing; this distorts the drawing and necessitates finding and deleting the resulting **[HRt]** code to correct the problem. Use the DOWN ARROW key instead.

If you prefer to type the text first—which is sometimes easier, because the text can serve as a visual guide as you draw—then a **[HRt]** code must end every line of text. You must therefore not allow word wrap to work. Also, because line drawing overwrites text (it works in the Typeover mode, not the Insert mode), you need to be sure to insert enough spaces around the text, on all sides, to leave room for the drawing.

Keep in mind that Line Draw can't draw lines around indented, justified, or aligned text, and it won't extend beyond a column. However, you can use the Advance feature (described in Chapter 7) to get around these limitations—by typing your text, advancing back to the top of the page, and then using Line Draw. If you wish to use Line Draw around centered text, draw the line near the left margin by inserting spaces with the SPACEBAR before the **[Cntr]** code that precedes the centered text; then, use Line Draw to draw through the spaces only.

Tip: *Use the ESC (REPEAT VALUE) key to draw quickly.*

You learned in Chapter 3 about the Repeat Value feature (accessed via the ESC key), which repeats a character a specified number of times. The ESC key is invaluable when using Line Draw to draw across or down the screen. Not only does it save time, but it can also ensure that boxes you draw (such as for an organizational chart) are all the same size.

Suppose you wish to draw 20 double lines across the screen:

1. Position the cursor where you wish to start drawing.
2. Press SCREEN (CTRL + F3).
3. Select Line Draw (2 or L).
4. Select 2 to draw with a double line.
5. Press ESC. WordPerfect responds

   Repeat Value = 8

6. Type **20**.
7. Press RIGHT ARROW. The result is as if WordPerfect had pressed RIGHT ARROW 20 times for you.

Tip: *Relocate a drawing by defining a rectangular block of text.*

In Chapter 6 you learned how to move or copy a rectangular block of text by using the Block feature. This feature is quite handy when you use Line Draw, if you wish to move or copy one chunk of a drawing. For example, suppose you used Line Draw to create the organizational chart shown in Figure 17-7. Now you wish to reposition the "Vice President Marketing" box without affecting the other boxes.

1. Use the Block command to highlight the "Vice President Marketing" box, as shown in Figure 17-8. WordPerfect also highlights the adjacent box, assuming that you wish to move a block.

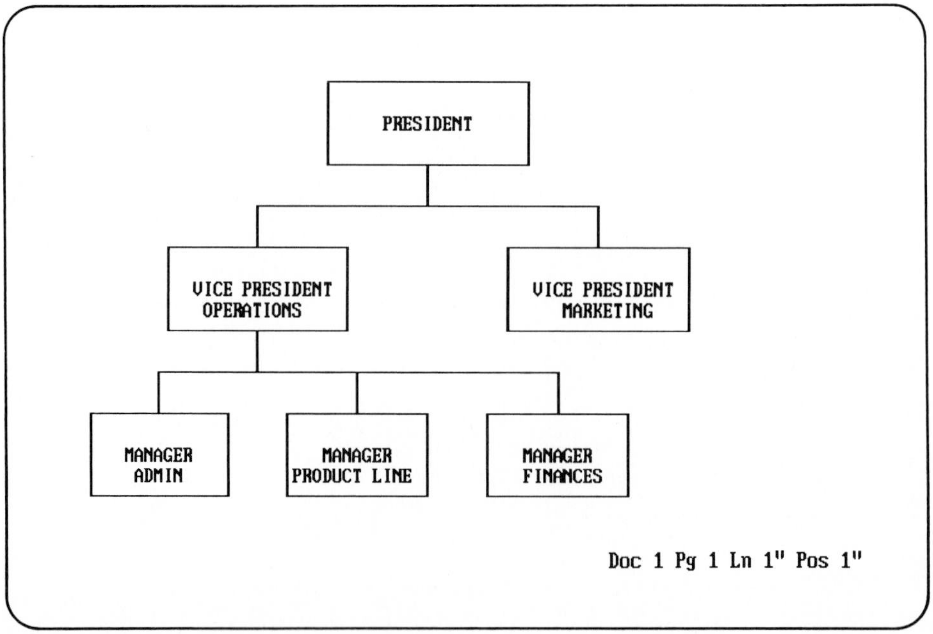

Figure 17-7. An organizational chart created using Line Draw

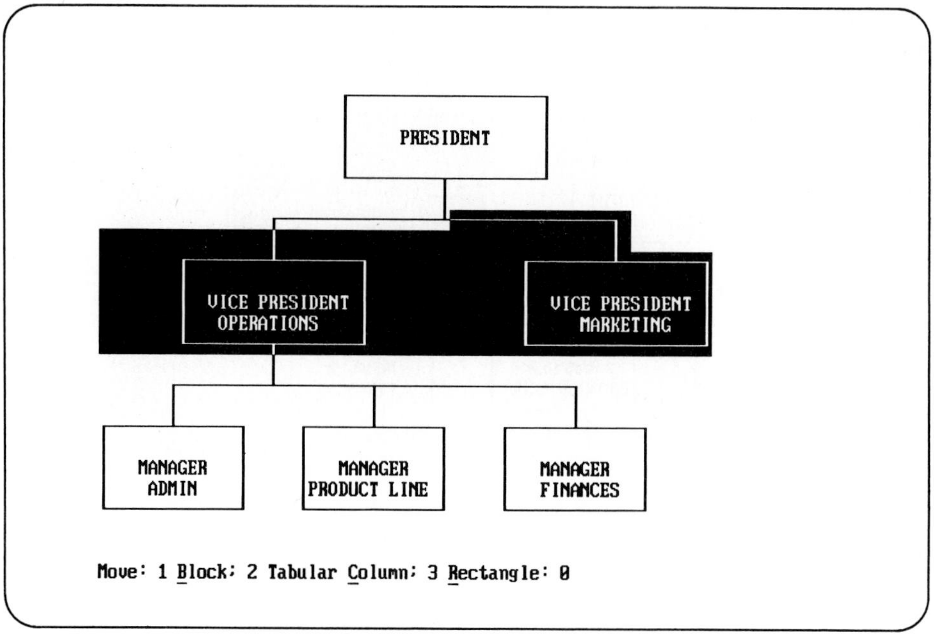

Figure 17-8. A highlighted block containing the "Vice President Marketing" box

2. Press MOVE (CTRL + F4).
3. Select Rectangle (3 or R) from the Move menu. Now, WordPerfect highlights only the rectangle defined by the cursor's beginning and endpoint, as shown in Figure 17-9.
4. Select Move (1 or M). The rectangle is erased from the screen.
5. Reposition the cursor where you wish the box to reappear.
6. Press ENTER to retrieve the rectangle.

Figure 17-10 shows where the "Vice President Marketing" box is now located, so that this officer appears to be almost as critical in the company hierarchy as the president is.

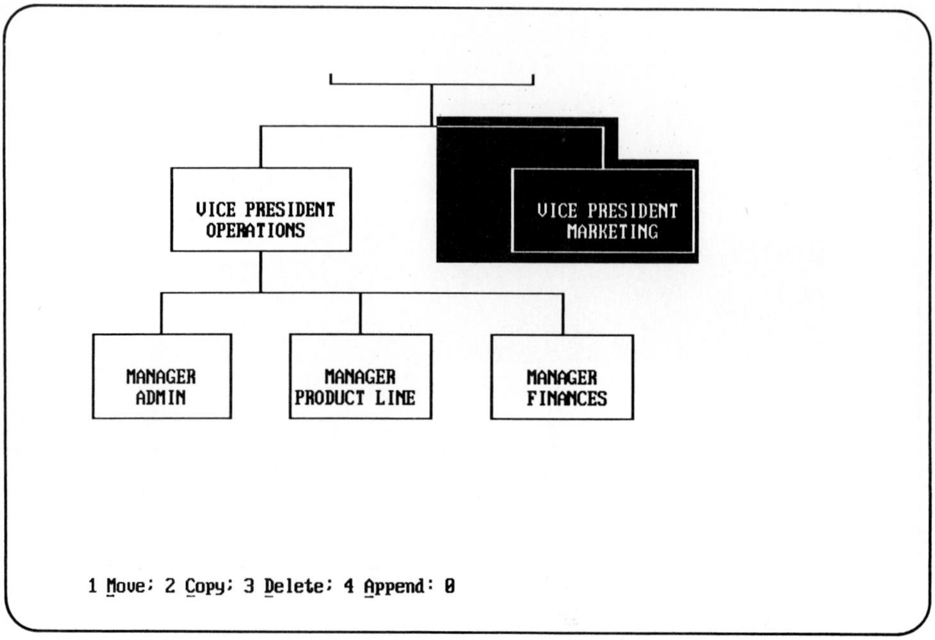

Figure 17-9. A rectangular block

Trap: *Beware of margins when you move or copy drawings.*

You can fit on a line only as many characters as will fit in the current margins. This includes characters drawn using the Line Draw feature. If you try to move a drawing to a space that isn't wide enough, you'll get a jumble of unmatched lines, as shown in Figure 17-11.

It is a good idea to save a drawing to disk before you attempt to move or copy it to another location; that way, if the result is not what you expected, you can retrieve the original drawing and start over.

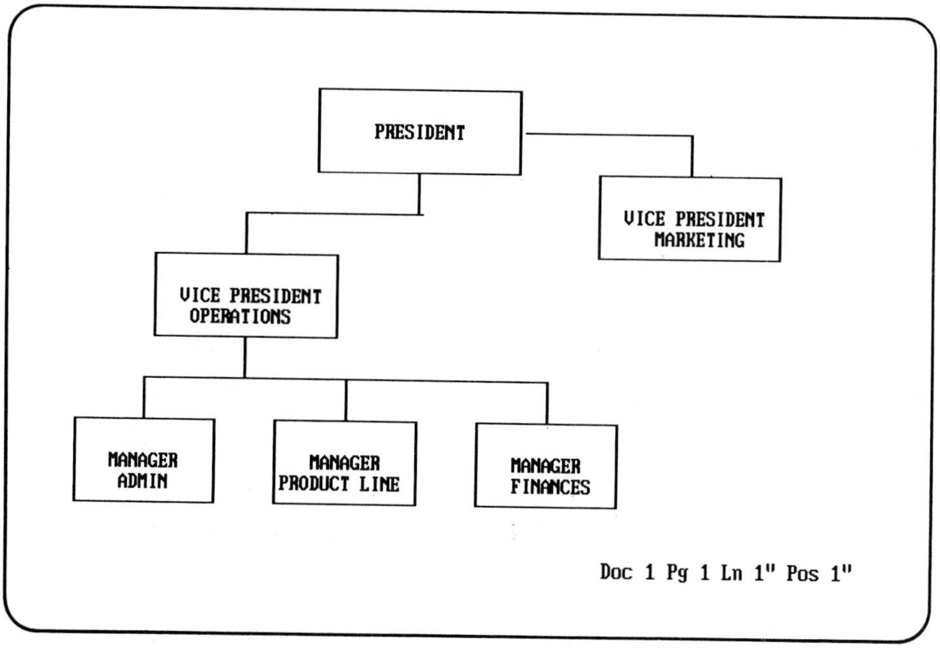

Figure 17-10. The rectangular block moved to a new position in the organizational chart

Tip: *Reveal codes to view the WordPerfect character number that corresponds to a certain draw character.*

The characters used in Line Draw, like other special characters, are assigned WordPerfect character numbers (which you learned about in the first section of this chapter, "Special Characters on the Screen"). All the draw characters are assigned to WordPerfect's character set number 3, Box Drawing. You can decipher a draw character's WordPerfect character number by revealing codes and placing the cursor on a draw character. For example, Figure 17-12 shows the Reveal Codes

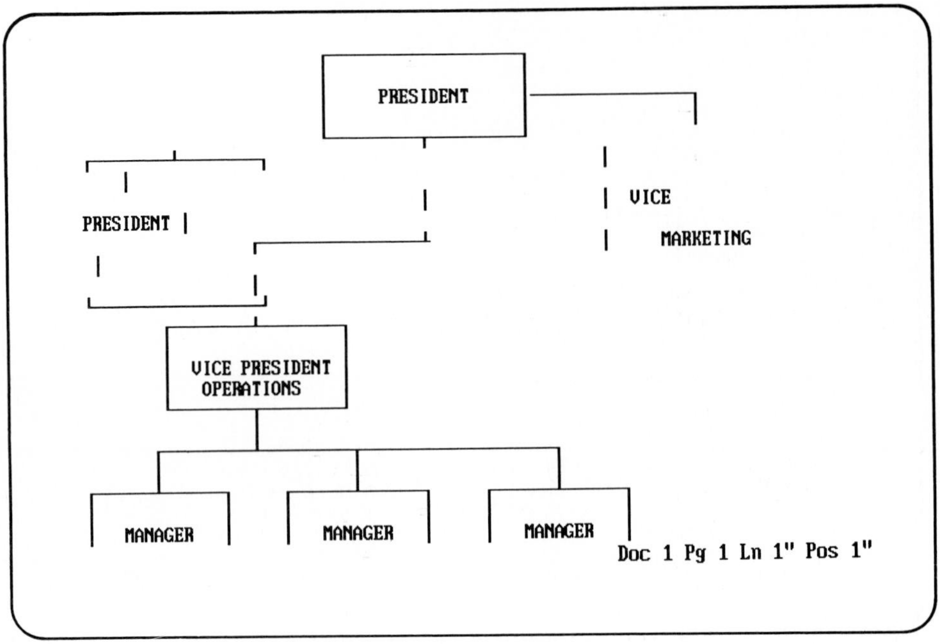

Figure 17-11. *The result of moving a box so there are more characters than can fit in the margins*

screen with the cursor on a draw character. The bottom window on the screen shows the WordPerfect character number for that draw character is 3,9.

Tip: *The tiny arrows on screen won't print with a line drawing.*

Whenever you draw using the single or double line, WordPerfect displays tiny arrows to lead you as you draw. These arrows remain in the text (unless they cross over an existing line, as when you complete the last corner of a box drawing, in which case they disappear). Tiny arrows in your line drawing will not appear on

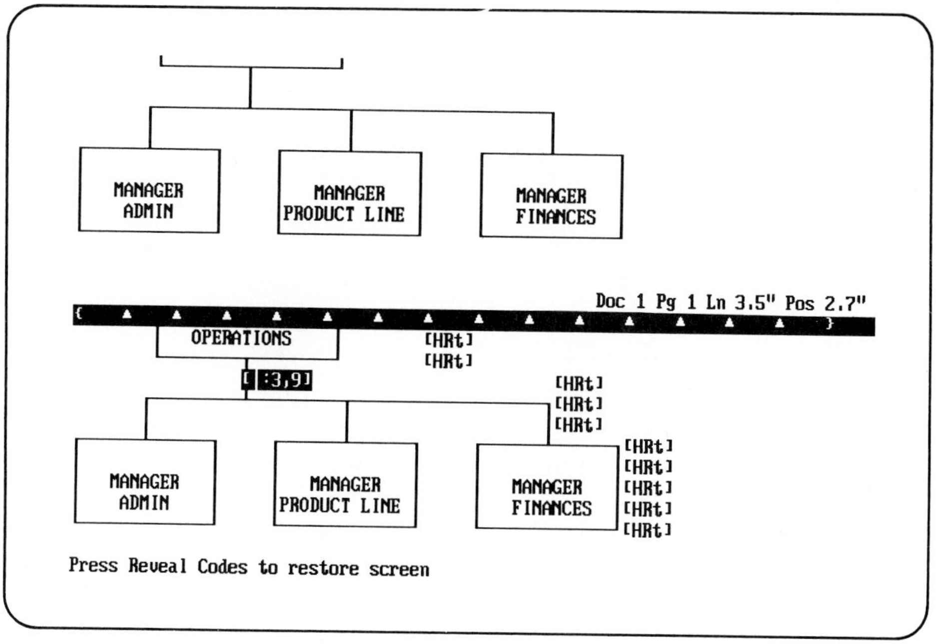

Figure 17-12. *The Reveal Codes screen showing a draw character's WordPerfect character number*

the printed page. (For instance, the arrows shown bordering the single and double lines in Figure 17-6 will not appear when this graph is printed.)

But, depending on your printer, if you print out your line drawing and a dash or some other character *does appear* in place of tiny arrows, then all arrows should be deleted from your line drawing. An easy way to do so is to switch into Typeover mode (by pressing INS so that the prompt **Typeover** appears on the status line), position the cursor on a tiny arrow, and press the SPACEBAR. In this way, you erase an arrow without distorting the line drawing. Once you've deleted all the arrows, print out the line drawing again.

Trap: *What you draw on the screen with Line Draw does not necessarily print as drawn.*

As you learned in the preceding section of this chapter, "Special Characters at the Printer," each printer has its own set of characteristics and prints a certain number of special characters. The characters it can print affect Line Draw. To understand how Line Draw works with your printer, you must perform some tests.

To print with a single or double line with sharp corners, or to print using certain other draw characters, your printer must be able to produce some of the special characters in WordPerfect's Box Drawing Character Set 3. Check your CHARMAP.TST printout to see which characters your printer can print. (CHARMAP.TST is discussed in the previous section of this chapter.) In addition, another way to check the Line Draw feature with your printer is to print another test file on the Conversion disk, named PRINTER.TST (mentioned in Chapter 15). This file contains a footer with line drawings usings the single- and double-line characters.

If a particular font won't print certain draw characters properly, then another font might; you must experiment by printing out line drawings with each of the various fonts that are available to you. Refer to Chapter 7 for the procedure for changing the font used to print out all or part of a document. And keep in mind that line drawings won't print out properly if you use a proportionally spaced font, so be sure to select a font that is monospaced. (Some printers offer a font especially for line draw, with a font name such as "Solid Line Draw"; check your list of fonts on the Base Font screen, as described in Chapter 7, to see if your printer has a special font for drawing, and check your printer manual to see if you can purchase a line draw font.)

Also, your printer might work best in printing a line drawing if you change certain format settings (as described in Chapter 8). Some printers print best, for example, if you change the line-spacing setting to half-line spacing rather than single spacing. (Line drawings will look odd if printed with double spacing or a larger spacing.) Other printers work better if you change the line-height setting. Test these variables on your printer.

You may find that your printer is incapable of printing many of the special symbols used with the Line Draw feature. If that's the case, draw with the asterisk (*), the plus sign (+), the minus sign (−), or the broken line (¦)—characters that all printers can produce. Your lines may not look as smooth, but this is better than having no line drawing at all. Figure 17-13 shows two boxes, one printed by a printer using special characters and one printed by a printer that can't use special characters.

Tip: *Line Draw is a convenient way to "draw" with words or numbers.*

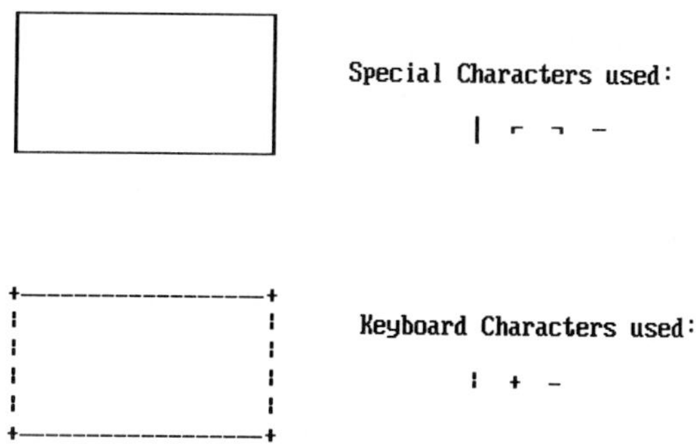

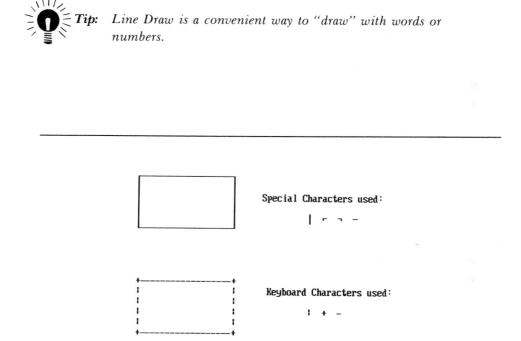

Figure 17-13. *Two boxes created by Line Draw—with and without special characters*

When you use Line Draw, the cursor moves in any direction you choose without constantly returning to the left margin. You can attain the same freedom when you wish to type intricate designs or mathematical formulas, by first employing Line Draw's Move option to fill lines with spaces by using a procedure called space fill.

After you fill lines with spaces, you can press LEFT ARROW and RIGHT ARROW (rather than the SPACEBAR) to move horizontally, and UP ARROW and DOWN ARROW (rather than ENTER) to move vertically. This saves time and energy when typing on different lines and in different positions on the screen. Figure 17-14 illustrates two instances in which Line Draw would come in handy.

To easily produce word and number "drawings" such as these, follow this procedure:

1. If right justification is on, turn it off before you use space fill; otherwise, your text shifts to the left and right to align against the margins as you type.
2. Move the cursor to the left margin of the first line on which you wish to type.
3. Press SCREEN (CTRL + F3), and select Line Draw (2 or L).
4. Select 6, Move. You are now ready to use space fill.
5. Press RIGHT ARROW (use it in combination with ESC to make the job quicker) until you have enough horizontal space between the left margin and the cursor for what you wish to type.
6. Press DOWN ARROW (use it in combination with ESC) until you have enough vertical space between the first line and the cursor for what you wish to type.
7. Press EXIT to clear the Line Draw feature.
8. Press INS to switch to the Typeover mode.

Now you are ready to move your cursor freely, by using the arrow keys within the defined space, and to type text— without pressing the SPACEBAR or ENTER to move, and without having the cursor jump down a line or to the left margin as it

Our pyramid of winners in the sales contest:

Marie
John Paul Saul
Pam Denise Peter Jacob Tomas
Maria Gail Anthony Jonathon Barb
Angelique Deborah Cathy David Joe Bonnie

$$N = \frac{D^2 + R^{\beta^2} F^{1/4}}{½¶ - ¼Q + D_2F_2}$$

Figure 17-14. Line Draw used to create graphic arrangements of words or letters

hits hidden hard return codes. (You may also wish to change to half-spacing before typing mathematical formulas.)

Tip: *Use another WordPerfect feature to draw straight lines or to integrate a graphics image into a WordPerfect document.*

If your printer is capable of printing graphics, then there's a feature—in addition to Line Draw—that will allow you to insert lines in your text. The Graphics feature, described in Chapter 18, allows you to place straight horizontal or vertical lines or shaded boxes in a document. The lines won't show on the Typing screen, as they do with Line Draw. However, lines created when using the Graphics feature can be placed at specific locations on the page (such as at the left margin or centered), they can be defined as a certain width and length, and they can even be shaded. Thus, the Graphics feature may be more convenient to use if you want to insert a border around pre-existing text.

This feature also allows you to incorporate into WordPerfect a detailed graphics image that you create with a graphics package (such as Harvard Graphics or Lotus 1-2-3 or PC Paintbrush). Be sure to read Chapter 18 if you wish to get fancy when integrating graphics with text.

Tip: *(When upgrading from 4.2.) The Line Draw feature operates in basically the same way.*

Line Draw works basically as it did previously, except that in version 5 (1) a tiny arrow leads you when you draw with the single or double line, and (2) you can discover a draw character's WordPerfect character number on the Reveal Codes screen, so that you can test a certain character to see if your printer supports it.

Tips and Traps Summary

Special Characters on the Screen

Tip: The Compose feature produces no on-screen prompt.

Tip: Use CTRL + V to insert a special character if you prefer to see an on-screen prompt.

Tip: Use a shortcut to insert digraphs and diacritical marks in your documents.

Tip: Once you've inserted a special character on screen, reveal codes to reference its WordPerfect character number.

Tips and Traps Summary (*continued*)

Tip: In addition to CHARACTR.DOC, a file named CHARMAP.TST provides WordPerfect character numbers.

Tip: Keep track of the WordPerfect character numbers for special characters you use often.

Tip: If you consistently use certain special characters, be sure to create a keyboard definition for them.

Tip: You can use special characters in either the search or the replace string.

Tip: You can type certain special characters in your document using ASCII decimal value conventions.

Tip: Depending on your monitor and graphics card, you may be able to view as many as 512 characters on screen.

Trap: Special characters you see on the screen might not be what you get on your printout.

Tip: You can create a user-definable character set for your printer.

Tip: (When upgrading from 4.2.) The method for inserting special characters has changed.

Special Characters at the Printer

Tip: Your printer may support more than one set of characters.

Tip: Use the Superscript/Subscript feature to produce certain raised or lowered symbols that your printer might not otherwise produce.

Tips and Traps Summary (*continued*)

Tip: Use the Overstrike feature to produce special characters that your printer might not otherwise produce.

Tip: (When upgrading from 4.2.) The Overstrike feature has been enhanced.

Line Drawing

Trap: Be cautious as you combine text with a line drawing on screen.

Tip: Use the ESC (REPEAT VALUE) key to draw quickly.

Tip: Relocate a drawing by defining a rectangular block of text.

Trap: Beware of margins when you move or copy drawings.

Tip: Reveal codes to view the WordPerfect character number that corresponds to a certain draw character.

Tip: The tiny arrows on screen won't print with a line drawing.

Trap: What you draw on the screen with Line Draw does not necessarily print as drawn.

Tip: Line Draw is a convenient way to "draw" with words or numbers.

Tip: Use another WordPerfect feature to draw straight lines or to integrate a graphics image into a WordPerfect document.

Tip: (When upgrading from 4.2.) The Line Draw feature operates in basically the same way.

18

Integrating Graphics into Documents

WordPerfect's ability to combine text and graphics images in one document brings it soundly into the world of desktop publishing. The Graphics feature enables you to integrate into your document graphics images from a variety of sources—such as PlanPerfect, Lotus 1-2-3, AutoCAD, and Windows Paint. As a result, you can incorporate fancy figures, logos, or pictures—as needed—in a report, a newsletter, or instructional materials.

This chapter describes the three basic steps involved in creating a graphics box: deciding on your box style—whether a figure, table, text, or a user-defined style; creating the box around which the text on the page wraps; and retrieving a graphics image or text into the box. Next, the chapter tells how to change WordPerfect's default graphics settings so that you can enhance the sizing and positioning of a graphics box and, ultimately, its appearance on the printed page. The end of the chapter describes how the Graphics feature also allows you to insert in your document both horizontal and vertical lines, as well as shaded boxes.

Creating a Graphics Box Using WordPerfect Defaults

You can insert any number of graphics boxes in a document. WordPerfect numbers graphics boxes automatically when they appear in the body of a document. If you insert a new box or delete an old one, the box numbers are updated.

When you're ready to insert a graphics box into your text, you must decide what you want to place inside that box. You can leave a box blank, insert text in it, or insert a graphics image in it. WordPerfect supports many graphics programs, including standard graphing programs, painting/scanner programs, drawing/CAD programs, or clip art programs. Table 18-1 lists the graphics programs that have been tested with WordPerfect and are directly supported by it. (WordPerfect Corporation constantly tests new graphics programs, so your graphics program may have been recently added to the list shown in Table 18-1; check with WordPerfect Corporation. Also, see the Tips later in this section for methods to import images from other graphics programs not listed in Table 18-1. In one way or another, WordPerfect can import files from almost any PC-compatible graphics program.) If it is a graphics image that you wish to insert into a graphics box in a document, that image must already be stored on disk.

The following are the graphics parameters that WordPerfect assumes as defaults when you insert a graphics box in your document:

- There will be no caption placed near the graphics box when it is printed.
- The graphics box will be defined as the paragraph type. This means that the box stays with its surrounding text, even if the text is edited later on.

Table 18-1. Graphics Programs Directly Supported by WordPerfect

AutoCAD
Dr Halo II
GEM Paint
GEM SCAN
Lotus 1-2-3
MacPaint
PC Paintbrush
PC Paint Plus
PicturePaks
Professional Plan
Symphony
Windows Paint

But, if the paragraph is so close to the bottom of the page that the graphics box can't fit on that page, the box is moved to the top of the next page. A graphics box code is placed at the beginning of the paragraph that the cursor is in when you create the graphics box.

- The graphics box will be positioned vertically so that the top starts on the line where the cursor was located when you created the box (or the next line below).
- The graphics box will be positioned horizontally with its right edge at the right margin.
- Text will be wrapped on the left side of the graphics box.
- The width and height of the graphics box are calculated automatically by WordPerfect based on the size of the original graphics image (making sure to maintain the image's proportions), or, if the box will contain text, based on the amount of text to be inserted in the box.

Figure 18-1 shows an example of a page that combines text and graphics, where the graphics box containing a map of the United States was created by using the default settings. If you wish to create a graphics box by using the default settings, proceed as follows:

1. Position the cursor at the beginning of a specific line in the paragraph where you want the box to appear. For example, position the cursor at the beginning of the paragraph to create a box so that the top is even with the first line of the paragraph.
2. Press the GRAPHICS (ALT + F9) key. The following menu is displayed:

   1 Figure; 2 Table; 3 Text Box; 4 User-defined Box; 5 Line: **0**

   The first four items represent the four box styles you can create.
3. Type the number or mnemonic character that represents the style of box that you wish to create. The choices are

   - **Figure (1 or F)** Useful when inserting graphics images or diagrams. As a default, WordPerfect places a single-line box around the image when printed (as shown in the U.S. map in Figure 18-1).
   - **Table (2 or T)** Useful when creating tables of numbers, maps, and statistical data. As a default, WordPerfect places a thick line above the image and another thick line below it when printed.
   - **Text Box (3 or B)** Useful when inserting quotes or sidebars, or any special text that is set off from the rest of the document (often referred to

MEMORANDUM

TO:	All Regional Sales Offices
FROM:	Jamie Hurwitz Marketing Department, Headquarters Office
DATE:	January 12, 1989

It is time once again to produce ABCD Company's annual report. For 1988, there is much enthusiasm, since sales increased by 14% over last year's figures. We plan to publish our annual report by the middle of March, so I need sales figures for 1988 from each regional sales office by the end of January.

The southwestern and western regions will be the focus of the 1988 report, since these two regions showed the greatest gains last year. I need these two regions to submit a short description of growth in sales over the past five years. Make sure to discuss any changes in the size of the sales staff and of your product line since 1983. Also, can you break down the sales figures by state? That way, we can focus on those states where we show the strongest presence. I suggest that Todd Sheller write the description for the southwestern region, and that Mary Janowitz write the description for the western region. Please feel free to call on me if you have any questions as you begin writing your descriptions. I'll be happy to help. Thank you.

Figure 18-1. A document integrating text and graphics

as a "call-out" in an article). As a default, WordPerfect places a thick line above the image and another thick line below it when printed.

- **User-defined Box (4 or U)** Useful when creating a box that doesn't fit into the other categories. As a default, WordPerfect places no border around the image when printed.

Once you select a graphics box style, a menu for that box style appears. For instance, if you selected Figure (1 or F), WordPerfect displays

Figure: 1 Create; 2 Edit; 3 New Number; 4 Options: 0

The other box styles display menus with the same four items.

4. Select Create (1 or C). WordPerfect displays a full-screen Graphics Definition menu. If the box style is "Figure," for example, then the menu shown

in Figure 18-2 is displayed. The other box styles display Graphics Definition menus with the same eight items for defining your box.

5. If you wish to retrieve a file into the graphics box, select Filename (1 or F). WordPerfect prompts

   Enter filename:

   Enter the name of a file containing a WordPerfect document or containing a graphics image, preceded by the drive or directory in which that file is stored, if it is not in the default drive/directory. The filename appears on screen, along with an indication of whether the file contains text "(Text)" or a graphics image "(Graphics)."

   Or, if you wish to type text directly into the box, select Edit (8 or E). A clear screen is displayed, on which you can type the text and then press EXIT (F7) to return to the Graphics Definition menu. The message "(Text)" appears on screen.

6. Press EXIT (F7) to return to your document.

```
Definition: Figure

     1 - Filename

     2 - Caption

     3 - Type                          Paragraph

     4 - Vertical Position             0"

     5 - Horizontal Position           Right

     6 - Size                          3.25" wide x 3.25" (high)

     7 - Wrap Text Around Box          Yes

     8 - Edit




Selection: 0
```

Figure 18-2. The Figure Graphics Box Definition menu

WordPerfect moves the cursor to the beginning of the paragraph (even if your cursor was in the middle of the paragraph when you first pressed the GRAPHICS key), and a graphics box code is placed at the beginning of the paragraph. The code indicates which box style you chose, the number of the box, and the graphics image you inserted in the box (if any). Each box style is numbered separately. For example, if you just defined your first figure-style graphics box in your document, and you inserted a graphics image contained in a file named USAMAP.WPG, then the code inserted is **[Figure:1;USAMAP.WPG;]**. Or, if you just defined your first text-style graphics box, and you inserted text into that box, then the code inserted is **[Text Box:1;;]**. Or, if you just defined your second table-style graphics box (meaning that you previously created another table-style graphics box closer to the top of the document), and you inserted a graphics image contained in a file named BOOK.WPG, then the code inserted is **[Table:II;BOOK.WPG;]**. (Boxes defined as table style are, by default, numbered with Roman rather than Arabic numerals.)

An outline of the graphics box appears on screen only after you begin typing text following the graphics box code or after you move the cursor. The top of the box outline indicates the box style and number. For example, Figure 18-3 shows a

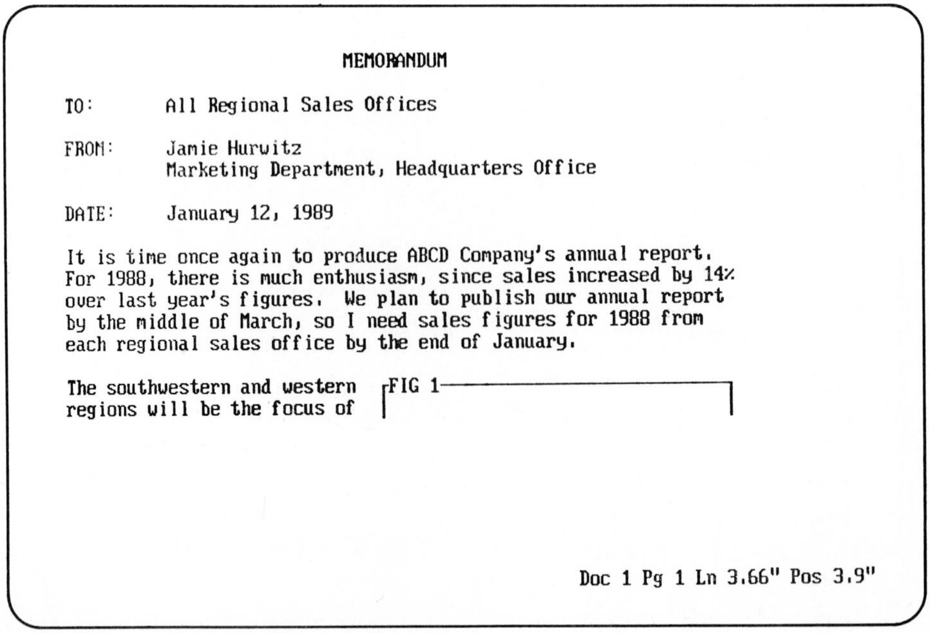
MEMORANDUM
TO: All Regional Sales Offices
FROM: Jamie Hurwitz
Marketing Department, Headquarters Office
DATE: January 12, 1989
It is time once again to produce ABCD Company's annual report. For 1988, there is much enthusiasm, since sales increased by 14% over last year's figures. We plan to publish our annual report by the middle of March, so I need sales figures for 1988 from each regional sales office by the end of January.
The southwestern and western regions will be the focus of
FIG 1
Doc 1 Pg 1 Ln 3.66" Pos 3.9"

Figure 18-3. The top portion of a figure box outline

```
FROM:      Jamie Hurwitz
           Marketing Department, Headquarters Office

DATE:      January 12, 1989

It is time once again to produce ABCD Company's annual report.
For 1988, there is much enthusiasm, since sales increased by 14%
over last year's figures.  We plan to publish our annual report
by the middle of March, so I need sales figures for 1988 from
each regional sales office by the end of January.

The southwestern and western  ┌FIG 1──────────────────────────┐
regions will be the focus of  │                               │
the 1988 report, since these  │                               │
two regions showed the        │                               │
greatest gains last year.  I  │                               │
need these two regions to     │                               │
submit a short description of │                               │
growth in sales over the past │                               │
five years.  Make sure to     │                               │
discuss any changes in the    │                               │
size of the sales staff and of└───────────────────────────────┘
your product line since 1983.  Also, can you break down the sales
figures by state?  That way,  we can focus on those states where
                                        Doc 1 Pg 1 Ln 5.5" Pos 7.4"
```

Figure 18-4. A fully expanded figure box outline

box outline for the first figure-style graphics box after you've typed two lines following the graphics box code.

As you type, a box outline expands to its full size. Figure 18-4 shows a box outline after additional text is typed. Now you can see the full size of the graphics box, so you can tell how much space will be occupied by the contents of the box when it is printed.

Trap: *The Typing screen does not show the contents of a graphics box.*

On the Typing screen, you can view the outline of the graphics box, but not the contents of the box. In order to view the contents of the box, you can use the View Document feature on the Print menu (a feature described in Chapter 14). If your monitor does not support a graphics display, then the image will be rough; consider purchasing a graphics card if you wish to work more effectively with the graphics capabilities of WordPerfect.

Or, rather than using the View Document feature, you can print out the page where the graphics box code is located to see your printed result.

Trap: *Your printer must be able to support graphics in order to print images properly.*

Some printers can print both text and graphics, while others can print only text. Try printing a document that contains a graphics image to see whether your printer can print it properly. You may wish to change your font (see Chapter 7) and try printing the document again to see if the image can be printed with better resolution.

If you have a LaserJet printer, you need to have adequate memory in your printer if you wish to print sophisticated, full-page graphics; 1MB of memory is usually sufficient. Because the standard is less than 1MB, you may wish to purchase additional memory. (The HP LaserJet Series II, for example, comes standard with only 512KB of memory.)

In addition, when you print a graphics image, keep in mind that you can use the Print menu to select the quality of the printed graphics—either draft, medium, high, or "Do Not Print" (in which case only the text on the page is printed); see Chapter 14 for details.

Tip: *WordPerfect can wrap text around a maximum of 20 boxes on a page.*

You can create an unlimited number of graphics boxes on a page. If two boxes are created in such a way that they will overlap on some of the same lines, then WordPerfect alters the size of the second box so that it can fit in the space allotted. An example is shown in Figure 18-5, where the figure-style box was created first, and the text box second. You can insert any number of graphics boxes on a page; however, the text won't wrap around more than the first 20.

Tip: *Graphics can be placed in more than just the main body of your document.*

Graphics boxes can be inserted in headers, footers, footnotes, and endnotes. (However, refer to the next section, "Changing the Graphics Definition Defaults for One Box," for certain limitations when used in footnotes and endnotes.) You might consider creating a header to be used as your standard letterhead, including text and a graphics image in the header. Graphics boxes can also be inserted into text that is formatted into columns, so that you can created professional looking newsletters containing your company logo or other graphics. Moreover, if a graphics box you create is empty or if it contains text, that box can be inserted as part of a style. (See Chapter 10 for procedures for creating styles.)

However, a graphics box cannot always be inserted. For example, a box cannot be inserted in a table of authorities, inside another graphics box, or in document comments.

Tip: *The graphics box style you select has more to do with the system for numbering a graphics box than with the contents of the box.*

There is no functional difference between the four graphics box styles. You could, for example, create a graphics box as figure style even though it will contain text, or you could create a box as text style even though it will contain an image.

What is different is the numbering of the graphics boxes, since the graphics boxes for each style are numbered separately from the other styles. For instance, if

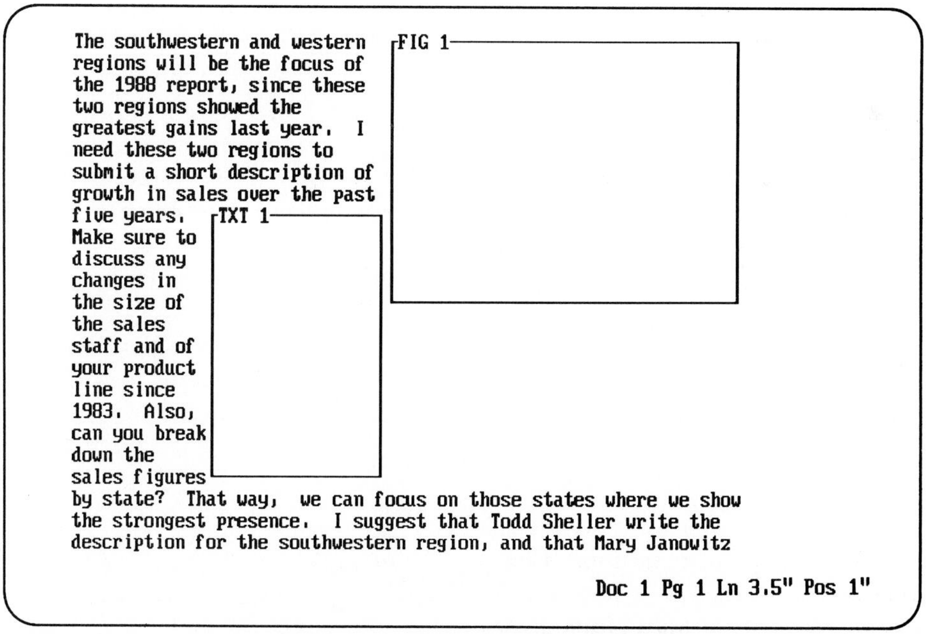

Figure 18-5. Two adjacent box outlines on a page

you create four graphics boxes in a document, two as table style and two as figure style, then the boxes are numbered as Tables I and II (by default, tables are numbered with Roman numerals) and as Figures 1 and 2. But, if you create all four graphics boxes as table style, then the boxes are numbered Tables I through IV. Therefore, if you wish to number all graphics boxes *sequentially* in a document, continue to select the same graphics style for each box that you create.

The other difference is in how WordPerfect assumes that you want the graphics boxes to appear when printed. For example, figure-style graphics boxes are assumed to have a single line bordering the image, while table-style graphics boxes are assumed to have a thick line along only the top and bottom edges. But these can be changed; see the section of this chapter entitled "Changing Graphics Options for a Box Style," to alter the default settings for a particular graphics box style.

Tip: *Refer to the Graphics Definition menu to view WordPerfect's assumptions for a particular graphics box.*

WordPerfect makes certain assumptions, as previously described, about the graphics box you are creating. For example, menu items 2 through 7 in Figure 18-2 indicate that the particular graphics box specified on that screen will

- Contain no caption.
- Be of the paragraph type.
- Be positioned vertically 0 inches from the top of the paragraph (meaning *even* with the first line of the paragraph). This assumption was made by WordPerfect because the cursor was located at the beginning of the paragraph when the GRAPHICS key was pressed. If the cursor had been in the middle of the paragraph when the GRAPHICS key was pressed, then the vertical position would have a different value, such as 0.32 inch or 0.48 inch. (WordPerfect translates your current cursor position to a value in inches based on the line-height setting in your document.)
- Be positioned horizontally at the right margin.
- Be 3.25 inches wide by 3.25 inches high. The size of the graphics box will change depending on the dimensions of the graphics image you retrieve or the text you type into the graphics box.
- Have text wrapped around it.

All of these assumptions can be changed. For instance, you can insert a caption below the graphics box. Or you can change the vertical or horizontal position of the box. See the section "Changing Graphics Options for a Box Style," later in this chapter for the procedure to alter the graphics box defaults.

Tip: *You can change the graphics box style or edit a graphics box definition.*

After creating a graphics box, you can change the box style. For example, you can change a figure-style graphics box into a table-style graphics box. Or you can edit any item on the Graphics Definition menu for a particular graphics box. To do so:

1. Position the cursor anywhere in your document.
2. Press the GRAPHICS (ALT + F9) key. The following menu is displayed:

   1 Figure; **2** Table; **3** Text Box; **4** User-defined Box; **5** Line: **0**

3. Type the number or mnemonic character that represents the style of box you wish to change.
4. Select Edit (2 or E). WordPerfect responds by asking for the number of the box you wish to edit. For example, if you choose to edit a figure, the prompt reads

   Figure number?

   and suggests the number of the next figure-style box ahead of the current position of the cursor in the text.
5. Press ENTER if the correct number is suggested, or type in the number of the box you wish to edit and press ENTER. The Graphics Definition menu for that graphics box appears on screen.
6. To change an item on the Graphics Definition screen, select the appropriate item and make the change. If you select Filename (1 or F), then WordPerfect prompts for a filename. Enter in a new filename if you want a different image to be inserted in the graphics box. Then WordPerfect asks for verification that you wish to replace the existing image. Type **Y** to continue, or type **N** to leave the old filename. (Items 2 through 8 are described in detail in the following section of this chapter, "Changing the Graphics Definition Defaults for an Individual Graphics Box.") Any changes made are reflected on the Graphics Definition screen.

Or to change the graphics box style, press the GRAPHICS (ALT + F9) key. The following menu appears at the bottom of the screen:

1 Figure; **2** Table; **3** Text Box; **4** User-defined Box: **0**

Select the desired box style. The change is then reflected at the very top of the Graphics Definition screen.

7. Press EXIT (F7) to return to your document.

If you changed to another graphics box style, the abbreviation on screen for the style of box changes to reflect the new style. For example, if you switched from a figure to a table style, the screen would now read "TAB I" rather than "FIG 1."

Tip: *You can delete the contents of a box without deleting the box itself.*

If you wish to remove a graphics box from your document, you must delete the graphics box code that defines that box—just as you delete any WordPerfect code.

However, if you wish to delete the contents of the box without deleting the box itself, then follow steps 1 through 5 for editing a box, described in the preceding Tip. Then select Filename (1 or F), from the Graphics Definition menu. WordPerfect prompts

Enter filename:

and suggests the filename that you entered previously (or indicates no filename if you typed text directly into the graphics box). Now press DELETE EOL (CTRL + END) and ENTER to erase the filename from the prompt line (or simply press ENTER if no filename is suggested). WordPerfect prompts

Clear contents? (Y/N) No

Type **Y** to clear the contents of the box, or type **N** to abort the command.

Tip: *You can reset graphics box numbers.*

In a new document, WordPerfect starts numbering graphics boxes for each style (figure, table, text, and user-defined box), beginning at number 1. But you can override that numbering system for a specific style by inserting a code in the document where you want the new numbering to start.

Suppose you want the table-style graphics boxes in the document to begin numbering at 11 (perhaps because a previously created document already contains ten table-style graphics boxes). Position the cursor where you want the next box renumbered. For example, to begin the box renumbering for the entire document, position the cursor at the top of that document. Then (1) press GRAPHICS (ALT + F9), (2) select a graphics box style, such as Table (2 or T), (3) select New Number (3 or N), and (4) enter the new number.

WordPerfect inserts a hidden code in the text. For instance, if you specified that the next table-style graphics box be numbered as 11, then the following code is inserted: **[New Tab Num:XI]** (tables are numbered by default with Roman numerals rather than Arabic numerals). Or, if you specified that the next figure-style graphics box be numbered as 5, then the following code is inserted: **[New Fig Num:5]**. All graphics boxes for that particular style will be numbered sequentially, starting with the new number you specified.

Trap: *You can't retrieve two files into one box, but you can superimpose two or more images at the printer.*

Whenever you retrieve a graphics image or a text file into a box, it replaces the current contents of that box. Therefore, two graphics images cannot be placed in the same box.

If you wish to overlay two images on top of each other when a document is printed, you can create two or more boxes at the same location on the page, each with its own image or text. Only one of the boxes should have the "Wrap Text Around Box" option (shown in Figure 18-2) set to "Yes." See the next section for more on this option.

Laser printers offer the ability to print anywhere on a page before ejecting that page of text from the printer. As a result, if you have a laser printer, you can also take advantage of the Advance feature to print two boxes in the same location. For example, you can insert a graphics box starting at the top of the page, use the Advance feature to move the cursor back to the top of the page, and then create a second graphics box. If you don't have a laser printer, you can create two graphics boxes on separate pages on screen. Insert the same piece of paper twice—once to print the first graphics box, and a second time to print a second box in the same position on the page.

Tip: *Thirty graphics images are included in the WordPerfect package so you can start using the Graphics feature immediately.*

To assist you in taking advantage of the Graphics feature right away, a sampling of graphics images is included with each WordPerfect package. On the WordPerfect Fonts/Graphics disk are housed 30 Publisher's PicturePaks images, created by Marketing Graphics Inc. (MGI). The images are stored in WordPerfect's own graphics format, with the filename extension .WPG. For example, one image is stored under the filename BOOK.WPG, and another under the filename CHECK.WPG. These images are ready to be inserted into any WordPerfect document, using the procedure described at the beginning of this chapter for retrieving a graphics image into a graphics box.

Figure 18-6 illustrates the 30 MGI Clip-art images included on the Fonts/Graphics disk. If you plan to use any of these images in a graphics text box, remember that in creating a graphics box (as outlined at the beginning of this section), you must specify on the Graphics Definition screen the complete filename, including its extension, as well as the drive/directory where the graphics file is housed if different from the default. For instance, if you've stored the files from the Fonts/Graphics disk on the hard disk in the directory \WPER, and you wish to retrieve the file named BOOK.WPG into a document, then enter the filename as **C: \WPER \BOOK.WPG**. If you enter the filename as **BOOK.WPG** or as **C: \WPER \BOOK**, WordPerfect will be unable to locate the graphics file for you.

Publisher's PicturePaks for WordPerfect is a library of three editions from what MGI calls its Eye Opener Series: Executive & Management, Sales & Marketing, and Finance & Administration. The series offers a total of 565 business-related images. The editions can be purchased collectively ($250) or separately ($99.95). For more information, or to order the series directly from MGI, call the company at (804) 788-8844.

Trap: *You cannot insert a graphics image that is not created by a WordPerfect-supported program.*

If you attempt to retrieve a graphics image into a box and an error message is displayed, then you created the image in a program that is not supported by WordPerfect. However, there are two alternatives to try if this message is displayed. See the following two Tips for details.

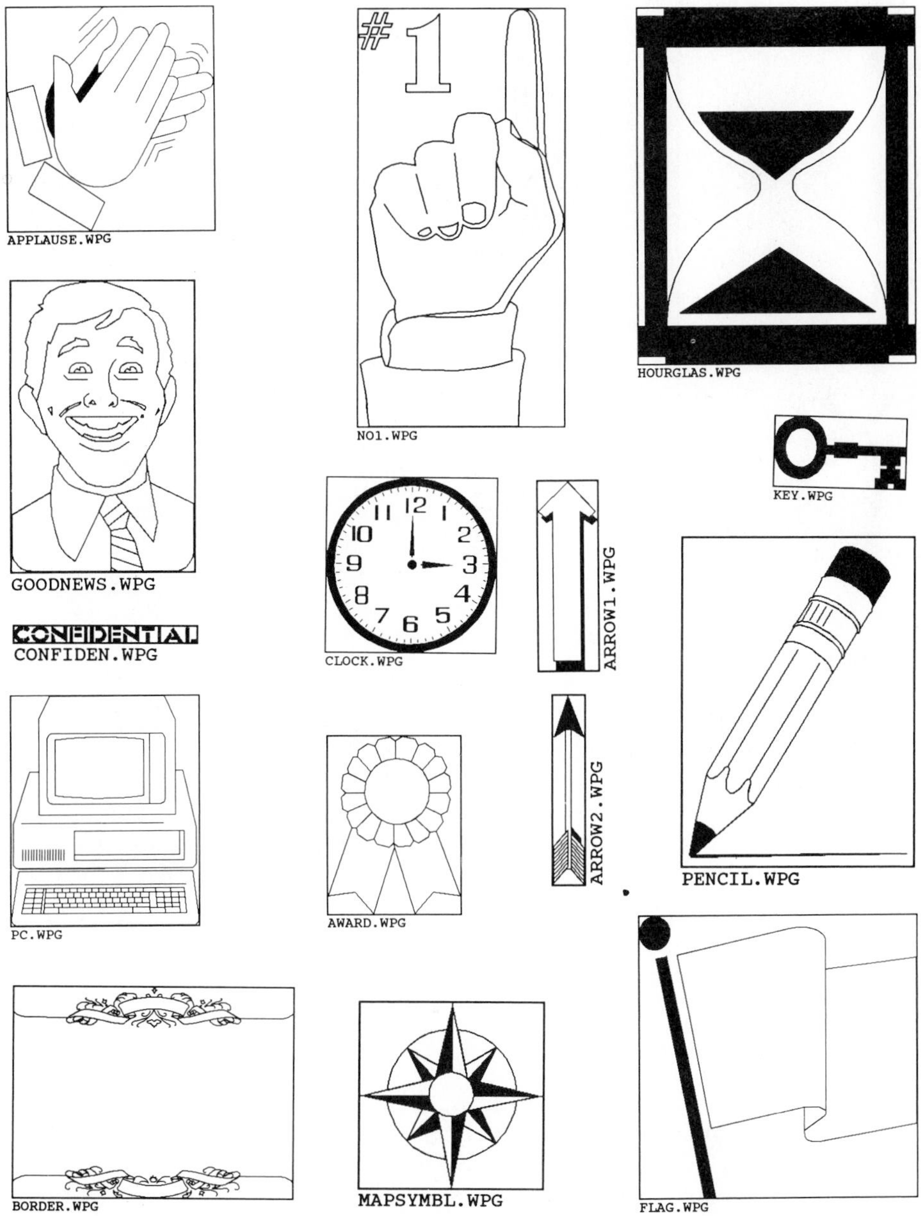

Figure 18-6. MGI Clip-art images included with WordPerfect

Figure 18-6. MGI Clip-art images included with WordPerfect (continued)

Tip: *You can insert a graphics image into a WordPerfect document even when using a graphics program not directly supported by WordPerfect.*

There are numerous graphics programs that are not directly supported by WordPerfect that can be retrieved into a WordPerfect document if converted into one of the WordPerfect-supported graphics formats. Table 18-2 lists the graphics programs that have been tested with WordPerfect and that can be retrieved into a WordPerfect document if you convert a graphics image into one of WordPerfect's supported graphics formats.

Note that WordPerfect Corporation constantly tests new graphics programs, so your graphics program may have been recently added to the list shown in Table 18-2; check with WordPerfect Corporation. The supported formats include the following:

- **CGM (Computer Graphics Metafile)** Fonts are converted to either Courier, Helvetica, or Times Roman WordPerfect vector fonts. Pattern conversions depend on what is available in WordPerfect graphics. Multiple pictures within a single file are superimposed. Color conversion depends on the color and graphics capabilities of your display.

  Graphics files created when you are using PlanPerfect 3.0 can be converted into CGM format with a graphics driver named META.SYS (a proprietary product of Graphics Software Systems, Inc.), which is housed on the Conversion disk. (On some version 5 releases, META.SYS is not on the Conversion disk; contact WordPerfect Corporation if you wish to receive that graphics driver.) The output of your graph is stored in a file named METAFILE.DAT, which can be retrieved into WordPerfect. This CGM format file can be converted into WordPerfect Graphics format and then retrieved into WordPerfect directly; see the last bullet below (WPG) for details.

- **DHP (Dr Halo PIC format)** Supported up to Dr Halo II. Area cut pictures are not supported.

- **DXF (AutoCAD format)** The following attributes are not converted: shape entities, tapering widths in polylines, text obliquing, curve fitting, and 3D rendering. DXF files can be converted into WordPerfect Graphics format and then retrieved into WordPerfect directly; see the last bullet below (WPG) for details.

- **EPS (Encapsulated PostScript)** An EPS file should conform to version 2.0 of the Adobe PostScript document-structuring conventions. The file may

Table 18-2. Graphics Programs Supported after Converting to a WordPerfect Graphics Format

Graphics program	WordPerfect-supported graphics format
Adobe Illustrator	EPS
AutoCAD	DXF, HPGL
Boeing Graph	IMG
CCS Designer	HPGL
CHART-MASTER	HPGL
CIES (Compuscan)	TIFF
DFI Handy Scanner	IMG, TIFF
DIAGRAM-MASTER	HPGL
Digraph	HPGL
Dr Halo II	DHP
EnerGraphics	IMG, TIFF
Freelance Plus	CGM
GEM Paint	IMG, TIFF
GEM SCAN	IMG, TIFF
Generic CADD	HPGL
Graph-in-the-Box	HPGL
Graphwriter	CGM
Harvard Graphics	HPGL, CGM, EPS
HP Graphics Gallery	TIFF, PCX
HP Scanning Gallery	TIFF, PCX
IBM CADAM	HPGL
IBM CATIA	HPGL
IBM CBDS	HPGL
IBM GDDM	HPGL
IBM GPG	HPGL
Lotus 1-2-3	PIC
MacPaint	PNTG
Microsoft Chart	HPGL
PC Paintbrush	PCX
PC Paint Plus	PPIC
PicturePaks	WPG, CGM, PCX
PlanPerfect	CGM
Quattro	PIC, EPS
SIGN-MASTER	HPGL
SlideWrite Plus	HPGL, TIFF, PCX
SuperCalc 4	PIC
Symphony	PIC
VersaCAD	HPGL
VP Planner	PIC
Windows Paint	MSP
Word & Figures	PIC

begin with either the standard 30-byte header or either of the following strings, which indicate a PostScript-only file: "%!PS-Adobe" or "%%PS-Adobe". It will usually have a graphics screen representation that may be manipulated and displayed in WordPerfect. (If contained within the file, only TIFF bitmap images are supported.) If no graphics screen representation is available, the image will be represented as an empty box on the Graphics Edit and View Document screens.

- **HPGL (Hewlett-Packard Graphics Language Plotter File)** Fonts are converted to Helvetica. Several graphics programs can create HPGL plotter files by redirecting the output to a disk file instead of directly to the plotter. Select the HP 7475A plotter if given the choice. (Not all plotters support the same HPGL commands, but the most commonly used commands are supported.)
- **IMG (GEM Paint Format)** GEM Draw pictures and files with a .GEM filename extension are not supported.
- **MSP (Microsoft Windows Paint Format)** The images are saved as a full page.
- **PCX (PC Paintbrush Format)** PC Paintbrush files are created by using the Save As option.
- **PIC (Lotus 1-2-3 PIC Format)** After a graph is created in Lotus 1-2-3, a file with a .PIC filename extension is saved with the /GS command.
- **PNTG (Macintosh Paint Format)** You must use a network or another communication link to transfer the data fork of the Macintosh file to the IBM PC. Pictures are transferred as full pages. Images conforming to the size of the Macintosh screen are produced in the upper left-hand corner of the page. The Macintosh screen grabber output is also compatible. It is activated by pressing SHIFT + COMMAND + 3. The file created is named SCREEN# (where # represents the number of the file created).
- **PPIC (PC Paint Plus Format)** With PC Paint 1.5, both packed and unpacked picture file formats are supported. With PC Paint Plus 2.0, packed picture file format is supported. BSAVE format is not supported (PC Paint 1.0 or 1.01).
- **TIFF (Tagged Image File Format)** Both the modified CCITT/3 (standard compression) and PackBits compression formats are supported.
- **WPG (WordPerfect Graphics Format)** This is the internal graphics format used by WordPerfect. All graphics formats directly supported by WordPerfect, as well as DXF format (which is not directly supported), can

be converted into WPG format and then retrieved into WordPerfect. To transform a graphics file into WPG format, you must access a utility program named GRAPHCNV.EXE, which is housed on the Conversion disk.

To use the Graphics conversion utility, you must know the name of the graphics file that you wish to convert. When a graphics file is converted using GRAPHCNV.EXE, a new extension of .WPG is assigned. Once you know the name of the graphics file you wish to convert:

1. You must be in DOS. If you are in WordPerfect, exit the program.
2. Floppy disk users should place the Conversion disk in drive A. Also, make sure that the default is drive A. If not, type **A:** and press ENTER. Place the disk containing the graphics file in drive B.

   Hard disk users should have the file called GRAPHCNV.EXE on the hard disk. Make sure that the default is the directory in which that file is housed. (If you installed according to the instructions in Appendix A, GRAPHCNV.EXE is in the \WPER directory.)
3. At the DOS prompt, type **GRAPHCNV** (in uppercase or lowercase letters). WordPerfect will prompt for the name of the graphics file you wish to convert.
4. Type the name of the file to be converted, preceded by the drive or directory where the file is stored, if different from the default, and press ENTER. WordPerfect will prompt for the name of the file that will be transferred into WPG format.
5. Type in the new filename, and press ENTER.

WordPerfect will convert the file for you, providing the file with the extension .WPG. That file is now ready to be inserted into a graphics box in a WordPerfect document.

To know how to create a particular format, you must check your graphics package's manual; each has a different method for doing so. For example, if you wish to insert a graph created in Lotus 1-2-3 into a WordPerfect document, you would save that graph in Lotus 1-2-3 by using the /GS command; a file with a .PIC extension is created. Then, you would load WordPerfect and retrieve the PIC file into a graphics box in your WordPerfect document.

As another example, if you wish to insert a graph created in Harvard Graphics (version 2.0), you could save that graph in Harvard Graphics by selecting 5, Import/Export, from Harvard Graphics' main menu, and then selecting 7, Export Matafile; a file with a .CGM extension is created. Then, you would load Word-

Perfect and retrieve the CGM file into a graphics box in your WordPerfect document.

Tip: *You can insert a graphics image into a WordPerfect document by first saving it with WordPerfect's Screen Capture Utility program.*

GRAB.COM is a Screen Capture utility that is provided on the WordPerfect Fonts/Graphics disk. This utility copies an image that is displayed on screen into

Table 18-3. Graphics Programs That Can Be Used with WordPerfect's Screen Capture Utility

Auto CAD
CHART-MASTER
DFI Handy Scanner
DIAGRAM-MASTER
Dr Halo II
Enable
EnerGraphics
Framework II
Freelance Plus
GEM Paint
GEM SCAN
Generic CADD
Graphwriter
Harvard Graphics
HP Graphics Gallery
Javelin
Lotus 1-2-3
MathCAD
Microsoft Chart
PC Paintbrush
PC Paint Plus
PlanPerfect
Printmaster
Professional Plan
Quattro
Silk
SlideWrite Plus
SuperCalc 4
Symphony
TWIN
VP Planner
Words & Figures

a file, which can then be used with WordPerfect's Graphics feature. It is a TSR (terminate and stay resident) program, meaning that it remains in memory while you are working with another software package. Table 18-3 lists those graphics programs whose images can be captured with GRAB.COM.

Note: WordPerfect Corporation constantly tests new graphics programs, so your graphics program may have recently been added to the list shown in Table 18-3; check with WordPerfect Corporation.

If given a choice, use WordPerfect-supported graphics formats (see the preceding Tip) rather than GRAB.COM. GRAB.COM captures images of a lesser quality than those created in a WordPerfect-supported format because GRAB.COM captures data only in the resolution of the screen.

To use GRAB.COM, you must load it into your computer's memory *before* you load either WordPerfect or any other software package. You must do so each time you turn on your computer. Floppy disk users will proceed as follows:

1. Make sure that you have loaded DOS so that the A> prompt appears on screen.
2. Insert the Fonts/Graphics disk into drive A.
3. At the DOS prompt, type **GRAB** and press ENTER.

If you're a hard disk user, proceed in this manner:

1. Make sure that you have loaded DOS so that a prompt, such as C: or C:\>, appears on screen.
2. Issue the CD (Change Directory) command to switch to the hard disk directory where the WordPerfect GRAB.COM program is stored. Suppose, for example, that GRAB.COM is located in the directory called \WPER. At the DOS prompt, type **CD \WPER** and press ENTER.
3. Type **GRAB** and press ENTER.

Now you are ready to use the Screen Capture utility, as follows:

1. Load the graphics program that you wish to use to create and store an image.
2. Display the image you want to capture on screen.
3. Press ALT + SHIFT + F9 to activate the Screen Capture utility. A two-toned chime indicates that the utility is ready to capture the image. A box is displayed on screen. (A low-pitched buzz indicates that you are not in

Graphics mode or that you have a monitor that is not supported by the utility, so that you cannot use GRAB.COM.)

4. Use the directional arrow keys to move the box. Use the combination SHIFT + an arrow key to resize the box. Press the INS key to switch between fine and coarse increments when you are moving or sizing the box.

5. Once the box is properly positioned over the image that you wish to capture, press ENTER to capture the image; the two-toned chime again sounds when the captured image has been stored on disk. Or press ESC to abort the capture command.

   If you do capture the image, it is stored in the default disk/directory in a file named GRAB.WPG. If a file by this name exists, then the file is named GRAB1.WPG. If GRAB1.WPG exists, then the file is named GRAB2.WPG. The Screen Capture utility can name files up to GRAB9999.WPG.

You can now load WordPerfect and retrieve the file named GRAB.WPG (or GRAB1.WPG and so on) into a graphics box, as described earlier in this chapter.

Depending on your needs, you may wish to store the captured files in a drive/directory other than the default. Or you may wish to store the files under a different filename. Both options are available to you if you load the Screen Capture Utility program in a slightly different way. Instead of typing GRAB to load the utility, you can add the slash symbol (/), followed by various letters.

At the DOS prompt, you can type **GRAB/D=path**, where "path" is the pathname (up to 80 characters in length) used to indicate where you want to store a captured file. For example, type **GRAB/D=C: \WPER \IMAGE** and press ENTER to load the utility and to store all the screens that you capture in the directory \WPER \IMAGE on the hard disk (assuming this directory has been created on your hard disk).

Or, you can type **GRAB/F=filename**, where "filename" is the filename for the captured files. The filename can be up to four characters long. For example, type **GRAB/F=MAP** and press ENTER to load the utility and to store all the screens that you capture under the filenames MAP.WPG, MAP1.WPG, MAP2.WPG, and so on.

You can also remove the Screen Capture Utility program from memory. Suppose you loaded GRAB.COM and then you loaded another program. Exit the other program and return to the DOS prompt. Now type **GRAB/R** and press ENTER. The utility is no longer in memory.

For additional information on WordPerfect's Screen Capture utility, you can type **GRAB/H** at the DOS prompt.

You may find that GRAB.COM conflicts with some other TSR programs that you may use. If this is the case, you may want to load only the Screen Capture utility into memory, capture various screens, exit the utility by typing **GRAB/R** at the DOS prompt, and then load your other TSR programs.

Tip: *If you have Shell, you can retrieve text or a graphics image from the Clipboard.*

If you use Shell, a program packaged in a separate software package named WordPerfect Library, you can retrieve text or graphics from the Shell Clipboard. On the Graphics Definition screen, when you select Filename (1 or F) and are ready to enter the name of a file, instead press the SHELL (CTRL + F1) key and type **Y** to retrieve the image or text contained in the Clipboard.

Tip: *You can list files in order to retrieve a file into a graphics box.*

When you want to retrieve a document onto the Typing screen but have forgotten that document's filename, you can use the LIST FILES (F5) key to refresh your memory and to retrieve the file. The same feature is also available when you are viewing the Graphics Definition screen, ready to retrieve a file into a graphics box. Each time that you wish to insert a file containing either text or an image into a graphics box, you have two alternatives.

If you know the correct drive/directory and filename where the graphics image is stored, then after you've pressed GRAPHICS (ALT + F9) and selected a box style, you would select Create (1 or C) and enter the appropriate filename—preceded by the drive or directory where it is stored if different from the default.

If you can't remember a filename, then, after pressing Create (1 or C), you would (1) press the LIST FILES (F5) key, (2) enter a drive or directory to view a list of files, (3) position the cursor on the filename of the graphics image you wish to insert into the graphics box, and (4) select Retrieve (1 or R).

Tip: *Store your graphics images in the same directory or on the same disk.*

Consider storing all your graphics images together in the same directory or on the same disk. For instance, hard disk users can store all graphics images in a directory named \WPER\GRAPHS. That way, you'll always know the drive/directory where the graphics images are stored; you won't have to keep hunting through numerous directories or disks to locate the filename of a graphics image you wish to insert in your document. (See chapter 13 for a discussion on how to create new directories and copy or move files between directories.)

Tip: *(When upgrading from 4.2.) The Graphics feature is brand-new in version 5.*

The Graphics feature is one of the most dramatic, welcome additions to version 5 of WordPerfect. You can now retrieve images directly into a document, or retrieve text that will be surrounded by a border. You therefore have a much greater ability to have drawings displayed in a document than you had in version 4.2 with the Line Draw feature (as discussed in Chapter 17).

Changing the Graphics Definition Defaults for an Individual Graphics Box

When creating a graphics box, as described in the preceding section of this chapter, "Creating a Graphics Box Using WordPerfect Defaults," none of WordPerfect's default settings on the Graphics Definition screen (as shown in Figure 18-2 for a figure style) were changed. You learned only how to create a graphics box and how to insert a graphics image or text into the box.

The other items on the Graphics Definition screen allow you to place and size a graphics box on the page in a manner different from that assumed by WordPerfect. You can display this screen either when you first create a graphics box, or when you choose to edit that box. The other items available—in addition to Filename (1 or F), which was explained previously—are used to size and place the box on the page as follows.

Caption (2 or C)

This feature allows you to insert a caption near the box. WordPerfect assumes that you want *no* caption accompanying a graphics box; however, if you choose this feature, then WordPerfect assumes that you desire a caption and *automatically* inserts the default caption for the box style that you selected. You are placed on a Caption Typing screen, the top of which is blank except for the default caption. For instance, if you are creating your first figure-type graphics box and you select Caption (2 or C), you will see the following at the top of the Caption Typing screen: **Figure 1**.That is the default caption for a figure-type graphics box. Or for your second figure-type graphics box, you will see the following: **Figure 2**. Or for your first table-type graphics box, you will see the following: **Table I**. (See the following section, "Changing Graphics Options for a Box Style," to learn the default captions for each of the four box styles.) If you reveal codes on the Caption Typing screen, you will discover that what WordPerfect inserts is actually the code **[Box Num]**, which specifies the caption that is the default. It is because of this code that the captions can be numbered sequentially for each graphics box type.

If you want the caption to remain as the default, simply press F7 (EXIT) to return to the Graphics Definition screen. Or before pressing EXIT, you can insert additional text around the default caption (which, remember, is actually a hidden code), or you can even erase the default caption by erasing the **[Box Num]** code and insert your own caption. The caption will be aligned with the left edge of the graphics box (although it may not appear as such on the Caption Typing screen), unless you use the CENTER or FLUSH RIGHT key to align the text differently.

Should you wish to change the text of the default caption for *all* graphics boxes of the same type in a document, then you should use the Graphics Options feature, described in the next section, "Changing Graphics Options for a Box Style." (WordPerfect makes an assumption as to whether the caption will be placed above or below the box and inside or outside the box borders; also look to the next section if you wish to change these assumptions.)

Type (3 or T)

This feature defines the type of graphics box you desire; it is the *type* that determines how the graphics box will be treated in relation to text on the page. The three types you can choose from are

- **Paragraph (1 or P)** This is the default setting, and it specifies that the box stay with its surrounding text. The graphics box is inserted on the line where your cursor was located when you pressed GRAPHICS to create the box (or on the next line) and the code is placed *at the beginning of the paragraph*. If the paragraph is so close to the bottom of the page that the graphics box can't fit on that page, the box is moved to the top of the next page.
- **Page (2 or A)** This specifies that the graphics box remain at a fixed position on the page. When creating the graphics box, place the cursor at the top of the page *before* any text you want to wrap around the box; other-

wise, the box is moved to the next page. The code is placed at the current cursor position.

- **Character (3 or C)** This specifies that the graphics box be treated as a single character, regardless of the box size. The graphics box code is placed *at the current cursor position.* When a line containing a graphics box code is wrapped, the next line starts below the box.

Vertical Position (4 or V)

This feature specifies where the box will sit vertically on the page. Your choices are dependent on the type of box you defined.

For a paragraph type, WordPerfect provides the following prompt:

Offset from top of paragraph:

and suggests the default setting, which depends on the location of your cursor in the paragraph when you created the graphics box. You would enter an offset measurement *from the top line* of the paragraph where the graphics box has been inserted— in inches (such as 0″), centimeters (such as 2c), points (such as 16p), or in WordPerfect 4.2 units (such as 3v). A setting of 0″, for example, places the box even with the paragraph's first line. If the paragraph is close to the bottom of the page, WordPerfect may need to alter the offset measurement setting to keep the box within the paragraph.

For a page type, WordPerfect provides the following menu:

Vertical Position: **1** Full Page; **2** Top; **3** Center; **4** Bottom; **5** Set Position: **0**

You can select Full Page (1 or F) to have the graphics box fill the page area within the top and bottom margins, meaning that the box will be on a page by itself. Or you can align the box at the top (first line), center, or bottom (last line, excluding footers and footnotes) by selecting options 2 through 4. Or you can select Set Position (5 or S) and enter an offset measurement from the top of the page (meaning from the very top edge of the form). The default setting is Top (2 or T).

For a character type, WordPerfect provides the following menu:

Align Text with: **1** Top of Box; **2** Center of Box; **3** Bottom of Box: **0**

Using this menu, you can indicate whether you wish the rest of the text on the line to align with the top, center, or bottom of the box. The default setting is Bottom of Box (3 or B).

Horizontal Position (5 or H)

This feature specifies where the box will sit horizontally on the page. Your choices are dependent on the type of box you defined.

For a paragraph type, WordPerfect provides the following menu:

Horizontal Position: 1 Left; **2** Right; **3** Center; **4** Both Left & Right: **0**

You can select to have the box centered or aligned with the left or right edge of the area where the text wraps. Or select Both Left & Right (4 or B) to have the box fill the area from left to right. All indents, columns, and graphics boxes are honored. The default setting is Right (2 or R).

For a page type, WordPerfect provides the following menu:

Vertical Position: 1 Margins; **2** Columns; **3** Set Position: **0**

You can select Margins (1 or M) and then decide whether you wish to align the box with the left margin or right margin, center it between the margins, or expand the box to fill the page between the margins. Or you can select Columns (2 or C), enter a range of columns (such as 1-3), and then decide whether you wish to align the box with the left column or right column, to center it between the columns, or to expand the box to fill the page from the first to the last column indicated. Or you can select Set Position (3 or S), and enter an offset measurement from the left edge of the form. The default setting is to align the box with the right margin.

For a character type, you do not enter a horizontal position; the box is positioned immediately following the character to its left.

Size (6 or S)

This feature sets the width and/or height of the graphics box. The default setting depends on the cursor position and the shape of the image or text that you inserted in the graphics box.

WordPerfect provides the following menu:

1 Width (auto height); **2** Height (auto width); **3** Both Width and Height: **0**

Select Width (1 or W) if you wish to define a particular width, but you want WordPerfect to calculate the height of the box automatically to preserve the graphics image's original shape.

Select Height (2 or H) if you wish to define a particular height, but you want WordPerfect to calculate the width automatically in order to preserve the graphics image's original shape.

Select Both Width and Height (3 or B) to specify both measurements yourself, in which case the image could change its proportions based on the measurements you indicate.

Wrap Text Around Box (7 or W)

This feature determines whether WordPerfect wraps text around the box you create or whether it ignores the box and continues to print text from the left to the right margin, over the graphics box. The default setting is "Yes," to wrap text around the box.

Edit (8 or E)

This feature not only allows you to insert text directly into a graphics box (as described in the previous section of this chapter, "Creating a Graphics Box Using WordPerfect Defaults"), but if you inserted an image in the box, it allows you to

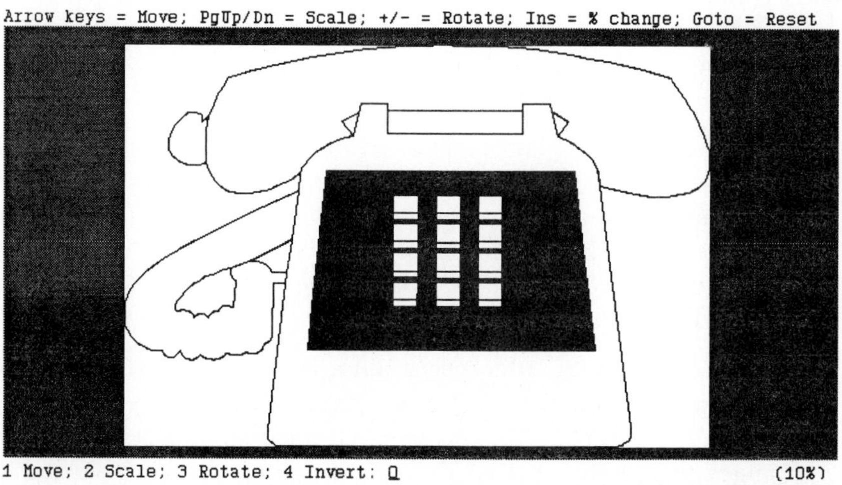

Figure 18-7. Graphics Edit screen with an image of a telephone (PHONE.WPG)

rotate, scale, and move that image within the box. Figure 18-7 shows the Graphics Edit screen after an image was inserted in the graphics box. You can

- *Move* the image horizontally and vertically in the box. Use the directional arrow keys to move the figure around the box by a certain percentage, as displayed in the lower right-hand corner of the screen.

  Or select 1, Move, from the menu at the bottom of the screen and enter horizontal and vertical measurements in positive or negative numbers.

- *Scale* the image, which expands or contracts it. Press the PGUP key to expand the image horizontally and vertically and press the PGDN key to contract the image horizontally and vertically by a certain percentage, as displayed in the lower right-hand corner of the screen. This maintains the same vertical and horizontal proportions of the figure.

  Or select 2, Scale, from the menu at the bottom of the screen and enter vertical (X) and horizontal (Y) scale factors. For example, to keep the vertical scale as it is and to reduce the horizontal scale by half, enter scale X as **100** and scale Y as **50**.

- *Rotate* the image in a circle. Use the MINUS key (on the numeric keypad) to rotate the image in a clockwise direction or the PLUS key (on the numeric keypad) to rotate the image in a counterclockwise direction by a certain percentage, as displayed in the lower right-hand corner of the screen.

  Or select 3, Rotate, and enter the number of degrees that you want to rotate the figure. For example, 180 degrees means that the image will be rotated so that it is upside down. Then, type **Y** to mirror the image, or type **N** if you do not want to mirror it. For example, if the image consists of a hand pointing to the right, and you mirror the image, the hand will point to the left.

- *Invert* a bitmap image so that the complementary color of each dot in the image is displayed—black becomes white and white becomes black. This item has no effect on line drawings, but only on bitmap images (where images are depicted as a matrix of black dots, and where what appears as white on black will print the opposite of what's shown on screen). Graphics files that are bitmapped include files imported using GRAB.COM, as well as HPGL files and PIC files.

- Indicate a *% Change,* which determines the extent to which the cursor movement keys, the PGUP and PGDN keys, and the MINUS and PLUS keys affect an image for moving, scaling, and rotating. The percentage can be changed to 1, 5, 10, or 25%. The default setting, as shown in the lower right-hand corner of Figure 18-7, is 10%. To change this percentage, press the INS key until the desired percentage appears in the lower right-hand corner of the screen.

- *Reset* the image to its initial appearance on the Graphics Edit screen before you attempted to move, scale, or rotate the image. Press GOTO (CTRL + HOME) to reset the image.

Once you have altered as many of these menu items as you desire, press EXIT (F7) to return to your document. The graphics box code that you inserted registers all the changes that you made.

Tip: *Inserting a caption alters the look of the graphics box code.*

When you choose to insert the default caption near a graphics box, the code **[Box Num]** is inserted not only on the Caption Typing screen (shown when you reveal codes), but *within* the graphics box code as well. For instance, if you defined your first figure-style graphics box with an image from the file USAMAP.WPG and with a caption, then the code inserted is **[Figure:1;**USAMAP.WPG;**[Box Num]]**. Or, if you just defined your first user-style graphics box with an image from APPLAUSE.WPG and with a caption, where the caption will be preceded by the word "Picture," then the code inserted is **[Usr Box:1;**APPLAUSE.WPG;Picture **[Box Num]]**.

The code **[Box Num]** represents the numbering, along with the default caption, for whichever graphics box style you selected (see the next section of this chapter, "Changing Graphics Options for a Box Style," for ways to change that default caption).

Trap: *Only certain graphics box definitions are allowed for boxes placed in headers, footers, footnotes, and endnotes.*

Captions cannot be created for graphics boxes that are placed in headers, footers, footnotes, and endnotes. For example, when you create a header A (as described in Chapter 9), as you insert a graphics box into that header, if you select Caption (2 or C) from the Graphics Definition menu, WordPerfect ignores your command.

In addition, the only boxes that are allowed inside footnotes or endnotes are character-type boxes.

Tip: *Use the GRAPHICS key to insert a caption number erased from the Caption Typing screen.*

If you are typing or editing a caption on the Caption Typing screen, you can erase the **[Box Num]** code (shown when you reveal codes) with the BACKSPACE or the DEL key. If you inadvertently erase the box-numbering code, don't just type in a new caption and number from the keyboard; WordPerfect will be unable to number the graphics boxes properly. Instead, position the cursor where you want the code reinserted and press GRAPHICS (ALT + F9). WordPerfect inserts a **[Box Num]** code, and the proper box number is inserted for you.

Tip: *If you create captions for your graphics boxes, WordPerfect can generate lists of the boxes that are contained in your document.*

Chapter 22 describes how you can instruct WordPerfect to automatically generate various lists for a document. A separate list can be generated for each graphics box style in your document, providing that you create a caption for each box of a given style. For instance, if your document contains six figure-style graphics boxes and ten text-style graphics boxes, WordPerfect can generate two separate lists. One will list the six figure captions and the pages on which they are found; the other will list the ten text box captions and their corresponding page numbers. See Chapter 22 for details on the Lists feature.

Tip: *Where a box appears in the text depends on the box type and position you selected.*

You have control over exactly where a box will appear—in two ways. First, you can specify a box type, as paragraph, page, or character. This determines where the box will appear relative to the text on the page. Second (and only after specifying a box type), you can indicate the vertical and horizontal positions of the box, since these positions are dependent on the choice you made for the box type.

Remember to position the cursor carefully if you will change from a paragraph type to another box type. Whereas you can position the cursor anywhere in a paragraph to insert a graphics box at the beginning of the paragraph, you must position the cursor more precisely if you select a page or character type. And, when defining a page type, be sure to place the cursor *at the top of the page,* before any text you want to wrap around the box, or the box will be moved to the next page.

Keep in mind that if you change your font after creating a graphics image defined as character type, the box might wind up in a different location if that new font results in characters of a different pitch.

Tip: *Position character type graphics boxes just as you position text in your document.*

Character type graphics boxes can be separated and positioned using spaces, tabs, and hard returns. In addition, they can be placed in precise locations using the Advance feature (as described in Chapter 7). As a result, these graphics boxes can be used when positioning various boxes in precise positions on the page. Or, character type boxes can be used to create organizational charts (where you use the Graphics Line feature, discussed later in this chapter, to connect the boxes with a line).

Tip: *How a box outline displays on screen depends on the box type and position selected.*

As you learned previously, with the default Graphics Definition menu settings, a box outline on screen indicates the space that the graphics box will occupy in the printed document. This is not always the case if you change the box type or position. If you change to a character box type, then the Typing screen shows the location of the graphics box by a shaded rectangle which is the size of one character of text. Or, if you select the horizontal position of a graphics box as left to right, then only the top of the box outline will appear on screen. Thus, you must use the View Document feature on the Print menu, or print out your document, to see exactly how much space the graphics box will occupy.

Trap: *If you don't wrap text, then the box outline is not shown on the Typing screen.*

When you choose not to wrap text around a graphics box, text that you type on the same line as a box will overlap the box when the page is printed. It is easy to forget about a box and overlap a box with text because, when you select not to wrap text around a graphics box, the box outline is hidden from view. To view the page, use the View Document feature (described in Chapter 14).

Tip: *Wrap text around both sides of a graphics box using the Text Columns feature and defining a page type box.*

When you insert a graphics box into a document, text will flow only around the left or only around the right side of the graphics box (even if you select the horizontal position as center). But if you are using newspaper columns, you can wrap text around both sides of a graphics box.

Chapter 19 describes the Text Column feature, with which you can create newspaper columns with text that flows down one column and then starts at the top of the next. To create a page on which text flows around both sides of the graphics box, create newspaper columns as discussed in Chapter 19. Then, create a graphics box where you define it as page type and set the horizontal position of the box to be centered between two specific columns (such as between columns 1 and 2). You can even center the graph from top to bottom by setting a vertical position (probably a value somewhere between 2″ and 4″, depending on the box size, your page size, and your top and bottom margin settings).

Trap: *Not all images can be rotated or scaled.*

Depending on the type of image you integrated into your WordPerfect document, you may not be able to rotate or scale it. For example, you can't rotate a PCX file imported from PC Paintbrush.

Trap: *For a box containing only text, you can select only certain size options.*

If you wish to size a box that contains only text, you can set the box width or set both the width and height. However, you cannot choose to set just the height of the text box, because the height is calculated according to the number of lines of text in the box.

Tip: *You can select to edit on the Graphics Definition menu even if the graphics box contains only text.*

You learned previously that item 8, Edit, on the Graphics Definition menu, allows you to rotate, scale, and/or move an image in a graphics box. If the graphics box contains text rather than an image, this option enables you to rotate the text. From the Graphics Edit screen, you would press GRAPHICS (ALT + F9). The following menu is displayed:

Rotate text: 1 0° ; **2** 90° ; **3** 180° ; **4** 270° : **1**

Type the number that corresponds to the amount you wish to rotate the text. For example, a 90° rotation means that the text will be printed sideways on the page (and is available only on the printed page if your printer supports sideways printing, also referred to as landscape printing). The rotation will appear if you use the View Document feature or print out the document.

Tip: *The HOME key extends a Search or Replace command to text boxes and graphics box captions.*

In Chapter 4 you learned about the Search feature, which finds phrases in your text. Similarly, the Replace feature (Chapter 6) finds a character string and substitutes another in a document's text. When you wish to broaden the use of these features to graphics boxes containing text or to graphics box captions, (as well as to headers, footers, footnotes, and endnotes) in addition to the document text, perform an Extended Search or Extended Replace. Press HOME before pressing the →SEARCH, ←SEARCH, or REPLACE key. That way, you can locate and/or replace a string should it occur in a text box or caption.

Changing Graphics Options for a Box Style

The Graphics Options feature is used to adjust settings for a specific style of graphics box: figure, table, text, or user-defined. When you change a graphics option, you change the option for *every* box of that style that is created from that point forward in the text of that document. This is quite different from the settings you learned about in the preceding section of this chapter, "Changing the Graphics Definition Defaults for an Individual Graphics Box," where you learned how to change certain defaults related to placement and size for a particular graphics box. To change a graphics option for a box style:

1. Position the cursor at the location in the document where you want to change the graphics option for a particular style.
2. Press the GRAPHICS (ALT + F9) key. The following menu is displayed:

   1 Figure; **2** Table; **3** Text Box; **4** User-defined Box; **5** Line: **0**

3. Type the number or mnemonic character that represents the style of box you wish to edit.

4. Select Options (4 or O). The Options menu appears for that particular style. Figures 18-8 through 18-11 show the Options menu for the four different graphics box styles. From these menus, you can view the default settings for each of these styles, and make any changes you desire. Each setting is described below:

   - **Border Style** Sets the style individually for all four borders of your graphics box. The choices are None, Single line, Double line, Dashed line, Dotted line, Thick line, or Extra Thick line. For example, the default setting for the figure-style graphics box is for a single line on all sides of the box, as indicated in Figure 18-8.
   - **Outside Border Space** Sets the amount of space individually between each border of your box and the text *outside* the box. Enter a distance, in inches, centimeters, points, or version 4.2 units. For example, the default setting for the figure-style graphics box is for 0.16 inch of space on all sides of the box, as indicated in Figure 18-8.
   - **Inside Border Space** Sets the amount of space individually between each border of your box and the image or text *inside* the box. Enter a

```
Options:    Figure

     1 - Border Style
              Left                                  Single
              Right                                 Single
              Top                                   Single
              Bottom                                Single
     2 - Outside Border Space
              Left                                  0.16"
              Right                                 0.16"
              Top                                   0.16"
              Bottom                                0.16"
     3 - Inside Border Space
              Left                                  0"
              Right                                 0"
              Top                                   0"
              Bottom                                0"
     4 - First Level Numbering Method               Numbers
     5 - Second Level Numbering Method              Off
     6 - Caption Number Style                       [BOLD]Figure 1[bold]
     7 - Position of Caption                        Below box, Outside borders
     8 - Minimum Offset from Paragraph              0"
     9 - Gray Shading (% of black)                  0%

Selection: 0
```

Figure 18-8. Figure Graphics Box Options menu

```
Options:    Table

     1 - Border Style
              Left                        None
              Right                       None
              Top                         Thick
              Bottom                      Thick
     2 - Outside Border Space
              Left                        0.16"
              Right                       0.16"
              Top                         0.16"
              Bottom                      0.16"
     3 - Inside Border Space
              Left                        0.16"
              Right                       0.16"
              Top                         0.16"
              Bottom                      0.16"
     4 - First Level Numbering Method     Roman
     5 - Second Level Numbering Method    Off
     6 - Caption Number Style             [BOLD]Table 1[bold]
     7 - Position of Caption              Above box, Outside borders
     8 - Minimum Offset from Paragraph    0"
     9 - Gray Shading (% of black)        0%

Selection: 0
```

Figure 18-9. Table Graphics Box Options menu

```
Options:    Text Box

     1 - Border Style
              Left                        None
              Right                       None
              Top                         Thick
              Bottom                      Thick
     2 - Outside Border Space
              Left                        0.16"
              Right                       0.16"
              Top                         0.16"
              Bottom                      0.16"
     3 - Inside Border Space
              Left                        0.16"
              Right                       0.16"
              Top                         0.16"
              Bottom                      0.16"
     4 - First Level Numbering Method     Numbers
     5 - Second Level Numbering Method    Off
     6 - Caption Number Style             [BOLD]1[bold]
     7 - Position of Caption              Below box, Outside borders
     8 - Minimum Offset from Paragraph    0"
     9 - Gray Shading (% of black)        10%

Selection: 0
```

Figure 18-10. Text Graphics Box Options menu

```
Options:   User-defined Box

     1 - Border Style
              Left                           None
              Right                          None
              Top                            None
              Bottom                         None
     2 - Outside Border Space
              Left                           0.16"
              Right                          0.16"
              Top                            0.16"
              Bottom                         0.16"
     3 - Inside Border Space
              Left                           0"
              Right                          0"
              Top                            0"
              Bottom                         0"
     4 - First Level Numbering Method        Numbers
     5 - Second Level Numbering Method       Off
     6 - Caption Number Style                [BOLD]1[bold]
     7 - Position of Caption                 Below box, Outside borders
     8 - Minimum Offset from Paragraph       0"
     9 - Gray Shading (% of black)           0%

Selection: 0
```

Figure 18-11. User-defined Graphics Box Options menu

distance, in inches, centimeters, points, or version 4.2 units. For example, the default setting for the figure-style graphics box is for 0 inches of space, as indicated in Figure 18-8.

- **First and Second Level Numbering Method** Sets the numbering for a box. The choices are Off, Numbers (Arabic), Letters, or Roman Numerals. For example, the initial setting for the figure-style graphics box is for Numbers as a first level and Off as a second level, as indicated in Figure 18-8. Thus, figure one would be numbered "1," and figure two would be numbered "2." The number displays on the top line of the box outline on screen when you create a graphics box.

  Letters and roman numerals are inserted in uppercase when used for first-level numbering and lowercase when used for second-level numbering. If, for instance, you selected roman numerals as the first level and letters as the second level, then figure one would be numbered "I,a," and figure two would be numbered "I,b."

- **Caption Number Style** Sets the style for a caption that you may wish to insert near the graphics box when printed. (See the preceding section, "Changing the Graphics Definition Defaults for an Individual Graphics Box," for the procedure to insert a caption near a graphics box.) Enter the number **1** where you wish the first level number to display. Enter **2** where you wish the second level number to display. In addition, you can include text or font attributes, such as boldface and underline, in the style. For example, the initial setting for the figure-style graphics box is for a caption to read "Figure 1" in boldface letters, where "1" represents the first-level number, as indicated in Figure 18-8. Thus, the caption for figure one (assuming that the level one numbering style is for numbers) would read "Figure 1," and the caption for figure two would read "Figure 2."

If you've defined both a first and second numbering level, then to include them both in a caption, insert the numbers **1** and **2**. For example, if you selected Roman numerals as the first level and letters as the second level, then if you enter a caption number style as **[UND]Figure No. 1-2[und]**, the caption for figure one would read "Figure No. I-a."

- **Position of Caption** Sets the position of the caption—either above or below the box, and either outside or inside the box borders. For example, the initial setting for the figure-style graphics box is for the caption to be located below and outside the box, as indicated in Figure 18-8.
- **Minimum Offset from Paragraph** Sets the limit as to how much WordPerfect can reduce an offset measurement you specify for a paragraph type (as described in the preceding section of this chapter, "Changing the Graphics Definition Defaults for an Individual Graphics Box"). The default setting for all graphics box styles is 0 inches; this means that the offset measurement is honored unless the paragraph is too close to the bottom of the page so that the box cannot fit on the page; in this case, the box is moved to the top of the next page. The larger the minimum offset value, the more the offset measurement is able to be reduced in an attempt to keep the paragraph and the box together on the same page.
- **Gray Shading** Sets the shading within the graphics boxes of a certain style, where 100% means black. For example, the initial setting for the figure-style graphics box is for 0% shading (for no shading), as indicated in Figure 18-8, while the setting for the text-style graphics box is for 10% shading, as indicated in Figure 18-10.

5. Press EXIT (F7) to return to your document.

A graphics options code is placed at the current cursor position, affecting all graphics boxes of the style you specified from the position of the cursor forward in the document (or until the next code of its type appears). For example, if you altered the graphics options for the figure-style box, then the code inserted is **[Fig**

Opt]. Or, if you altered the options for the table-style box, the code inserted is **[Tab Opt]**.

Tip: *You can change your graphics options at any time before or after you insert graphics boxes in the text.*

A graphics options code will take effect for all boxes that follow the code. If you have already included graphics boxes in the text, and then change graphics options at the top of the document for a specific style, the graphics boxes corresponding to that style will be automatically updated to reflect the change, as the cursor moves past those boxes and rewrites the screen.

Trap: *Your printer may be unable to support different line thicknesses and shading intensities.*

Your printer may not be able to support some of the options for the border around your text. In addition, it may not be able to support various shading intensities. Test these options on your printer. If your printer can support only one shading level, then enter **100%** to shade the box.

Tip: *Change the graphics option defaults by using the Setup menu.*

If you find that you constantly change the default options in the same way each time you type a document with a certain graphics box style, you can change the defaults permanently. (Refer to Appendix B, which describes how to do this through the Initial Settings option on the Setup menu.)

Drawing Lines and Shaded Boxes

The Graphics menu offers a special box-type option, Line, which allows you to place horizontal or vertical lines and shaded rectangles on a page. Thus, the Line option is not actually a box. Yet the feature is offered on the Graphics menu because your printer must support graphics in order to print these lines and rectangles. An example of graphics lines is shown in Figure 18-1. Two horizontal lines were inserted to set off the "To:," "From:," and "Date:" headings from the rest of the text. To create a graphics line:

1. Position the cursor where you wish to create a line.
2. Press the GRAPHICS (ALT + F9) key. The Graphics menu is displayed:

   1 Figure; **2** Table; **3** Text Box; **4** User-defined Box; **5** Line: **0**

3. Select Line (5 or L). The following menu appears

   1 Horizontal Line; **2** Vertical Line: **0**

4. Select Horizontal Line (1 or H). Or select Vertical Line (2 or V).

   WordPerfect displays a Graphics Line menu. The menu displayed after you choose to create a vertical line is shown in Figure 18-12. The menu displayed after you choose to create a horizontal line is the same, except that item 2, Vertical Position, is not on the menu, so that there are four, rather than five, menu items to choose from. The items are as follows:

   - **Horizontal Position** When creating a vertical line, this enables you to position the line: (1) Left, to the left of the left margin; (2) Right, to the right of the right margin; (3) Between columns, between any two

```
Graphics: Vertical Line

     1 - Horizontal Position              Left Margin

     2 - Vertical Position                Full Page

     3 - Length of Line

     4 - Width of Line                    0.01"

     5 - Gray Shading (% of black)        100%




Selection: 0
```

Figure 18-12. Vertical Line Graphics menu

columns (you specify the column number of the first column to the left); or (4) Set Position, at a specific horizontal offset from the left edge of the form. The default setting is "Left Margin."

When creating a horizontal line, this enables you to position the line: (1) Left, beginning against the left margin; (2) Right, ending against the right margin; (3) Center, centered between the margins; (4) Both Left & Right, filling the area from the left to the right margin; or (5) Set Position, beginning at a specific horizontal position on the line where the cursor is located, measured from the left edge of the form. The default setting is "Left & Right."

- **Vertical Position** When creating a vertical line, this enables you to position the line: (1) Full Page, across the full length of the page from the top to the bottom margin; (2) Top, beginning against the top margin; (3) Bottom, ending against the bottom margin; (4) Center, centered between the top and bottom margins; or (5) Set Position, beginning at a specific vertical position (absolute measurement) from the top of the form. The default setting is "Full Page."

  When creating a horizontal line, the vertical position always aligns to the bottom of the current line of text. Therefore, there is no menu item available.

- **Length of Line** Allows you to specify the length of the line in inches, centimeters (such as 2c), points (such as 16p), or WordPerfect 4.2 horizontal or vertical units (such as 8h or 3v).

  For a vertical line, the default line length is calculated based on the vertical position setting (see the preceding bullet). You can enter any length that fits within the current top and bottom margins. If the vertical position setting is "Full Page," the line length is calculated automatically.

  For a horizontal line, the default line length is calculated based on the horizontal position setting (see the first bullet). You can enter any length that fits within the current left and right margins. If the horizontal position setting is "Left & Right," the line length is calculated automatically.

- **Width of Line** Allows you to specify the thickness of the line in inches, centimeters, points, or WordPerfect 4.2 units. The default setting is 0.01 inches. If you select a thick line, then you will actually be defining a shaded rectangle, rather than a line.

- **Gray Shading** Allows you to specify how much of the line should be shaded; the higher the percentage, the more the box is shaded. 100% means the line is black. The default setting is "100%."

5. Press EXIT (F7) to return to the document.

Once you create a graphics line, a graphics line code is inserted in the text at the current cursor position. The code indicates the line options you selected. For example, if you create a vertical line starting at the left margin, centered vertically on the page, 5 inches in length, 0.01 inch in width, and with 100% shading (meaning black), then the code inserted is

[Vline:Left Margin,Center,5",0.01",100%]

Or, if you create a horizontal line extending from the left margin to the right, 6.5 inches in length (the automatic setting based on a form 8 1/2 inches wide and with one-inch margins), 0.02 inch in width, and with 100% shading, then the code inserted is

[Hline:Left & Right,6.5",0.02",100%]

The graphics line will not display on screen; however, you can see how the line will appear when printed by using the View Document feature (as described in Chapter 14).

Tip: *Use the Graphics Line feature to quickly create a fill-in-the-blanks form.*

The Graphics Line feature is convenient when you wish to create a pre-printed form with lines to indicate where information should be filled in on a page. To do this, you could insert a horizontal line, and copy the **[Hline:]** code down the page to produce the number of lines that you desire.

For instance, one section of the form might appear as follows:

```
List all previous employers:  ______________________________
____________________________________________________________
____________________________________________________________
____________________________________________________________
```

To create this part of the form, you could: (1) type **List all previous employers:**, and press the SPACEBAR twice, (2) insert a **[Hline:]** code that begins at the current cursor position and extends to the right margin (see the next Tip), (3) on the next line, insert a **[Hline:]** code that extends from the left to the right margin, and (4) copy the code created in step 3 two more times, down to the next two lines.

Tip: *Position the cursor precisely if you wish a line to begin or end at a specific horizontal or vertical position.*

Instead of inserting a line at the left or right or centered on a page, you may wish to begin a line at a precise vertical or horizontal location on the page, according to text already typed. If you position the cursor where you want the line to *begin* before pressing the GRAPHICS key, WordPerfect will automatically assume that you want the line to begin at the current cursor position (unless you specify otherwise).

For example, suppose that you are producing the section of a fill-in-the-blanks form, as discussed in the preceding Tip. You want to begin a horizontal line just after the phrase "List all previous employers:." To do so, you would position the cursor just past this phrase, press GRAPHICS (ALT + F9), select Line (5 or L), and then select Horizontal Line (1 or H). Once on the Horizontal Line Graphics menu, you would select Horizontal Position (1 or H) and then select Right (2 or R). As a result, WordPerfect assumes that you wish to begin the line at the current cursor position and to end it at the right margin, so it calculates the proper line length for you. (Or you could also select Set Position (5 or S), in which case WordPerfect again assumes that you wish to begin the line at the current cursor position and to end it at the right margin.)

Similarly, you can position the cursor where you want the line to *end* before pressing the GRAPHICS key so that WordPerfect can assume that you want the line to end at the current cursor position. For instance, to create a horizontal line, you could select a horizontal position of Left (1 or L). In this case, WordPerfect assumes that you wish to begin the line at the left margin and to end the line at the current cursor position, so it calculates the proper line length for you. Thus, without having to calculate specific horizontal or vertical settings yourself, the line is inserted correctly for you.

Trap: *Text does not wrap or adjust around graphics lines.*

Text does not wrap around graphics lines that you create to border your text. As a result, however, it is quite possible to set a vertical or horizontal position that results in a line printing over text in your document. If you insert a line within the text, make sure that you leave sufficient room so that the line and your text aren't printed in the same location. For example, if you place a horizontal line on the same line as text, the line may overwrite the bottom of each character of text.

Keep in mind that if you do wish to insert graphics lines around text based on your current cursor position, a horizontal line is placed on the *baseline* (bottom edge) of the line where the cursor is located, as shown here:

HORIZONTAL LINE PLACED ON THE LINE ABOVE THIS TEXT

HORIZONTAL LINE PLACED ON THE LINE BELOW THIS TEXT

Thus, adjustments may be necessary when bordering text. One solution would be to use the Advance feature (described in Chapter 7) to position each line at a precise vertical position.

Trap: *Graphics line codes cannot be edited.*

Unlike a graphics box code, a graphics line code cannot be edited. To change the size or position of a graphics line, you must delete the graphics line code and insert a new one.

Trap: *When inserting graphics lines, your printer may be unable to support different line thicknesses and shading intensities.*

The same limitation holds for graphics lines as for the borders around graphics boxes: your printer may not be able to support certain line thicknesses or shadings. Test these options on your printer. If your printer can support only one shading level, then, to shade a box, enter **100%**.

Tip: *Use another WordPerfect feature to draw straight lines that are shown on the Typing screen.*

The Line Draw feature, described in Chapter 17, allows you to draw lines and boxes using a variety of draw characters, such as a line, a double line, or the asterisk. You use the cursor movement keys to draw directly on the screen and the drawings created with Line Draw are displayed on the Typing screen.

Tips and Traps Summary

Creating a Graphics Box Using WordPerfect Defaults

Trap: The Typing screen does not show the contents of a graphics box.

Trap: Your printer must be able to support graphics in order to print images properly.

Tip: WordPerfect can wrap text around a maximum of 20 boxes on a page.

Tip: Graphics can be placed in more than just the main body of your document.

Tip: The graphics box style you select has more to do with the system for numbering a graphics box than with the contents of the box.

Tip: Refer to the Graphics Definition menu to view WordPerfect's assumptions for a particular graphics box.

Tip: You can change the graphics box style or edit a graphics box definition.

Tip: You can delete the contents of a box without deleting the box itself.

Tip: You can reset graphics box numbers.

Trap: You can't retrieve two files into one box, but you can superimpose two or more images at the printer.

Tip: Thirty graphics images are included in the WordPerfect package so you can start using the Graphics feature immediately.

Trap: You cannot insert a graphics image that is not created by a WordPerfect-supported program.

Tip: You can insert a graphics image into a WordPerfect document even when using a graphics program not directly supported by WordPerfect.

Tip: You can insert a graphics image into a WordPerfect document by first saving it with WordPerfect's Screen Capture Utility program.

Tips and Traps Summary (*continued*)

Tip: If you have Shell, you can retrieve text or a graphics image from the Clipboard.

Tip: You can list files in order to retrieve a file into a graphics box.

Tip: Store your graphics images in the same directory or on the same disk.

Tip: (When upgrading from 4.2.) The Graphics feature is brand-new in version 5.

Changing the Graphics Definition Defaults for an Individual Graphics Box

Tip: Inserting a caption alters the look of the graphics box code.

Trap: Only certain graphics box definitions are allowed for boxes placed in headers, footers, footnotes, and endnotes.

Tip: Use the GRAPHICS key to insert a caption number erased from the Caption Typing screen.

Tip: If you create captions for your graphics boxes, WordPerfect can generate lists of the boxes that are contained in your document.

Tip: Where a box appears in the text depends on the box type and position you selected.

Tip: Position character type graphics boxes just as you position text in your document.

Tip: How a box outline displays on screen depends on the box type and position selected.

Trap: If you don't wrap text, then the box outline is not shown on the Typing screen.

Tip: Wrap text around both sides of a graphics box using the Text Columns feature and defining a page type box.

Trap: Not all images can be rotated or scaled.

Trap: For a box containing only text, you can select only certain size options.

Tips and Traps Summary (*continued*)

Tip: You can select to edit on the Graphics Definition menu even if the graphics box contains only text.

Tip: The HOME key extends a Search or Replace command to text boxes and graphics box captions.

Changing Graphics Options for a Box Style

Tip: You can change your graphics options at any time before or after you insert graphics boxes in the text.

Trap: Your printer may be unable to support different line thicknesses and shading intensities.

Tip: Change the graphics option defaults by using the Setup menu.

Drawing Lines and Shaded Boxes

Tip: Use the Graphics Line feature to quickly create a fill-in-the-blanks form.

Tip: Position the cursor precisely if you wish a line to begin or end at a specific horizontal or vertical position.

Trap: Text does not wrap or adjust around graphics lines.

Trap: Graphics line codes cannot be edited.

Trap: When inserting graphics lines, your printer may be unable to support different line thicknesses and shading intensities.

Tip: Use another WordPerfect feature to draw straight lines that are shown on the Typing screen.

19

Creating Text Columns

By placing text in columns, you can enhance a document's appearance and make it easier to read—thus making the words easier to comprehend. Your daily newspaper provides a good example of text columns in action. When creating columns with a standard typewriter, your only choice is to position text on tab stops. For charts or tables, such tabular columns work well. But when words extend beyond one line, as in paragraphs of text in a newspaper, tab stops are cumbersome. And if you add just one word at the top of an already-typed column, you might have to adjust dozens of lines.

Fortunately, WordPerfect gives you the ability to create columns in which words are automatically wrapped to the next line within the column. You can add or delete text just as you do when typing the full width of the page; WordPerfect adjusts the text to fit in the column. This chapter describes the steps you take to create text columns: define your column layout, turn columns on, type your text, and turn columns off. You'll also learn how to edit text that is in column format. You'll soon see that the Column feature is quite sophisticated.

Defining Text Columns

You cannot use the Column feature until you define your column layout. What kind of column do you desire? How many columns do you want across the page?

How wide should they be? How far apart should they be? All this must be decided first.

There are three kinds of text columns you can choose from, depending on the document you are producing:

- **Newspaper columns** These are for newsletters or other documents in which text flows down one column and, after reaching the bottom of the page, starts at the top of the next column. Each column is independent of the others, and when you edit, text might flow into another column. An example of newspaper columns is shown in Figure 19-1. Notice that there are two columns of equal width, with one-half inch of space separating them.

CAREER CORNER

Since our last newsletter, many of you expressed an interest in information about careers in the computer industry. Today's "Career Corner" article will be the first of three parts on the computer education field.

Those of you who have recently learned how to use a computer undoubtedly see the need for computer education. A computer is not something you become comfortable with in a day, any more than you can learn to drive a car in that same amount of time. As a result, there are numerous opportunities in the computer education field.

To teach computers in schools, it is often necessary to know some programming—such as BASIC or C. But many jobs require no such programming knowledge. Software companies are often interested in people who have used their product or a similar one and can share their expertise with new users.

There are also training companies specifically devoted to teaching people how to use computers and various software. Computer retailers often hire trainers to provide assistance to their customers.

A related field is technical writing. Employers are looking for people who can write hardware and soft ware documentation. They want clear, organized writing and an in-depth understanding of computer jargon.

Figure 19-1. Newspaper-style columns

EMPLOYEE PROMOTIONS—YEAR-TO-DATE

NAME	ADDRESS	JUSTIFICATION
John Caldwell Sales Manager, Eastern Div.	3345 Cypress Creek Blvd. Pompano Beach, FL 33436 (305) 734-4432	Increased sales 120% as manager in Florida. 10 years with the company.
Paula Chin Sales Rep.	9000 Rillips Street Chicago, IL 60616 (312) 833-2233	Sales apprentice for 13 months. Strong marks and excellent recommendations from P. Smith and N. Begley.
Phyllis Reimer (formerly Carrington) Sales Rep.	12330 Algonquin Rd. Des Plaines, IL 60622 (312) 630-3388	Asst. to N. Begley for 6 years. Strong recommendation.
Rick Tanquez Sales Rep.	123 Fillmore Street Apartment 305 San Francisco, CA 94123 (415) 563-9933	Sales apprentice for 12 months. Strong marks and excellent recommendations from L. Larell and P. Berger.

Figure 19-2. Parallel columns

- **Parallel columns** These are for inventory lists, address lists, glossaries, interrogatories, or other documents in which related information varies in length but must remain together in adjacent columns. A related group is kept together, side by side in columns, and text from one column does not flow into the next column when you add or delete information. Each group of parallel columns is separated from the next group by a blank line. An example is shown in Figure 19-2. Here there are four groups, each with entries in three columns: "NAME," "ADDRESS," and "JUSTIFICATION." Notice that the first column is narrower than the other two. One-half inch of space separates the columns.

- **Parallel-with-Block-Protect columns** These are similar to parallel columns, except that WordPerfect will not allow any column of a group of to be separated by a page boundary. If a group of columns spans a page break, the entire group moves to the top of the next page. This style of column is appropriate for documents with short columns, but not for documents like interrogatories in legal briefs, where information must be typed in adjacent columns and where entries in one column can be pages long.

You can select anywhere from 2 to 24 columns in WordPerfect. If you want columns of equal width with consistent spacing between them (as in Figure 19-1), WordPerfect can automatically calculate each column's margins for you during the column layout process. WordPerfect takes into account (1) the width across the page (the distance between the left and right margins), (2) the number of columns you want, and (3) the distance you want between columns. If you wish to use columns that vary in width, you must set each column's margins manually. Define your column layout as follows:

1. Position the cursor at the left margin, where you want the columns to begin.
2. Press the MATH/COLUMNS (ALT + F7) key. WordPerfect responds with the Math/Columns menu:

   1 Math On; **2** Math Def; **3** Column On/Off; **4** Column Def: **0**

3. Select Column Def (4 or D). The Text Column Definition screen appears, as shown in Figure 19-3. As a default, WordPerfect assumes that you desire two newspaper-style columns of equal width, with 0.5 inches between them.
4. Select a column definition option, and enter your response. The options are as follows:

   Select Type (1 or T) to define a type of column (if other than newspaper style). WordPerfect responds with:

   Column Type: 1 Newspaper; **2** Parallel; **3** Parallel with Block Protect: **0**

   Choose a column type.

   Select Number of Columns (2 or N), to define the number of columns if other than two columns). Type in a number and press ENTER.

```
Text Column Definition

     1 - Type                                          Newspaper

     2 - Number of Columns                             2

     3 - Distance Between Columns

     4 - Margins

     Column    Left      Right     Column    Left      Right
      1:       1"        4"        13:
      2:       4.5"      7.5"      14:
      3:                           15:
      4:                           16:
      5:                           17:
      6:                           18:
      7:                           19:
      8:                           20:
      9:                           21:
     10:                           22:
     11:                           23:
     12:                           24:

Selection: 0
```

Figure 19-3. The Text Column Definition screen

Select Distance Between Columns (3 or D) to define the spacing between columns (if other than 0.5 inch). Type in the number that represents the amount of space to be used between columns and press ENTER.

Select Margins (4 or M) to define column margins (if other than the margins suggested by WordPerfect). Type in the first column's left margin location (as measured from the left edge of the page), press ENTER, and continue until all left/right margins have been redefined for each column.

5. Press EXIT (F7) or ENTER to accept all the settings. You are then returned to the Math/Columns menu (so that you can switch on the Column feature, if you're ready to begin typing in columns, as described in the next section of this chapter, "Entering Text in Columns").

A column definition code has been inserted in your text at the current cursor position. Suppose that you defined 2 columns, the first with margins of 1″ and 3.5″, the second with margins of 4.5″ and 7.5″. The code inserted is **[Col Def: 2,1″,3.5″,4.5″,7.5″]**.

Tip: *You can set column margins that are wider or narrower than the document margins.*

When you are establishing the column margins on the Text Column Definition screen, the left margin of the first column and the right margin of the last column can be changed to create columns that are wider or narrower than the document margins. For example, suppose that the document margins are currently at the default settings—that is, the left and right margins are both one inch. When you define the left margin for your first column, you can set it to begin before one inch (such as at .5″), even though the left margin for the document, when not in Column mode, is one inch.

Trap: *You cannot overlap columns.*

If you choose your own margin settings for each column, remember that columns cannot overlap. For example, set one column's right margin at 5″ and the next column's left margin at 4.5″ and WordPerfect responds

ERROR: Text columns can't overlap

A less obvious example would be when you set one column's right margin at 5″ and the next column's left margin also at 5″. WordPerfect offers no error message, but when you print, you'll be unable to tell where one column stops and another starts.

When you select new column margins, be sure to take into account the space that is required between the columns.

Tip: *Spacing between columns is an important consideration.*

Columns are intended to enhance the presentation of information and thus make it easier to read. If the spacing between columns is too narrow, the columns will be hard to read. Conversely, if the spacing between columns is too wide, the columns will be so narrow as to be difficult to read. Three to six character spaces (0.3 to 0.6 inch) is usually an appropriate distance between columns.

Trap: *The column definition code provides no indication of column style.*

You can often decipher every detail of the format you choose by revealing hidden codes. But once you insert a column definition code in the text, you cannot tell whether it dictates newspaper, parallel, or parallel-with-Block-Protect-type columns until you start entering text into the columns. The column codes for all three types are identical.

Therefore, you must either make a mental note of your choice of column style, or review the Text Column Definition screen. That is, position the cursor after the **[Col Def:]** code and, as if you're about to define columns, press MATH/COLUMNS and choose Column Def (4 or D). The Text Column Definition screen appears, showing you the layout that you specified in the **[Col Def:]** code. Now press CANCEL (F1) twice to exit this screen without inserting another code in the text.

Tip: *You can define your column layout in inches, centimeters, points, or version 4.2 units of measure.*

As a default setting, WordPerfect displays format settings in inches and expects you to enter any changes using inches as the unit of measure. In previous chapters, you learned that you can also indicate formatting changes by using other units of measure: centimeters, points, or version 4.2 units. The same applies when defining your column layout.

As a default setting, WordPerfect indicates your column margins and the distance between columns in inches. But, if you want the distance between columns to be two centimeters, for example, then select the Distance Between Columns item on the Text Column Definition screen and type **2c**. Or, if you want the left margin of a column to begin at position 50, type **50h** (where the "h" stands for horizontal WordPerfect version 4.2 units). When you press ENTER, WordPerfect converts your selection into inches.

If you want to continue working in centimeters, points, or version 4.2 units, then you can change the default setting for WordPerfect's unit of measure. For example, suppose you change the default to centimeters. Then WordPerfect converts all your selections into centimeters; even the column definition code shows your column margins in centimeters. (Appendix B describes how to change the default unit-of-measure settings on the Setup menu.)

Tip: *You may wish to type using tabular columns rather than parallel columns if only the last column on the page has multiple lines.*

Using parallel columns is effective when a group of parallel columns must be kept side by side and when the columns contain multiple lines so that word wrap can make sure the column margins are maintained. If the last column in a group is the only column containing more than one line, however, then it may be easier to type in tabular columns, using the → INDENT (F4) key to align text within the last column. For instance, suppose you wish to type this inventory list:

Product	**Quantity**	**Comments**
No. 2 pencils	100	Staff uses approximately 20 per month. Reorder in March
Legal pads	148	Staff uses approximately 35 per month. Reorder in February (stock no. is H-443)

Rather than employ the Column feature to type this inventory list, you could set tab stops where each column is to start (as described in Chapter 8). Then proceed as follows:

1. Type the first product entry at the left margin.
2. Press TAB or →INDENT (F4) to position the cursor in the second column, and type the quantity entry (whether you press TAB or →INDENT makes no difference, since the entries in the second column are only one line long).
3. Press →INDENT (F4) to position the cursor in the third column, and type the "Comments" entry.

4. Press ENTER to position the cursor at the left margin, and begin typing in the next product entry. Continue until you've completed typing the product list.

By using the →INDENT (F4) key, every line of the third column is word wrapped between the boundaries of the tab stop and the right margin, until a **[HRt]** code ends that entry. (Chapter 7 discusses the →INDENT key, as well as other keys that align text on a tab stop.)

Tip: *Place a column definition code in the Document Initial Codes screen to reduce the clutter at the top of the document.*

You can alter a setting for a whole document either at the top of the document or on the Document Initial Codes screen. The advantage of doing the latter is that it reduces the potential jam-up of codes at the top of the document and protects the codes from being moved or erased accidentally. Consider placing a column definition code on the Document Initial Codes screen (as discussed in Chapter 8) if you wish to begin columns starting at the top of the document.

Tip: *You can create a style for text columns.*

You may find yourself repeatedly using the same column layout for a specific type of document. For instance, perhaps you produce a monthly newsletter for which you always set three newspaper-type columns. Consider incorporating the column definition code into a Style so that you can access the column layout quickly and easily every time you're ready to create a new issue of the newsletter (the Styles feature is described in Chapter 10).

Tip: *(When upgrading from 4.2.) The biggest change in version 5 is the ability to define parallel columns that can extend beyond a page boundary.*

In version 5, you have a choice between two types of parallel columns: (1) standard parallel columns, where a group of related columns will be broken by a page break; and (2) parallel columns with Block Protect, where a group of related columns will never be broken by a page break. Previously, only the parallel columns with Block Protect were available. Thus, with version 5, you can use parallel columns even when an entry in a column spans more than one page.

The Text Column Definition screen has also been modified, so that establishing a column layout is more straightforward. On this screen, you are now able to set the left margin of the first column and the right margin of the last column to be wider or narrower than the document margins; in version 4.2, you had to change document margins before defining columns if you wanted columns to be wider than the document margins. Moreover, on this screen, you can now define your column layout in various units of measure—inches, centimeters, points, or version 4.2 units.

Entering Text in Columns

Once a column definition code is embedded in the text, you are ready to type text into columns. You must switch Column mode on, enter the text, and then remember to switch Column mode off. Text is entered quite differently in newspaper columns than in parallel columns.

If you are using newspaper-style columns, think of each newspaper column as an independent page, and proceed as follows:

1. Position the cursor to the right of or below the **[Col Def:]** code and press the MATH/COLUMNS (ALT + F7) key. (If you just finished defining your columns, then the Math/Columns menu will already be displayed on the screen.)

2. Select Column On/Off (3 or C). WordPerfect inserts a **[Col On]** code in the text, turning on Column mode. You'll know that you're in Column mode because the status line now has a column indicator, such as:

   Col 1 **Doc** 1 **Pg** 4 **Ln** 1″ **Pos** 1″

3. Start typing. All the standard typing keys work the same as they do in other modes. TAB moves the cursor to the first tab stop in a column, ENTER ends a paragraph or a short line of text, and word wrap keeps text within the right margin of the column.

   After a column is filled with text, WordPerfect inserts a soft page code **[SPg]** and automatically wraps the cursor to the top of the next column. In that way, text flows from column to column. After you fill the last column on a page,

WordPerfect inserts a **[SPg]** code and displays a page bar (a dashed line), the cursor jumps to the top of the first column on a new page, and you are ready to continue.

4. You must turn Column mode off after you've finished working with newspaper-style columns. To do so, press MATH/COLUMNS (ALT + F7).

5. Select Column On/Off (3 or C). WordPerfect inserts a **[Col Off]** code in the text, switching the Column mode off. The cursor moves down to the left margin of the next line, ready for you to type text that is no longer governed by your column layout. The "Col" indicator disappears from the status line.

If you are using parallel columns (either with or without Block Protect), think of entries that are side by side (parallel) across the page as one group to be kept together. The next row of entries below is a second group, independent of the group above. For example, in Figure 19-2 the three entries across the top of the page, concerning John Caldwell, make up one group of three columns; the three entries regarding Paula Chin make up a second group. You type one group of parallel columns, and then move on to type a new group. To type parallel column entries, proceed as follows:

1. Position the cursor to the right of or below the **[Col Def:]** code and press MATH/COLUMNS (ALT + F7). (If you just finished defining your columns, then the Math/Columns menu will already be displayed on the screen.)

2. Select Column On/Off (3 or C). If you're working in parallel columns with Block Protect, WordPerfect places two codes in the text: **[Block-Pro:On]**, which turns on the Block Protect feature for the first group of entries so they will be kept together and not separated by a page break; and **[Col On]**, which turns on Column mode for the first group of columns. (The block protect code is discussed in Chapter 9.)

   Or, if you're working in parallel columns without Block Protect, WordPerfect places one code in the text: **[Col On]**, which turns on Column mode for the first group of columns.

   You'll know that you're in Column mode because the status line now has a column indicator, such as:

   Col 1 Doc 1 Pg 4 **Ln 1" Pos** 1"

3. Start typing the first entry. All the standard typing keys work the same as they do in other modes. TAB moves the cursor to the first tab stop in a

column, ENTER ends a paragraph or a short line of text, and word wrap keeps text within the right margin of a column.

4. After completing the first entry in a group, press HARD PAGE (CTRL + ENTER). WordPerfect inserts a hard page code **[HPg]** and moves the cursor to the next column.

   For example, in the "NAME" column, type the entry related to John Caldwell (as shown in Figure 19-2), and then press HARD PAGE. The cursor jumps to the "ADDRESS" column. Type his address and press HARD PAGE; the cursor moves to the "JUSTIFICATION" column.

5. After you type the last entry in one group of parallel columns, again press HARD PAGE. WordPerfect inserts several codes in the text. If you're working in parallel columns with Block Protect, the first two codes—**[BlockPro:Off]** and **[Col Off]**—turn off both the Block Protect feature and the Column mode for that group. The cursor then jumps back to the first column, skips a line of space below the first group by inserting a **[HRt]** code, and, to prepare for the next group of parallel columns, two other codes—**[BlockPro:On]** and **[Col On]**—are automatically inserted. Block Protect and Column mode are thus turned on again for the next entry.

   Figure 19-4 illustrates where the hidden codes are inserted in parallel columns with Block Protect. Notice how WordPerfect considers the information about John Caldwell as one distinct group, with codes marking its beginning and end like bookends. Also notice how WordPerfect automatically skips one line below the longest entry in the first group before preparing for the first entry in the next group.

   If you're working in parallel columns without Block Protect, then only the **[Col Off]**, **[HRt]**, and **[Col On]** codes are inserted.

6. Continue to type entries and to press HARD PAGE between each entry.

7. You must turn Column mode off after you've finished working with parallel columns. To do so, press MATH/COLUMNS (ALT + F7).

8. Select Column On/Off (3 or C). WordPerfect inserts two codes in the text if you're working with Block Protect— **[BlockPro:Off]** and **[Col Off]**—to switch off Column mode.

   Or, if you're not using Block Protect, then only a **[Col Off]** code is inserted.

[BlockPro:On][Col On]		
John Caldwell	3345 Cypress Creek Blvd.	Increased sales 120%
Sales Manager	Prompano Beach, FL 33436	as manager in Florida.
Eastern Div.**[HPg]**	(305) 734-4432**[HPg]**	10 years with the
[HRt]		company.
[BlockPro:On][Col On]		**[BlockPro:Off][Col Off]**
Paula Chin		
Sales Rep.		

Figure 19-4. Where hidden codes are inserted in parallel columns (with Block Protect)

The cursor moves down to the left margin of the next line, ready for you to type text that is no longer governed by your column layout. The "Col" indicator disappears from the status line.

Trap: *You cannot turn Column mode on without a Column definition code.*

The location of the cursor is critical when you are switching on Column mode. You should switch on Column mode only when the cursor is forward in the text from a column definition code and in the place where you want to start typing a column.

If WordPerfect cannot locate a **[Col Def:]** code backward in the text from the current cursor position, you cannot enter Column mode. Instead, WordPerfect responds

ERROR: No text columns defined

If you haven't yet defined your columns, you must do so. If you've already defined columns and you receive an error message, then you may need to position the cursor farther down in the text. Reveal codes to find the **[Col Def:]** code and position the cursor after that code.

Tip: *Switch in and out of Column mode as often as you like.*

When you press MATH/COLUMNS (ALT + F7) and then select Column On/Off (3 or C), you are working with a toggle switch; press it once to turn Column mode on; press it again to turn Column mode off. The codes inserted define the upper and lower boundaries of your text columns.

In fact, once you've inserted a **[Col Def:]** code in the text, you can go in and out of Column mode as often as you like. Figure 19-5 shows an example. A column layout was defined just below the heading "EMPLOYEE PROMOTIONS." Column mode was turned on to type in columns. It was then turned off to type several sentences across the full width of the page. Column mode was then turned on to again type in columns.

You can tell if the cursor is located between a **[Col On]** code and a **[Col Off]** code by checking the status line. If you see the column indicator, as in

Col 1 Doc 2 Pg 7 Ln 1" Pos 1"

then you are between the codes and thus in Column mode.

Tip: *You can change a column definition after you type text.*

After typing in columns, you may find that one column is not wide enough or that the spacing between columns is too narrow. You can change the layout of columns by inserting a new column definition code in the text. Reveal codes and position the cursor just to the right of the **[Col Def:]** code already created. Then press MATH/COLUMNS and create a new column definition. But make sure that you retain the same number of columns, or the result will be a jumble.

Once the new code is embedded, press DOWN ARROW and the columns are aligned to the new column layout. Don't forget to again reveal codes and erase the original **[Col Def:]** code—the one to the left—so that you erase unnecessary codes and thereby tidy up your document.

EMPLOYEE PROMOTIONS

John Caldwell Sales Manager, Eastern Div.	3345 Cypress Creek Blvd. Pompano Beach, FL 33436 (305) 734-4432	Increased sales 120% as manager in Florida. 10 years with the company.

Three Sales Representatives will be promoted this year, as compared to five last year. Two are in the chicago office, while one is in the San Francisco office:

Paula Chin Sales Rep.	9000 Rillips Street Chicago, IL 60616 (312) 833-2233	Sales apprentice for 13 months. Strong marks and excellent recommendations from P. Smith and N. Begley.
Phyllis Reimer (formerly Carrington) Sales Rep.	12330 Algonquin Rd. Des Plaines, IL 60622 (312) 630-3388	Asst. to N. Begley for 6 years. Strong recommendation.
Rick Tanquez Sales Rep.	123 Fillmore Street Apartment 305 San Francisco, CA 94123 (415) 563-9933	Sales apprentice for 12 months. Strong marks and excellent recommendations from L. Larell and P. Berger.

Figure 19-5. The results of switching in and out of Column mode

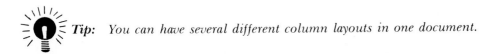

Tip: *You can have several different column layouts in one document.*

You can place more than one **[Col Def:]** code in a document when you want to create different column layouts in different parts of the document. A second **[Col Def:]** code must be located farther forward in the text, following a **[Col Off]** code.

Tip: *A ruler line can display the width of your columns as you type.*

If you wish to keep track of the width of your text columns as you type, you can insert a ruler line at the bottom of the screen, which will indicate left and right margins for each column. With your cursor anywhere on the screen:

1. Press the SCREEN (CTRL + F3) key.
2. Select Window (1 or W).
3. Type the number of lines in the window as **23** (unless your monitor is not of standard size, in which case enter one less than the number of lines that your monitor can display on the WordPerfect Typing screen).
4. Press ENTER.

In the ruler line shown in Figure 19-6, there are three sets of left and right margin indicators, marking the width of each column. A square bracket [or] represents a column margin setting, while a curved brace { or } represents a point at which both a margin setting and a tab stop are located. (The triangles represent the locations of tab stops only.) (See Chapter 12 for more on the Window features.)

If you wish to remove the ruler line later, repeat steps 1 through 4, but type the number of lines in the window as **24**.

Tip: *Shorten the length of newspaper columns by increasing the top or bottom margins.*

WordPerfect is preset with one-inch top and bottom margins, as discussed in Chapter 8. If you want to lengthen or shorten the length of columns automatically, then position the cursor above the **[Col Def:]** code and change the top or bottom margin setting by using the FORMAT (SHIFT + F8) key. WordPerfect will then adjust its **[SPg]** codes accordingly, for newspaper-style columns.

Tip: *In newspaper columns, you can force an individual column to end before the bottom of the page.*

```
               EMPLOYEE PROMOTIONS -- YEAR-TO-DATE

       NAME                  ADDRESS                 JUSTIFICATION

John Caldwell      3345 Cypress Creek Blvd.     Increased sales 120%
Sales Manager,     Pompano Beach, FL 33436      as manager in
Eastern Div.       (305) 734-4432               Florida.  10 years
                                                with the company.

Paula Chin         9000 Rillips Street          Sales apprentice for
Sales Rep.         Chicago, IL  60616           13 months.  Strong
                   (312) 833-2233               marks and excellent
                                                recommendations from
                                                P. Smith and N.
                                                Begley.

Phyllis Reimer     12330 Algonquin Rd.          Asst. to N. Begley
(formerly          Des Plaines, IL 60622        for 6 years.  Strong
Carrington)        (312) 630-3388               recommendation.
Sales Rep.

Rick Tanquez       123 Fillmore Street          Sales apprentice for
                                                Col 1 Doc 1 Pg 1 Ln 2" Pos 1"
{  ▲   ▲   ]▲  [▲   ▲   ▲   ▲   ▲ ]  ▲[  ▲   ▲   ▲   ▲ ]  ▲   ▲
```

Figure 19-6. A ruler line indicating column margins

If you want a newspaper column to end before it is filled with text to the bottom of the page, press HARD PAGE (CTRL + ENTER). This causes the cursor, along with the subsequent text, to jump to the next column.

Tip: *For newspaper-style columns, you can turn Column mode on before or after you type text.*

Typically, you define columns, turn on Column mode, type text, and then turn the feature off. But if you've already typed text, you can later place it into newspaper-style columns. Position the cursor above the text to be reformatted into columns. Press MATH/COLUMNS, define columns, and then turn on columns. Press

DOWN ARROW continuously to move through the text and the text is readjusted within the columns that you set. Now move to the bottom of the text and turn columns off.

Tip: *You can retrieve text into newspaper-style columns.*

Once you've created a newspaper column layout and turned on Column mode, you can retrieve text into that column. Position the cursor where you wish to retrieve the text, making sure that the **[Col On]** code precedes the cursor. Then use the RETRIEVE (SHIFT + F10) key or LIST FILES (F5) key to bring into the column the text that has already been typed. Or use the MOVE key to move/copy text into the column. Now press DOWN ARROW until the text is aligned within the column layout you defined.

Tip: *With parallel columns, you can insert more than one blank line between each group of entries.*

As you are typing parallel columns, WordPerfect automatically inserts one blank line between groups of entries. However, you may want more than one blank line. Suppose that you want three blank lines between entries. If so, then when you are typing the longest entry in a group, press ENTER twice before pressing HARD PAGE. This adds two extra lines to that entry. When WordPerfect inserts another line automatically to separate groups of parallel columns, you will have three lines between entries.

Or, you may decide to insert extra blank lines between groups of parallel columns after you have typed them. To do this, use the REVEAL CODES (ALT + F3) key to view the column codes. Position the cursor between the **[Col Off]** code of the first group of parallel columns and the **[Col On]** code of the next group. For instance, position the cursor so that it is highlighting the **[HRt]** code that separates the two groups. Now you can press ENTER as many times as you desire to insert extra blank lines. Continue to position the cursor between the column codes and press ENTER until you've added extra lines between each group of columns in your document.

Tip: *Create empty parallel columns for information that you will be typing in at a later date.*

If you're typing in parallel columns and you don't yet have the information for a certain entry, press HARD PAGE anyway. This inserts a **[HPg]** code and leaves a column open. When you wish to enter the missing information, position the cursor in the correct column, highlighting the **[HPg]** code, and begin typing.

Tip: *Block Protect is ended if a column entry spans more than one page.*

Parallel columns with Block Protect are used with entries that are shorter than one page. If, however, you type an entry that turns out to be longer than one page, then Block Protect is automatically canceled at the bottom of the page for that one group of parallel columns.

Trap: *Parallel columns are not as flexible as newspaper-style columns.*

With parallel columns, you must press the HARD PAGE key to insert a code or codes between each entry, and it must be inserted with Column mode on. Otherwise, WordPerfect doesn't know when one entry is complete, or which group to keep together. As a result, parallel columns are less flexible than free-flowing newspaper columns. Thus, you can use the RETRIEVE or the MOVE key to bring text into a column, but only as one single entry in one group of parallel columns.

Trap: *Turn off columns before pressing HARD PAGE or you'll insert unnecessary codes.*

As you've learned, whenever you press HARD PAGE after typing the last entry in a group of parallel columns, codes are inserted which (1) turn off columns for that one group, (2) insert a blank line, and (3) turn on columns once again for the next group. For example, for parallel columns with Block Protect, five codes are inserted: **[BlockPro:Off]**, **[Col Off]**, **[HRt]**, **[BlockPro:On]**, and **[Col On]**.

If you've completed the *last* group of entries and are ready to leave Column mode for good, don't press HARD PAGE or you'll insert a trail of unnecessary codes. Instead, with the cursor at the end of the last entry, simply turn columns off by pressing MATH/COLUMNS and selecting option 3 to turn columns off. Now, you've inserted only two codes, **[BlockPro:Off]** and **[Col Off]**, or only **[Col Off]** if the column type is parallel columns without Block Protect. In this way, you avoid a string of unnecessary codes after typing in parallel columns.

Tip: *(When upgrading from 4.2.) Enter text in columns as you did in previous versions.*

Type text into newspaper or parallel columns as you did with version 4.2. One nice enhancement is that if you retrieve text into columns, you'll no longer be bombarded by hyphenation questions if WordPerfect needs to squeeze long words into a narrow space. Instead, WordPerfect inserts invisible soft return **[ISRt]** codes in the text so that word wrap takes effect, even within words. Because of another enhancement, you no longer have to face a **Divide Overflow** error message if text spans more than a page when you are typing in parallel columns with Block Protect; instead, Block Protect is disabled for that column.

Moving the Cursor/Editing Text in Columns

In order to edit text, you must first become comfortable with maneuvering the cursor within and between columns. The cursor movement keys, for moving up and down in a document, work in the same way, whether or not your document contains columns. For example, PGUP moves the cursor up to the previous page. HOME + UP ARROW moves the cursor to the top of the screen. HOME, HOME, UP ARROW moves the cursor to the top of the document.

The cursor movement keys for moving left and right in a single column work as usual. For example, press RIGHT ARROW to move one character to the right. Press HOME, RIGHT ARROW or press END to move to the end of a line within a column. At the end of a line, pressing RIGHT ARROW wraps the cursor to the first character on the next line within a column.

However, the cursor movement keys for moving up and down a column are a bit different. If the cursor is on the last character in a column, then RIGHT ARROW moves the cursor to the top of the *next* column. DOWN ARROW moves the cursor to the top of the *same* column on the next page. (In parallel columns, DOWN ARROW moves the cursor to the same column in the *next group of entries.*) This is illustrated as follows.

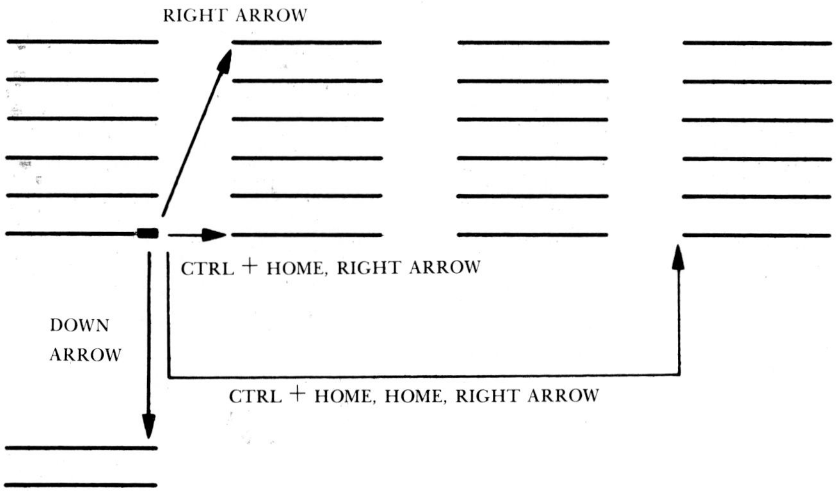

Also a quick way to move to the top or bottom of the column in which your cursor is located involves use of the GOTO (CTRL + HOME) key:

Key Combination	**Cursor Movement**
CTRL + HOME, UP ARROW	Top of column
CTRL + HOME, DOWN ARROW	Bottom of column

Be aware that in parallel columns, you'll move to the top or bottom of the column for only one group of entries, and not for the entire page.

To move quickly *between* columns, you can again take advantage of the GOTO (CTRL + HOME) key:

Key Combination	**Cursor Movement**
CTRL + HOME, LEFT ARROW	Preceding column (to the left)
CTRL + HOME, RIGHT ARROW	Next column (to the right)
CTRL + HOME, HOME, LEFT ARROW	First column
CTRL + HOME, HOME, RIGHT ARROW	Last column

The standard editing keys work within a column. For instance, to add text, position the cursor and simply start typing; when you press DOWN ARROW, the text is readjusted to fit within the column's margins. Or, to erase text from the cursor to the end of a line within a column, you can press DELETE EOL (CTRL + END). You can also use the BLOCK key to mark the boundaries of a portion of text within a column, and then delete it or move or copy that text to another location or another column—just as you do when you move text between pages.

Most of the special features work in Column mode as well. For example, use CENTER (SHIFT + F6) to center text in a column, or FLUSH RIGHT (ALT + F6) to position text against the right margin of a column. Use UNDERLINE (F8) or BOLD (F6), or change fonts within a column, by using FONT (CTRL + F8). The Conditional EOP or the Block Protect feature work in newspaper-style columns to stop text from splitting between two columns; if a number of lines that you specify cannot fit at the bottom of one column, they will be moved to the top of the next.

Trap: *Be cautious when blocking a column of text.*

When deleting, copying, or moving a block in a column, be careful as you highlight text. If the block is a group of entries in a parallel column with Block Protect, be sure to include in the block the **[BlockPro:On][Col On]** and the **[BlockPro:Off][Col Off]** codes that surround that group. Otherwise, the columns will not align properly as you delete, copy, or move text. It is often easier, therefore, to block within text columns after revealing codes.

In a related situation, be cautious when you're highlighting text at the bottom of a column. If you're on the last line of a newspaper-style column or the last line of an entry in a parallel column, pressing DOWN ARROW will highlight all the other columns to the right on that page. Press RIGHT ARROW instead, if you want to highlight only a part of the next column.

Trap: *Do not use the Tabular Column feature to move or copy in text columns.*

You learned in Chapter 6 how you can move or copy a column that is aligned on a tab stop by blocking text, pressing MOVE (CTRL + F4), and then choosing option 2, Tabular Column. The Move/Copy command does not apply when working in newspaper-style or parallel-style columns. Block the text, press MOVE (CTRL + F4), and select option 1, Block, when working within text columns.

Tip: *Position the cursor carefully when you wish to insert a new group of parallel columns.*

Suppose you've typed six groups of parallel columns and now wish to insert a new group in the middle. You can insert an entire group of parallel columns. To do so, position the cursor in the last column of the group that will *precede* your inserted columns. Make sure that you are working on the Reveal Codes screen, so that you can place the cursor on the **[BlockPro:Off]** code if you're working with Block Protect, or on the **[Col Off]** code if you're working without Block Protect. Now press HARD PAGE (CTRL + ENTER) and begin to type your first entry of the new group. Press HARD PAGE again and type your second entry. Continue until you've typed your last entry (but don't press HARD PAGE after typing the last entry; the **[HPg]** code is already there from the preceding column).

Tip: *Text columns are each right-justified individually.*

WordPerfect right-justifies not just the last column on a page, but every column—so that the left and right margins of each column are even—as long as right justification is turned on. Figure 19-1 shows examples of how WordPerfect justifies text columns when printed. If you want to turn off right justification, place a **[Just Off]** code in the text above where the columns begin, as described in Chapter 8. Remember that right justification appears only on the printed page and not on the screen.

Trap: *The Reveal Codes screen shows only one column at a time.*

If you wish to view the Reveal Codes screen while working with columns, you'll be able to see only one column at a time. That column will appear at the left side of the bottom window, which at first can look confusing. Figure 19-7 shows an example of the Reveal Codes screen with the cursor positioned in the second of two newspaper-style columns.

If a column is short or if the cursor is at the bottom of a column when you press REVEAL CODES, you may also see the top of the next column on the Reveal Codes screen. For example, Figure 19-8 shows a Reveal Codes screen with the cursor on the second entry in a group of parallel columns. Notice that the first, the second, and part of the third column are displayed. Become comfortable with the way Reveal Codes displays columns so that if you encounter a problem when trying to format columns, you can turn on the Reveal Codes screen to help uncover that problem.

Tip: *You can speed up operations when working with columns.*

As you work with columns, you'll notice that WordPerfect slows down. It takes more time for WordPerfect to display columns side by side and to readjust text between columns as you edit.

There are two ways to speed up this process if you find it too slow. One way is to turn off the Automatic Format and Rewrite feature (formerly called the Auto-rewrite feature). WordPerfect is initially set with this feature on, meaning that after being edited, text readjusts very quickly to fit within the margins, often without the need to press DOWN ARROW. If you turn off this feature, WordPerfect won't automatically realign your text, so you won't have to wait while Word-Perfect adjusts your text after each change you make. When you've typed some text and made editing changes, you can then readjust the text either by pressing

```
     Since our last newsletter,      as BASIC or C.  But many jobs
many of you expressed an             require no such programming
interest in information about        knowledge.  Software companies
careers in the computer              are often interested in people
industry.  Today's "Career           who have used their product or
Corner" article will be the          a similar one and can share
first of three parts on the          their expertise with new users.
computer education field.
                                     _    There are also training
     Those of you who have           companies specifically devoted
                                                  Col 2 Doc 1 Pg 1 Ln 2.5" Pos 4.5"

their expertise with new users. [SRt]
[HRt]
[Tab]There are also training[SRt]
companies specifically devoted[SRt]
to teaching people how to use[SRt]
computers and various software. [SRt]
Computer retailers often hire[SRt]
trainers to provide assistance[SRt]
to their customers.[HRt]
 [HRt]

Press Reveal Codes to restore screen
```

Figure 19-7. The Reveal Codes screen showing part of one column

```
Sales Manager,    Pompano Beach, FL 33436     as manager in
Eastern Div.      (305) 734-4432              Florida.  10 years
                                              with the company.

Paula Chin        9000 Rillips Street         Sales apprentice for
Sales Rep.        Chicago, IL  60616          13 months.  Strong
                  (312) 833-2233              marks and excellent
                                              recommendations from
                                              P. Smith and N.
                                              Begley.

                                       Col 2 Doc 1 Pg 1 Ln 2.66" Pos 2.87"

[Col On]Paula Chin[HRt]
Sales Rep.[HPg]
9000 Rillips Street[HRt]
Chicago, IL  60616[HRt]
(312) 833[-]2233[HPg]
Sales apprentice for[SRt]
13 months.  Strong[SRt]
marks and excellent[SRt]
recommendations from[SRt]
P. Smith and N.[SRt]

Press Reveal Codes to restore screen
```

Figure 19-8. The Reveal Codes screen showing three short columns

DOWN ARROW through every line of the text that needs adjustment, or by pressing SCREEN (CTRL + F3) and—since WordPerfect suggests option 0, Rewrite—by pressing ENTER. The text is readjusted for you.

A second alternative to speed up operations when working with columns is to turn off the side-by-side display of columns. WordPerfect is initially set with side-by-side display on. If you turn it off, you'll see each column on a separate page. However, when the document is printed, columns will be printed side by side.

Both features are changed under the Display option in the Setup menu, which is discussed in detail in Appendix B.

Tip: *Change the display pitch if text looks awkward in columns on screen.*

As described in Chapter 7, the Display Pitch feature alters the amount of space that one character occupies on screen. By default, the display pitch is set to automatic, which may cause text on screen to appear as if there is extra space between columns. Or columns may appear to overlap each other. If the columns don't seem to align properly on screen, use the FORMAT (SHIFT + F8) key to turn the display pitch automatic setting to N (for "No") on the Document Format menu and change the width of the display pitch on this menu. Decrease the pitch to expand the document, or increase the pitch to contract the document. For instance, increase the display pitch to 0.2" to show the columns closer together. Keep in mind that the Display Pitch feature affects text only on screen, and not on the printed page. (See Chapter 7 for the precise keystroke to use if you want to change the display-pitch setting.)

Tip: *The Graphics feature allows you to place graphics images in columns or to draw borders around or between columns.*

Chapter 18 describes how you can insert graphics images into any WordPerfect document by using the Graphics feature. Also described is how to insert horizontal or vertical lines anywhere on a page. Both graphics images and lines can be combined with the Column feature to create professional-looking documents.

For example, suppose you use newspaper-style columns to create a company newsletter. You can place a vertical line between each column on a page to visually separate columns, and then insert a horizontal line at the top and bottom of each page to border the text. And you can insert a graphics image (such as your company logo) on page 1 of the newsletter. Be sure to refer to Chapter 18 for details on the Graphics feature.

Trap: *While many features operate within columns, other features are inoperative.*

You can use a variety of features when working in columns, such as changing fonts, altering line spacing, resetting tabs, inserting endnotes, numbering lines down a page, or even inserting graphics into a column.

However, you cannot change margins, insert footnotes, or perform a sort when in Column mode. Also, document comments won't display when created within a column. In addition, you cannot create a new column definition when Column mode is on. Column mode must be off before you can create a new definition.

Tip: *(When upgrading from 4.2.) Edit text in columns as you did in previous versions.*

Edit text as you did previously. In version 5, features such as Line Spacing and Line Numbering are now allowed in Column mode. Remember, too, that you can now edit text on the Reveal Codes screen, which is convenient because columns (especially parallel columns) are overrun with codes, and the placement of the cursor is often critical when editing in columns.

If you wish to turn off Automatic Format and Rewrite or the side-by-side display of columns, you will now find these features on the Setup menu.

Tips and Traps Summary

Defining Text Columns

Tip: You can set column margins that are wider or narrower than the document margins.

Trap: You cannot overlap columns.

Tip: Spacing between columns is an important consideration.

Trap: The column definition code provides no indication of column style.

Tip: You can define your column layout in inches, centimeters, points, or version 4.2 units of measure.

Tip: You may wish to type using tabular columns rather than parallel columns if only the last column on the page has multiple lines.

Tip: Place a column definition code in the Document Initial Codes screen to reduce the clutter at the top of the document.

Tip: You can create a style for text columns.

Tip: (When upgrading from 4.2.) The biggest change in version 5 is the ability to define parallel columns that can extend beyond a page boundary.

Entering Text in Columns

Trap: You cannot turn Column mode on without a column definition code.

Tip: Switch in and out of Column mode as often as you like.

Tip: You can change a column definition after you type text.

Tips and Traps Summary (*continued*)

Tip: You can have several different column layouts in one document.

Tip: A ruler line can display the width of your columns as you type.

Tip: Shorten the length of newspaper columns by increasing the top or bottom margins.

Tip: In newspaper columns, you can force an individual column to end before the bottom of the page.

Tip: For newspaper-style columns, you can turn Column mode on before or after you type text.

Tip: You can retrieve text into newspaper-style columns.

Tip: With parallel columns, you can insert more than one blank line between each group of entries.

Tip: Create empty parallel columns for information that you will be typing in at a later date.

Tip: Block Protect is ended if a column entry spans more than one page.

Trap: Parallel columns are not as flexible as newspaper-style columns.

Trap: Turn off columns before pressing HARD PAGE or you'll insert unnecessary codes.

Tip: (When upgrading from 4.2.) Enter text in columns as you did in previous versions.

Moving the Cursor/Editing Text in Columns

Trap: Be cautious when blocking a column of text.

Tips and Traps Summary (*continued*)

Trap: Do not use the Tabular Column feature to move or copy in text columns.

Tip: Position the cursor carefully when you wish to insert a new group of parallel columns.

Tip: Text columns are each right-justified individually.

Trap: The Reveal Codes screen shows only one column at a time.

Tip: You can speed up operations when working with columns.

Tip: Change the display pitch if text looks awkward in columns on screen.

Tip: The Graphics feature allows you to place graphics images in columns or to draw borders around or between columns.

Trap: While many features operate within columns, other features are inoperative.

Tip: (When upgrading from 4.2.) Edit text in columns as you did in previous versions.

20

Performing Math

When you use WordPerfect to type a billing statement, a table of values, or an income statement, it is convenient to have the word processor figure totals as well. Why run off to a calculator, figure out a sum, and then type that sum into the document? WordPerfect calculates and places the results in the text wherever you specify. In fact, for a word processor, WordPerfect has quite an impressive math ability. You can either calculate vertically down columns or horizontally across lines (rows). Calculating down columns is quick and easy, but it is limited to adding numbers.

The first two sections in this chapter describe how to total down columns. Calculating across rows, discussed in the third section, involves more planning and more work, although the benefits are the ability to add, subtract, multiply, divide, or average numbers.

Totaling Columns

You can add up to 24 math columns on a page, where a *math column* is a column of numbers aligned on tab stops. Column A is the first tab stop, Column B is the second, and so on. Any values sitting flush against the left margin are not considered in a math column, because they are not on a tab stop.

All math columns in WordPerfect have initial column definitions. These defaults are as follows:

- Calculations occur down the page vertically, but not across a line horizontally.
- The only calculation performed is addition (but it can include positive or negative numbers).
- The three levels of calculation allowed are *subtotal,* which adds the numbers above it; *total,* which adds the subtotals above it; and *grand total,* which adds the totals above it.
- Each math column contains numbers only, and they are aligned with their decimal points at the tab stop.
- Results of calculations show two digits after the decimal point (such as 50.00 or 175.32).
- Calculations that result in negative values are displayed with parentheses around the values rather than a minus sign in front of them: (50.49) rather than −50.49.

If these defaults are acceptable to you, the Math feature will be quick and easy, because WordPerfect has predefined the math columns for you. Figure 20-1 shows the printed result for two math columns, where none of the defaults were altered, and two levels of calculations were used—subtotals and totals. To create a document such as this, proceed as follows:

1. In your mind or on paper, design your math columns layout. Think about how many columns there will be (up to 24), how wide they must be, and how they will be positioned on the page. Any characters typed at the left margin are not considered as a math column, since they aren't aligned on a tab stop. Therefore, it is convenient to design columns so that text descriptions appear at the left margin, labeling each row.
2. Position the cursor where you want the math columns to appear, and below any titles or headings that label the math columns. (The math columns can be a part of a larger document or they can be a document on their own.)

ABC Company—Budget by Department		
	Marketing	Legal
Salaries	44,555.00	56,333.00
Taxes	9,356.54	10,444.54
Overtime	6,400.00	9,500.00
Personnel	60,311.54	76,277.54
Rent	4,333.66	6,444.55
Utilities	978.44	1,066.55
Supplies	1,097.10	445.01
Materials	6,409.20	7,956.11
TOTAL	66,720.74	84,233.65

Figure 20-1. Printout of a math document created by using standard defaults

3. Use the FORMAT (SHIFT + F8) key to set flush left tab stops for the math columns you will use, according to the layout you designed. (Refer to Chapter 8 for the procedure to reset tabs.) A **[Tab Set:]** code is inserted in the text.

4. Press MATH/COLUMNS (ALT + F7). The following menu appears:

   1 Math On; **2** Math Def; **3** Column On/Off; **4** Column Def: **0**

5. Select Math On (1 or M). WordPerfect embeds a **[Math On]** code in the text, turning on the feature. In addition, the message **Math** appears in the lower left portion of the screen, signifying that you are in a math area.

6. Begin typing data, pressing TAB to move to each math column (or ENTER to end a line). Each time you press TAB, the bottom of the screen reads

   Align char = . Math

   All tab stops become decimal tabs when the Math feature is turned on; numbers are aligned on their decimal point, or aligned flush right if they contain no decimal point. WordPerfect inserts tab align codes around each number preceding the decimal on a tab stop. For instance, if you press TAB and type **55.33**, then the hidden codes inserted are **[Align]**55**[C/A/Flrt]**.33.

7. When the cursor is positioned with the TAB key at a place where you want a calculation to appear, type in one of the following math operators:

Operator	**Calculation**	**Description**
+	Subtotal	Numbers directly above the operator are added
=	Total	Subtotals above the operator are added
*	Grand Total	Totals above the operator are added

The math operator appears on screen. In addition, WordPerfect embeds a hidden code in the document containing the math operator that you inserted. For example, if you type the plus sign (+) to add the numbers above and then press REVEAL CODES (ALT + F3) to view hidden codes, you'll see that WordPerfect inserted the code [+] in the text.(Three additional math operators are described in the Tips and Traps that follow.)

8. Continue to type in data and math operators. After you've completed typing the math columns, your math document should look like Figure 20-2, with numbers entered and math operators situated where you want totals calculated.

9. Press MATH/COLUMNS (ALT + F7). A different Math/Columns menu appears when you are in a math area:

   1 Math Off; **2** Calculate; **3** Column On/Off; **4** Column Def: **0**

10. Select Calculate (2 or A). WordPerfect responds

    * **Please Wait** *

    In seconds, calculation results are displayed next to the math operators, as shown in Figure 20-3.

11. Position the cursor below the last row of numbers, and press the MATH/COLUMNS (ALT + F7) key.

12. Select Math Off (1 or M). WordPerfect embeds a **[Math Off]** code in the text, turning off the feature. In addition, the message **Math** disappears from the lower left portion of the screen. You have defined the end boundary of the math area.

Tip: *Switch to the numeric keypad for easy number typing.*

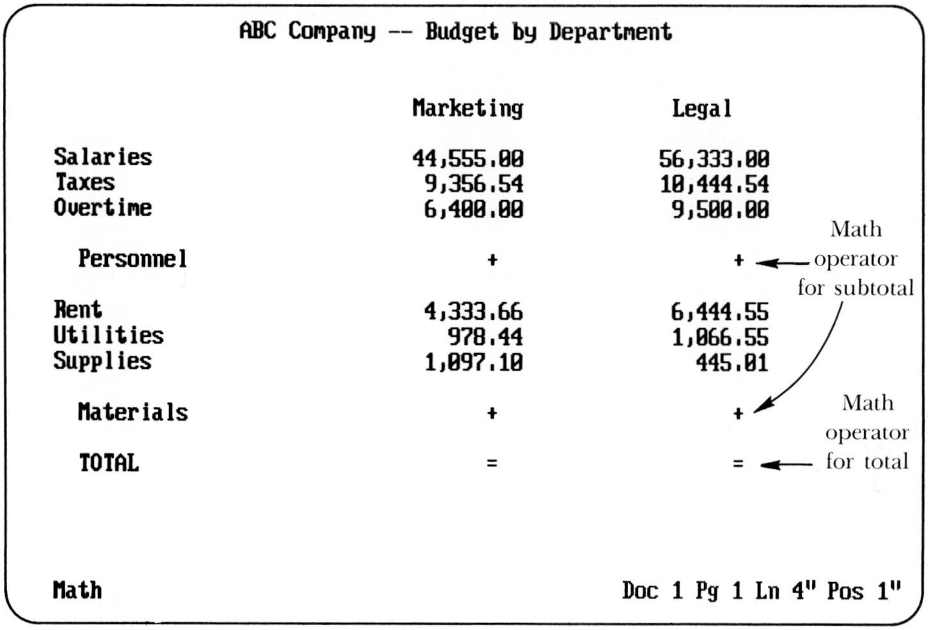

ABC Company -- Budget by Department

	Marketing	Legal
Salaries	44,555.00	56,333.00
Taxes	9,356.54	10,444.54
Overtime	6,400.00	9,500.00
Personnel	+	+
Rent	4,333.66	6,444.55
Utilities	978.44	1,066.55
Supplies	1,097.10	445.01
Materials	+	+
TOTAL	=	=

Math Doc 1 Pg 1 Ln 4" Pos 1"

Figure 20-2. A math document before calculations have been performed

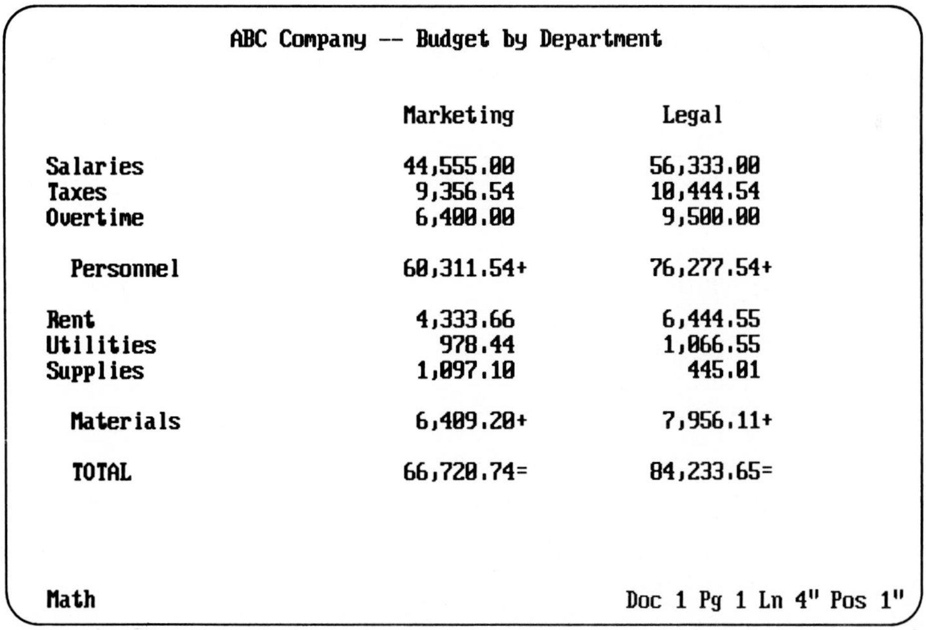

ABC Company -- Budget by Department

	Marketing	Legal
Salaries	44,555.00	56,333.00
Taxes	9,356.54	10,444.54
Overtime	6,400.00	9,500.00
Personnel	60,311.54+	76,277.54+
Rent	4,333.66	6,444.55
Utilities	978.44	1,066.55
Supplies	1,097.10	445.01
Materials	6,409.20+	7,956.11+
TOTAL	66,720.74=	84,233.65=

Math Doc 1 Pg 1 Ln 4" Pos 1"

Figure 20-3. A math document after calculations have been performed

When you're typing columns of numbers, it is often more convenient to do so by turning the cursor movement keypad at the far right of the keyboard into a numeric keypad.

With the Math feature, this is easily done. You don't require the cursor movement keys when typing numbers, because TAB takes you from column to column and ENTER takes you from line to line. If the numeric keypad is not active, press NUM LOCK; now you will be able to use the right side of the keyboard to type numbers. You'll know that the numeric keypad is active because the position indicator on the status line ("Pos") blinks. After you've finished entering your data, you can press NUM LOCK again to turn off the numeric keypad.

Tip: *Dollar signs or other symbols are easily inserted.*

If you want a dollar sign to appear in front of a value, simply tab to the column, type the dollar sign, and then type the value. This applies to a calculated total as well; type the dollar sign before you type a math operator, such as **$+** or **$=**.

You can also include a symbol after a value. Press TAB to jump to that column, type the value, and then type the symbol, such as **44%**.

Tip: *Use a ruler line to keep track of tab stop locations.*

It may be convenient for you to keep track of your tab stop locations as you type math columns. To do so, you can insert a ruler line (also called a tab ruler) at the bottom of the screen, which shows current margin and tab settings. With your cursor anywhere on the screen:

1. Press SCREEN (CTRL + F3).
2. Select Window (1 or W). WordPerfect prompts

   Number of lines in this window: 24

3. Type **23** as the number of lines in the window. (If your screen displays something other than 24 lines as the default setting, then enter a value that is one line less than what WordPerfect suggests.)

The ruler line remains until you again use the SCREEN key to reset the window to 24 lines. (For more on the Window feature, refer to Chapter 12.)

Trap: *Don't insert column headings in the same way that you insert values and math operators in math columns.*

Notice in Figure 20-3 that the two math columns were labeled with the headings "Marketing" and "Legal." If you want to label each math column as in the example shown in Figure 20-3, then don't attempt to insert headings as if they were values in the math columns; if you do, problems may result.

Suppose that your cursor is currently within a math area, following a **[Math On]** code. If you press the TAB key to position the cursor and then type the heading, WordPerfect will treat the heading like a value and will attempt to align it on the decimal (if there is a decimal in your heading), or will otherwise make it flush right. You may be unable to position the heading in the place that you desire.

Moreover, inserting column headings as if they were values may cause your calculations to be incorrect. If you include numbers (such as a date) in the headings, those numbers will be included in the calculation result. And, if you include the characters +, =, *, t, T, or N in a heading, WordPerfect treats those characters as math operators and inserts math operator codes in the text.

To avoid these problems, consider inserting the column headings above the **[Math On]** code. Or, if you do insert column headings within a math area, don't use the TAB key to position the cursor before typing. Instead, use the SPACEBAR or the →INDENT key. That way, WordPerfect knows that these entries are not values to be involved in the math calculations.

Tip: *At the left margin in a math area, you can insert titles or text to label rows.*

As previously described, any values or text typed at the left margin in a math area are not considered in a math column because they are not aligned on a tab stop. Therefore, use the column at the left margin to include titles or text that label each line (row) in the math area. For instance, in Figure 20-3, the entries "Salaries," "Taxes," and so on, were all typed starting at the left margin so that they would label each row.

Tip: *Math operators work backward and only until a math operator of the same kind is encountered.*

Subtotal, total, and grand total operators add in the math column in which they are located, and only up to the similar operator that precedes them. For example, if two subtotal operators (+) are in one column, the top operator adds all values above it and the bottom operator adds values above it up to the previous subtotal operator.

Calculations Result Like This:	But NOT Like This:
10	10
10	10
20+	20+
10	10
10	10
20+	40+

Tip: *Two additional math operators, T and t, enable you to include a known subtotal or total in a math column.*

There are times when you will know a value that you want to have treated as a subtotal or a total during calculations. To treat a value as a subtotal, precede the value with a lowercase t. To treat a value as a total, precede the value with an uppercase T.

For example, Figure 20-4 shows a category called "SPECIAL PROJECTS." These values are to be treated as totals; notice that a T was typed before the values were typed. When WordPerfect calculated grand totals, it treated the special projects values as totals. Otherwise, the special project numbers would only be treated as regular values, and would not be added in to produce the grand total result.

Like the math operators +, =, or *, the t and T are considered to be codes, so WordPerfect inserts **[t]** or **[T]** in the document.

ABC Company -- Budget by Department

	Marketing	Legal
Salaries	44,555.00	56,333.00
Taxes	9,356.54	10,444.54
Overtime	6,400.00	9,500.00
Personnel	60,311.54+	76,277.54+
Rent	4,333.66	6,444.55
Utilities	978.44	1,066.55
Supplies	1,097.10	445.01
Materials	6,409.20+	7,956.11+
TOTAL	66,720.74=	84,233.65=
SPECIAL PROJECTS	T32,448.55	T10,333.99 ← Known totals
GRAND TOTAL	99,169.29*	94,567.64*

Math Doc 1 Pg 1 Ln 4" Pos 1"

Figure 20-4. A math document with known totals inserted

Tip: *You can force WordPerfect into performing subtraction by using the minus sign or parentheses, or with the math operator N.*

WordPerfect only calculates totals down a column. However, you can change the addition into subtraction simply by adding negative numbers to positive ones. Negative numbers are typed by placing the number in parentheses or preceding it with a minus sign: (50.00) or −50.00. When a calculation results in a negative value, WordPerfect by default displays the result in parentheses. (See the next section of this chapter, "Enhancing Totals Down Columns," for the method to have WordPerfect display negative numbers with minus signs.)

You can also turn a calculated sum into a negative number for further calculations. Place the math operator N in front of the subtotal, total, or grand total operator. For example:

	Before Calculating	**After Calculating**
	55.6	55.6
	44.2	44.2
Amount Owed	+	99.80+
	5.3	5.3
	12.3	12.3
Amount Paid	N+	N17.60+
Balance	=	82.20=

Notice how the amount paid (17.60) is shown as a positive calculation, but when used to calculate the balance, it is treated as a negative.

As with the math operators, WordPerfect inserts hidden codes in the text when you enter the math operator N. The hidden code is **[N]**.

Tip: *Math operators do not appear on the printed document.*

The math operators (+, =, *, t, T, and N) act like other codes, except that they do not "hide." They are displayed on the Typing screen, informing you as to the type of calculation that appears at that position. But the math operators will *not* appear on the printed page.

Trap: *Calculations will be inaccurate if each value and math operator isn't aligned properly on a tab stop.*

The following conditions must be met before you type a value or math operator in a math column:

- The message **Math** must appear on the lower left-hand corner on the screen, signifying that you are in a math area.

- You must position the cursor on a tab stop by pressing the TAB key.
- You must see the prompt **Align char = . Math**.

Don't type a value or a math operator into a math column unless all three conditions have been met—or the calculations will be incorrect.

Also remember not to use the other keys that work with tab stops, such as →INDENT or →INDENT←, to move the cursor to a math column; if you do, the **Align char = . Math** prompt will not appear. (Pressing →INDENT will allow you to left-justify entries on a tab stop in a math column when you don't want calculations performed on those entries.)

Trap: *Overlapping numbers cause incorrect calculations.*

Make sure your tab stops are spaced so that numbers do not extend beyond their column boundaries. Take into account that the decimal point, not the number, will be aligned on the tab stop. If your numbers overlap into another column, calculations will be inaccurate and you will have to reset your tab stops.

Tip: *One nice advantage of the Math feature is that you can change numbers in a column and then recalculate.*

You can change any number within a math document at any time, and have WordPerfect recalculate for you. Make sure that when you edit a value, that the value is still aligned properly on a tab stop. Then recalculate the totals. To do so, move the cursor below the **[Math On]** code, so that the message **Math** appears on the screen. Press the MATH/COLUMNS (ALT + F7) key and select Calculate (2 or A). Every math operator positioned between that **[Math On]** code and the next **[Math Off]** code will recalculate. Remember, however, that your cursor must be within a math area in order to choose the calculation option. If your cursor is positioned before the **[Math On]** code, then the Calculate option is not displayed on the Math/Columns menu.

Tip: *Use the Move feature to delete or relocate an entire math column.*

Chapter 6 describes how you can use the BLOCK (ALT + F4) key to highlight a column and then press MOVE (CTRL + F4) to move, copy, delete, or append a tabular column, which is a column aligned on tab stops. This is a convenient method to use when you wish to remove or relocate a math column.

Trap: *Page breaks do not define the boundaries of distinct math areas.*

A math area is considered to be the space between a **[Math On]** and a **[Math Off]** code. If you have different sets of calculations, then create more than one math area. They can use the same column layout, but each will act independently. Page bars do not indicate a separate math area. A math code, not a page break, separates math areas.

For example, set tab stops and then turn on the Math feature to calculate this year's budget for your company. At the bottom of the budget (whether it is one, two, or many pages long), turn Math off. Skip several lines and then turn Math on again, type in and calculate next year's budget, and turn Math off again. You have two distinct math areas in which the calculated totals are unrelated.

Tip: *(When upgrading from 4.2.) Total columns as you did previously.*

The procedure for totaling columns has not changed. A minor enhancement is that now the math operators +, =, *, t, T, and N are shown on the Reveal Codes screen in square brackets, like other codes. Now, for example, if you press REVEAL CODES (ALT + F3), you may see [+], rather than simply +.

You can retrieve a math document created in version 4.2 into version 5; the calculations will work properly. (For more information on converting documents into version 5 format, see Chapter 28.)

Enhancing Totals Down Columns

You are not limited to WordPerfect's initial math definitions when adding down a math column. You have the flexibility to alter certain elements.

- You can display from 0 to 4 digits after the decimal place in your calculations. WordPerfect rounds off where necessary (numbers 5 through 9 are rounded up to the next whole number). WordPerfect assumes you wish to display 2 digits unless you specify otherwise.
- You can display negative results with a minus sign rather than parentheses.
- You can create four types of math columns. *Numeric columns* are those that contain only values to be calculated down a column. WordPerfect assumes that all columns in a math area are numeric columns unless you specify otherwise. *Total columns* contain the calculated results of the values in columns to their immediate left. For example, one column might contain values representing different types of expenses. A total column to its right could contain the subtotal, total, and grand total calculations of those expenses. *Text columns* contain descriptions or headings. When you press TAB to move the cursor to a text column, an entry that you type is left-justified on the tab stop, rather than aligned on a decimal. *Calculation columns* are used to calculate across lines, based on specified formulas (this type of column is described in the next section of this chapter, "Calculating Across Lines").

Figure 20-5 shows a math document enhanced by creating new math column definitions, thus overriding WordPerfect's preset definitions. Notice that there are three types of columns: the first column (Column A) is a numeric column; the second (Column B) is a total column; and the third (Column C) is a text column. Also notice that totals are rounded to the nearest whole number.

You create new column definitions to allow for these special enhancements *after* setting tab stops but *before* turning Math on. Therefore, you create new definitions between steps 4 and 5, as described at the beginning of the previous section of this chapter, "Totaling Columns." When you're ready to set math column definitions (after step 4), proceed as follows:

1. When the Math/Columns menu is displayed, select Math Def (2 or E). WordPerfect displays the Math Definition screen, shown in Figure 20-6. On this screen you can change the definition for each math column.

   Notice that columns are labeled A through X, representing 24 potential math columns. (Remember that any text or numbers positioned at the left margin—not on a tab—are not counted as a math column.) Also

ABC Company Budget, Marketing Department

	Column A: Numeric	Column B: Total	Column C: Text
Salaries	$44,555.00		Approved
Taxes	9,356.54		Approved
Overtime	6,400.00		

Personnel		60,312+	
Rent	4,333.66		Approved
Utilities	978.44		Approved
Supplies	1,097.10		Pending

Materials		6,409+	
TOTAL		66,721=	
SPECIAL PROJECTS		T32,448	Pending

GRAND TOTAL		99,169*	

Math   Doc 1 Pg 1 Ln 4" Pos 1"

Figure 20-5. A math document with three types of math columns

notice that each column is defined as a numeric column, that negative calculations are shown in parentheses, and that each column is defined with two places to the right of the decimal point; these are the initial settings. The cursor is located on the "Type" definition for Column A.

2. Select a number corresponding to how you desire the first math column to be defined. A key showing which number stands for which type of column is at the bottom of the screen, under the heading "Type of Column."

   The cursor jumps to the next column. Continue to select numbers until all the math columns you will use have been defined. For example, for the math document in Figure 20-5, select 2 for Column A, 3 for Column B, and 1 for Column C.

3. Press DOWN ARROW to move to the "Negative Numbers" definition. Change the left parenthesis to a minus sign in those columns where you wish negative calculations to be displayed with a minus sign.

4. Press DOWN ARROW to move to the "Number of Digits" definition. Change the number of digits to any number between 0 and 4 in each column, depending on how many digits you want to appear after the decimal in

```
Math Definition        Use arrow keys to position cursor

Columns                A B C D E F G H I J K L M N O P Q R S T U V W X

Type                   2 2 2 2 2 2 2 2 2 2 2 2 2 2 2 2 2 2 2 2 2 2 2 2

Negative Numbers       ( ( ( ( ( ( ( ( ( ( ( ( ( ( ( ( ( ( ( ( ( ( ( (

Number of Digits to    2 2 2 2 2 2 2 2 2 2 2 2 2 2 2 2 2 2 2 2 2 2 2 2
  the Right (0-4)

Calculation    1
  Formulas     2
               3
               4

Type of Column:
     0 = Calculation    1 = Text      2 = Numeric     3 = Total

Negative Numbers
     ( = Parentheses (50.00)          - = Minus Sign  -50.00

Press Exit when done
```

Figure 20-6. The Math Definition screen

your calculations. To produce Figure 20-5, for example, the number **0** is entered for Column B.

5. Press EXIT (F7) to clear the Math Definition screen. You are returned to the Math/Columns menu. WordPerfect inserts a math definition code **[Math Def]** into the text to override the initial math settings.
6. Select Math On (1 or M), type in the data, calculate, and then turn Math off as described in steps 5 through 12 at the beginning of the previous section of this chapter, "Totaling Columns."

Trap: *Math definitions do not determine the appearance of numbers entered by you.*

When you set math definitions, you are determining how WordPerfect displays the result of calculations. These definitions do not, however, determine how values that you enter will appear. If you type numbers with two digits after the decimal, those digits remain, regardless of how you defined the column. Only calculation totals abide by the definition.

Tip: *You can total numbers that do not include decimal points.*

If you specify that calculations contain no digits after the decimal point, then you probably will type in your values with no decimal points, as well. You don't necessarily have to type a decimal point when entering values, even though the prompt **Align char = .** appears. Press TAB to move to a column, type the value, and, rather than typing a decimal point (period), simply press TAB again to move to the next column. The number you typed is aligned flush right against the tab stop and will be included in the calculation.

Tip: *The decimal/align and thousands' separator characters affect math documents.*

In a math document, the *decimal/align character* is the symbol—such as a decimal point (period), comma, or space—used to separate decimal units from whole numbers. It is this character on which the values you enter are aligned in a math document. (As described in Chapter 8, this character also affects how values are aligned when you use the TAB ALIGN key.) The *thousands' separator* is the symbol used to separate decimal units from whole numbers in the math area. The initial settings are the decimal point as the alignment character and the comma as the thousands' separator. Therefore, numbers align on the decimal point and are displayed as follows:

```
 44,555.00
109,000.88
```

Using the Decimal/Align and Thousands' Separator Character feature, you can change one or both of these characters. To change the initial setting in a math area:

1. Position the cursor above the math area.
2. Press the FORMAT (SHIFT + F8) key to view the Format menu.

3. Select Other (4 or O), to display the Other Format menu.
4. Select Decimal/Align character (3 or D) and type the character you want your numbers aligned on. The cursor moves down to the thousands' separator heading.
5. Type the character you want to use to separate hundreds from thousands.
6. Press EXIT (F7) to return to your math document.

WordPerfect inserts a code in your text. For example, if you select the decimal character as a comma and the thousands' separator as a decimal point, then the code inserted is **[Decml:Algn Char:,,.]**. Now, when you press TAB to move to a math column, the following message displays:

Align char = , Math

Each value will now align on the comma, and your numbers will appear as follows:

 44.555,00
109.008,88

Trap: *Do not confuse text columns in a math area with those created by using the Column feature.*

Chapter 19 describes how to create text columns to type text as found in a newspaper. This is not the same as the text column in a math area. In a math area a text column enables you to left-align text. But text that extends beyond the width of the column is not wrapped down to the next line of the column. Text on one line in a math column must not extend beyond the boundaries of the column.

Trap: *Math operators must be placed in total columns in order for calculations to appear in those columns.*

A total column can set apart values from their subtotal, total, or grand total. The values are in the numeric column to the left. The calculations are in the total column to the right. But to instruct WordPerfect to place a calculation in a total column, you must do more than define the column types. You must also place the values in the numeric column. And you must place the math operators (+, =, *) in the total column. Calculations appear only where the math operators are located.

Tip: *You can create different math definitions in different math areas.*

There should be no more than one **[Math Def]** code in each math area. The code must be situated between the tab set code and math-on code, as follows:

[Tab Set:][Math Def][Math On]

At the end of the math area you must also include a **[Math Off]** code.

Farther down in the document, you can create a second math area and an entirely new math definition. Perhaps you want one budget sheet showing values to the nearest penny and another rounded to the whole number. Create one math area with a math definition for two digits after the decimal point and then create a second math area with a definition for zero digits. Each math area is a separate unit, with independent subtotals, totals, and grand totals.

Tip: *(When upgrading from 4.2.) The Math Definition screen hasn't changed, but the method for defining the alignment character has.*

Proceed to create a math definition as you did previously. If you wish to change the decimal/align character, this is now done on the Other Format menu. In addition, you have an option, which was unavailable in version 4.2, that enables you to define a thousands' separator other than the comma.

Calculating Across Lines

When you set up your own math definitions, overriding the initial math settings, you have more options than just enhancing your columns. You can also calculate across columns. The calculations can include sophisticated formulas for addition, subtraction, multiplication, division, and averaging.

In addition to totals down columns, the printed math document in Figure 20-7 shows some line-by-line calculations, where the third column, titled "Increase ($)," equals the result of the first minus the second column. The fourth column represents the percentage increase of the first column over the second for selected lines.

Calculating across lines involves using the math definition procedure to establish a fourth type of column, called a calculation column. You can have up to four calculation columns in a math area, out of a total of 24 possible math columns. You must type in formulas to inform WordPerfect of what calculations will apply for every line in that column. In a formula, you can use four basic operators:

+	addition	*	multiplication
−	subtraction	/	division

The formula can contain values and letters that refer to other math columns. The calculations *proceed from left to right* unless the formula contains a set of parentheses to change the order of calculations; those values inside parentheses are calculated first. Table 20-1 lists some sample formulas and results. In addition to formulas containing the four basic operators, you can use four special formulas, also shown in Table 20-1. These special formulas must be entered on their own; they cannot be typed as part of a larger formula.

You can write formulas when you create a math definition. Remember that this occurs after you set tab stops but before you turn math on (as explained in the previous section). While on the Math Definition screen,

1. For each column that will result in a calculation based on other columns, select 0, Calculation column, as the "Type" definition. For example, if Column C is to be a calculation across lines, move the cursor to the "Type" definition in Column C and choose 0. WordPerfect moves the cursor down to the "Calculation Formulas" definition area and places the column letter next to the first unoccupied formula number.
2. Type in a formula, which can include values or letters that reference other columns by letter. For example, to subtract Column B from A, type **A−B**. Upper- or lowercase letters make no difference.
3. Press ENTER. The cursor returns to the "type" definition for the next column. Continue until formulas have been inserted for all calculation columns.

Table 20-1. Sample Formulas for Calculating Across Lines

Formula	Result Across One Line
18−8	10
3+5*8	64
3+(5*8)	43
18−A	18 minus the value in column A, which is the first math column
3+5*B	8 multiplied by the value in column B, which is the second math column
3+(5*B)	5 multiplied by the value in column B, plus 3
A−B/B*100	percentage increase of the value in column A over the value in column B
+	adds the numbers in all numeric columns
+/	calculates the average in all numeric columns
=	adds the numbers in all total columns
=/	calculates the average in all total columns

4. If you wish to alter the "Number of Digits" or "Negative Numbers" definitions for any of the calculation columns, move the cursor to those columns and type in a new number or symbol. The Math Definition screen for the result in Figure 20-7, for example, is shown in Figure 20-8.
5. After you finish defining all the math columns, press EXIT (F7) to clear the Math Definition screen. WordPerfect inserts a **[Math Def]** code in the text and returns you to the Math/Columns menu.
6. Select Math On (1 or M), and type in data.

Each time you tab to a calculation column, a new math operator appears—an exclamation point (!)—and the hidden code **[!]** is inserted. This signifies that a calculation will be performed across columns and the result will appear in that spot. Where you want a calculation to appear, simply press TAB to move to the next column (or ENTER if you're at the last column across the page). Where you want no calculation to appear, press BACKSPACE to erase the exclamation point before moving to the next column.

ABC Company, Marketing Department	Current Year	Past Year	Increase ($)	Increase (%)
Salaries	$44,555	$41,005	3,550	
Taxes	9,356	8,448	908	
Overtime	6,400	9,555	−3,155	
Personnel	60,311	59,008	1,303	2
Rent	4,333	4,333	0	
Utilities	978	1,000	−22	
Supplies	1,097	1,445	−348	
Materials	6,408	6,778	−370	−5
TOTAL	66,719	65,786	933	1

Figure 20-7. Printout of math documents with calculations across lines

```
Math Definition          Use arrow keys to position cursor

Columns                  A B C D E F G H I J K L M N O P Q R S T U V W X

Type                     2 2 0 0 2 2 2 2 2 2 2 2 2 2 2 2 2 2 2 2 2 2 2 2

Negative Numbers         - - - - ( ( ( ( ( ( ( ( ( ( ( ( ( ( ( ( ( ( ( (

Number of Digits to      0 0 0 0 2 2 2 2 2 2 2 2 2 2 2 2 2 2 2 2 2 2 2 2
  the Right (0-4)

Calculation   1      C   A-B
  Formulas    2      D   C/B*100
              3
              4

Type of Column:
     0 = Calculation     1 = Text      2 = Numeric     3 = Total

Negative Numbers
     ( = Parentheses (50.00)          - = Minus Sign  -50.00

Press Exit when done
```

Figure 20-8. The Math Definition screen for a document with calculations across lines

ABC Company, Marketing Department

	Current Year	Past Year	Increase ($)	Increase (%)
Salaries	$44,555	$41,005	!	
Taxes	9,356	8,448	!	
Overtime	6,400	9,555	!	
Personnel	+	+	!	!
Rent	4,333	4,333	!	
Utilities	978	1,000	!	
Supplies	1,097	1,445	!	
Materials	+	+	!	!
TOTAL	=	=	!	!

Math operators for a formula

Math Doc 1 Pg 1 Ln 4" Pos 1"

Figure 20-9. A math document containing formula operators before calculating

After you type in data within a math area and before you calculate, the screen appears as shown in Figure 20-9. Calculate the results, insert a **[Math Off]** code below the last row in the math area—if one is not already in the text—and the results appear, as shown in Figure 20-10. As is the case for other math operators, the exclamation points do not print at the printer.

Trap: *Don't use parentheses to denote a negative number in a formula definition.*

In a formula, parentheses are used to change the order of a calculation, but not to signify a negative number. Write your formula as −6+3, not as (6)+3.

Trap: *You cannot nest parentheses in a formula, and no spaces can be included at all.*

ABC Company, Marketing Department

	Current Year	Past Year	Increase ($)	Increase (%)
Salaries	$44,555	$41,005	3,550!	
Taxes	9,356	8,448	908!	
Overtime	6,400	9,555	-3,155!	
Personnel	60,311+	59,008+	1,303!	2!
Rent	4,333	4,333	0!	
Utilities	978	1,000	-22!	
Supplies	1,097	1,445	-348!	
Materials	6,408+	6,778+	-370!	-5!
TOTAL	66,719=	65,786=	933!	1!

Math　　　　Doc 1 Pg 1 Ln 4" Pos 1"

Figure 20-10. A math document with formula operators after calculating

In a formula, you are limited to only one set of parentheses to change the order of a calculation. If you use two sets, such as:

(1+A)/(3*B)

WordPerfect will ignore the first set; only the second set of parentheses will be considered, so that the formula becomes

1+A/(3*B)

Nor will WordPerfect accept formulas in which parentheses are nested. The following is an example of a formula that is disallowed:

9*((A−B)/3)

Finally, do not insert spaces when typing a formula; if you press the SPACEBAR, the effect is as if you pressed the ENTER key, and your cursor moves back up to the "Type" definition on the Math Definition screen. No spaces are allowed in a formula.

Trap: *Don't type an exclamation point from the keyboard as a calculation operator.*

WordPerfect will insert a calculation at an exclamation point only if you tab to a calculation column and the program inserts that math operator. If you insert an exclamation point from the keyboard, WordPerfect will ignore that symbol when calculating.

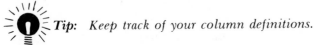

Tip: *Keep track of your column definitions.*

Your column definitions can become quite complicated—numeric columns, total columns, and calculation columns with different formulas in each. It is often difficult to keep track of each of your column definitions as you work in a math area.

There are two alternatives to help you out. One is to make a written copy of the column definitions to keep beside your keyboard. The other is to periodically view the Math Definition screen. Reveal codes and position the cursor between the **[Math Def]** and **[Math On]** codes. Next, press MATH/COLUMNS (ALT + F7) and select Math Def (2 or E). The Math Definition screen appears, showing the column definitions you created. (You can even turn on the printer and press SHIFT + PRTSC to print a copy of the screen on paper.) After examining the screen, press CANCEL (F1) to clear it without inserting an extraneous code.

Tip: *Check your formulas before you enter data.*

A mistake in one formula can ripple through an entire math document and distort your calculations. It's a good idea, therefore, to verify that your formulas are correct before you rely on them to balance your books or bill a client. Test your formulas with dummy numbers. For example, place the number 1 in every column that the formula depends on and calculate. Does the formula produce the number you would expect? Then try with another small, whole number. Once you know that you can trust the formulas you entered, go ahead and enter the real data.

Tip: *You can change the formula in a column.*

After you've defined each column and entered your data, you may discover that you want to change the definition. Perhaps you placed the wrong formula in a column or you prefer two, rather than zero, digits after the decimal point.

To change the column definitions, you must create a new **[Math Def]** code. But there's no need to start from scratch. Reveal codes and position the cursor between the **[Math Def]** and **[Math On]** codes. Next, press MATH/COLUMNS (ALT + F7) and select Math Def (2 or E). The Math Definition screen appears showing the column definitions you created. Change any of the column definitions.

If you plan to edit a formula, position the cursor at the "Type" definition in the column that you wish to edit. The number 0 should be at that location. Type **0** so that the cursor moves to the formula. Now use the cursor movement and the deletion keys to make any changes in the formula, and press ENTER. Once you've made all appropriate changes on the Math Definition screen, press EXIT to clear that screen, and press CANCEL (F1) to clear the Math/Columns menu.

You have just created a second code. Reveal codes and you will find the following:

[Math Def][Math Def][Math On]

Since it is good practice to always erase extraneous codes, you should now delete the old **[Math Def]** code—the code to the far left. Then move inside the math area (to the right of the **[Math On]** code), and press MATH/COLUMNS (ALT + F7) and select 2, Calculate, to activate the newly created math definition.

Tip: *Another WordPerfect product can assist you with sophisticated spreadsheet applications.*

You may find that you require a program that offers more sophistication than WordPerfect provides. WordPerfect is first and foremost a word processor, so its math capabilities are limited. When you find yourself wanting to build a completed spreadsheet to perform complex number-crunching, then consider purchasing PlanPerfect, another program manufactured by WordPerfect Corporation. PlanPerfect is a full-fledged spreadsheet, with statistical, trigonometric, and financial functions. It also provides the capability to produce graphs for visual representations of the spreadsheets you create. Any PlanPerfect spreadsheet or graph can be easily incorporated into a WordPerfect document. For more information on PlanPerfect, see your computer dealer or contact WordPerfect Corporation directly.

Tip: *(When upgrading from 4.2.) Calculate across columns as you did previously.*

The procedure for inserting a formula to calculate across columns has not been modified.

Tips and Traps Summary

Totaling Columns

Tip: Switch to the numeric keypad for easy number typing.

Tip: Dollar signs or other symbols are easily inserted.

Tip: Use a ruler line to keep track of tab stop locations.

Trap: Don't insert column headings in the same way that you insert values and math operators in math columns.

Tip: At the left margin in a math area, you can insert titles or text to label rows.

Tip: Math operators work backward and only until a math operator of the same kind is encountered.

Tip: Two additional math operators, T and t, enable you to include a known subtotal or total in a math column.

Tip: You can force WordPerfect into performing subtraction by using the minus sign or parentheses, or with the math operator N.

Tips and Traps Summary (*continued*)

Tip: Math operators do not appear on the printed document.

Trap: Calculations will be inaccurate if each value and math operator isn't aligned properly on a tab stop.

Trap: Overlapping numbers cause incorrect calculations.

Tip: One nice advantage of the Math feature is that you can change numbers in a column and then recalculate.

Tip: Use the Move feature to delete or relocate an entire math column.

Trap: Page breaks do not define the boundaries of distinct math areas.

Tip: (When upgrading from 4.2.) Total columns as you did previously.

Enhancing Totals Down Columns

Trap: Math definitions do not determine the appearance of numbers entered by you.

Tip: You can total numbers that do not include decimal points.

Tip: The decimal/align and thousands' separator characters affect math documents.

Trap: Do not confuse text columns in a math area with those created by using the Column feature.

Trap: Math operators must be placed in total columns in order for calculations to appear in those columns.

Tip: You can create different math definitions in different math areas.

Tip: (When upgrading from 4.2.) The Math Definition screen hasn't changed, but the method for defining the alignment character has.

Tips and Traps Summary (*continued*)

Calculating Across Lines

Trap: Don't use parentheses to denote a negative number in a formula definition.

Trap: You cannot nest parentheses in a formula, and no spaces can be included at all.

Trap: Don't type an exclamation point from the keyboard as a calculation operator.

Tip: Keep track of your column definitions.

Tip: Check your formulas before you enter data.

Tip: You can change the formula in a column.

Tip: Another WordPerfect product can assist you with sophisticated spreadsheet applications.

Tip: (When upgrading from 4.2.) Calculate across columns as you did previously.

21

Numbering Outlines, Paragraphs, Lines, and References Automatically

WordPerfect gives you the ability to automatically number portions of your document. First, WordPerfect can number outlines or paragraphs. For example, perhaps you wish to create a book outline, where topics are denoted as I., II., III., subtopics as A., B., C., and so on. If you use the Outline or the Paragraph Numbering feature to number your items, then when you later insert, move, copy, or delete outline items, WordPerfect will renumber the entire outline accordingly. Because numbering and outlining are a constantly changing, fluid process, the ability to renumber items automatically is the key reason for letting WordPerfect insert paragraph and outline numbers for you, rather than doing so manually.

Second, WordPerfect can number each line, along the left margin of the page, for reference purposes. It can simulate the preprinted pleading paper used in legal offices, and is useful anytime you find it necessary to refer to specific lines in your documents.

Third, with the Automatic Reference feature, WordPerfect can number references for you. For instance, perhaps the book that you are writing contains many references to figures, or to other pages, such as, "For more on the greenhouse effect, see page 14." Use automatic referencing so that when you edit the document, your reference numbers change accordingly.

All these numbering features are addressed in turn in this chapter. You learn how to number paragraphs, how to create outlines, and then how to change the numbering style (such as from I., II., III. to 1., 2., 3.) for paragraphs and outlines. Next, you learn about line numbering, and finally, about the Automatic Reference feature.

Paragraph Numbering

Paragraph numbers are inserted in the text one at a time. The type of number WordPerfect places in the text depends on which numbering style you have chosen, and which tab stop the cursor is located on. By default, WordPerfect assumes that you want to use what it refers to as the *outline numbering* style, with the following eight numbering levels:

```
Level 1 I.
Level 2    A.
Level 3       1.
Level 4          a.
Level 5             (1)
Level 6                (a)
Level 7                   i)
Level 8                      a)
```

Level 1 is at the left margin, with each successive tab stop representing the next numbering level. An example of this style, using levels 1 and 2, is shown in Figure 21-1.

Every time you want WordPerfect to insert a paragraph number in outline numbering style, follow this procedure:

1. Position the cursor on the line where you want a paragraph number to appear.
2. Position the cursor on the tab stop that corresponds to the level number that you want to use. For example, to insert a level 1 code, leave the cursor

RESIDENTIAL AGREEMENT

The terms of this residential rental agreement are between the Landlord and each signatory jointly and severally.

I. The Landlord leases to the Tenant, and the Tenant rents from the Landlord the premises, where the terms of the lease commence on __________ 19 ____ and end on __________ 19 ____. This agreement will continue on a year-by-year basis until either party shall terminate the same by giving the other party 30 days written notice.

II. Tenant shall be responsible for the payment of:

A. A rent charge of __________ per year in equal monthly installments, payable by the fifth day of each month.

B. All utilities and services in addition to the rent charge.

III. The premises shall be sued exclusively for a residence, by no more than 2 persons. Tenant shall maintain the premises in a clean manner at his own expense.

Figure 21-1. Paragraphs numbered using standard defaults

at the left margin. To insert a level 2 code, press TAB or →INDENT (F4) to jump to the first tab stop.

3. Press the DATE/OUTLINE (SHIFT + F5) key. The following menu appears

   1 Date Text; **2** Date Code; **3** Date Format; **4** Outline; **5** Para Num; **6** Define: **0**

4. Select Para Num (5 or P). WordPerfect responds

   Paragraph Level (Press Enter for Automatic):

5. Press ENTER to insert a paragraph number. The paragraph number you insert is actually an automatic paragraph number code **[Par Num:Auto]**. The code is *automatic* because WordPerfect automatically determines the

numbering level based on your cursor position. You can view the code on the Reveal Codes screen.

6. Press the SPACEBAR to insert spaces, and then start typing the text.

   Or press TAB, →INDENT (F4), or one of the other keys that jump to the next tab stop and then type the text. (If you use →INDENT, remember that all lines of text will be indented to the tab stop until the next **[HRt]** code.)

7. Repeat steps 1 through 6 each time you wish to insert another paragraph number in your document.

You can insert a paragraph number at any time, even after your text has been typed, by positioning the cursor and then following the steps above. You can delete a paragraph number by erasing it like you would any other character—by positioning the cursor on the number and pressing DEL, or by positioning the cursor just to the right of the number and pressing BACKSPACE. Both the number and the hidden code disappear. Or you can copy or move a paragraph number along with its accompanying text. When you edit your document, either to insert a new paragraph number or to delete, copy, or move an existing paragraph number, all subsequent paragraph numbers are updated automatically. Notice, for example, that if paragraph I. is erased from Figure 21-1, the result is a correctly renumbered outline, as shown in Figure 21-2.

RESIDENTIAL AGREEMENT

The terms of this residential rental agreement are between the Landlord and each signatory jointly and severally.

I. Tenant shall be responsible for the payment of:

A. A rent charge of ____________ per year in equal monthly installments, payable by the fifth day of each month.

B. All utilities and services in addition to the rent charge.

II. The premises shall be used exclusively for a residence, by no more than 2 persons. Tenant shall maintain the premises in a clean manner at his own expense.

Figure 21-2. Paragraphs renumbered after an entry is deleted

Tip: *Sometimes you must rewrite the screen before paragraph levels are renumbered.*

If you erase, copy, or move a paragraph number, the number may not update immediately. Simply press DOWN ARROW or another cursor movement key to scroll the cursor down past the number; it will then be updated properly. Or press the SCREEN (CTRL + F3) key and select Rewrite (0 or R) to renumber all the following paragraphs quickly.

Tip: *You can change the level of the paragraph number after you type the paragraph.*

You may find that after you've inserted paragraph numbers and typed some paragraphs, a paragraph number is at the wrong level. To increase a paragraph number's level—for example, from level 2 to level 3—position the cursor on the paragraph number and press TAB until the number is moved to the desired tab stop. Then press DOWN ARROW to update the number automatically. To decrease a paragraph number's level—for example, from level 4 to level 3—position the cursor on the paragraph number and press BACKSPACE to the desired tab stop. Then press DOWN ARROW, if necessary.

Trap: *Don't type some paragraph numbers on your own, while having WordPerfect insert others.*

WordPerfect can renumber paragraphs correctly because it keeps track of all the **[Par Num:Auto]** codes that are placed in the text. If you type one paragraph number on your own—such as typing an uppercase I followed by a period—instead of allowing WordPerfect to do this for you, the numbering sequence will be incorrect.

If you have a numbering sequence problem, press REVEAL CODES (ALT + F3). On the bottom window of the Reveal Codes screen you should see the **[Par Num:Auto]** codes, but no actual paragraph numbers. If you see a number, then you inserted it yourself. Erase it and use the DATE/OUTLINE key to have WordPerfect insert the number for you. The numbering sequence should correct itself.

Tip: *You can assign a specific numbering level to any tab stop location.*

With automatic paragraph numbering, the numbering level is based on your tab stop location, and changes if you move the number to another tab stop. At the left margin, for example, the numbering style is level 1—uppercase Roman numerals. Press TAB and the style is level 2—uppercase letters, as in this example:

I. Paragraph

  A. Paragraph

  B. Paragraph

II. Paragraph

As an alternative, you can specify a particular numbering level, *no matter which tab stop* the cursor is on. This is referred to as *fixed paragraph numbering.* When WordPerfect prompts for a paragraph level, type in the number (from 1 through 8) that represents the level you want to use, and then press ENTER.

For example, suppose that all your paragraphs will begin at the left margin. But instead of numbering them by using level 1 (I., II., III., and so on), as WordPerfect would typically use, you want all paragraphs numbered as level 5, that is, (1), (2), (3), and so on. Position the cursor at the left margin, press DATE/OUTLINE (SHIFT + F5), and select Para Num (5 or P). Then, when WordPerfect responds

Paragraph Level (Press Enter for Automatic):

type **5** and press ENTER. The code inserted is **[Par Num:5]**, meaning that the paragraph numbering was set as level 5 by you, rather than automatically by WordPerfect. If you continue to select level 5 for each paragraph, you can create paragraphs that are numbered as follows:

(1) Paragraph

(2) Paragraph

(3) Paragraph

Now, even if you move the paragraph numbers to a different tab stop location, the numbering will remain at level 5, because you have fixed the paragraph number as such.

Tip: *You can align paragraph numbers on the decimal point.*

Typically, all paragraph numbers are aligned flush left on a tab, as shown here:

I.   Paragraph
II.   Paragraph
III. Paragraph
IV.   Paragraph

If you prefer, you can align them on an align character, such as the decimal point (used here as a period), which produces the following:

  I. Paragraph
 II. Paragraph
III. Paragraph
IV.   Paragraph

To align numbers on the decimal point, you must align each paragraph number by using the TAB ALIGN (CTRL + F6) key, which adds one extra step to the paragraph numbering procedure. Follow these steps:

1. Position the cursor on the line where you want a paragraph number to appear.
2. Position the cursor just *before* the tab stop where you want the paragraph number to appear. (For example, position the cursor on the preceding tab stop.)
3. Press the TAB ALIGN (CTRL + F6) key. The cursor jumps to the next tab stop, and the following message is displayed:

   Align char = .

4. Press the DATE/OUTLINE (SHIFT + F5) key.
5. Select Para Num (5 or P). WordPerfect responds

   Paragraph Level (Press Enter for Automatic):

6. Press ENTER to insert a paragraph number or type in a specific numbering level (see the preceding Tip), and press ENTER.

7. Press TAB or →INDENT to align the paragraph number on the period, and then type the text.
8. Repeat steps 1 through 7 each time you wish to insert in your document another paragraph number that is aligned on the decimal point.

Notice in step 2 that you position the cursor before the tab stop where you want the paragraph number to appear. This is because the cursor jumps a tab stop when you press TAB ALIGN. Also, step 7 is critical; if you don't press TAB or →INDENT to align the paragraph number before typing your text, WordPerfect assumes that the text should be aligned as well, and the text will move beyond the left margin and out of sight.

Tip: *Numbered paragraphs are useful in paragraph libraries.*

It is often convenient to create a library of commonly used paragraphs, each stored in its own separate file. You can then retrieve separate paragraphs to create a new document, with little typing involved. If you often number paragraphs after retrieving them, let the Paragraph Numbering feature save you time. Save each paragraph in its own file, preceded by a paragraph number code. When you retrieve paragraphs, in whatever order, WordPerfect automatically renumbers the paragraphs correctly. In moments, you have a document with paragraphs numbered sequentially.

Tip: *Create a style or a macro to insert paragraph numbers.*

The procedure for inserting a paragraph number code in the text is cumbersome in relation to the modest result. You use at least three keystrokes to insert just one paragraph number, and you use many more keystrokes to align that paragraph number on the decimal point.

At first glance, therefore, it may seem that paragraph numbering is more trouble than it's worth. Reconsider this verdict, however. By using the Styles feature (described in Chapter 10), you can include a paragraph number code along with other formatting codes in a style, and in that way you can quickly number paragraphs while also handling other formatting. And, by using the Macro feature (described in Chapter 27), you can direct WordPerfect to insert a paragraph number with one keystroke (such as by pressing ALT + P), or number all the paragraphs of an existing document in an instant. Thus, WordPerfect can bear the burden of many of the chores associated with inserting a paragraph number. And you'll then have the benefit of WordPerfect's ability to maintain the correct paragraph numbering sequence as you edit a document.

Trap: *The Search and Replace features cannot find a specific paragraph number.*

You cannot use the Search or the Replace feature as a quick way to move the cursor to a specific paragraph number inserted by WordPerfect. This is because WordPerfect does not recognize the number; instead, the program recognizes it as a **[Par Num]** code. You can thus search for or replace a **[Par Num]** code, but not a specific paragraph number.

To search for a paragraph numbering code, press →SEARCH (F2) and, at the prompt, press DATE/OUTLINE (SHIFT + F5). WordPerfect provides a menu of possible codes. Select option 2 and the search string reads

→Srch: [Par Num]

Press →SEARCH (F2) and the cursor jumps to the next paragraph number code in the text. The same procedure applies when using the ←SEARCH (SHIFT + F2) and the REPLACE (ALT + F2) keys. More information on the Search feature and the Replace feature is provided in Chapters 4 and 6, respectively.

Tip: *You can define a different numbering style or restart the numbering scheme.*

You may not necessarily want to use the default paragraph numbering style. For example, in legal documents, the numbering scheme often resembles this example:

1 Paragraph

2 Paragraph

  2.1 Paragraph

  2.2 Paragraph

Or you may wish to insert symbols, such as the bullet, rather than actual numbers. You can change the default numbering style to meet your own specifications.

You can also restart paragraph numbers in the middle of a document, so that you have two independent groups of paragraphs, each starting, for example, at roman numeral I., in the same document. Refer to a later section of this chapter "Changing the Paragraph or Outline Numbering Style," for details.

Tip: *(When upgrading from 4.2.) The procedure for inserting individual paragraph numbers is housed on a different function key.*

In version 5, the Paragraph Numbering feature is accessed via the DATE/OUTLINE (SHIFT + F5) key, rather than the MARK TEXT key, as in version 4.2. Also, you'll notice that WordPerfect now offers eight numbering levels, rather than seven.

Outline Numbering

Outlining is similar to paragraph numbering in three ways. First, the default numbering style is the same: I., A., 1., a., and so on. An example of this numbering style within an outline is shown in Figure 21-3. Second, the numbering codes are identical; when you create an outline, what's hidden behind each outline number is the code **[Par Num:Auto]**. Third, if you later edit the text so that you insert, delete, copy, or move a numbering code, the outline is automatically updated for you.

However, the process in outlining is very different from paragraph numbering. Instead of inserting numbers one at a time, you switch into Outline mode. When you do, four keys perform specific functions to aid in producing an outline:

- The ENTER key moves the cursor down to the left margin of the next line and inserts a level 1 number on that line. With the cursor just to the right of an outline number, the ENTER key moves the number down to the next line. (Also, if you press CTRL+ENTER to insert a hard page code, a level 1 number is inserted below the hard page code.)
- With the cursor just to the right of an outline number, the TAB key moves an outline number one tab stop to the right, changing the numbering style to the next level.
- With the cursor just to the right of an outline number, the →INDENT (F4) key moves the cursor one tab stop to the right *without* moving the outline number, and indents the text that follows the number up to the next **[HRt]** code.
- With the cursor just to the right of an outline number, the ←MARGIN RELEASE (SHIFT + TAB) key moves the outline number one tab stop to the left and changes the numbering style to that of the preceding level.

I. Definition of Air Pollution

II. Types of Pollutants

  A. Carbon Monoxide

    1. Sources

      a. Automobiles, which contribute over 50% of the total
      b. Power Plants
      c. Miscellaneous Sources

    2. Harmful Effects

      a. Greenhouse effect on the environment, with a
         gradual heating of the atmosphere
      b. Health Issues

  B. Hydrocarbons

Figure 21-3. An outline numbered using standard defaults

With these four keys in mind, you can switch into Outline mode and create an outline, as follows:

1. Position the cursor *one line above* where you want the first outline number to appear.
2. Press the DATE/OUTLINE (SHIFT + F5) key. The following menu appears:

   1 Date Text; **2** Date Code; **3** Date Format; **4** Outline; **5** Para Num; **6** Define: **0**

3. Select Outline (4 or O). The Date/Outline menu clears. WordPerfect displays the message **Outline** in the lower left-hand corner of the screen to remind you that you are in Outline mode. No code is inserted in the text when you switch on Outline mode, but the ENTER, TAB, →INDENT, and ←MARGIN RELEASE keys take on their special functions.
4. Press ENTER. The cursor moves down one line and the first outline level number (I.) appears at the left margin, just to the left of the cursor.
5. If you want outline level 1, then you are ready to begin typing. Press the SPACEBAR or the →INDENT (F4) key to move the cursor, and begin typing.

   Or, if you want to change the outline level before typing, press TAB to jump to succeeding tab stops or press ←MARGIN RELEASE to jump to preceding tab stops until the correct outline number appears. Then press the SPACEBAR or the →INDENT key, and begin typing.
6. Repeat steps 4 and 5 until you've finished typing the outline. Remember that to insert a blank line between outline entries, press ENTER once to insert an outline level number and then as many additional times as you desire to position the outline number farther down the page.
7. Press DATE/OUTLINE (SHIFT + F5) and select Outline (4 or O). The message **Outline** disappears from the screen, indicating that you have exited Outline mode. Now when you press ENTER, an outline number will no longer be inserted.

In Outline mode, each time the ENTER key places an outline number on the screen, the hidden code **[ParNum:Auto]** is inserted at that spot in the text. Remember that a paragraph number and an outline number use the same code.

To delete an outline number, erase it as you would any other character—by pressing BACKSPACE or DEL. The hidden code **[Par Num:Auto]** is then erased, along with the number. After you insert, erase, copy, or move an outline number code, all the outline numbers that follow are renumbered automatically. The correct numbering sequence of your outline is maintained.

Tip: *Sometimes you must rewrite the screen before outline levels are renumbered.*

If you insert a new outline number, or delete, copy, or move an entry with its accompanying outline number, the outline might not renumber immediately. Simply press DOWN ARROW to scroll through the text and the outline will be renumbered correctly. Or press the SCREEN (CTRL + F3) key and select Rewrite (0 or R) to renumber the entire outline quickly.

Trap: *Don't forget to exit Outline mode when you've finished typing an outline.*

The ENTER key conveniently inserts an outline number automatically when you want to create an outline, but it can be annoying when you wish to type straight text. Remember to exit Outline mode after completing an outline, or you'll continue to insert outline numbers you no longer want. Also, WordPerfect automatically exits Outline mode when you use the EXIT (F7) key to clear the screen.

Tip: *You can change the level of an outline number after you've typed it.*

You may find that after you've inserted outline numbers and typed some entries, an outline number is at the wrong level. It is easy to rectify this situation, however.

Whether or not you're in Outline mode, you can increase an outline number's level—for example, from level 2 to level 3—by positioning the cursor on the outline number and pressing TAB. Then press DOWN ARROW, if the number needs to be updated by WordPerfect. You can decrease an outline number's level—

for example, from level 4 to level 3—by positioning the cursor on the outline number and pressing BACKSPACE. Press DOWN ARROW if necessary. (When in Outline mode, you can also increase the outline level by pressing TAB or decrease the outline level by pressing ←MARGIN RELEASE (SHIFT + TAB) with the cursor just to the right of the outline number.)

Tip: *You can use the paragraph numbering method in an outline when you're not in Outline mode.*

You may create an outline, exit Outline mode, and then realize that you want to insert a new item. You don't necessarily have to switch back into Outline mode to insert a new outline number. Position the cursor at the tab stop you desire and then follow the paragraph numbering procedure (described in the preceding section, "Paragraph Numbering"). Since you have inserted the same numbering code, the outline numbers are readjusted automatically.

In fact, if you prefer, you can create an outline by inserting each number individually using the paragraph numbering procedure, rather than switching into Outline mode.

Tip: *You can define a different numbering style for your outline or create two or more outlines in one document.*

You may not necessarily want to use the default numbering style for outlines. For example, you may want your outline to be numbered as follows:

1. Topic
   a. Subtopic
   b. Subtopic
2. Topic

Or, you may wish to insert symbols such as the bullet, rather than actual numbers. You can change the default numbering style to meet your own specifications.

You can also restart outline numbers in the middle of a document, so that you have two independent outlines, each beginning, for example, with Roman numeral I. Refer to the following section of this chapter for details.

Tip: *(When upgrading from 4.2.) The procedure to switch into Outline mode is housed on a different function key.*

In version 5, the Outline feature is accessed via the DATE/OUTLINE (SHIFT + F5) key, rather than the MARK TEXT key, as in version 4.2. Also, you'll notice that WordPerfect now offers eight numbering levels, rather than seven.

Changing the Paragraph or Outline Numbering Style

As with any WordPerfect default setting, you can change the default style for your paragraph or outline numbers. Besides the outline numbering style, which you are now familiar with and which is the default whether you insert paragraphs individually or switch to Outline mode to insert numbers, there are three more preset styles. They are the *paragraph* numbering style, the *legal* numbering style, and the *bullets* numbering style. All four predefined styles are shown together in Figure 21-4. Moreover, as a fifth option, you can devise your own style.

WordPerfect also allows you to restart the numbering and to specify the number and/or level that you wish to use. Restarting numbering is particularly useful if you wish to create two or more sets of numbered paragraphs in one document, each starting with number 1. or I. or whatever, depending on your numbering style.

To specify a style different from outline numbering, or to restart numbering:

1. Position the cursor in your document *before* the location where you want the outline or the set of paragraphs to appear.
2. Press the DATE/OUTLINE (SHIFT + F5) key. The following menu appears

   1 Date Text; **2** Date Code; **3** Date Format; **4** Outline; **5** Para Num; **6** Define: **0**

Outline Numbering Style

Level 1	I. II. . . .
Level 2	A. B. . . .
Level 3	1. 2. . . .
Level 4	a. b. . . .
Level 5	(1) (2) . . .
Level 6	(a) (b) . . .
Level 7	i) ii) . . .
Level 8	a) b) . . .

Paragraph Numbering Style

Level 1	1. 2. . . .
Level 2	a. b. . . .
Level 3	i. ii. . . .
Level 4	(1) (2) . . .
Level 5	(a) (b) . . .
Level 6	(i) (ii) . . .
Level 7	1) 2) . . .
Level 8	a) b) . . .

Legal Numbering Style

Level 1	1 2. . . .
Level 2	1.1 1.2 . . .
Level 3	1.1.1 1.1.2. . . .
Level 4	1.1.1.1 1.1.1.2 . . .
Level 5	1.1.1.1.1. 1.1.1.1.2 . . .
Level 6	1.1.1.1.1.1 1.1.1.1.1.2 . . .
Level 7	1.1.1.1.1.1.1 1.1.1.1.1.1.2 . . .
Level 8	1.1.1.1.1.1.1.1 1.1.1.1.1.1.1.2 . . .

Bullets Numbering Style

Level 1	●	(bullet)
Level 2	○	(hollow bullet)
Level 3	-	(hypen)
Level 4	■	(square bullet)
Level 5	*	(asterisk)
Level 6	+	(plus)
Level 7	•	(small bullet)
Level 8	x	(lowercase x)

Figure 21-4. The four predefined numbering styles

3. Select Define (6 or D). WordPerfect responds with the Paragraph Number Definition screen, shown in Figure 21-5.

   The current numbering style definition is indicated in the middle of the screen, next to the heading "Current Definition." If you have not yet changed from the default, then the current style is the outline numbering style.

4. Should you wish to select one of the predefined numbering styles that isn't the current definition, type the corresponding option number or mnemonic. For example, to select the bullets style of numbering, type **5** or **B**, for Bullets.

   Or, to devise a numbering scheme of your own, type **6** or **U**, for User-defined. The cursor will move to the level 1 number under the heading "Current Definition." You can leave the level 1 style as is by pressing ENTER; the cursor moves to the next level. Alternatively, you can change the level 1 style by pressing the DEL key to delete the existing style and by

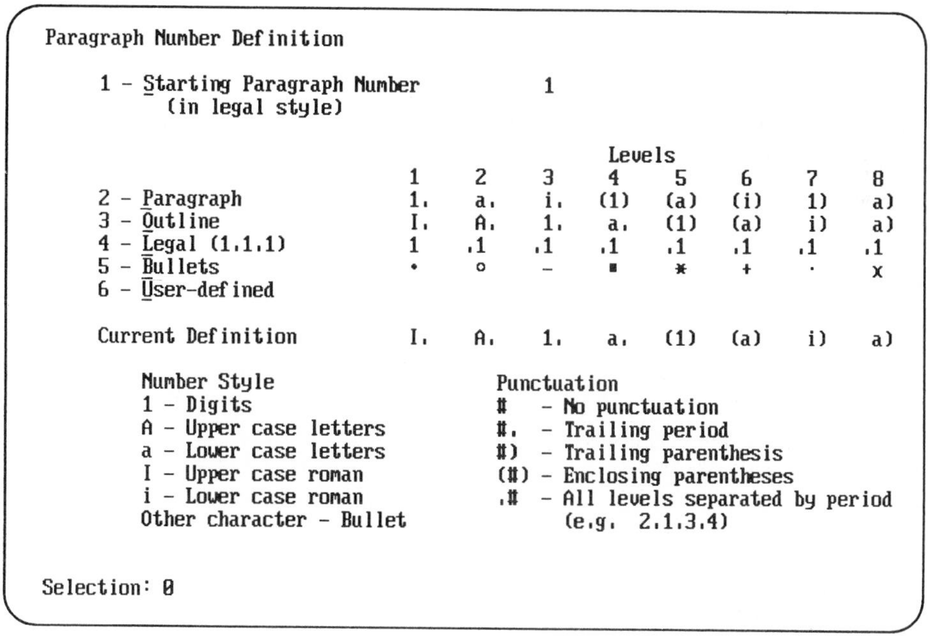

Paragraph Number Definition
1 - Starting Paragraph Number 1
(in legal style)
Levels
1 2 3 4 5 6 7 8
2 - Paragraph 1. a. i. (1) (a) (i) 1) a)
3 - Outline I. A. 1. a. (1) (a) i) a)
4 - Legal (1.1.1) 1 .1 .1 .1 .1 .1 .1 .1
5 - Bullets • o - ■ * + · x
6 - User-defined
Current Definition I. A. 1. a. (1) (a) i) a)
Number Style
1 - Digits
A - Upper case letters
a - Lower case letters
I - Upper case roman
i - Lower case roman
Other character - Bullet
Punctuation
- No punctuation
#. - Trailing period
#) - Trailing parenthesis
(#) - Enclosing parentheses
.# - All levels separated by period
(e.g. 2.1.3.4)
Selection: 0

Figure 21-5. The Paragraph Number Definition screen

typing in a style of your own. At the bottom of the Paragraph Number Definition screen is a list of the available number and punctuation options. For instance, if you want lowercase Roman numerals followed by a period as level 1, then type **i.** and press ENTER; the cursor moves to the next level. Continue until all levels have been defined and the cursor returns to the bottom of the screen.

5. If you wish to restart numbering at a location other than the beginning (that is, other than 1. or I., and so forth), select Starting Paragraph Number (1 or S) and enter a number, following the legal style format, to indicate the number and/or level at which to start the numbering.

   For example, assume that you will be using the outline numbering style. Then, type 4 and press ENTER to begin numbering where level 1 starts at IV. and all the other levels start at the beginning. Or type **4.2** and press ENTER to begin numbering where level 1 starts at IV. and level 2 starts at B. Or type **4.1.3** and press ENTER to begin numbering where level 1 starts at IV., level 2 starts at A., and level 3 starts at 3.

6. Press EXIT (F7) or ENTER to return to your document. The Date/Outline menu remains at the bottom of the screen.

7. Select another item from the Date/Outline menu, or press CANCEL (F1) or ENTER to clear the menu from the screen.

WordPerfect inserts a **[Par Num Def]** code in the text, which affects the restart number and the style of all paragraph numbering codes from that point to the end of the document, or until the next **[Par Num Def]** code is encountered.

Tip: *You can insert a paragraph numbering definition code before or after numbering your text.*

You can insert a paragraph numbering definition code before you type your numbered paragraphs or outline—or you can do it afterward. After completing an outline, for example, you may find that you want a different numbering style. If so, move the cursor above the outline and insert a **[Par Num Def]** code. As you press DOWN ARROW, all the numbers are adjusted to the new style that you set. Or press the SCREEN (CTRL + F3) key and select Rewrite (0 or R) to update the screen.

Tip: *Insert a new paragraph numbering definition code for each outline or set of numbered paragraphs.*

Even if you wish to retain the same numbering style, insert a **[Par Num Def]** code preceding the second and all succeeding outlines or sets of numbered paragraphs in your document. That way, you will make sure that each one starts at the beginning number.

Tip: *A numbering style can include any special characters that your printer can print.*

If you wish to use the bullets numbering style in your document, make sure that your printer is capable of printing the bullet and other special characters included in this style. Turn to Chapter 17 to learn about special characters.

Chapter 17 also describes how you can insert in your text special characters not found on the standard keyboard. You press the COMPOSE (CTRL + 2) key, type in the WordPerfect character number assigned to the special character that you wish to insert, and press ENTER. You can use the COMPOSE key to insert a special character at a certain level when creating a user-defined numbering style. For instance, Chapter 17 describes how the bullet symbol is listed in Character Set 4, with a WordPerfect character number 4,0. To insert the bullet as part of a style, follow steps 1 through 7 as shown at the beginning of this chapter section; when you're at step 4 and creating a user-defined style, make sure the cursor is at the level for which you wish to define a special character. Then, follow these steps:

1. Press the COMPOSE (CTRL + 2) key.
2. Type the WordPerfect character number.
3. Press ENTER. The special character appears on the Paragraph Number Definition screen at the current cursor position.

The WordPerfect character number for some special characters that you may wish to employ in a user-defined numbering style are as follows:

Character Name	**WordPerfect Character Number**	**Symbol**
Bullet	4,0	●
Hollow bullet	4,1	○
Square bullet	4,2	■
Small bullet	4,3	•
Left double guillemets	4,9	≪
Right double guillemets	4,10	≫

However, remember that your printer may not be able to produce all of these special characters. Be sure to refer to Chapter 17 for further information, if you wish to use special characters in your numbering style.

Trap: *A user-defined style is restricted.*

When you define your own numbering style, you are restricted to using one of the following as a given level style:

- A digit (an Arabic number, such as 1, 2, 3), a letter (upper- or lowercase), or a roman numeral (upper- or lowercase), followed by a punctuation mark — including a trailing period, a trailing parenthesis, enclosing parentheses, or another special character. For example, type **1.** to number a level as 1., 2., 3., and so on. Or type **I*** to number a level as I*, II*, III*, and so on. Or type **(a)** to number a level as (a), (b), (c), and so on.

  Any special character by itself—such as the bullet, the hollow bullet, the dash, or the asterisk.

  The level being appended to the previous level by inserting a period as the first character. For example, if level 1 is defined as uppercase letters (regardless of what you define as the punctuation mark for level 1), and if for level

2, you type **.1**, then for level 2, the numbering will appear as A.1, A.2, A.3, and so on.

Tip: *Place a paragraph number definition code on the Document Initial Codes screen to reduce the clutter at the top of a document.*

In Chapter 8, you learned that you can alter a setting for a whole document by placing a code either at the top of the document itself or on the Document Initial Codes screen. The advantage of the latter is that it reduces the potential jumble of codes at the top of a document, and it also protects the codes from being erased or accidentally moved as you edit the text. If you're changing a numbering style for a whole document, consider doing so on the Document Initial Codes screen.

Tip: *Change the paragraph numbering definition permanently on the Setup menu.*

You may find that the default setting—outline numbering style—is a numbering system that you rarely use. For example, you may find yourself consistently switching to the bullets style. Or, if you work in a law office, you may use the legal style most often. If that's the case, then you can change the default permanently. To do so, alter the initial settings on the Setup menu (refer to Appendix B for details).

Tip: *(When upgrading from 4.2.) The ability to change the paragraph numbering style has been enhanced.*

Changing a paragraph numbering style is now done through the DATE/OUTLINE key, rather than the MARK TEXT key. Each style now has eight levels, rather than seven.

In version 5, WordPerfect offers the ability to number outlines or paragraphs not only with numbers and letters, but also with special characters. There is a predefined bullets style. Or, you can include any special character when creating your own user-defined style (the user-defined style was referred to as "Other" in version 4.2).

Line Numbering

With the Line Numbering feature, you can print line numbers on a page and start and stop those numbers as often as desired. The numbers appear down the left margin of the page, as shown in the legal document in Figure 21-6. Numbers also print on lines that contain footnotes and endnotes, but not on header and footer lines.

WordPerfect assumes that you desire no line numbering, but that if you choose to turn on this feature, then the default settings for line numbering are as follows: blank lines (lines containing no text) are included in the line count; every line is numbered; the numbers are positioned 6/10 of an inch from the left

---

Plaintiff THE MARINER INSURANCE COMPANY submits the following Trial Brief for the assistance of the Court:

I. <u>FACTUAL BACKGROUND</u>

This litigation arises out of a first-party insurance claim made by the defendant IAN S. COOPER ("Cooper") under an insurance policy issued to him by THE MARINER INSURANCE COMPANY ("TMIC").

The insured property is located at 445 West Kalarama Blvd, Sacramento, California. It is a 75-year-old structure which includes a first-floor living room, a deck, and a basement.

Figure 21-6. A legal document with line numbering down the left margin of the page

edge of the page; the numbering starts at number 1 (even if you begin line numbering halfway down the page); and a new line count starts on each succeeding page (so that the first line of each page starts at number 1).

Proceed as follows to turn on line numbering and change any of the defaults, or to turn off line numbering:

1. Position the cursor at the left margin on the line where you want the numbering to begin if it is currently off, or to end if it is currently on.
2. Press the FORMAT (SHIFT + F8) key. WordPerfect displays the Format menu.
3. Select Line Format (1 or L) to display the Line Format menu, as shown in Figure 21-7. Next to the heading "Line Numbering," WordPerfect indicates whether line numbering is on ("Yes") or off ("No").

```
Format: Line

     1 - Hyphenation                    Off

     2 - Hyphenation Zone - Left        10%
                            Right       4%

     3 - Justification                  Yes

     4 - Line Height                    Auto

     5 - Line Numbering                 No

     6 - Line Spacing                   1

     7 - Margins - Left                 1"
                   Right                1"

     8 - Tab Set                        0", every 0.5"

     9 - Widow/Orphan Protection        No


Selection: 0
```

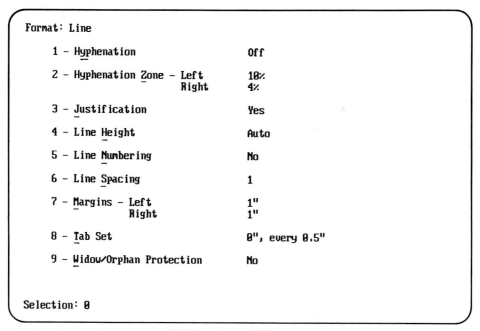

Figure 21-7. The Line Format menu

4. Select Line Numbering (5 or N).

5. Type **Y** to turn line numbering on, or **N** to turn it off. If you turn numbering on, WordPerfect provides the Line Numbering menu, shown in Figure 21-8.

6. If you've turned line numbering on, then, to change any default setting, select an option from the Line Numbering menu as follows:

   If you want to exclude—rather than include—blank lines from the line count, select Count Blank Lines (1 or C) and type **N**.

   If you want a style other than every line being numbered, select Number Every n Lines (2 or N) , type a number, and press ENTER. For example, type **2** and press ENTER to print numbers on every other line.

   If you want to position the line numbers at a distance other than 0.6 inch from the left edge of the paper, select Position of Number from Left

```
Format: Line Numbering

     1 - Count Blank Lines                          Yes

     2 - Number Every n Lines, where n is           1

     3 - Position of Number from Left Edge          0.6"

     4 - Starting Number                            1

     5 - Restart Numbering on Each Page             Yes









Selection: 0
```

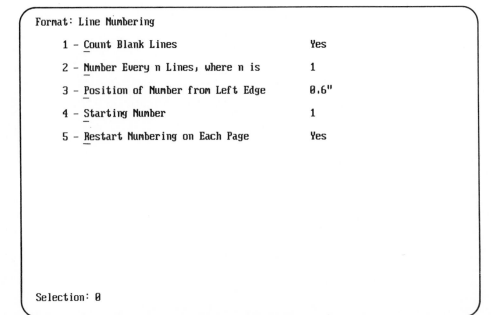

Figure 21-8. The Line Numbering menu

Edge (3 or **P**), type a number, and press ENTER. For example, type **.5** and ENTER to print numbers half an inch from the left edge.

If you want to start numbering with a number other than 1, select Starting Number (4 or S), type a number, and press ENTER. For example, type **6** and press ENTER to print the first line number as "6".

If you want to continue numbering across page breaks rather than restart numbering at 1 on each printed page, select Restart Number on Each Page (5 or **R**) and type **N**.

7. Press EXIT (F7) to return to your document.

WordPerfect inserts a hidden line numbering code in the text at the current cursor location, which turns line numbering on or off from that point forward in the text, with the codes **[Ln Num:On]** or **[Ln Num:Off]**.

Trap: *Line numbering does not appear on the Typing screen.*

If you turn on line numbering, you do not see the numbers as you type text; instead, you will see the result on the printed page. You can get a preview of how the document will appear with line numbers by using the View Document feature, which is accessed through the PRINT (SHIFT + F7) key (this feature is described in Chapter 14). But be warned that line numbers *always* restart at number 1 for each page on the View Document screen, even if you change the default for option 5 on the Line Numbering menu so as *not* to restart numbering on each page when printed.

Trap: *Not all printers support line numbering.*

You must test your printer to see whether line numbering is supported properly. Either insert a **[Ln Num:On]** code in your text and print, or use the PRINTER.TST file provided by WordPerfect (this file is described in Chapter 15).

Trap: *Line numbering is dependent on the line spacing that you establish in your document.*

For single-spaced text, the Line Numbering feature counts each line (or it counts every line containing text if you select not to count blank lines). If you change your spacing, then the line numbering changes as well. For example, switch to double spacing for a portion of your document, and the line numbers will also be double spaced in that portion of the document. (Also see the following Tip.)

Tip: *You can choose to have one spacing setting for line numbering and another for text.*

As described in the previous Tip, the spacing for line numbering depends on the spacing of your document. This can make the line numbering look awkward if your document constantly changes its spacing setting. You may want to number lines with one line-spacing setting, and type your text with another line-spacing setting. For example, perhaps you want line numbering to appear consistently as double spaced, even though the text on the page may be single spaced in some sections and double spaced in others. An example is shown in Figure 21-9; notice that the line numbering is double spaced, even where the text is single spaced, such as at the very top of the document.

One way to produce a document like the one shown in Figure 21-9 is to first print out pages with nothing but line numbers on them and then print out your document on those pages:

1. On a clear Typing screen, insert a double-spacing code **[Ln Spacing:2]** (see Chapter 8 for more information on using the Line Spacing feature).
2. Insert a **[Ln Num:On]** code, as described earlier in this section.
3. Continually press ENTER to insert **[HRt]** codes all the way to the end of the page.
4. Print out that page as many times as you need pages with numbers along the left margin; each page will be blank, except that every other line will be numbered.
5. Reinsert those pages into the printer.
6. Print out your document on the pages containing line numbers.

You have another alternative, if you use a laser printer. Laser printers can print anywhere on a page, before ejecting that page of text. As a result, you can take advantage of the Advance feature to print two sections of text—the document text and then the line numbers—in the same location. To do so, follow steps 1 through 3, as just described. Then, follow these additional steps:

4. Position your cursor at the bottom of the page and turn off line numbering.
5. Insert a **[Ln Spacing:1]** code that returns the document to single spacing.

HINCKLER & HAINES
4 California Street, Suite 1200
San Francisco, Ca 94111
(415) 334-2234

Attorneys for Plaintiff
ABC Company

SUPERIOR COURT OF THE STATE OF CALIFORNIA

FOR THE COUNTY OF CONTRA COSTA

ABC COMPANY, Plaintiff, vs. RON J. SMITH, Defendant. ________________________	)))))))))))	NO. 5545677-23 DEFENDANTS' NOTICE OF MOTION AND MOTION FOR SUMMARY JUDGMENT

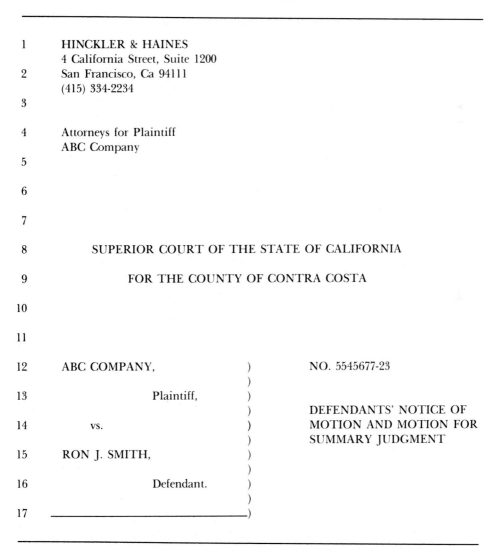

Figure 21-9. A legal document with line number spacing different from the spacing of the text

6. Insert an advance code, which directs the printer to move back up to the top of the page. For instance, if your top margin is one inch, then insert the code **[AdvToLn:1″]** (see Chapter 7 for more information on using the Advance feature).
7. Now, type the text of that page (or retrieve it from another file).
8. Print out the page.

This procedure must be repeated for each successive page in your document; that is, you would copy all the codes starting at the top of the previous page (up to the actual text) onto the new page, and then type the text of that new page.

Use the Advance feature with line numbering only after you've completed your final draft of the document, because editing changes alter the location of page breaks and will shift the location of the codes you inserted. Also, be sure to retain a copy of your document without all the line numbering and advance codes, so that you are later able to edit the text.

Tip: *Draw a vertical line to separate the line numbers from the body of the text.*

You may wish to print a vertical line down the left margin of your document to isolate the line numbers from the body of your text. Legal pleading paper usually has such a line on the page, but WordPerfect can also produce this effect. After you turn on line numbering, use the Graphics Line option on the GRAPHICS (ALT + F9) menu to direct WordPerfect to insert a vertical line—which you can specify as any length or thickness (see Chapter 18 for details). If the Graphics Line option doesn't work on your printer, then try the Line Draw feature to draw a vertical line; however, you must be in single spacing in order for the line to be drawn unbroken when printed (but you can get around this limitation—see the preceding Tip).

Tip: *Line numbering can be useful whenever you wish to count lines.*

If you find yourself manually counting lines in a document, consider using the Line Numbering feature to help. For example, when filling out predesigned forms, it often becomes necessary to count lines in order to know exactly where on the page to print. Instead, let the Line Numbering feature do the counting for you. Insert a predesigned form in the printer and, on that form, print out a page that contains only the **[Ln Num:On]** code, followed by a page full of **[HRt]** codes. You'll discover which line corresponds to which item on the form.

Or, if it is important to keep track of how many lines comprise a document, turn on line numbering at the beginning of the document, and change the default setting for Restart Numbering on Each Page from "Yes" to "No." When you print the document, WordPerfect will perform the line count for you. Then, you can always delete the **[Ln Num:On]** code and print the document again, without the line numbers.

Trap: *Don't position the line numbers beyond the left margin.*

When you set the position of the line numbers from the left edge of the page, make sure that the numbers are printed within the left margin, and not within the body of your text (unless you want to do so). For example, if your margin is set at one inch and you choose to have numbers appear two inches from the left edge of the paper, your numbers will appear beyond the left margin and will thus overwrite your text.

Tip: *You may set the position of line numbers from the left edge by using units of measure other than inches.*

WordPerfect assumes that you will indicate the position of the line numbers from the left edge of the page in inches. Thus, if you enter a position number as **.5**, WordPerfect assumes you mean 0.5 inches. However, you can also use three other units of measure: centimeters, points, or version 4.2 units. Type in the position setting followed by a letter that represents the unit of measure you desire. To position the numbers two centimeters from the left edge of the page, for example, type **2c**. To position numbers 24 points from the left edge, type **24p**. To position numbers at horizontal position 5 (the unit of measure used in WordPerfect version 4.2), type **5h**. WordPerfect converts your entry into inches.

If you wish, you can also request that WordPerfect assume a unit of measure other than inches. You can change the unit of measure on the Setup menu (as described in Appendix B).

Tip: *(When upgrading from 4.2.) You can now specify a starting number with the Line Numbering feature.*

The Line Numbering feature is now accessed via the FORMAT (SHIFT + F8) key, and is housed on the Line Format menu. An enhancement has been added so that you can specify a starting number if you want WordPerfect to begin numbering with a number other than 1; in version 4.2, WordPerfect always started at number 1.

Automatic Number Referencing

When producing a large document such as a book or a report, it is common to include references to other pages or to footnotes or figures. For instance, one sentence of referring text might read, "Refer to footnote number 6." Another might read, "See page 24 for a detailed discussion of projected income." But, what if you edit your document so that footnotes are renumbered, or the description of projected income is found on page 27 rather than page 24? If you use the Automatic Reference feature, your referring text can be updated automatically.

To create an automatic reference, you must tie the referring text to the text being referred to, called the *target.* You do this by inserting a reference code, with a *target name,* in the referring text wherever the target is mentioned. You also insert a target code, with the *same* target name, in the text being referred to. For example, the reference code would be inserted in place of the number "24" in the sentence, "See page 24 for a detailed discussion of projected income." The target code would be inserted wherever the discussion on projected income begins, because the discussion of projected income is the target. Both could be marked with the target name "income," to link them together permanently.

You can place a reference code in regular text, in a header, a footer, a footnote, an endnote, a graphics box caption, or in a graphics text box. A target code can be inserted within regular text on a page, next to a paragraph or outline number (described earlier in this chapter), in a footnote, in an endnote, or in a graphics box caption.

When the referring text and the target are both present and in the same document, you insert the reference and target codes in the same operation, as follows:

1. Position the cursor within the referring text. For instance, type **See Page** and press the SPACEBAR. You can be typing regular text, or be in the middle of creating or editing a header, footer, footnote, endnote, graphics box caption, or graphics text box.
2. Press the MARK TEXT (ALT + F5) key to display the Mark Text menu:

   1 Auto Ref; 2 Subdoc; 3 Index; 4 ToA Short Form; 5 Define; **6** Generate: **0**

3. Select Auto Ref (1 or R). The menu shown in Figure 21-10 is displayed.

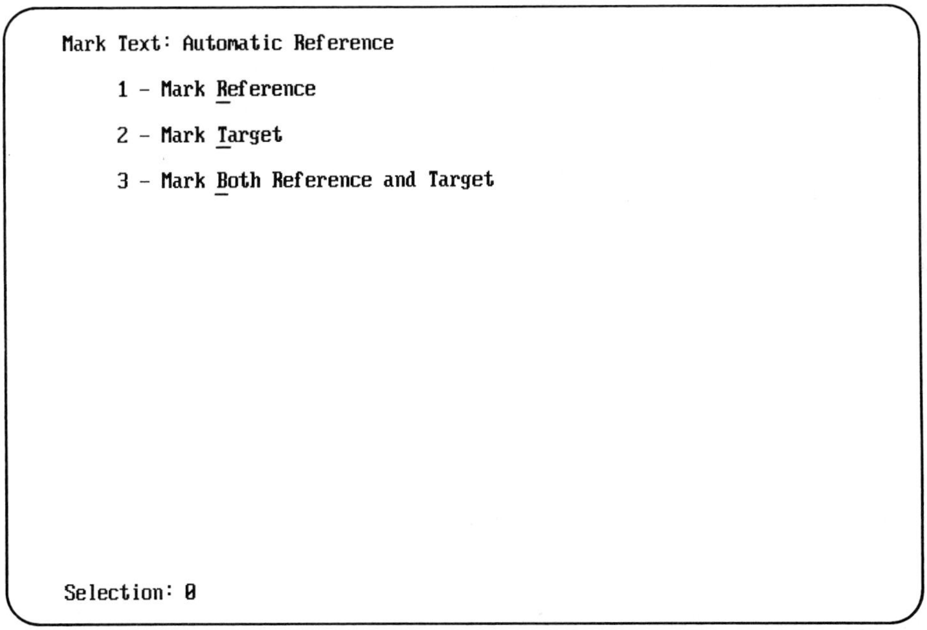

Mark Text: Automatic Reference
1 - Mark Reference
2 - Mark Target
3 - Mark Both Reference and Target
Selection: 0

Figure 21-10. The Automatic Reference menu

```
Tie Reference to:

     1 - Page Number

     2 - Paragraph/Outline Number

     3 - Footnote Number

     4 - Endnote Number

     5 - Graphics Box Number

After selecting a reference type, go to the location of the item you want to
reference in your document and press Enter to mark it as the "target".





Selection: 0
```

Figure 21-11. *The Tie Reference menu*

4. Select Mark Both Reference and Target (3 or B). The menu shown in Figure 21-11 appears.

5. Select the location of the target. For example, select Page Number (1 or P), if the target is a page number. Or select Footnote Number (3 or F), if the target is a footnote. Or select Graphics Box Number (5 or G), if the target is a graphics box number. (If you are referring to a graphics box number, then you will also be prompted to indicate the style of graphics box you wish to target — such as a figure, a table, and so on).

   Now WordPerfect prompts you to go to the target location. For example, if you selected a page number, the prompt reads

   Press Enter to select page.

   Or, if you selected a footnote, the prompt reads

   Press Enter to select footnote.

6. Move the cursor just past the target location and press ENTER. For example, if the target is a page number, position the cursor on that page where the discussion to which you are referring is located, just past the begin-

ning text of the discussion, and press ENTER. Or, if the target is a footnote, use the FOOTNOTE (CTRL + F7) key to view the Typing screen for the target footnote (see Chapter 23), position the cursor just after the footnote number, and press ENTER. Or, if the target is a figure-style graphics box, then use the GRAPHICS (ALT + F9) key to view the Caption Typing screen for the target figure (see Chapter 18), position the cursor just after the caption, and press ENTER.

WordPerfect prompts, asking for a target name (and suggesting a previous name if you have already inserted a reference code in your text).

Target Name:

7. Enter a target name, which links the referring text and target together. For example, type **income** and press ENTER if tying a page number to a discussion on projected income.
8. Finish typing the phrase begun in step 1, if necessary. For example, type **for a detailed discussion of projected income.**

WordPerfect inserts a reference code in the text wherever your cursor was located when you pressed the MARK TEXT key in step 2, above. The reference code indicates the target name in parentheses, as well as the target to which it refers. For instance, the reference code for targeting a page number, where the target name is INCOME and the target is located on page 24, would be **[Ref**(INCOME)**:Pg** 24]. The code is not visible on the Typing screen; instead, you see the reference number, such as "24." As another example, the reference code for targeting a footnote, where the target name is JONES and assuming that the target is currently footnote number 1, would be **[Ref**(JONES)**:Ftn** 1]. The reference code for targeting an endnote would be **[Ref**(JONES)**:End** 1].

WordPerfect also inserted a target code whenever you pressed ENTER in step 6, above. The target code also indicates the target name in parentheses. For example, the target code may read **[Target**(INCOME)] or **[Target**(JONES)].

If you later edit your document, the location of the text being referred to may change. The discussion of income projections may now be on page 27, for example, rather than page 24. In order to update all the references in your document, you must direct WordPerfect to regenerate the automatic references. Do so before you print out your document, as follows:

1. The cursor can be positioned anywhere in your document.
2. Press the MARK TEXT (ALT + F5) key to display the Mark Text menu.
3. Select Generate (6 or G). The Generate Mark Text menu appears, as shown in Figure 21-12.

```
Mark Text: Generate

     1 - Remove Redline Markings and Strikeout Text from Document

     2 - Compare Screen and Disk Documents and Add Redline and Strikeout

     3 - Expand Master Document

     4 - Condense Master Document

     5 - Generate Tables, Indexes, Automatic References, etc.

Selection: 0
```

Figure 21-12. The Generate Mark Text menu

4. Select Generate Tables, Indexes, Automatic References, etc. (5 or G). WordPerfect prompts for verification that you wish to continue.
5. Type **Y** to begin generating (updating) the references (at the same time, lists, tables, and indexes will also be generated, as described in Chapter 22). A counter at the bottom of the screen indicates WordPerfect's progress in generating the references.

   Or type **N** to abort the command and return to your document.

Trap: *Don't mark both the target and the reference if you're placing a reference in a graphics box caption.*

Chapter 18 describes how you can create a graphics box caption to accompany a graphics box. If you are creating such a caption and wish to insert a reference code, mark the reference separately. Later, mark the target. WordPerfect will not allow you to mark both the referring text and the target in the same operation if the *reference* code is placed on the Caption Typing screen. (The reverse is not true, however; if the *target* code is being inserted in a graphics box caption, then both the reference and target codes can be marked in the same operation.) See the following Tip for the procedure to mark referring text and targets in separate operations.

Tip: *References can be marked separately from targets.*

You can mark referring text even if the target has not yet been typed into your text. For example, you may be typing the introduction to a report, and wish to refer to a discussion farther on in the report that you haven't yet written. In this case, to insert a reference code:

1. Position the cursor in the phrase where you want to create the reference. For instance, move the cursor to the space after "See page" in the regular text; in a header, footer, footnote, or endnote; in a graphics box caption; or in a graphics text box. (Remember that a reference code can be inserted in any of these locations.)
2. Press the MARK TEXT (ALT + F5) key. WordPerfect displays the Mark Text menu.
3. Select Auto Ref (1 or R). The menu shown in Figure 21-10 is displayed.
4. Select Mark Reference (1 or R). A menu appears, with the same options as those shown in Figure 21-11.
5. Select the location of the target.
6. Enter a target name, which will link the reference and target together.
7. Finish typing the phrase, if necessary. For example, type **for a detailed discussion of projected income.**

WordPerfect inserts a reference code in the referring text which indicates the target name in parentheses, and it inserts a question mark to represent the target to which it refers. For example, the reference code for targeting a page number where the target name is SMITH may be [**Ref**(SMITH):**Pg** ?]. On the Typing screen, only a question mark is shown, so that you may view a phrase such as

"Refer to page ? for more information on Mr. Smith's account."

Later, when you type the rest of the report, you will insert the corresponding target code, as follows:

1. Move the cursor just past the target location. For example, if the target is a page number, position the cursor on that page where the discussion to which you are referring is located, just past the beginning text of the discussion. Or, if the target is a footnote, display the Footnote Typing screen for that footnote and position the cursor just past the footnote number. (Remember that the target can be a page number, a paragraph or outline number, a footnote, an endnote, or a graphics box caption.)
2. Press the MARK TEXT (ALT + F5) key. WordPerfect displays the Mark Text menu.
3. Select Auto Ref (1 or R). The menu shown in Figure 21-10 is displayed.
4. Select Mark Target (2 or T).
5. Enter a target name that will link the reference and target together (such as SMITH). (And, if you're on a special typing screen such as the Footnote Typing screen, press EXIT (F7) to return to your document.)

WordPerfect inserts a target code in the text which indicates the target name in parentheses, such as **[Target**(SMITH)**]**.

You must then remember to generate references, so that the question mark in the reference code is replaced by the proper reference number.

Tip: *Multiple references can be created for a single target.*

There may be instances when you wish to refer to the same target several times in a document. Because you can mark referring text and targets separately (as described in the preceding Tip), you can have many references linked to just one target code. For example, perhaps there are three places in a document where you say "Refer to the chart on page 6." If this is the case, then you would insert three separate reference codes in your document, all referring to the chart. Next, you would insert just one target code, which you would insert on the same page as the chart. All four of these codes—three reference codes and one target code—would use the *same* target name. Then if you edited the text so that the chart moved from page 6 to page 8, all the references to that chart would update once you regenerated.

Even if the references are of different types, they can still refer to the same target. For instance, a sentence might read, "A summary of the results is found on page 16, footnote 9." There are two references in this sentence, but they are different types of references—one to a page number where a footnote is located, another to a footnote number. Yet you can still use the same target code, even though the references are different. You would insert two different reference codes in the sentence, one referencing a page number and another referencing a footnote number. Then you would insert a target code in footnote 9. All three codes would use the same target name.

Tip: *Multiple targets can be created for a single reference.*

There may be instances when you wish to refer to different targets in the same reference in a document. Because you can mark references and targets separately (as described in a preceding Tip), you can have many targets linked to just one reference code. For example, perhaps you wish to insert the reference "(See the discussion on company expansion plans, pages 12, 13, 20, 44.)". If this is the case, then you would insert just one reference code, after the word "pages." Next, insert four different target codes, on pages 12, 13, 20, and 44. All five codes—one reference code and four target codes—would use the *same* target name. When you generated references, the reference numbers in the sentence "(See the discussion on page . . .)" would be separated by a comma and one space.

Trap: *Be sure to edit the target name when creating a new target or reference, or you'll have a mismatch.*

When marking a reference or a target, WordPerfect always suggests the target name that you last indicated. Be sure you change the target name that WordPerfect suggests if you are creating a new reference/target pair.

Tip: *Automatic referencing is convenient in connection with the Master Document feature.*

Chapter 12 describes the Master Document feature, whereby you can connect smaller files together into a comprehensive document. Automatic referencing operates properly when you've created a master document, whether the reference and target codes are in the master document or in one of the master file's subdocuments. When you generate references, the reference numbers are updated correctly.

Trap: *If you edit your text and forget to generate references, your printed document will be incorrect.*

If you edit your document, don't forget to generate references by using option 6, Generate, on the Mark Text menu; otherwise, WordPerfect won't update the references, and some of your references may be inaccurate. In fact, if you attempt to print when there's a reference or target code in your text, WordPerfect reminds you that you should consider whether or not a new generation is required, displaying this prompt:

Document may need to be generated. Print? (Y/N) No

Type **Y** if you recently generated automatic references and have not edited the text since then. Or, type **N** or press ENTER to cancel the print command so that you have the chance to generate your document.

Trap: *You could find a question mark instead of a reference number, even after you generate.*

Each reference code must have a corresponding target code in the text, with the same target name. For example, if you insert the reference code [**Ref**(INCOME):**Pg** ?], then the target code [**Target**(INCOME)] must also be in the text. When you mark the reference and target in the same operation, WordPerfect inserts the same target name in both codes.

However, if you mark the reference and target separately, then you must remember to insert the *same target name,* spelled the same way. The reference code contains a question mark until you generate. If, after you generate references, the reference code still contains a question mark, then the problem is most likely that the target name in the reference code doesn't match the target name in the corresponding target code (or that you forgot to insert a corresponding target code in the text). Check to make sure that a target code with the same target name exists, and that you spelled the target name the same in both codes.

Tip: *Generate endnotes when you are referencing an endnote's page number.*

As previously described, you can place a target code inside an endnote. The reference code in the text to which it corresponds can cite the endnote number, as in "Refer to endnote number 3 for details," and/or the page number where it is located, as in "Refer to endnote number 3 on page 14." As described in the preceding Tip, you would insert two reference codes into the sentence and one target code into the endnote text. If the reference is to a page number, be sure to generate the endnotes so that the page number can appear in the reference (see Chapter 23 for the procedure to generate endnotes). Generating endnotes is accomplished the same way as generating automatic references.

Also, if you insert a target code next to an endnote number in your text rather than in the endnote itself, then any reference to the endnote's page number will reference where the endnote *number* appears in the text, not where the actual endnote text is printed.

Tip: *(When upgrading from 4.2.) Automatic referencing is a new feature in version 5.*

Automatic referencing is a brand new feature in version 5, and a welcome one if you frequently create long reports and often refer to various pages, figures, paragraph numbers, footnotes, endnotes, or graphics boxes.

Tips and Traps Summary

Paragraph Numbering

Tip: Sometimes you must rewrite the screen before paragraph levels are renumbered.

Tip: You can change the level of the paragraph number after you type the paragraph.

Trap: Don't type some paragraph numbers on your own, while having WordPerfect insert others.

Tip: You can assign a specific numbering level to any tab stop location.

Tip: You can align paragraph numbers on the decimal point.

Tip: Numbered paragraphs are useful in paragraph libraries.

Tip: Create a style or a macro to insert paragraph numbers.

Trap: The Search and Replace features cannot find a specific paragraph number.

Tip: You can define a different numbering style or restart the numbering scheme.

Tip: (When upgrading from 4.2.) The procedure for inserting individual paragraph numbers is housed on a different function key.

Outline Numbering

Tip: Sometimes you must rewrite the screen before outline levels are renumbered.

Trap: Don't forget to exit Outline mode when you've finished typing an outline.

Tip: You can change the level of an outline number after you've typed it.

Tips and Traps Summary (*continued*)

Tip: You can use the paragraph numbering method in an outline when you're not in Outline mode.

Tip: You can define a different numbering style for your outline or create two or more outlines in one document.

Tip: (When upgrading from 4.2.) The procedure to switch into Outline mode is housed on a different function key.

Changing the Paragraph or Outline Numbering Style

Tip: You can insert a paragraph numbering definition code before or after numbering your text.

Tip: Insert a new paragraph numbering definition code for each outline or set of numbered paragraphs.

Tip: A numbering style can include any special characters that your printer can print.

Trap: A user-defined style is restricted.

Tip: Place a paragraph number definition code on the Document Initial Codes screen to reduce the clutter at the top of a document.

Tip: Change the paragraph numbering definition permanently on the Setup menu.

Tip: (When upgrading from 4.2.) The ability to change the paragraph numbering style has been enhanced.

Line Numbering

Trap: Line numbering does not appear on the Typing screen.

Trap: Not all printers support line numbering.

Tips and Traps Summary (*continued*)

Trap: Line numbering is dependent on the line spacing that you establish in your document.

Tip: You can choose to have one spacing setting for line numbering and another for text.

Tip: Draw a vertical line to separate the line numbers from the body of the text.

Tip: Line numbering can be useful whenever you wish to count lines.

Trap: Don't position the line numbers beyond the left margin.

Tip: You may set the position of line numbers from the left edge by using units of measure other than inches.

Tip: (When upgrading from 4.2.) You can now specify a starting number with the Line Numbering feature.

Automatic Number Referencing

Trap: Don't mark both the target and the reference if you're placing a reference in a graphics box caption.

Tip: References can be marked separately from targets.

Tip: Multiple references can be created for a single target.

Tip: Multiple targets can be created for a single reference.

Trap: Be sure to edit the target name when creating a new target or reference, or you'll have a mismatch.

Tip: Automatic referencing is convenient in connection with the Master Document feature.

Trap: If you edit your text and forget to generate references, your printed document will be incorrect.

Trap: You could find a question mark instead of a reference number, even after you generate.

Tips and Traps Summary (*continued*)

Tip: Generate endnotes when you are referencing an endnote's page number.

Tip: (When upgrading from 4.2.) Automatic referencing is a new feature in version 5.

22

Generating Lists, Indexes, Tables of Contents, and Tables of Authorities

Once you complete a report, dissertation, book, or other long document, you may wish to prepare reference aids for the reader. These aids can include a table of contents; lists of illustrations, maps, pictures, and graphics boxes; and/or an index of key words for easy reference. In addition, if you are preparing a legal document, you may wish to include a table of authorities listing various cases, statutes, and regulations cited in the text.

WordPerfect can drastically change the way you compile these reference aids. If you specify which words or phrases to include, WordPerfect does the work for you; it copies those phrases from the text into the list, index, or table, and inserts page number references. And once you create a list, index, or table, WordPerfect can update it after you make changes in your text.

This chapter explains the three steps you must follow to create a reference aid: (1) mark the phrases in your document that are to be included, (2) provide WordPerfect with a definition of how the reference aid should be generated, and (3) generate.

Marking Phrases for a List, Table, or Index

When you want WordPerfect to do the work of generating a reference aid, you must mark each phrase to be included. Before you begin marking phrases, it is good practice to visualize how you want that reference aid to appear once generated, so that you will know how to mark the phrases which will comprise it. WordPerfect provides certain parameters around which you must plan.

- **List** Figure 22-1 shows an example of a list that WordPerfect can generate for you. WordPerfect can create a maximum of nine separate lists per document. Each contains phrases from the body of the document, listed in the order in which they appear in the document. When you create a list, you must decide which phrases to include, and on which list they should be included. For example, if you are writing a report on Impressionism, perhaps you will provide lists of the illustrations by each artist that are included in the report. You might have one list of Renoir paintings, another of Monet paintings, another on Morisot, and so on.

  Notice that the list in Figure 22-1 contains page numbers flush against the right margin, indicating on which page each illustration can be found. You have other page numbering options, as well, for each list. You can have WordPerfect insert no page numbers, place page numbers next to each entry, place page numbers in parentheses next to each entry, or place page

RENOIR PAINTINGS	PAGE
The Swing	1
Camille Monet and Her Son	18
Dance at Bougival	21
Portrait of Madame Charpentier and Her Children	25

Figure 22-1. A list

numbers at the right margin with dot leaders that draw your eye from an entry to the page number. All five numbering styles are shown in Figure 22-2.

- **Index** Figure 22-3 shows an example of part of an index generated by WordPerfect. The purpose of an index is to provide references to the pages on which specific topics are discussed, and therefore, it can list multiple

---

No page numbers

The Swing
Camille Monet and Her Son
Dance at Bougival

Page numbers follow entries

The Swing 1
Camille Monet and Her Son 18
Dance at Bougival 21

Page numbers in parentheses follow entries

The Swing (1)
Camille Monet and Her Son (18)
Dance at Bougival (21)

Flush right page numbers

The Swing	1
Camille Monet and Her Son	18
Dance at Bougival	21

Flush right page numbers with leaders

The Swing 1
Camille Monet and Her Son 18
Dance at Bougival 21

Figure 22-2. Different numbering styles for a list, index, or table of contents

Paris 3, 7, 10
Post-Impressionism 16, 17
Renoir
    childhood years 4
    established painter 7, 8
    later years 11, 12
    marriages 6
    painting techniques 8, 9
Salon
    acceptance by 12, 15
    etiquette 4, 5, 7
    rules 13, 15, 19
Seurat
    childhood years 6
    established painter 3-5
    later years 6
Sisley 12, 14, 16
Sponsors 3, 19

Figure 22-3. An index

pages for one topic. You can also have a heading and a subheading entry. A heading—the main reference to a topic—appears at the first tab stop (which can be the left margin). A subheading is positioned at the next tab stop. Headings are alphabetized by WordPerfect, and subheadings are alphabetized under each heading.

Notice the organization of headings and subheadings in Figure 22-3. The subheadings under "Renoir" include "childhood years" and "established painter." A reader would look under the name Renoir to find the pages related to a particular aspect of his life. In planning an index, you must decide how to organize topics into headings and subheadings that are logical and useful to the reader.

For an index, you have the same five page-numbering options as you have for lists or for a table of contents (as shown in Figure 22-2). Notice in Figure 22-3 that the numbering style is that of page numbers following

Note: If you specify a level in wrapped format, only the first three numbering styles shown in Figure 22-2 are allowed for that level.

- **Table of authorities** Figure 22-6 shows an example of a table of authorities. You can divide a table into as many as 16 sections—one for cases, another for statutes, a third for treaties, and so on. Two sections are shown in Figure 22-6. A table of authorities is automatically sorted alphanumerically within each section when it is generated.

  You can select from two numbering styles in a table of authorities. In Figure 22-6, the numbering style places the numbers flush against the right margin, with dots leading the eye from an authority to the page number. You can also choose not to include dot leaders. Scattered page references for authorities are separated by a comma and a space (for example, 2, 4, 6). Inclusive page references (three or more consecutive pages) are separated by a hyphen (for example, 1-4).

<u>Cases</u> <u>Page(s)</u>

Austero v. National Gas Co. (1978) 84 Cal.App.3d 1 [148 Cal.Rptr. 653]..............5

C&H Foods Company v. Hartford Ins. Co. (1984) 163 Cal.App.3d 1055, 1066-67 [211 Cal.Rptr. 765] 1-4

Neal v. Farmers Insurance Exchange (1978) 21 Cal.3d 910 [148 Cal.Rptr. 389].... 2, 4, 6

Zurn Engineers v. Eagle Start Ins. Co. (1976) 61 Cal.App.3d 493 [132 Cal.Rptr. 206] 1, 2

<u>Statutes</u> <u>Page(s)</u>

Witkin, 4 Summary of California Law (Eighth Edition) Torts SS657-667, pages 2937-2948 2

Figure 22-6. A table of authorities

Once you've visualized your reference aid, you are ready to mark phrases so that WordPerfect knows what to include. You mark each phrase individually. To mark one phrase:

1. Position the cursor on the first character of the phrase (a word or group of words) that you want to include in the list, index, or table.
2. Use the BLOCK (ALT + F4) key to highlight the phrase.
3. With **Block on** flashing, press MARK TEXT (ALT + F5). WordPerfect responds

   Mark for: 1 To<u>C</u>; **2** <u>L</u>ist; **3** <u>I</u>ndex; **4** To<u>A</u>: **0**

4. Now select the number or mnemonic character corresponding to the reference aid you are marking the text for and follow WordPerfect's prompts, as follows:

   If you select *ToC* (1 or C)—where ToC is the abbreviation for Table of Contents—WordPerfect prompts

   ToC Level:

   Type in the level at which that phrase should appear. For example, if the phrase is a chapter subhead, then, to create a table with subheads at level 2, type **2**.

   The highlighting disappears. WordPerfect places a pair of codes around the phrase to mark it as a part of the table of contents, which indicates the phrase's level number. For example, if a phrase will be a level 2 entry, the codes surrounding the phrase will be **[Mark:ToC,2]** Phrase**[EndMark:ToC,2]**.

   If you select *List* (2 or L), WordPerfect prompts

   List Number:

   Type in the number of the list in which this phrase will appear. For example, if the phrase is the title of a Renoir painting, and Renoir paintings will make up list 1, type the number **1**.

   The highlighting disappears. WordPerfect places a pair of codes around the phrase to mark it as part of a specific list number, as in this example: **[Mark:List,1]**Phrase**[EndMark:List,1]**.

   If you select *Index* (3 or I) WordPerfect prompts with a suggestion for the highlighted phrase as an index heading. Suppose, for example, that the highlighted phrase is "Childhood years." Then the prompt reads

Index Heading: Childhood years

When the phrase suggested is to be a *heading,* press ENTER. WordPerfect provides a blank subheading prompt:

Subheading:

Press ENTER to indicate no subheading, or type in a subheading before pressing ENTER.

Or, when the phrase suggested is to be a *subheading,* type in a new heading (such as **Renoir**) and press ENTER. WordPerfect provides a prompt suggesting the highlighted phrase as a subheading, such as

Subheading: Childhood years

Press ENTER to accept the subheading, or type in a new subheading before pressing ENTER.

The highlighting disappears. WordPerfect embeds one code at the end of the phrase, which indicates the heading and subheading. For example, if the heading will be "Childhood years" with no subheading, then the code inserted is [**Index:**Childhood years]. As another example, if the heading is to be "Renoir," and the subheading is to be "Childhood years," then the code will be [**Index:**Renoir;Childhood years].

If you select *ToA* (4 or A)—where ToA is the abbreviation for Table of Authorities—WordPerfect prompts

ToA Section Number (Press Enter for Short Form only):.

The first time that an authority occurs in your text, you must mark the authority with what's called its *full form,* meaning that you are indicating to WordPerfect the full text of that citation. Thereafter, you can mark the same authority in *short form,* as a shortcut for marking the same, often lengthy citation over and over again.

When marking the full-form text, enter the correct section number. For example, if all cases will be in section 1 and the authority you are currently highlighting is a case, type **1** and press ENTER. WordPerfect provides the highlighted text on the Table of Authorities Editing screen; an example is shown in Figure 22-7. If the text is as you want it to appear in the table when it is generated, simply press EXIT (F7). Or, if you want to edit the text, use the standard editing keys. The text can be up to 30 lines long and can include enhancements such as underlining, boldface, or italic. After editing the text, press EXIT (F7). WordPerfect responds with the prompt:

Short Form:

followed by the first 40 characters of the highlighted text. If the citation appears only once in the text, you need not bother with a short form. Simply press ENTER. Or, if the citation appears more than once, edit WordPerfect's suggestion, creating a short-form name that will serve as a nickname to represent that citation. Press ENTER.

When marking the short-form text (meaning that a full form has previously been inserted in the text), simply press ENTER to bypass having to define the full text of the citation. WordPerfect responds with the prompt:

Short Form:

followed by up to the first 40 characters of the highlighted text. Edit WordPerfect's suggestion so that the short-form name is the same as the name you indicated when you marked the full-form text.

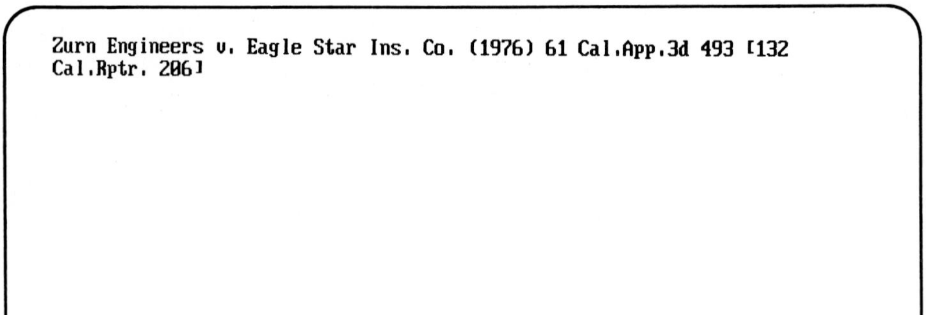

Zurn Engineers v. Eagle Star Ins. Co. (1976) 61 Cal.App.3d 493 [132
Cal.Rptr. 206]
Press Exit when done
Ln 1" Pos 1"

Figure 22-7. The Table of Authorities Editing screen showing the full form of a citation

The highlighting disappears. WordPerfect embeds one code at the beginning of the phrase. A code for a full form includes the section number in which it will be generated and the short-form name. For instance, if you marked a citation for a section 1 entry, and the short form is, "Zurn," then the full-form code inserted is **[ToA:1;**Zurn;**Full Form]**. A code for a short form indicates only what the short-form name is, such as **[ToA:**;Zurn;]. A short-form code and full-form code are linked together when they have the same short-form name.

If you mark a phrase to be included in a reference aid and then decide you do not want that reference, delete the code you inserted, as you would any WordPerfect code.

Trap: *Poor planning means an ineffective reference aid for the reader.*

You should design your reference aid to be as helpful as possible to the reader, and then mark your text using that design. For example, you must think about how a reader will look up topics before you plan an index. An index that listed "Childhood years" as a heading would make less sense to a reader than one that listed that topic as a subheading under a specific artist's name.

Tip: *Use a shortcut to mark text for an index or for the short form in a table of authorities.*

The code inserted when you mark text for an index or the short form in a table of authorities is a single code, and not a code pair. As a result, it is not necessary to use the BLOCK (ALT + F4) key before marking text for an index or a short form, which means that you can mark text for an index or a table of authorities very quickly.

To mark text for an index, position the cursor on any character in the word or the space just to the right. Then press MARK TEXT (ALT + F5). When Block is off, a different menu appears than with Block on:

1 Auto Ref; **2** Subdoc; **3** Index; **4** ToA Short Form; **5** Define; **6** Generate: **0**

Select Index (3 or I) for an index entry; WordPerfect prompts for a heading, suggesting the word just to the left of the cursor. Type the heading and subheading you desire and press ENTER. An index code is inserted.

To mark for a short form in a table of authorities, position the cursor on the first character of the citation and press MARK TEXT. Now select ToA Short Form (4 or A) for a table of authorities citation's short form; WordPerfect prompts for a short-form name, suggesting the last short-form name that you typed previously. Type in the short-form name and press ENTER. A table of authorities short-form code is inserted. (To mark for a full form in a table of authorities, however, you must use the BLOCK key, as outlined in the steps above.)

Trap: *The same occurrence of a phrase cannot be marked for more than one list.*

You cannot mark the same text for inclusion in more than one list. WordPerfect simply ignores the second instance you mark. (However, you *can* mark a phrase for *one* list and also for an index or table.) Of course, if a certain phrase is repeated elsewhere in the document, you can mark its first occurrence for list 1 and its second occurrence for list 2.

Tip: *There's no need to mark text in a graphics box caption for inclusion in a list.*

Chapter 18 describes the Graphics feature, whereby you can insert graphics boxes in your text. There are four possible box styles: figure, table, text, and user-defined. You can also choose to create box captions that will be inserted near each graphics image.

WordPerfect is set up so that when you insert graphics boxes with captions in your text, the captions will automatically be included in a list, should you decide to generate one. WordPerfect will generate a separate list for each box style without requiring that you mark each caption manually. The captions from any figure-style boxes in a document are included as part of list 6; table-style as part of list 7; text-style as part of list 8; and user-defined-style as part of list 9. Or course, you can mark other text to be included in list 6, 7, 8, or 9. But graphics box captions should not be marked by you; WordPerfect recognizes their existence without your input.

In other words, suppose that you want WordPerfect to generate up to four lists (numbers 6, 7, 8 and 9) in a document, and those lists contain only graphics box captions. In that case, you can ignore the step of marking phrases (as discussed in this section) and move directly to the step of inserting list definition codes (as described in the next section) for these four lists.

Tip: *You can include enhancement codes in the phrases you mark for a list or a table.*

When you block text to be marked for inclusion in a list or table, you can also include codes—for underlining, boldfacing, and so on—in the block. That way the phrase retains the enhancement when it appears in the generated list or table. For instance, if all your table of contents heads are boldface in the text, then if you include in the highlighted block the **[BOLD]** and **[bold]** codes that surround each heading, those headings will be boldfaced in the table of contents when it is generated.

You can also include paragraph number codes when marking a phrase. For example, if chapter heads and subheads are preceded by paragraph numbers, include those numbers in the highlighted block. That way your table of contents will be numbered as well.

However, don't include boldface and other types of codes in a highlighted block if you don't want those enhancements to appear in the reference aid when it is generated. (As you'll see in the following section of this chapter, the one enhancement you can specifically request to delete in a table of authorities is underlining. For any list or table, if you inadvertently include an enhancement code in the highlighted block, you can always rid the list or table of that enhancement later by using the Replace feature.)

One exception: you cannot include enhancement codes when marking for an index; the code inserted will not allow boldface or underlining. If you wish to enhance text in an index, you must do so after the index is generated.

Trap: *Watch out for uppercase and lowercase when marking phrases.*

A phrase appears in a list or table in whatever form it was in when marked in the text. When you mark a phrase for an index, however, WordPerfect suggests that the heading be capitalized, whether or not it was typed that way in the text. Accept WordPerfect's suggestion, or type in a phrase of your own, in which case you must supply your own capital letter. On the other hand, when WordPerfect suggests a subheading, the first letter is not automatically capitalized. If you want subheadings to be capitalized, you must edit WordPerfect's suggestion.

Tip: *You are not limited to phrases in the text when marking index entries or table of authorities entries.*

In a list or a table of contents, the pair of codes that mark the text surround a particular phrase. Therefore, each entry appears in the list or table in exactly the same way as it is phrased in the text.

This is not the case for an index or a table of authorities, however. With an index only one code is inserted, and the code itself contains the phrase to be used. You can therefore reword the phrase. And you can insert more than one index code in the same spot.

For example, suppose that in the text there's a sentence that relates to Renoir as an established painter, to his marriages, and to his sponsors. You can position the cursor within the sentence and create three index marks in a row: one with the heading "Renoir" and the subheading "established painter"; one with the heading "Renoir" and the subheading "marriages"; and one with the heading "Sponsors." All three will then be referenced to the same page. There is no limit to the number of index marks associated with a particular portion of text.

Similarly, with a table of authorities, you are provided the ability to edit the citation when entering the table's full-form code; you are not limited to the phrase actually found in the document.

Tip: *Keep a list of the short-form names of each citation in a table of authorities.*

It is easy to forget the short-form name of an authority. If you made editing changes and now have to mark another place where an authority is cited, you would need to reveal codes and find an existing code for the same authority in order to discover the short-form name assigned to that authority. Instead, consider keeping a list of short forms in the same or another document, or on a notepad at your desk, so you'll have them at your fingertips when needed.

Trap: *Make sure that the short-form names are unique for each citation in your document, or the table of authorities will be generated inaccurately.*

Be sure to mark the same citation with the same short-form name throughout your text. The first time a citation appears in the text it must be marked with a table of authorities full-form code. Each subsequent occurrence of that citation must be marked with a table of authorities short-form code, using the same short-form name. For example, for the case *Zurn Engineers v. Eagle Star Ins. Co.,* suppose that you establish the short form as "Zurn." Make sure that each subsequent marking of that case is a short-form code also using "Zurn" as the short-form name. The short-form name must be spelled exactly the same way each time it is cited; otherwise WordPerfect will be unable to link the full-form code and short-form codes when it generates. Use a short-form name that is easy to type and easy to remember.

Tip: *You can edit a citation to be included in a table of authorities.*

After marking a citation for a table of authorities, you may wish to alter the way you marked it. You may wish to change the full form or section number in which the citation should be included when generated. You can do so by editing the full-form code, as follows:

1. Position the cursor just to the right of the table of authorities full-form code for that citation.
2. Press MARK TEXT (ALT + F5). The following menu is displayed:

   1 Auto Ref; **2** Subdoc; **3** Index; **4** ToA Short Form; **5** Define; **6** Generate: **0**

3. Select Define (5 or D). The Define Mark Text menu appears, as shown in Figure 22-8.

```
Mark Text: Define

     1 - Define Table of Contents

     2 - Define List

     3 - Define Index

     4 - Define Table of Authorities

     5 - Edit Table of Authorities Full Form




Selection: 0
```

Figure 22-8. The Define Mark Text menu

4. Select Edit Table of Authorities Full Form (5 or E). The citation is displayed on screen for editing (as shown in Figure 22-7).
5. Edit the authority and then press EXIT (F7) to save the changes. WordPerfect prompts for a section number.
6. Type in the section number that this authority should be included in when the table of authorities is generated, and press ENTER. You are automatically returned to your document.

Tip: *You can indent all but the first line of a citation in a table of authorities.*

A common table of authorities format involves a hanging paragraph style for each authority in the table, with the first line starting at the left margin and all subsequent lines starting at the first tab stop. Here are two examples:

Neal v. Farmers Insurance Exchange (1978) 21 Cal.3d 910 [148 Cal.Rptr. 389] 2,4,6

Zurn Engineers v. Eagle Star Ins. Co. (1976) 61 Cal.App.3d 493 [132 Cal. Rptr. 206] 1,2

WordPerfect does not automatically indent all subsequent lines in an authority (see Figure 22-6), but you can create this effect when you edit the full form of an authority as it is displayed on screen for editing. Move the cursor where you want the first line of the authority to end and press ENTER. At the beginning of the second line, press →INDENT (F4). This procedure must be followed each time you edit the full form of an authority. Or, move the cursor to the first character of an authority and press →INDENT, and then ←MARGIN RELEASE (SHIFT + TAB). The first method is useful if you wish to control where the cursor wraps to the second line for each authority in the table; the second is easier if you will be editing the full form of the authority later, because word wrap is still in effect.

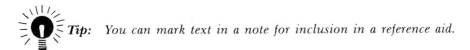

Tip: *You can mark text in a note for inclusion in a reference aid.*

If you wish a table of authorities or index to include a reference to a footnote or endnote, you can mark the phrase on the Footnote or Endnote Typing screen, just as you mark a phrase within the body of the text. (Chapter 23 discusses notes.)

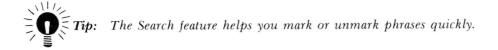

Tip: *The Search feature helps you mark or unmark phrases quickly.*

The Search feature can aid you in finding a phrase in a document so that it can be marked. This feature is especially useful for finding all references to a specific topic for an index, or all of the same citations in a legal document. For example, search for all occurrences of the word *"Renoir,"* and you'll be sure not to miss a reference to that name.

Similarly, the Search feature can aid you in finding those phrases that are already marked. Perhaps you wish to check all your list markings or all your index markings. Rather than reveal codes to find them, use the Search feature to move the cursor to each, one at a time, as follows.

1. Position the cursor at the top of the text.
2. Press →SEARCH (F2).
3. Press MARK TEXT (ALT + F5). WordPerfect responds

   1 ToC/List; **2** Endmark; **3** Index; **4** ToA; **5** Defs and Refs;
   6 Subdocs: **0**

4. To search for a list mark code or table of contents mark code (the two are not distinguishable), select ToC/List (1 or C or L). The search prompt reads

   →Srch: [Mark]

   To search for an index code, select Index (3 or I). The search prompt reads

   →Srch: [Index]

   To search for a table of authorities code, whether short form or full form, select ToA (4 or A). The search prompt reads

   →Srch: [ToA]

5. Press →SEARCH (F2). The cursor moves just to the right of the first mark specified.
6. Press →SEARCH (F2) again to initiate a move to the next mark code of the same type.

You can use the Extended Search feature to include footnotes and endnotes in the search. And you can use the ←SEARCH (SHIFT + F2) key to move backward rather than forward in the text (Chapter 4 describes the Search feature in detail).

However, also see the following Tips if you wish to mark the same phrase repeatedly for an index or a table of authorities.

Tip: *Create a style or a macro to mark phrases for you.*

Chapter 10 describes the Styles feature, which you can use to enhance various elements in your text. A style can also include codes to mark text for a reference aid. For example, design a style so that all your headings are underlined, boldfaced, and marked as level 1 entries for a table of contents. This streamlines the mark text process. (See Chapter 10 for more on the Styles feature.) As an alternative, you can create a macro to help in the marking process. For instance, define a macro to find and mark all short forms of a certain citation. (Chapter 27 discusses the Macro feature.)

Tip: *For an index, create a concordance file if the same phrases appear on multiple pages.*

Certain phrases might occur many times in a document, requiring a reference in the index for each occurrence. The Concordance feature frees you from having to mark each phrase individually.

You list common phrases in a *concordance file* which is a standard WordPerfect file with one phrase listed on each line. Then, when you generate the index, WordPerfect searches the document for phrases in the concordance file and includes the corresponding page numbers in the index. Creating a concordance file does not prevent you from also marking phrases individually in the text; WordPerfect will compile both into an index that is generated.

To create a concordance file, type each phrase on a separate line. Each phrase must be separated by a hard return code **[HRt]**. Whether you use uppercase or lowercase doesn't matter, but the phrase must be spelled exactly as found in the document. The concordance file may contain just a few words, listed as follows:

etiquette
paris
salon
sponsors

If you want all these phrases to be headings, then do nothing more. If you want some to be listed as subheadings when found in the document, then you must mark those phrases as such in the concordance file—just as you mark phrases in a document. For example, if you want "etiquette" to be a subheading of "Salon," then insert an index code just to the right of the word "etiquette." With codes revealed, the concordance file would then resemble the following:

etiquette**[Index:**Salon;etiquette**][HRt]**
paris**[HRt]**
salon**[HRt]**
sponsors**[HRt]**

Save this concordance file as you would any standard WordPerfect file. It will be accessed when you define the index's structure (as described in the next chapter section).

When creating a concordance file, keep three factors in mind. First, an index is generated faster if the concordance file phrases are in alphabetical order. Chapter 26 describes the Sort feature, which can alphabetize a concordance file for you.

Second, don't include in a concordance file those phrases that should sometimes be listed under one heading and sometimes under another. For example, the phrase "established painter" might apply to the heading "Renoir" when found on page 4, and "Monet" when found on page 10. Only you can judge the context of a phrase and mark it accordingly. Thus, use a concordance file only for phrases that will be marked the same way each time they occur in the text, with the same heading and subheading.

Third, WordPerfect may be unable to process all the words in the concordance file when an index is generated. This depends on the random access memory (RAM) available during generation. If all the words cannot be indexed, WordPerfect will prompt you. This is addressed further in the last section of this chapter, "Generating a List, Table of Contents, or Index."

Tip: *Reference aids can be marked in subdocuments, and then generated in a master document.*

Chapter 12 describes the Master Document feature, whereby you can connect smaller files together into a comprehensive document. The generation of reference aids operates properly when you've created a master document, regardless of whether the text is marked in the subdocuments, and the reference aid is generated in the master document. Therefore, if your book, report, or other document is a long one, mark phrases in individual documents. Then, be sure to use the Master Document feature to link these files together, and to generate your tables, lists, and/or indexes in the master document. In that way, you can, for example, store each chapter of your book in a separate subdocument and, at the same time, generate a comprehensive table of contents for all the chapters.

Trap: *Phrases are easily separated from mark codes when you edit your document.*

After you mark phrases for inclusion in a reference aid, do not forget about the mark codes surrounding them. If you later edit the text, reveal codes to check for these codes. For example, if you are moving a chapter subhead that has been marked for a table of contents to another location in your document, be sure to include the accompanying codes along with the subheading in the block before you move it. Otherwise, the **[Mark:ToC]** and/or **[End Mark:ToC]** codes could be separated from the subhead, and the table will be incorrect when it is generated.

Tip: *(When upgrading from 4.2.) The method for marking text has not changed, but new features can aid in the process.*

Mark text for inclusion in a reference aid as you did previously. But now, you can mark text for up to nine lists, rather than just five, as in version 4.2. And keep in mind that the Styles feature is available to make the job of marking text easier, especially for a table of contents; the Styles feature, new in version 5, is described in Chapter 10.

Also, a major enhancement is that you can now mark text in various subdocuments, and then generate your reference aids by using the Master Document feature, also new to version 5 and described in Chapter 12. Previously, a reference aid could be generated exclusively for one document, and, thus, if you separated a long document into separate files, you were forced to combine the separate files together manually before generating.

Defining a List, Table of Contents, or Index

After you mark phrases, you must tell WordPerfect where you want the table of contents, index, and each list to appear. In addition, you must indicate what the structure of the reference aids will be, and indicate a numbering style for each. To do this, you embed a definition code in the text.

You must insert a definition for each reference aid you wish to create. For example, to create one table of contents and three lists, you must provide WordPerfect with four separate definitions.

Define a list, index, table of contents, or table of authorities, as follows:

1. Position the cursor where you want the list, index, or table to be placed when generated. For example, you'll want the index to be located at the end of the document, so that's where you should position your cursor.

2. Press MARK TEXT (ALT + F5). The following menu appears

   1 Auto Ref; **2** Subdoc; **3** Index; **4** ToA Short Form; **5** Define;
   6 Generate: **0**

3. Select Define (5 or D). The Define Mark Text menu appears, as shown in Figure 22-8.

4. Select the number or mnemonic character corresponding to the reference aid you wish to define. Then, follow WordPerfect's prompts:

   If you select *Define Table of Contents* (1 or C), the menu shown in Figure 22-9 is displayed. There are three items to define:

   - Select Number of Levels (1 or N) and enter the number of levels in your table. For instance, if you marked heads for level 1 entries and subheads for level 2 entries, but did not mark any text for levels 3, 4, or 5, then enter the number **2**.
   - Select Display Last Level in Wrapped Format (2 or D) and type **N** to create a table as shown in Figure 22-4 or **Y** to create a table as shown in Figure 22-5.
   - Select Page Number Position (3 or P). WordPerfect displays a menu listing the five numbering style options. For each level to be included in your table, select from among the five page numbering options; these different numbering styles are illustrated in Figure 22-2. (For a level specified in wrapped format, only the first three styles are possible.) Press the DOWN ARROW key after defining the numbering style for each level.

   Press EXIT (F7) twice to return to your document. WordPerfect inserts a definition mark code in the text indicating the number of levels you want in the table and the numbering style for each. For example, for a table with three levels, all defined for a numbering style without page numbers (which is option 1), the hidden code inserted is **[Def Mark:ToC,3:1,1,1]**.

   If you select *Define List* (2 or L), WordPerfect prompts

   List Number (1-9):

```
Table of Contents Definition

     1 - Number of Levels                    1

     2 - Display Last Level in               No
           Wrapped Format

     3 - Page Numbering - Level 1            Flush right with leader
                          Level 2
                          Level 3
                          Level 4
                          Level 5





Selection: 0
```

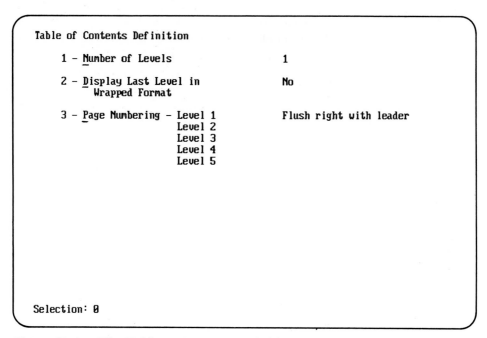

Figure 22-9. The Table of Contents Definition menu

Type in the number of the list that you are defining. WordPerfect then provides a menu of the five numbering style options, which are illustrated in Figure 22-2. Type in a number corresponding to the numbering style you desire. You are automatically returned to your document.

WordPerfect places a definition mark code in the text that indicates the list that you defined and the numbering style that you selected. For example, the definition code for list 1, where the numbering style will be flush right page numbers (which is option 4), is as follows: **[Def Mark:List,1:4]**

If you select *Define Index* (3 or I), WordPerfect prompts

Concordance Filename (Enter=none):

If you have not created a concordance file (as described in the previous section of this chapter, "Marking Phrases for a List, Table, or Index"), then press ENTER. Or type in the name of the concordance file and press ENTER.

WordPerfect then provides a menu of the five numbering style options, which are illustrated in Figure 22-2. Type in a number corresponding to the numbering style you desire. You are automatically returned to your document.

WordPerfect places a definition mark code in the text that indicates the numbering style for the index and the name of the concordance file (if any). For example, suppose that you decided on page numbers following entries (which is option 2), and that your concordance file is named CONCORD.RPT. Then the code inserted is **[Def Mark:Index,2:CONCORD.RPT]**.

If you select *Define Table of Authorities* (4 or A), WordPerfect prompts

Section Number (1-16):

Type in the number of the section you are defining and press ENTER. WordPerfect displays the Definition for Table of Authorities menu, as shown in Figure 22-10. (The section that you are defining is indicated at the top of the screen; it is section "1" in Figure 22-10). There are three options to define.

- Whether or not you want dot leaders preceding the numbers that will be aligned at the right margin in the table. Type **Y** or **N**. The default setting is "Yes" (an example is shown in Figure 22-6).
- Whether or not you want underlining allowed in the table of authorities when generated. Type **Y** or **N**. The default setting is "No."
- Whether or not you want blank lines inserted between each authority when the table is generated. Type **Y** or **N**. The default setting is "Yes."

Press ENTER or EXIT (F7) and you are returned to your document. WordPerfect places a definition mark code in the text that indicates which section number you have just defined. For example, the definition code for section 1 is **[Def Mark:ToA,1]**.

Tip: *Insert a definition mark code for each list and each section for a table of authorities.*

```
Definition for Table of Authorities 1

     1 - Dot Leaders                          Yes

     2 - Underlining Allowed                  No

     3 - Blank Line Between Authorities       Yes
```

Figure 22-10. The Definition for Table of Authorities menu

You must insert a separate definition mark code for each list you wish to create. For example, if you marked text for three separate lists, then be sure to insert three separate list definition codes in your text. And, make sure that you insert definition codes for lists 6, 7, 8, and 9 if you wish to have WordPerfect generate lists of graphics box captions for figure, table, text, and user-defined box styles, respectively (as discussed in the previous section). You also must insert a separate definition mark code for each section of a table of authorities.

Tip: *You can set up the page where a list, table, or index will be generated.*

The point at which you insert a definition mark code is the point at which a reference aid will be generated. Therefore, you can prepare that location. For example, precede and follow a definition mark code with a hard page code **[HPg]** so that the list, table, or index prints on its own page.

In addition, you can type in a title above the point where a definition code mark will be placed (but place the title after the first **[HPg]** code). For example, above the table of contents definition code, center "Table of Contents." Or set up a page for three sections of a table of authorities, as follows:

[HPg]

Table of Authorities

Cases

[Def Mark:ToA,1]

Statutes

[Def Mark:ToA,2]

Treaties

[Def Mark:ToA,3]

[HPg]

Of course, you can also insert headings and page breaks after the reference aids are generated.

Trap: *Index marks are recognized only if they precede the index definition mark code.*

When WordPerfect generates an index, it looks backward in the text for marked phrases. Any marked phrases subsequent to the definition mark code are excluded. Therefore, place the cursor at the *end* of the document before inserting an index definition code.

Trap: *You must safeguard against incorrect numbering for a table of authorities.*

The definition code for a table of authorities can be located anywhere in the text.

But you must be careful to place the table where it won't disrupt the correct referencing of pages. For example, if you place the table of authorities definition code on page 1 followed by a page break, and then the rest of the document, when WordPerfect creates the table, all references to page 1 of text will be listed as if on page 2.

When you want the table generated on page 1, to ensure correct page numbering you must press the FORMAT (SHIFT + F8) key to insert a **[Pg Num]** code to renumber page 2—the first page of actual text—as page 1. Also, the page where the table of authorities will be generated can be renumbered as page i (the procedure for renumbering pages is described in Chapter 9).

WordPerfect reminds you about this potential page numbering error. During generation, when it finds no **[Pg Num]** code between the **[Def Mark:ToA]** code and the first citation marked for inclusion in the table of authorities, the program prompts with a warning message. Heed the prompt's warning if the table definition code is at the beginning of the file. Insert a **[Pg Num]** code and then regenerate the table to ensure proper page number references in your table. (Generating is discussed in the next chapter section.)

Alternatively, simply decide that you'll position the table of authorities definition code at the end of the text, in which case there's no need to renumber the document.

Trap: *You must safeguard against incorrect numbering for a table of contents or for lists.*

As with a table of authorities, a definition code for a table of contents or a list can, technically, be positioned anywhere in the text. And, just as for a table of authorities, this can create incorrect numbering. Suppose, for example, that you place the table of contents definition code on page 1, with a page break following. The text begins on page 2. When WordPerfect generates the table, the first page of actual text will be considered as page 2. The numbering will be incorrect, because the first page of text should be page 1.

There are two solutions. The first is to use the FORMAT (SHIFT + F8) key to renumber pages (as described in Chapter 9). For instance, the page on which the table of contents will appear can be numbered as page i, and the first page of text as page 1. (If you are generating many reference aids at the beginning of a document, such as a table of contents, and various lists, then all of them can be numbered with Roman numerals, and the text can be numbered with Arabic numbers;

you will thus have two separate numbered sections in your text.) Another solution is to place definition codes at the end of the text, so as not to create incorrect reference numbers.

Note: WordPerfect does not warn you of a potential numbering error, as it does for a table of authorities, if no **[Pg Num]** code is found in the text when a table of contents or list is generated.

Tip: *Use the Setup menu to change the defaults for a table of authorities definition.*

If you find yourself continually altering WordPerfect's suggestions for how the table of authorities is defined (the defaults are shown in Figure 22-10), you can change the defaults permanently. Refer to Appendix B, which tells how to do this by using the Setup menu.

Tip: *(When upgrading from 4.2.) The procedure for defining a reference aid is basically the same.*

You insert a definition code for a reference aid as you did in version 4.2, although the prompts are slightly different. The code that you insert indicates the numbering style that you selected; in version 4.2, you could not ascertain the numbering style by revealing codes.

Generating a List, Table of Contents, or Index

There is a fair amount of preliminary work involved in the creation of a list, a table, or an index. But once you are at the generation stage, just press a few keys and sit back and watch WordPerfect do the compilation for you. It will create a reference aid for every definition code you have embedded in the text.

The cursor can be positioned anywhere in the text when you are ready to generate reference aids:

1. Press MARK TEXT (ALT + F5) to display the Mark Text menu:

    1 Auto Ref; **2** Subdoc; **3** Index; **4** ToA Short Form; **5** Define; **6** Generate: **0**

2. Select Generate (6 or G). The menu shown in Figure 22-11 appears.
3. Select Generate Tables, Indexes, Automatic References, etc. (5 or G). WordPerfect warns that existing tables, indexes, and lists will be replaced if you generate a new one, and prompts you for verification that you wish to continue.
4. Type **N** to abort. You are returned to the text; no new reference aids are generated.

    Or type **Y** to continue. WordPerfect erases any reference aids previously generated—but not the definition code. It begins to generate all new reference aids, and the following message appears:

    Generation in progress: Pass 1; Page 1

```
Mark Text: Generate

     1 - Remove Redline Markings and Strikeout Text from Document

     2 - Compare Screen and Disk Documents and Add Redline and Strikeout

     3 - Expand Master Document

     4 - Condense Master Document

     5 - Generate Tables, Indexes, Automatic References, etc.
```

Figure 22-11. The Generate Mark Text menu

The counter increases until the process is complete. The reference aids are generated, and WordPerfect places an end definition code **[End Def]** at the end of each reference aid it creates.

Once reference aids are generated, you can edit them as you would edit text in WordPerfect. For instance, you may wish to underline certain table of contents entries. Or you may wish to insert headings and extra blank spaces between sections in the table of authorities just generated. Or you may wish to format an index into columns by using the Text Column feature.

Tip: *How reference aids are indented depends on your tab stop locations.*

WordPerfect generates a reference aid based on the tab stops that you set. For example, the left margin is where WordPerfect places lists, index headings, and table of contents level 1 entries. The first tab stop is where WordPerfect places index subheadings and table of contents level 2 entries. The second tab stop is where WordPerfect places table of contents level 3 entries. Therefore, make sure you have tabs set in appropriate locations before you generate.

Trap: *Don't forget to regenerate all reference aids if you later edit text in the document.*

After you generate reference aids, you may edit your text, perhaps inserting text that causes the page numbers to change, or marking new phrases for inclusion in a list, index, or table, or deleting certain mark codes. Be sure to regenerate after editing your document, because a reference aid does not update automatically when you make a change in the document. In fact, when you attempt to print when there's a definition code in your text, WordPerfect reminds you that you should consider whether or not a new generation is required, displaying the prompt:

Document may need to be generated. Print? (Y/N) No

Type **Y** if you recently generated tables, indexes, and so forth, and have not edited the text since then. Or, type **N** or press ENTER to cancel the print command so that you have the chance to generate your document.

It doesn't matter that other reference aids have not been changed. When WordPerfect regenerates, it erases the old reference aids and creates new ones—some identical to the previous version, others incorporating new marked phrases.

Tip: *You can change the basic structure of a reference aid after you have generated it.*

After you generate a reference aid, you may decide that you don't like the way the page numbers appear. In that case, you can insert a new **[Def Mark:]** code with a different page numbering style specified, and then regenerate. But you must remember to delete the old definition mark code before generating again. There is no need to also erase the text of the reference aid or the **[End Def]** code inserted by WordPerfect when you first generated; these are updated automatically when you regenerate.

Tip: *Delete both the begin and end definition codes to preserve a reference aid as you regenerate.*

Once you generate so that a **[Def Mark:]** code precedes and an **[End Def]** code follows a reference aid, the reference aid will be automatically regenerated by WordPerfect each time you select option 5, Generate Tables, Indexes, Automatic References, etc., from the Generate Mark Text menu. You can delete these two codes if you want the reference aid to be untouched the next time you select option 5.

Suppose, for example, that you generate a table of contents and an index. You then add certain enhancements to the table— such as boldfacing the heads and inserting extra blank lines between heads. Later, you mark additional entries for the index, and you wish to regenerate. However, you don't want to regenerate the table of contents, which does not need regeneration and which you already edited. The solution is to delete the **[Def Mark:]** and **[End Def]** codes that surround the table. When you generate, WordPerfect has no indication that there's a table of contents to be generated, and thus does not tamper with the table. Be sure, however, to delete *both* codes (see the following Trap for related information).

Trap: *WordPerfect won't generate if an end definition code is found in the text without an accompanying definition mark code.*

If you generate reference aids, and later edit your text to erase a **[Def Mark:]** code without inserting a new one, then you must also remember to erase the accompanying **[End Def]** mark that WordPerfect created; otherwise, the next time you attempt to generate, WordPerfect will prompt

ERROR: [End Def] code does not have matching [Def Mark:]

WordPerfect will not regenerate until you either erase the **[End Def]** code or insert a new **[Def Mark:]** code above.

Trap: *A concordance file may be so large that WordPerfect is unable to generate an index for you.*

The number of phrases that can be processed in a concordance file during the generation of an index depends on the RAM available in your computer. If you reach the memory limit during generation, WordPerfect responds

Not enough memory to use entire concordance file. Continue? (Y/N)

Type **Y** to build an index using only part of the phrases in the concordance file. Type **N** to stop generating an index. You may have to reduce the size of the concordance file. Make sure that when you generate, you have only one document in memory (that is, that the Doc 2 screen is clear). That leaves more RAM available for the generation process.

Tip: *WordPerfect warns you during generation if there is a potential page numbering problem with a table of authorities.*

When WordPerfect finds no **[Pg Num]** code between the **[Def Mark:ToA]** code and the first citation marked for inclusion in the table, then, during generation, the program prompts with a warning message. In this case, the page number references may not be accurate. As discussed in the previous section of this chapter, "Defining a List, Table of Contents, or Index," you may need to insert a **[Pg Num]** code and then regenerate the table to ensure proper page number references in your table. Or, if you decide to generate the table of authorities at the end of the text and thus have placed the definition code at the end of the text, then there's no need to renumber the document.

Trap: *An asterisk in the generated table of authorities means there's a problem with short forms.*

If you generate a table of authorities and one or two asterisks appear at the top of a section of the generated table, then either one short-form name is associated with two distinct authorities, or a short-form code has no full-form code preceding it.

As an example, suppose a full-form code in the text reads **[ToA:1;**Zurn;**Full Form]**, and that you made a typographical error when inserting the short-form code that is supposed to refer to that same citation, so that it reads **[ToA:;**Xurn;**]**. Notice here that the short-form names do not match — "Zurn" and "Xurn." Thus, during generation, when WordPerfect encounters the short-form code, it can find no full-form code with the short-form name "Xurn." Not having a citation for the short-form code, WordPerfect inserts asterisks in the table of authorities to warn you of the problem.

If asterisks appear in a generated table of authorities, reveal codes and check all full-form codes and their corresponding short-form codes to find out where the problem lies. Delete and insert new codes as necessary, and regenerate the table.

Tip: *(When upgrading from 4.2.) The procedure for generating a reference aid is basically the same.*

Although the precise keystrokes are different, the general procedure for generating reference aids is the same in version 5 as it was in version 4.2.

Tips and Traps Summary

Marking Phrases for a List, Table, or Index

Trap: Poor planning means an ineffective reference aid for the reader.

Tip: Use a shortcut to mark text for an index or for the short form in a table of authorities.

Trap: The same occurrence of a phrase cannot be marked for more than one list.

Tip: There's no need to mark text in a graphics caption box for inclusion in a list.

Tip: You can include enhancement codes in the phrases you mark for a list or a table.

Trap: Watch out for uppercase and lowercase when marking phrases.

Tip: You are not limited to phrases in the text when marking index entries or table of authorities entries.

Tip: Keep a list of the short-form names of each citation in a table of authorities.

Trap: Make sure that the short-form names are unique for each citation in your document, or the table of authorities will be generated inaccurately.

Tip: You can edit a citation to be included in a table of authorities.

Tip: You can indent all but the first line of a citation in a table of authorities.

Tip: You can mark text in a note for inclusion in a reference aid.

Tip: The Search feature helps you mark or unmark phrases quickly.

Tips and Traps Summary (*continued*)

Tip: Create a style or a macro to mark phrases for you.

Tip: For an index, create a concordance file if the same phrases appear on multiple pages.

Tip: Reference aids can be marked in subdocuments, and then generated in a master document.

Trap: Phrases are easily separated from mark codes when you edit your document.

Tip: (When upgrading from 4.2.) The method for marking text has not changed, but new features can aid in the process.

Defining a List, Table of Contents, or Index

Tip: Insert a definition mark code for each list and each section for a table of authorities.

Tip: You can set up the page where a list, table, or index will be generated.

Trap: Index marks are recognized only if they precede the index definition mark code.

Trap: You must safeguard against incorrect numbering for a table of authorities.

Trap: You must safeguard against incorrect numbering for a table of contents or for lists.

Tip: Use the Setup menu to change the defaults for a table of authorities definition.

Tip: (When upgrading from 4.2.) The procedure for defining a reference aid is basically the same.

Tips and Traps Summary (*continued*)

Generating a List, Table of Contents, or Index

Tip: How reference aids are indented depends on your tab stop locations.

Trap: Don't forget to regenerate all reference aids if you later edit text in the document.

Tip: You can change the basic structure of a reference aid after you have generated it.

Tip: Delete both the begin and end definition codes to preserve a reference aid as you regenerate.

Trap: WordPerfect won't generate if an end definition code is found in the text without an accompanying definition mark code.

Trap: A concordance file may be so large that WordPerfect is unable to generate an index for you.

Tip: WordPerfect warns you during generation if there is a potential page numbering problem with a table of authorities.

Trap: An asterisk in the generated table of authorities means there's a problem with short forms.

Tip: (When upgrading from 4.2.) The procedure for generating a reference aid is basically the same.

23

Inserting Footnotes and Endnotes

Footnotes and endnotes provide source citations, which contain various types of detailed information, for the reader. Footnotes are placed at the bottom of the pages to which they refer, whereas endnotes are located together, usually at the end of a document (although you can specify that endnotes appear in another location). You can have both footnotes and endnotes in one document. Each can contain thousands of lines—certainly no limit at all.

WordPerfect numbers footnotes and endnotes automatically in the body of the text. When you insert a new note (footnote or endnote) or delete an old one, note reference numbers are updated. This chapter describes the process, which is almost identical for footnotes and endnotes. You learn how to create and edit notes and then how to change the options for how footnotes and endnotes appear on the printed page.

Creating and Editing Notes

WordPerfect is set with defaults that determine how footnotes and endnotes appear in the printed text. Both are referenced numerically, and each separately, so that it is possible to have both footnotes and endnotes in one document. As a default, footnotes are positioned two lines below the text on a page, and are separated from it by a two-inch horizontal line. The first line of each footnote is indented, the footnote number is superscripted, and a blank line is inserted between each footnote. An example is shown in Figure 23-1. Endnotes are positioned at the end of the text (unless you specify otherwise, as is described shortly). Each endnote number is followed by a period, and a blank line is inserted between each endnote, as shown in Figure 23-2. For both endnotes and footnotes, note reference numbers in the body of their text are superscripted above the line when printed (provided that your printer supports superscripted characters; if not, note reference numbers appear within the line).

You can insert a note (footnote or endnote) either while you are typing a document or after you have finished. You insert the text of the note; WordPerfect numbers that note for you. To insert a note:

1. Position the cursor in the body of the text where you want the note reference number to appear.
2. Press FOOTNOTE (CTRL + F7). WordPerfect displays the Footnote menu:

   1 Footnote; **2** Endnote; **3** Endnote Placement: **0**

3. Select Footnote (1 or F). Or select Endnote (2 or E). If you chose to insert a footnote, then the Footnote menu appears

   Footnote: 1 Create; **2** Edit; **3** New Number; **4** Options: **0**

   The Endnote menu contains the same four items.

4. Select Create (1 or C) to insert a note. WordPerfect displays a Footnote or an Endnote Typing screen, which is blank except for a note number that appears in the upper left-hand corner of the screen and a prompt at the bottom, which reads

   Press **Exit** when done

   Your cursor is positioned just to the right of the note number.

And what truly happened to the former slaves? How did they adjust to their newfound freedom? According to Mr. Don Samuelson: "There was mass confusion. Even though Congress set up a Freedman's Bureau in March of 1865, exploitation of the freed slaves did not stop. In most cases, it became worse."[1]

Who oversaw the country during the turbulent years that followed? Andrew Johnson ascended to the presidency after the shocking assassination of Abraham Lincoln. But he was not to stabilize the country. The House voted for Johnson's impeachment on February 24, 1868.[2] Though he barely escaped conviction, he

[1]Don Samuelson, History of the United States—1492 to 1900. Panish-Clark Publishers, 1970, p. 321.

[1]Lois Hinderman, The Reconstruction Period in U.S. History. Bolling, Klyde and Marx Co., Inc., 1956, p. 51.

Figure 23-1. The lower portion of a printed page showing footnotes

1. Larry Fletcher, The War Between the States, Fifth Edition. New York: Huxter Book Co., Inc., 1982, page 57.

2. Alicia Smith-Hayes, Political Ways and Institutions. Parker Publishing, 1955, pages 3-6.

3. Tony Stephano, The U.S. in International Trade during the Eighteenth and Nineteenth Century. New York: Cleaver & Strauss Co., Inc., 1945, page 192.

4. David Kahn, Modern Concepts in Politics. Manners Publishing, 1980, pages 56-64.

Figure 23-2. A printed page containing endnotes

5. Press the SPACEBAR or the TAB or →INDENT key, depending on how you want the text of the note indented after the note number, and then type in the text.
6. Press EXIT (F7) to return to the Typing screen.

You are returned to your document. On the Typing screen, a note reference number is displayed at the current cursor position. When viewing the Reveal Codes screen, you can see a code embedded in the text that, if displayed on the Reveal Codes screen, shows up to the first 50 characters of the note's text. For example, the code for footnote number 2 might read

[Footnote:2;[Note Num]first 50 characters of footnote text...]

The full text of the notes appears on the printed page.

When you wish to review the entire text of a note (more than the first 50 characters), or if you wish to edit a note, follow these steps:

1. Position the cursor anywhere in the text.
2. Press FOOTNOTE (CTRL + F7).
3. Select either Footnote (1 or F) or Endnote (2 or E).
4. Select Edit (2 or E). WordPerfect responds, asking for the number of the note you wish to edit, for example

   Footnote Number?

   and suggests the number of the next note that follows the cursor position.
5. Press ENTER if the correct number is suggested, or type in the footnote or endnote number you wish to view, and press ENTER.
6. Edit the note. The standard editing keys work when you are viewing the Footnote or Endnote Typing screen, as do the BLOCK and MOVE keys.
7. Press EXIT (F7) to store the editing changes and return to the text of your document.

   The cursor is now located in the body of the text, to the right of the note you just edited.

When a page with footnotes is printed, WordPerfect attempts to keep the footnotes on the same page as their reference numbers in the text. If this is not possible for a long footnote, then by default the first half-inch of footnote text is kept together and the rest of the footnote is printed on the next page. Moreover, if not even 0.5 inch of the footnote will fit, both the footnote and the line containing the footnote number are positioned on the next page.

By default, endnotes are normally placed after the last page of the document, and thus are printed only when you print an entire document or the last page of one. However, you can insert endnotes anywhere in the text by using the Endnote Placement feature. To specify a location where endnotes should be printed:

1. Position the cursor where you wish endnotes to appear in the text when printed.
2. Press FOOTNOTE (CTRL + F7). WordPerfect displays the Footnote menu:

   1 Footnote; **2** Endnote; **3** Endnote Placement: **0**

3. Select Endnote placement (3 or P). WordPerfect prompts

   Restart endnote numbering? (Y/N) Yes

   WordPerfect is asking whether you wish to restart endnote numbering at 1 for all endnotes that *follow* the endnote placement code. The default is to restart numbering.

4. Type **Y** or restart numbering. Type **N** or press ENTER to continue with consecutive numbering.

WordPerfect inserts an **[Endnote Placement]** code in the text, followed by a **[HPg]** code, so that additional text starts at the top of the next page. And, if you elected to restart endnote numbering for endnotes below this code, then WordPerfect inserts a third code, **[New End Num:1]**. This means that the next endnote will have a new endnote number, which will be number 1.

On the Typing screen, WordPerfect displays a comment box wherever the **[Endnote Placement]** code is located; this comment is shown in Figure 23-3.

You are able to insert more than one endnote placement code in each document; for each code, WordPerfect generates endnotes for references that have been created above that code up to the previous endnote placement code in the text (or to the beginning of the document, if there is no previous code). For instance, if you place a first endnote placement code at the bottom of page 12 and a second at the end of the document, all endnotes from the beginning of the document through page 12 will be generated at the bottom of page 12; the remaining endnotes will be generated at the end of the document.

```
     Andrew Johnson ascended to the presidency after the shocking
assassination of Abraham Lincoln on April 14, 1865.  He continued
Lincoln's basic policies.1
     Then, in 1868, Ulysses S. Grant was elected president, during
a time when the country was in the midst of massive change and
reconstruction.2
     Hayes, the governor from Ohio, succeeded Grant as another
Republican president in 1876.  He was capable, yet unpopular during
his time in office.3

 Endnote Placement
 It is not known how much space endnotes will occupy here.
 Generate to determine.

================================================================================

                                                Doc 1 Pg 1 Ln 1" Pos 1"
```

Figure 23-3. An Endnote Placement comment

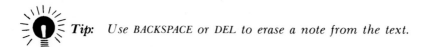

Tip: *Use BACKSPACE or DEL to erase a note from the text.*

Any time you wish to erase a note, simply position the cursor on the note reference number in the text and press DEL, or position the cursor just past the note number and press BACKSPACE. If you're working on the Typing screen, WordPerfect prompts you for confirmation that you want to erase the note. Type **Y** and the number and the text of the note are deleted. All notes that follow will be automatically renumbered.

Trap: *Sometimes you must rewrite the screen before notes are renumbered.*

If you erase or move a footnote or endnote number in the main text, the other footnote or endnote numbers may not update immediately. Press DOWN ARROW or another cursor movement key to scroll the cursor down past the number and it will be updated. Or press the SCREEN (CTRL + F3) key and select Rewrite (0 or R) to update the note numbers.

Trap: *The only way to exit from the Footnote or Endnote Typing screen is to press EXIT (F7).*

Once you choose to create or edit a note and WordPerfect displays the Footnote or Endnote Typing screen, the only way to exit is to press the EXIT key. The CANCEL (F1) key will not exit you from the screen. Therefore, if you entered the screen inadvertently, press EXIT and then BACKSPACE to erase the note created.

Tip: *Use the FOOTNOTE key to insert a note number erased accidentally from the Footnote or Endnote Typing screen.*

If you are typing or editing a note on the Footnote or Endnote Typing screen and inadvertently erase the note number, don't just type in a new number from the keyboard; WordPerfect will be unable to properly number the notes that follow. Instead, position the cursor before the text of the note and press FOOTNOTE (CTRL + F7). WordPerfect inserts a **[Note Num]** code, and the proper note number is inserted for you.

Tip: *Insert a hard page code to place endnotes on their own page.*

Endnotes located below the last endnote placement code in a document normally print after the last page of a document (if there are no endnote placement codes, then *all* endnotes are printed at the end). To place endnotes on a separate page, insert a hard page code **[HPg]** at the very end of the document. Then the endnotes will be printed on their own page. You can also insert a heading for the endnote page—for example, center the word "Endnotes" just below the **[HPg]** code that you insert.

Similarly, if you use the Endnote Placement feature to have endnotes printed within a document, precede the **[Endnote Placement]** code with a hard page code if you want the endnotes to be generated on their own page in the middle of a document.

Tip: *WordPerfect can determine how much vertical space endnotes will occupy.*

Once you've inserted endnote placement codes in the text, you can direct WordPerfect to calculate how much space the resulting endnotes will occupy on the printed page. To do so:

1. With the document on screen, press the MARK TEXT (ALT + F5) key.
2. Select Generate (6 or G).
3. Select Generate Tables, Indexes, Automatic References, etc. (5 or G).
4. Type **Y** to begin the generation.

WordPerfect replaces each Endnote Placement Comment box with a new Comment box, as shown in Figure 23-4. The status line now reflects the amount of space that will be taken up by endnotes on the printed page. Position the cursor just before the Endnote Placement Comment box and check the "Ln" indicator on the status line to see the position where the endnotes will begin printing. Then, press RIGHT ARROW to position the cursor just after the Comment box and check the "Ln" indicator to see the position where the endnotes will end printing. That way, you can tell how much vertical space the endnotes will occupy. For instance, notice that with the cursor positioned just after the Comment box in Figure 23-4, the status line shows that the endnotes will end 4.66 inches from the top of the printed page.

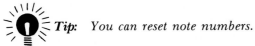

Tip: *You can reset note numbers.*

WordPerfect starts numbering footnotes and endnotes at number 1 for each document. But you can override that numbering system by inserting a code in the document where you want the new numbering to start.

Suppose, for example, that you split a 100-page document into two separate

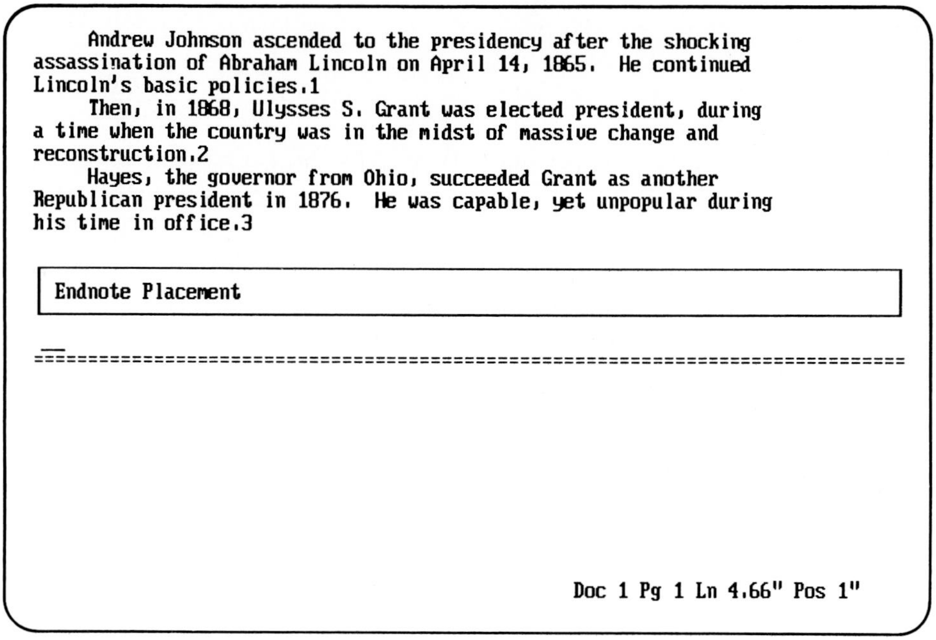

Andrew Johnson ascended to the presidency after the shocking
assassination of Abraham Lincoln on April 14, 1865. He continued
Lincoln's basic policies.1
Then, in 1868, Ulysses S. Grant was elected president, during
a time when the country was in the midst of massive change and
reconstruction.2
Hayes, the governor from Ohio, succeeded Grant as another
Republican president in 1876. He was capable, yet unpopular during
his time in office.3
Endnote Placement
Doc 1 Pg 1 Ln 4.66" Pos 1"

Figure 23-4. An Endnote Placement comment after generating

files and you want the footnotes and endnotes in the second file to begin numbering where the first file stopped. Move to where you want the next note renumbered. For example, to begin the note renumbering for the second file, position the cursor at the top of the first page of the second document. Then:

1. Press the FOOTNOTE (CTRL + F7) key.
2. Select Footnote (1 or F) or select Endnote (2 or E).
3. Select New Number (3 or N).
4. Enter the new number.

WordPerfect inserts a hidden code in the text. For instance, if you wish the next footnote to be numbered as 26, then the code **[New Ftn Num:26]** is inserted. All footnotes are now numbered consecutively, starting at number 26. (You may need to press DOWN ARROW to move through the text, or select Rewrite (0 or R) on the Screen menu, to have WordPerfect renumber for you.)

Tip: *It is possible to preview how footnotes or endnotes will appear on the printed page.*

While footnotes and endnotes are not displayed on the Typing screen, the View Document feature can show you your footnotes and endnotes and how they will be positioned in a document when printed. Simply press PRINT (SHIFT + F7), and choose View Document (6 or V). (This is only a preview, however; you cannot make editing changes on the View Document screen.)

After a few moments, the preview displays on the screen. Move through the document and you will be able to see footnotes at the bottom of a page or endnotes at the end of the document (or wherever you inserted an endnote placement code). To exit the View Document screen, press EXIT (F7). (See Chapter 14 for more on the View Document feature.)

Tip: *Footnotes reduce the number of lines of text on a page.*

When WordPerfect inserts an automatic soft page, it takes into account all lines of each footnote, a blank line separating the footnotes from the body of the text, and a blank line preceding the text of each footnote on a page. (It also takes into account all lines of a header and one line of a footer, as described in Chapter 9.) Therefore, if footnotes are present on a page, WordPerfect will start the next page earlier than you might expect.

For example, say that you created one footnote, which is five lines in length. The blank line between the footnote and the body of the page counts as one, and the footnote counts as five, so the soft page break will be inserted six lines earlier than if the page contained no footnote.

Tip: *You can alter the format of footnotes/endnotes in several ways.*

You learned in Chapter 8 that unless you specify otherwise, a document will be printed using the default format settings (such as left/right margins of 1″). WordPerfect will use these same format settings when printing footnotes and endnotes.

You can, however, alter the format used to print your footnotes/endnotes by making a change on the Document Initial Codes screen (also described in Chapter 8). When you insert a format code on the Document Initial Codes screen, this code alters the entire document, including footnotes/endnotes. In fact, if you then insert format codes in the document itself, starting at the top of the document, you effectively create one set of formatting codes on the Document Initial Codes screen for the footnotes and endnotes and another set for the body of the text.

Note: Line spacing is one format setting that will not affect footnotes or endnotes even if the line-spacing code is inserted on the Document Initial Codes screen. The spacing within footnotes and endnotes is instead controlled by the Footnote or Endnote Options menu, as described in the next section.

You can also alter the format used for one particular footnote or endnote. Just make sure that the cursor is in the Footnote/Endnote Typing screen, positioned before the actual text of the footnote/endnote. Then, change the format for that footnote/endnote. Only that one footnote or endnote will abide by the format change.

Tip: *You can specify that footnotes/endnotes be printed using a particular font.*

You learned in Chapter 7 that unless you specify otherwise, a document will be printed using the default font you designated for your printer (as described in the section "Selecting Your Printer" in Appendix A). WordPerfect will use this same font when printing footnotes/endnotes.

You can, however, alter the font used to print your footnotes/endnotes. Change the font using the Document Initial Font feature, accessed via the FORMAT (SHIFT + F8) key (also described in Chapter 7). When you change the initial font of a document, this alters the entire document, including the font used to print footnotes/endnotes. In fact, if you then use the FONT (CTRL + F8) key to insert a base font change code in the document itself, starting at the top of the document, you effectively direct WordPerfect to print footnotes and endnotes with the font indicated as the Document Initial Font and to print the body of the text with the font indicated by the base font change code.

You can also alter the font or alter the font attribute (such as to large or fine type size) for one particular footnote or endnote. Just make sure that the cursor is in the Footnote/Endnote Typing screen, positioned before the actual text of the footnote/endnote. Then, use the FONT (CTRL + F8) key to change the font or attribute for that footnote/endnote. Only that one footnote or endnote will abide by the base font or attribute change.

Tip: *Use the Move feature to copy or move the text of a note to another location.*

Many footnotes, as well as endnotes, typically refer to the same source a number of times in one document. Instead of typing in the same information every time you refer to the same source, use the Copy feature.

For example, if you want footnote number 6 to contain the same text as number 5, you would use the Move feature, as follows:

1. Press FOOTNOTE (CTRL + F7) and select Edit (2 or E) from the Footnote menu to view footnote number 5.
2. Press the BLOCK (ALT + F4) key to highlight the text of the note, and press the MOVE (CTRL + F4) key to copy the text.
3. Press EXIT (F7) to exit the Footnote Typing screen.
4. Position the cursor where the note number for footnote 6 will appear.
5. Select Create (1 or C) from the Footnote menu.
6. On the Footnote Typing screen, retrieve the copied text.
7. Press EXIT (F7) to exit the Footnote screen.

Using a similar method, you can convert a footnote to an endnote or vice versa. The Move command allows you to do this with relative ease. For example, to convert footnote number 1 to an endnote, you could follow the steps above, but create an endnote rather than a footnote in step 5. (Also see the following Trap, which discusses a quick way to convert all footnotes to endnotes quickly.)

Trap: *Footnotes are not allowed in text columns.*

When you format text into columns with the Column feature (described in Chapter 19), you can insert endnotes in the text. But footnotes are not allowed in columns. If Column mode is on, and you select Create (1 or C) from the Footnote menu, WordPerfect aborts the command and clears the menu from the screen.

In fact, if you have previously typed a document that contains footnotes and you later format that document into text columns, WordPerfect converts every footnote into an endnote. This turns out to be useful if you wish to transform all your footnotes into endnotes; format the text into newspaper columns by inserting a column definition and a column-on code and, as soon as the footnotes are converted, delete the two codes, thus eliminating the column format. But this turns out not to be useful if you don't want your footnotes to be converted; so remember that footnotes are not allowed when employing the Column feature to format text.

Tip: *Notes can be created in subdocuments and then compiled in a master document.*

Chapter 12 describes the Master Document feature, whereby you can connect smaller files together into a comprehensive document. If footnotes and endnotes are created in subdocuments, they will be assembled and numbered properly after the master document to which the subdocuments are linked is expanded.

Tip: *The HOME key extends a Search or Replace command to footnotes and endnotes.*

In Chapter 4 you learned about the Search command, which can locate specific phrases in your text. Similarly, the Replace command (discussed in Chapter 6) can find a phrase and substitute another. You can search through footnotes and endnotes, and headers and footers—as well as the body of your text—in what is referred to as an Extended Search. To activate an Extended Search, press the HOME key before pressing the →SEARCH (F2), or ←SEARCH (SHIFT + F2) key. Or, to activate an Extended Replace, press HOME: before pressing the REPLACE (ALT + F2) key. Now WordPerfect will check footnotes and endnotes for a character string during a Search or Replace command.

Tip: *You can check spelling for each note along with the whole document or individually.*

In Chapter 16 you learned that when you check spelling for a page or for a document, WordPerfect also checks any headers, footers, footnotes, or endnotes located on that page or document.

Alternatively, you can check spelling for just a footnote or endnote without checking the body of your text. For example, to check spelling for a footnote, display the footnote on the Footnote Typing screen. Next, press SPELL (CTRL + F2). Then choose 2, Page, or 3, Document, to check spelling for only that one footnote.

Tip: *(When upgrading from 4.2.) Footnotes and endnotes have been separated on the Footnote menu, and new features have been added.*

In version 5, you still insert footnotes and endnotes by using the FOOTNOTE (CTRL + F7) key. However, the menu that displays is quite different. You must first choose whether you wish to work with footnotes or endnotes; then you choose whether you wish to create, edit, and so on.

A brand-new feature is Endnote Placement. In version 4.2, endnotes were always printed at the end of a document. In version 5, you can situate endnotes anywhere in the document by inserting an endnote placement code at the appropriate location. Endnotes up to that point in the text will be printed at that location.

There are also several minor improvements in version 5. First, an existing footnote's or endnote's margins will automatically update when you change document margins on the Document Initial Codes screen. In version 4.2, you had to edit each note or perform a spelling check to have WordPerfect readjust the note margins. Second, if you press TAB on the Footnote or Endnote Typing screen, a **[TAB]** code is inserted, so that if you change tabs for the document, notes will reformat to the new tab settings. In version 4.2, the TAB key positioned the cursor at the next tab stop, but it inserted spaces rather than a tab code. Also, you can change the font used to print footnotes and endnotes, either for all footnotes/endnotes on the Document Initial Font menu or for an individual footnote/endnote within the text of the footnote or endnote itself.

Changing Footnote or Endnote Options

You can change the set of assumptions that WordPerfect uses when printing footnotes and endnotes, thereby tailoring the format to meet your specific needs. Your choices fall into several categories: the spacing within and between notes, the type of note numbering you use, and the way the note numbers appear in the text and in the notes themselves. To change an option:

1. Position the cursor in the location where you want the new options to take effect. For example, to reset options for the entire document, you can position the cursor on the Document Initial Codes screen (as discussed in Chapter 8). Or, to reset options starting at page 3, position the cursor at the top of page 3.
2. Press FOOTNOTE (CTRL + F7).
3. Select Footnote (1 or F). Or select Endnote (2 or E). If you choose to insert a footnote, then the Footnote menu appears:

   Footnote: 1 Create; **2** Edit; **3** New Number; **4** Options: **0**

   The Endnote menu has the same four items.
4. Select Options (4 or O). Assuming that you chose Options for footnotes, WordPerfect provides the Footnote Options menu shown in Figure 23-5. The Endnote Options menu, which contains fewer options, is shown in Figure 23-6.
5. Select a number or mnemonic corresponding to the option you wish to change, type that selection, and press ENTER.
6. Press EXIT (F7) to save the changes and return to the Document Initial Codes screen or to the document, depending on your cursor location in step 1.

When you make changes on the Footnote Options menu or on the Endnote Options menu, you insert a code in the text—**[Ftn Opt]** for a change in footnotes, or **[End Opt]** for a change in endnotes. This code affects all footnotes or endnotes

```
Footnote Options

     1 - Spacing Within Footnotes              1
                 Between Footnotes             0.16"

     2 - Amount of Note to Keep Together       0.5"

     3 - Style for Number in Text              [SUPRSCPT][Note Num][suprscpt]

     4 - Style for Number in Note                 [SUPRSCPT][Note Num][suprscpt]

     5 - Footnote Numbering Method             Numbers

     6 - Start Footnote Numbers each Page      No

     7 - Line Separating Text and Footnotes    2-inch Line

     8 - Print Continued Message               No

     9 - Footnotes at Bottom of Page           Yes


Selection: 0
```

Figure 23-5. The Footnote Options menu

from the current cursor position to the end of the document. The options for both footnotes and endnotes are as follows:

- **Spacing within notes** This is preset at 1, for single spacing. You can enter **0.5** for half spacing, **1.5** for one and a half spacing, **2** for double spacing, and so on.
- **Spacing between notes** This is preset at 0.16″ so that there is one blank line, one-sixth inch in height, between notes. You can change that setting: for example, to 0.17″ for slightly more space between notes. (You can also enter the spacing in another unit of measure, such as **15p** for 15 points, or **0.5c** for **0.5** centimeter.)
- **Amount of note to keep together** This is preset to keep 0.5 inch of a long note on a page before continuing it onto the next page (only if WordPerfect needs to split the text of the note). It can be reset in inches, or entered in another unit of measure.
- **Style for number in text** This is preset for both footnotes and endnotes as superscript preceding the note reference number, meaning that the number

```
Endnote Options

     1 - Spacing Within Endnotes            1
                 Between Endnotes           0.16"

     2 - Amount of Endnote to Keep Together 0.5"

     3 - Style for Numbers in Text          [SUPRSCPT][Note Num][suprscpt]

     4 - Style for Numbers in Note          [Note Num].

     5 - Endnote Numbering Method           Numbers







Selection: 0
```

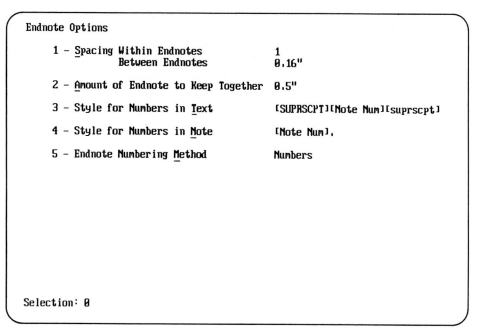

Figure 23-6. The Endnote Options menu

in the text is raised up one-half line from the rest of the text. The string of codes shown on the Footnote or Endnote Options menu when you select this item appears as: **[SUPRSCPT][Note Num][suprscpt]**.

You can create a new style. For instance, you can remove the superscript codes, choose to enhance the note number with attributes such as underline or boldface, or precede or follow the reference number with other characters. Then press ENTER to save the string of codes.

- **Style for number in note** This is preset for *footnotes as* a five-space indent and superscript preceding the note reference number, meaning that the number where the footnote text is actually printed will be indented five spaces and raised up one-half line from the text of the footnote. The string of codes on the Footnote Options menu when you select this item looks just like the setting for the "style for number in text," above, except that five spaces precede the first code.

  This is preset for *endnotes* as the note reference number followed by a period. The string of codes on the Endnotes Options menu appears as: **[Note Num]**.

You can create a new style and then press ENTER to save the string of codes on the Footnote or Endnote Options menu.

- **Note numbering method** This is preset to numbers, meaning footnote and endnote references will be marked with superscripted numbers (1, 2, and so on). If you select this option, WordPerfect offers two other superscript choices: you can select letters (^{a}, ^{b}, and so on), or characters (*, $^{@}$, $^{\#}$, $^{+}$, or whatever symbol you wish). If you choose Characters as the note-numbering method, then type in the character you wish to use. If you type an asterisk, for example, an asterisk will appear to mark the first note, two asterisks will mark the second note, and so on.

The following choices are available only on the Footnote Options menu:

- **Start footnote numbers each page** This is preset to "No," meaning that notes are numbered sequentially without regard to page breaks. It can be set to "Yes" by typing **Y**, so that footnote numbering restarts after each page break. (For example, if your footnotes use numbers, the first footnote on every page will be number 1.)
- **Line separating text and footnotes** This is preset for a two-inch line separating the body of the text from the footnotes. Your other options are to select no line, or a line that extends from the left margin to the right margin.
- **Print Continued Message** Preset to "No," where no message is printed if a footnote is split between two pages. This can be changed to "Yes," so that a "(Continued...)" message is printed on the last line of a footnote on the page on which the first part of the footnote appears. And, a "(...Continued)" message is printed on the first line of the second part of the footnote on the following page.
- **Footnote at bottom of page** This is preset to "Yes," meaning that the footnote is printed at the bottom of the page, even if the text does not fill the whole page. It can be set to "No," so that the footnote is printed just below the text, whether or not a page is full.

Tip: *You can use up to five different characters when marking notes.*

If you select characters as the note-numbering method, you are not limited to only one character. You can use up to five. To use different characters, type in the characters you would like to use. WordPerfect will use them each one time, then double each character, then triple each one, and so on.

For example, suppose that you choose the following three characters as your note-numbering symbols: +#*. The first footnote will be marked +, the second #, and the third *. The fourth will be marked ++, the fifth ##, the sixth**, the seventh +++, and so on.

Tip: *Insert codes in a numbering style by pressing the key combination that typically inserts that code in the text.*

A note style determines how a note is marked in the text and in the note itself. You can use a variety of codes in a note string such as **[SUPRSCPT]**, **[UND]**, **[Note Num]**, or **[BOLD]**. You enter these by pressing the key combination that typically inserts that code. For instance, use the FONT (CTRL + F8) key to insert **[SUPRSCPT]** and **[suprscpt]** codes. In addition, you can use any characters in the string.

For example, suppose that you want a note reference mark for a first endnote next to the note itself to be Note #1/, for a second endnote, Note #2/, and so on. Therefore, you want the style to be **[UND]**Note #**[Note Num]**/**[und]**. To accomplish this:

1. On the Endnote Options menu, select option 4, Style for Numbers in Note (4 or N). WordPerfect prompts

   Replace with: **[Note Num]**

2. Press UNDERLINE (F8). The prompt now reads

   Replace with: **[UND]**

3. Type **Note #**.

4. Press FOOTNOTE (CTRL + F7), select Endnote (2 or E), and then select 2, Number Code. The prompt now reads

   Replace with: **[UND]**Note #**[Note Num]**

5. Type a slash (/).

6. Press UNDERLINE. The prompt should now read

   Replace with: **[UND]**Note #**[Note Num]**

7. Press ENTER. The Endnote Options menu should now reflect the change. (However, because of space limitations, you can view only part of the string of codes on the menu.)

Tip: *Change the note option defaults by using the Setup menu.*

If you find that you constantly change the default options in the same way each time you type a document with footnotes or endnotes, you can change the defaults permanently. Refer to Appendix B, which describes how to do so through the Initial Settings option on the Setup menu.

Tip: *(When upgrading from 4.2.) Footnotes and endnotes each have an options menu.*

You can now set formatting options separately for footnotes and endnotes, and thus have greater control over how they appear on the printed page.

In addition, you have greater variety in determining the style for notes in the text and in the notes themselves. In version 4.2, you could not use codes other than **[Note Num]**, **[UND]**, and **[SUPRSCPT]** in a note style. In version 5, you can use other font attributes as well, such as bold.

Tips and Traps Summary

Creating and Editing Notes

Tip: Use BACKSPACE or DEL to erase a note from the text.

Trap: Sometimes you must rewrite the screen before notes are renumbered.

Trap: The only way to exit from the Footnote or Endnote Typing screen is to press EXIT (F7).

Tip: Use the FOOTNOTE key to insert a note number erased accidentally from the Footnote or Endnote Typing screen.

Tip: Insert a hard page code to place endnotes on their own page.

Tips and Traps Summary (*continued*)

Tip: WordPerfect can determine how much vertical space endnotes will occupy.

Tip: You can reset note numbers.

Tip: It is possible to preview how footnotes or endnotes will appear on the printed page.

Tip: Footnotes reduce the number of lines of text on a page.

Tip: You can alter the format of footnotes/endnotes in several ways.

Tip: You can specify that footnotes/endnotes be printed using a particular font.

Tip: Use the Move feature to copy or move the text of a note to another location.

Trap: Footnotes are not allowed in text columns.

Tip: Notes can be created in subdocuments and then compiled in a master document.

Tip: The HOME key extends a Search or Replace command to footnotes and endnotes.

Tip: You can check spelling for each note along with the whole document or individually.

Tip: (When upgrading from 4.2.) Footnotes and endnotes have been separated on the Footnote menu, and new features have been added.

Changing Footnote or Endnote Options

Tip: You can use up to five different characters when marking notes.

Tip: Insert codes in a numbering style by pressing the key combination that typically inserts that code in the text.

Tips and Traps Summary (*continued*)

Tip: Change the note option defaults by using the Setup menu.

Tip: (When upgrading from 4.2.) Footnotes and endnotes each have an options menu.

24

Merging with the Keyboard

The Merge feature helps you produce repetitive documents—of which there are many in an office environment. For example, you may find yourself typing a similar letter over and over to different clients. Or filling out the same standard form for different products in stock. Or writing the same interoffice memo to different employees. Each document must be personalized for the individual involved, although only a small amount of the text in the document actually varies. Yet it does vary somewhat, so the document cannot simply be photocopied; it must be produced over and over.

Before the advent of computers, a document had to be retyped as many times as there were people to receive the letter or products about which to write. With WordPerfect, you type a basic document—called a *primary file*—only once. Then the Merge feature takes over, incorporating variable information into the primary file for every new document generated.

The Merge feature works with what are called *merge codes*—fourteen in all. Using the merge codes, you can choose one of two basic ways to insert variable information in a document. One way is for WordPerfect to read the variable information from a file stored on disk—a procedure discussed in Chapter 25.

The other way to insert variable information is to type directly from the keyboard during the merge process. During a merge, WordPerfect displays the primary file (the basic document) on screen and moves to the first location where variable information is to be typed, waiting for input from the keyboard. After you enter text, the cursor moves to the second spot, and so on, until you've completed the document. In that way, you type only the variable information to create the document. Print the document and then start the merge process again.

If the variable information constantly changes, so that you don't need to save it for future use, then merging from the keyboard is the easiest and most productive method for you. This chapter first describes how to create a primary file, then the steps in a merge, and finally, the various options available to enhance the merge process so it meets special needs.

Creating a Primary File for a Keyboard Merge

A primary file is the same basic document that you want to create over and over again for different clients, products, or employees—with one exception. In every place where the text is to be personalized, you instead enter a merge code in the text. The merge code you insert is ^C (pronounced "control C"), where C stands for console (keyboard). ^C marks the spot where the cursor pauses for you to type variable information—whether a number, word, sentence, or many paragraphs—from the console (keyboard). The ^C thus acts like a stop marker.

Figure 24-1 shows an example of a primary file. It is a standard memo requesting new employees of the ABC Company to attend an orientation seminar. Notice how the body of the text is typed just like a standard WordPerfect file. But wherever there is variable information—information that changes from memo to memo—a ^C code occupies that space. The phrase "Welcome to ABC Company, ^C!" will become "Welcome to ABC Company, John!" or "Welcome to ABC Company, Mary!" depending on the name you type when WordPerfect stops at that point.

To create a primary document:

1. Clear the WordPerfect screen and set up margins, tabs, and other format settings just as you would to type a standard document.

2. Begin typing the basic document until your cursor is at the exact spot in the document where the first variable phrase would be typed.

3. Press the MERGE CODES (SHIFT + F9) key. WordPerfect responds with a menu of 13 possible merge codes:

```
To:    ^C

From:  Jennie Chin, Personnel Department


     Welcome to ABC Company, ^C!

     I would like you to join me in our ABC Orientation Seminar,
held once a month for new employees.  This month's Seminar will
be on ^C, from 9:30 to 12:00, in Room ^C.

     I've attached some forms that you must fill out and return
to me.  Just bring them along to the Seminar.  The forms that you
must fill out include: ^C

     I look forward to meeting you at the seminar.  You'll enjoy
learning about ABC Company and all that we have to offer you.




                                          Doc 1 Pg 1 Ln 1" Pos 1"
```

Figure 24-1. A primary file

^C; ^D; ^E; ^F; ^G; ^N; ^O; ^P; ^Q; ^S; ^T; ^U; ^V:

4. Select C. The menu clears and WordPerfect inserts a ^C code in the text at the current cursor position.
5. Continue to type the document, following steps 3 and 4, to insert ^C codes wherever variable information belongs.
6. Save the file under a unique filename that reminds you that this is a primary file. For example, you may decide that all primary files will be named with the extension .PRI, so that the primary file in Figure 24-1 could be stored under the filename ORSEM.PRI—for orientation seminar, primary document.

Tip: *Check the primary document carefully for spelling and grammatical mistakes.*

It is critical that the primary file contain no errors, since this document will be the basis for many others. Perform a spelling check and then proofread for any content errors. The extra time is worth it; if you plan to personalize the primary file for 50 people and the file has a spelling mistake, that mistake will appear in 50 letters!

Tip: *You can use CTRL + C to produce ^C when typing in merge codes.*

You do not necessarily have to press MERGE CODES to produce the ^C. Instead, you can press CTRL + C to produce the same code.

Trap: *Don't use the caret key when typing in merge codes.*

When you are typing in **^C**, do not type the caret (^), usually located on the number 6 key at the top of the keyboard, and then type a C. Although the result looks the same on the Typing screen, it is not the same to WordPerfect, and thus WordPerfect won't pause for keyboard input.

When you're unsure as to whether you inserted ^C properly, reveal codes. On the Reveal Codes screen, merge codes such as ^C are boldfaced like all other WordPerfect codes. (When your cursor is on the code, WordPerfect highlights both the caret and the C that make up the code.)

Thus, if the ^C is boldfaced, then it is, in fact, a merge code that WordPerfect will recognize as a pause for input from the keyboard. If, however, the ^C is not boldfaced on the Reveal Codes screen, then you mistakenly inserted a caret and the letter C. Erase these characters and insert the merge code correctly.

Tip: *Print out a primary file as you would any WordPerfect document.*

If you want a printed copy of a primary file, simply print it out as you would any other WordPerfect document. The result will show the merge codes (^C and the like) exactly where they appear on screen.

Tip: *(When upgrading from 4.2.) The* MERGE CODES *key has switched positions.*

In version 5, the MERGE CODES key is now SHIFT +F9, whereas it was previously housed under the ALT + F9 key combination. To insert the ^C merge code, you now press SHIFT + F9 and type **C**. Other than that, there have been no changes in how you create a primary file for a keyboard merge.

Merging on the Screen

Once you have created and saved a primary file, you are ready to begin the merge process to create personalized documents. To merge with the keyboard:

1. Make sure the Typing screen is completely blank. If not, press the EXIT (F7) key to clear it.
2. Press the MERGE/SORT (CTRL + F9) key. WordPerfect responds

   1 Merge; **2** Sort; **3** Sort Order: **0**

3. Select Merge (1 or M). WordPerfect prompts

   Primary file:

4. Type in the name of the primary file (preceded by a path if the file is not in the default drive/directory). Then press ENTER. WordPerfect prompts

   Secondary file:

5. Since you are merging with the keyboard and not with a secondary file, simply press ENTER. WordPerfect retrieves the primary file to screen, positions the cursor at the first ^C code, erases the code, and waits for input.

   In addition, the message * **Merging** * appears at the bottom of the screen, reminding you that you are in the midst of a merge procedure. The appearance of the screen is illustrated in Figure 24-2.

6. Type in the variable information that belongs in that location. Use the ENTER key, the BOLD key, the UNDERLINE key, and keys for other text enhancements, just as you would in typing a standard document.

```
To: _

From:  Jennie Chin, Personnel Department


     Welcome to ABC Company, ^C!

     I would like you to join me in our ABC Orientation Seminar,
held once a month for new employees.  This month's Seminar will be
on ^C, from 9:30 to 12:00, in Room ^C.

     I've attached some forms that you must fill out and return to
me.  Just bring them along to the Seminar.  The forms that you must
fill out include: ^C

     I look forward to meeting you at the seminar.  You'll enjoy
learning about ABC Company and all that we have to offer you.






* Merging *                                Doc 1 Pg 1 Ln 1" Pos 1.7"
```

Figure 24-2. The screen during a merge

7. Press the MERGE R (F9) key. The cursor jumps to the next ^C, erases the code, and pauses again for the keyboard input. (If you inadvertently press ENTER rather than MERGE R, press BACKSPACE to erase the **[HRT]** code you inserted and then press MERGE R.)

8. Repeat steps 6 and 7 until the cursor reaches the bottom of the document, having paused at all the ^C codes in the document. The message * **Merging** * disappears from the screen.

The merge process is complete, and so is the memo. The variable information that you typed has replaced the ^C codes. You are now ready to print the memo to get a result similar to that shown in Figure 24-3, or to save this document, clear the screen, and start the merge process again. Or simply insert a hard page code at the bottom of the document and start the merge again.

Trap: *Sometimes the merging message disappears, even when you're in the midst of a merge.*

When you begin a merge, the message * **Merging** * appears at the bottom of the screen. However, after you type text from the keyboard and press MERGE R (F9) to jump your cursor to the next ^C code, this message temporarily disappears. You are, nonetheless, still within the merge. Type text from the keyboard (text that extends beyond the right margin) and the message reappears.

As a result, don't rely on the message * **Merging** * to indicate whether a merge is still in effect. Remember that you're in the middle of the merge process, so continue to press MERGE R. If the cursor jumps to the next ^C code, you are still processing a merge; continue to insert text and press MERGE R until the cursor reaches the end of the document. If, when you press MERGE R, WordPerfect inserts the code ^R, followed by a hard return, then the merge with the keyboard is no longer active. Erase the ^R code, and proceed to print or save your document. (The merge code ^R is explained in Chapter 25, "Merging with a File," because this merge code relates to a merge with a file.)

Trap: *Certain features don't operate when you're in the midst of a merge.*

```
To:       Hank Turner, Engineering Department

From:     Jennie Chin, Personnel Department


     Welcome to ABC Company, Hank!

     I would like you to join me in our ABC Orientation Seminar,
held once a month for new employees.  This month's Seminar will be
on Thursday, April 30th, from 9:30 to 12:00, in Room 225.

     I've attached some forms that you must fill out and return to
me.  Just bring them along to the Seminar.  The forms that you must
fill out include:

          Tax Information Form
          Pension Plan Form
          Non-Disclosure Clause
          Medical Insurance Form

     I look forward to meeting you at the seminar.  You'll enjoy
learning about ABC Company and all that we have to offer you.
```

Figure 24-3. A merged document

As you are merging with the keyboard, specific features are inoperative. For instance, when merging, you cannot elicit help by pressing HELP (F3), switch to the second document screen by pressing SWITCH (SHIFT + F3), work with the Column or the Math feature by pressing MATH/COLUMNS (ALT + F7), or print a document by pressing PRINT (SHIFT + F7)—although you can view the Control Printer screen to check the status of print jobs or create a macro by pressing MACRO DEFINE (CTRL + F10). Press any of these keys while merging, and WordPerfect will ignore your request. You must either complete the merge or abort the merge (as described in the following Tip) to again have access to these features.

Tip: *Select the ^E code to stop the merge process.*

You can abort the merge procedure. If the cursor is paused, ready to accept information from the keyboard, and the message * **Merging** * is on the screen, press MERGE CODES (SHIFT + F9) and type **E** to select the ^E code. This effectively ends the merge. The message * **Merging** * disappears. You are now free to clear the screen and to start another merge.

Trap: *When WordPerfect pauses, don't move the cursor down past the next ^C code in the text.*

When WordPerfect pauses for input, the cursor can be moved anywhere. You might type information and then realize, for example, that you forgot to insert something up above. Just move the cursor up to correct the mistake and then move it back to its previous position.

Do not, however, move the cursor below another ^C code, and then press MERGE R to continue. WordPerfect looks for the next merge code ahead of the cursor and thus skips past any ^C codes positioned above the cursor.

Tip: *When WordPerfect pauses during a merge, you can retrieve another file.*

When WordPerfect pauses for input, you don't necessarily have to type in the information yourself. You can retrieve a file from disk. This is especially handy if you have standard paragraphs saved in files by themselves.

Suppose, for example, that WordPerfect pauses where you want to insert a standard paragraph. That paragraph is stored in a file called PARA1. Press RETRIEVE (SHIFT + F10), type **PARA1** as the filename, and press ENTER. The paragraph is inserted in the text. Now, simply press MERGE R to move the cursor to the next ^C, continuing the merge.

Further, you can have WordPerfect retrieve a file automatically—without having to use the RETRIEVE key and/or without pausing. To do this, you use a merge code pair, ^P^P, to indicate that you want a file by a specified name brought in during the merge. Refer to the following section of the chapter for more on the ^P^P merge code.

Trap: *Don't save a merged document under the same name as the primary file.*

A primary file should always contain merge codes so that it can be used over and over. Once you execute a merge to fill in a document with personalized information, save that document under a unique filename.

Tip: *(When upgrading from 4.2.) Merge with the keyboard as you did previously, but convert 4.2 primary files to version 5 before you use those old files in a merge.*

The procedure for initiating a merge from the keyboard has not changed. Note, however, that if you wish to stop a merge, in version 5 you must press the MERGE CODES (SHIFT + F9) key and select E. Previously, you could press the MERGE E key, which no longer exists as a separate function key in version 5.

You can use a primary file created in version 4.2 in a version 5 merge; however, make sure you first retrieve that primary file onto the screen when version 5 is loaded. That way, the file is converted to version 5 format. Resave the document, and you're ready to begin a merge using that primary file. For more information on converting version 4.2 documents for use in version 5, see Chapter 28.

Enhancing the Merge Process

When you merge with the keyboard, you can attain flexibility in the process by using merge codes other than ^C. For example, you can include a merge code that inserts the current date for you or that prints the document automatically when the merge is complete. Some merge codes are inserted one at a time, while others must be inserted in pairs. Figure 24-4 shows an example of a primary file containing five different merge codes: ^C, ^D, ^O^O, ^T, and ^P^P. Each of these codes (except for ^C, which was discussed previously) is explained below. (Some of the merge codes found on the Merge Codes menu are used only when merging with a file; a complete list of *all* the merge codes is included in Chapter 25.)

```
                                                                  ^D
To:    ^OEmployee's full name, department^O^C

From:  Jennie Chin, Personnel Department

     Welcome to ABC Company, ^OEmployee's first name^O^C!

     I would like you to join me in our ABC Orientation Seminar,
held once a month for new employees.  This month's Seminar will
be on ^OSeminar date (day of week, month date)^O^C, from 9:30 to
12:00, in Room ^ORoom number of seminar^O^C.

     I've attached some forms that you must fill out and return
to me.  Just bring them along to the Seminar.  The forms that you
must fill out include: ^OList forms, each on a separate line^O^C

     I look forward to meeting you at the seminar.  You'll enjoy
learning about ABC Company and all that we have to offer you.

^T^P^P
                                         Doc 1 Pg 1 Ln 1" Pos 1"
```

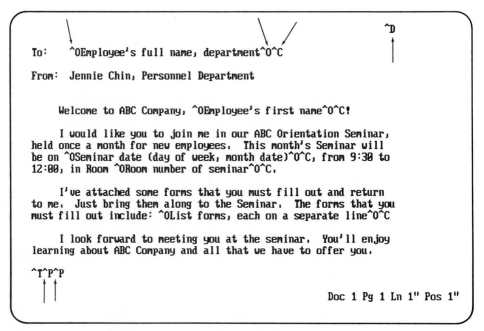

Figure 24-4. A primary file with various merge codes

^D The *date* code inserts the current date in your document, in place of the ^D code, during a merge. Notice that this code exists in the upper right-hand corner of the primary document in Figure 24-4.

^O^O The *output to the screen* code pair prompts, at the bottom of the screen, with a message of your own design. This code pair is used most often before the ^C code as a reminder of what variable information needs to be inserted at a given location. The message that you want to have displayed can be up to 37 characters in length, and must be sandwiched between the code pair, as in ^Omessage^O. For example, suppose that you want to be prompted with the message **First Name** while WordPerfect pauses for you to type in information during a merge. Where you want to insert a first name in the primary file, enter

^OFirst Name ^O^C

This will cause WordPerfect to prompt **First Name** at the bottom of the screen when it pauses for your input; this string of codes will disappear from the screen as the message is displayed.

Notice that the message between the first ^O^O pair in Figure 24-4 is **Employee's full name, department**. Figure 24-5 shows the screen after the merge has begun, when WordPerfect pauses for input at the first ^C code. That message is now at the bottom of the screen. You would type in the employee's name and department as prompted, and then press MERGE R (F9) to continue. A new message would appear when WordPerfect encountered the next ^O^O pair.

^T The *type text to the printer* code instructs WordPerfect to print the text that has merged up to where the ^T code is located. The printed text is then erased from the screen, and the merge continues. In general, place the ^T code at the *bottom* of a primary file so that a complete document is printed. And, make sure that you turn on your printer before initiating a merge that contains a ^T code.

Notice the ^T code at the bottom of Figure 24-4 (along with the code pair **^P^P**, as described below). The ^T code will cause WordPerfect to automatically print the document and clear the

```
                                          August 18, 1988

To:_

From:  Jennie Chin, Personnel Department


     Welcome to ABC Company, ^OEmployee's first name^O^C!

     I would like you to join me in our ABC Orientation Seminar,
held once a month for new employees.  This month's Seminar will be
on ^OSeminar date (day of week, month date)^O^C, from 9:30 to
12:00, in Room ^ORoom number of seminar^O^C.

     I've attached some forms that you must fill out and return to
me.  Just bring them along to the Seminar.  The forms that you must
fill out include: ^OList forms, each on a separate line^O^C

     I look forward to meeting you at the seminar.  You'll enjoy
learning about ABC Company and all that we have to offer you.

^T^P^P


Employee's full name, department              Doc 1 Pg 1 Ln 1.33" Pos 1.7"
```

Figure 24-5. A prompt, generated by a merge code, during a merge

screen after you have typed all the variable information into the document.

^P^P The *primary file* code pair instructs WordPerfect to recall a primary file to the screen and then continue the merge process. The name of the primary file you want to have retrieved is sandwiched between each of the two ^P codes, as in ^P*filename*^P. For instance, suppose that you want to retrieve a file named FORMS to the screen during a merge. Where you want the text of FORMS retrieved to the screen, enter

^PFORMS^P

This will cause WordPerfect to automatically retrieve the file named FORMS when these codes are encountered during the merge. Then the merge continues.

If you want WordPerfect to reuse the same primary file that it is currently using during a merge, then specify no filename; just type ^P^P. In essence, then, ^P^P with no filename creates a loop whereby the merge continues to use the same primary file. If, at the bottom of a primary file, you insert a hard page followed by ^P^P, you can produce any number of similar letters in a row, each on a separate page, without having to begin the merge over again before creating each letter. WordPerfect just starts the merge again, as soon as you complete one letter, pausing at the first ^C in the primary file. This will continue endlessly, so after you've completed all the memos to new employees during one computer session, press MERGE CODES (SHIFT + F9) and type **E** to end the repeating merge.

If you use ^P^P in conjunction with ^T, this directs WordPerfect to print a document, clear the screen, and then retrieve the same primary file for another merge. Notice the ^T^P^P codes located at the bottom of Figure 24-4 (and Figure 24-5). They will cause WordPerfect to print a document after all the variable information is typed and then begin the merge again (thus, no hard page is required above the ^T^P^P combination). This will also continue endlessly, so press MERGE CODES and type **E** when you're ready to end the merge.

Whether you use ^D, ^O^O, ^T, or ^P^P in a primary file, all of these merge codes are inserted in the text in the same way that the ^C merge code is inserted: position the cursor, press the MERGE CODES (SHIFT + F9) key, and then type the letter that corresponds to the code you wish to insert. Remember that ^O^O and ^P^P must be inserted in pairs, so you'll have to use the MERGE CODES key twice to correctly insert each pair in a primary file.

Trap: *Matched-pair merge codes should not be inserted alone.*

Always be sure to use ^O in pairs. Always insert two ^O codes, with a message in between. Similarly, always use ^P in pairs. If you don't, the merge will work improperly. (If you should inadvertently insert a single ^O in a primary file and then try a merge, press MERGE CODES (SHIFT + F9) and type **E** to end the merge and get out of the predicament.)

Tip: *You can use the CTRL key to produce certain merge codes.*

As is the case when inserting ^C, you do not necessarily have to press MERGE CODES (SHIFT + F9) to produce ^D, ^O, ^T, or ^P. Instead, hold the CTRL key down and, while holding it down, type the letter that corresponds to the code you wish to insert. For example, press CTRL and type **D**. Make sure, however, that you don't use the caret (^) as a shortcut. The result looks the same on screen, but WordPerfect will not treat a caret followed by a letter as a merge code.

Trap: *The ^D code works improperly if your computer is unaware of today's date.*

How does WordPerfect know the current date? In one of two ways. Either the computer has an internal clock, or, when you turned on the computer, you responded to the prompt

Current date is Tues 1-01-1980
Enter new date:_

by entering the current date. (That procedure is described in Chapter 1.) If, however, you have no internal clock and you bypassed this question, WordPerfect does not know the correct date, and therefore the ^D codes will insert the wrong date during a merge.

You can correct the situation by returning to DOS either by exiting WordPerfect or exiting temporarily by pressing SHELL (CTRL + F1), as described in Chapter 13. At the DOS prompt (A>, B>, or C>), type **DATE**. The screen displays

A>DATE

Press ENTER. Type the correct date and press ENTER. Now return to WordPerfect. The computer keeps track of the correct date until you turn it off. And now you can take advantage of the ^D code in a merge.

Trap: *Don't use ^T if you want to save a merged document to disk.*

Keep in mind that ^T not only prints all text merged to that point, but also erases that text from the screen. If you want to save a merged document to disk, do not include a ^T code in the primary file. Instead, complete the merge, save the letter, and then send it to the printer. Or complete a number of merges in a row, separating each letter with a hard page break; save the letters in a file and then send them to the printer.

Tip: *As an alternative to the ^O^O code pair, you can insert document comments into a primary file.*

Chapter 3 describes the Document Comment feature, whereby you can insert comments, in a double-line box, that appear on screen but not on the printed page. You can insert a document comment as an alternative to using the ^O^O merge code pair. In that way, rather than having the prompt appear on the status line at the bottom of the screen, the prompt appears within a box in the text. Since document comments are never printed, the text will print correctly.

Be aware, however, that a comment in the text can seem confusing on screen if it is inserted in the middle of a line, because text before the comment appears on a line separate from the text after the comment. Because of this potential confusion, it is best to insert comments at the left margin of a line where the ^C code is located. On screen, the comment will appear on the line just above the ^C code. Examples are shown in Figure 24-6. (Refer to Chapter 3 for more details on the Document Comment feature.)

Tip: *Use merge codes and the Advance feature to make it easier to fill in preprinted forms.*

Some of the repetitive documents that you type may be preprinted forms on which you must fill in the blanks. You can set up a primary document with merge codes at the positions corresponding to the same blank positions on the form. Then you can perform a merge, place the preprinted form in the printer, and print.

The trick is to place the ^C merge codes in positions in the primary file that correspond to the correct placement on the preprinted form. To do this, you can determine the exact location of the blank lines on the form by measuring, and then use the tab stops and/or Advance feature to appropriately position the cursor

```
                                                          ^D

  Enter the employee's full name and department

To:  ^C

From:  Jennie Chin, Personnel Department

  Enter employee's first name

     Welcome to ABC Company, ^C!

     I would like you to join me in our ABC Orientation Seminar,
held once a month for new employees.  This month's Seminar will be

                                          Doc 1 Pg 1 Ln 1" Pos 1"
```

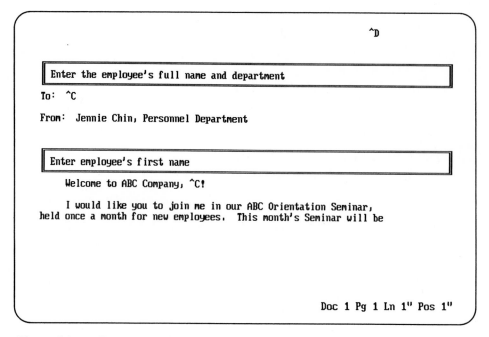

Figure 24-6. Document comments inserted in a primary file

in the primary file. In addition, the ^O^O merge code pair can be used, so that the primary file prompts for, and thus identifies, the needed information.

For example, suppose that the preprinted form is a job application and the first blank is for inserting an applicant's name. On a clear Typing screen, you would

1. Measure the distance from the top of the form to the blank line, and then measure the distance from the left edge of the form to that same blank line.

2. Insert advance codes that position the cursor in the appropriate vertical and horizontal position (see Chapter 7 for a discussion of the Advance feature). Tabs can also be used to position the cursor horizontally.

3. Just to the right of the advance codes, insert a ^O*message*^O code pair, such as **^OApplicant's Name^O**.

4. Just to the right of the ^O^O codes, insert a ^C merge code. Or continue with steps 1 through 4 until you've inserted the advance and ^C codes

```
^OApplicant's Name^O^C

^OApplicant's Address^O^C

^OApplicant's ZIP Code^O^C

^OHire Date^O^C
^ODepartment Name^O^C                    ^ODepartment Code Number^O^C



                                        Doc 1 Pg 1 Ln 2.5" Pos 1"
```

Figure 24-7. A primary file corresponding to a preprinted form

needed to complete the primary file. The result on screen could look like the example shown in Figure 24-7.

Save your primary document. Every time you wish to fill out one of the preprinted forms, perform a merge from the keyboard and type the information as prompted. When the merge is complete, place a preprinted form in the printer and print out the merged document. Finding the correct coordinates for where to place merge codes may be time-consuming, but if you type the same preprinted form over and over, the time savings will soon be apparent.

Tip: *Use the Advance command to put two long prompts on one line.*

You may find that you want to place two pauses for input on the same line, as in

^Omessage^O^C^Omessage^O^C

This could easily be necessary with preprinted forms. But what if the first message is so long that it extends beyond the point at which the second message must be placed? In that case, you can take advantage of the Advance feature (described in Chapter 7), which instructs the printer to place text at a specified location. In this way, you can place two messages on separate lines *on screen,* but have the information you type appear on the same line *when printed.*

To do this, position the cursor at the correct location for the first pause and type in the first message, such as:

^OFirst name and middle initial^O^C

Now press ENTER to move down one line and indicate that you want to advance up one line, as follows:

1. Press the FORMAT (SHIFT + F8) key.
2. Select Other Format (4 or O).
3. Select Advance (1 or A).
4. Select Line (3 or L).
5. Enter the value that corresponds to the line above. For example, if the line above is at 1.68", then type **1.68** and press ENTER.
6. Press EXIT to return to your document.

Next, position the cursor at the correct horizontal location for the second pause and type in the second message. Your screen may appear as follows:

```
^OFirst name and middle initial^O^C
              ^OLast name^O^C
```

On screen it looks as if the two messages are on separate lines. However, once you merge, and assuming that you type **Samuel J.** at the first pause and **Peterson** at the second pause, the result, when printed, will be

```
Samuel J.     Peterson
```

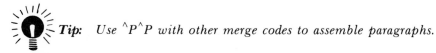

Tip: *Use ^P^P with other merge codes to assemble paragraphs.*

In the previous section of the chapter, "Merging on the Screen," you learned that you can press RETRIEVE and bring in text stored in another file when WordPerfect pauses for keyboard input during a merge. By using the merge code combination ^P^C^P, you don't need to bother with the RETRIEVE key—just type in the filename, and that file will be brought in.

For example, suppose that you have stored standard paragraphs on disk, each in a separate file. Create a primary file and place the merge code combination ^P^C^P in various locations in the primary file where you want the standard paragraphs to appear in the final merged document. When you merge with the primary file, WordPerfect will pause at the ^C, and, when you type in a filename and press MERGE R (F9) to continue the merge, that filename will be inserted between the ^P^P code pair. For instance, type in **CLOSE** and this is interpreted as ^PCLOSE^P. Press MERGE R and the file named CLOSE will be retrieved on screen during the merge. Then WordPerfect moves on to the next merge code and waits for you to enter another filename.

To go further, you can also have WordPerfect prompt to remind you that it has paused for you to type the filename of a paragraph. In creating the primary file, include the following wherever you want a standard paragraph to be inserted:

^OEnter a paragraph name^P^C^P^O

(Notice in this code combination that the other merge codes are inside the ^O^O code pair.) When you merge with the primary file, WordPerfect will prompt with **Enter a paragraph name** at the bottom of the screen. Type in a filename and press MERGE R (F9) to continue the merge; that file will be automatically retrieved.

Sometimes, depending on how intricate the merge codes in a primary file are, it is necessary to precede a long merge code combination with the *update merge code* ^U. This code rewrites the screen so that it shows the current status of the merge. For a complicated merge, if your screen does not update properly when WordPerfect pauses for input, precede the merge code combination with ^U, as in

^U^OEnter a paragraph name^P^C^P^O

Now you can be sure that the screen will be updated when WordPerfect pauses for your input.

Trap: *Using* ^Pfilename^*P causes a new primary file to be active.*

During a merge, keep in mind that once you retrieve another document into a primary file by using the ^P^P code pair, WordPerfect considers that retrieved paragraph as the new, active primary file. For example, if you include ^POPENING^P in a primary file, when WordPerfect retrieves the file named OPENING, that file becomes the active primary file. If the next merge code is ^PPARA1^P, then when PARA1 is retrieved, that file becomes the active primary document. If the next merge code is ^P^C^P, when WordPerfect pauses and you type in a filename, that file now becomes the active primary file.

Thus, if you wish to loop back to repeat the merge with the *original* primary file—the one that began the merge in the first place, you cannot simply insert ^P^P at the bottom of the original primary file (as was the case in Figure 24-4). Instead, the filename of the *original* primary file must be sandwiched between the last ^P^P code pair at the very bottom of the document. For example, if the primary file containing all the ^P*filename*^P and ^P^C^P merge codes is named MEMO1.PRI, then, after a merge is complete, if you wish to print out the document, clear the screen, and then loop back to begin the same merge again, you must insert the following at the bottom of the primary file:

^T^PMEMO1.PRI^P

Tip: *WordPerfect can automatically execute a macro when a merge is complete.*

As described in Chapter 27, a macro is basically a group of keystrokes that you can store and then play back in sequence. You can direct WordPerfect to begin executing a macro after the merge process is complete by inserting a Goto macro pair of codes, ^G^G, anywhere in the text of the primary file. The name of the macro must be typed between the code pair: ^G*macroname*^G. The macro executes as soon as the merge ends, no matter where you place the ^G^G merge codes in the primary file.

For instance, suppose you wrote a macro named OKPRINT that selects your Okidata printer, send to that printer two copies of the document currently on the screen, and then saves that document on disk. To activate that macro after the merge is complete, type the following anywhere in the primary file used in that merge:

^GOKPRINT^G

(If you wrote such a macro, then you would obviously not want to include a ^T code in the primary file; the macro handles the printing for you.)

You can even have WordPerfect prompt you for the macro that you wish to execute. Place the following at the bottom of the primary file:

^OEnter macro name^G^C^G^O

Once the merge is complete, WordPerfect will prompt with **Enter macro name**. Type in a macro name and press MERGE R; the macro will execute.

Tip: *(When upgrading from 4.2.) Enhance the merge process just as you did previously.*

The merge codes that allow you to enhance the merge process are the same as they were previously. Remember, however, that the MERGE CODES key is now SHIFT + F9.

Tips and Traps Summary

Creating a Primary File for a Keyboard Merge

Tip: Check the primary document carefully for spelling and grammatical mistakes.

Tip: You can use CTRL + C to produce ^C when typing in merge codes.

Trap: Don't use the caret key when typing in merge codes.

Tip: Print out a primary file as you would any WordPerfect document.

Tip: (When upgrading from 4.2.) The MERGE CODES key has switched positions.

Tips and Traps Summary (*continued*)

Merging on the Screen

Trap: Sometimes the merging message disappears, even when you're in the midst of a merge.

Trap: Certain features don't operate when you're in the midst of a merge.

Tip: Select the ^E code to stop the merge process.

Trap: When WordPerfect pauses, don't move the cursor down past the next ^C code in the text.

Tip: When WordPerfect pauses during a merge, you can retrieve another file.

Trap: Don't save a merged document under the same name as the primary file.

Tip: (When upgrading from 4.2.) Merge with the keyboard as you did previously, but convert 4.2 primary files to version 5 before you use those old files in a merge.

Enhancing the Merge Process

Trap: Matched-pair merge codes should not be inserted alone.

Tip: You can use the CTRL key to produce certain merge codes.

Trap: The ^D code works improperly if your computer is unaware of today's date.

Trap: Don't use ^T if you want to save a merged document to disk.

Tip: As an alternative to the ^O^O code pair, you can insert document comments into a primary file.

Tip: Use merge codes and the Advance feature to make it easier to fill in preprinted forms.

Tip: Use the Advance command to put two long prompts on one line.

Tip: Use ^P^P with other merge codes to assemble paragraphs.

Tips and Traps Summary (*continued*)

Trap: Using ^*Pfilename*^P causes a new primary file to be active.

Tip: WordPerfect can automatically execute a macro when a merge is complete.

Tip: (When upgrading from 4.2.) Enhance the merge process just as you did previously.

25

Merging with a File

There are two ways to fill a form letter with variable information. One way, which you learned about in Chapter 24, is to merge with the keyboard. You learned how to create a primary file containing text and merge codes. During the merge, WordPerfect pauses at each ^C merge code so you can type in variable information — the text that personalizes each document. In this way, you produce similar documents without typing them over and over.

But if the variable information is also used repeatedly, merging with the keyboard does not automate the process sufficiently. There is a second alternative — merging with a file. You create not only a primary file, but also a secondary merge file. The *secondary file* stores the information that personalizes each document. When you merge, WordPerfect combines the primary file with the secondary file. You don't type the basic document or the variable information more than once. For example, you might send out a letter to people on your mailing list once a month. Store the mailing list in a secondary file and then merge it with a new primary file every month.

This chapter first describes how to set up a secondary file of variable information. It then describes how to create a primary file, such as a form letter, that will extract the corresponding variable information. You learn the steps to merge the two files and, finally, the various options available to enhance the merge process.

Creating a Secondary Merge File

A secondary file is not standard text. It can be thought of as a database containing all the variable information that can personalize a document. For example, suppose you work for M & D Motors and you plan to send promotional letters to your clients offering discounts on service to their cars. A sample of the promotional letter is shown in Figure 25-1. The information that changes for each letter is circled. A secondary file for this letter would include each client's name, company name, address, percent discount, and car make. Figure 25-2 shows a part of a secondary file used to create personalized letters for M & D Motors.

In a secondary file, there are two categories of data: records and fields. A *record* is one set of related information. Each record is separated by the merge code

---

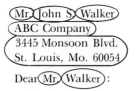

Mr. John S. Walker
ABC Company
3445 Monsoon Blvd.
St. Louis, Mo. 60054

Dear Mr. Walker:

We are pleased to announce a deal that will save you money. Between now and August 15th, you will receive a 20% discount for any service on your Mazda.

We have top mechanics and genuine Mazda replacement parts, so that we can give you the service you expect.

To make an appointment, just give us a call.

Sincerely,

M & D Motors

Figure 25-1. A promotional letter containing variable information (circled copy)

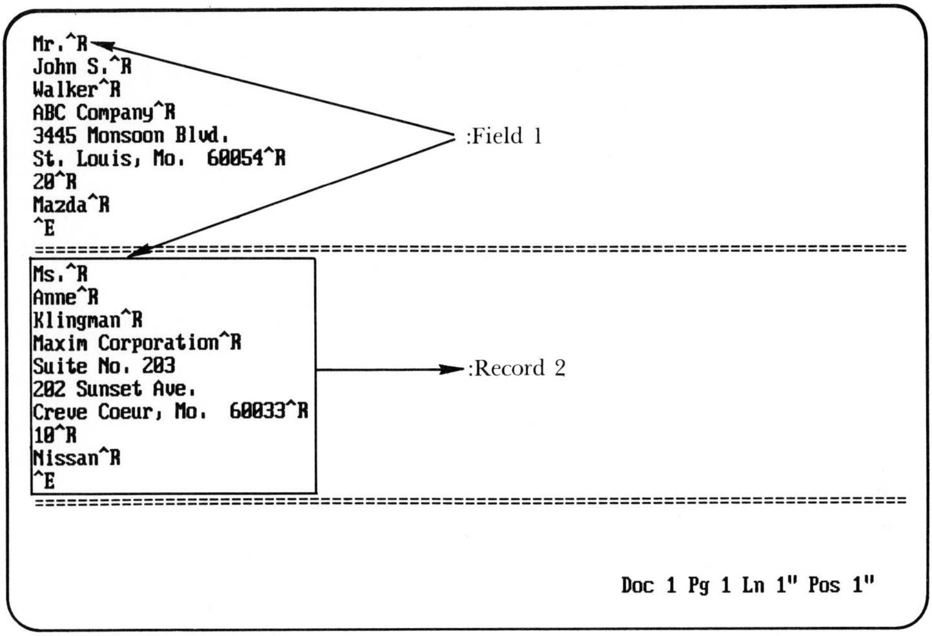

Figure 25-2. Secondary file for a promotional letter

^E (pronounced "control E," signifying the end of the record) and a hard page code. In Figure 25-2 you can see two records. Each record represents a different client at M & D Motors. The number and size of records in a secondary file are limited only by disk space.

A *field* is one category within a record, which can contain text or numbers. Each field is separated by the merge code ^R (pronounced "control R," signifying a merge return). You can include any number of fields in a record. In Figure 25-2 there are seven fields in each record.

WordPerfect keeps track of fields based on their order in each record. So the title "Mr." in Figure 25-2 is field 1, first name and middle initial are field 2, and last name is field 3. The same applies for each record. You must have the same number of fields, in the same order, for each record. However, the length of each field can differ. Notice in Figure 25-2, for example, that field 5, which contains addresses, is two lines long for Mr. Walker and three lines for Ms. Klingman.

To create a secondary file, follow these steps.

1. Clear the Typing screen.
2. Type in the first field of the first record, just as you want it to be inserted in the final document.
3. Press MERGE R (F9). WordPerfect inserts the ^R merge code and a hard return, wrapping the cursor to the next line.
4. Type in the second field and press MERGE R. Continue to type in all the fields in a record.
5. At the end of the first record, press MERGE CODES (SHIFT + F9). WordPerfect displays a menu of 13 merge codes:

   ^C; ^D; ^E; ^F; ^G; ^N; ^O; ^P; ^Q; ^S; ^T; ^U; ^V:

6. Select E. WordPerfect inserts a ^E merge code in the text, followed by a hard page code.
7. Continue with steps 2 through 6 until all records have been typed.
8. Save the file under a unique filename that reminds you that this is a secondary file. For example, you can name the file so it starts with the letters SEC, or use SEC in the filename extension, as in CLIENTS.SEC.

Tip: *Type your variable information accurately.*

Each field must contain characters that appear exactly as you want them in the document. For example, in the secondary document, you must capitalize the first letter of a name in order for it to be capitalized in the merged document.

Tip: *You can use CTRL when typing in the ^R and ^E merge codes.*

You can create merge codes by pressing CTRL instead of using the function keys. Instead of pressing MERGE R (F9) to produce ^R, you can press CTRL + R. But then you must press ENTER to move to the next line. Thus, it seems easier to use the MERGE R key to insert the ^R.

In the case of ^E, you've learned to press MERGE CODES (SHIFT + F9) and type **E** to produce ^E. An alternative is to press CTRL + E and then press CTRL + ENTER to insert a hard page code. It is a toss-up as to which is easier: SHIFT + F9, E, or CTRL + E, CTRL + ENTER. Try each set of keystrokes and decide for yourself.

A merge will operate correctly even if the ^E merge codes in a secondary file are followed by a hard *return* code rather than a hard *page* code. So, if you dislike the look of a page bar below each record, press CTRL + E, ENTER to insert ^E in a secondary merge file to end a record.

Trap: *Don't use the caret when typing in merge codes.*

When you are typing in a merge code such as ^R, do not type the caret (^)—usually located on the number 6 key at the top of the keyboard—and then type **R**. Although the result looks the same on the screen, it is not the same to WordPerfect, and thus WordPerfect won't recognize each field and record correctly.

When you're unsure as to whether you inserted ^R or ^E properly, reveal codes. On the Reveal Codes screen, merge codes such as ^R are boldfaced like all other WordPerfect codes. (When your cursor is on the code, WordPerfect highlights both the caret and the R that compose it.)

So if the ^R is boldfaced, then it is, in fact, a merge code that WordPerfect will recognize as a pause for input from the keyboard. If, however, the ^R is not boldfaced on the Reveal Codes screen, then you mistakenly inserted a caret and the letter R. Erase these characters and insert the merge code correctly.

Trap: *Don't insert extra hard returns or spaces between fields.*

When WordPerfect merges, it assumes that a field includes every character from the first all the way to a ^R code. Don't insert a hard return before the ^R unless you want one inserted in the text during the merge. You do *not* want to type the following into a secondary file:

```
Mr. ^R
John S.
^R
Walker
^R
3445 Monsoon Blvd.
St. Louis, Mo. 60054^R
```

If you did create such a record, the letter's inside address would read

Mr. John S.
Walker

3445 Monsoon Blvd.
St. Louis, Mo. 60054

Similarly, don't include extra spaces before ^R or ^E code. If you do, extra spaces will be inserted in your merged document.

Trap: *Empty fields cannot be skipped.*

Records cannot have different numbers of fields. Thus, even if a field is blank for one record, you must insert a ^R merge code at the appropriate place. Otherwise, WordPerfect can't keep track of fields in the correct order.

For example, if you had no knowledge of Ms. Klingman's company name for the secondary file, you could not just skip it entirely. You would leave the field empty, but end it with a merge code. The record would read

Ms. ^R
Anne ^R
Klingman ^R
^R
Suite No. 203
202 Sunset Ave.
Creve Coeur, Mo. 60033^R
10^R
Nissan^R
^E

Tip: *Design records to be flexible but efficient.*

You can type a field of any size—it can be one word or three paragraphs. But how do you break up variable information into separate fields? It's a trade-off. You want to make that information as flexible as possible to merge correctly with your primary document. At the same time, you don't want to break up a record into so many fields that typing the records is cumbersome and inefficient.

For example, because each client's name is broken up into separate fields in Figure 25-2, you are able to mix and match the fields. You can have the address at the top read "Mr. John S. Walker," but you can address the letter to "Dear Mr. Walker." You could even split the city, state, and ZIP code into separate fields for added flexibility, although they were not separated in Figure 25-2.

But there are extremes. A setup like the following might be considered too inflexible:

```
Mr. John S. Walker
ABC Company
3445 Monsoon Blvd.
St. Louis, Mo. 60054^R
20^R
Mazda^R
^E
```

Broken into only three fields, it would not allow you to separate a name from an address, and thus you could not have WordPerfect insert "Mr. Walker" as a salutation (unless you included the salutation as a separate field in this file—a convenient method if you wish to address clients you know personally by their first name and clients you don't know by using the formal "Mr. Walker" or "Ms. Klingman"). On the other hand, the following might be too flexible—too extreme a breakdown of information based on the letter that needs to be produced.

```
Mr.^R
John S.^R
Walker ^R
ABC Company^R
3445^R
Monsoon^R
Blvd.^R
St. Louis^R
Mo.^R
60054^R
20^R
Mazda^R
^E
```

Tip: *Plan ahead for future merges.*

When you create a secondary file, you do so because you will use the variable information it contains more than once—otherwise, a secondary file would not be worth creating. A secondary file can contain more fields than will be used in the first primary document you use it with. When you design the secondary file, think about how the variable information will be used in future merges. Perhaps a future form letter will contain each client's phone number. In that case, include phone number as a field when creating the secondary file. The secondary file can thus hold the data concerning your clients; it can become your database, whether or not you use the information in all fields in every merge.

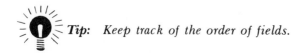

Tip: *Keep track of the order of fields.*

As you'll see in the next section, you must know exactly what information each field contains and the order of those fields when you create a primary file. Therefore, either (1) keep a written note of what is contained in each field in your secondary files (for example, you would jot down that "field 1 = title, field 2 = first name," and so on); (2) print out a copy of the first record in a secondary file and keep that nearby; or (3) retrieve the secondary file to the Doc 2 screen when you are in the process of creating your primary file on the Doc 1 screen, so that you can continuously refer to the secondary file.

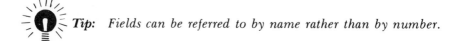

Tip: *Fields can be referred to by name rather than by number.*

As previously discussed, when you create secondary files, like those in Figure 25-2, WordPerfect keeps track of each field by number from top to bottom in a record. For example, the field containing the title "Mr." or "Ms." is considered field 1, the field containing the first name (and middle initial, if any) is field 2, the field containing the last name "Walker" or "Klingman" is field 3, and so on. When you later create a primary file (as discussed in the next chapter section), you reference each field by a number.

But rather than reference fields by number, you can reference them by name. For instance, you can assign field 1 to the name "Title," field 2 to "First," field 3 to "Last," and so on.

You assign names to fields by including a special record as the *first* record in the secondary file. That record must start with a ^N merge code. Next, each field name must appear on a separate line, each boldfaced individually. The last field name should be followed by: a ^R merge code, a hard return code, a ^E merge code, and a hard page code. Here's an example of the first record that assigns names—with codes revealed:

^N[HRt]
[BOLD]Title**[bold][HRt]**
[BOLD]First**[bold][HRt]**
[BOLD]Last**[bold][HRt]**
[BOLD]Company**[bold][HRt]**
[BOLD]Address**[bold][HRt]**
[BOLD]Percentage**[bold][HRt]**
[BOLD]Car Make**[bold]^R[HRt]**
^E[HPg]

Figure 25-3 shows how this first record appears on screen as the first record in the secondary file. To insert the ^N merge code in this first record, either press MERGE

```
^N
Title
First
Last
Company
Address
Percentage
Car Make^R
^E
===============================================================================
Mr.^R
John S.^R
Walker^R
ABC Company^R
3445 Monsoon Blvd.
St. Louis, Mo.  60054^R
20^R
Mazda^R
^E
===============================================================================
Ms.^R
Anne^R
Klingman^R
Maxim Corporation^R
                                                     Doc 1 Pg 1 Ln 1" Pos 1"
```

Figure 25-3. Secondary file in which the first record assigns field names

CODES (SHIFT + F9) and select N, or simply press CTRL + N. Insert the ^R and ^E merge codes as you would for any other record.

You may decide to assign names to some of the fields, but not to all fields. In this case, the fields that are unassigned must be represented by codes ^N^R. Suppose, for example, that you wish to assign names to the first five fields in the preceding example, but not to the last two fields. In that case, the first record would appear in the secondary merge file as follows (again, with codes revealed):

^N[HRt]
[BOLD]Title**[bold][HRt]**
[BOLD]First**[bold][HRt]**
[BOLD]Last**[bold][HRt]**
[BOLD]Company**[bold][HRt]**
[BOLD]Address**[bold][HRt]**
^N^R[HRt]
^N^R[HRt]
^E[HPg]

If you decide to reference fields by name, be sure to keep track of the exact spelling of those field names for when you create a primary file.

Trap: *Don't make your secondary file too large.*

If your secondary file becomes gigantic, with thousands of records, the Merge feature will be cumbersome to use and the computer may be unable to merge that many records. The size that your computer can handle depends on the random access memory (RAM) in your computer and the available disk storage space.

When a secondary file is larger than your computer can handle, an error message will display during the merge. You can avoid such error messages by planning ahead—keep your secondary files small from the start. For example, if your computer is not equipped with a hard disk, consider maintaining separate secondary files, each no larger than 64,000 bytes (64K) in size. (Refer to Chapter 13 to see how to keep track of the size of your files.)

Tip: *Several other WordPerfect products can help you manage secondary files.*

Depending on your database needs, you may want to consider purchasing two other programs offered by WordPerfect Corporation: Notebook and DataPerfect. Notebook is included in the WordPerfect Library, a file-organizing and utility program. Notebook allows you to create and manage secondary merge files without needing to insert ^R and ^E merge codes. It also allows you to view many records at once in rows and columns (similar to a spreadsheet format), or one record at a time as if it were a form. But Notebook imposes size restrictions; depending on the size of each record, a file can hold from 500 to 1000 records. DataPerfect is a full-fledged database program, in which each file can support more than 16 million records.

Records created in either Notebook or DataPerfect can be transferred directly into WordPerfect.

Tip: *You can convert records from other software programs into WordPerfect secondary files.*

You may already have created records using another software package, such as Lotus 1-2-3 or dBASE III. It is possible to convert those records into a secondary merge file. Refer to Chapter 28 for the procedures.

Tip: *(When upgrading from 4.2.) ^E is inserted differently and records are each separated by a hard page code in version 5.*

In version 5, SHIFT + F9 is no longer called the MERGE E key; instead, it is now the MERGE CODES key. When you press MERGE CODES (SHIFT + F9), the ^E code is listed, along with 12 other merge codes. You insert a ^E code by pressing the MERGE CODES (SHIFT + F9) key and typing **E**.

Another difference is that when you insert ^E, WordPerfect inserts ^E and a hard *page* code, rather than a hard *return* code. Thus, each record is visually separated on screen by a page bar. (However, if you find the page bars between records distracting, you can always substitute the **[HRt]** codes for **[HPg]** codes, so that secondary merge files look as they did in version 4.2. The merge will still operate correctly. See a later section in this chapter, "Merging on the Screen," to learn about using 4.2. secondary merge files in the merge process.)

An enhancement in version 5 allows you to assign names to each field, so that fields can be referenced by name rather than by number.

Creating a Primary File for a File Merge

A primary file is the basic document that you want to type for each person on your list, except that merge codes are inserted in those spots where variable information is to appear. Figure 25-4 shows an example of a primary file that will produce the promotional letter to M & D Motors' customers. Notice how the body of the text is typed just like a standard WordPerfect file, with the appropriate spacing and punctuation. In every place where variable information is to be inserted, you enter a ^F merge code in the text, where F stands for field.

The ^F merge code you insert should specify a field number so that WordPerfect knows which field to pull information from in the secondary file. For example, in Figure 25-4, ^F7^ is placed wherever the make of car must be inserted. Figure 25-2, which shows the corresponding secondary file, has a car make in

```
^F1^ ^F2^ ^F3^
^F4^
^F5^

Dear ^F1^ ^F3^:

     We are pleased to announce a deal that will save you money.
Between now and August 15th, you will receive a ^F6^% discount
for any service on your ^F7^.

     We have top mechanics and genuine ^F7^ replacement parts, so
that we can give you the service you expect.

     To make an appointment, just give us a call.

Sincerely,

M&D Motors



                                        Doc 1 Pg 1 Ln 1" Pos 1"
```

Figure 25-4. Primary file for a promotional letter

field 7 of every record. Similarly, ^F3^ is placed where a person's last name belongs, since field 3 contains a last name in each record.

To create a primary document:

1. Clear the typing screen and set margins, tabs, and other format settings, just as you would to type a standard document.
2. Begin typing the basic document until the cursor is at the exact spot in the document where the first variable phrase would be typed.
3. Press MERGE CODES (SHIFT + F9). WordPerfect responds with a menu of 13 merge codes:

   ^C; ^D; ^E; ^F; ^G; ^N; ^O; ^P; ^Q; ^S; ^T; ^U; ^V:
4. Select F. WordPerfect responds with:

   Field:

5. Type in the number that corresponds to that field in the secondary file (for example, to insert a last name in that spot, type 3) and press ENTER. The menu clears and WordPerfect inserts ^F3^ in the text at the current cursor position.
6. Continue to type the document, following steps 3 through 5 to insert a ^F merge code wherever variable information belongs.
7. Save the file under a unique filename that reminds you that this is a primary file. For example, the primary file in Figure 25-4 could be stored under the filename PROMO1.PRI, for promotional letter 1, primary document.

> ***Tip:*** *You can insert and edit a merge field code without using MERGE CODES.*

The merge code ^F1^ is made up of three parts: the ^F code, a field number, and an ending caret (^). If you insert a field number and then realize that the number is incorrect, you do not have to erase the entire merge code and start again. Instead, position the cursor under the field number, press DEL, and type in the new number. In fact, an entire merge code can be typed without using MERGE CODES. Instead, you can do the following:

1. Press CTRL + F.
2. Type the field number.
3. Type a caret.

Tip: *You can insert a ^F code with a name rather than a number.*

When you insert a ^F code in a primary file, you can type in a field name instead of a field number. This is of significance only if you assigned names to fields with a special record (as described in the previous section), or if you used the Notebook in the WordPerfect Library to create secondary merge files, where each field can have a name.

Suppose that you created a secondary file in which the fifth field is assigned to the field name "Address" (as shown in Figure 25-3). Then, when you want to insert the ^F merge code in a primary document in WordPerfect, you can insert ^F5^ or ^FAddress^. Press MERGE CODES (SHIFT + F9) and type **F**. Then, at the prompt

Field:

type **5** or **Address** and then press ENTER.

Figure 25-5 shows an example of a primary file in which all fields were referenced by name.

Tip: *Check the primary document carefully for spelling, grammatical, and numbering mistakes.*

It is critical that the primary file contains no errors because this document is the basis for all the merged documents. Perform a spelling check and then reread for any content errors. The extra time is worth it, since an error in the body of this letter means an error in all of the merged letters.

Further, make sure that field numbers correspond to the correct fields in the secondary file. Otherwise, you may get a letter that begins "Dear Mr. Mazda." And remember that a space should often precede or follow a ^F merge code; otherwise, you could wind up with "DearMr.Mazda."

```
^FTitle^ ^FFirst^ ^FLast^
^FCompany^
^FAddress^

Dear ^FTitle^ ^FLast^:

     We are pleased to announce a deal that will save you money.
Between now and August 15th, you will receive a ^FPercentage^%
discount for any service on your ^FCar Make^.

     We have top mechanics and genuine ^FCar Make^ replacement
parts, so that we can give you the service you expect.

     To make an appointment, just give us a call.

Sincerely,

M&D Motors



                                          Doc 1 Pg 1 Ln 1" Pos 1"
```

Figure 25-5. *Primary file where fields are referenced by name rather than by number*

Tip: *Print out a primary file as you would any WordPerfect document.*

If you want a printed copy of a primary file, simply print it out as you would any other WordPerfect document. The result shows the merge codes (^F and the like) exactly where they appear on screen.

Tip: *The ^F codes can be inserted in any order and as many times as desired.*

The ^F codes may be inserted in a document as many times as you wish and in any order. You can use ^F3^ four times to sprinkle a person's name throughout a document. Or you may not use a certain ^F code at all in a primary document. In Figure 25-4, for example, ^F1^, ^F3^, and ^F7^ are each used twice.

Tip: *Place underline, bold, and other word enhancements in the primary document.*

You may find that you want to underline variable information as it is inserted in the primary file. There are two approaches. One is to enhance the information in the secondary file. For example, you could underline field 4, the company name, in each record of Figure 25-2.

But the alternative is easier. Underline the merge code itself in the primary file, just as you underline any word: ^F4^. The company name will thus be underlined for every letter by underlining only once. The same applies for other enhancements, such as boldface or font changes.

Tip: *(When upgrading from 4.2.) Create a primary file as you did previously.*

The method for inserting ^F merge codes in a document is the same; thus, create a primary file containing ^F codes in version 5 as you did in version 4.2. However, remember that the MERGE CODES key is now assigned to SHIFT + F9, rather than to ALT + F9 as in version 4.2.

Merging on the Screen

Once you have created and saved a primary file and a secondary file, you are ready to begin the merge process. The merge process is automatic. That is, WordPerfect creates a personalized document for each record in the secondary file. Also, a hard page break **[HPg]** is inserted between each personalized document. Because so much is automated for you, this can be thought of as a *simple merge*.

To perform a simple merge with one primary and one secondary file:

1. Make sure the Typing screen is clear of all documents.

2. Press MERGE/SORT (CTRL + F9). WordPerfect responds

   1^Merge; **2**^Sort; **3**^Sort Order: **0**

3. Select Merge (1 or M). WordPerfect prompts

   Primary file:

4. Type in the name of the primary file and press ENTER. WordPerfect prompts

   Secondary file:

5. Type in the name of the secondary file and press ENTER. The message

   *** Merging ***

   appears at the bottom of the screen, reminding you that you are in the midst of a merge procedure.

One by one WordPerfect creates a document for each record in the secondary file. Text is automatically readjusted to fit properly within the margins. When the merge is complete, the merging message disappears. The cursor is positioned at the bottom of the file on the last document merged. You are now ready to review the documents, save them on disk, print them, or do any combination of these.

Tip: *Press CANCEL (F1) to stop the merge process.*

You can cancel the procedure while files are merging by pressing CANCEL (F1). The merging message disappears. You are now free to clear the screen and to start another merge.

Trap: *The merge will stop if your computer runs out of room.*

If you merge by using a very large secondary file, the merge may stop when it runs out of RAM or disk space. An error message will display on the screen. You have several choices to help you out of the predicament. First, you can break up the secondary file into separate files. (For an easy way to do this, see the discussion in Chapter 11 on saving a block of text on screen to disk.) Then you can merge each of these smaller secondary files separately.

Second, you can expand memory or disk storage. Before merging, make sure that your second document screen (such as the Doc 2 screen) is clear. In this way, you maximize the amount of RAM available. You also may wish to purchase more RAM for your computer and/or a larger-capacity hard disk.

Third, you can use the ^T merge code, described in the following section of this chapter, to send each merged document directly to the printer.

Tip: *Primary and secondary files can be mixed and matched.*

After you create a primary file, you can use it with any secondary file. For example, you may have two secondary files, one listing clients in Missouri, and another listing clients in Illinois. Perform two merges in which you use the same primary document twice—once to merge with Missouri clients, and a second time with Illinois clients.

Conversely, you can use one secondary file with many primary files. For example, send a form letter to all your Missouri clients and send a follow-up letter two weeks later using the same secondary file in the merge. Or one primary file can produce a letter, and the second primary file can produce envelopes. (The procedure to create a primary file for envelopes is described in the next section.)

Trap: *Don't save a merged document under the same name as the primary or the secondary file.*

If you save a merged document on disk, make sure you use a unique filename, and not the name of the primary or secondary file. That way, you can always perform another merge.

However, think again if you plan to store the merged result in a separate file. This new merged document will take up space on disk even though it can easily be reproduced later by simply performing the merge again. Consider printing out the merged result and then clearing the screen rather than storing the final merged document on disk.

Tip: *The Sort and Select features offer powerful complements to the merge process.*

It is possible to sort records before a merge! Perhaps you wish to sort by ZIP code before you print, or to sort alphabetically by last name. This is possible by using the Sort command, described in Chapter 26. You sort the secondary merge file before merging.

Chapter 26 also describes the procedure for selecting which records to include in a merge. Suppose you have a secondary file listing clients, but you wish to send letters only to those clients who drive a Mazda. You can select from the secondary file those records in which the car make is Mazda, and place those limited records in a separate secondary file to be used in the merge.

Tip: *Use the question mark to eliminate blank lines when a field is empty.*

You may have some records that contain no information in a certain field, as in the following example:

```
Ms.^R
Anne^R
Klingman^R
^R
Suite No. 203
202 Sunset Ave.
Creve Coeur, Mo. 60033^R
```

This record will cause a blank line during the merge in place of the ^F4^ code:

Primary Document	**Result**
^F1^ ^F2^ ^F3^	Ms. Anne Klingman
^F4^	
^F5^	Suite No. 203
	202 Sunset Ave.
	Creve Coeur, Mo. 60033

Luckily, you have the ability to suppress blank lines that are created when a field is empty. Place a question mark in the primary file where certain fields may be empty, as in this example:

^F1^ ^F2^ ^F3^
^F4?^
^F5^

Notice that the question mark is inside the code. It can be entered at the same time you type in the field number at WordPerfect's prompt. Or it can be inserted after the code has been created by positioning the cursor on the second caret (^) and typing the question mark. WordPerfect evaluates that field for each record. If a field is blank, WordPerfect will eliminate the blank line that would otherwise result.

There is one caution to consider when using the question mark: don't use it in a ^F merge code followed by other ^F merge codes on the same line; the other codes will be ignored if the first field is blank. For example, ^F1^ ^F2?^ ^F3^ causes WordPerfect to bypass both field 2 and field 3 if field 2 is blank for a particular record.

Tip: *(When upgrading from 4.2.) Merge with a file as you did previously, but convert 4.2 files to version 5 before you use those old files in a merge.*

The procedure for initiating a merge from a file has not changed. Moreover, you can use a primary or a secondary merge file created in version 4.2; however, make sure to first retrieve the file onto the screen when version 5 is loaded. That way, it is converted to version 5. Resave the document. Repeat this for all primary and secondary merge files. Then you're ready to begin a merge using those primary and secondary files.

When you retrieve a 4.2 secondary file into version 5, WordPerfect does not insert hard page codes below each record. This is of no concern; the merge will work properly anyway. You can, if you wish, change all the **[HRt]** codes that follow each ^E into **[HPg]** codes so that there's a page break between each record, but this is up to you. (The Replace feature can replace ^E**[HRt]** with ^E**[HPg]** quickly; see Chapter 6 for details on Replace.)

Chapter 28 discusses the general topic of converting version 4.2 documents for use in version 5.

Enhancing the Merge Process

You can take more control of the merge process, tailoring a merge to meet your needs. For example, you can direct WordPerfect to pause during the merge, to retrieve another file during the merge, or to print each document as it is merged. Or have WordPerfect print out envelopes, mailing labels, or a report listing each record in the secondary file.

To tailor a merge, you can use 11 merge codes, in addition to ^R, ^E, and ^F in primary and secondary files. A description of each of the merge codes follows. Some are inserted individually, while others must be inserted in pairs. All merge codes (except ^R) are inserted in a primary or a secondary file just as ^F and ^E are—by pressing MERGE CODES (SHIFT + F9) and selecting the appropriate letter.

^C — This code governs input from the *console*. It allows for a temporary pause during the merge process so you can enter variable information from the keyboard. Press MERGE R (F9) to continue the merge process. Also see Chapter 24 for details on ^C

^O^O — This code pair governs *output* to the screen. It creates prompts at the bottom of the screen with a message of your own design (specified as ^O*message*^O). Also see Chapter 24 for details on ^O

^D — The *date* code inserts the current date in the document, in place of the ^D code, during a merge. For example, place ^D in the upper right-hand corner of your primary file and the correct date will be inserted there each time a merged document is created (provided that you entered the current date at the the start of the computer session). If the date is incorrect, exit to DOS and input the correct date

^T — This code prints (*types*) directly to the printer—so that it prints the text that has been merged up to the place where the ^T code is located. The printed text is then erased from the screen and the merge continues. ^T improves speed and performance when merging with a large secondary file

^P^P — The *primary file* code pair retrieves a primary file to the screen and then continues the merge process (with the filename specified as ^P*filename*^P). If no filename is specified (^P^P), the most recently used primary file is assumed

^S^S The *^secondary file^* code pair continues the merge process by switching to another secondary file (specified as ^S*secondary filename*^S). Every ^F code encountered from that point on is filled in by records from that new secondary file

^N The *next record* code uses the next record in the secondary file to continue the merge. After the last record is processed, the merge ends automatically. (^N is also employed when assigning names to fields, as described in the first section of this chapter, "Creating a Secondary File.")

^U This code *updates* the screen, rewriting the screen so that it shows the current status of the merge. This code is useful for complicated merges (using many merge codes) that require you to rewrite the screen, such as when WordPerfect pauses for keyboard input

^Q This code *quits* the merge, stopping the merge process. If you have 100 records in a secondary file but want to merge only to the first 15, place this code after the fifteenth record. The merge stops when it encounters the code

^V^V This code pair *inserts additional merge codes,* transferring them into the text during a merge without acting upon them, as if those codes were just standard text. It is specified as ^V*codes*^V

^G^G This code pair tells WordPerfect to *goto a macro.* It initiates a macro at the end of the merge (specified as ^G*macroname*^G). As described in Chapter 27, a macro houses a series of keystrokes and/or programming statements under a filename. If you insert ^GSAVEF^G somewhere in a primary file, for example, the keystrokes stored under the macro named SAVEF will be executed when the merge is complete

There are two merge codes that you cannot use alone when merging with a file: ^P^P and ^S^S. The reason is that when you use them in a primary file, you leave the simple merge process behind. Instead, you are entering the arena of the *manual merge.* This means that rather than having WordPerfect automatically insert page breaks and repeat the merge for the next record, you must direct the program to do so. If you do not use merge code combinations along with these codes, the merge could end or use the wrong primary or secondary file each time a new document is created. Effective combinations using these two codes, as well as other effective combinations, are described in the following Tips and Traps.

Tip: *You can use CTRL when typing in most of the codes that enhance a merge.*

You insert most of the merge codes by pressing CTRL instead of using the function keys. For instance, press CTRL + D to insert ^D, or CTRL + U to insert ^U, or CTRL + S to insert ^S.

If you decide to insert codes like ^D or ^U or ^P by bypassing MERGE CODES, don't press SHIFT + 6 to insert the caret (^) and then type a letter. This looks like a code on the Typing screen, but it's not, so WordPerfect won't act on it properly during a merge. Use the CTRL key instead.

However, there is one merge code that cannot be inserted with the CTRL key, and that is ^V. If you press CTRL + V, WordPerfect prompts **Key =**, which allows the opportunity, among other things, to insert certain special characters in the text in a search string (as discussed in Chapter 17). You must only use the MERGE CODES key to insert ^V codes in the text.

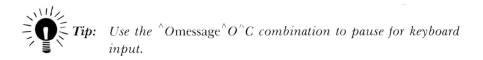

Tip: *Use the* ^Omessage^*O*^*C combination to pause for keyboard input.*

You can merge from a file and at the same time pause for input from the keyboard. Either ^C alone or ^C preceded by the ^O^O merge code pair can be inserted in the primary file. For example, you might desire to type a personal closing sentence at the end of each letter from M & D Motors. At the end of the last paragraph of the primary file, type

^OInsert a closing sentence^O^C

As each letter is merged, WordPerfect pauses at the last paragraph and prompts

Insert a closing sentence

You can then type in a sentence and press MERGE R (F9) to continue the merge. To end a merge at any time when WordPerfect is paused for input, press MERGE CODES (SHIFT + F9) and type **E**. See Chapter 24 for further details on ^C and ^O.

Tip: *Use ^N^P^P to merge records onto the same page or to continue the merge.*

^N^P^P creates a loop so that WordPerfect will begin the merge again. ^N instructs WordPerfect to begin using the next record in the secondary file but to stop the merge when there are no more records. **^P^P** instructs WordPerfect to use the most recently used primary document again.

This merge code combination is implicit in the simple merge. The difference between inserting this code combination, which switches you to a manual merge, and letting WordPerfect perform a simple merge is that this combination does *not* create a hard page break between each merge cycle. You can thus have all the resulting documents printed on one page.

Why would you want to suppress the hard page break? Why print each merged document on the same page? To produce lists and reports—a telephone list of all clients in your secondary file, an address list, or a list of those people to whom you just sent form letters.

For example, perhaps you wish to print out a report of the names of all the people you sent the M & D Motors letter to, one name after another. A primary document for that report would look like this:

```
^F1^ ^F2^ ^F3^

^F4^
^N^P^P
```

In this primary document, a blank line is inserted between the ^F codes and the **^N^P^P** combination so that a blank line will be inserted between the clients' names. The result, when this primary file is merged with a secondary merge file (for just two records), is

Mr. John S. Walker
ABC Company

Ms. Anne Klingman
Maxim Corporation

Imagine how convenient this would be when printing out a list of 200 clients. You can even add one more code, ^U, to see the report being generated on screen. The code combination to use would be ^U^N^P^P.

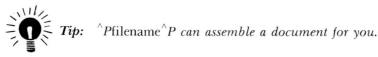

Tip: *^Pfilename^P can assemble a document for you.*

^P*filename*^P tells WordPerfect to retrieve another primary file to the screen during the merge. This is convenient when you want to insert specific text during the merge—perhaps a paragraph—that has been saved in its own file.

You can assemble an entire document by using this combination. For example, suppose that you have four standard paragraphs to be included in a letter in four separate files: OPENING, INTRO, REASON, and CLOSE. Then create a document that includes the ^P*filename*^P sequence, as shown in Figure 25-6. This figure assumes that the primary file is called LET.PRI.

Notice the page break at the bottom of Figure 25-6 (denoted by a page bar consisting of a row of equal signs), followed by the ^N^Plet.pri^P merge combi-

```
^F1^ ^F2^ ^F3^
^F4^
^F5^

Dear ^F1^ ^F3^:

     ^Popening^P

     ^Pintro^P

     ^Preason^P

     ^Pclose^P

Sincerely,

M&D Motors

=================================================================
^N^Plet.pri^P

                                         Doc 1 Pg 1 Ln 1" Pos 1"
```

Figure 25-6. Primary file for document assembly using ^P^P and ^N merge codes

nation. These codes must also be provided if you use ^P*filename*^P and wish to continue the merge for all records in the secondary file. This is because the first ^P merge code that WordPerfect encounters switches the merge to a manual one. The combination at the bottom of the page tells WordPerfect to first insert a hard page break between each document. Then ^N tells WordPerfect to continue with the next secondary record; ^Plet.pri^P tells the program to start at the primary document, LET.PRI, all over again. As a result, the merge continues looping, creating a letter for each record in the secondary file.

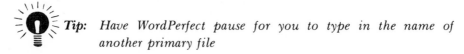

Tip: *Have WordPerfect pause for you to type in the name of another primary file*

You can add sophistication to ^P*filename*^P (described in the previous Tip) with additional merge codes. The combination ^P^C^P causes WordPerfect to pause during the merge with the prompt **Primary File:**, enabling you to type the filename of any other file you wish to use during the merge. Then, press MERGE R (F9) or ENTER to retrieve that new primary file. You can also precede this merge code combination with ^U, so that the string of merge codes is ^U^P^C^P. In this way, you can see the letter currently being merged on screen and can specify a particular filename depending on the record that WordPerfect is currently merging with.

For further sophistication, you can have WordPerfect prompt for the name of a primary file with a message of your own design by using the combination ^U^O*message*^P^C^P^O. For example, the combination

^U^OType paragraph filename^P^C^P^O

causes WordPerfect to pause and prompt **Type paragraph filename**. The filename you specify (by typing the filename and pressing MERGE R or ENTER) will then be retrieved into the document.

The primary file you retrieve may have its own merge codes, such as pauses for keyboard input or another ^P^C^P combination. The merge can become quite complicated and intertwined. It is a good idea, therefore, to precede this combination with ^U to ensure that the screen is being updated in front of you as you type responses for input. This merge code combination is also described in Chapter 24.

Don't forget that if you use the ^P^P merge code pair in a primary document and, after one record is merged, you wish to perform the same merge again, you must place a hard page code and the combination ^N^P*filename*^P—where *filename* is the name of the original primary file—at the bottom of the original primary file (as described in the previous Tip).

Tip: *Prepare a primary file to produce multiple envelopes or mailing labels.*

You can create a primary file to print envelopes or mailing labels for all the names (records) in a secondary file. To print envelopes, the primary file should contain those fields that correspond to each person's name and address in the secondary file you plan to use. For example, if the secondary file is set up as shown in Figure 25-2, then the codes inserted in the primary file should appear as follows:

```
^F1^  ^F2^  ^F3^
^F4^
^F5^
```

No other text is inserted in the primary file. Save this primary document to disk and then perform a merge, using this primary file along with the secondary file containing the address list. Once you perform the merge, a page break appears between each address on screen.

As a final step before printing, you must alter the format of the merged document so that the addresses print in the proper position on each envelope. Assuming you use a 9 1/2- by 4-inch envelope (with your return address already printed in the upper left-hand corner), you will typically want to print the address 2.5 inches from the top and 4.5 inches from the left edge of the envelope. Thus, insert the following codes at the top of the merged document (depending on your printer, you may need to adjust some settings):

- **Paper Size/Type** Envelope size; envelope type (see Appendix A for methods to define the envelope form for your printer)
- **Left margin** 4.5 inches
- **Right margin** 0 inches (to allow room for a lengthy line in an address).
- **Top margin** 2.5 inches
- **Bottom margin** 0 inches (to allow room for an address with numerous lines)

Now print out the merged document onto your envelopes. (Whether or not WordPerfect pauses for you to insert each envelope is determined by how you defined the envelope type—you indicate either that the envelopes are initially present and at a particular location (bin number), meaning that the envelopes are fed automatically, or that they will be fed manually. Methods to define form types are described in Appendix A.)

When you wish to produce labels, the primary file will contain the same ^F merge codes in the same order as when you are printing envelopes. What differs is how you format the document for labels, which depends on your labels and whether or not you are printing on a laser printer.

If you use a dot matrix or letter-quality printer and if the labels are continuous and one across, perform a merge as described previously for printing envelopes. Once you perform the merge, a page break will appear between each address on screen. You must then format the merged document for labels. Insert the following codes at the top of the merged document (depending on your printer and the size of your labels, you may need to adjust some settings):

- **Paper Size/Type** Labels size; Labels type (See Appendix A for methods to define the label form for your printer. If your labels are 4 inches by 1 7/8 inches in size, for example, then this is the size you would specify when defining the label form.)
- **Left margin** 0.5 inch
- **Right margin** 0 inches (to allow room for lengthy line in an address)
- **Top margin** 0.25 inch
- **Bottom margin** 0 inches (to allow room for an address with numerous lines)

Now, print out the merged document onto the labels.

If you use a dot matrix or letter-quality printer and if the labels are on standard 8 1/2- by 11-inch sheets with two or three labels across a sheet, perform the merge as described previously, and also format the merged document by inserting the paper size/type and top and bottom margins codes as described above. (However, when you define the label form for your printer, as described in Appendix A, specify the labels size as 8.5″ wide rather than the actual width of each label because you will be printing from sheets that contain two or three labels across the sheet.)

Next, you must format the labels into columns and delete any double hard page codes that sometimes result. Position the cursor at the top of the document and format the document into text columns by using the MATH/COLUMNS (ALT + F7) key. (Chapter 19 discusses the step-by-step procedure for formatting text into columns.) Set the type of columns as newspaper. Set the number of columns as 2 or 3, depending on the sheets you use. Set the distance between columns as 0, to provide the maximum room for each line of the addresses. Set the column margins to correspond to the location of the labels on each sheet. For example, for three columns across, try these settings:

- **First column** Left margin of 0.25″, right margin of 3″
- **Second column** Left margin of 3″, right margin of 5.75″
- **Third column** Left margin of 5.75″, right margin of 8.5″

Once you insert the column definition and column-on codes, the labels are shown on screen, three across the page with a hard page break after each set of three.

Now use the Replace feature (described in Chapter 6) to search for **[HPg][HPg]** and replace with **[HPg]**. To do so:

1. Position the cursor at the top of the document.
2. Press REPLACE (ALT + F2) and type **N** for a replace with no confirmation.
3. Press CTRL + ENTER twice to insert the search string **[HPg][HPg]**, and then press →SEARCH (F2) to register the search string.
4. Press CTRL + ENTER once to insert the replace string **[HPg]**, and then press →SEARCH (F2) to initiate the command.

You are now ready to send each page of labels to the printer.

If you use a laser printer, then you use labels on standard 8 1/2- by 11-inch sheets that can be fed through the printer. **[HPg]** codes are unacceptable in the final merged document; otherwise, only one set of labels across the page will be printed on each sheet. Instead, you must insert formatting codes in the primary file rather than in the merged document. First, position the cursor at the top of a blank Typing screen and change the top and bottom margins to 0.25″. Next, insert codes to format the document into text columns by using the MATH/COLUMNS (ALT + F7) key. (Chapter 19 discusses the step-by-step procedure for formatting text into columns.) Set the type of columns as parallel with Block Protect. Set the number of columns as 4—even though there are only three labels across a sheet. The extra column is used to ensure that each row of three labels in the merged document contains the same number of lines. Set the distance between columns as 0, to provide the maximum room for each line in the addresses. Set the column margins to correspond to the location of the labels on each sheet. For example, for three columns across, try these settings:

- **First column** Left margin of 0.25″, right margin of 0.3″
- **Second column** Left margin of 0.3″, right margin of 3.05″
- **Third column** Left margin of 3.05″, right margin of 5.8″
- **Fourth column** Left margin of 5.8″, right margin of 8.5″

Once you insert the column definition and column-on codes, you must insert the appropriate text and merge codes:

- **First column** Enter as many hard returns as the longest address that can fit on a label. For example, if the longest address that can fit on a label is five lines long, press ENTER five times. Then press HARD PAGE (CTRL + ENTER) to move to the second column.
- **Second column** Insert those fields that correspond to each person's name and address in the secondary file you plan to use. The last line should contain a ^N merge code, so that WordPerfect will continue the merge with the next record. For example, if the secondary file is set up as shown in Figure 25-2, then the codes inserted in the primary file should appear as follows:

```
^F1^ ^F2^ ^F3^
^F4^
^F5^
^N
```

Now press CTRL + ENTER to move to the third column.

- **Third column** Insert codes identical to those inserted in the second column.

- **Fourth column** Insert codes identical to those inserted in the second and third columns, but do not insert the ^N as the last line. Instead, use the MATH/COLUMNS (ALT + F7) key to turn off columns.
- Once columns are off and the cursor returns to the left margin on screen, type in the merge codes ^N^P^P so that the merge will start again, continuing with the next record in the same primary file.

Figure 25-7 shows an example of how a primary file for mailing labels might appear, showing the second, third, and fourth columns. (The first column is invisible since it contains only hard returns. Also, depending on your monitor, you may be unable to see all the columns at one time on screen.) Save this document under a name that reminds you that it is a primary file for mailing labels on a laser printer—such as MLLASE.PRI (Mailing Labels, LASEr, PRImary document). Next, you are ready to merge this primary file with a secondary file and

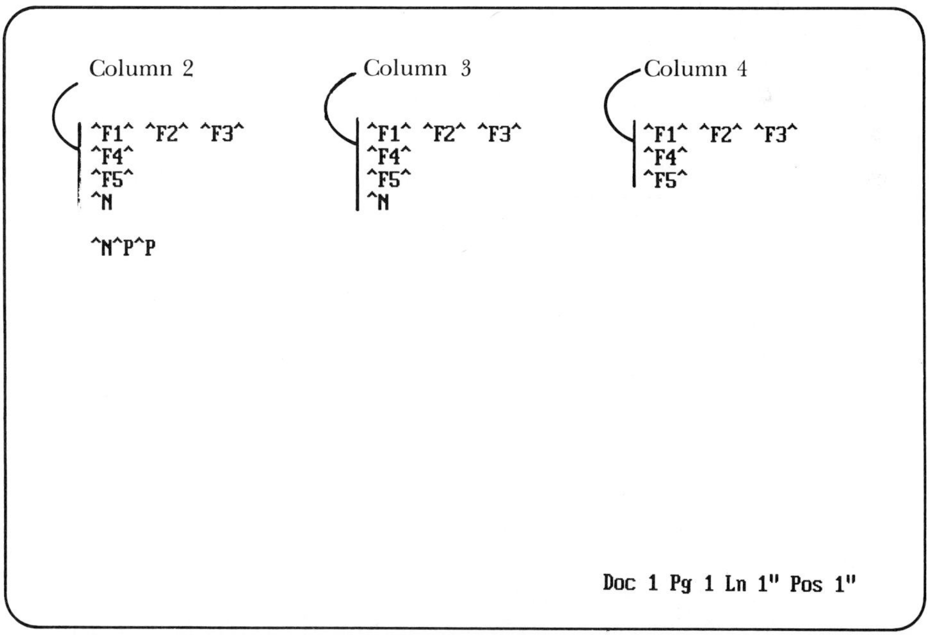

Figure 25-7. Primary file for mailing labels to be printed on a laser printer

create the label file. After the merge, no hard page breaks are visible, and you are ready to send the file to the printer.

Setting up a primary file for envelopes or labels takes time in the beginning (especially if you are printing labels on a laser printer). But remember that once this primary file is stored on disk, it can be used every time you wish to print out envelopes or labels for any address list in a secondary merge file.

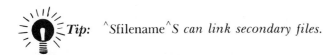

Tip: ^Sfilename^*S can link secondary files.*

^*Sfilename*^S tells WordPerfect to switch to another secondary file as it continues the merge. This is a useful combination if you have many small files you wish to link together in one merge process. For example, you may wish to merge the same primary document with two secondary files called SEC1 and SEC2. Include this code combination at the very end of SEC1: ^SSEC2^S. Once WordPerfect merges with all the records in SEC1, it automatically continues with SEC2 records.

If you use ^*Sfilename*^S in a secondary file, you do not have to insert any other code combination. If you insert ^*Sfilename*^S in a primary document, however, you must include another combination in the primary document if you wish to continue the merge for a new record in the original secondary file—just as with the ^P*filename*^P combination.

Trap: *Don't use ^T alone to print directly to the printer when you merge with a file.*

^T can be easily inserted in a document to print directly to the printer if you are merging exclusively with the keyboard, a procedure described in Chapter 24. But don't use ^T by itself if you are merging from a secondary file. The reason is that ^T prints the document and advances the paper to the next page (just as when you print a document using the PRINT key). At the same time, a file merge automatically creates a hard page break between each document. Thus, if you insert ^T in a file merge, WordPerfect will produce one sheet of blank paper for every printed page—a waste of time and paper.

Instead, in a file merge, insert the combination ^T^N^P^P at the bottom of the primary file. This combination initiates a manual merge and tells WordPerfect to print the text up to where the ^T is located and to loop back to continue the merge. It circumvents the problem of wasting one sheet of paper for each page printed.

Trap: *Don't use ^T at all if you want to save a merged document to disk.*

Keep in mind that ^T not only prints all text merged to that point, but also erases that text from the screen. If you want to save a merged document to disk, do not include a ^T code in the primary file. Rather, complete the merge, save the merged document, and then send the letters to the printer.

Tip: *Stop sending a merge to the printer just as you stop sending a standard document.*

If you've started a merge that sends documents directly to the printer (using ^T^N^P^P) and you must stop the process, first stop the merge by pressing CANCEL (F1). Then, to stop the printer, use the same procedure as when you stop any WordPerfect document from printing, as described in Chapter 14.

Tip: *You can automatically execute a macro when a merge with a file is complete.*

You can direct WordPerfect to begin executing a macro after the merge process is complete by inserting ^G*macroname*^G in the primary file. The macro executes as soon as the merge ends, no matter where you place the ^G^G merge codes in the primary file.

In addition, you can even have WordPerfect prompt you for the macro that you wish to execute with a message of your own design. For example, type the following in the primary file:

^OEnter macro name ^G^C^G^O

Once the merge is complete, WordPerfect will prompt with **Enter macro name**. Type in a macro name and press MERGE R; the macro will execute. (For more on macros, refer to Chapter 27.)

Tip: *Use ^U^F^C^ to specify a field number during the merge process.*

^F^C causes WordPerfect to pause, allowing you to specify which field you would like to have brought in at this point in the merge. WordPerfect pauses in the merge and prompts

Field:

Type in the corresponding field number and press ENTER. WordPerfect continues the merge. Precede this combination with ^U so that the screen is rewritten before you type at the pause. The complete merge combination is thus ^U^F^C^. To insert this merge code combination in a primary file, position the cursor and press CTRL + U, CTRL + F, CTRL + C, and then the caret (SHIFT + 6).

Suppose, for example, that M & D Motors adjusts car prices, depending on the season. The company has a secondary file in which each record represents a car make. For each record there are four fields. Field 1 is the car's price in the winter, field 2 is its price in the spring, field 3 is its price in the summer, and field 4 is its price in the fall. The primary file could, in part, read

Now is the time of year when you can buy that new car for as little as $^U^F^C^!

For every merge WordPerfect would pause for a field number. Depending on the season, you could choose the appropriate field number and press MERGE R to continue the merge. WordPerfect would insert the correct price.

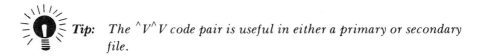

Tip: *The ^V^V code pair is useful in either a primary or secondary file.*

If you create a primary or a secondary file that contains ^V^V code pairs, then any other merge codes in between will be inserted in the merged document during a merge. This is handy in a primary file for automating the process of creating new records in secondary files.

For example, suppose that you've created a secondary file for M & D Motors, as shown in Figure 25-2. Now you have many more records to add to that secondary file. Type a primary document as follows:

^OMr. or Ms.?^O^C^V^R^V
^OFirst Name^O^C^V^R^V
^OLast Name^O^C^V^R^V
^OCompany^O^C^V^R^V
^OAddress^O^C^V^R^V
^OPercent Discount Offered^O^C^V^R^V
^OCar Make^O^C^V^R^V
^V^E^V

Notice that the ^R and ^E merge codes are surrounded by ^V codes. As a result, the ^R and ^E codes will remain intact during the merge process, as if they were characters instead of codes.

When creating this primary file, you will want to insert ^R codes without having them followed by a hard return; to do so, either press CTRL + R to insert the ^R merge code or press MERGE R (F9) and then press BACKSPACE to erase the **[HRt]** inserted. Similarly, you will want to insert ^E without having it followed by a hard page; to do so, either press CTRL + E to insert the ^E merge code or press MERGE CODES (SHIFT + F9), type **E**, and then press BACKSPACE to erase the **[HPg]** inserted.

Once you've finished typing this short primary file, save the file and clear the screen. Next, merge the primary file just created with the secondary file that you completed previously. At the bottom of the screen WordPerfect prompts

Mr. or Ms.?

Type in the appropriate response (such as **Mr.**) and then press MERGE R to continue. The following appears on the Typing screen in place of the first line in the primary file:

Mr.^R

WordPerfect does not act upon the ^R code, but places it on screen. Next, WordPerfect prompts

First Name

Type in the appropriate response (such as **John**) and then press MERGE R. The following appears on the Typing screen in place of the second line in the primary file:

John^R

Continue until one record has been completed. Then, since this is a merge with a file, a hard page will be inserted and the primary file will be used again, ready to process a new record. The merge will repeat as many times as you have records in the secondary file. Enter as many records as you wish. When you want to end the process, press MERGE CODES (SHIFT + F9) and type **E**. Erase from the primary file any extraneous lines at the bottom of the screen. Now you can use the Append feature (discussed in Chapter 12) to add these new records to the secondary file already on disk.

Note: Remember to append these added records to the secondary file. WordPerfect does not do so for you. The reason you requested that the merge involve the secondary file was so that WordPerfect would continue to repeat the primary file over and over for you.

The ^V^V code pair is also handy in a secondary file when you wish to merge with records that may contain variable information. For example, suppose that you frequently type contracts that are combinations of 20 paragraphs. One contract may contain only six paragraphs, while another contains 19. The order varies for every contract. All paragraphs must be numbered correctly in the contract. Also, variable information must be typed into many of the contracts. For instance, the first paragraph of one contract may read

1. The term hereof shall commence on March 1, 1989, and continue until March 1, 1990, between Elliot Matthews, hereinafter referred to as Tenant, and Rachel Patt, hereinafter referred to as owner.

In another contract, the same paragraph may be positioned third and read

3. The term hereof shall commence on December 5, 1989, and continue until December 5, 1990, between Carol White, hereinafter referred to as Tenant, and David Michaels, hereinafter referred to as Owner.

A solution is to create a secondary file containing one record, where each of the 20 standard paragraphs is a separate field; use the Paragraph Numbering feature to insert **[Par Num:Auto]** codes that number each paragraph sequentially; and place ^C merge codes where the customized information should be typed from the keyboard, and ^V^F*n*^^V codes where variable information repeats itself from record to record. Two fields in a secondary file could read

1. The term hereof shall commence on ^C and continue until ^C, between ^V^F1^^V, hereinafter referred to as Tenant, and ^V^F2^^V, hereinafter referred to as Owner.^R

2. The Tenant, ^V^F1^^V, can terminate this contract by giving the Owner, ^V^F2^^V, a 30-day written notice.^R

The primary file to assemble the records into a contract can be as simple as the following, which creates a contract by assembling paragraphs 1, 2, 9, and 10:

CONTRACT

^F1^
^F2^
^F9^
^F10^

During a merge, WordPerfect pauses for you to type information where the ^C codes are situated. Meanwhile, the ^F1^ and ^F2^ codes remain intact, since they are protected by the ^V codes. So, the first part of the merged document could read

CONTRACT

1. The term hereof shall commence on June 1, 1989, and continue until June 1, 1990, between ^F1^, hereinafter referred to as Tenant, and ^F2^, hereinafter referred to as Owner.

2. The Tenant, ^F1^, can terminate this contract by giving the Owner, ^F2^, a 30-day written notice.^R

Next, create a new secondary file that contains one record composed of two fields—the name of the tenant as field 1 and the name of the owner as field 2. Perform a second merge, using the merged document created from the *first* merge as the primary file. Now, the tenant's and owner's names are inserted wherever the ^F1^ and ^F2^ merge codes are found in the primary file. This might seem like quite a lot of work at the start, but it will definitely pay for itself in the long run if you must repeat the same variable information over and over in the same contract.

Tip: *(When upgrading from 4.2.) Enhance the merge with file process just as you did previously.*

The merge codes that allow you to enhance the merge process operate the same as they did in version 4.2. Remember, however, that in version 5 the MERGE CODES key is SHIFT + F9.

Tips and Traps Summary

Creating a Secondary Merge File

Tip: Type your variable information accurately.

Tip: You can use CTRL when typing in the ^R and ^E merge codes.

Trap: Don't use the caret when typing in merge codes.

Trap: Don't insert extra hard returns or spaces between fields.

Trap: Empty fields cannot be skipped.

Tip: Design records to be flexible but efficient.

Tip: Plan ahead for future merges.

Tip: Keep track of the order of fields.

Tip: Fields can be referred to by name rather than by number.

Trap: Don't make your secondary file too large.

Tip: Several other WordPerfect products can help you manage secondary files.

Tip: You can convert records from other software programs into WordPerfect secondary files.

Tip: (When upgrading from 4.2.) ^E is inserted differently and records are each separated by a hard page code in version 5.

Tips and Traps Summary (*continued*)

Creating a Primary File for a File Merge

Tip: You can insert and edit a merge field code without using MERGE CODES.

Tip: You can insert a ^F code with a name rather than a number.

Tip: Check the primary document carefully for spelling, grammatical, and numbering mistakes.

Tip: Print out a primary file as you would any WordPerfect document.

Tip: The ^F codes can be inserted in any order and as many times as desired.

Tip: Place underline, bold, and other word enhancements in the primary document.

Tip: (When upgrading from 4.2.) Create a primary file as you did previously.

Merging on the Screen

Tip: Press CANCEL (F1) to stop the merge process.

Trap: The merge will stop if your computer runs out of room.

Tip: Primary and secondary files can be mixed and matched.

Trap: Don't save a merged document under the same name as the primary or the secondary file.

Tip: The Sort and Select features offer powerful complements to the merge process.

Tip: Use the question mark to eliminate blank lines when a field is empty.

Tips and Traps Summary (*continued*)

Tip: (When upgrading from 4.2.) Merge with a file as you did previously, but convert 4.2 files to version 5 before you use those old files in a merge.

Enhancing the Merge Process

Tip: You can use CTRL when typing in most of the codes that enhance a merge.

Tip: Use the ^O*message*^O^C combination to pause for keyboard input.

Tip: Use ^N^P^P to merge records onto the same page or to continue the merge.

Tip: ^P*filename*^P can assemble a document for you.

Tip: Have WordPerfect pause for you to type in the name of another primary file.

Tip: Prepare a primary file to produce multiple envelopes or mailing labels.

Tip: ^S*filename*^S can link secondary files.

Trap: Don't use ^T alone to print directly to the printer when you merge with a file.

Trap: Don't use ^T at all if you want to save a merged document to disk.

Tip: Stop sending a merge to the printer just as you stop sending a standard document.

Tip: You can automatically execute a macro when a merge with a file is complete.

Tip: Use ^U^F^C to specify a field number during the merge process.

Tips and Traps Summary (*continued*)

Tip: The ^V^V code pair is useful in either a primary or a secondary file.

Tip: (When upgrading from 4.2.) Enhance the merge with file process just as you did previously.

26

Sorting and Selecting

In WordPerfect there are two features controlled by the Sort command: Sort and Select. The Sort feature enables you to rearrange information in either numerical or alphabetical order. Perhaps a mailing list must be organized by ZIP code. Or a glossary must be organized from A through Z. Or a product list must be organized with the least expensive item mentioned first and the most expensive one mentioned last. Instead of organizing before you type, simply type the information and then let WordPerfect put it in order for you.

The second feature is Select, which enables you to extract specific information from a file. For example, request that WordPerfect select only those people from your mailing list who reside in Pennsylvania. Request that it select only those products that cost more than $100. Request that it include only those glossary terms that start with the letter S.

WordPerfect's ability to sort and select is quite flexible, as long as you have the text in one of three formats: lines, paragraphs, or secondary merge files. This chapter explains how to quickly sort by lines using the WordPerfect default settings. Next, you learn how to alter the line sort defaults. You then learn how to sort paragraphs and secondary files, and finally, how to select information—whether in lines, paragraphs, or secondary merge files.

Quickly Sorting by Line Using WordPerfect Defaults

The following are the sort parameters that WordPerfect assumes as defaults:

- The sort is performed line by line.
- The sort is based on the first word in each line.
- The sort is done in ascending order, that is, A, B, C for letters and 1, 2, 3 for numbers.
- The sort is for the entire document. No lines will be specially selected.

Figure 26-1 is an example of a file for which the default settings would be appropriate. The default settings would result in each line being sorted by last name, from A through Z.

The way the information is set up in Figure 26-1 is also the way it must be set up to perform any line sort. Each line represents a distinct group of related information and ends at a soft or a hard return. Each line is called a record; there are ten records in Figure 26-1. The records are broken up into separate categories

Field 1

Wurman	Connie	New York, NY	(212)-336-9000	$234.00
Haber	Lisa	New York, NY	(212)-445-5565	$1,900.00
Davis	John	San Francisco, CA	(415)-563-9887	$45.55
Wild	Tony	Palm Beach, FL	(305)-559-5559	$2,555.50
Davis	Bonnie	Los Angeles, CA	(213)-445-5567	$32.50
Leonard	Steve	Seattle, WA	(206)-334-4210	$23.99
Akman	Anita	New York, NY	(212)-333-0097	$255.97
Davis	Bonnie	Seattle, WA	(206)-332-5443	$344.55
Wild	Anne	Palm Beach, FL	(305)-755-2333	$9.77
Helford	Cathy	Chicago, IL	(312)-445-7771	$1,000.66

Record 10

Figure 26-1. Format of text for a line sort

called fields. Each field is separated by one tab or one →INDENT. In Figure 26-1 there are five fields. Notice that there are the same number of fields in each record, positioned in the same order. For example, the first field for every record makes up a column containing last names. A field can contain one or more words; words are separated by a space. Notice in Figure 26-1 that field 3 contains more than one word in each record.

To sort a file such as Figure 26-1 using the default settings:

1. Retrieve the file to the screen.
2. Locate the cursor anywhere in the file.
3. Press MERGE/SORT (CTRL + F9). WordPerfect responds

   1 Merge; 2 Sort; 3 Sort Order: 0

4. Select Sort (2 or S). WordPerfect assumes that the file you wish to sort is on screen, and prompts

   Input file to sort: (Screen)

5. Since the file is on screen, press ENTER. WordPerfect assumes that you want the result of the Sort command displayed on screen as well, and prompts

   Output file for sort: (Screen)

6. To see the results on screen, press ENTER. The screen splits in half, as shown in Figure 26-2. The top half of the screen shows the first ten lines of the file you wish to sort. The middle of the screen displays the ruler line, showing the current margin and tab settings. The bottom half shows the Sort by Line menu. (This menu reflects the default settings and is explained further in the next section of the chapter.) The last line on the screen displays seven options to choose from.
7. Select Perform Action (1 or P). WordPerfect prompts with the number of records being sorted. In seconds the Sort by Line menu disappears. Every line on screen is sorted in ascending order, according to the first word in the first field.

Trap: *Be careful of hidden codes being sorted along with records.*

Delete all extraneous codes before you begin a sort, including hard returns on blank lines or hard page codes. Otherwise, these codes will be considered records

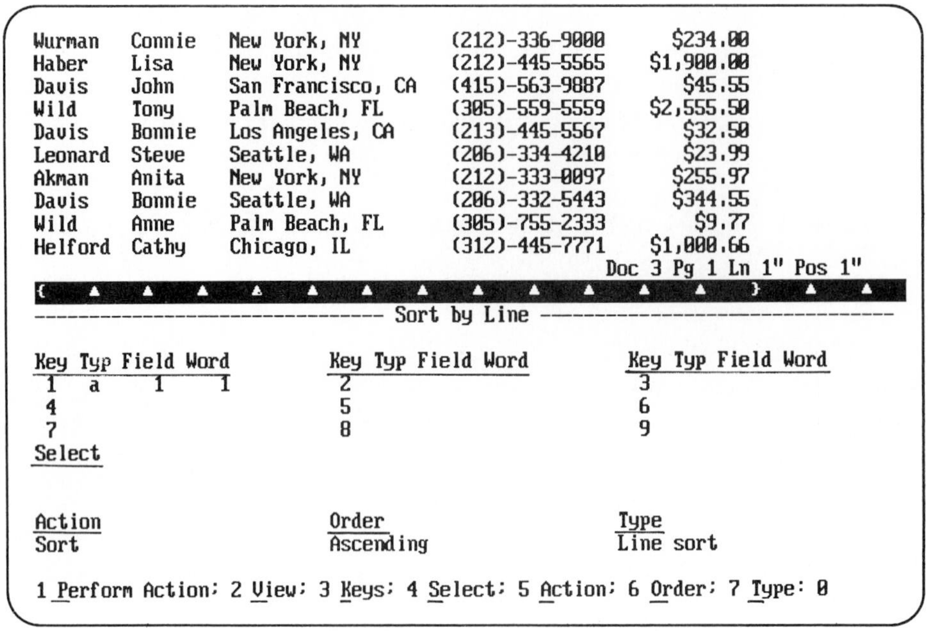

Figure 26-2. Sort by Line screen

and sorted along with the text. If sorted in ascending order, for example, extra hard return codes that insert blank lines will be moved to the top of the file during a sort.

Further, make sure that the **[Tab Set:]** code is at the beginning of the file you wish to sort. If a hard return or a hard page code precedes the **[Tab Set:]** code, the code might be sorted along with the line it is on.

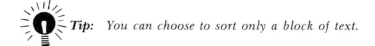

Tip: *You can choose to sort only a block of text.*

WordPerfect cannot distinguish between records and other information in a file. It sorts every word, even text you may not wish to sort. As an alternative you can use the Block command to highlight a block before initiating the sort. The block is sorted on screen.

For example, suppose that the file you wish to sort contains headings, as in the following example:

Last	**First**	**Location**	**Phone #**	**Amount Owed**
Wurman	Connie	New York, NY	(212)336-9000	$234.00
Haber	Lisa	New York, NY	(212)445-5565	$1,900.00
Davis	John	San Francisco, CA	(415)563-9887	$45.55
Wild	Tony	Palm Beach, FL	(305)559-5559	$2,555.50

To exclude the headings from the sort, first press BLOCK (ALT + F4) and highlight the portion of text to be sorted. Then, with Block on, press MERGE/SORT (CTRL + F9). WordPerfect assumes that you wish to sort to the screen; select Perform Action (1 or P). The headings and the line below the headings are not sorted along with the records. If you do not block out the records but rather sort the entire file, you will get awkward results, such as:

Davis	John	San Francisco, CA	(415)563-9887	$45.55
Haber	Lisa	New York, NY	(212)445-5565	$1,900.00
Last	**First**	**Location**	**Phone #**	**Amount Owed**
Wild	Tony	Palm Beach, FL	(305)559-5559	$2,555.50
Wurman	Connie	New York, NY	(212)336-9000	$234.00

Tip: *You can sort information directly from or directly to a file.*

You can request that WordPerfect sort a file not currently on screen. When WordPerfect prompts

Input file to sort: (Screen)

you can replace the "screen" suggestion by typing in the name of the file stored on disk (preceded by the filename's path if not found in the default drive/directory). When WordPerfect displays the Sort by Line menu, you will see the first ten lines of the file you named.

If you type in a filename, be sure that file contains only information to be sorted. Don't forget that WordPerfect sorts every line in a file. To sort only part of a file, you must retrieve that file to screen and use the BLOCK key before you invoke the Sort command.

Similarly, you can request that WordPerfect place the sorted result directly into a file. When WordPerfect prompts

Output file for sort: (Screen)

you can replace the "Screen" suggestion by typing in a new filename. If the name you type is already on disk, WordPerfect will ask whether you wish to replace the old version with the sorted result.

If you choose to output the results of the sort directly into a file, make sure that the name you provide is not that of the original copy safely stored on disk. Otherwise, you will be unable to retrieve the unsorted file in the event that you dislike the sort results. And if you choose to output the results directly into a file, you will need to retrieve that output file in order to see the results of the sort.

Trap: *Never sort a file on screen without first saving a copy to disk.*

Once you sort a file on screen, you cannot return it to its original order. A sort rearranges the order of your records, and there is no "undo" command that will place it in its previous form (unless the original was typed in ascending or descending order). Therefore, *always* make sure a copy of the file to be sorted is stored safely on disk before you sort using the screen as both the input file and the output file. That way, you can retrieve the copy if you wish to return to the original order.

Tip: *You can temporarily view your file from the Sort by Line menu.*

The Sort by Line menu enables you to view only ten lines of the document to be sorted at any one time. If you wish to check records in your file from the Sort by Line menu before you perform the sort, select View (2 or V) on the Sort by Line menu. The cursor jumps up to the top of the screen. You can use the cursor movement keys to move around in the text. You cannot make any editing changes, however. Press EXIT (F7) when you are through scrolling through your text and you wish to continue with the sort.

Tip: *Change the sort order if you are using a Scandinavian language.*

Scandinavian languages contain some accented letters not found in the English or Western European languages, and thus the sort order is different. WordPerfect assumes as the default order to sort according to the US/European alphabet. To sort properly in Scandinavian languages, press MERGE/SORT (CTRL+F9), select Sort Order (3 or O), and then select Scandinavian (2 or S). Then you are ready to follow the standard procedure for sorting your file. Remember to change the sort order back to US/European (1 or U) if you later wish to sort a document that has not been created in a Scandinavian language.

Tip: *(When upgrading from 4.2.) The Sort by Line feature has not changed.*

Sort a line just as you did when using version 4.2.

Changing the Sort Pattern

In the quick line sort described in the previous section of the chapter "Quickly Sorting by Line Using WordPerfect Defaults," none of WordPerfect's initial settings were changed. There are two defaults that you may want to change often as you sort different records line by line: the key on which the file is sorted and the order in which the sort occurs.

A *sort key* is a word in each record that is the basis for the sort. Key 1 is the primary key—the first word that the records are sorted on. You can change the primary key to be any word within any field that you wish. Perhaps you wish to sort numerically on dollar amount, for example, or alphabetically on city.

To define a new Key 1, you must provide three items of information to WordPerfect:

- The type of key you are defining. There are two possibilities: alphanumeric (a) and numeric (n). An *alphanumeric key* contains text—letters, numbers, or special characters. Numbers must be of equal length, such as telephone numbers or ZIP codes. Fields 1 through 4 in Figure 26-1 would be alphanumeric keys.

A *numeric key* contains numbers that represent values, such as dollar amounts. Numbers can be of unequal length, and will still be considered numeric keys if they contain dollar signs, commas, and periods. Field 5 in Figure 26-1 would be a numeric key. WordPerfect assumes that a key is alphanumeric unless you specify otherwise.

- The field where the key resides. Fields are counted consecutively from left to right. Field 1 is at the left margin, field 2 is on the next tab stop, and so on.
- The word within the field that will serve as the key. Words are counted left to right with positive numbers; the first word on the tab stop is word 1, the second word is word 2, and so on.

For example, notice in Figure 26-2 that Key 1 is defined as:

Typ	Field	Word
a	1	1

These are default settings, which means that the records will be sorted alphanumerically based on last name—the first word of the first field.

To sort based on city, the key would instead be defined as:

Typ	Field	Word
a	3	1

To sort based on dollar amount, the key would be defined as:

Typ	Field	Word
n	5	1

Notice in Figure 26-2 that there are options to define Key 2 through Key 9 as well. Why define more that Key 1? So that WordPerfect knows how to break a tie if there are multiple occurrences in the primary key. For example, notice in Figure 26-2 that two people have the last name Wild and two have the last name Davis. If Key 1 is the last name field, you can define Key 2 as the first name field. This will determine which Davis will be listed first, and which Wild will be listed first. If no Key 2 is defined, then the order of the Wild and Davis records is arbitrary.

If there are multiple occurrences in the second key, then you may want to sort on Key 3. For example, notice in Figure 26-1 that two people have the name Bonnie Davis. You can define a Key 3 as the dollar amount field. This will determine which Bonnie Davis will be listed first. When you define keys, the order determines which takes precedence. Always define the primary key as Key 1, the secondary key as Key 2, and so on. You can define up to a maximum of nine keys. Once you define new sort keys, these keys remain defined until you change them or until you exit WordPerfect.

Suppose that you wish to sort Figure 26-1 based on last name. If two last names are the same, you wish to sort based on first name. If two first names are the same, you wish to sort based on dollar amount. You specify this on the Sort by Line menu. Thus, follow steps 1 through 6 in the preceding section. Then, on the Sort by Line menu,

1. Select Keys (3 or K). The cursor is positioned for you to define Key 1, under the heading "Typ," which stands for type. It is defaulted at "a" for alphanumeric. A Type menu appears at the bottom of the screen:

   Type: a = Alphanumeric; n = Numeric; Use arrows; Press **Exit** when done

2. Press RIGHT ARROW or ENTER to accept last name as an alphanumeric key. The cursor moves to the "Field" heading. It is defaulted at 1.
3. Press RIGHT ARROW or ENTER, since last name is field 1. The cursor moves to the "Word" heading. It is defaulted at 1.
4. Press RIGHT ARROW or ENTER, since last name is the first (and only) word in that field. The cursor moves to Key 2, automatically placing an "a" under the "Type" heading.
5. Press RIGHT ARROW or ENTER, since the first name column is, in fact, alphanumeric. The cursor moves to the "Field" heading. WordPerfect inserts the number 1 as the next two entries.
6. Type **2**, and press RIGHT ARROW or ENTER to indicate that first name is field 2. The cursor moves to the "Word" heading.
7. Type **1**, and press RIGHT ARROW or ENTER to indicate that first name is the first (and only) word of field 2. (Since the number 1 was inserted automatically as a default, you could simply press RIGHT ARROW or ENTER.)

8. Type **n** to indicate that the dollars column is numeric. WordPerfect inserts the number 1 as the next two entries.

9. Type 5, and press RIGHT ARROW or ENTER to indicate that the dollars column is field 5.

10. Type **1** to indicate that the dollars amount is the first and only "word" in that field. (The number 1 was inserted automatically, so this step is unnecessary.) You've finished defining the three keys, and the result is shown in Figure 26-3.

11. Press EXIT (F7) because you've finished defining the three keys.

12. Select Perform Action (1 or P). In moments, the Sort by Line menu disappears. Every line on screen is sorted in ascending order according to Key 1, then Key 2, and finally Key 3. The results are shown in Figure 26-4.

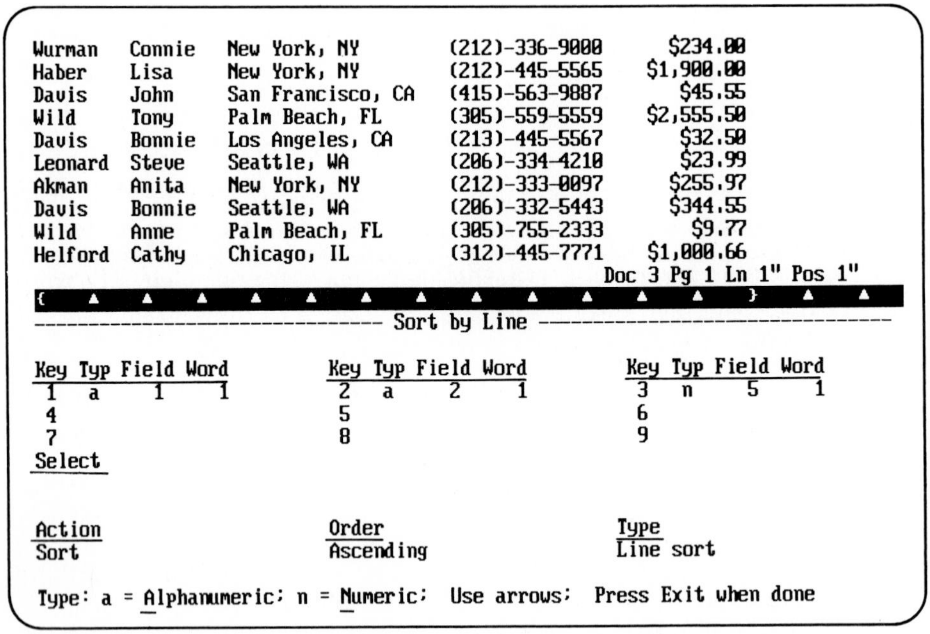

Figure 26-3. *Three keys defined on the Sort by Line menu*

Akman	Anita	New York, NY	(212)-333-0097	$255.97
Davis	Bonnie	Los Angeles, CA	(213)-445-5567	$32.50
Davis	Bonnie	Seattle, WA	(206)-332-5443	$344.55
Davis	John	San Francisco, CA	(415)-563-9887	$45.55
Haber	Lisa	New York, NY	(212)-445-5565	$1,900.00
Helford	Cathy	Chicago, IL	(312)-445-7771	$1,000.66
Leonard	Steve	Seattle, WA	(206)-334-4210	$23.99
Wild	Anne	Palm Beach, FL	(305)-755-2333	$9.77
Wild	Tony	Palm Beach, FL	(305)-559-5559	$2,555.50
Wurman	Connie	New York, NY	(212)-336-9000	$234.00

Figure 26-4. Lines sorted based on three keys

Notice how WordPerfect sorted the three people with the last name Davis. The name "Davis, Bonnie" precedes the name "Davis, John" in the sorted file, since you defined Key 2 as first name, which is field 2. The "Davis, Bonnie" who owes "$32.50" precedes the "Davis, Bonnie" who owes "$344.55," since you defined Key 3 as dollar amount, which is field 5.

Besides changing the sort keys, you can also change the direction of the sort before performing the action. WordPerfect assumes that all keys are sorted in ascending order—A through Z or smallest number to largest. The reverse is referred to as descending order.

To choose descending order, select Order (6 or O) on the Sort by Line menu. WordPerfect responds

Order: 1 Ascending; 2 Descending: **0**

Select Descending, (2 or D). WordPerfect displays "Descending" under the "Order" heading on the Sort by Line menu, affecting the sort order of every key defined. If you had already defined Key 1, Key 2, and Key 3 as instructed previously, you would change to descending order on the Sort by Line menu and again select Perform Action (1 or P) to switch the order of records. For instance, rather than being sorted to the top of the list, as shown in Figure 26-4, "Akman, Anita" (and the three fields that follow that name) would be sorted to the bottom of the list.

Trap: *The sort won't work properly unless there's only one tab per field.*

When you set up records, you must make sure that every field begins after the same number of tab codes in each record. Otherwise, the records will not sort properly.

For example, suppose that you typed in the four names shown here. In order to line up the last name in this list, some last names are preceded by one tab code, and others by two tab codes, depending on the length of the first name.

Jonathan[**Tab**]Smith
Bert[**Tab**][**Tab**]Brown
Benjamin[**Tab**]O'Leary
Mary[**Tab**][**Tab**]Johnson

Thus, some of the last names are in field 2, while others are in field 3. A sort on last names will work improperly.

Instead, reset tabs so that they are farther apart to accommodate the fields with longer first names. All the last names will thus follow a single tab code, and the sort will work properly when you define last names as field 2.

Jonathan [**Tab**]Smith
Bert [**Tab**]Brown
Benjamin [**Tab**]O'Leary
Mary [**Tab**]Johnson

Tip: *Edit the sort keys by using BACKSPACE or DEL.*

You can edit key definitions at any time by choosing Keys (3 or K) on the Sort by Line menu. Then use RIGHT ARROW to move the cursor to the heading of the key definition you wish to alter and type in the new definition. If you wish to erase one single heading for a particular key definition, move the cursor to that heading and press BACKSPACE.

If you wish to erase all the headings for a particular key, position the cursor under any of the headings for that key and press DEL. If an "a" remains under the "Typ" heading for that definition, the "a" will disappear as soon as you press LEFT ARROW to move to the previous key definition. The only definition that you cannot erase is the default setting for Key 1.

Tip: *WordPerfect follows a specific sort order, depending on whether the key is defined as alphanumeric or numeric.*

If the key to be sorted on is defined as alphanumeric, then WordPerfect looks at the first character of the key in each field. In an ascending sort, words starting with special symbols are placed first, followed by numbers, followed by letters. In addition, if two words are identical in two records except that one is lowercase and the other is uppercase, lowercase will be placed first. If two words start with the same letter, then the second letter in the word is examined for the sort order. Here is a sorted example:

```
*smith
1Jones
danners
davis
Davis
Johnson
Peters
```

The descending sort produces just the opposite result.

If the key is defined as numeric, then in an ascending sort all words that contain no numbers are placed first. Words containing numbers are then sorted numerically, no matter where in the word that number is found. Here is a sorted example:

```
Jones
R15
J142
155.99
```

$179
1111 Jones
P2994
*2555

Tip: *Use negative numbers to indicate word positions from right to left.*

In addition to recognizing word positions from left to right, WordPerfect recognizes them from right to left. To count from right to left, precede the word number by a hyphen to make it negative (such as -1 or -2). This enables you to pinpoint words in fields where the word count varies.

For example, suppose that you wish to define a key as the state in each record shown in Figure 26-1. The state is in field 3, but in different positions. For New York, NY, the state is word 3. But, for Seattle, WA, the state is word 2. This would cause a problem if you counted from left to right. Instead, count from right to left. The state is field 3, word -1 of every record.

Tip: *Use a hard space to treat two words as one.*

WordPerfect defines a word as a group of characters separated by spaces. You may have typed two words that you want to have considered as one word during your sort. For instance, you may want WordPerfect to treat "Johnson, M.D." or "Berg, Esq." or "St. Louis" as one word. To do so, insert a hard space between the words, which is the key combination HOME, SPACEBAR. When a hard space separates two words, they are treated as one.

Tip: *(When upgrading from 4.2.) Change the sort pattern as you did previously*

The default settings on the Sort by Line menu and the method for changing the defaults are the same as in version 4.2.

Sorting Paragraphs or Secondary Merge Files

Once you are comfortable with the Sort by Line menu, sorting paragraphs or merge files is easy to understand. All the same procedures apply, but you must add another step—redefining the type of sort you desire.

Use a paragraph sort if records occupy different numbers of lines. Each record in your file must end with two or more hard returns or a page break. If the paragraph contains more than one field, each field is separated by a tab or →INDENT. Figure 26-5 shows an example of a glossary that is in the appropriate format for a paragraph sort. There are three fields in each record, each occupying a different number of lines.

Choose a merge sort if your records are organized in a secondary file, which must be set up as follows: each field ends with a ^R merge code; each record ends with a ^E merge code; each record contains the same number of fields; and the fields must be placed in the same order. Figure 26-6 shows an example of a secondary file that WordPerfect can sort; the three records contain four fields each.

You change the type of sort on the Sort menu. Select Type (7 or T). WordPerfect responds

Type: 1 Merge; 2 Line; 3 Paragraph: 0

Field 1

Ch. 1	Ecosystem	System of living organisms through which they exchange energy and matter.
Ch. 1	Cell	Basic component of all living things.
Ch. 2	Atmosphere	Mixture of gases surrounding the surface of the earth.
Ch. 3	Ecology	Science dealing with the interactions between living organisms and their environment.
Ch. 3	Pollution	Poisons and heat that enter an ecosystem faster than the ecosystem can naturally process and distribute them.

Record 5

Figure 26-5. Format of text for a paragraph sort

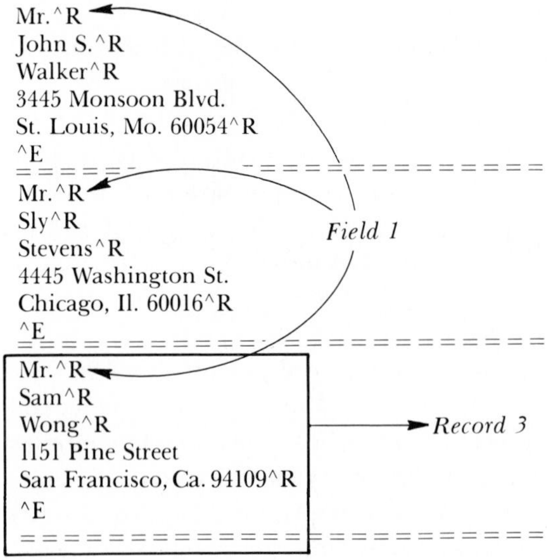

Figure 26-6. Format of text for a merge sort

If you choose Paragraph (3 or P), the bottom portion of the screen now displays the Sort by Paragraph menu, as shown in Figure 26-7. Notice that the heading below the ruler line now reads "Sort by Paragraph" and that the type of sort in the lower right-hand corner reads "Paragraph Sort."

If you choose Merge (1 or M), the bottom portion of the screen displays the Sort Secondary Merge File menu, as shown in Figure 26-8. Now the heading below the ruler line reads "Sort Secondary Merge File" and type of sort is listed as "Merge Sort."

The menus are almost identical to the Sort by Line menu, except in the area where each key is defined. For a paragraph or merge sort, a record can occupy more than one line. As a result, you must also indicate a line when defining keys in order to pinpoint a word location. Lines are counted consecutively from top to bottom.

For example, in Figure 26-5 there is a different number of lines in each record. If you wish to sort this file alphabetically by glossary term, you must

```
Ch. 1      Ecosystem       System of living organisms through which
                           they exchange energy and matter.

Ch. 1      Cell            Basic component of all living things.

Ch. 2      Atmosphere      Mixture of gases surrounding the surface
                           of the earth.

Ch. 3      Ecology         Science dealing with the interactions
                           between living organisms and their
                                              Doc 3 Pg 1 Ln 1" Pos 1"
{  ▲  ▲  ▲  ▲  ▲  ▲  ▲  ▲  ▲  ▲  ▲  ▲  }  ▲  ▲
------------------------------ Sort by Paragraph ------------------------------

Key Typ Line Field Word    Key Typ Line Field Word    Key Typ Line Field Word
 1   a    1    1    1       2                          3
 4                          5                          6
 7                          8                          9
Select


Action                     Order                      Type
Sort                       Ascending                  Paragraph sort

1 Perform Action; 2 View; 3 Keys; 4 Select; 5 Action; 6 Order; 7 Type: 0
```

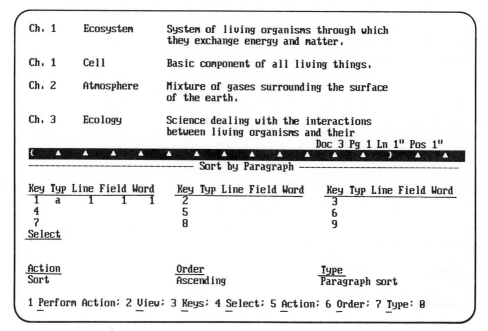

Figure 26-7. The Sort by Paragraph menu

indicate that the terms (Ecosystem, Cell, and so on) are on line 1 in field 2. Define Key 1 as

Key	Typ	Line	Field	Word
1	a	1	2	1

In Figure 26-6, field 4 in each record of the secondary file is composed of two lines. If you wish to sort Figure 26-6 by city, then the sort key would be defined as

Key	Typ	Field	Line	Word
1	a	4	2	1

Or, to define the sort key by ZIP code, specify the following:

Key	Typ	Field	Line	Word
1	a	4	2	-1

```
Mr.^R
John S.^R
Walker^R
3445 Monsoon Blvd.
St. Louis, Mo.  60054^R
^E
================================================================================
Mr.^R
Sly^R
Stevens^R
                                                    Doc 3 Pg 1 Ln 1" Pos 1"
---------------------------- Sort Secondary Merge File -------------------------

Key Typ Field Line Word    Key Typ Field Line Word    Key Typ Field Line Word
 1   a    1     1    1      2                          3
 4                          5                          6
 7                          8                          9
Select


Action                     Order                     Type
Sort                       Ascending                 Merge sort

1 Perform Action; 2 View; 3 Keys; 4 Select; 5 Action; 6 Order; 7 Type: 0
```

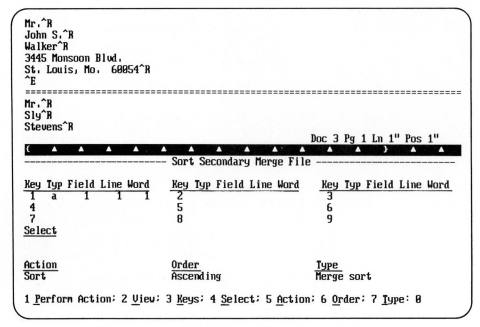

Figure 26-8. The Sort Secondary Merge File menu

(Remember from the previous section, "Changing the Sort Pattern," that you can count words from right to left by counting with negative numbers.) To initiate a paragraph or merge sort, select Perform Action (1 or P), just as you do for a line sort.

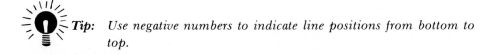

Tip: *Use negative numbers to indicate line positions from bottom to top.*

Just as you can count words from right to left by preceding the word "number" with a hyphen, you can count lines from bottom to top with a hyphen. This enables you to pinpoint lines in fields where the line count varies. For example, the field that contains addresses in a secondary file might have two lines in some records and three in others:

4445 Washington St.
Chicago, Il. 60016^R

Apartment 405
1151 Pine Street
San Francisco, CA. 94109^R

To specify the bottom line of the field, use line number -1.

Trap: *Paragraph and merge sort keys are defined in a different order.*

The Sort by Paragraph and Sort Secondary Merge File menus are the same except for the order in which the key definition headings are listed. Notice in Figure 26-7 that the line is defined *before* the field for paragraphs, whereas in Figure 26-8 the line is defined *after* the field for a merge file. Be aware of this difference as you define keys to sort different types of files.

Trap: *Don't forget that an indented paragraph is considered to start at field 2.*

If you are sorting paragraphs that are not separated into fields, then you have one field only. It will be field 1 if the paragraphs are flush against the left margin. However, if the paragraphs are indented to the first tab stop, the sort key will be field 2. For example, consider this table of authorities:

Herne v. Deyoung (1901) 132 Cal 357 [64 P. 576]

Austero v. National Cas. Co. (1978) 84 Cal.App.3d 1 [148 Cal.Rptr.653]

C&H Foods Company v. Hartford Ins. Co. (1984) 163 Cal.App.3d 1055, 1066-67[211 Cal.Rptr.765]

Johansen v. California State Automobile Association Inter-Insurance Bureau (1975) 15 Cal.3d 9, 19[538 P.3d 744,123 Cal.Rptr.288]

Zurn Engineers v. Eagle Star Ins. Co. (1976) 61 Cal.App.3d 493 [132 Cal.Rptr.206]

To sort by the first word of each paragraph, the key definition should be

Key	Typ	Line	Field	Word
1	a	1	2	1

Tip: *Numbered paragraphs are automatically renumbered after a sort.*

Chapter 21 describes how you can have WordPerfect number paragraphs for you by using the MARK TEXT (ALT + F5) key. If you then sort those paragraphs, they will be renumbered after the sort.

Trap: *Don't sort without first checking* all *settings on a Sort menu.*

Just as WordPerfect remembers previous key definitions, it remembers previous type and order definitions. Be sure to check the settings that you have chosen on a Sort menu before you select Perform Action (1 or P). Otherwise, you might not get the sort that you desire. For example, if you are sorting paragraphs but the menu indicates the "Type" as a line sort, your paragraphs will be torn apart during the sort as WordPerfect sorts each line separately.

Tip: *(When upgrading from 4.2.) Sort paragraphs and secondary merge files as you did previously.*

Sort a paragraph or a secondary merge file just as you did when using version 4.2.

Selecting Records

In addition to sorting records, you are also able to select from among a group of records. The Select feature is available, regardless of whether the records are in lines, paragraphs, or secondary files. You can select on any key once that key has been defined. You do so by writing a selection statement on the Sort menu. Then you can decide whether you want to select those records or to both select and sort at the same time. To proceed from the Sort menu:

1. Choose Select (4 or S) from the Sort menu. The cursor moves under the "Select" heading. A Select menu appears at the bottom of the screen:

   +(OR), *(AND), =, <>, >, <, >=, <=; Press **EXIT** when done

   This menu shows the eight comparison symbols you can use in an equation. They are each described in Table 26-1.

2. Write a select statement as if you were writing an equation. For example, suppose you wish to select only records with a ZIP code of 60054. Suppose ZIP code has been defined as Key 1. The equation that you type is

   key1=60054

   For a merge sort the screen would resemble Figure 26-9; notice that the equation has been inserted beneath the "Select" heading.

   As another example, suppose that you wish to select only those records with a ZIP code not equal to 60054. The equation that you type is

   key1<>60054

   You can also connect equations in a select statement by using the * (AND) or + (OR) symbols as described in Table 26-1, as long as you insert a space before and after the * or +. Suppose that you wish to select only those records with ZIP codes equal to 60054 *and* with the name Walker. Assume that Last Name has been defined as Key 2. The statement that you type is

   key1=60054 * key2=Walker

   As another example, suppose that you wish to select records with a ZIP code equal to 60054 *or* with the last name Walker. Either condition can be met in order for that record to be selected. The statement that you type is

   key1=60054 + key2=Walker

   Finally, suppose that you wish to select records where ZIP codes start with the number 6. This means that you want to select a range of numbers greater than or equal to 60000 *and* less than 70000. The statement that you type is

   key1>=60000 * key1<70000

```
Mr.^R
John S.^R
Walker^R
3445 Monsoon Blvd.
St. Louis, Mo.  60054^R
^E
================================================================================
Mr.^R
Sly^R
Stevens^R
                                                     Doc 3 Pg 1 Ln 1" Pos 1"
{    ▲    ▲    ▲    ▲    ▲    ▲    ▲    ▲    ▲    ▲    ▲    ▲    ▲    }    ▲    ▲
------------------------- Sort Secondary Merge File -------------------------

Key Typ Field Line Word    Key Typ Field Line Word    Key Typ Field Line Word
 1   a    4    -1   -1      2                          3
 4                          5                          6
 7                          8                          9
Select
key1=60054

Action                     Order                      Type
Sort                       Ascending                  Merge sort

+(OR), *(AND), =, <>, >, <, >=, <=;  Press Exit when done
```

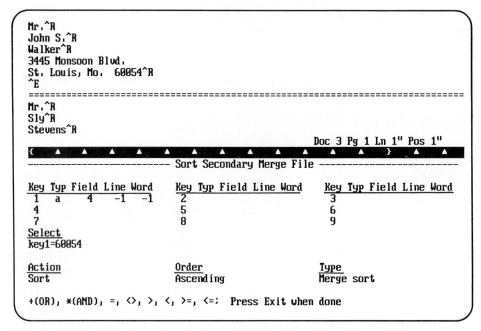

Figure 26-9. Selecting records from the Sort Secondary Merge File menu

Table 26-1. Comparison Symbols in a Selection Statement

Comparison Symbol	Description
=	Equal to
<>	Not equal to
>	Greater than
>=	Greater than or equal to
<	Less than
<=	Less than or equal to
+	OR (Connects two key conditions together in an equation so that *either* can be true for a record to be selected)
*	AND (Connects two key conditions together in an equation so that *both* must be true for a record to be selected)

3. Press EXIT (F7) after writing the statement.
4. Choose Action (5 or A). WordPerfect responds

   Action: 1 Select and Sort; **2** Select Only: **0**

5. If you want to select based on the selection statement and then sort those selected records based on the order of the defined keys, choose Select and Sort (1 or S).

   Or, if you want to select only, without rearranging the order of the records, choose Select Only (2 or O).
6. Choose Perform Action (1 or P). All records are deleted except those that meet the selection statement.

Trap: *Once records are deleted, they cannot be resurrected.*

If you have a file on screen with hundreds of records, those that are erased because they do not meet the selection statement are erased from the screen and from RAM. (If you chose to place the output in a file, then the results will be found only in the output file.) The only way to retrieve them is to retrieve the original copy of the records—another reason to make sure that you have a file on disk before you attempt a Sort or Select command where both the input and output are on screen.

Tip: *You can edit the selection statement.*

If you wish to edit a selection statement, choose Select (4 or S) on the Sort menu. You can then edit the statement by using the cursor movement, DEL, and BACKSPACE keys, or by pressing DELETE EOL (CTRL + END) to erase the whole statement and start again.

Trap: *Don't forget to erase the selection statement before performing a new sort.*

Just as WordPerfect retains in memory your key definitions until you change them or exit WordPerfect, the program retains your selection statement. Therefore, proceed with caution if you want to sort a new file after selecting on a previous file. Erase the old selection statement before you perform the next sort.

Trap: *You cannot choose an action until you write a selection statement.*

WordPerfect will not allow you to choose Action (5 or A) on a Sort menu until you first choose Select (4 or S) and write a selection statement. If you choose Action (5 or A) first, WordPerfect will ignore your request. If no selection statement is written, then you can only sort your records.

Tip: *When you write a selection statement, WordPerfect assumes that you wish to both sort and select.*

The first time that you type in a selection statement, WordPerfect automatically changes the "Action" heading to read "Select and Sort." Unless you want to change that setting, you don't have to choose Action (5 or A) before selecting Perform Action (1 or P).

Tip: *When you both sort and select, define the sort keys first.*

If you are performing only a select on a file, WordPerfect ignores the order in which you defined keys. If you are performing both a sort and a select, the order in which you defined keys is critical. Define the sort keys first, in the order that you want the file sorted. You may wish to select on the same keys, in which case you don't need to define additional keys. But some of the keys on which you want to select may not be the same as the sort keys. In that case, define selection keys later.

For example, suppose that you defined Key 1 and Key 2 as sort keys. Then any *additional* keys you need to define for a selection statement should be defined as Key 3, Key 4, and so on.

Tip: *You can specify a range of letters in a selection statement.*

You can select words starting with a certain letter, or starting with letters in a certain range, similar to the way you work with numbers. A is considered less than Z.

For example, to find only last names that start with A, assuming that Last Name is defined as Key 1, the equation is

key1<B

Or, to find only last names that start with A through L, the equation is

key1<M

Or, to find only those last names that begin with P or Q, the statement contains two equations:

Key1>P * key1<R

Tip: *You can combine all the comparison symbols into one selection statement.*

Your selection statements can become quite intricate. You can use any of the eight comparison symbols in one statement, and you can use parentheses to change the meaning of the statement. Selection is performed from left to right unless parentheses are present. For example, where Key 1 is defined as Last Name and Key 2 as City, assume that you wish to select only those people whose last names begin with an S *and* who either live in Cincinnati *or* Chicago. The selection statement is

(key1>S * key1<T) * (key2=Cincinnati + key2=Chicago)

If parentheses were not used, then WordPerfect would select those people whose last names begin with an S *and* who live in Cincinnati, *or* WordPerfect would select those people who live in Chicago regardless of their last names.

Tip: *If you include "keyg" in a selection statement, you don't need to define keys first.*

The only time that you can write a selection statement without first defining the appropriate key is when you use "keyg" in a selection statement. This executes what's called a *global select.* WordPerfect checks every word of every record.

For example, suppose that you wish to select only those records of people with the last name of James. You don't have to define that key first. You can write the selection statement as

keyg=James

WordPerfect then performs a global select. If James appears in a record, that record will be selected. But follow one precaution in a global select: remember that WordPerfect looks at every word in every record. If someone in the file has the *first* name of James, then that record will be selected as well.

Tip: *WordPerfect can select on an empty field.*

You can select all records where a certain field is empty. For example, suppose that you have a secondary file with the names and addresses of your clients. Field 4 represents the client's company name. You have a company name for some records, but not for others. Select those records with no company name listed by first defining field 4 as key 1 and then writing the selection statement as

key1=

This ability to select on an empty field can come in handy in a variety of circumstances—such as when you wish to select all those records for which payment has not yet been received.

Tip: *The Sort and Merge commands form an effective alliance.*

The Select feature is very powerful when used with the Merge feature. You can store a list of all your clients in one large secondary file. That file can serve as your master client list. Then you can select certain records from that master list at will every time that you plan a merge with a form letter.

For example, suppose that you wish to target only your clients with businesses in Pennsylvania. Select from the master list only those clients with an address in Pennsylvania. Store the selected records in another secondary file. Now perform a merge on that smaller number of clients, creating letters to only that select group. Chapter 25 tells how to merge with a file.

Tip: *(When upgrading from 4.2.) The Select feature has not changed.*

Select specific records in lines, paragraphs, or in a secondary merge file just as you did when using version 4.2.

Tips and Traps Summary

Quickly Sorting by Line Using WordPerfect Defaults

Trap: Be careful of hidden codes being sorted along with records.

Tip: You can choose to sort only a block of text.

Tip: You can sort information directly from or directly to a file.

Trap: Never sort a file on screen without first saving a copy to disk.

Tip: You can temporarily view your file from the Sort by Line menu.

Tip: Change the sort order if you are using a Scandinavian language.

Tips and Traps Summary (*continued*)

Tip: (When upgrading from 4.2.) The Sort by Line feature has not changed.

Changing the Sort Pattern

Trap: The sort won't work properly unless there's only one tab per field.

Tip: Edit the sort keys by using BACKSPACE or DEL.

Tip: WordPerfect follows a specific sort order, depending on whether the key is defined as alphanumeric or numeric.

Tip: Use negative numbers to indicate word positions from right to left.

Tip: Use a hard space to treat two words as one.

Tip: (When upgrading from 4.2.) Change the Sort Pattern as you did previously.

Sorting Paragraphs or Secondary Merge Files

Tip: Use negative numbers to indicate line positions from bottom to top.

Trap: Paragraph and merge sort keys are defined in a different order.

Trap: Don't forget that an indented paragraph is considered to start at field 2.

Tip: Numbered paragraphs are automatically renumbered after a sort.

Trap: Don't sort without first checking *all* settings on a Sort menu.

Tip: (When upgrading from 4.2.) Sort paragraphs and secondary merge files as you did previously.

Tips and Traps Summary (*continued*)

Selecting Records

Trap: Once records are deleted, they cannot be resurrected.

Tip: You can edit the selection statement.

Trap: Don't forget to erase the selection statement before performing a new sort.

Trap: You cannot choose an action until you write a selection statement.

Tip: When you write a selection statement, WordPerfect assumes that you wish to both sort and select.

Tip: When you both sort and select, define the sort keys first.

Tip: You can specify a range of letters in a selection statement.

Tip: You can combine all the comparison symbols into one selection statement.

Tip: If you include "keyg" in a selection statement, you don't need to define keys first.

Tip: WordPerfect can select on an empty field.

Tip: The Sort and Merge commands form an effective alliance.

Tip: (When upgrading from 4.2.) The Select feature has not changed.

27

Automating Repetitive Tasks with Macros

A macro can make a short, easy task out of what would otherwise be a lengthy keyboard process. Even if you've never heard the term "macro," you've probably been exposed to the concept—if you use speed dialing on your telephone, for example. With speed dialing, your telephone records a certain phone number that you frequently dial and plays it back when you press one or two buttons. This saves you time, frees you from having to look up or memorize phone numbers, and gives your fingers a rest.

WordPerfect macros are identical in concept. A macro is a set of keystrokes that WordPerfect stores once and later executes at your command. For example, if you type the same phrase in one letter after another, you can record that phrase and let WordPerfect type it for you. If you print the same document every day, you can let WordPerfect record the process and print the document for you. To play back the keystrokes, just press a few keys.

WordPerfect enables you to create two types of macros. *Keyboard macros* are basic macros that you create when you type characters and select menu functions and features from the keyboard. *Programming language macros* are a set of recorded keystrokes linked by programming statements that chain operations together; these complex macros go beyond menu selections, and can perform conditional logic tests, branch to macro subroutines, or help you establish your own customized menus.

Like speed dialing, macros are not a necessity. You can use WordPerfect quite effectively without ever creating one. But as with speed dialing, once you begin to rely on macros, it becomes burdensome and time-consuming to perform repetitive tasks without them.

Read on to learn how macros can bear the burden of your routine tasks. You learn how to create keyboard macros, how to chain and nest keyboard macros, how to insert special keyboard macro commands, and how to edit macros and use the Macro Programming Language. If you're new to macros, start by creating simple keystroke macros. If you're used to programming, then you'll appreciate the sophistication of the Macro Programming Language, which allows you to customize the WordPerfect program to your own needs and habits.

Creating and Executing a Keyboard Macro

To create a keyboard macro, you must assign that macro a name. The macro will be stored on disk and, like a document you store on disk, it can be accessed during any future computer session—today, tomorrow, or next month. Macros on disk can be distinguished from documents because WordPerfect assigns macros the extension .WPM (for *W*ord*P*erfect *M*acro) when they are saved on disk. A macro can be named by using

- **The ALT key along with a letter** For example, assign a macro to ALT + A. It is stored on disk with the name ALTA.WPM.
- **The ENTER key** A macro named with the ENTER key is stored on disk as WP{WP}.WPM.
- **One to eight characters** These are the same characters you can use to name a document, including letters, numbers, or special symbols such as: !, @, #, $, %, or (. For example, assign a macro to the name PRINT1, $AMT, or PARA. A macro named PARA will be stored on disk as PARA.WPM.

A keyboard macro is created by typing a set of keystrokes exactly as you want them recorded. To create a macro, follow these steps:

1. Prepare the screen so that you are ready to perform the task that you are asking WordPerfect to record. For example, if you want the macro to underline a sentence, make sure that a sentence appears on the Typing

screen, and that the cursor is located in the appropriate spot to begin creating the macro. If the macro prints a document, make sure that the printer is turned on and that there's a document available for you to print.

2. Press MACRO DEFINE (CTRL + F10) to turn on the Keystroke Recording feature. WordPerfect responds with a prompt at the bottom of the screen:

   Define macro:

   WordPerfect is prompting you to assign a name to the macro that you are about to define (record).

3. Type in a macro name. For example, press ALT + M. Or press ENTER. Or type **PARA** (either uppercase or lowercase is acceptable). Then, if you named the macro with one to eight characters, press ENTER.

   When you name a macro with the ALT key or with one to eight characters, WordPerfect prompts

   Description:

   When you name a macro by simply pressing the ENTER key, no such prompt appears.

4. For a macro named with the ALT key or with one to eight characters, you can keep track of the macro's purpose by typing a description of up to 39 characters in length and then pressing ENTER. Or, if you want no description, press ENTER without typing a comment. (Macros named with the ENTER key do not allow for a description.) The following message starts blinking on the screen:

   Macro Def

5. Enter in the series of keystrokes exactly as you want them recorded.

6. Press MACRO DEFINE (CTRL + F10) to stop recording the keystrokes. The blinking **Macro Def** message disappears. The macro is stored on disk in the default drive or directory with the extension .WPM.

How you execute a macro you've created depends on whether or not you named the macro with the ALT key. If you used ALT, then when you're ready to execute the macro:

1. Locate the cursor in the proper position for execution. For example, if the macro inserts a phrase, position the cursor where you want the phrase to appear. If the macro capitalizes a word assuming that the cursor is posi-

tioned anywhere in that word, place the cursor within a word that you wish to capitalize.

2. Press ALT + the character with which you named the macro. For example, to execute the macro that you named with ALT and A, press ALT + A.

Or, if you named a macro with the ENTER key or one to eight characters:

1. Locate the cursor in the proper position for execution.
2. Press MACRO (ALT + F10).
3. Type in the macro name, such as **PARA** (unless the macro was named with the ENTER key).
4. Press ENTER.

Once executed from disk, a macro remains in memory and is accessed faster for the rest of the current working session and from then on.

Macros 1 through 4 below provide the keystroke-by-keystroke procedures for recording and executing four different macros. Practice with all four and you will become comfortable with the macro definition and execution process. You'll see that a macro can perform a task in a fraction of the time it would take you to do it manually.

Macro 1

Suppose that you work for the ABC Company and thus type the company name hundreds of times each month. Create a macro that types "ABC Company" on command. Name the macro ALT + A. Keystroke by keystroke, you type the following:

1. Press MACRO DEFINE (CTRL + F10).
2. Press ALT + A to name the macro.
3. Press ENTER, signifying that you won't provide a description for this macro.
4. Type **ABC Company**.
5. Press CTRL + F10.

To practice executing the macro, position the cursor in another location and press ALT + A. "ABC Company" appears on screen as quickly as lightning.

Macro 2

Suppose that for certain reports you type, you reset your left margin to 1.5 inches, your right margin to 1.5 inches, and you use double spacing. You can create a macro to do this job. Name the macro REPORTS.

1. Press MACRO DEFINE (CTRL + F10).
2. Type **REPORTS** to name the macro.
3. Press ENTER to register the macro name.
4. Type the following description: **Margins 15,75; Double spacing.**
5. Press ENTER to register the description.
6. Enter the following keystrokes:

   FORMAT (SHIFT + F8)

   L, **M**, **1.5″**, ENTER—to define the left margin setting

   1.5″, ENTER—to define the right margin setting

   S, **2**, ENTER—to indicate double spacing

   EXIT (F7)
7. Press CTRL + F10.

To see the macro in action, clear the screen. Next press ALT + F10, type **REPORTS**, and then press ENTER. Now you can type some text to examine the format in which it appears.

Macro 3

Suppose that in a long report you are numbering certain paragraphs. Create a macro that will automatically insert a paragraph number wherever the cursor is positioned. Name the macro PARA.

1. Press MACRO DEFINE (CTRL + F10).
2. Type **PARA** to name the macro.
3. Press ENTER to register the macro name.
4. Type the following description: **Insert automatic paragraph number.**
5. Press ENTER to register that description.
6. Enter the following keystrokes:

   DATE/OUTLINE (SHIFT + F5)

   P—to insert a paragraph number

   ENTER—to specify that the paragraph number will be automatic

   Two spaces—to create a gap separating a paragraph number from the text

7. Press CTRL + F10.

To execute this macro, position the cursor in a location where you want a paragraph number to appear. Then press ALT + F10, type **PARA**, and press ENTER.

Macro 4

Suppose that you just wrote a report but forgot to place in uppercase letters certain words sprinkled throughout the document. Create a macro named with the ENTER key that will switch a word to uppercase when the cursor is positioned anywhere in that word.

1. Position the cursor on any character of a word that's currently in lowercase letters on the screen.
2. Press MACRO DEFINE (CTRL + F10).
3. Press ENTER to name the macro.
4. Enter the following keystrokes:

   CTRL + RIGHT ARROW, CTRL + LEFT ARROW— to position the cursor on the first character of that word

   BLOCK (ALT + F4)

CTRL + RIGHT ARROW—to highlight the word

SWITCH (SHIFT + F3)

U—to select uppercase

5. Press CTRL + F10.

To execute this macro, position the cursor in another word, press ALT + F10, and then press ENTER.

Tip: *When you create a macro, you are performing the task at hand.*

When you define a macro, you are actually pressing the keys once so that WordPerfect can record them. For example, if you write a macro to erase the screen, you'll lose the text on your screen. If you write a macro to sort lines in alphabetical order, you will alphabetize the lines on your screen. Therefore, define a macro only when the keys you press will not harm the text currently on screen. In fact, it's a good idea to type sample text onto the screen to use when defining the macro.

Tip: *Define the macro so that it operates correctly in as many situations as possible.*

You should design a macro so that it can work no matter what the situation. For example, in Macro 4, the keystrokes used to highlight an entire word are CTRL + RIGHT ARROW, so that it never matters how many letters comprise the word to be switched to uppercase. As another example, suppose that you write a macro to change the font in your document. You should use the Name Search feature on the Base Font screen to move the cursor to a particular font, rather than using the DOWN ARROW key; that way, WordPerfect will seek the correct font even if the order of fonts listed on the Base Font screen changes.

Trap: *Don't press extraneous keys when recording a macro.*

Once you press MACRO DEFINE (CTRL + F10) to start recording, WordPerfect records every keystroke until you turn it off. It is easy to forget that a macro is being recorded, especially when you press a function key that causes WordPerfect to prompt for further information or to display a menu, and the flashing **Macro Def** temporarily disappears from the screen.

Make a mental note that you're in the midst of a macro definition. And be sure to turn the macro recording by pressing MACRO DEFINE (CTRL + F10) a second time, before you start performing another task.

Trap: *Don't write macros for tasks you perform only once, or once in a while.*

Macros occupy room on your disk just as documents do. Create macros only for repetitive tasks. For instance, if you hardly ever use WordPerfect's Speller feature, you won't want to write a macro to start a spelling check. On the other hand, if you merge the same primary file with the same secondary file frequently to print out mailing labels, write a macro to accomplish this task for you. Or, if you will be typing the same phrase 12 times in one day, write a macro to insert that phrase for you.

Tip: *A macro can be created that forces WordPerfect into Typeover or Insert mode.*

You can make WordPerfect change to either Typeover or Insert mode regardless of the current setting. The keystrokes for Forced Typeover mode are HOME, INS. The keystrokes for Forced Insert mode are HOME, HOME, INS.

For example, suppose that to draw the reader's attention, you wish to insert a line drawing containing the phrase "Action Required" in various locations throughout a report:

```
ACTION REQUIRED
```

Because you must be in Typeover mode to position text in an already existing box (as described in Chapter 17), you must force WordPerfect into Typeover mode before inserting the phrase. By using the keystrokes HOME, INS (rather than just INS) when recording the macro, you can make sure that WordPerfect switches into Typeover mode when the macro is executed, regardless of whether WordPerfect is in Insert mode or Typeover mode before you execute.

Tip: *A macro description can be displayed in two different situations.*

As described earlier, when you create a macro named with the ALT key or with one to eight characters, WordPerfect offers the opportunity to insert a 39-character description of the macro's function. Imagine creating 20 macros named ALT + A, ALT + B, ALT + C, and so on, and trying to keep track of the function performed by each. The description serves just that purpose—to remind you of the tasks that the macros perform.

A description does not appear when you execute a macro. Rather, the description appears in two other instances. First, the description appears if you use the LIST FILES (F5) key to display the List Files screen, position the cursor on a macro filename (remember that all macros are named with the extension .WPM), and type **6** or press ENTER to invoke the Look feature. Second, the description appears on the Macro Edit screen, the screen that is displayed as you edit a macro (described in the last section of this chapter, "Editing a Macro and Using the Macro Programming Language").

It is a good idea to enter a description for your macros. That way you can check, either on the List Files screen or as you edit the macro, to see what each macro accomplishes.

Trap: *Once you begin creating a macro, the only method for ending the definition is with the MACRO DEFINE key.*

When you press MACRO DEFINE (CTRL + F10) to define a macro and then wish to back out of the command, you can press CANCEL (F1). But once you name the macro, type a description, and the **Macro Def** message begins flashing on screen, CANCEL (F1) won't back you out. Instead, press MACRO DEFINE to stop recording.

Now you can press MACRO DEFINE (CTRL + F10) to start the recording process again. Give the macro the same name when redefining it, and WordPerfect will allow you to either replace the macro or to edit it. Alternatively, you can delete the macro from the disk by using the LIST FILES key. (See the following two Tips for more on replacing, editing, or deleting a macro that you've created.)

Tip: *You can replace or edit a macro already stored on disk.*

When you press MACRO DEFINE (CTRL + F10) and type in a name for a macro at the **Define Macro:** prompt, WordPerfect checks to see if a macro by that name already exists on disk (for all macros except a macro named with the ENTER key, as described further on in this section). If so, WordPerfect prompts you to decide whether you wish to replace the macro already on disk or to edit that macro. For instance, if that macro is named PARA, WordPerfect prompts

PARA.WPM is Already Defined. 1 Replace; **2** Edit: **0**

Select Replace (1 or R), and you can type in a new description and a brand-new set of macro keystrokes. The old macro is replaced by the one you now create.

Or, select Edit (2 or E) and you can edit the macro description and/or the keystrokes stored in the macro. The Edit option is also convenient if you've forgotten the tasks that a macro can perform; the macro keystrokes are displayed for you. As you edit a macro, you can, at the same time, use the Macro Programming Language. (For more on editing and the programming language, refer to the last section of this chapter, "Editing a Macro and Using the Macro Programming Language.")

Tip: *In general, macro files can be managed on disk like document files.*

If you record a macro so that it is stored on disk and then decide that you want to rename, copy, delete, or move it, you can do so on the List Files menu (accessed through the LIST FILES (F5) key), just as you can rename, copy, delete, or move a WordPerfect document stored on disk. You can also use the Look feature on the List Files menu to view the macro description (as described in a previous Tip).

However, you cannot use the Retrieve option or the Print option on the List Files menu to retrieve or print a macro. If you try, WordPerfect will prompt

ERROR: Incompatible file format

and will ignore your request.

Trap: *Don't use the ENTER key to name a macro that is complicated and may require editing.*

A macro named with the ENTER key operates differently than a macro named with ALT key or with one to eight characters. First, when you initially create a macro named with the ENTER key, WordPerfect provides no opportunity to type a description of the macro's purpose. WordPerfect skips over the "Description" prompt, and you begin defining the macro immediately. The macro you define is saved on disk in a file named WP{WP}.WPM.

Second, you cannot edit a macro named with the ENTER key. WordPerfect assumes that you always wish to replace a macro named with the ENTER key. If you press MACRO DEFINE (CTRL + F10) and press ENTER, the **Macro Def** message begins flashing immediately—even if a macro file named WP{WP}.WPM is already stored on disk.

Because of these differences, consider naming a macro with the ENTER key when you wish to create a macro that (1) you want to be easy to execute, (2) will require no editing once created, and (3) will become obsolete quickly, making the ENTER key available for creating another "quick-and-dirty" macro.

Trap: *Don't name a destructive macro with ALT.*

An ALT macro is easier to execute, so reserve this for frequently used macros. In general, name a macro with one through eight characters if the macro is used less often.

Be aware, however, that if you use ALT when defining a macro that erases the screen or rearranges an entire document, you run the risk of executing it by accident. As you learned, a macro named with ALT is executed easily—you simply press ALT and the letter key. It is quite easy to press the wrong key by mistake. Perhaps you meant to press SHIFT + R but instead pressed ALT + R. If ALT + R is a macro that erases the screen, you've lost your document. Therefore, assign a name other than ALT to destructive macros.

Tip: *When creating or executing a macro, you can specify a drive or directory different from the default.*

WordPerfect saves macros onto the default drive or directory (unless you specified a macro/keyboard directory, as described in the following Tip). When you invoke a macro, WordPerfect first looks on the default drive or directory and, if the macro is not found, checks the directory where the WordPerfect program file WP.EXE is stored.

You can, however, override these assumptions. You can save a macro into another drive or directory by specifying a path when naming the macro. For example, suppose you wish to create a macro named PARA and store it in the directory \WPER\BUD on the hard disk. When you press MACRO DEFINE (CTRL + F10) and WordPerfect prompts

Define macro:

you can type **C:\WPER\BUD\PARA** and press ENTER. The macro that you create will be named PARA, and will be stored in \WPER\BUD. Or, suppose that you wish to store that macro in the directory \WPER, where the WordPerfect program files are housed. Then you would type **C: \WPER\PARA**. Or, to store it on drive A, type **A:PARA**.

Similarly, you can execute a macro stored in a drive or directory other than the default by specifying a path when invoking the macro. For example, suppose that you wish to execute a macro named PARA stored in the directory \WPER\BUD. When you press MACRO (ALT + F10) and WordPerfect prompts

Macro:

you can type **C:\WPER\BUD\PARA** and press ENTER. Remember that if you store a macro in the directory where the WordPerfect program file WP.EXE is housed, then even if the default is another directory, you can still invoke it simply by specifying the macro name, without a path. That's because if a macro is not found in the default, WordPerfect checks the directory where WP.EXE is located. (See the following Tip for related information.)

Tip: *Store macros on the drive or directory that will make them most accessible.*

As described in the preceding Tip, WordPerfect assumes that you wish to save macros in the default drive or directory. This causes a problem if you later change the default; WordPerfect will be unable to find the macro. If you use certain macros often and in many documents, you will want to store your macros in a location in which they will always be available to you.

If you use floppy disks only, you have two options. One option is to store macros on the WordPerfect system disk in drive A. This is because WordPerfect checks for macros in both the default drive and the drive in which the WordPerfect program is housed. You have enough room available to store a limited number of macros on the WordPerfect disk that resides in drive A. To store macros on the WordPerfect system disk, either switch the default to drive A before defining a macro, or precede the macro name with A: (for example, A:REPORTS), as described in the preceding Tip. In time, however, you may run out of room to store additional macros on the WordPerfect disk.

The second option is to store your macros on one data disk that serves as your macro library. Then, every time you format a new data disk for storing new document files, copy all the macros from the macro library onto that data disk. That way the macros will always be accessible to you, no matter which data disk is inserted in drive B.

Hard disk users have three options. First, you can store macros in the same directory where the WordPerfect program file WP.EXE is stored (which would be \WPER if you followed the installation procedures in Appendix A). WordPerfect automatically checks that directory if the macro isn't found in the default directory.

Alternatively, hard disk users can create a directory just for macros, perhaps one called \WPER\MACS. Then you would switch the default to that directory whenever you wished to create or execute a macro, or you could precede the macro name by \WPER\MACS, as described in the Tip above.

The third option is often the most effective of all. You can create a directory just for macros (such as \WPER\MACS) and then inform WordPerfect about this special directory by using the Location of Auxiliary Files option on the Setup menu. (The options on the Setup menu are discussed in Appendix B.) Once you inform WordPerfect of the existence of this directory, all macros you create will be automatically saved into that special directory. And, when you execute a macro, WordPerfect looks first in that special directory (rather than in the default directory) to locate it; if the macro is not found, WordPerfect then checks the directory where the WordPerfect program file WP.EXE is stored.

Tip: *The Keyboard Layout feature allows you to map a macro to any key and to group macros together.*

The Keyboard Layout feature, which is accessed from the Setup menu (as described in Appendix B), offers the ability to create keyboard definitions, which essentially remap the keyboard to your needs. Using this feature, you can assign a macro to any key within a keyboard definition. To execute the macro, you simply press the key that the macro was assigned to (providing that the appropriate keyboard definition is active).

Using keyboard definitions to name macros is not for everyone. For instance, if the 26 easily accessed macros available with ALT + a letter are sufficient for you, then you may not wish to bother with keyboard definitions.

Yet there are times when assigning macros to a keyboard definition is advantageous. For example, suppose that you rely heavily on macros and have created 50 of them. By using keyboard definitions, you are not limited to naming an easily executed macro—one that is executed without first pressing the MACRO key—with ALT + a letter. You can name a macro with virtually any key combination, such as with CTRL + a letter or with ALT + a number, or with any function key combination, such as F2, or SHIFT + F4, or CTRL + F6, or F12 (providing your keyboard has 12 function keys).

Keyboard definitions also allow you to group macros together. For instance, you can create one keyboard definition that contains macros you use only when writing legal documents, another that contains macros that you use only when writing reports, and a third that contains macros that you use to produce your company newsletter. Then, depending on the document you are typing, you can activate a specific keyboard definition. In that way, you have control over exactly when macros are available to you. If you activate a macro keyboard definition, the macros it contains are all available; if you return to the original keyboard definition (that is, to the standard keyboard assignments established by WordPerfect

Corporation), they are not. (Refer to Appendix B for more on the Keyboard Layout feature.)

Tip: *Consider using the Styles feature, rather than the Macro feature, for certain tasks.*

Chapter 10 describes how the Styles feature allows you to define the look of certain elements in your document, such as headings, subheadings, and paragraphs, and to have WordPerfect format or enhance those elements for you. In this way, you can set up the appearnce of your text quickly and easily.

When you are considering a macro that formats or enhances text in a document, consider whether the Styles feature might prove more effective. For instance, suppose you wish to have WordPerfect do the work of inserting a paragraph number in front of each document heading and then boldfacing the heading text. You could create a macro to do so. But one advantage to creating a style instead is that if you later decide to change the way the headings appear (for example, changing the boldfacing to underlining), you can simply change the style; all headings will be changed automatically. You can even define macros that insert style codes at specified locations in your document. Turn to Chapter 10 for more on the Styles feature.

Tip: *Stop macro execution by pressing CANCEL.*

If you press MACRO (ALT + F10) to execute a macro and then realize that the cursor is incorrectly positioned, press CANCEL (F1) to abort the macro command. Reposition the cursor and then press MACRO to initiate the execution.

Further, you can press CANCEL (F1) to abort a macro that is in the process of executing—although a macro containing only a few keystrokes will often execute even before you have the chance to press CANCEL. (By using the Macro Programming Language described in the last section of this chapter, "Editing a Macro and Using the Macro Programming Language," you can disable the CANCEL key from stopping a macro execution.)

Tip: *Remember your original assumptions when executing a macro.*

It is very important to know how a macro has been recorded. When activated, does it begin by assuming that the cursor is on the first character of a word? Does it assume that the cursor is at the top of the document (or is that step included in the macro)? Does it assume that the screen is clear? Does it assume that the cursor is on the Typing screen or the Reveal Codes screen? Make sure that the stage is correctly set before you ask a macro to take over for you.

Tip: *Use the Repeat Value feature to execute a macro a specified number of times.*

You can repeat a macro any number of times in a row by using the Repeat Value feature, accessed with the ESC key (discussed in Chapter 3). For example, suppose that you have five words in a row that you wish to change into uppercase letters. You could use Macro 4, which performs this task for one word and is named with the ENTER key. Invoke this macro five times, as follows:

1. Place the cursor anywhere within the first word to be changed into uppercase.
2. Press ESC. WordPerfect responds

   Repeat Value = 8

3. Type 5. Now the prompt reads

   Repeat Value = 5

   You are ready to execute the macro.

4. Press MACRO (ALT + F10). WordPerfect responds

   Macro:

5. Press ENTER (since the macro is named with the ENTER key). In seconds, WordPerfect capitalizes five words in a row for you.

Tip: *A macro ends when a search string is not found.*

The Search or Replace command can be included in a macro. For instance, you may wish to create a macro that searches for a certain phrase or sequence of codes in your document. If the search string is found, then the macro will continue executing. If that phrase is not found, however, then the macro terminates.

Including a search string in a macro allows you the flexibility to create looping macros, where a macro repeats only if the search string is found. This is described in the next section, "Chaining and Nesting Keyboard Macros."

If you use the Macro Programming Language to create a programming language macro, then you can alter WordPerfect's assumption that a macro ends when a search string is not found. For instance, you can specify that if the search string is not found, the macro executes a certain subroutine of keystrokes. See the last section of this chapter for details on the Macro Programming Language.

Trap: *If a macro is created to begin a merge, the merge must be the last macro step.*

You can use a macro to perform a merge; the macro can automatically initiate the merge and insert the names of the primary and secondary files that you wish to use. But the command that starts the merge must constitute the final keystrokes of the macro. A macro automatically ends when a merge is begun (unless you use the Macro Programming Language, as described in the last section of this chapter, "Editing a Macro and Using the Macro Programming Language").

Tip: *You can execute a macro after a merge is completed.*

In Chapters 24 and 25 you learned about merge codes that can be inserted in primary merge files. One such code pair is ^G^G. Place the codes ^G^G in a primary document, with a macro name between the pair, and that macro will be executed when the merge ends. If the macro you wish to execute is named PRINTX, for example, insert ^GPRINTX^G. PRINTX will be executed when the merge is completed.

Tip: *You can create a full-screen menu of available macros by employing the Merge feature.*

Suppose that one of your responsibilities is to produce monthly reports, and you plan to create seven macros to make the job easier. Using the Merge feature, you can create a customized menu of your seven macros. You can then execute any of the macros by selecting from the menu, just like you execute a WordPerfect feature by selecting from a WordPerfect menu.

What you do is create a primary file for a merge with the keyboard (a process discussed in Chapter 24), such as the one shown in Figure 27-1. In that primary file, you insert the text of the menu—many lines long and listing each macro—between two ^O merge codes. This is followed by a ^C merge code, and the instructions to execute each macro between two ^G merge codes.

Creating such a macro menu requires these basic steps:

1. Establish a pattern for naming the macros that will comprise the macro menu. Each of the macro names should start with the character that corresponds to its selection number on the menu, followed by the same set of one to seven characters.

```
^O              MENU FOR MONTHLY REPORTS


1.          Standard Report Margins and Spacing

2.          Insert Report Graphics Figure and Logo

3.          Insert Introductory Paragraph

4.          Number Paragraphs with Roman Numerals

5.          Pause for Base Font Change

6.          Insert Market Share Paragraph

7.          Insert Closing Paragraph



MAKE A SELECTION (1-7) AND PRESS ENTER:   ^G^CCHOICE^G^O
                                          Doc 1 Pg 1 Ln 1" Pos 1"
```

Figure 27-1. Primary file containing a menu of macros

For example, notice in Figure 27-1 that the macro which inserts margins and spacing codes in a report is listed as number 1. That macro could be named 1CHOICE, in which case the macro that inserts a certain graphics figure and logo would be named 2CHOICE, the next macro would be named 3CHOICE, and so on. Or the first macro could be assigned to the name 1XX, in which case the second macro would be assigned 2XX, and so on.

2. Create each macro separately, using the filename pattern that you devised, and store all of the macros in the same drive/directory.
3. Create the macro menu as follows:

   Clear the Typing screen and, at the very top of the screen, insert a ^O merge code. Remember from Chapter 24 that to insert this merge code you can press CTRL + O, or you can press MERGE CODES (SHIFT + F9) and select O.

   Type the text of the menu exactly as you want it to appear, but without any enhancements such as centering, underlining, boldfacing, tabs, or indents. Between the ^O^O merge codes you can insert only characters, hard returns, and spaces.

   Where you want the cursor to pause for keyboard input, type in ^G^C, then the characters that each macro name have in common, and then ^G^O.

   For example, if each of the macros were named 1CHOICE, 2CHOICE, and so on, the merge codes inserted at the end of the menu would be ^G^CCHOICE^G^O. Or, if you named each macro 1XX, 2XX, 3XX, and so on, the merge code combination would be ^G^CXX^G^O. Figure 27-1 shows the primary file in the case where each macro was named 1CHOICE, 2CHOICE, and so on.

4. Save the menu to disk with a name that reminds you that it is a primary file containing a macro menu (such as REPMENU.PRI, which stands for REPort MENU, PRImary file).

Once a macro menu has been created, you are ready to use it whenever you want to execute one of the macros it contains. The macro will take effect at the end of the document that is currently on screen. Therefore, if the macro you are about to invoke will retrieve a paragraph, for example, make sure that the document into which you wish to retrieve that paragraph is on screen, and that the cursor is at the end of the document. Then proceed as follows (of course, you can also write a macro that automatically performs the following four steps):

1. Press MERGE/SORT (CTRL + F9).
2. Select Merge (1 or M).
3. Type in the name of the primary file (such as REPMENU.PRI) containing the menu of macros, and press ENTER.
4. Press ENTER when asked for a secondary filename—since the input will be from the keyboard and not another file. WordPerfect displays all the text that you had inserted between the merge codes in the primary file, as shown in Figure 27-2.

Now you are ready to select a macro by number and to press ENTER. Whichever number you type will be substituted for the ^C code. For example, if you type

```
                MENU FOR MONTHLY REPORTS

1.          Standard Report Margins and Spacing
2.          Insert Report Graphics Figure and Logo
3.          Insert Introductory Paragraph
4.          Number Paragraphs with Roman Numerals
5.          Pause for Base Font Change
6.          Insert Market Share Paragraph
7.          Insert Closing Paragraph



MAKE A SELECTION (1-7) AND PRESS ENTER:
```

Figure 27-2. Menu of macros during a merge

2, the merge codes would read ^G2CHOICE^G. When you then press ENTER, the menu clears and the macro indicated will be executed (such as the macro named 2CHOICE).

Or, if you wish to clear the menu from the screen without executing any of the macros, press MERGE CODES (SHIFT + F9) to end the merge. The menu clears without invoking any of the macros it contains.

Note: If you decide to delve into the Macro Programming Language, discussed in the last section of this chapter, "Editing a Macro and Using the Macro Programming Language," you'll find that you can create even slicker, more sophisticated menus than the one shown in Figure 27-2.

Tip: *You can create a temporary macro if the sole task of the macro is to insert text.*

As you'll learn in the last section of this chapter, "Editing a Macro and Using the Macro Programming Language," variables are used when you are creating a sophisticated macro using the Macro Programming Language and you need to pass values (either text values or numeric values) to a specific subroutine. But if you don't mind using up variables, or if you have no intention of using the Macro Programming Language, then take advantage of variables to create *temporary* macros, which are stored not on disk, but in the computer's random access memory (RAM). A temporary macro remains in effect only for the current working session and is deleted as soon as you exit WordPerfect.

A temporary macro can be used only when the task for that macro is to insert text. For example, suppose that you're writing a letter in which you frequently refer to "The Tree Growers and Tree Planters Association of America." That's a long name to type. You can create a temporary macro which inserts this name for you whenever you request it. You cannot, however, create a temporary macro to change margins or to initiate a spelling check.

When you create a temporary macro, you do *not* use the MACRO DEFINE key; instead, use the key combination CTRL + PGUP. Then assign your text to any of ten variables which must consist of the numbers 0 through 9 located above the letter keys on the keyboard. There are two alternatives for doing this: type in the text directly (it can be up to 120 characters in length), or use the Block feature. (When assigned to a variable, most codes in a highlighted block are ignored, except for the following codes: Tab, →Indent, Hard Return, Hard Page, and Required Hyphen. Also Soft Return codes and Soft Page codes are converted into spaces.)

To type in the text directly, create a temporary macro as follows:

1. With the cursor positioned anywhere on the Typing screen, press CTRL + PGUP. WordPerfect prompts

   Variable:

2. WordPerfect is prompting for a number that the text will be assigned to. Type a number from 0 through 9. WordPerfect prompts

   Value:

3. Type your text, up to 120 characters in length. The text appears at the bottom of the screen.

4. Press ENTER to assign the text to the variable you specified.

Or, if the text is already on screen, use the Block feature to create a temporary macro:

1. Use the BLOCK (ALT + F4) key to highlight the text in reverse video. The message **Block on** flashes on screen.

2. Press CTRL + PGUP. WordPerfect prompts:

   Variable:

3. WordPerfect is prompting for a number that the text will be assigned to. Type a number from 0 through 9. The reverse video and the **Block On** message clear.

When you wish to execute a temporary macro, whether or not you used the Block feature to assign the variable, follow these steps:

1. Position the cursor where you want the text to appear.

2. Press ALT + the number you named with it. For example, to execute the macro that you stored as variable 1, press ALT + 1.

Remember that as soon as you exit WordPerfect, temporary macros are erased from RAM. Therefore, if you wish to write a macro that inserts text during any

WordPerfect session, be sure to use the MACRO DEFINE key to create a permanent macro, as the example in Macro 1 illustrates. (Or you can write a macro, using the MACRO DEFINE key, that will assign text to a number key. Execute that macro, and then you can employ ALT + a number for the rest of the working session.)

Tip: *Use a startup option to automatically invoke a macro when WordPerfect is loaded.*

Chapter 1 describes various slash options that are available when you load WordPerfect. One such startup option is /M, which directs WordPerfect to execute a macro as soon as WordPerfect is loaded. This is a handy feature to use if you want WordPerfect to perform the same tasks whenever you start the program.

For instance, suppose that you share a computer with office mates. Whenever you load WordPerfect—but before you begin to type, edit, or print documents—you always perform three tasks: change the default directory to the one where you alone store files; select a specific dot matrix printer; and change the text quality on the Print menu to draft mode. Suppose that you create a macro to perform these tasks for you, which you store under the name SUE. You can load WordPerfect so that the macro named SUE is executed, as soon as the program is loaded, by typing **WP/M-SUE** at the DOS prompt. (Or, if you created your own batch file to automatically load WordPerfect with the options you desire, then you can include the command WP/M-SUE in the batch file. Appendix A describes how to create a batch file to load WordPerfect.)

Tip: *(When upgrading from 4.2.) The basics of the Macro feature remain the same, although it has been substantially enhanced and version 4.2 macros must be converted to operate in version 5.*

The fundamental method for creating and executing a macro has not changed in version 5; the MACRO DEFINE (previously called MACRO DEF) and MACRO keys work as they did before. There are, however, some modifications. First, you can now provide a macro description before you begin defining a macro named with the ALT key or with one to eight characters. Second, you can now specify a path to indicate which drive or directory a macro should be stored on or executed from.

Also, macros are stored on disk with the extension .WPM, rather than the extension .MAC. And, you can now rename macros by using the List Files screen.

But in version 5 you no longer create a temporary macro by naming a macro with one letter or with the ENTER key, as in version 4.2; these macros now become permanent. Instead, you can create a temporary macro that inserts text by assigning a text value to a variable, as described in an earlier Tip.

As you'll learn in the last section of this chapter, "Editing a Macro and Using the Macro Programming Language," additional enhancements include the ability to edit a macro or to use the Macro Programming Language to write sophisticated routines.

As a version 4.2 user, you may have already recorded a variety of macros that you wish to use in version 5. You cannot use version 4.2 macros in version 5 unless you first convert them to version 5 by using the macro conversion program, MACROCNV.EXE. This program converts all text, all cursor movement functions, and those features that are accessed using the same keys as in version 4.2. Keystrokes that it cannot convert will be flagged with comments, and those you will have to correct manually by using the Macro Edit feature (also described in the last section of this chapter). To use this conversion program, refer to Chapter 28.

Keep in mind that version 5 offers some features that were unavailable in version 4.2 that may make your old macros either obsolete or too cumbersome to be performed in version 5. Therefore, for each macro, consider whether it makes sense to convert it, or to replace it with a brand-new macro that performs the same task in a more elegant, efficient manner using the new version 5 features.

Chaining and Nesting Keyboard Macros

You can define macros in such a way that they are linked to one another. Then, invoking one macro can create a chain reaction, as if you knocked over one domino and many others fell down, too. There are three methods you can use to link macros together. You can define a macro so that it executes the following:

- **A simple chain** This type of chain executes another macro. To create a simple chain, define one macro that, in its final keystrokes, executes another macro. In other words, when recording a macro, for the last macro keystrokes press MACRO (ALT + F10) and enter the name of the next macro. Then press MACRO DEFINE (CTRL + F10) to finish defining the macro. Macro 5, below, provides an example of a simple chain.

- **A repeating, or looping, macro** This type of macro repeats itself. You will need to insert a Search command in this type of macro. The macro automatically repeats itself until the search string is not found, thus preventing an endless loop in which a macro won't stop executing itself. To create a looping macro, instruct the macro, as the final step in its creation, to execute itself again. In other words, as the last keystrokes during the recording of the macro, press MACRO (ALT + F10) and enter the name of the macro that you are currently recording. Then press MACRO DEFINE (CTRL + F10) to end the macro definition. Macro 6, below, provides an example of a repeating macro.
- **A nesting macro** This type of macro executes one macro inside another macro. Unlike chained macros, the nested macro is not executed when the first macro is completed, but rather at the point at which it is encountered in the macro. After the completion of the nested macro, the original macro continues to execute. To create a nesting macro, begin defining the original macro. When you come to the point at which you wish to execute a second macro, press ALT + the letter of the macro that will be nested. Then continue to define the first macro. Only a macro named with the ALT key can be nested inside another macro. The ALT macro must be defined before it can be placed in another macro. Macro 7, below, provides an example of a nesting macro.

Macro 5

At the beginning of the chapter, in the Macro 3 example, you learned how to create a macro named PARA that automatically inserts a paragraph number wherever the cursor is placed. Suppose that every time you execute this macro, you then want to execute another macro called ABC, which inserts the words "ABC Company agrees to." You can create a variation on Macro 3 by replacing the old macro named PARA with a new macro with the same name. Then you can create the macro called ABC. To replace the PARA macro:

1. Press MACRO DEFINE (CTRL + F10).
2. Type **PARA** to name the macro.
3. Press ENTER to register the macro name.
4. Select Replace (1 or R) to indicate that you wish to replace the macro with a new one.

5. Type the following description: **Insert paragraph number and execute ABC.**
6. Press ENTER to register the description.
7. Enter the following keystrokes:

   DATE/OUTLINE (SHIFT + F5)

   P—to insert a paragraph number

   ENTER—to specify that the paragraph number will be automatic

   Two spaces—to create a gap that separates the paragraph number from the text

8. Press ALT + F10 to signal that another macro should be executed.
9. Type **ABC** and press ENTER to signal that the macro called ABC will be executed.
10. Press CTRL + F10.

To create the macro called ABC:

1. Press CTRL + F10.
2. Type **ABC**—to name the macro.
3. Press ENTER—to register the macro name.
4. Press ENTER—to signify that you will not provide a description.
5. Type the following: **ABC Company agrees to**.
6. Press CTRL + F10.

Now two macros are chained together. When you are ready to execute the macros, press MACRO (ALT + F10), type **PARA**, and press ENTER. First PARA, and then ABC, will be executed.

Note: ABC can still be executed on its own without the PARA macro by pressing ALT + F10, typing **ABC**, and pressing ENTER.

Macro 6

Suppose that you wish to number every paragraph in a document all at once, rather than just one paragraph at a time as described in Macro 3. Paragraphs are separated by one blank line, which means that two hard return codes precede each paragraph (one **[HRt]** concluding the paragraph above, and another **[HRt]** on the blank line). You can use the Search command to position the cursor in front of a paragraph and then number that paragraph. And because the macro contains a Search command, you can loop it back onto itself, so that it executes over and over until the search string is not found. Call this new macro PARALL (meaning PARagraph numbers for ALL paragraphs).

1. Press MACRO DEFINE (CTRL + F10).
2. Type **PARALL** to name the macro.
3. Press ENTER to register the macro name.
4. Type the following description: **Insert para number in front of each paragraph.**
5. Press ENTER to register that description.
6. Enter the following keystrokes:

   →SEARCH (F2), ENTER, ENTER—to insert a search string

   →SEARCH (F2)—to execute the search

   DATE/OUTLINE (SHIFT + F5)

   P—to insert a paragraph number

   ENTER—to specify that the paragraph number will be automatic

   Two spaces—to create a gap that separates the paragraph number from the text

7. Press ALT + F10 to signal that another macro should be executed.
8. Type **PARALL** and press ENTER to signal that the same macro should be executed, creating a loop.
9. Press CTRL + F10.

When you're ready to execute, move the cursor to the top of a document of paragraphs and press MACRO (ALT + F10), type **PARALL**, and press ENTER. Paragraph numbers are inserted in front of each paragraph until the search string is no longer found.

Macro 7

Suppose that you wish to create a macro that sorts every line in a document on screen alphabetically based on the first word of each line (an example of a document that would be appropriate for this type of sort can be found in Chapter 26, "Sorting and Selecting," in Figure 26-1). In addition, you wish to create a separate macro that sorts every line, then inserts a certain title at the top of the document, and then prints the document. You can create the sort macro first, and name it ALT + S. Then you can create a second macro, named FINAL, that executes the ALT + S macro and then inserts the title "Product List" and prints. You'll need two macros.

To create the macro named ALT + S:

1. Press MACRO DEFINE (CTRL + F10).
2. Type ALT + S to name the macro.
3. Type the following description: **Sort all lines on screen**.
4. Press ENTER to register the description.
5. Enter the following keystrokes:

   MERGE/SORT (CTRL + F9)

   S, ENTER, ENTER—to sort from and to the screen

   3, **A**, **1**, ENTER, **1**, ENTER—to define Key 1 as the first word

   EXIT (F7)

   S, CTRL + END—to erase any selection statement that may have been previously defined

   EXIT (F7)

   O, **A**—to select ascending order

   T, **L**—to select a line sort

P—to perform the sort

6. Press CTRL + F10.

Now that you've created the ALT + S macro, it can be nested into a macro named FINAL:

1. Press MACRO DEFINE (CTRL + F10).
2. Type **FINAL** to name the macro.
3. Press ENTER to register the macro name.
4. Type the following description: **Execute ALTS.WPM, insert title, print.**
5. Press ENTER to register the description.
6. Press ALT + S to execute the macro named ALT + S as the first step in the macro.
7. Enter the following keystrokes:

   HOME, HOME, UP ARROW—to move to the top of the document

   ENTER, ENTER—to insert blank lines at the top

   HOME, HOME, UP ARROW—to move back up to the top

   CENTER (SHIFT + F6)—to center the title

   Product List—to type in the title

   PRINT (SHIFT + F7), **F**—to print out the full document

8. Press CTRL + F10.

When you are ready to execute the macro named FINAL, make sure that a document to be sorted line by line is on screen. Also, make sure that the printer is on. When you are ready to execute the macros, press MACRO (ALT + F10), and type **FINAL**, and press ENTER. ALT + S will be executed as part of the macro.

Note: ALT + S can still be executed on its own without the FINAL macro—simply by pressing ALT + S.

Tip: *Chained macros rarely do what you want them to the first time around.*

As the tasks for the macros you create become more complicated, so does the process of defining the macros. Therefore, be prepared if a macro does not work properly. Try executing the macro on a test document before you use it with your actual work. And, if it doesn't work properly, you can either create it again, or you can edit the macro as described in the last section of this chapter, "Editing a Macro and Using the Macro Programming Language."

Trap: *An endless loop can lock up the computer.*

A repeating macro should contain a Search command. If it doesn't, the macro continues to repeat itself, like a mouse on a treadmill, and you run the risk of locking up the computer. CANCEL (F1) sometimes stops the macro before the system locks.

Trap: *You can't define a nesting macro until you've created the ALT macro to nest.*

When you record a nesting macro and you press ALT + a letter, WordPerfect executes the ALT macro, even during the macro definition. The ALT macro must therefore be defined before it can be used in another macro.

Tip: *(When upgrading from 4.2.) The nesting macro is new in version 5.*

Previously, your only choice when linking macros was to begin another macro only when the first one had finished execution. In version 5, you can define a macro so that another macro named with ALT executes at any time; WordPerfect does not wait until the first macro is complete before executing the nesting macro. After the nesting macro is entirely executed, the first macro resumes execution.

In version 4.2, you could create a conditional macro, where one macro executed if a search condition was found, and another executed if a search condition was not found. In version 5, you must use the Macro Programming Language to create a conditional macro (as described in the last section of this chapter, "Editing a Macro and Using the Macro Programming Language").

Inserting Special Keyboard Macro Commands

As you gain confidence in creating macros, it is helpful to know about four special macro commands that can be inserted in the macro as you are recording it: Pause, Display, Assign, and Comment. To access these commands, you press CTRL + PGUP while **Macro Def** is flashing on the screen (meaning that you're in the middle of creating a macro). If you are viewing the Typing or the Reveal Codes screen when you press CTRL + PGUP, the following menu appears

1 Pause; 2 Display; 3 Assign; 4 Comment: **0**

Or, if you are viewing a WordPerfect menu or are in the middle of a WordPerfect feature when you press CTRL + PGUP, the following shorter menu appears

1 Pause; 2 Display: **0**

You would then select one of these items, enter the appropriate information, and continue to create your macro.

The purpose and use of each of these four special macro commands are as follows:

- **Pause** Enables you to bring the macro to a complete stop (pause) during macro execution so that you can type text and/or commands from the keyboard and then press ENTER to complete the macro execution.

  When you are defining the macro and you want to insert to a pause, you would press CTRL + PGUP and select Pause (1 or P).

  After indicating a pause, you may then need to type in a sample of what will be entered during the pause once the macro is executed. Type in a sample of the text to be entered. Next, press ENTER again to continue defining the macro. The sample keystrokes to be entered at the pause will not be recorded as part of the macro. Or, if you do not need to include sample keystrokes (because, for example, the pause is simply to allow the user to read the screen), simply press ENTER.

  Now you can continue to define the macros. When you execute a macro and WordPerfect encounters a pause, it stops executing and allows you to enter keystrokes from the keyboard. Type the necessary keys and then press ENTER so the macro will resume execution.

  For example, Macro 2, in the first section of this chapter, "Creating and Executing a Keyboard Macro," describes how to create a macro named

REPORTS that changes margins and spacing. Suppose that you want to replace that macro with a new one that pauses when prompted for a right margin, so that you can indicate different right-margin settings depending on the format of the report. Macro 8 (shown at the end of this list) provides the steps with which to do this.

- **Display** Allows you to select whether you want the macro to display as it is executed. The default is for Display to be off, meaning that the display of the macro execution is turned off so that it is invisible. You can instead select to turn the display on.

  When you are recording the macro and you want to turn the display on or off, you would press CTRL + PGUP and select Display (2 or D). If Display is currently off, the following prompt appears:

  Display execution? (Y/N) No

  Type **Y** to turn on the display of the macro execution. Or type **N** or press ENTER to leave Display off.

  If Display is currently on, the following prompt appears:

  Display execution? (Y/N) Yes

  Type **N** to turn off the display of the macro execution. Or type **Y** or press ENTER to leave Display on.

  Now you can continue to define the rest of the macro. You can turn Display on or off many times in the same macro.

- **Assign** Gives a value to a variable. This is useful when you are creating a sophisticated macro using the Macro Programming Language (described in the following section of this chapter) and you need to pass a text or numeric value to a specific macro subroutine. The variables to which you can assign values are the number keys 0 through 9.

  When you are recording the macro and you want to assign a variable, you would press CTRL + PGUP and select Assign (3 or A). WordPerfect prompts

  Variable:

  Type in a number from 0 through 9. Next, WordPerfect prompts

  Value:

  Type in the value that you wish to assign to the variable.

  Alternatively, you can assign a variable by using the Block feature. When you are recording the macro, use the BLOCK (ALT + F4) key to highlight the text that is to be assigned to a number key. Then press CTRL + PGUP and select Assign (3 or A). WordPerfect prompts

Variable:

Type in a number from 0 through 9. The highlighted text is assigned to that number, and the reverse video clears.

- **Comment** Inserts a comment into the macro which is ignored when the macro is executed. The comment is usually an explanation of a certain set of keystrokes that you have just typed to define the macro.

  When you are recording the macro and you want to insert a comment, press CTRL + PGUP and select Comment (4 or C). WordPerfect prompts

  Comment:

  Type in a comment of any length, and press ENTER. Now continue to record the macro. You can include any number of comments in the same macro.

  Comments are shown only when you choose to edit the macro, as discussed in the following section of this chapter.

Macro 8

At the beginning of the chapter, in the Macro 2 example, you learned how to create a macro called REPORTS that changes margins and spacing. Suppose that you've already created the macro named REPORTS, but you want to replace it with a new macro that pauses when prompted for a right margin. This way you can indicate different right-margin settings, depending on the format of the report. To replace the REPORTS macro:

1. Press MACRO DEFINE (CTRL + F10).
2. Type **REPORTS** to name the macro.
3. Press ENTER to register the macro name.
4. Select Replace (1 or R) to indicate that you wish to replace the macro with a new one.
5. Type the following description: **Margins 1.5",?; Double spacing.**
6. Press ENTER to register the description.

7. Enter the following keystrokes:

   FORMAT (SHIFT + F8)

   L, **M**, **1.5"**, ENTER—to define the left-margin setting

8. Press CTRL + PGUP to view a menu of special macro commands.
9. Select Pause (1 or P).
10. Type **1.25"**—to indicate a sample response so that you can continue typing the macro. The number 1.25 will not be recorded.
11. Press ENTER—to signal the end of the pause.
12. Enter the following keystrokes:

    ENTER—to register whatever right-margin setting you type at the pause

    S, **2**, ENTER—to indicate double spacing

    EXIT (F7)

13. Press CTRL + F10.

When you are ready to execute, position the cursor. Then press MACRO (ALT + F10), type **REPORTS**, and then press ENTER. WordPerfect stops for you to type in a right-margin setting. Type a right-margin setting and press ENTER to signal WordPerfect to complete the macro.

Trap: *Only by pressing ENTER can you continue a macro that is stopped for keyboard input.*

Remember that when a macro comes to a temporary stop for keyboard input, the macro resumes only after you press ENTER. For example, if the macro is paused for you to type in a search string, type the string and press ENTER. Don't press →SEARCH (F2) after typing in the search string, as you normally would if not executing a macro.

Tip: *You can assign a variable even when you've finished creating a macro.*

In addition to assigning a text or numeric value to a variable during the recording of a macro, there are other times when you can do so. If you are viewing the

Typing or the Reveal Codes screen but are *not* currently defining a macro, then pressing CTRL + PGUP allows you to assign variables manually (or to create temporary macros), as described in the first section of this chapter, "Creating and Executing a Keyboard Macro." And if you are editing a macro, you can also assign variables, a task described in the following section of this chapter.

Tip: *Comments are useful when you're creating a long, complicated macro.*

If you insert comments when recording a macro, they are never displayed on screen when you execute; they are ignored. So, why include comments in a macro? Because they are useful if you are writing a long macro that will probably require editing later to make it work properly. By inserting comments, you break the keystrokes up into separate chunks, making it easier to decipher the keystrokes when you edit them. The procedure for editing macros is described in the following section of this chapter.

Tip: *(When upgrading from 4.2.) You slow down or pause a macro differently in version 5.*

In version 4.2, you indicated a pause during macro definition by pressing CTRL + PGUP, and then either by pressing ENTER to signal a pause, or by typing in a delay value to make the macro visible at a certain speed and pressing ENTER. In version 5, pressing CTRL + PGUP brings up a menu of four items. You can pause the macro by selecting the first option, Pause, or make it visible by selecting the second option, Display. To slow the macro to a certain speed, you must employ the Macro Programming Language, as described in the following section of this chapter.

Editing a Macro and Using the Macro Programming Language

When recording a macro, it is easy to inadvertently press the wrong key. And the more complicated the macro, the greater the chance that it won't work properly when first created. With the Macro Edit feature, you can correct a typing mistake, and add or delete keystrokes. In addition, this feature provides access to the Macro Programming Language, which does not limit you to the WordPerfect menus and features, but instead allows you to write complicated macros, as you can with any programming language.

In order to edit a macro or to access the programming language for that macro, the macro must already be stored on disk. It makes no difference what is currently on the Typing screen. Proceed as follows:

1. Press MACRO DEFINE (CTRL + F10).
2. Type in the name of the previously defined macro (and, if the macro was named with one through eight characters, press ENTER). For instance, type ALT + S, or type **PARA** and press ENTER.

   A new prompt appears. For example, if you pressed the macro ALT + S, then WordPerfect prompts

   ALTS.WPM is Already Defined. 1 Replace; **2** Edit: **0**

3. Select Edit (2 or E). A Macro Edit screen, like the one shown in Figure 27-3 appears. (Figure 27-3 shows the macro keystrokes for the macro named ALT + S, which you created if you followed the instructions in Macro 7.)

   The top of the Macro Edit screen lists the name of the macro file. Next is the "Description" heading, displaying the description that you inserted when creating the macro; if you did not type a description, then no description appears. Finally, under the "Action" heading is a double-line box that contains each of the keystrokes recorded for that macro. Each keystroke you used while defining the macro is displayed. Any keystroke that corresponds to a function key or to an editing key is represented by the key name, surrounded by curved brackets and with the first letter of major words capitalized. For instance, {Merge/Sort} signifies the MERGE/SORT (CTRL + F9) key, and {Del to EOL} signifies the DEL EOL (CTRL + END) key combination.

   Note: Notice that the first keystroke shown in the Action box in Figure 27-3 is {DISPLAY OFF}. This is one of the commands in the Macro Command Language, and is automatically inserted because WordPerfect assumes that you wish macro execution to be invisible unless you edit the macro. The Macro Command Language is described later in this chapter section.

4. If you wish to edit the description, select Description (1 or D), and use the standard cursor movement and editing keys to change the text of the de-

```
Macro: Edit

     File              ALTS.WPM

  1 - Description      Sort all lines on screen

  2 - Action

     {DISPLAY OFF}{Merge/Sort}s{Enter}
     {Enter}
     3a1{Enter}
     1{Enter}
     {Exit}s{Del to EOL}{Exit}oatlp

Selection: 0
```

Figure 27-3. The Macro Edit screen

scription. Remember that a description can be up to 39 characters in length. Then press EXIT (F7) or ENTER.

If you wish to edit the keystrokes themselves, select Action (2 or A). The cursor moves inside the Action box. Now, while the cursor is inside the Action box, you can

- Position the cursor by using the standard cursor movement keys. For instance, press RIGHT ARROW to move the cursor one keystroke to the right, or press END to move the cursor to the end of the line. The cursor is on a function or editing keystroke when it is on the keystroke's left curved bracket {.
- Delete keystrokes by using the standard editing keys. For example, delete a keystroke by positioning the cursor on the keystroke (or on the left curved bracket if the keystroke is in curved brackets) and pressing DEL. Or position the cursor just to the right of the keystroke and press BACKSPACE. Or delete all keystrokes from the current cursor position to the end of the line by pressing CTRL + END.
- Insert a character or a key name at the current cursor position by pressing that key. For instance, type **ABC** and WordPerfect inserts

those characters at the current cursor position. Press the SPACEBAR to insert spaces (the space character appears on the Macro Edit screen as a dot, for clarity). Press CENTER (SHIFT + F6) and WordPerfect inserts {Center}. Press GRAPHICS (ALT + F9) and WordPerfect inserts {Graphics}.

- Separate the keystrokes into more readable chunks by positioning the cursor and pressing TAB to move keystrokes that follow the cursor five spaces to the right, or press ENTER to move keystrokes that follow the cursor down to the next line.
- Press ALT + any number from 0 through 9 to insert the value previously assigned to that variable. For example, if you assigned the text value "Print" to number 3, then press ALT + 3 to insert the the word "Print."
- Press CANCEL (F1) or ESC to abort any changes you made to the keystrokes. WordPerfect prompts

  Cancel changes? (Y/N) N

  Type **Y** and the keystrokes that you inserted or deleted since you last saved the macro keystrokes will be aborted; the macro will return to the original keystrokes it had before you began editing it. The cursor remains in the double-line box.

  Or type **N** or press ENTER to abort the Cancel command. The cursor remains in the double-line box.
- Press EXIT (F7) to register your editing changes. The cursor leaves the Action box and returns to the bottom of the screen.
- Press MACRO DEFINE (CTRL + F10) to switch on a toggle enabling you to enter the literal keystrokes for all the editing keys mentioned in the bulleted paragraphs above—keys that are otherwise reserved for normal editing. When you press MACRO DEFINE, a message appears in the bottom of the Action box:

  Press **Macro Define** to enable editing

  Now if you press a cursor movement key, it will cause that keystroke to appear, rather than moving the cursor. For instance, press RIGHT ARROW, and {Right} appears. Or, if you press an editing key, it will make that keystroke appear rather than editing that keystroke. For example, press BACKSPACE, and {Backspace} appears.

Similarly, press TAB to insert {Tab}, press INS to insert {Typeover}, press ENTER to insert {Enter}, press CANCEL (F1) to insert {Cancel}, or press EXIT (F7) to insert {Exit}.

In addition, if you press ALT + a number from 0 through 9, that variable—rather than its current value—is inserted. For instance, press ALT + 3 to insert {Var 3}.

When you're ready to re-enable normal editing, again press MACRO DEFINE. The message disappears, and now you can edit the keystrokes further.

- Press CTRL + PGUP to display a double-line box in the upper right-hand corner of the screen which contains a list of the Macro Programming Language commands, as shown in Figure 27-4. A cursor that is the width of the Command box rests on the first command in the list. There are 39 commands in all, but only seven are shown at one time. To view additional commands, use the cursor movement keys (UP ARROW, DOWN ARROW, PGUP, PGDN, and so

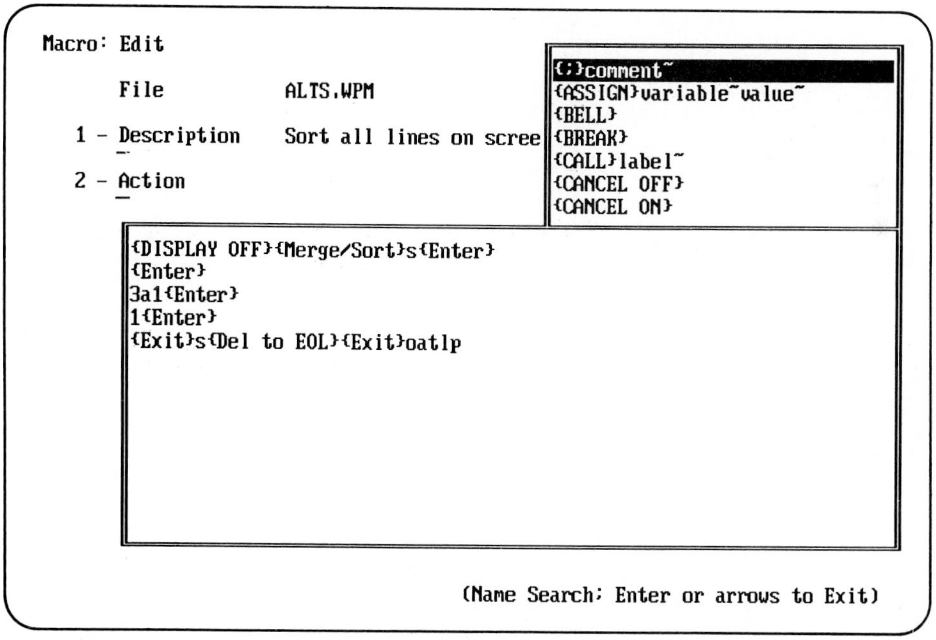

Figure 27-4. Command box displayed after pressing CTRL + PGUP on the Macro Edit screen

on), or type the beginning of one of the commands until the cursor moves to that command (analogous to how you use the Name Search feature on the List Files screen). Table 27-1 provides an alphabetical list of those commands, and the functions that each performs.

To insert a command, position the cursor on that command and press EXIT (F7) or ENTER. The command is inserted in uppercase letters and within curved brackets wherever the cursor was located in the Action box *before* you pressed CTRL + PGUP. For example, position the cursor on the command "{BELL}" and press EXIT to insert {BELL} in the Action box. Or position the cursor on the command "{CALL}label~" and press ENTER to insert {CALL} in the Action box. The cursor automatically returns to the Action box after a command is inserted there.

To return the cursor to the Action box without inserting a command, press CANCEL (F1) or ESC.

When you return the cursor to the Action box, the Command box remains on screen. To return the cursor to the Command box, simply press CTRL + PGUP again.

5. Once you press EXIT (F7) to move the cursor from the Action box to the bottom of the screen, press EXIT (F7) again to return to your document on the Typing screen.

With the macro edited—whether or not you employed the Macro Programming Language—you are now ready to test the macro on a document, and re-edit if necessary.

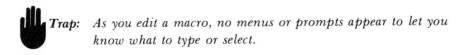

Trap: *As you edit a macro, no menus or prompts appear to let you know what to type or select.*

If you're in the Action box on the Macro Edit screen and you press a function key, remember that the menu or prompt that normally appears when you're on the Typing screen does not appear in place of the Macro Edit screen. For example, press MARK TEXT (ALT + F5) and WordPerfect inserts {Mark Text}; it does not display the Mark Text menu.

Therefore, you must know the exact keystrokes that you wish to insert before you begin to edit the macro. Because it is almost impossible to know by heart the exact keystrokes needed to execute a command, the best alternative is to perform the keystrokes on the Typing screen and record them on paper before entering the Macro Edit screen. See the related Tip that follows.

Table 27-1. Macro Programming Language Commands

Command	Function
{;}comment~	Inserts a comment in the text that is ignored during macro execution
{ASSIGN}variable~value~	Assigns a text or numeric value to a variable, where the variable is any number from 0 through 9
{BELL}	Sounds a beep
{BREAK}	Moves to the end of the IF structure (that is, past the {END IF} command), or, if the macro is currently not in an IF structure, moves to the end of the macro
{CALL}label~	Branches to a label to execute a subroutine inside the macro
{CANCEL OFF}	Disables the use of the CANCEL (F1) key to stop the execution of a macro
{CANCEL ON}	Allows the CANCEL (F1) key to stop the execution of a macro
{CASE}value~case1~label1 ~case2~...	Compares the value to each case. If an exact match is found, goes to the label associated with that match. If no match is found, continues execution with the next command following the {CASE} command
{CASE CALL}value~ case1~label1~case2~...~	Compares the value to each case. If an exact match is found, goes to the label associated with that match to execute a subroutine, and then execution returns to the next command following the {CASE CALL} command. If no match is found, goes directly to the next command following the {CASE CALL} command. Commands beginning with label1, label2, and so on, are subroutines and should end with the {RETURN} command
{CHAIN}file~	Executes the macro file indicated when the current macro is complete. If macros are nested, one macro can be chained at each level
{CHAR}variable~message~	Prompts the user with a message on the status line for input of a single character, which is then assigned to a variable

Table 27-1. Macro Programming Language Commands (continued)

Command	Function
{DISPLAY OFF}	Turns off the display of the macro as it is executing. (This is a default setting for all macros)
{DISPLAY ON}	Turns on the display of macro execution
{ELSE}	Used with the {IF} command. Inserted after an {IF} command, the {ELSE} command is executed when the IF condition is false, or is ignored when the IF condition is true
{END IF}	Ends the IF structure. Placed after the last command in the {ELSE} command sequence, or, if no {ELSE} command is used, after the last command in the {IF} sequence
{GO}label~	Goes to a label that executes a subroutine inside the current macro
{IF}value~	If the value is not 0 or is a non-numeric string, continues executing sequentially. If the string equals 0 or there is no value, skips to the next {ELSE} or {END IF} command
{IF EXISTS}variable~	If the variable has been assigned a value, then returns a true condition. Otherwise, returns a false condition
{LABEL}label~	Label that will be used to execute a subroutine in a {GO}, {CALL}, {CASE}, or {CASE CALL} command. Labels can be of any length, and can include any characters
{LOOK}variable~	If a character has been input by the user, assigns that character to the variable indicated. If not, continues the macro execution without stopping. Useful in combination with the {IF EXISTS} command
{NEST}file~	Immediately executes the file macro specified, and then continues executing the current macro
{ON CANCEL}action~	After this command is executed, indicates what should happen next. The actions allowed are {QUIT}, {BREAK}, {RESTART}, {RETURN}, {RETURN ERROR}, {RETURN NOT FOUND}, {GO}, {CALL}, and {RETURN CANCEL}. {RETURN CANCEL} is the default if no {ON CANCEL} command is executed
{ON ERROR}action~	When an error is detected in macro execution, in normal WordPerfect operations, or in DOS, indicates what should happen next. See {ON CANCEL} for actions

Table 27-1. Macro Programming Language Commands (continued)

Command	Function
	allowed. {RETURN ERROR} is the default if no {ON ERROR} command is executed
{ON NOT FOUND}action~	When a search, word search, or name search fails, indicates what should happen next. See {ON CANCEL} for actions allowed. {RETURN NOT FOUND} is the default if no {ON NOT FOUND} command is executed
{ORIGINAL KEY}	Returns the original (unmapped) value of the last key entered at the keyboard before the macro started
{PAUSE}	Stops macro execution for keyboard input (unprompted). The pause terminates when the user presses ENTER
{PROMPT}message~	Displays a message on the status line
{QUIT}	Terminates all macro execution
{RESTART}	Terminates all macro execution after the complete execution of the current subroutine or macro
{RETURN}	Returns from {CALL} or {CASE CALL} subroutines, or leaves the macro
{RETURN CANCEL}	Returns from the current level of macro execution (subroutine or macro) and indicates a cancel at the next highest level—which can be tested with an {ON CANCEL} command at the next level
{RETURN ERROR}	Returns from the current level of macro execution (subroutine or macro) and indicates an error condition at the next highest level. That level will then perform commands specified by its {ON ERROR} condition
{RETURN NOT FOUND}	Returns from the current level of macro execution (subroutine or macro) and indicates a not-found condition at the next highest level. That level will then perform commands specified by its {ON NOT FOUND} condition
{SPEED}100ths~	Slows down macro execution, waiting the amount of time indicated (in 100ths of a second) between each key input
{STATE}	Returns a number that indicates the current state of WordPerfect. All conditions that apply are added together. (See Table 27-2 for conditions)
{STEP OFF}	Turns off single-step execution of a macro. (This is a default setting for all macros)

Table 27-1. Macro Programming Language Commands (continued)

Command	**Function**
{STEP ON}	Turns on single-step execution of a macro
{TEXT}variable~message~	Prompts the user with a message on the status line for input of a value of up to 120 characters, which is then assigned to a variable
{WAIT}10ths~	Delays further execution of the macro, waiting the amount of time indicated (in 10ths of a second) before continuing the macro execution

Tip: *Map out your macro keystroke by keystroke before you attempt to edit it on the Macro Edit screen.*

When you are editing a macro, and especially when you are planning to use the programming language to perform a complicated and intricate series of events, be sure to map out your macro keystrokes first. There are two stages in this process.

First, you need to figure out the logical flow of the macro—the basic structure that it will take. For sophisticated macros, you will want to separate the macro into a main section and subroutines. When the main section calls for branching to a subroutine, the subroutine is executed (by its label) until the subroutine ends or until it encounters a command to return to the main section. You may wish to draw a flow chart to help you design the macro's basic structure. Proper design is important if you wish to have an organized macro program.

Second, you must write up the detailed instructions that tell the computer to perform each task in the macro. This will include both programming language codes and WordPerfect menu commands—and can be quite tedious. For the menu commands, perform the task at hand and jot down each step, keystroke by keystroke.

Then, and only then, are you ready to display the Macro Edit screen and begin entering the programming language commands and keystrokes to build the macro.

Tip: *The Macro Programming Language is not for everyone.*

The Macro Programming Language is not for novices; you should have some basic programming knowledge in order to use the programming commands properly. Even sophisticated users may not find a need for the programming language, since the WordPerfect menus and features have been so well constructed.

How do you know when to stay with the WordPerfect menus and commands and when to start using the programming language? Whenever possible, rely on WordPerfect's commands; they have already been programmed for you. When you want to accomplish a task that the menu commands cannot handle, then you need to start the hard work of programming. If you've never programmed before but you see the need to use the programming language, you will want to start with macros that contain only a few programming commands, and build from there. Also consider gaining some background knowledge in the art of programming (and it is an art!) by attending a class, researching the topic, or being tutored by someone with programming experience, before you attempt to create complicated macros.

Tip: *Besides MACRO DEFINE, another key combination enables you to insert the keys used for editing as keystrokes.*

You learned that, when in the Action box, you can press MACRO DEFINE to type in keys used typically in editing as actual keystrokes. For instance, pressing BACKSPACE in normal editing in the Action box erases the character to the left of the cursor, but if you press the MACRO DEFINE key, pressing BACKSPACE inserts {Backspace}. This also applies to other editing keys, cursor movement keys, ESC, TAB, EXIT, and CANCEL. But you must remember to press MACRO DEFINE to turn this feature off when you wish to return to normal editing. (It is easy to forget to turn this feature off and to inadvertently insert something like {Left}{Left}{Left}{Left}{Left}.)

An alternative, if you wish to insert just one of those keys as the actual keystroke, is to press the key combination CTRL + V and then press that key. CTRL + V turns the toggle on for that one keystroke only, and then turns it off again. For example, when the cursor is in the Action box, position it where you want the keystroke {Exit} to appear. Next, press CTRL + V, and then press EXIT (F7). {Exit} is inserted. But press EXIT again, and this key returns to its normal editing functions. Or press CTRL + V and press LEFT ARROW to insert {Left}; if you next press LEFT ARROW, the cursor moves one space to the left.

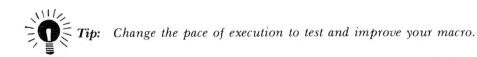

Tip: *Change the pace of execution to test and improve your macro.*

When you wish to debug a macro, it is helpful to start the macro with the commands {DISPLAY ON} and {STEP ON}. With {STEP ON} activated, the macro is executed one step at a time—and only when you press a key will WordPerfect execute the next step. This command conveniently tells you which key or command will be executed next. If the next step is a normal character, that character is displayed at the bottom of the screen. For example, when the next keystroke will press the number 4, then "4" is displayed. If the next step is a command, then the command is displayed at the bottom of the screen—first its type and then a number or letter, as follows:

- KEY CMD # = normal keystroke command, where # represents the decimal value of that command. Examples of keystroke commands include {Backspace} or {Left} or {Macro} or {Mark Text}.
- MACRO CMD # = Macro Programming Language command, where # represents the decimal value of that command. Examples of macro commands include {IF} or {STATE}.
- ALT L = ALT macro execution, where L represents the letter of that command. An example of an ALT command is {ALT D}.
- VAR # = variable execution, where # represents the variable number (0 through 9). An example of a variable command is {VAR 1}.

If you wish to debug only a certain section of the macro, then insert {STEP ON} where you want step-by-step execution, and insert {STEP OFF} where you wish to return to normal execution.

Tip: *Use the {WAIT} or {PAUSE} command for print macros or computer-generated presentations.*

The {WAIT} and {PAUSE} commands are critical in macros that contain keystrokes to issue a "go" to the printer to start printing. For instance, you might want to define a macro to help you print addresses on envelopes when you have previously defined your envelope form to feed the envelopes manually. The macro would contain the keystrokes to issue the print command and to display the Printer Control menu. Then, in order to work properly, the macro must contain either a {WAIT} or {PAUSE} in the macro before each keystroke that sends a "go" ("g") to the printer to start printing a new envelope.

The {WAIT} and {PAUSE} commands are also useful in creating a macro that provides a computer-generated presentation—a presentation that retrieves information from document files to the screen in a specific sequence. For example, you could define a macro that retrieves a document containing an outline, graphics images, and line drawings, and then moves from page to page in specified time intervals using the {WAIT} command. Or, to control the speed of the presentation from the keyboard, you can have the macro move from page to page only on your signal—when you press the ENTER key—by using the {PAUSE} command. As the macro moves from page to page, you can turn off the display of the screen so that no distracting prompts appear. To accomplish this, one line in the macro would read: {DISPLAY OFF}{Pgdn}{DISPLAY ON}{PAUSE}. This line could be repeated many times, to match the number of pages that comprise the presentation.

Of course, you could add other features. You could insert the {BEEP} command, so a beep sounds when WordPerfect is pausing for input. Or design the macro so that a line drawing is created on screen as the audience watches. If certain screens contain graphics images, you will want the macro to switch to the Preview screen at the appropriate points in the presentation.

Tip: *The {STATE} command allows you to check the status of WordPerfect and perform certain keystrokes based on that status.*

The {STATE} command can check to determine whether the cursor is currently on the Typing screen or on the Reveal Codes screen, or if WordPerfect is prompting with a yes/no question, such as **Save document? (Y/N) Yes**. Numbers that corre-

Table 27-2. Conditions to Be Used in the {STATE} Command

Number	Current State Indicated
3	Document number (Doc 1, 2, or 3)
4	Typing screen (also referred to as the Document Editing screen)
8	Editing structure other than the main Typing screen (such as when a menu is active and you're editing a header, footer, footnote, endnote, or style)
16	Macro execution active
32	Macro execution active (always set)
64	Merge active
128	Block active
256	Typeover active
512	Reveal Codes screen
1024	Yes/no question active

spond to specific status conditions are shown in Table 27-2. You would use the AND operation (using &) to evaluate the condition. For example, if you wish to determine whether the current state of WordPerfect is that of displaying the Typing screen, then the command to use is {STATE}&4.

When the state is evaluated, the value 0 will be assigned if the statement is false, and the value specified will be assigned if the statement is true.

Then you can have the macro execute one way or another, based on that status. This command is useful when it precedes commands such as {IF}, {CASE}, {CASE CALL}, and {ASSIGN}.

For example, suppose that you wish to capitalize a word (similar to the example in Macro 4 at the beginning of the chapter), but only if that word is on the Typing screen with no prompts or menus appearing. The macro could include these commands:

```
{IF}{STATE}&4~
{Word Right}{Word Left}
{Block}{Word Right}
{Switch}U
{Word Right}
```

Commands can be used together to evaluate one or more conditions. For instance, the command STATE&12 will return one of the following: 0, meaning that some menu is active; 4, meaning that the Typing screen is displayed; 8, meaning that a menu is active and you are editing on a special editing screen, such as the Footnote Editing screen; 12, meaning that the Typing screen is active and you are editing on a special editing screen.

Tip: *Numerous macro commands affect the flow of macro execution.*

The most basic and often-used set of commands to specify the flow of the execution of a macro is {IF} and {END IF}. There can be numerous {IF} statements in one macro.

For example, suppose that you wish to create a macro that saves a document on screen to disk and then clears the screen. You want the opportunity to type in a new filename, or, if the file has previously been saved, either to save it under the current name or to indicate a different filename. Here's a macro that can do this:

{IF}{STATE}&4~	(1) Checks to see if the Typing screen is currently displayed without any special features or commands being active. If so, the macro continues. Otherwise, the macro stops (because there is no {ELSE} command after the {END IF} in step 7, below, to indicate an alternative action).
{Save}{PAUSE}{Enter}	(2) Pauses for you to either press ENTER if WordPerfect suggests a filename that you wish to accept, or to type in a new filename and press ENTER.
{IF}{STATE}&1024~	(3) Checks to see if WordPerfect is prompting with a yes/no question (in this case, the yes/no question would be whether or not to replace the file currently on disk). If so, the macro continues. Otherwise, the macro moves to step 6.
Y	(4) Selects Y (Yes) to replace.
{END IF}	(5) Ends the {IF} statement begun in step 3.
{EXIT}nn	(6) Clears the screen.
{END IF}	(7) Ends the {IF} statement begun in step 1.

Other macro commands that alter the flow of execution include: {BREAK}, {CALL}, {CASE}, {CASE CALL}, {CHAIN}, {ELSE}, {GO}, {LABEL}, {NEST}, {ON CANCEL}, {ON ERROR}, {ON NOT FOUND}, {QUIT}, {RESTART},

```
Macro: Edit

      File            X.WPM

   1 - Description    Save document and clear the screen

   2 - Action

      {IF}{STATE}&4~                {;}Continue·only·if·on·Typing·screen~
      {Save}{PAUSE}{Enter}          {;}Save·document~
          {IF}{STATE}&1024~             {;}Confirm·for·replace·if·file·exists~
          y
          {END IF}
      {Exit}nn                      {;}Clear·screen~
      {END IF}

Selection: 0
```

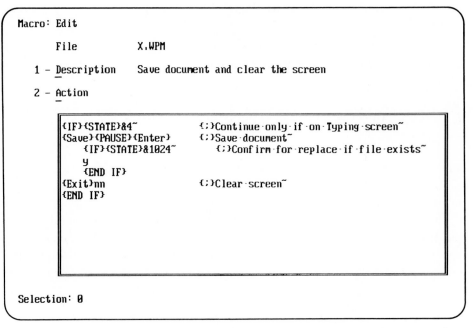

Figure 27-5. *An easy-to-read macro that employs comments, the* ENTER *key, and the* TAB *key*

{RETURN}, {RETURN CANCEL}, {RETURN ERROR}, {RETURN NOT FOUND}, and {IF EXISTS}. Examples of other macros that use these commands are found in the following Tips.

Tip: *Create structured, easy-to-read macros.*

The {;} programming language command inserts a comment into the macro. Combined with the use of the ENTER key and TAB key, the Comment command allows you to write a macro that is easy to read and to decipher later, when you wish to edit or debug the macro. The {;}, the ENTER key, and the TAB key have no effect on the execution of the macro, and therefore can be used freely. They enable the user to structure the macro on screen, while visually indicating where the routines and subroutines take effect, and what each task accomplishes.

Figure 27-5 shows an example of a structured, organized macro, which is easy to read (this macro is described in the preceding Tip). This is so much easier

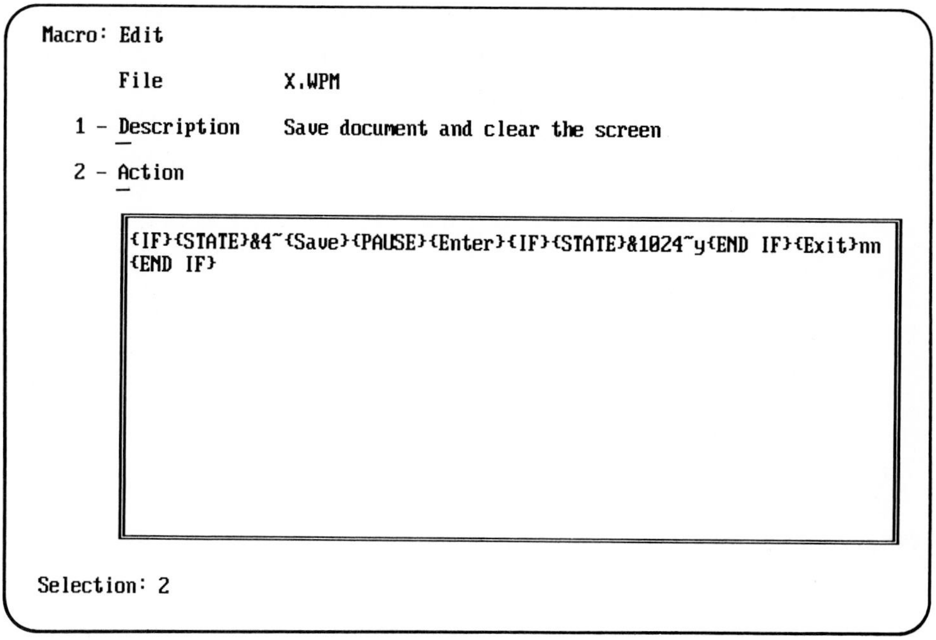

Figure 27-6. A macro that is difficult to interpret

to decipher than Figure 27-6, where the keystrokes and commands are the same, but where they were inserted one after another without using ENTER, TAB, or comments.

Note that you can also insert a comment during macro execution; see the preceding section of the chapter, "Inserting Special Keyboard Macro Commands," if you wish to do this.

Tip: *You can prompt the user for input during a macro using fancy enhancements.*

With the {CHAR}, {TEXT}, and {PROMPT} commands, a macro can prompt a user with a message on the screen. With the {CHAR} and {TEXT} commands, the information that the user inputs is assigned to the variable that you specify, as in this example:

{TEXT}1~Type in the appropriate filename: ~

The filename typed would then be assigned to variable number 1.

The {PROMPT} command can be used to instruct the user during a pause operation (without using up a variable). It should be preceded by a {DISPLAY ON} command so that message displays and should be followed by a {PAUSE} command so that the macro pauses in order for the user to read the message. The user then presses ENTER to continue the macro execution. You could then also insert a {DISPLAY OFF} command to again make the macro invisible. Here's an example:

```
{DISPLAY ON}
{PROMPT} Position cursor on page to be printed and press Enter.~
{PAUSE}
{DISPLAY OFF}
```

In addition, by inserting certain control characters in the message string, you can control the exact appearance of that message. For example, you can underline the prompt, or turn on reverse video. Or, instead of a prompt that appears on the status line (which is WordPerfect's assumption), it can be displayed anywhere on screen, such as at the top. The control characters that can be used in combination with {TEXT}, {PROMPT}, and {CHAR} are listed in Table 27-3. To insert any of these characters, you press CTRL + the letter indicated. In other words, press CTRL + A to insert {^A}.

For instance, if as part of a macro you wish to prompt the user with the {PROMPT} command, and have the message appear in the upper left-hand corner of the screen when the macro is executed, you would insert the command {PROMPT}{Home}*message*~, as in the following:

```
{PROMPT}{Home}Make sure the printer is on!~
```

(Notice in Table 27-3 that to insert {Home}, you must include ^H, which means you press CTRL + H.)

Or, if you wish to use the {TEXT} command to assign a value to variable 1, and have the message underlined, and then display a prompt containing underlining, the command you insert could read {TEXT}1~{^T}*message*{^U}~, such as in the following:

```
{TEXT}1~{^T}Type in the appropriate filename:{^U} ~
```

Moreover, with extra keystrokes, you can even specify the attributes used, such as small caps or italics (providing that your computer monitor can display these attributes). The attribute characters are listed in Table 27-4, but operate only

Table 27-3. Control Characters That Can Be Used in the Message

Character	Display in the Macro Editor Action Box	Action
^H	{Home}	Position cursor to upper left
^J	{Enter}	New line
^K	{Del to EOL}	Clear to end of line
^L	{Del to EOP}	Clear full screen and position to upper left
^M	{^M}	Position to beginning of line
^N	{^N}	Turn on display attribute (followed by attribute character)*
^O	{^O}	Turn off display attribute (followed by attribute character)*
^P	{^P}	Position cursor (followed by two characters: column, then row)
^Q	{^Q}	Turn off all display attributes
^R	{^R}	Turn on reverse video
^S	{^S}	Turn off reverse video
^T	{^T}	Turn on underline
^U	{^U}	Turn off underline
^V	{^V}	Turn on mnemonic attribute
^W	{UP}	Position cursor up one line
^X	{RIGHT}	Position cursor right one character
^Y	{LEFT}	Position cursor left one character
^Z	{DOWN}	Position cursor down one line
^\	{^\}	Turn off bold
^]	{^]}	Turn on bold

*Attribute characters are shown in Table 27-4.

if you first employ the ^N or ^O control characters from Table 27-3. For instance, if you wish to prompt the user for a filename with the {TEXT} command and have the prompt shown in very large characters, the command you insert could read

{TEXT}1~{^N}{^A}Type in the appropriate filename:{^O}{^A} ~

Trap: *It is all too easy to forget to insert the one tilde, or sometimes two, that a macro command may require.*

The majority of macro command languages require that you insert a tilde (~) after specifying a certain action, file, label, message, value, or variable (as indicated in Table 27-1). It is easy to forget to insert the tilde, and if you do, the macro won't operate properly. Thus, make sure you check your macro to ensure that the tildes are in place.

In some circumstances, two tildes in a row are required. For instance, suppose that you wish to insert a command specifying that if a search string is not found, the macro should go to the subroutine labeled "sub" in the current macro. Both the {ON NOT FOUND} and {GO} commands require a tilde after the label, so the command sequence should be {ON NOT FOUND}{GO}sub~~. The same applies to combinations such as {ON NOT FOUND}{CALL}, {ON CANCEL}{GO}, {ON CANCEL}{CALL}, {ON ERROR}{GO}, and {ON ERROR}{CALL}.

Table 27-4. Attribute Characters That Can Be Used in Conjunction with the ^N and ^O Control Characters

Character	Display in the Macro Editor Action Box	Attribute
^A	{^A}	Very large
^B	{^B}	Large
^C	{^C}	Small
^D	{^D}	Fine print
^E	{^E}	Superscript
^F	{^F}	Subscript
^G	{^G}	Outline
^H	{Home}	Italics
^I	{Tab}	Shadow
^J	{Enter}	Redline
^K	{Del to EOL}	Double underline
^L	{Del to EOP}	Bold
^M	{^M}	Strikeout
^N	{^N}	Underline
^O	{^O}	Small caps
^P	{^P}	Blinking
^Q	{^Q}	Reverse video

Tip: *Values can be passed to variables during a macro execution, and then can be accessed with the {VAR} command.*

The commands {ASSIGN}, {LOOK}, {CHAR}, and {TEXT} can pass a text or numeric value along to a specific variable during the execution of a macro. This allows the macro to act on the variable, either via a macro command such as {IF EXISTS}, or by activating that variable with {VAR}.

For example, suppose that you want to create a macro that prompts the user for the number of copies to print of the document on screen and then sends that job to the printer. Here's a macro to perform that task:

{TEXT}1~How many copies? ~	(1) Prompts the user for the number of copies, and assigns that value to the variable 1.
{Print}N	(2) Displays the Print menu and selects the Number of Copies option.
{VAR 1}{Enter}F	(3) Passes the value in variable 1 (inserted by the user) as the number of copies to be printed, and prints out the full document that number of times.

Tip: *You can assign values and insert them into a macro in a variety of ways.*

As described in the preceding Tip, the commands {ASSIGN}, {LOOK}, {CHAR}, and {TEXT} can pass a text or a numeric value along to a specific variable during the execution of a macro. There are other times when you can assign a value to a variable, in addition to when commands are inserted in a macro during editing. One such time is when you are on the Typing screen, during normal operations. Here, you can press CTRL + PGUP, type in a number from 0 through 9, and type in the value that you want to assign to the variable. Or, still on the Typing screen, you can use the BLOCK key to highlight the characters that you want as the value for the variable, press CTRL + PGUP, and type in a number from 0 through 9. (These methods are also described in the first section of this chapter, "Creating and Executing a Keyboard Macro," as a way to create temporary macros if you don't plan to use all ten variables with the Macro Programming Language.)

Another method for assigning a variable is to do so while you are recording a macro's keystrokes. When **Macro Def** is flashing on screen, you can press CTRL + PGUP to display a menu of options, where one option enables you to assign a value. (This method is described in the preceding section of the chapter, "Inserting Special Keyboard Macro Commands.")

Once you've assigned a variable, you can use that variable in a macro that employs the Macro Command Language. In addition, you can access a variable by pressing ALT + the variable number at any point when working with WordPerfect. When pressed, the variable contents are executed like a macro.

Tip: *For specialized macro applications, you can assign expressions to variables.*

Table 27-5 shows possible expressions that may be assigned to variables. The majority are arithmetic expressions (binary-based computer arithmetic) that you

Table 27-5. Values that Can Be Assigned to Variables

Value	**Operation**
!value	Assign the logical not (bitwise) of the value to the variable, where the bitwise value is the string of 16 bits in binary with a value between 0 and 65,535. For instance, since 128 = 0000000010000000, then !128 = 1111111101111111, which is also equal to 65,407
−value	Assign the negative of the value to the variable
v1+v2	Add v1 and v2 and assign the result to the variable
v1−v2	Subtract v2 from v1 and assign the result to the variable
v1*v2	Multiply v1 by v2 and assign the result to the variable
v1/v2	Divide v1 by v2 and assign the *integer* result to the variable
v1%v2	Divide v1 by v2 and assign the *remainder* to the variable
v1$v2	Logical *and* (bitwise) v1 with v2
v1¦v2	Logical *or* (bitwise) v1 with v2
v1=v2	If the values are equal, assign −1 to the variable. Otherwise, assign 0 to the variable
v1!=v2	If the values are *not* equal, assign −1 to the variable. Otherwise, assign 0
v1>v2	If v1 is greater than v2, assign −1 to the variable. Otherwise, assign 0
v1<v2	If v1 is less than v2, assign −1 to the variable. Otherwise, assign 0

might assign and that are extremely specialized. Others are useful as text strings as part of If statements, including v1=v2, v1!=v2, v1>v2, and v1<v2.

In a binary string operation, the pair " " or ' ' are used as string delimiters. For instance, "string1"="string2" means that if the two strings are identical, the variable is assigned the value −1; otherwise, it is assigned the value 0. For example, suppose that you create a macro that has the user indicate his department code number (such as 440 or 680), and different subroutines are executed based on what the user entered. The macro commands could, in part, read

```
{TEXT}2~Enter your department number: ~
{IF}"{VAR 2}"="440"~
{CALL}marketing~
{IF}"{VAR 2}"="68"~
{CALL}sales~
```

Later in the macro, you would have defined a subroutine with the label "marketing," and another with the label "sales," and so on.

Tip: *You can create a line menu or a full-screen menu by using the programming language.*

You can create a prompt, a line menu, or a full-screen menu that has the look and feel of a WordPerfect menu. For example, suppose that you're writing a macro with which you will prompt the user to ask whether the document on screen should be printed. Perhaps the prompt will look like this:

Do you wish to print? (Y/N) No

To do so, here's the basic structure of the macro, where a value is assigned to variable number 1 when the user types in a response:

```
{CHAR}1~Do you wish to print? (Y/N) No~
{CASE CALL}{VAR 1}~y~printit~Y~printit~
{ELSE}~
......
```

```
{LABEL}printit~
......
```

If the user responds with Y (in either uppercase or lowercase), then the macro branches to a subroutine named printit. If the user responds with another key, then the macro continues at the {ELSE} command. The "...." entries represent an appropriate subroutine or a continuation of the macro keystrokes and commands.

Or, suppose that your computer is hooked up to three different printers. Rather than have all the users learn how to select a new printer, as part of a macro you can write a menu that allows the user to select a printer. Perhaps the menu will look like this:

```
Select Printer: 1 Laser; 2 Epson; 3 Diablo: 0~
```

Shown below is the basic structure of the macro, where a value is assigned to variable number 1 when the user makes a menu selection, and based on that selection, the macro branches to a subroutine:

```
{CHAR}1~ Select Printer: 1 Laser; 2 Epson; 3 Diablo: 0
{CASE CALL}{VAR 1}~1~laser~2~epson~3~diablo~~
{RETURN}

{LABEL}laser~
......
{RETURN}

{LABEL}epson~
......
{RETURN}

{LABEL}diablo~
......
{RETURN}
```

With this macro, the user can enter the number 1 to execute the subroutine named laser, or 2 to execute epson, or 3 to execute diablo. The "...." entries represent an appropriate subroutine for each of the three printers.

You can also add enhancements to a menu. Perhaps you want the user to be able to choose not only a number to make a selection, but also a mnemonic character, in either uppercase or lowercase. You also want to boldface the numbers and use the mnemonic attributes (that is, whatever you have selected as the menu letter display by using the Setup menu). Then you'll have a line menu that is indistinguishable from a WordPerfect menu, such as:

Select Printer: 1 Laser; **2** Epson; **3** Diablo: **0**

Here's what the basic structure of the macro would look like:

```
{CHAR}1~ {^N}{Del to EOP}Select Printer:{^Q}
    {^N}{Del to EOP}1{^Q} {^V}L{^Q}aser;
    {^N}{Del to EOP}2{^Q} {^V}E{^Q}pson;
    {^N}{Del to EOP}3{^Q} {^V}D{^Q}iablo:
    {^N}{Del to EOP}0{^Q}~
{CASE CALL}{VAR 1}~
    1~laser~L~laser~l~laser~
    2~epson~E~epson~e~epson~
    3~diablo~D~diablo~d~diablo~~
{RETURN}

{LABEL}laser~
......
{RETURN}

{LABEL}epson~
......
{RETURN}

{LABEL}diablo~
......
{RETURN}
```

The {^N}{Del to EOP} are control characters that turn on the boldface (refer to

Tables 27-3 and 27-4) attribute, the {^Q} turns off all display attributes, and the {^V} turns on the mnemonic attribute. Hard returns and tabs were inserted to make the macro commands more readable; remember from previous discussions that hard returns and tabs do not affect macro execution.

Tip: *A macro can also be edited and the Macro Programming Language employed with the Keyboard Layout feature.*

As discussed in the first section of this chapter, "Creating and Executing a Keyboard Macro," the Keyboard Layout feature lets you create a keyboard definition in which you change key assignments for tasks. You make a keyboard definition active by selecting it when using the Setup menu.

With the Keyboard Layout feature, you can assign a macro to any key. Then you can create or edit the macro on the Key Edit screen, which is almost identical to the Macro Edit screen. The Macro Programming Language is accessed by pressing CTRL + PGUP, just as on the Macro Edit screen. When you have finished editing the macro, you can choose options to either save it in a macro file (to which WordPerfect assigns the file extension .WPM, as with any other macro), leave it attached to a key in a keyboard definition, or both.

One benefit of working on macros in the Keyboard Layout feature is that you don't have to have an already created macro to access the Key Edit screen (unlike the Macro Edit screen). You can simply choose a key to attach the macro to, and the Key Edit screen appears. Other benefits, as discussed previously, include the following: you are not limited to naming an easily executed macro—one that is executed without first pressing the MACRO key—with ALT + a letter; macros can be grouped together within a keyboard definition; and macros are accessed only when you select the keyboard definition they are attached to. (Refer to Appendix B for more on the Keyboard Layout feature).

Tip: *The WordPerfect program contains useful macros that provide additional examples of programming commands in action.*

As described previously, macros can be assigned to keys as part of a keyboard definition. WordPerfect's Conversion disk contains three keyboard definitions. One of the keyboard definitions is named MACROS and contains many useful macros. For instance, one macro creates a calculator that works with integers, while another prints a document's address to an envelope. These macros are available for use right away. In addition to executing these macros, you should examine the commands that make up the macros as examples of how to use various programming commands. Refer to Appendix B for the method to activate the keyboard definition named MACROS and to view a macro on the Key Edit screen.

Tip: *Consider purchasing WordPerfect Library if you need more sophistication in macro editing.*

WordPerfect Library, a collection of programs for WordPerfect users which is packaged separately from WordPerfect, has a program called Macro Editor with which you can edit macros. If you're an avid macro user, this program will come in handy. It offers several advantages over the Macro Edit feature in WordPerfect, including the ability to:

- Edit two macros at the same time, analogous to how, in WordPerfect, you can edit two documents at the same time in the Doc 1 and Doc 2 screens.
- Move or copy a highlighted block of keystrokes.
- Print out a copy of a macro easily.

The WordPerfect Library is purchased separately from your computer dealer or through WordPerfect Corporation.

Tip: *(When upgrading from 4.2.) The Macro Edit feature and the Macro Programming Language are new to version 5.*

If your macro didn't work properly or if you accidentally pressed the wrong key in recording a version 4.2 macro, your only alternative was to begin the macro process all over again. This is not the case with version 5. The easy-to-use Macro Edit feature allows you to debug a macro or to erase that one keystroke that you pressed inadvertently. If you create a variety of macros, you'll truly welcome this feature.

If you constantly bumped up against the macro limitations in version 4.2, or if you're a programmer at heart, then WordPerfect 5 offers what you've been craving—the sophistication of true programming so that you can create menus and command keys just like those built in to WordPerfect itself.

Tips and Traps Summary

Creating and Executing a Keyboard Macro

Tip: When you create a macro, you are performing the task at hand.

Tip: Define the macro so that it operates correctly in as many situations as possible.

Trap: Don't press extraneous keys when recording a macro.

Trap: Don't write macros for tasks that you perform only once, or once in a while.

Tip: A macro can be created that forces WordPerfect into Typeover or Insert mode.

Tip: A macro description can be displayed in two different situations.

Trap: Once you begin creating a macro, the only method for ending the definition is with the MACRO DEFINE key.

Tip: You can replace or edit a macro already stored on disk.

Tip: In general, macro files can be managed on disk-like document files.

Trap: Don't use the ENTER key to name a macro that is complicated and may require editing.

Trap: Don't name a destructive macro with ALT.

Tip: When creating or executing a macro, you can specify a drive or directory different from the default.

Tip: Store macros on the drive or directory that will make them most accessible.

Tip: The Keyboard Layout feature allows you to map a macro to any key and to group macros together.

Tip: Consider using the Styles feature, rather than the Macro feature, for certain tasks.

Tip: Stop macro execution by pressing CANCEL.

Tip: Remember your original assumptions when executing a macro.

Tips and Traps Summary (*continued*)

Tip: Use the Repeat Value feature to execute a macro a specified number of times.

Tip: A macro ends when a search string is not found.

Trap: If a macro is created to begin a merge, the merge must be the last macro step.

Tip: You can execute a macro after a merge is completed.

Tip: You can create a full-screen menu of available macros by employing the Merge feature.

Tip: You can create a temporary macro if the sole task of the macro is to insert text.

Tip: Use a startup option to automatically invoke a macro when WordPerfect is loaded.

Tip: (When upgrading from 4.2.) The basics of the Macro feature remain the same, although it has been substantially enhanced and version 4.2 macros must be converted to operate in version 5.

Chaining and Nesting Keyboard Macros

Tip: Chained macros rarely do what you want them to the first time around.

Trap: An endless loop can lock up the computer.

Trap: You can't define a nesting macro until you've created the ALT macro to nest.

Tip: (When upgrading from 4.2.) The nesting macro is new in version 5.

Inserting Special Keyboard Macro Commands

Trap: Only by pressing ENTER can you continue a macro that is stopped for keyboard input.

Tips and Traps Summary (*continued*)

Tip: You can assign a variable even when you've finished creating a macro.

Tip: Comments are useful when you're creating a long, complicated macro.

Tip: (When upgrading from 4.2.) You slow down or pause a macro differently in version 5.

Editing a Macro and Using the Macro Programming Language

Trap: As you edit a macro, no menus or prompts appear to let you know what to type or select.

Tip: Map out your macro keystroke by keystroke before you attempt to edit it on the Macro Edit screen.

Tip: The Macro Programming Language is not for everyone.

Tip: Besides MACRO DEFINE, another key combination enables you to insert the keys used for editing as keystrokes.

Tip: Change the pace of execution to test and improve your macro.

Tip: Use the {WAIT} or {PAUSE} command for print macros or computer-generated presentations

Tip: The {STATE} command allows you to check the status of WordPerfect and perform certain keystrokes based on that status.

Tip: Numerous macro commands affect the flow of macro execution.

Tip: Create structured, easy-to-read macros.

Tip: You can prompt the user for input during a macro using fancy enhancements.

Trap: It is all too easy to forget to insert the one tilde, or sometimes two, that a macro command may require.

Tip: Values can be passed to variables during a macro execution, and then can be accessed with the {VAR} command.

Tips and Traps Summary (*continued*)

Tip: You can assign values and insert them into a macro in a variety of ways.

Tip: For specialized macro applications, you can assign expressions to variables.

Tip: You can create a line menu or a full-screen menu by using the programming language.

Tip: A macro can also be edited and the Macro Programming Language employed with the Keyboard Layout feature.

Tip: The WordPerfect program contains useful macros that provide additional examples of programming commands in action.

Tip: Consider purchasing WordPerfect Library if you need more sophistication in macro editing.

Tip: (When upgrading from 4.2.) The Macro Edit feature and the Macro Programming Language are new to version 5.

28

Transferring Files from One Software Package to Another

Just like people, software packages speak different languages. WordPerfect recognizes what you mean when you insert a code such as **[L/R Mar:1",1.5"]** or **[Ln Spacing:1]** in the text, but other software packages do not. In fact, even WordPerfect version 4.2 won't recognize certain new version 5 codes.

If you use another software package in addition to WordPerfect version 5 on your computer, you may wish to transfer the contents of the files from that other package into WordPerfect, or vice versa. For instance, if you're upgrading from WordPerfect version 4.2, you'll want to convert your version 4.2 documents for use in version 5. Or you may wish to transfer all the files you created in WordStar into WordPerfect format. Or perhaps you wish to convert a database file created in dBASE into a WordPerfect secondary file for use in a merge operation. How you transfer files depends on which other formats ("languages") WordPerfect recognizes, and which other formats the other software package recognizes.

This chapter first describes how to convert WordPerfect version 4.2 files—including document files, macros, dictionary files, and merge files—into version 5. Then the two alternatives for transferring information between WordPerfect and other software packages are described: using the Convert program, which is a utility provided with WordPerfect, or using ASCII (DOS) text files as an intermediary.

Working Within WordPerfect

If you've recently upgraded from an earlier version of WordPerfect to version 5, no special process is required to transfer a basic document file. The file may have been created in version 4.2 or an earlier version, such as 4.1, 4.0, or 3.0. Just retrieve that file with version 5 loaded. The following message appears at the bottom of the screen:

Document conversion in progress

After a few seconds, the file appears on screen; the conversion is complete. Edit the document if you wish and then resave it; the document will now be stored on disk in version 5.0 format. See the Tips that follow, however, for information on transferring documents containing features that have been modified in version 5 (such as with font changes), or for information on transferring special WordPerfect files, such as supplemental dictionaries or macros, into version 5.

A special process *is* required to transfer version 5 files into 4.2. Why would you want to convert from the more recent WordPerfect version to the older one? This would be useful, for example, if you wanted to provide a document on disk to another user who has not yet upgraded to version 5. To save the version 5 document file in 4.2 format:

1. The document you wish to save in 4.2 format should be on screen.
2. Press the TEXT IN/OUT (CTRL ± F5) key. WordPerfect provides the following menu:

   1 Dos Text; **2** Password; **3** Save Generic; **4** Save WP 4.2; **5** Comment: **0**

3. Select Save WP 4.2 (4 or W). WordPerfect prompts

   Document to be saved (WP 4.2):

   and suggests the current filename if the file has previously been saved.
4. Type in a filename (preceded by a drive or directory if you wish to store the file in a drive/directory different from the default), and press ENTER.

Now you can exit WordPerfect version 5, load version 4.2, and retrieve the file that you just saved in WP 4.2 format.

Tip: *WordPerfect version 5 may be unable to convert certain codes from earlier WordPerfect versions.*

Many features of earlier WordPerfect versions have been replaced in version 5 by different features. For example, you no longer change the pitch and font in the middle of a document by using what was the PRINT FORMAT key in version 4.2, but instead select a font by name from the Base Font menu via the FONT (CTRL + F8) key. And you no longer specify a bin number by using the PRINT FORMAT key, but instead indicate a bin number when you insert a paper type/size code in the text, where that paper type has been previously assigned a bin number.

Because of the enhancements to version 5, you might find that after you retrieve a version 4.2 document into version 5, certain codes have been converted in a way that you do not desire. For instance, margins and tab stop settings are converted into fixed measurements (for example, in inches, if you have not altered the default setting), assuming a paper size of 8 1/2 x 11 inches. However, the margins in your version 4.2 document may have been set for a different page length, and therefore the margins will convert incorrectly. You will then need to erase the code inserted by WordPerfect and insert the correct margin setting code.

In other cases, you will find that WordPerfect inserts comments that indicate which codes it could not convert. For instance, suppose that your version 4.2 document contained a font change code that altered the text to 12-pitch, font 3, and to proportional spacing (with an asterisk after the pitch specification). In that case, when you retrieve that file with version 5 loaded, WordPerfect will insert the following comment, which will be displayed in a double-line box on screen, wherever the font change code was located in the version 4.2 document:

Note: The change to pitch (12*) and font (3) must be converted manually.

You will then need to insert manually a font change code (as described in Chapter 7), delete the comment, and resave the file.

As an alternative to inserting and deleting fonts manually, you can use a file named STANDARD.CRS to instruct WordPerfect on how to convert font change and other codes. Then, when you retrieve a file created with version 4.2 into

WordPerfect 5, the codes can be converted automatically in the way that you desire. See the following Tip for details.

Tip: *When converting a document, a conversion resource file can instruct WordPerfect on how to convert some codes.*

Because features such as font selection, sheet feeder bin numbers, and paper size/type are accessed differently in version 5, WordPerfect has a difficult time knowing how to convert certain codes contained in files created in version 4.2. The program thus makes a "guess." But the Conversion disk contains a file named STANDARD.CRS, with which you can instruct WordPerfect on how to convert certain codes without guesswork.

Figure 28-1 shows the first part of the STANDARD.CRS (which stands for STANDARD Conversion ReSource) file. The file is composed of "equals to" statements, one statement on each line. Commands that represent 4.2 codes are

```
FO 1,10 =
  This was Font/Pitch 1,10 - On.

FF 1,10 =
  This was Font/Pitch 1,10 - Off.

FO 2,10 =
  This was Font/Pitch 2,10 - On.

FF 2,10 =
  This was Font/Pitch 2,10 - Off.

FO 2,12 =
  This was Font/Pitch 2,12 - On.
                                      Doc 1 Pg 1 Ln 1" Pos 1"
```

Figure 28-1. Part of the STANDARD.CRS conversion resource file on screen

located on the left side of each equal sign, followed by a comment in a double-line box indicating which version 4.2 code the command represents. Your job is to insert version 5 codes on the right side of each statement (either preceding or in place of the **[Comment]** code) and, in that way, to specify for WordPerfect how certain codes should be converted in your documents. For example, you can indicate that a font change code for and pitch 10 font 1 in a version 4.2 document should be replaced with a **[Font:Tms Rmn 10pt]** code when a document is converted to version 5.

There are three types of "equals to" statements included in the STANDARD.CRS file:

- **Font change (on and off) statements** This type of statement is necessary for each different font change code found in version 4.2 documents. You should specify both a Font Change On and a Font Change Off "equals to" statement for each font change.

  Version 4.2 font-change-on codes are represented on the left side of the "equals to" statement by FO, followed by a space, the font number, a comma, and the pitch number (and an asterisk if the pitch was proportionally spaced). The version 5 font-change-on codes that you insert on the right side of the statement can be for a specific font change, such as **[Font: Courier 10 pitch]**, or for an attribute, such as **[BOLD]** or **[LARGE]**.

  Version 4.2 font-change-off codes are represented by FF, followed by the same information as the FO statement. Version 5 font-change-off codes that you insert can be a specific font change or an attribute.

  Each FO statement where the version 4.2 font change code will be converted into an *attribute* code should be directly followed by an FF statement on the next line. Although version 4.2 documents contain no font-change-off codes, you must include an FF statement so that when WordPerfect encounters the next font-on-code, it can insert a code to turn off the attribute before inserting the font-on-code for the new font or attribute. For example, suppose you complete two "equals to" statements in the STANDARD.CRS file to read as follows (assuming you erased the **[Comment]** code in each statement):

  FO3,13*= **[LARGE][HRt]**
  FF 3,13*= **[large][HRt]**

  In this case, during the conversion to version 5, when WordPerfect encounters a **[Font Change:3,13*]** code in the version 4.2 document, it substitutes a **[LARGE]** code instead. Then, if WordPerfect encounters

[large] code *before* converting the next font change code. (See Chapter 7 for instructions on how to insert WordPerfect 5 font and attribute codes.)

- **Bin number statements** This type of statement is necessary if sheet feeder bin number codes are contained in the version 4.2 document, such as **[Bin#:2]**. In the "equals to" statement, version 4.2 bin number codes are represented by BN followed by a space and the bin number. The right side of the statement should contain the appropriate version 5 paper size/type code. For example:

  BN 2=**[Paper Sz/Type:9.5"x4",Envelope][HRt]**

  (See Chapter 8 for instructions on how to insert WordPerfect 5 paper size/type codes.)

- **Paper size statements** This type of statement is necessary if margin or page length codes are contained in the version 4.2 document. In order to calculate left, right, top, and bottom margins correctly, WordPerfect must know the size of paper you assume for printing the document. The left side of the statement simply reads SZ. The right side should contain the appropriate paper size/type code, such as:

  SZ=**[Paper Sz/Type:8.5"x11",Standard][HRt]**

  (See Chapter 8 for instructions on how to insert WordPerfect 5 paper size/type codes.)

In STANDARD.CRS, you can edit the phrases representing WordPerfect version 4.2 codes in the same way that you would edit text in a WordPerfect document. Version 5 codes, always on the right side, are inserted or deleted in the same way that you would insert those codes in a standard document. For instance, to insert a **[BOLD]** code in a Font On statement and a **[bold]** code in the Font Off statement, use the BLOCK (ALT + F4) key to highlight the text to be surrounded by these codes, and then press the BOLD (F6) key.

You edit STANDARD.CRS and create a new file containing your modifications *before* you retrieve a version 4.2 file into WordPerfect 5. Here are the steps involved in using STANDARD.CRS:

1. With version 5 loaded, retrieve the file named STANDARD.CRS to the screen just as you would retrieve any WordPerfect document. Press the RETRIEVE (SHIFT + F10) key, and when WordPerfect prompts for a filename, floppy disk users should type **A:STANDARD.CRS** (assuming that the Conversion disk is in drive A) and press ENTER. Hard disk users

should precede the filename with the directory where STANDARD.CRS is stored; for example, if that file is in the directory \WPER, then type **C:\WPER\STANDARD.CRS** and press ENTER.

2. Modify the file as desired, editing the "equals to" statements as described above. Make sure that the version 5 codes you insert precede the **[Comment]** code in each statement. Or you can delete the **[Comment]** code from all the statements. It is best to complete the statements while viewing the Reveal Codes screen.

3. Save the file on the same drive or directory where the WordPerfect program file WP.EXE and your printer files are stored. Also, you must assign the file the same filename as the Printer Selection file that you wish to use, and with an extension of .CRS. For example, suppose that you plan to retrieve a version 4.2 document into version 5 with the HP LaserJet Series II as the selected printer. The HP LaserJet's Printer Selection filename is HPLASEII.PRS. Thus, you must resave the STANDARD.CRS file under the name HPLASEII.CRS. In this way, you link the Conversion Resource File (.CRS) to a specific Printer Resource File (.PRS). (See Appendix A for the method to list your printer files, so that you use the appropriate filename.)

4. Clear the screen.

5. Make sure that the correct printer is selected for that .CRS file. (Appendix A describes how to select different printers.)

6. Retrieve the version 4.2 document. Because of the new .CRS file you created, WordPerfect will convert all font change, bin number, page length, and margin codes, as you specified.

7. Resave the file, which is now in version 5 format.

Repeat steps 6 and 7 for each version 4.2 file that you wish to convert using the .CRS file you created. Or repeat steps 1 through 7 if you wish to convert other files using a *different* .CRS file for the *same* printer, in which case you will replace the current .CRS file with the new file. Or repeat steps 1 through 7 if you wish to convert other files using a *different* .CRS file for a *different* printer, in which case the new .CRS file you create will be named differently.

Tip: *Convert many version 4.2 files at once to version 5 using the Convert program.*

Although no special process is necessary to retrieve a version 4.2 document into version 5, you'll notice that the document conversion process takes several seconds each time you retrieve a version 4.2 document. To save time, you can use the Convert program, a utility provided on the WordPerfect Conversion disk. One option in the Convert program allows you to transfer version 4.2 documents into version 5.

By using the Convert program, you can convert a number of WordPerfect version 4.2 document files into 5 and then, when you retrieve one of those files into version 5, there will be no delay before the file is retrieved. As you use the Convert program, WordPerfect will prompt, asking for the name of the .CRS file you created, which is a conversion file that instructs WordPerfect on how to convert certain codes (see the preceding Tip for the method to create a .CRS file).

Employing Convert is especially useful if the files you wish to transfer into version 5 have a common filename pattern. For example, if the files you wish to convert all have the file extension .RPT, then you can convert all the files at once, specifying *.RPT as the name of the "input file." (The Convert program is described in the following section of the chapter.)

Tip: *Convert version 4.2 primary and secondary files into version 5 before you attempt a merge in version 5 using these files.*

If you're a longtime version 4.2 user, you've probably created various primary and secondary files for use with the Merge feature. These files can be used in a version 5 merge, but first they must be converted. When version 5 is loaded, retrieve and then separately resave each primary and secondary file that you wish to employ in a merge. Then proceed with the merge (the merge procedure is discussed in Chapters 24 and 25). Or, if all your primary and secondary files have a common filename pattern, you can use the Convert program to quickly transfer these merge files into version 5 format. For instance, perhaps you named all your primary files with the extension *.PRI. In that case, you can use Convert and specify *.PRI as the name of the "input file." See the following section of the chapter for details on Convert.

Tip: *Convert dictionaries into version 5 so they can be used with the version 5 Speller feature.*

If you frequently used the Speller feature in version 4.2, then you may have created one or more supplementary dictionaries containing words found in your documents that are not included in WordPerfect's own dictionary. As long as these supplementary dictionaries were saved in a separate file, they can be converted into version 5 format.

When you used version 4.2, WordPerfect created a file named {WP}LEX.WP and stored all words in that file when you selected the Add Word option on the Not Found menu. (The Not Found menu appears when you activate the Speller feature and a word on screen is not found in the dictionary; see Chapter 16 if you wish to review the Speller feature.) This file served as your primary supplementary dictionary. In version 5, WordPerfect instead creates a file named WP{WP}EN.SUP.

Check to see if your Speller disk (floppy disk users) or the WordPerfect 4.2 subdirectory (hard disk users) contains a file named {WP}LEX.WP. If it does, when version 5 is loaded, retrieve {WP}LEX.SUP onto a clear screen; it will be converted to version 5 format. Next, resave this supplement under the name WP{WP}EN.SUP—and it will now serve as your supplement. Words in this file will be checked, along with words in WordPerfect's main dictionary when you activate the Speller feature. And, when you select the Add Word option, the highlighted word will be added to WP{WP}EN.SUP.

If, while you used version 4.2, you created additional supplementary dictionaries, be sure to convert these files as well. Retrieve each one into version 5, and then resave it. You can resave it under the same name that you used when you used version 4.2, and then, when you're ready to use it during a spelling check, switch to this new supplemental dictionary name on the Spell menu, as described in Chapter 16. You can also convert supplementary dictionaries into version 5 using the Speller Utility, as described in Chapter 16.

In addition to creating supplementary dictionaries in version 4.2, you may have altered WordPerfect's main dictionary, which is named LEX.WP in version 4.2, by adding words directly to the LEX.WP file. As of this writing, a special conversion program for version 4.2 main dictionaries is in the works at WordPerfect Corporation. You will need the conversion program only if you added a large number of words to the version 4.2 LEX.WP file using the Speller Utility and you no longer have a separate list of those added words. Contact WordPerfect Corporation for details on this main dictionary conversion program.

Tip: *Version 4.2 macros can be converted into version 5.*

WordPerfect offers a utility program named MACROCNV.EXE, which converts WordPerfect version 4.2 macro files to WordPerfect version 5 macros. The utility converts into version 5 all text, all cursor movement functions, and the features that are accessed with the same keys in version 4.2. Keystrokes that it cannot convert will be flagged with comments; these you will have to correct manually, using the Macro Edit feature (as described in Chapter 27). Large macros will be split up into separate, chained macros.

To use the Macro Conversion utility, you must know the name of the version 4.2 macro that you wish to convert. All version 4.2 macros are named with the extension .MAC. When a macro is converted using MACROCNV.EXE, the name stays the same, but a new extension of .WPM (which stands for *W*ord*P*erfect *M*acro) is assigned, since all version 5 macros are named with the extension .WPM. Use the List Files screen to study the names of your macros and to decide which ones you wish to convert. Once you know the name of a macro you wish to convert, follow these steps to convert it:

1. You must be in DOS. If you are in WordPerfect, exit the program or exit temporarily by using the SHELL (CTRL + F1) key (as described in Chapter 13).
2. Floppy disk users should place the Conversion disk in drive A. Also, make sure that the default is drive A. If not, type **A:** and press ENTER.

   Hard disk users may have the file called MACROCNV.EXE on the hard disk and should change the default to the directory in which MACROCNV.EXE is housed. (If you installed according to the instructions in Appendix A, MACROCNV.EXE is in the \WPER directory.) Otherwise access the file from the Conversion disk as if you use floppy disks only.
3. At the DOS prompt, type **MACROCNV** (in either uppercase or lowercase letters), press the SPACEBAR, and then type the name of the macro to be converted, preceded by the drive or directory where the macro is stored, if different from the default.

   For example, suppose that you wish to convert a file stored on drive B and named ALTA.MAC (meaning that you invoke the macro by pressing ALT + A). Then, type

   MACROCNV B:ALTA.MAC

   Or suppose that you wish to convert a file stored in the directory \WP \MACROS on the hard disk and named REPORT.MAC. Then, type

   MACROCNV C:\WP\MACROS\REPORT.MAC
4. Press ENTER.

WordPerfect will convert the file, indicating how many characters, control characters, and functions have been processed. WordPerfect will also display a message indicating whether this macro will work with or without major modifications. The new file, named with the extension .WPM, is stored in the same drive or directory as the macro that you just converted. Repeat this procedure for all macros that you wish to convert.

You can use two wildcard symbols—? and *—to convert a whole group of macro files at once. The question mark represents any one character, whereas the asterisk represents any number of characters.

For example, suppose you have ten macro files, all on the same disk in drive B, that you wish to transfer to WordPerfect format. At the DOS prompt, you would type

MACROCNV B:*.MAC

Or, suppose you wish to convert all your macro files named with the ALT key that are stored in a directory named \WP\MACROS. At the DOS prompt, you would type

MACROCNV C:\WP\MACROS\ALT?.MAC

Whenever you use the Macro Conversion utility and a version 5 macro already exists with the name that WordPerfect is planning on converting the 4.2 macro into, WordPerfect prompts asking if you wish to replace the existing macro. For instance, if you're converting REPORT.MAC and REPORT.WPM already exists, then a prompt appears for a replacement decision. Type **Y** to overwrite the existing macro with the new converted one, or type **N** to abort the conversion. You can instead put the Conversion utility into Override mode, where any .WPM macro files are replaced without confirmation, by using the /O switch. For instance, suppose you wish to convert all macros named with the ALT key on the B drive, even though version 5 macro files named ALTA.WPM and ALTR.WPM also exist there. Then, execute the conversion by typing

MACROCNV B:ALT?.MAC /O

If a macro that you convert contains more than simple text and cursor movement keys, chances are that the macro will not operate correctly unless you edit it (as described in Chapter 27). There are two aids in pinpointing which sections of a macro will require editing to work properly in version 5. First, when you perform the actual conversion, you can request that WordPerfect output ("print") the conversion process on screen by using the /P switch. Suppose, for example, that the macro you are about to convert is named REPORT.MAC and is housed in the hard disk directory named \WP\MACROS. Then, at the DOS prompt, type

MACROCNV C:\WP\MACROS\REPORT.MAC /P

When you press ENTER, WordPerfect will begin the conversion, listing each keystroke in the macro. Print this screen by turning on your printer and using SHIFT + PRTSC to get a printout. Or, if the macro is long and the output will occupy more than one screen display, redirect the output to the printer by using the >PRN: command. For instance, type

MACROCNV C:\WP\MACROS\REPORT.MAC /P > PRN:

That way, you'll have a written record of the codes that you must edit manually.

The second aid in pinpointing the sections of a macro that must be manually edited is on the Macro Edit screen, the screen you view while editing the macro you just converted. Notice in Figure 28-2, for example, that for the macro named REPORT, the Macro Edit screen displays the comment **Bad?** in two places where WordPerfect assumes that the macro will not work properly. You can use the type of information shown in Figure 28-2 to assist in editing the macro until it works properly. (The procedure to edit macros is described in detail in Chapter 27.)

For additional information on WordPerfect's Macro Conversion utility, you can use the /H switch. Type **MACROCNV /H** at the DOS prompt.

Keep in mind that version 5 offers certain features, which were unavailable in version 4.2, that may make your old macros either obsolete or too cumbersome to be performed in version 5. Therefore, consider whether it makes more sense to write a brand-new macro, which can accomplish a task more elegantly using new version 5 features, or to convert the version 4.2 macro.

Tip: *Convert customized printer definitions that you created in an earlier WordPerfect version into version 5 format.*

Earlier versions of WordPerfect stored character maps and proportional spacing tables in files called WPFONT.FIL and WPFONT.ALL. WordPerfect 5 stores this

```
Macro: Edit

       File             \WPER\MACROS\REPORT.WPM

   1 - Description      WP 4.2 Converted Macro

   2 - Action

       {DISPLAY OFF}{Format}{;}     Bad?  ~315{Enter}{;}
       ~70{Enter}{;}
       ~{Center}MONTHLY·SALES·FIGURES{Enter}{;}
       ~Sales·Figures·by·region·are·as·follows:{Enter}{;}
       ~{;}■■■■·■■?{;}  Bad?  ~1{Enter}{;}
       ~2{Enter}{;}
       ~{Enter}{;}
       ~

Selection: 0
```

Figure 28-2. The Macro Edit screen indicating potential macro conversion problems

information either with the rest of a single printer definition in a file with the extension .PRS or as part of a collection of printer definitions in a file with the extension .ALL.

If you previously created your own customized WPFONT.FIL or WPFONT.ALL files, all of the information they contain can be converted into a new .ALL file in version 5 format by using the File Converter utility, FC.EXE. In other words, you don't have to re-create your character maps and proportional spacing tables.

FC.EXE is found on the Conversion disk, along with a file named FC.DOC that contains the FC.EXE documentation. The File Conversion utility works as follows:

1. You must be in DOS. If you are in WordPerfect, exit the program or exit temporarily by using the SHELL (CTRL + F1) key (as described in Chapter 13).

2. Floppy disk users should place the Conversion disk in drive A and the file containing the WPFONT file in drive B. Also, make sure that the default is drive A. If not, type **A:** and press ENTER.

   Hard disk users may have the file called FC.EXE on the hard disk. Change the default to the directory where FC.EXE is housed. Or, access FC.EXE from the floppy disk.

3. At the DOS prompt, type **FC**, press the SPACEBAR, type the name of the existing 4.2 file, press the SPACEBAR, and then type a name for the new version 5 printer file. For example, enter

   FC B:WPFONT.FIL B:NEW5.ALL.

The new file that is created contains the character maps and proportional spacing tables that have now been converted to version 5 format.

As a final step, you must use the Printer program PTR.EXE to actually select, edit, and expand this new file, thus producing your own printer definition. You would execute PTR.EXE (as described in Chapter 15), and retrieve the new file you just created. Next, use the F4 key to view the character maps that you converted, and copy those into a specific .PRS or .ALL file. (For instance, if the maps are for the HP LaserJet Series II, and if you have already defined the LaserJet as your printer, then copy those into the file on disk named HPLASEII.PRS.) Then use the F6 key to view the proportional spacing tables that you converted, and copy those into a specific .PRS or .ALL file. Finally, save and clear that new file from the Printer program and retrieve the .PRS or .ALL file into which you copied the character maps and proportional spacing tables, so that you can edit that file, creating fonts that will use the proportional spacing tables. (See Chapter 15 for a discussion of the Printer program.)

Trap: *Remember that you can't retrieve version 5 documents into version 4.2.*

If you try to retrieve a version 5 document while using version 4.2, WordPerfect will respond

ERROR: Incompatible file format

Remember that when you are working with version 5, save files into version 4.2 format before you attempt to retrieve them when using version 4.2.

Trap: *When you save from version 5 to 4.2 format, you may lose features, and extra codes may appear.*

If you save a version 5 file into version 4.2, any version 5-specific features will be lost. For example, if a file contains a graphics text box, this will be removed when you save the file in version 4.2 format.

As a result, if you're saving a file in version 4.2 format, save it twice—once using the SAVE (F10) key to preserve the version 5 features, and a second time, under a separate filename, in version 4.2 format. That way you can use the file in either version of WordPerfect and not lose version 5-specific features that you created when using version 5.

Also, after you convert to version 4.2, be sure to check to see how the conversion proceeded. Load version 4.2 and retrieve the converted file. Examine your document to see if WordPerfect inadvertently inserted any extra codes. You may want to move the cursor through the entire document, including footnotes or endnotes, to see if WordPerfect will delete those extra codes as it automatically rewrites the document. (A quick way to do this is by using the Extended Search feature to search for a search string that doesn't exist in the file, or by performing a spelling check.) Also, see if the formatting codes were correctly converted. If not, you will need to manually edit the file. Use the Search feature (see Chapter 4) and the Replace feature (see Chapter 6) to aid in this process.

Tip: *It's a good idea to convert a whole office at once to version 5.*

Since version 4.2 cannot read a version 5 document unless you specifically save in version 4.2 format, it's a good idea to convert your entire office to version 5 at the same time. That way, you won't have to keep track of which format a file was saved in.

Changing a File's Format Using the Convert Program

The WordPerfect package contains the Convert program, housed on the Conversion disk with the filename CONVERT.EXE, which enables you to transfer files from other software packages into WordPerfect version 5 format, or vice versa.

Using the Convert program, the following document files can be converted into WordPerfect 5 format:

- Revisable-Form-Text (DCA). IBM word processing packages on IBM mainframes and microcomputers use this format to transfer documents between these systems. This format can also be used as an intermediary to WordPerfect. For example, DisplayWrite and DisplayWrite 3 document files can both be transferred into Revisable-Form-Text format and then transferred into WordPerfect format by using the Convert program.
- Navy DIF Standard. This is a standard DIF (Data Interchange Format) developed by the United States Navy and most often used by the Navy for document transfer.
- WordStar 3.3.
- MultiMate 3.22.
- WordPerfect 4.2.

The following database files can be transformed into WordPerfect secondary merge file format with the Convert program:

- Mail Merge. This is a standard data file. A WordStar Mailmerge document is an example of a standard data file. In addition, programs such as dBASE allow you to transfer a dBASE data file into Mail Merge (standard data) format so that it can then be used with the Convert program.
- Spreadsheet DIF (Data Interchange Format). Programs such as Lotus 1-2-3 allow data files to be transferred into spreadsheet DIF format and can then be converted using CONVERT.EXE. Cells become fields and rows become records.

Conversely, WordPerfect 5 document files can be converted into the following with the Convert program:

- Revisable-Form-Text or Final-Form-Text (IBM DCA Format)
- Navy DIF Standard
- WordStar 3.3
- MultiMate 3.22
- ASCII (DOS) text (for more on ASCII text files, see the following section of the chapter)

You can also convert WordPerfect secondary merge files into spreadsheet DIF formats with CONVERT.EXE. Fields become cells and records become rows, so that a merge file can then be retrieved into a program such as Lotus 1-2-3.

Finally, the Convert program helps when sending a WordPerfect document electronically. WordPerfect codes use eight bits when transferring over a modem. But if the modem or line you wish to use transfers in seven bits, the document sender can use CONVERT.EXE to translate a WordPerfect file into seven-bit format so that it can be sent with all codes intact. After the file is sent over the modem, the receiver of the file can then use CONVERT.EXE to translate the file back into eight-bit format. The file will not lose any of its formatting codes this way.

If you wish to convert files to or from WordPerfect 5 format, then use the Convert program, as follows:

1. If you are importing a file into WordPerfect format, you must have the file on disk in one of the other formats handled by Convert (that is, Revisable-Form-Text, Navy DIF, WordStar, MultiMate, seven-bit transfer, WordPerfect 4.2, Mail Merge, or spreadsheet DIF).

   If you are exporting a WordPerfect file into another format, you must have the WordPerfect file already stored on disk. The WordPerfect file can contain either a WordPerfect document or WordPerfect secondary merge data.

2. You must be in DOS. If you are in WordPerfect, exit the program or exit temporarily by using the SHELL (CTRL + F1) key (as described in Chapter 13).

3. Floppy disk users should make sure that the default is drive B, where the file you wish to convert is stored. The DOS prompt should read B>. If the DOS prompt reads A>, type **B:** and press ENTER. Next, place the Conversion disk in drive A.

   Hard disk users should have the file called CONVERT.EXE on the hard disk. Make sure that the default is the directory where CONVERT.EXE is housed. (If you installed WordPerfect according to the instructions in Appendix A, CONVERT.EXE is in the \WPER subdirectory.)

4. At the DOS prompt, floppy disk users should type **A:CONVERT** (in either uppercase or lowercase letters). The screen reads

   B>A:CONVERT

   Hard disk users should type **CONVERT**. The screen reads

   C>CONVERT or C:\WPER>CONVERT

5. Press ENTER. WordPerfect loads the CONVERT.EXE file. In a few moments, WordPerfect prompts

   Name of Input File?

6. Type in the name of the file on disk that you wish to convert into another format, and press ENTER. (Hard disk users: If the file is in a location other than the default directory, you must indicate the file's path as well, such as \WPER\DATA\MEMO.) WordPerfect prompts

   Name of Output File?

7. Type in the name of the file where the converted document will be stored and press ENTER. The output filename *must be different* from the name of the input file. (If you wish to store that file in other than the default drive or directory, you must indicate the output file's path.)

   WordPerfect then displays a list of possible input file format types, as shown in Figure 28-3.

```
Name of Input File? B:\610727A.WP
Name of Output File? B:\610727A.MM


1 WordPerfect to another format
2 Revisable-Form-Text (IBM DCA Format) to WordPerfect
3 Navy DIF Standard to WordPerfect
4 WordStar 3.3 to WordPerfect
5 MultiMate 3.22 to WordPerfect
6 Seven-Bit Transfer Format to WordPerfect
7 WordPerfect 4.2 to WordPerfect 5.0
8 Mail Merge to WordPerfect Secondary Merge
9 WordPerfect Secondary Merge to Spreadsheet DIF
A Spreadsheet DIF to WordPerfect Secondary Merge

Enter number of Conversion desired
```

Figure 28-3. The CONVERT.EXE Input File menu

8. Type in the number corresponding to the format of the file to be converted and press ENTER.

   For example, if the file is a WordPerfect document that you wish to convert to another format, select 1. Or, if the file is a WordPerfect secondary merge file that you wish to convert to a spreadsheet DIF file, choose 9.

   Or the file may not be in WordPerfect format. If the file is a WordStar document (meaning that you want to import the file into WordPerfect), select 4. If the file is a MultiMate file, choose 5. If the file is a Lotus 1-2-3 spreadsheet that will be converted to a WordPerfect secondary merge file, select A.

9. What happens next depends on your response in step 8:

   If you chose number 1 from the Input File menu, meaning that the input file is in WordPerfect document format, you must indicate which format the file should be converted to. A list of possible output file format

```
Name of Input File? B:\610727A.WP
Name of Output File? B:\610727A.MM


1 Revisable-Form-Text (IBM DCA Format)
2 Final-Form-Text (IBM DCA Format)
3 Navy DIF Standard
4 WordStar 3.3
5 MultiMate 3.22
6 Seven-Bit Transfer Format
7 ASCII text file

Enter number of output file format desired
```

Figure 28-4. The CONVERT.EXE Output File menu

types, as shown in Figure 28-4, is displayed. Type in the number that corresponds to the format of the output file and press ENTER. For example, select 4, WordStar, to convert the file to WordStar document format. Or select 6, Seven-Bit Transfer Format, if you wish to prepare the WordPerfect file to be sent over a modem that requires seven-bit transfer. The document is converted into the format that you specify.

If you chose any number from 2 through 6 from the Input File menu, the conversion process begins and a WordPerfect version 5 document is generated.

If you chose number 7 from the Input File menu, meaning that you are converting a WordPerfect version 4.2 file into version 5, Convert would prompt, requesting the name of a .CRS file containing instructions for how you wish certain font change and other 4.2 codes to be converted. Type in the correct filename (such as HPLASEII.CRS) and press ENTER, or press ENTER if you have not created a .CRS file. (The preceding section of this chapter, "Working Within WordPerfect," discusses the procedure for creating a .CRS file and explains that you don't necessarily need to use Convert; with WordPerfect version 5 loaded, you can simply retrieve a version 4.2 document.)

If you chose number 8 from the Input File menu, Convert would prompt you to specify the field delimiter and record delimiter used by the particular Mail Merge file you wished to convert, so that it could remove those delimiters and insert the ^R and ^E codes. WordPerfect would also prompt you if there were any other characters used in the Mail Merge file that need to be removed.

For example, WordStar Mailmerge files are nondocument files where the field delimiter is a comma, the record delimiter is a hard return, and quotation marks are the extra characters that surround certain field entries. And dBASE can produce a similar data file format using a comma as the field delimiter, a hard return as the record delimiter, and quotation marks around certain field entries.

Consider how you would specify delimiters for a dBASE file you wished to convert. Two records in a standard data file could be

```
"Wolf","Steven J.",19551223
"Panos","Carl P.",19460415
```

In this example, when Convert prompts for a field delimiter, type in a comma (,). When Convert prompts for a record delimiter, you must indicate a hard return, which is a return plus a line feed. The decimal value you enter should be in curved braces { }. Enter the following: **{13}{10}**. When Convert prompts for any extra characters that should be stripped, type quotation marks ("). This database file would be converted to a secondary merge file, where the result is

Wolf^R
Steven J.^R
19551223^E
Panos^R
Carl P.^R
19460415^E

If you chose number 9 from the Input File menu, a spreadsheet DIF file is generated.

If you chose item A from the Input File menu, a WordPerfect secondary merge file is generated.

A message appears after the conversion is complete and you are returned to DOS. For example, if you converted a file on drive B called MEMO into an output file called MEMO2.CON, the following message would appear after a successful conversion:

B: \MEMO converted TO B: \MEMO2.CON

If you converted to WordPerfect version 5, you would be ready to load WordPerfect and retrieve the output file as a standard WordPerfect file. (Once you retrieve a converted file, you may find that there are extraneous characters you must delete or slight formatting problems you must correct.) If you converted to another program, you would now load the other software program to use the output file.

Trap: *Convert is automatically aborted if the input file is not found or has the same name as the output file.*

The Convert program may be unable to convert a file for you. Perhaps the file you indicated as the input file cannot be found on the drive or directory you indicated. Or perhaps the file you wish to convert is not in the format you specified. If that's the case, Convert is aborted. For example, suppose that you make a typing mistake when prompted for the input filename. An error message indicates that the file is nonexistent, another message indicates that the file has not been converted, and you are returned to DOS. You must reload Convert in order to try the conversion again.

Further, WordPerfect will abort Convert if you don't specify that the output filename is different from the input filename. The Convert program has been designed so that when a file is transferred into a different format, the input file remains intact. Convert creates a second, separate file. That's why the input file and the output file must have different filenames. You need to change only one character, or just the filename extension, to make the output filename different. For instance, if the input filename is MEMO, you can name the output file MEMO1. Or, if the input filename is MEMO.DOC, you can name the output file MEMO.WP.

Tip: *For certain formats you must use another software package's built-in facility in addition to Convert.*

Formats such as Revisable-Form-Text or spreadsheet DIF are intermediaries. You must use another software package's built-in conversion facility in addition to WordPerfect's Convert program. For example, suppose that you wish to convert a DisplayWrite 3 file into WordPerfect. You must first use Document Utilities (item J on the Text Task Selection menu) in the DisplayWrite 3 program to convert a DisplayWrite 3 file into Revisable-Form-Text. Then, and only then, are you ready to switch to DOS and use the Convert program.

As another example, suppose that you wish to convert a Lotus 1-2-3 spreadsheet containing an address list to a WordPerfect secondary merge file. You must use the Translate program on the Lotus Access menu to transfer the spreadsheet into a spreadsheet DIF file. Then you are ready to use Convert to transfer the DIF file into WordPerfect secondary merge file format.

Or suppose that you wish to convert a dBASE file into WordPerfect. You must first use dBASE's COPY TO and DELIMITED commands to transfer the database into the Mail Merge (standard data file) format. Then you can use Convert.

Tip: *Type in ASCII codes if the delimiter you wish to indicate is a control code such as a hard return.*

As described previously in this chapter section, when you choose option 8, Mail Merge, from the Convert program menu, the program prompts for three additional pieces of information: a field delimiter, a record delimiter, and any extra characters that should be removed from the file. This is because different data files use different delimiters to denote the end of a field or record.

A field delimiter is often a symbol such as the comma (,). But a record delimiter is often a hard return, which is a carriage return and a line feed. To specify a hard return as the record delimiter, you must type in each control code's decimal values between curved braces { }. Thus, if the record delimiter is a hard return, you must type in the following: **{13}{10}**. This applies when you transfer WordStar files or other standard data files.

Trap: *You cannot change WordPerfect secondary merge files into standard Mail Merge files with Convert.*

Although you can convert Mail Merge files into WordPerfect secondary merge files with Convert, the reverse is not the case. If you want to erase the ^R codes and ^E codes and put in delimiters that work with another software package, you cannot rely on Convert. But you can erase the ^R and ^E codes and put in the correct delimiters yourself. Depending on how you wish to alter the file, you should consider using either the Replace feature (see Chapter 6) or the Macro feature (see Chapter 27) to automate this task, letting WordPerfect do the work. Be sure to then save such a file using the generic word processor format, as described in the following section of this chapter.

Tip: *You can convert more than one file at the same time.*

You can use two wild card symbols—? and *—to convert a whole group of files at once. The question mark represents any one character, whereas the asterisk represents any number of characters.

For example, suppose that you have ten MultiMate files, all on the same disk in drive B, which you wish to transfer to WordPerfect format. MultiMate files all have the extension DOC. Therefore, when Convert requests an input file, type **B:*.DOC** and press ENTER. When Convert requests an output file, type an asterisk to represent the filename but use another extension; for example, type **B:*.2** and press ENTER or, type **B:*.WP** and press ENTER. Finally, when Convert requests an input file format, select number 5, MultiMate format. All ten files are converted from MultiMate into WordPerfect format, each with the same filename and with a different extension.

Or, suppose that you have ten WordStar files, all in the directory named \WPER\SUE, with names such as MEMO1, MEMO2, MEMO3, and so on. When Convert requests an input file, type **C:\WPER\SUE\MEMO?**. When Convert requests an output file, you can type **C:\WPER\SUE\MEMO?.WP**. Then, when you select number 4, WordStar format, as the input file form, Convert creates new files with names such as MEMO1.WP, MEMO2.WP, and so on.

Tip: *You can convert files without viewing the Convert menu.*

Once you become comfortable with the Convert program, you can translate files quickly without going through the Convert menus. Instead of typing **CONVERT** at the DOS prompt, you type all the information that the program needs on the same line, with each item separated from the next by one space.

- The format to convert any document format, except Mail Merge files, to a WordPerfect 5 document format is

  CONVERT *input_filename output_filename input_file_type*

  The input_file_type number is derived from the Input File menu, as shown in Figure 28-3. For example, the figure indicates that option 4 is the number for WordStar format. Therefore, to convert a file from WordStar to WordPerfect, where the WordStar file is called MEMO and the WordPerfect file will be called MEMO.WP, type **CONVERT MEMO MEMO.WP** 4 and press ENTER.

- The format to convert Mail Merge format to a WordPerfect secondary merge file is

  CONVERT *input_filename output_filename input_file_type field_delimiter record_delimiter characters_to_be_stripped*

  The input_file_type number will always be number 8, which is the option for converting Mail Merge to WordPerfect format, as shown in Figure 28-3. The output_file_type number is derived from the Output File menu, as shown in Figure 28-4.

- The format to convert WordPerfect to another format is

  CONVERT *input_filename output_filename input_file_type output_file_type*

  The input_file_type will always be number 1, which is the option for converting WordPerfect files into another format, as shown in Figure 28-3.

Trap: *Even after using Convert, you may need to manually edit your new file.*

Once you retrieve a converted file, you may find that there are extraneous characters that you must delete or slight formatting problems that you must correct. If the file has been converted into WordPerfect format, let WordPerfect features help you clean up the document. For instance, take advantage of the Replace feature (see Chapter 6) to delete certain unwanted characters that appear in the document.

Tip: *(When upgrading from 4.2.) The Convert program operates in the same way as in the previous version.*

Use the Convert program in version 5 as you did previously. One new item appears on the Input File menu: converting version 4.2 documents to version 5. With this option, you can convert documents before you load WordPerfect, or you can convert many documents at one time if they have a common filename pattern. However, as described in the preceding section of this chapter, "Working Within WordPerfect," using the Convert feature is not necessary; when version 5 is loaded, you can simply retrieve a version 4.2 file and it will automatically convert for you.

One new item also appears on the Output File menu: converting WordPerfect 5 files into ASCII text file format. You can thus convert documents to ASCII text without having WordPerfect loaded, and you can convert many documents at one time if they have a common filename pattern. However, as discussed in the following section of this chapter, you can also convert a file on screen into ASCII format without using Convert.

Converting Files Using ASCII (DOS) Text Files

WordPerfect enables you to save or retrieve an ASCII (DOS) text file. ASCII stands for American Standard Code for Information Interchange, a set of codes used as a basic standard language of communication between computers. Transferring files into ASCII text is a sound alternative if using Convert does not support the software package which you wish to involve in the transfer of files.

Be aware, however, that when you transfer information into an ASCII file, special formatting is lost in the process. An ASCII text file contains text, spaces, and carriage returns, so that all you basically have in an ASCII text file is raw data and a few control codes.

To export a WordPerfect document into ASCII format, stripping it of all special formatting so that the file can then be imported into another software package, follow these steps:

1. Make sure the document is on the Typing screen.
2. Press TEXT IN/OUT (CTRL + F5). The following menu appears:

   1 Dos Text; **2** Password; **3** Save Generic; **4** Save WP 4.2; **5** Comment: **0**

3. Select Dos Text (1 or T). The DOS Text menu appears:

   1 Save; **2** Retrieve (CR/LF to [HRt]); **3** Retrieve (CR/LF to [SRt] in HZone): **0**

4. Select Save (1 or S). WordPerfect prompts

   Document to be saved (Dos Text):

5. Type in a filename (preceded by a drive or directory if different from the default) and press ENTER.

WordPerfect converts the file into ACSII format, replacing all **[SRt]** codes with carriage return/line feeds (CR/LF), which are ASCII codes that end a line and move the cursor to the beginning of the next line. →Indent←, center, tab align, flush right, and margin codes are converted into spaces. Tab codes are retained and →Indent codes are converted into tab codes. Date, soft hyphen, and paragraph numbering codes are converted to ASCII text. But special formatting is not retained. For instance, text within headers, footers, footnotes, and endnotes is not converted, and column format is not converted. The file is now ready to be imported into another software package.

You can also retrieve a document that is in ASCII format, importing the text in two different ways. You can retrieve the file in such a way that all CR/LF codes are converted into hard returns, so that each line ends with a **[HRt]** code. Or you can retrieve the files in such a way that the CR/LF codes are converted into soft returns, so that **[SRt]** codes appear within WordPerfect's Hyphenation Zone (the Hyphenation Zone, discussed in Chapter 8, is the area that determines when WordPerfect will hyphenate). Any sequence of two or more CR/LF codes is converted to hard returns so that the document format is preserved. Using this second method, your file more closely matches WordPerfect format. Proceed as follows:

1. Press TEXT IN/OUT (CTRL + F5). The following menu appears:

   1 Dos Text; 2 Password; 3 Save Generic; 4 Save WP 4.2; 5 Comment: **0**

2. Select Dos Text (1 or T). The DOS Text menu appears:

   1 Save; 2 Retrieve (CR/LF to [HRt]); 3 Retrieve (CR/LF to [SRt] in HZone): **0**

3. Select Retrieve (CR/LF) to [HRt]) (2 or R), or select Retrieve (CR/LF to [SRt] in HZone) (3 or R). WordPerfect prompts

   Document to be retrieved:

4. Type in a filename (preceded by a drive or directory if different from the default) and press ENTER.

Trap: *Save a file in ASCII text under a different name or you'll lose the WordPerfect format.*

If you've already saved a file by using the SAVE (F10) key and then begin to save that WordPerfect file again into ASCII format by using the TEXT IN/OUT (CTRL + F5) key, WordPerfect suggests that the file be saved under the same filename. Type in a new filename, or the file formatted in WordPerfect will be overwritten.

For example, suppose that you wrote a document and saved it in WordPerfect under the name MEMO. When you then press TEXT IN/OUT and select Save (1 or S), WordPerfect responds

Document to be Saved: B:\MEMO

Type in a new filename, such as MEMODOS, and press ENTER. That way you'll save the document twice, once in WordPerfect format (MEMO), and a second time in ASCII format (MEMODOS).

Then be cautious. WordPerfect changes the name of the file on the status line to reflect the last file you saved. For example, the status line might now read **C:\WPER\DATA\MEMODOS.** Therefore, if you later edit the file and you wish to resave it as a WordPerfect file (and *not* as an ASCII text file), be sure that you type in the appropriate filename, or you'll accidentally overwrite the ASCII file with the WordPerfect document.

Tip: *Save many WordPerfect files into ASCII text in one command using the Convert program.*

It isn't necessary to have a file on the Typing screen in order to convert it to ASCII text format. By using the Convert program, you can convert WordPerfect document files directly from disk into ASCII text. Employing Convert is especially useful if the files that you wish to transfer into version 5 have a common filename pattern. For example, if the files you wish to convert all have the file extension .RPT, then you can convert all the files at once, specifying *.RPT as the name of the "input file." The Convert program is described in the preceding section of this chapter, "Changing a File's Format Using the Convert Program."

Tip: *Another option for importing a DOS text file is provided on the List Files menu.*

The Text In option on the List Files menu can also be used to retrieve a DOS text file. On the List Files screen, you would position the cursor on the DOS file that you wished to retrieve and then select Text In (5 or T). The file is retrieved with all CR/LF codes converted into hard returns, so that each line ends with a **[HRt]** code. Therefore, it is the same as selecting the second option, Retrieve (CR/LF to [HRt]), on the DOS Text menu.

If the Typing screen contains text when you select Text In (5 or T), WordPerfect prompts, asking you to verify that you wish to retrieve the ASCII file even though text is on the Typing screen. Type **Y** to retrieve the file, or **N** to abort the Text In command.

Tip: *Set WordPerfect's margins and tabs to match the DOS text file format when working with paragraphs of text.*

Standard format in a DOS text file is with lines 80 characters wide and tabs every eight spaces. With this in mind, you can create WordPerfect documents that contain the correct settings to properly retrieve or save a document in ASCII text. If you don't, you may find hard returns in the middle of paragraphs, which disrupt the appearance of the text.

For example, suppose that you plan to retrieve a DOS text file. Before you do, clear the screen and insert a **[L/R Mar Set:]** code and a **[Tab Set:]** code so that the screen conforms to ASCII format. Now retrieve the DOS text file. You should not experience margin and tab formatting problems.

Tip: *You can save WordPerfect files into generic word processing format, converting soft returns into spaces.*

As discussed earlier in this chapter section, when you save a WordPerfect file into DOS text format by using the Save option on the DOS Text menu, carriage return/line feed (CR/LF) codes are inserted at the end of every line.

As an alternative, you can instead save DOS Text files where soft returns are converted into spaces, tabs are converted to DOS tabs (which are eight spaces apart), and only those lines ending with hard returns are converted to a CR/LF. In addition, spaces are inserted in place of center, indent, and flush right codes. Thus, the layout of the text is maintained for a document that you will then import into another software package, and text will word wrap when imported into that other package. Generic word processing format is quite useful for retrieving WordPerfect documents into other word processing packages. With the WordPerfect document on screen, you would press the TEXT IN/OUT (CTRL + F5) key, select Save Generic (3 or G), and then enter a filename.

Tip: *You can print to an ASCII text file in a printer format.*

You can create an ASCII text file by using the Print feature, where you print a WordPerfect file not to a printer, but to a file. This is similar to using the DOS menu to save, except that more formatting codes are retained. The file will preserve centering, footnotes, endnotes, headers, footers, and columns by inserting spaces where appropriate. In addition, the file also contains those characters and codes that ordinarily are sent to the printer.

To print to disk, you would use the Select Printers option on the Print menu to redefine your printer definition so that files are sent to the disk rather than to the port to which the printer is connected. To print a file to disk:

1. Press PRINT (SHIFT + F7).
2. Choose S, Select Printers.
3. Position the cursor on the printer you wish to select.
4. Select Edit (3 or E).
5. Select Port (2 or P).
6. Select Other (8 or O).
7. Type in the name of the file in which you wish to "print" the file, preceded by a drive or directory if different from the default, and press ENTER.
8. Press EXIT (F7) to return to the Print menu.
9. Print the document by selecting Full Document (1 or F).

(For a more detailed discussion of the options on the Select Printers menu, refer to Appendix A.)

Once you print a file to disk, you can then send that file at any time to your selected printer directly from DOS by using the DOS PRINT command. Since all the printer codes are stored in the file, the document will print out properly. Thus, printing to disk is handy when, at a later date, you plan to print out that file without loading WordPerfect (for example, at another work station that doesn't have the WordPerfect program).

Note: Once you redefine your printer so that it will print to disk, you must remember to re-edit the printer definition to its original definition—with the port defined as the plug to which the printer is connected—if you later want to again send a document to the printer. If you plan to print to disk often, consider copying the original printer definition under a different name (such as copying HPLASEII.PRS to HPTODISK.PRS), changing the port for that new printer definition only (that is, changing the port for HPTODISK.PRS), and then always using the new definition for future printing to disk. Use the original definition to print to the printer.

Tip: *Use the DOS Text feature to retrieve text created in spreadsheet or database programs.*

The Convert program enables you to convert files from certain word processing packages into WordPerfect documents. And it permits you to convert spreadsheet or database program information into WordPerfect secondary merge format. However, what if you wish to convert a spreadsheet or database file into a standard WordPerfect document? For example, perhaps you use Lotus 1-2-3 to create a table of cost estimates and then wish to incorporate the table into a WordPerfect report. Or perhaps you use dBASE to produce a report and you want to use WordPerfect as an external word processor to enhance the appearance of the report. You can use ASCII as the intermediary in doing this.

In four basic steps, you can convert a document produced by a spreadsheet or database package into WordPerfect document format:

1. Create the document in the other software package. For example, develop your cost estimates using Lotus 1-2-3, or prepare a report using dBASE.
2. Transfer the document into a DOS text file. Most software packages enable you to send a file normally slated for the printer into a DOS text file instead. These files will contain the exact output used to create the printed document. By printing to disk, you are converting that document into standard ASCII format.

   For example, in Lotus 1-2-3 you usually print a file by typing /**PP** (the slash to bring up the Lotus commands, P for "print," and P for "printer"). Instead, type /**PF**, where the F signifies that you will be printing to a file instead of to the printer. On the Print to File menu, you can strip the Lotus 1-2-3 file of all its formatting by then selecting OOU (O for "options," O for "other," and U for "unformatted"). Then press ESC, select R to define your range, and finally select G for Go. You have thus created an ASCII file.

As another example, in dBASE you can format output from a database to a file by using the REPORT FORM command, where you print the report TO FILE. This produces an ASCII file that has the same structure and content as if you printed it on paper. (Also, SET ALTERNATE is frequently used in dBASE to create an ASCII text file of output.)

3. Load WordPerfect.
4. Retrieve the "printed" file by using the Text In/Out menu. (Unless you specify otherwise, Lotus 1-2-3 files are automatically saved with a .PRN extension, so if you print to disk a file called DATA, retrieve a file called DATA.PRN.)

Now you can manipulate the text as you wish, and add more text, and you can save it or print it as a WordPerfect file, or both.

Note: Graphics cannot be exchanged between programs in the same way that text can. If you wish to import a graph created in Lotus 1-2-3, for example, refer to Chapter 18.

Tip: *Write or edit a batch file in WordPerfect.*

A batch file is a sequence of DOS commands housed in a DOS text file (Appendix A discusses several batch files you can create to load WordPerfect easily). If you write or edit batch files, you will find WordPerfect to be an excellent vehicle for doing so.

To write a batch file, clear the WordPerfect Typing screen and type the batch file using the same syntax as you would if you were in DOS. The advantage to writing a batch file in WordPerfect is that you can insert or delete characters just as if you were creating a WordPerfect document. When you have completed the batch file, save it as an ASCII text file by pressing TEXT IN/OUT (CTRL + F5), selecting Dos Text (1 or T), and then selecting Save (1 or S).

To edit a DOS text file already on disk, retrieve the file by using TEXT IN/OUT, edit it as if it were a WordPerfect document, and then save it again as a DOS text file. By using WordPerfect, you can avoid using the EDLIN or the COPY CON: command.

Tip: *(When upgrading from 4.2.) Save files in ASCII text format as in the previous version.*

The Text In/Out menu has changed in version 5; it is now a line menu rather than a full-screen menu. While the specific keys you press are different, the same options are available as in version 4.2. You'll notice one difference in versions when saving a document as a DOS text file: tab codes are retained, and **→Indent** codes are converted into tab codes. In version 4.2, tabs and indents were converted into spaces.

Tips and Traps Summary

Working Within WordPerfect

Trap: WordPerfect version 5 may be unable to correctly convert certain codes from earlier WordPerfect versions.

Tip: When converting a document, a conversion resource file can instruct WordPerfect on how to convert some codes.

Tip: Convert many version 4.2 files at once to version 5 using the Convert program.

Tip: Convert version 4.2 primary and secondary files into version 5 before you attempt a merge in version 5 using these files.

Tip: Convert dictionaries into version 5 so they can be used with the version 5 Speller feature.

Tip: Version 4.2 macros can be converted into version 5.

Tip: Convert customized printer definitions that you created in an earlier WordPerfect version into version 5 format.

Trap: Remember that you can't retrieve version 5 documents into version 4.2.

Tips and Traps Summary (*continued*)

Trap: When you save from version 5 to 4.2 format, you may lose features, and extra codes may appear.

Tip: It's a good idea to convert a whole office at once to version 5.

Changing a File's Format Using the Convert Program

Trap: Convert is automatically aborted if the input file is not found or has the same name as the output file.

Tip: For certain formats you must use another software package's built-in facility in addition to Convert.

Tip: Type in ASCII codes if the delimiter you wish to indicate is a control code such as a hard return.

Trap: You cannot change WordPerfect secondary merge files into standard Mail Merge files with Convert.

Tip: You can convert more than one file at the same time.

Tip: You can convert files without viewing the Convert menu.

Trap: Even after using Convert, you may need to manually edit your new file.

Tip: (When upgrading from 4.2.) The Convert program operates in the same way as in the previous version.

Converting Files Using ASCII (DOS) Text Files

Trap: Save a file in ASCII text under a different name or you'll lose the WordPerfect format.

Tip: Save many WordPerfect files into ASCII text in one command using the Convert program.

Tips and Traps Summary (*continued*)

Tip: Another option for importing a DOS text file is provided on the List Files menu.

Tip: Set WordPerfect's margins and tabs to match the DOS text file format when working with paragraphs of text.

Tip: You can save WordPerfect files into generic word processing format, converting soft returns into spaces.

Tip: You can print to an ASCII text file in a printer format.

Tip: Use the DOS Text feature to retrieve text created in spreadsheet or database programs.

Tip: Write or edit a batch file in WordPerfect.

Tip: (When upgrading from 4.2.) Save files in ASCII text format as in the previous version.

Appendixes

A

Installing WordPerfect

The WordPerfect package offers too many features for the program to fit onto one, two, or even three disks. WordPerfect version 5 comes on twelve 5 1/4-inch (or six 3 1/2-inch) disks. Before you use any of those disks, you must prepare WordPerfect to work properly with your equipment. The installation process involves copying the WordPerfect files onto formatted disks if you are a two-drive floppy disk user, or onto your hard disk if you are a hard disk user—procedures which are described in the first two sections of this appendix.

The installation process also involves setting up WordPerfect to work in partnership with your printer(s). The last section of this appendix describes how to define and select the printer or printers that you have attached to your computer.

If you're upgrading from version 4.2, you'll find that in version 5 the procedure to install WordPerfect and select printers is quite different from version 4.2. Be sure to follow the instructions provided.

Installing WordPerfect on a Two-Drive Floppy Disk System

Floppy disk users need to perform the following tasks in order to install WordPerfect. (1) Format 14 blank disks (assuming that you are using 5 1/4-inch disks). Twelve will be formatted so that they can store a copy of all files on all disks, except for the main WordPerfect program file WP.EXE (which is stored on the original WordPerfect 1 disk). One disk will be formatted to serve as a data disk, which will store documents you create with WordPerfect (or you can format more disks so that you have many data disks available). The last disk will be formatted in a special way so that it is made "bootable," meaning that your computer's operating system (DOS) and WordPerfect can be started from the working copy of the WordPerfect 1 disk. The main WordPerfect program file (WP.EXE) will be copied onto this bootable disk. (2) Copy the diskettes in the WordPerfect package to the formatted disks, so that you create a working copy of the WordPerfect program. (3) Create a special file named CONFIG.SYS on the working copy of the WordPerfect 1 disk so that WordPerfect can be started properly. (4) Create a special file named AUTOEXEC.BAT on the working copy of the WordPerfect 1 disk so that WordPerfect can be started automatically whenever you place the working copy of the WordPerfect 1 disk in drive A and turn on your computer. (This is an optional step.)

When you are performing these tasks, you will frequently use the following two keys on the keyboard:

- **ENTER** Used when loading WordPerfect to send a command to the computer. Once WordPerfect is loaded, the ENTER key moves the cursor (the flashing light that serves as your pointer on screen) down to the next line. The ENTER key is marked on the keyboard with the word "ENTER" or "RETURN" or with a symbol of a bent arrow pointing to the left (↵).
- **BACKSPACE** Used to erase mistakes as you type, deleting the character to the left of the cursor. The BACKSPACE key is marked on the keyboard with the word "BACKSPACE" or with a symbol of a long arrow pointing to the left (←). BACKSPACE is often located above the ENTER key.

Note: The following instructions assume that you use a two-disk-drive system with 5 1/4-inch double-density disks, which hold approximately 360K of information. If you use 3 1/2-inch disks (which can hold twice as much information as 5 1/4-inch double-density disks), then you need to format half as many disks. Also, the 3 1/2-inch disks are named differently. For example, whenever the instructions refer to the WordPerfect 1 disk, you should read this as the WordPerfect 1/WordPerfect 2 disk. Or whenever the instructions refer to the Learning disk or the Fonts/Graphics disk, you should read this as the Learning/Fonts/Graphics disk.

Format Disks

To format 14 blank disks, proceed as follows:

1. Insert your DOS system disk into drive A (usually the drive on the left or on top) and turn on the computer.
2. If prompted to do so, type the correct date. Press ENTER. If prompted to do so, type the correct time. Press ENTER. (If you have never entered the date or time, see the first Tip in Chapter 1, which describes these procedures.) The following appears on the screen:

   A>
3. Insert a blank disk into drive B (usually the drive on the right or on the bottom) and close the disk drive door.
4. Type **FORMAT B:**. (Either uppercase or lowercase letters can be used when typing DOS commands.) The screen looks like this:

   A>FORMAT B:
5. Press ENTER. You are prompted to make sure that a blank disk is in drive B. Press ENTER a second time, and the computer begins formatting the disk in drive B.
6. When prompted to indicate whether you wish to format another disk, type **Y** and press ENTER. Insert a new blank disk in drive B and press ENTER again.
7. Repeat step 6 until you have formatted 13 disks. When asked if you wish to format another disk, type **N** and press ENTER. You are returned to the DOS prompt (A>).
8. Insert the final (fourteenth) disk into drive B, and type **FORMAT B:/S**. The /S will make this disk bootable. The screen looks like this:

   A>**FORMAT B:/S**

9. Press ENTER. You are prompted to make sure that a blank disk is in drive B. Press ENTER a second time, and the computer begins formatting the disk in drive B, making that disk bootable.
10. When asked whether you wish to format another disk, type **N** and press ENTER. You are returned to the DOS prompt (A>).

Copy the WordPerfect Files

Now you're ready to copy the files in the WordPerfect package onto the formatted disks so that you have working copies of the WordPerfect program. Table A-1 lists the files that are found on each of the disks provided in the WordPerfect package.

Table A-1. List of WordPerfect Files

WordPerfect 1 Disk	
WP.EXE	WordPerfect program
WPHELP.FIL	WordPerfect help file
WPHELP2.FIL	WordPerfect help file
WordPerfect 2 Disk	
KEYS.MRS	Keyboard macro resource file
STANDARD.PRS	Text mode preview and standard printer resource file
WP.FIL	Contains a part of the WordPerfect code
WP.MRS	Macro resource file
WPSMALL.DRS	Driver resource file
Speller Disk	
WP{WP}EN.LEX	Main and common word lists (English)
SPELL.EXE	Speller utility
Thesaurus Disk	
WP{WP}EN.THS	Thesaurus list (English)

Table A-1. List of WordPerfect Files (continued)

Learning Disk	
TUTOR.COM	Tutorial
LEARN.BAT	Batch file to initiate tutorial on floppy disk system
INSTALL.EXE	Auto-Install program
*.STY	Style examples
*.TUT	Tutorial files
*.WKB	Learning files
*.WPG	Graphics images for use with WordPerfect Workbook
*.WPM	Macro examples
PTR Program Disk	
PTR.EXE	Printer program
PTR.HLP	Printer program help file
Conversion Disk	
CURSOR.COM	Cursor utility
CHARACTR.DOC	WordPerfect character set documentation
CHARMAP.TST	Character set (map) printer test
CONVERT.EXE	Convert program
FC.EXE	Font conversion program
FC.DOS	Font conversion program documentation
GRAPHCNV.EXE	Graphics conversion program
LIBRARY.STY	Style library sample
MACROCNV.EXE	Macros conversion program (version 4.2 macros into version 5)
META.SYS	Meta file graphics conversion program (PlanPerfect 3.0 into CGM graphics format) (not all releases)
ORDERWPG.DOC	Graphics ordering information
PRINTER.TST	WordPerfect features printer test
README	DOS text file of updates to the WordPerfect manual

Table A-1. List of WordPerfect Files (continued)

README.WP	WordPerfect file of updates to the WordPerfect manual
STANDARD.CRS	Conversion resource file (version 4.2 documents into version 5)
*.WPK	WordPerfect keyboard definition examples
Fonts/Graphics Disk	
EGA*.FRS	Character sets for EGA monitors
HRF*.FRS	Fonts for Hercules RamFonts graphics cards
GRAB.COM	Screen capture utility
WP.DRS	Driver resource file (character set) for hard disk systems
*.WPD	Graphics driver file for various monitors
*.WPG	30 graphics (Clip-Art) images
Printer 1, 2, 3, 4 Disks	
*.ALL	Printer driver files
Auxiliary Files Created During a WordPerfect Session	
WP}WP{.*	Overflow, Print Buffer, Sort, and other temporary files that are stored on the drive where WP.EXE is located or on the drive specified with the /D option (see Chapter 1), which are deleted when you exit WordPerfect
*.BK!	Original Backup files
*.CRS	Document Conversion files
*.PRS	Printer Definition files
*.WPK	Keyboard Definition files
*.WPM	Macro files
WP{WP}*.HYL	Hyphenation module files
WP{WP}.BK#	Timed Backup files
WP{WP}EN.SUP	Supplementary Dictionary file (English)
WP{WP}.SET	Setup file, stored where WP.EXE is located

1. Insert the original WordPerfect 1 disk in drive A. The blank disk that is bootable should still be in drive B.

2. Type **COPY WP.EXE B:**. The screen looks like this:

   A>COPY WP.EXE B:

3. Press ENTER. The main WordPerfect program file named WP.EXE is copied onto the disk in drive B. Since the DOS system is also on the disk in drive B (to make it bootable), the disk in drive B has insufficient room to store the other two files that also reside on the original WordPerfect 1 disk.

4. Remove the disk in drive B, fill out a label for the new working copy of the WordPerfect disk (for example, write on the label "WordPerfect 1—Working Copy"), and affix the label to the disk. If the label is already on the disk, write gently, using a felt-tip pen, so as not to harm the disk.

5. Insert another blank disk in drive B. The original WordPerfect 1 disk should still be in drive A.

6. Type **COPY *.FIL B:**. The screen looks like this:

   A>COPY *.FIL B:

7. Press ENTER. The WordPerfect Help files (named WPHELP.FIL and WPHELP2.FIL) are copied onto the disk in drive B.

8. Remove the disks in both drives A and B, fill out a label for the new working copy of the Help files disk (for example, write on the label "WordPerfect 5—Help Files"), and affix the label to the disk. If the label is already on the disk, write gently, using a felt-tip pen, so as not to harm the disk.

9. Insert the WordPerfect 2 disk in drive A and another blank, formatted disk in drive B. (If you're a 3 1/2-inch disk user, then you would place back in drive B the working copy of the WordPerfect 1/WordPerfect 2 disk—the one onto which you recently copied WP.EXE—rather than a blank disk.)

10. Type **COPY *.* B:**. The screen looks like this:

    A>COPY *.* B:

    (If you're a 3 1/2-inch disk user, then you'll want to copy only selective files from the WordPerfect 1/WordPerfect 2 disk. Proceed as follows instead: type **COPY WP.FIL** and press ENTER; next, type **COPY *.?RS** and press ENTER. Now skip to step 12 below.)

11. Press ENTER. One by one, all the files from the WordPerfect 2 disk in drive A are copied to the disk in drive B.

12. Remove the disks in both drives A and B, fill out a label for the new working copy of the WordPerfect 2 disk (for example, write on the label "WordPerfect 2—Working Copy"), and affix the label to the disk. If the label is already on the disk, write gently, using a felt-tip pen, so as not to harm the disk.

13. Repeat steps 9 through 12 ten more times, until the rest of the WordPerfect disks have been copied onto formatted disks and the working disks have been labeled. (If you're a 3 1/2-inch disk user, also repeat steps 9 through 12, but ignore the information in parentheses in steps 9 and 10 for the rest of the WordPerfect disks.)

14. Place the 12 original WordPerfect disks in a safe place for storage. Use *only* the working copies with your computer from now on; if a working copy gets lost or wears out, you can always make a new working disk from the original.

15. Label the last formatted disk as your data disk. For instance, write on the label "Data Disk 1," and affix the label to the disk.

Create the CONFIG.SYS File

A file named CONFIG.SYS contains a set of commands to set up your computer system. WordPerfect operates properly only if you create a CONFIG.SYS file and only if that file contains the command FILES=20 (at least 20). This command tells DOS how many files can be open at one time. You will create this file on the working copy of the WordPerfect 1 disk (or on whatever disk is your startup disk):

1. Insert the working copy of the WordPerfect 1 disk (the disk that *you* labeled) into drive B.

2. Type **COPY B:CONFIG.SYS+CON B:CONFIG.SYS**. Be careful to type the command exactly as shown, making sure that spaces are in the proper places. Upper- or lowercase letters make no difference. The screen looks like this:

   A>COPY B:CONFIG.SYS+CON B:CONFIG.SYS

3. Press ENTER. WordPerfect responds with the message "CON."

4. Press ENTER again.

5. Type **FILES=20** and press the ENTER key.

    (You can also write a statement in the CONFIG.SYS file that speeds up the system, especially during operations such as a spelling check. To do so, you type **BUFFERS=15** and press ENTER. Now, the typing screen will read

    FILES=20

    BUFFERS=15

    Setting BUFFERS=15 is optional.)

6. Press CTRL+Z (which means that you hold down the CTRL key and, while holding it down, type **Z**).
7. Press ENTER. The filename CONFIG.SYS is saved on the disk in drive B (the working copy of the WordPerfect 1 disk).

Note: If you plan to load WordPerfect Library before you load WordPerfect, then you will want to make the WordPerfect Library disk bootable and to create the CONFIG.SYS file on the WordPerfect Library disk. You should set FILES=40, rather than FILES=20, in the CONFIG.SYS file to run both Library and WordPerfect program files.

Create the AUTOEXEC.BAT File

You are now ready to create a file named AUTOEXEC.BAT, which is a special batch file—a file that contains DOS commands and that is executed automatically as soon as DOS is loaded into your computer. Creating a batch file is optional; as Chapter 1 explains, you can load WordPerfect with or without a batch file. A batch file is effective because it allows you to automate the process of loading WordPerfect.

A basic AUTOEXEC.BAT file on the working copy of the WordPerfect disk might contain the following DOS commands:

```
DATE
TIME
B:
A:WP
A:
```

The batch file in this example automatically requests the current date and time when you turn on your computer with the WordPerfect disk in drive A (and it assumes that your computer is not equipped with an internal clock). It switches to drive B, so that your document files are saved to your data disk, and starts WordPerfect. When you exit WordPerfect, the default is automatically changed to drive A.

You can also enhance a basic batch file. You may wish, for example, to start WordPerfect with slash options (described in Chapter 1). If so, you can use the SET command to specify the option. Suppose that you wish to start up WordPerfect every time by executing both the /R option, to speed up the WordPerfect program, and the /M option, to execute a macro named TOC when WordPerfect is first loaded. Then the batch file would be

```
DATE
TIME
SET WP=/R/M-TOC
B:
A:WP
A:
```

Or suppose that you have an AST expansion board (which expands the memory in your computer and also comes with an internal clock). You want to set the clock, create a RAM drive (a portion of DOS partitioned to act like a disk drive) of 100K, include slash options so that the program speeds up, and be able to remove the WordPerfect disk by redirecting WordPerfect overflow files to the RAM drive (drive C). The batch file would be

```
ASTCLOCK
SUPERDRV C:/M=100
SET WP=/R/D-C:
B:
A:WP
A:
```

Note: The ASTCLOCK and SUPERDRV files must be copied onto the WordPerfect 1 disk for this batch file to operate correctly.

To create a batch file named AUTOEXEC.BAT (since you just created a CONFIG.SYS file, you should still be in DOS and the working copy of WordPerfect 1 disk should still be in drive B):

1. Type **COPY CON B:AUTOEXEC.BAT**. Be careful to type the command exactly as shown, making sure that spaces are in the proper places. Upper- or lowercase letters make no difference. The screen looks like this:

   A>COPY CON B:AUTOEXEC.BAT

2. Press ENTER.
3. Type the contents of the batch file (examples are provided above), with each command on a separate line—meaning that you end each line by pressing ENTER. For instance, to create a basic AUTOEXEC.BAT file, you would type **DATE** and press ENTER, type **TIME** and press ENTER, type **B:** and press ENTER, type **A:WP** and press ENTER, and type **A:** and press ENTER.
4. Press CTRL + Z (which means that you hold down the CTRL key and, while holding it down, type **Z**).
5. Press ENTER. The file named AUTOEXEC.BAT is saved on the disk in drive B (the working copy of the WordPerfect 1 disk).

You are now ready to explore the world of WordPerfect. Place your working copy of the WordPerfect 1 disk in drive A, your blank data disk in drive B, and press CTRL + ALT + DEL to restart your computer (or you can turn off your computer and then turn it on again). Be sure to turn to Chapter 1 for Tips for loading WordPerfect. Once you learn more about various startup options in Chapter 1, you may, in the future, wish to modify your file named AUTOEXEC.BAT. (You can do so from within WordPerfect, as described in Chapter 28, in the section "Converting Files Using ASCII (DOS) Text Files.")

When WordPerfect is loaded, turn to the section "Selecting Your Printer" in this appendix to guide you in setting up WordPerfect to work with the printer(s) attached to your computer.

Installing WordPerfect on a Hard Disk System

A hard disk, like a floppy disk, stores information. But a hard disk stores much more information. Hard disk users should perform the following tasks to install WordPerfect: (1) divide the hard disk into directories (which are comparable to separate file drawers in a filing cabinet), so that information is neatly organized, and then copy the diskettes in the WordPerfect package onto the hard disk; (2) create (or modify) a special file named CONFIG.SYS on the main (root) directory on the hard disk; (3) create a special batch file so that WordPerfect can be started automatically (an optional step) from DOS; and (4) change the AUTOEXEC.BAT file, if necessary, to indicate where the WordPerfect program files are stored.

Warning: Do not format your hard disk if it is already formatted (as has been assumed), or you will lose all the files currently on your hard disk!

When you are installing WordPerfect as described in the following sections, you will frequently use the following two keys on the keyboard:

- **ENTER** Used when loading WordPerfect to send a command to the computer. Once WordPerfect is loaded, the ENTER key moves the cursor (the flashing light that serves as your pointer on screen) down to the next line. The ENTER key is marked on the keyboard with the word "ENTER" or "RETURN" or with a symbol of a bent arrow pointing to the left (↵).
- **BACKSPACE** Used to erase mistakes as you type, deleting the character to the left of the cursor. The BACKSPACE key is marked on the keyboard with the word "BACKSPACE" or with a symbol of a long arrow pointing to the left (⟵). BACKSPACE is often located above the ENTER key.

Note: The following instructions assume that you use a system with 5 1/4-inch double-density disks, which hold approximately 360K of information. If you use 3 1/2-inch disks (which can hold twice as much information as 5 1/4-inch double-density disks), then the 3 1/2-inch disks are named differently. For example, whenever the instructions refer to the WordPerfect 1 disk, you should read this as the WordPerfect 1/WordPerfect 2 disk. Or whenever the instructions refer to the Learning disk or the Fonts/Graphics disk, you should read this as the Learning/Fonts/Graphics disk.

Create Directories and Copy the WordPerfect Files onto the Hard Disk

There are two methods for creating directories and copying the WordPerfect files. You can install WordPerfect manually, creating directories on your own in order to store the WordPerfect program files and then copying the WordPerfect files into those directories. Or you can use the Auto-Install program provided by

WordPerfect, which automatically creates directories named \WP50 and \WP50\LEARN to store the WordPerfect program files, and then prompts you with instructions for copying the WordPerfect files. Read both methods and decide which you prefer. Manual installation offers more flexibility in how you name directories and where you store files. The auto-install procedure is inflexible, but does most of the work of installing WordPerfect for you.

Manual Installation—Create Directories By manually installing the WordPerfect program on the hard disk, you can choose your directory names and where you want certain files stored. Table A-1 lists the files that are found on each of the disks provided in the WordPerfect package. Proceed as follows to install WordPerfect manually:

1. Turn on your computer.
2. If prompted to do so, type the correct date. Press ENTER. If prompted to do so, type the correct time. Press ENTER. (If you have never entered the date or time, see the first Tip in Chapter 1, which describes these procedures.) The following DOS prompt appears on the screen:

   C>

   Or you may see

   C:\>
3. At the DOS prompt type **CD **. (Either uppercase or lowercase letters can be used when typing DOS commands.) The screen looks like this:

   C>CD \
4. Press ENTER. This ensures that you are in the main (root) directory on the hard disk.
5. To create a new directory to house the WordPerfect files, type **MD \WPER**. The screen will look like this:

   C>MD \WPER

   (You can name your main WordPerfect directory as you wish—\WPER, \WP5, \WP50, or whatever. In fact, if you are upgrading from version 4.2 and you named your main WordPerfect 4.2 directory \WP or \WPER, then consider giving the version 5 directory another name, so that if disk space permits, you can keep the version 4.2 program files on disk in a separate directory until you become accustomed to the changes in version 5. Thus, you may wish to type **MD \WP5** or another name of your choosing.)
6. Press ENTER. A new directory, \WPER, is created.

7. To create a new subdirectory to house WordPerfect learning files, which include the tutorial program files as well as sample files that you can use along with the WordPerfect Workbook (an addition to the manual that comes with the WordPerfect package), type **MD \WPER\LEARN**. The screen looks like this:

   C>MD \WPER\LEARN

   (The sample files are stored in a subdirectory under \WPER so that all the WordPerfect files are grouped together. Again, if you named the directory in step 5 something other than \WPER, such as \WP5 or \WP50, then name its subdirectory accordingly, such as \WP5\LEARN or \WP50\LEARN. Or, if you do not plan to ever use the tutorial or WordPerfect Workbook, which are discussed in Appendix C, then you may find it unnecessary to create the \WPER\LEARN directory.)

8. Press ENTER. A new directory is created.

9. To create a new directory to house the data (document) files you create when working in WordPerfect, type **MD \WPER\DATA**. The screen looks like this:

   C>MD \WPER\DATA

   (Again, if you named the directory in step 5 something other than \WPER, such as \WP5 or \WP50, then name its subdirectory accordingly, such as \WP5\DATA or \WP50\DATA. And you can name the subdirectory something other than "DATA," such as \WPER\DOCS. In addition, it is recommended that as you begin creating numerous data files, you create more than one subdirectory under the \WPER directory to store different groups of your data files—such as the \WPER\DATA, \WPER\BUD, and \WPER\PERS subdirectories. Refer to Chapter 13 for the procedure to maintain an organized system of storing your data files.)

10. Press ENTER. A new directory is created.

Manual Installation—Copy WordPerfect Files Now, since you are installing WordPerfect manually, you are ready to copy some of the files from the WordPerfect disks to the \WPER directory and other files to the \WPER\LEARN directory. To copy these files:

1. Type **CD \WPER** to switch to the \WPER directory. The screen reads

   C>CD \WPER

2. Press ENTER.

3. Insert the WordPerfect 1 disk in drive A (usually the drive on the left or top—or the only floppy disk drive you have).

4. Type **COPY A:*.***. The screen reads

   C>COPY A:*.*

5. Press ENTER. All the program files on the floppy disk are copied to the hard disk.

6. Repeat steps 4 and 5 after inserting the WordPerfect 2 disk. Then repeat them again for the Fonts/Graphics disk, the Thesaurus disk, the Speller disk, the PTR Program disk, and the Conversion disk. The contents of seven disks have now been copied onto the hard disk.

   Note: You may find it unnecessary to keep a copy of all the files stored on the PTR and Conversion disk on your hard disk. Refer to the list of files in Table A-1 to see if there are any that you wish to delete from the hard disk.

7. If you have space to spare on your hard disk, you can copy the files stored on the Printer 1, Printer 2, Printer 3, and Printer 4 disks onto the hard disk as well. Repeat steps 4 and 5 after inserting each of these three disks, in turn. Once you select printers, you can then elect to erase the files on these disks (as described in the last main section of this appendix, "Selecting Your Printer.")

   If you have little space to spare on your hard disk, then do not copy the files stored on these four disks onto the hard disk.

8. If you created a directory named \WPER\LEARN to store the WordPerfect tutorial files, type **CD \WPER\LEARN** and press ENTER. You are switched to the \WPER\LEARN directory that you created so that you can copy the files from the Learning disk.

   If you chose not to create the \LEARN directory, then skip to step 13.

9. Insert the Learning disk in drive A. The Learning disk contains an assortment of files for use with the tutorial and WordPerfect Workbook (which are discussed in Appendix C).

10. Type **COPY A:*.***. The screen reads

    C>COPY A:*.*

11. Press ENTER. All the files on the Learning disk are copied to the hard disk.

12. One file that is copied from the Learning disk to the hard disk is named INSTALL.EXE, a file that runs the Auto-Install program. You can erase this file from the subdirectory, thereby saving disk space, by typing **ERASE INSTALL.EXE** and pressing ENTER.

    If you are a 3 1/2-inch disk user, you copied all the files on the Learning\Fonts\Graphics disk into both the \WPER and \WPER\ LEARN directories. You do not need the Learning files in the \WPER directory, and you do not need the Fonts/Graphics files (or the file named INSTALL.EXE) in the \WPER\ LEARN directory. You can erase these unnecessary files to save disk space. See Table A-1 for a complete list of files. Then you can also erase the unnecessary files by changing to the proper directory (for instance, by typing **CD \WPER**) and deleting those files (for instance, by typing **ERASE *.WKB** and pressing ENTER, by typing **ERASE *.TUT** and pressing ENTER, by typing **ERASE TUTOR.COM** and pressing ENTER, and so on).

13. Type **CD ** and press ENTER. You are returned to the main (root) directory.

14. Place all the original WordPerfect disks in a safe place for storage, to be used *only* as backups in the event that your hard disk malfunctions. However, if you did not copy the files stored on the Printer 1, 2, 3, and 4 disks to the hard disk, then keep these four disks available for when you select printers (a procedure described in the last main section of this appendix, "Selecting Your Printer").

If you wish, you can organize your hard disk in a manner different from that just described. For example, you can copy the Speller disk and the Thesaurus disk files into another directory. If you do, you must tell WordPerfect where these files are located by using the Setup menu (see Appendix B).

Automatic Installation Rather than installing WordPerfect manually, you can use the Auto-Install program, a file housed on the Learning disk and named INSTALL.EXE. By using Auto-Install, you enable WordPerfect to handle the following tasks for you: (1) creating a directory named \WP50 and another named \WP50\LEARN; (2) copying the files from certain disks into \WP50 (these disks include WordPerfect 1, WordPerfect 2, Speller, Thesaurus, Fonts/Graphics, and PTR Program); (3) copying the files from the Learning disk into \WP50\LEARN;

and (4) creating a CONFIG.SYS file so that WordPerfect runs properly (if you already have a file named CONFIG.SYS on your hard disk when you run the Auto-Install program, then that old CONFIG.SYS file is renamed CONFIG .OLD). To use Auto-Install:

1. Turn on your computer.
2. If prompted to do so, type the correct date. Press ENTER. If prompted to do so, type the correct time. Press ENTER. (If you have never entered the date or time, see the first Tip in Chapter 1, which describes these procedures.) The following DOS prompt appears on the screen:

   C>

   or you may see

   C:\>

3. Insert the WordPerfect Learning disk in drive A.
4. At the DOS prompt, type **A:**. The screen reads

   C>A:

5. Press ENTER. This changes the default drive to A. Now the DOS prompt on screen reads

   A>

   or you may see

   A:\>

6. Type **INSTALL** and press ENTER.
7. The Auto-Install program loads. You should now respond to the prompts as directed.
8. Once the WordPerfect program is installed, you will want to create a directory in which your WordPerfect data files will be stored, such as a directory named \WP50\DATA. To do so, see the earlier discussion under the heading "Manual Installation—Create Directories."
9. Once the WordPerfect program is installed, you may still wish to copy the files from the Conversion program (this is recommended) and the Printer 1, Printer 2, Printer 3, and Printer 4 disks into the \WP50 directory on your hard disk. To do so, see the earlier discussion under the heading "Manual Installation—Copy WordPerfect Files."

Create the CONFIG.SYS File

WordPerfect operates properly only if a special file, named CONFIG.SYS, exists in the main (root) directory on the hard disk and contains a FILES=20 (at least 20) command. This command tells DOS how many files can be open at one time.

You can ignore the instructions provided below if you used Auto-Install to install WordPerfect and you do not wish to alter the CONFIG.SYS file; skip to the next section, "Create a Batch File to Load WordPerfect." On the other hand, follow all the procedures below to create or modify the CONFIG.SYS file on your hard disk if:

- You installed WordPerfect manually and have no file named CONFIG.SYS on you hard disk (or just don't know whether or not that file exists), or
- You installed WordPerfect manually and have a file named CONFIG.SYS on your hard disk, but that file contains no FILES=20 (or more) command, or
- You installed WordPerfect using Auto-Install but wish to enhance the CONFIG.SYS with more than a simple FILES=20 command. For example, you may wish to include a BUFFERS=15 command that speeds up your computer system. (If you previously had a file named CONFIG.SYS on your hard disk, Auto-Install renamed it as CONFIG.OLD. You may still wish to modify the new CONFIG.SYS file, perhaps incorporating some of the commands from CONFIG.OLD.)

To create or modify the file named CONFIG.SYS in the root directory of the hard disk:

1. At the DOS prompt type **CD **. (Upper- or lowercase letters make no difference when typing DOS commands.) The screen looks like this:

   C>CD \

2. Press ENTER. This ensures that you are in the main (root) directory on the hard disk.

3. To see whether or not the CONFIG.SYS file currently exists on your hard disk, type **TYPE C: \CONFIG.SYS** and press ENTER.

   If a list of commands appears, and one of those commands reads

FILES=20 (or more), then your CONFIG.SYS needs no adjusting. You can skip to the next section of this chapter, "Create a Batch File to Load WordPerfect."

On the other hand, if the message "File Not Found" appears, or if a list of commands appears that does not include a FILES=20 (or more) command, then move on to step 4 below.

4. Type **COPY CONFIG.SYS+CON CONFIG.SYS**. Be very careful to type the command exactly as shown, making sure that spaces are in the proper places. Upper- or lowercase letters make no difference. The screen looks like this:

   C>COPY CONFIG.SYS+CON CONFIG.SYS

   or

   C:\>COPY CONFIG.SYS+CON CONFIG.SYS

5. Press ENTER. WordPerfect responds with the message "CON."
6. Press ENTER again.
7. Type **FILES=20** and press the ENTER key.

   (You can also write a statement in the CONFIG.SYS file that speeds up the system, especially during operations such as a spelling check. To do so, you type **BUFFERS=15** and press ENTER. Now, the Typing screen will read

   FILES=20
   BUFFERS=15

   Setting BUFFERS=15 is optional.)

8. Press CTRL+Z (which means that you hold down the CTRL key and, while holding it down, type **Z**).
9. Press ENTER. If no file named CONFIG.SYS existed, then one is created. If the file named CONFIG.SYS previously existed, then the FILES=20 command is added to the existing file.

Note: If you plan to load WordPerfect Library before you load WordPerfect, then you will want to make the WordPerfect Library disk bootable and create the CONFIG.SYS file on the WordPerfect Library disk. You should set FILES=40, rather than FILES=20, in the CONFIG.SYS file to run both Library and WordPerfect program files.

Create a Batch File to Load WordPerfect

You are now ready to create a file named WP5.BAT, which is a batch file (a file that contains DOS commands) that will load WordPerfect automatically for you when you type **WP5** at the DOS prompt. Creating a batch file is optional; as Chapter 1 describes, you can load WordPerfect with or without a batch file. A batch file is effective because it allows you to automate the process of loading WordPerfect.

A basic batch file might contain the following DOS commands (if you used Auto-Install, then substitute \WP50 wherever you read \WPER):

```
CD \WPER\DATA
WP
CD \
```

(or, optionally, use \WPER\WP instead of WP if you use DOS 3.0 or greater).

The batch file assumes that you have already created a directory called \WPER \DATA on the hard disk, and so it sets the default directory (the directory for saving and retrieving files when you start up WordPerfect) to \WPER\DATA. Then it starts WordPerfect. When you exit WordPerfect, the default is automatically changed back to the root directory.

You can also enhance a basic batch file. You may wish, for example, to start WordPerfect with a slash option (described in Chapter 1). If so, you can use the SET command to specify the option(s). Suppose you wish to start up WordPerfect every time by executing both the /R option (to speed up the WordPerfect program) and the /M option (to execute a macro named TOC when WordPerfect is first loaded). Then the batch file would be

```
CD \WPER\DATA
SET WP=/R/M-TOC
WP
CD \
```

(or, optionally, \WPER\WP instead of WP if you use DOS 3.0 or greater).

This batch file switches to the \WPER\DATA subdirectory, so that your document files are saved there, and starts WordPerfect with the two slash options. When you exit WordPerfect, the default is automatically changed to the hard disk's main (root) directory.

To create a batch file named WP5.BAT:

1. Since you just created a CONFIG.SYS file, you should still be in DOS and in the hard disk's root directory. (If not, then type **CD ** and press ENTER.)
2. Type **COPY CON WP5.BAT**. Be careful to type the command exactly as shown, making sure that spaces are in the proper places. Upper- or lowercase letters make no difference. The screen looks like this:

   C>COPY CON WP5.BAT

   or

   C:\>COPY CON WP5.BAT
3. Press ENTER.
4. Type the contents of the batch file (examples are provided above) with each command on a separate line—meaning that you end each line by pressing ENTER. For instance, to create a basic AUTOEXEC.BAT file, you would type **CD \WPER\DATA** and press ENTER, type **WP** and press ENTER, and type **CD ** and press ENTER.
5. Press CTRL + Z (which means that you hold down the CTRL key and, while holding it down, type **Z**).
6. Press ENTER. The batch file named WP5.BAT is saved on the hard disk.

Modify the AUTOEXEC.BAT File

Unless you specify a path, you cannot start WordPerfect from a directory other than the one where the WordPerfect program files (WP.EXE and WP.FIL) are housed—which, if you installed WordPerfect at set up above, is C:\WPER. Thus, if you wrote a batch file that changes the default directory and then loads WordPerfect, you should indicate to DOS where to find the WordPerfect program (WP.EXE and other program files). In addition, if you plan to use the tutorial (see Appendix C), you should also indicate where to find the tutorial program (TUTOR.COM) and learning files.

A PATH command provides DOS with a list of directories to search through for all executable program files—that is, files that end with the extension .EXE or .COM. It is convenient to include a PATH command in your AUTOEXEC.BAT file, which is a batch file that executes automatically as soon as DOS is loaded into your computer; otherwise, you must enter a PATH command each time you start your machine.

A basic AUTOEXEC.BAT file might contain the following DOS commands:

```
DATE
TIME
PATH C:\;C:\WPER;C:\WPER\LEARN
PROMPT $P$G
```

The first two lines prompt for the date and time when you first turn on the computer. The next line indicates the path to executable WordPerfect files. The fourth line tells DOS to display the current directory from the DOS command line. For example, if you enter **PROMPT PG** in your AUTOEXEC.BAT file and then type **CD \WPER** and press ENTER when in DOS, you will see C:\WPER> instead of C>.

If your computer is equipped with an internal clock, then there is no need for the date and time prompts when you turn on the computer. Then, the basic AUTOEXEC.BAT file would contain the following DOS commands:

```
PATH C:\;C:\WPER;C:\WPER\LEARN
PROMPT $P$G
```

It is likely that you already have a file named AUTOEXEC.BAT stored in the root directory of your hard disk. Thus, it is convenient to modify it from within WordPerfect (although you can also modify this file when in DOS, as described in your DOS manual). And if you don't have a file named AUTOEXEC.BAT on the root directory of your hard disk, you can create it from within WordPerfect. To do so:

1. Type **CD \WPER** (or type **CD \WP50** if you used Auto-Install) and press ENTER to switch to the directory where the WordPerfect program files are housed.
2. Type **WP**. The screen looks like this:

   C>WP

   or

   C:\WPER>WP
3. Press ENTER to load WordPerfect. Once WordPerfect is loaded, a clear Typing screen appears.
4. You will want to see if a file named AUTOEXEC.BAT already exists. To do so, press the TEXT IN/OUT (CTRL + F5) key. The following menu appears:

   1 DOS Text; 2 Password; 3 Save Generic; 4 Save WP 4.2; 5 Com-

5. Select Dos Text (1 or T). The DOS Text menu appears

   1 Save; 2 Retrieve (CR/LF to [HRt]); 3 Retrieve (CR/LF to [SRt] in HZone): **0**

6. Select Retrieve (2 or R). WordPerfect prompts

   Document to be retrieved:

7. Type **C:\AUTOEXEC.BAT** and press ENTER.

8. If an ERROR message appears, then a file named AUTOEXEC.BAT does not exist in the root directory on the hard disk, and you must create one. Press CANCEL (F1) to clear the prompt at the bottom of the screen. Then, on the blank WordPerfect Typing screen, type the contents of the AUTO-EXEC.BAT file, with each command on a separate line, meaning that you press ENTER after typing each command. For instance, to create the most basic AUTOEXEC.BAT file: type **PATH C:\;C:\WPER;C:\WPER\LEARN** and press ENTER, and then type **PROMPT PG** and press ENTER. Now, proceed with step 9 below.

   If text appears, then you are viewing the contents of the file named AUTOEXEC.BAT, which is stored in the root directory. Now, add or modify the PATH command so that, at minimum, it reads **PATH C:\;C\WPER;C:\WPER\LEARN**. Be sure to include in the path command any other directories that contain executable program files. Each directory is separated by a semicolon (;). Perhaps, for instance, when you retrieved the AUTOEXEC.BAT file, it read **PATH C:\;C:\DBASE;C:\LOTUS**. In that case, use the cursor movement keys to position the cursor on the C in C:\DBASE and type **C:\WPER;C:\WPER\LEARN;**. This modifies the command so that it reads **PATH C:\;C:\WPER;C: \WPER\LEARN;C:\DBASE;C:\LOTUS**.

9. Press the TEXT IN/OUT (CTRL + F5) key. The following menu appears

   1 DOS Text; 2 Password; 3 Save Generic; 4 Save WP 4.2; 5 Comment: **0**

10. Select Dos Text (1 or T). The DOS Text menu appears

    1 Save; 2 Retrieve (CR/LF to [HRt]); 3 Retrieve (CR/LF to [SRt] in HZone): **0**

11. Select Save (1 or S). WordPerfect prompts

    Document to be saved (Dos Text):

12. Type **C:\AUTOEXEC.BAT** (if the file already exists, then WordPerfect inserts the filename for you) and press ENTER. (Then type **Y**; if WordPerfect prompts asking whether you wish to replace this file, type **Y**.)

13. Now, clear the Typing screen and exit WordPerfect by pressing the EXIT (F7) key. WordPerfect prompts

    Save document? (Y/N) Yes

14. Type **N**. Now, WordPerfect prompts

    Exit WP? (Y/N) No

15. Type **Y**. You will be returned to DOS.

You are now ready to explore the world of WordPerfect. Press CTRL + ALT + DEL to restart your computer (or you can turn off your computer and then turn it on again). Be sure to turn to Chapter 1 for the Tips for loading WordPerfect. Once you learn more about various startup options in Chapter 1, you may in the future wish to modify your file named WP5.BAT. (You can do this the same way that you modify the AUTOEXEC.BAT file, as described above—from within WordPerfect. This procedure is also described in Chapter 28, in the section "Converting Files Using ASCII (DOS) Text Files.")

When WordPerfect is loaded, turn to the next section in this appendix, "Selecting Your Printer," to guide you in setting up WordPerfect to work with printer(s) attached to your computer.

Selecting Your Printer

WordPerfect can work with more than 100 brands of printers (and more are added all the time). You need to perform the following tasks in order to work with your printer(s): (1) create printer files, indicating to WordPerfect which printer or printers you plan to use; (2) edit WordPerfect's standard settings for each printer, adapting the printer file to your setup and equipment; and (3) mark a printer to select it as the active printer for the document(s) you are about to print. Once you create printer files and edit the settings, you can select a specific (and different) printer for each document you write.

Create Printer Files

Printer drivers, which tell WordPerfect how to operate with various printers, are housed on four disks—Printer 1, Printer 2, Printer 3, and Printer 4. The drivers are stored in files that have the extension .ALL as part of their filename. You must create a printer file for each printer you plan to use in your computer system with

WordPerfect. When you do, WordPerfect creates a file with a .PRS extension, which you then use whenever you wish to print a document using that printer.

To create new printer files for the printers you will use with WordPerfect:

1. For each printer attached to your computer, take note of both the printer's brand and model number. For example, don't note just Epson—look at the printer or the printer manual to see whether the model of Epson is FX-100, MX-100, or something else.

   Also, check your printer manual to find out whether your printer works with a parallel or a serial port. If your printer is serial, then you must gather information from your printer manual on (1) baud rate, (2) parity (none, odd, or even), (3) stop bits (1 or 2), and (4) data bits (7 or 8).

   Finally, decide how your paper (forms) will be fed to the printer: continuous, hand-fed, or via a sheet feeder. If you plan to use a sheet feeder, then you must know the sheet feeder's brand name and the number of paper bins it has. You may decide that sometimes you will hand-feed paper (such as your company stationary) into the printer, and other times you will use continuous forms.

2. Load WordPerfect so that the Typing screen displays.

3. If you use a floppy disk system, insert the Printer 1 disk into drive B.

   Or, if you use a hard disk system and have not copied the files from the Printer 1, 2, 3, and 4 disks onto the hard disk, then insert the Printer 1 disk in drive A or B.

   Or, if you use a hard disk system and have copied the files from the Printer 1, 2, 3, and 4 disks, then the files should already be stored in the same directory as the WordPerfect program files (in C: \WPER, if you followed the manual procedure described earlier).

4. Press PRINT (SHIFT + F7) to display the Print menu.

5. Choose S, Select Printer. The Select Printer Print screen appears, with the following menu displayed at the bottom of the screen:

   1 Select; **2** Additional Printers; **3** Edit; **4** Copy; **5** Delete; **6** Help: **1**

6. Select Additional Printers (2 or A) to view a list of printers supported by WordPerfect. The Additional Printers screen appears, like the screen shown in Figure A-1, with a new menu at the bottom of the screen:

   1 Select; **2** Other Disk; **3** Help; **4** List Printer Files; **N** Name Search: **1**

   Or, if WordPerfect can't find the files with the extension of .ALL, WordPerfect indicates that the printer files are not found. In that case, select Other Disk (2 or O), and WordPerfect prompts

```
Select Printer: Additional Printers

 Dataproducts LZR-1230
 Destiny Laseract I
 HP LaserJet
 HP LaserJet 2000
 HP LaserJet Series II
 HP LaserJet+, 500+
 Kyocera F-1000A/1010/2010/3010
 LaserImage 1000
 Mannesmann Tally MT910
 NEC Silentwriter LC-860+
 Okidata LaserLine 6
 Olympia Laserstar 6
 Panasonic KX-P4450 Laser Partner

1 Select; 2 Other Disk; 3 Help; 4 List Printer Files; N Name Search: 1
```

Figure A-1. The Additional Printers screen

Directory for printer files:

Type the name of the drive (such as **A:** or **B:**) or directory (such as \WPER \PTRS) where the printer files are located, and press ENTER.

7. Use the cursor movement keys (such as DOWN ARROW, UP ARROW, PAGE DOWN, or PAGE UP) to move the cursor (which highlights a printer name in reverse video) to the printer for which you want to create a .PRS file. Next, press ENTER to select that printer; a filename with the extension .PRS displays at the bottom of the screen.

   Alternatively, you can select N from the menu on the Additional Printers screen to initiate the Name Search option, and then begin typing the name of the printer; the cursor moves to that printer. Then press ENTER to leave the Name Search option, and press ENTER again to select that printer; a filename with the extension .PRS displays at the bottom of the screen.

   Or, if WordPerfect is reading the printer drivers from disk drive A or B and if your printer is not on the list of additional printers, insert another Printer disk (such as the Printer 2 disk), select Other Disk (2 or O), type in the name of the drive or directory where you inserted the other Printer disk, and press ENTER to view another list of printers. If the name of the printer is still not shown, repeat the process with another Printer disk (either the Printer 3 or the Printer 4 disk). Then position the cursor on the name of the printer for which you wish to create a .PRS file and press ENTER; a filename with the extension .PRS displays at the bottom of the screen.

Note: If your printer is not listed on *any* of the Printer disks, then you can try a printer definition for another printer—such as an Epson printer if you use a dot matrix printer, or a Diablo or NEC if you use a daisy wheel printer. Or you can create a printer definition for a standard printer, a procedure that is discussed at the end of this section. Or you can request that WordPerfect send you a driver for your printer. Send your name, address, and the name of your printer to:

Printer Diskette
81 North State Street
Orem, UT 84057

You can also change your printer specifications, thereby changing how WordPerfect Corporation set up your printer to operate with WordPerfect, by using the Printer program, described in Chapter 15.

8. Press ENTER to accept the displayed name of the printer definition file you are about to create, or enter a name of your own (with an extension of .PRS), and press ENTER. WordPerfect displays a Printer Helps and Hints screen.

9. Read over the Printer Helps and Hints screen and then press EXIT (F7). WordPerfect updates the fonts for that printer, and then displays the Select Printer Edit screen. An example of this screen is shown in Figure A-2.

10. Select the number corresponding to a printer setting option you wish to edit so that you can define the printer to meet your needs, adapting it to any special setup or equipment you may have, and enter the requested information. The printer setting options are discussed in the following section.

    Alternatively, you can edit the printer settings later (also discussed in the following section), and, for right now, you can continue with step 11 below.

11. Press EXIT (F7) to store the setting for the printer you just defined on disk

```
Select Printer: Edit

     Filename                         HPLASEII.PRS

  1 - Name                            HP LaserJet Series II

  2 - Port                            LPT1:

  3 - Sheet Feeder                    None

  4 - Forms

  5 - Cartridges and Fonts

  6 - Initial Font                    Courier 10 pitch (PC-8)

  7 - Path for Downloadable
        Fonts and Printer
        Command Files



Selection: 0
```

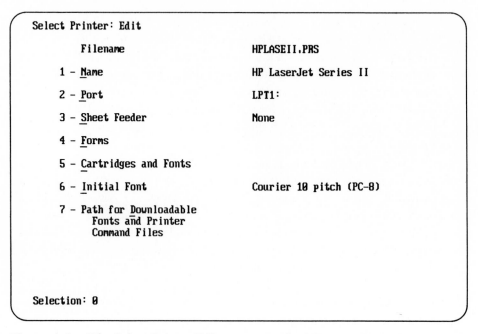

Figure A-2. The Select Printer Edit screen for the HP LaserJet Series II printer

in a file with the extension .PRS.

12. Repeat steps 6 through 11 for additional printers for which you wish to create printer files.

At any time you can view a list of the .PRS files that you created by returning to the Additional Printers screen (as in step 6 above), and by choosing List Printer Files (4 or L). One file shown on this list, STANDARD.PRS, is a file you did not create, but that resides on the WordPerfect 2 disk (and, if you are a hard disk user, you copied it onto the hard disk). This file contains a printer driver for a standard (or "vanilla") printer, allowing you to print out text on any printer (but not in proper format for your printer). You can select the standard printer by choosing Select (1 or S); the standard printer will be added to those listed on the Select Printer Print screen.

Edit Printer Settings

Once you have created a printer file for a certain printer, you should then review its standard settings and tailor them for your equipment. If you're not viewing the

Select Printer Edit screen for a particular printer (an example is shown in Figure A-2), then: (1) press PRINT (F7); (2) choose S, Select Printer; (3) position the cursor on the name of the printer file that you wish to edit; and (4) select Edit (3 or E). The options on the Select Printer Edit screen are as follows.

Name The name that is listed on the Select Printer Print screen. When you choose Name (1 or N), you can change this name by typing up to 36 characters and then pressing ENTER.

Port The type and number of the port (plug) on the back of the computer to which the printer is attached. When you select Port (2 or P), a Port menu appears, as follows:

> **Port: 1** LPT 1; **2** LPT 2; **3** LPT 3; **4** COM 1; **5** COM 2; **6** COM 3; **7** COM 4; **8** Other: **0**

LPT 1 through LPT 3 indicates a parallel printer, where the number indicates the parallel plug to which your printer is attached. If your printer is a parallel printer, generally it is plugged into LPT 1. COM 1 through COM 4 indicate a serial printer, where the number indicates the serial plug to which your printer is attached. When you specify a port for a serial printer, WordPerfect prompts for the printer's baud rate, parity, stop bits, character length, and whether the XON/XOFF protocol is on or off. See your printer manual for the appropriate settings. The Other (8 or O) option is useful if you wish to print a file to disk rather than to a printer, creating a DOS text file as described in Chapter 28; you must specify a device or a filename to which the file will be "printed."

Sheet Feeder The sheet feeder that automatically feeds paper into the printer. When you select Sheet Feeder (3 or S), a Sheet Feeder screen appears, listing possible sheet feeder brands for that printer. (If this screen does not appear, then it is because WordPerfect does not have access to the Printer disk containing the original driver for your printer, which is contained in the file with an extension of .ALL. WordPerfect prompts: **Directory for printer files:**. Insert the correct Printer disk in drive A or B, and then type **A:** or **B:** and press ENTER; or, if the printer file is on the hard disk, then type the correct directory name and press ENTER.) You must then move the cursor to the correct sheet feeder brand and press ENTER to select that brand. A Printer Helps and Hints screen appears for that brand of sheet feeder. Read the information provided, and then press the EXIT (F7) key to return to the Select Printer Edit screen. (You should then use the Forms option, described below, to indicate the location of the available forms in the sheet feeder.)

Forms Defines the characteristics of the forms you plan to use with the printer. WordPerfect uses this information when it encounters a paper size/type code in your document (as described in Chapter 8) and assumes the Standard form type if no such code is inserted in your document.

When you select Forms (4 or F), the Select Printer Forms screen appears, an example of which is shown in Figure A-3. Several forms have been defined for you (usually only the "Standard" and "[ALL OTHERS]" form types). You can delete a form by positioning the cursor and selecting Delete (2 or D). Or you can edit a form by positioning the cursor and selecting Edit (3 or E). Or you can add a form to that list by choosing Add (1 or A).

If you choose to add a form, then you must specify a "Form Type," that is, the type of form you are defining. It is this form type that carries with it a number of the characteristics of the form on which you will be printing. WordPerfect displays a menu that contains seven basic form types (such as "Standard" or "Envelope"), an "[ALL OTHERS]" option, which indicates the location of paper

```
Select Printer: Forms

                                        Orient Init              Offset
Form type               Size            P L    Pres Location   Top    Side

Standard                8.5" x 11"      Y Y    Y    Contin     0"     0"
[ALL OTHERS]            Width ≤ 8.5"           N    Manual     0"     0"











If the requested form is not available, then printing stops and WordPerfect
waits for a form to be inserted in the ALL OTHERS location.  If the requested
form is larger than the ALL OTHERS form, the width is set to the maximum width.

1 Add; 2 Delete; 3 Edit: 3
```

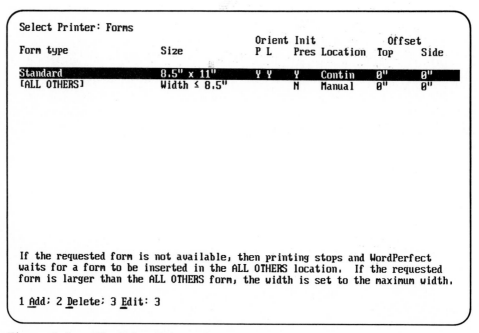

Figure A-3. *The Select Printer Forms screen*

types you plan to use that do not match any of the preset paper types, and an "Other" option, which enables you to indicate a form-type name of your choosing.

Then, whether you chose to add a form and indicated a form type or you chose to edit an existing form type, the Select Printer Forms menu appears—an example of which is shown in Figure A-4—for that specific form type. You now can specify the following characteristics for that form type:

- **Size** The dimensions of the paper you are defining. If you select this option, several commonly used dimensions are offered. Or select "Other," and enter a specific height and width of your choosing.
- **Orientation** The direction in which the characters will print, of importance for printers in which you are unable to insert the paper sideways. Portrait orientation prints lines parallel to how the form is inserted in the printer.

```
Select Printer: Forms

        Filename                    HPLASEII.PRS

        Form Type                   Standard

    1 - Form Size                   8.5" x 11"

    2 - Orientation                 Portrait, Landscape

    3 - Initially Present           Yes

    4 - Location                    Continuous

    5 - Page Offsets - Top          0"
                       Side         0"




Selection: 0
```

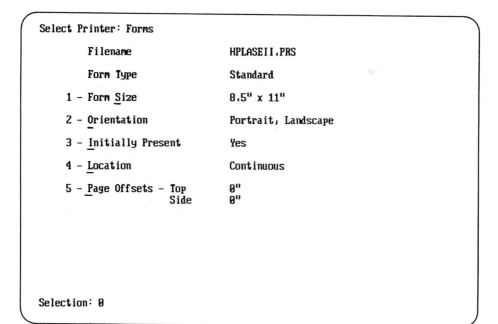

Figure A-4. The Select Printer Forms menu for a specific form type (Standard)

Landscape orientation prints lines perpendicular to how the form is inserted in the printer (sideways).

- **Initially Present** Whether the form is in the printer when you begin to print or you want WordPerfect to stop the print job and prompt you to insert the form.
- **Location** Where and how the form will be fed into the printer—either continuous feed, manual feed, or fed from a specific bin in a sheet feeder. For instance, select continuous if you use continuous-feed paper on a dot matrix or a daisy wheel printer, or if paper is fed through a tray on a laser printer. Select manual if you plan to feed each sheet of paper manually. Select sheet feeder if you defined a sheet feeder for use with your printer.
- **Page Offsets** Indicates if your forms are fed into the printer at different horizontal and vertical positions than WordPerfect otherwise assumes. For example, if envelopes are always fed in 2.5 inches from the normal starting position of the printhead, then you should specify that offset. You can specify a top-edge offset and/or a side offset, either in a positive number (such as 1″) for forms inserted with their top edge above the printhead or their left edge to the right of the printhead or a negative number (such as −1″) for forms inserted with their top edge below the printhead or their left edge to the left of the printhead.

Next, press ENTER or EXIT (F7) to return to the Select Printer Forms screen, which lists all forms defined for your printer, including the form you just defined or edited. You can define a number of forms for the same printer. For example, if you use a sheet feeder, you will want to define a form type and its characteristics for each sheet feeder bin. Or, if you plan to feed both envelopes and labels into your printer, create an Envelope form type and set the appropriate characteristics, and then a Label form type and its appropriate characteristics. (For example, on laser printers, the most common settings for envelopes include: the envelope size as 4″ by 9.5″, the orientation as "Landscape," initially present as "No," the location as "Manual," and the offsets as 0″.)

When you have defined all the forms you will use for your printer, press EXIT (F7) to return to the Select Printer Edit screen.

Cartridges and Fonts If your printer allows you to change fonts with different print cartridges, print wheels, or downloadable font files, list all possible cartridges or fonts you plan to use with your printer. WordPerfect uses this information when it encounters a font change code in your document (see Chapter 7).

use with your printer. WordPerfect uses this information when it encounters a font change code in your document (see Chapter 7).

When you select Cartridges and Fonts (5 or C), the Select Printer Cartridges and Fonts screen appears; an example is shown in Figure A-5. (If this screen does not appear, then it is because your printer does not support other cartridges or fonts, but WordPerfect does not have access to the Printer disk containing the original driver for your printer, which is contained in the file with an extension of .ALL, in which case, WordPerfect prompts **Directory for printer files:**. Insert the correct Printer disk in drive A or B, and then type **A:** or **B:** and press ENTER; or, if the printer file is on the hard disk, then type the correct directory name and press ENTER.) This screen indicates, under the heading "Font Category," whether your printer uses cartridge fonts, print wheels, and/or downloadable font files, each as a separate option. The information under the heading "Resource" indicates where the fonts are loaded from (such as from the printhead or from a cartridge slot), and the information under the heading "Quantity" indicates the number of slots available for cartridges, the print wheels that can be used, or the amount of memory available for downloadable font files.

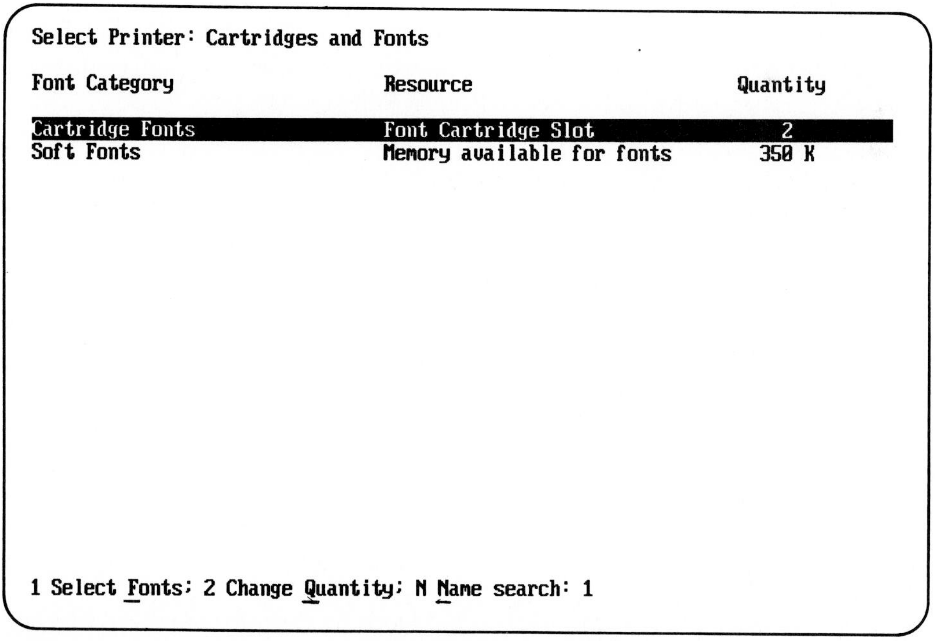

Figure A-5. The Select Printer Cartridges and Fonts screen

You can select Change Quantity (2 or Q) to indicate that you have added more slots or memory to your printer than are preset for your printer, and then enter the appropriate number.

Now you can move the cursor to the option of your choice (or select Name search, N, and begin typing to do so) and choose Select (1 or S), or simply press ENTER. A list of the available cartridges or fonts for that option appears. Move the cursor to a cartridge or font you want to use with your printer, and then, depending on the instructions at the bottom of the screen, choose one of these three courses of action. (1) Type an asterisk (*) to mark it as Present When Print Job Begins, which means that the cartridge or font is in a slot or in the printer memory when you start a print job. Fonts marked with this option are downloaded when you select the Initialize Printer option on the Print menu (see Chapter 14). Also, with printers for which fonts cannot be swapped, memory is automatically decreased when you mark a font with *. (2) Type a plus sign (+) to mark it as Can be Loaded (Unloaded) During Print Job, which means that WordPerfect will load (or unload) the font or ask you to insert (or remove) the cartridge during a print job. For printers in which fonts cannot be swapped, fonts can be loaded only during a print job or unloaded afterward. If fonts can be swapped, fonts can be loaded or unloaded during a print job. (3) Type both * and +, in which case WordPerfect downloads the font and, if necessary, unloads it to load another font. That font is then reloaded at the end of the print job. Continue to mark all fonts that you wish to use (or until memory is almost used up), and then press EXIT (F7) to return to the Select Printer Cartridges and Fonts screen. Press EXIT (F7) again to return to the Select Printer Edit screen.

Initial Font This setting specifies the default font for the printer you are defining. WordPerfect uses this font when it prints out a document, unless a font change code is inserted in the document to override the initial font (see Chapter 7).

When you select Initial Font (6 or I), the Select Printer Initial Font screen appears, which lists the possible fonts available for your printer (including built-in fonts and those you marked with the Cartridges and Fonts option, described above). Move the cursor to the font of your choice (or select Name search, N, and begin typing to do so) and choose Select (1 or S), or simply press ENTER. An asterisk appears next to that font, indicating that it has been chosen as the initial font, and you are automatically returned to the Select Printer Edit screen.

Path for Downloadable Fonts and Printer Command Files This setting indicates the drive/directory where WordPerfect should look for downloadable font files and printer command files. When you select Path for Downloadable Fonts and Printer

Command Files (7 or D), you should then enter a drive/directory. For instance, if all downloadable fonts are stored on the hard disk in a directory named \WPER\FONTS, then enter **C:\WPER\FONTS**.

Once you have changed the standard settings for one printer, press EXIT (F7) to return to the Select Printer Print screen. Now you can position the cursor on the name of the next printer file you wish to edit and select Edit (3 or E), and make any changes that are necessary to adapt that printer definition to your setup and equipment.

Three other related options on the Select Printer Print menu are (1) Copy (4 or C), which enables you to copy an existing printer definition to a file with a different filename (but also with the extension .PRS), so that the new file can be edited; (2) Delete (5 or D), which allows you to erase a printer definition from disk; or (3) Help (6 or H), which displays the Printer Hints and Helps screen for that printer (a screen that first displays when you create a .PRS file for your printer). See the following section for details of the first menu item, Select (1 or S).

Select a Printer

After you've defined the printer(s) you will be using with WordPerfect, you can select any defined printer for a particular print job. To do so, you would: (1) press the PRINT (SHIFT + F7) key; (2) choose S, Select Printer; (3) move the cursor to the name of the printer you want to use; (4) choose Select by selecting 1 or S or by pressing ENTER, in which case an asterisk is placed next to the selected printer and you are returned to the Print screen; and (5) either choose an option on the Print menu to print out your document, or press EXIT (F7) to exit the Print screen. The printer you selected remains as the currently selected printer until you select another printer.

Whenever you save a document, the currently selected printer's name is saved with that document. Then, when the document is printed, WordPerfect changes to the saved printer selection to print the document—even if the currently selected printer is now different. (See Chapter 14 for more information on printing documents.)

If you have not already done so, make sure you select a printer *before* you begin creating your very first document in WordPerfect. Press the PRINT (SHIFT + F7) key and choose S, Select Printer. If an asterisk does not appear in front of one of the printers listed, then no printer has been selected. You must position the cursor on a printer and choose 1 or S or press ENTER to select a printer. Then you are ready to turn to the beginning of this book and learn how to become an expert at using WordPerfect.

B

Using the Setup Menu

Whenever you start WordPerfect, the program works with a specific set of assumptions, or defaults. These defaults were preset by the designers of the WordPerfect program. However, you have the option to change WordPerfect's startup assumptions— thereby customizing the program for your equipment or for your special formatting needs—via the WordPerfect Setup menu.

You can access the Setup menu at any time while you are working on the Typing screen or the Reveal Codes screen. Simply press the SETUP (SHIFT + F1) key. The menu shown in Figure B-1 appears, with a list of eight options, which are all explained in this appendix. Once you alter the Setup menu and press EXIT (F7) to return to the Typing screen, your changes are saved on disk in a special file named WP{WP}.SET. These changes take effect for the current working session and each time thereafter that you start up WordPerfect.

If you are upgrading from version 4.2, you'll find that the version 5 Setup menu can be accessed *without* exiting the WordPerfect program, and that it offers many more options for changing defaults than previously allowed. In addition, several features that were previously found on function keys (such as the feature

```
Setup

     1 - Backup

     2 - Cursor Speed                      30 cps

     3 - Display

     4 - Fast Save (unformatted)           No

     5 - Initial Settings

     6 - Keyboard Layout

     7 - Location of Auxiliary Files

     8 - Units of Measure



Selection: 0
```

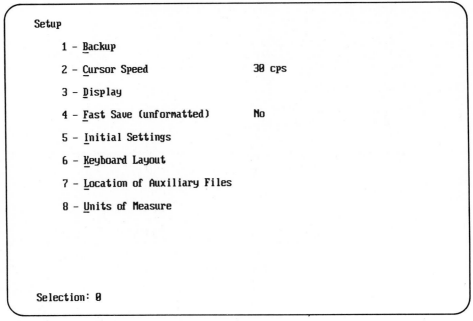

Figure B-1. The Setup menu

for setting screen colors) are now on the Setup menu. One feature that has been removed from the Setup menu is the option to set the size of your screen (if greater than 25 lines), which is now accessed by using a startup option (refer to Chapter 1 for details). You'll also discover that you can now change default settings without affecting previously created documents; in version 4.2, a change on the Setup menu affected all documents— both old and new.

Backup

Select Backup (1 or B) on the Setup menu and WordPerfect displays the screen shown in Figure B-2. On this screen, WordPerfect offers two features to help protect your documents from disaster: Timed Backup and Original Backup. Both are initially inactive. You can choose to activate one or both of them.

```
Setup: Backup

     Timed backup files are deleted when you exit WP normally.  If you
     have a power or machine failure, you will find the backup file in the
     backup directory indicated in Setup: Location of Auxiliary Files.

         Backup Directory

     1 - Timed Document Backup                    No
         Minutes Between Backups                  30


     Original backup will save the original document with a .BK! extension
     whenever you replace it during a Save or Exit.

     2 - Original Document Backup                 No







Selection: 0
```

Figure B-2. The Setup Backup menu

Timed Backup instructs WordPerfect to save whichever document is currently on screen (and thus in random access memory, or RAM) to a temporary backup file on disk at specified time intervals. Consider activating this feature if you are not in the habit of periodically saving your documents to disk by using the SAVE (F10) key. This feature prevents you from losing your text due to a power or machine failure—when all information in RAM disappears.

Turn on the Timed Document Backup option by selecting Timed Document Backup (1 or T) and then typing **Y**. WordPerfect inserts the word "Yes" next to the heading "Timed Document Backup," and then moves down to the heading "Minutes Between Backups," which suggests 30 minutes. Type in a number and press ENTER (or simply press ENTER if you wish to leave the backup at 30-minute intervals). Then press ENTER to return to the Backup screen, or press EXIT (F7) to return to the Typing (or Reveal Codes) screen.

Once the Timed Backup feature is active, text on the Doc 1 Typing screen is stored at the time interval specified in a temporary file named WP{WP}.BK1. Or, if you're currently working on a document in the Doc 2 Typing screen, that text is stored in a temporary file named WP{WP}.BK2. After the first backup, a document is saved again at the time interval specified only if the document is modified. For example, suppose that you have chosen the time interval of every 30 minutes and are now typing a memo on the Doc 1 screen. After 30 minutes, WordPerfect backs up the document in the Doc 1 screen, creating a file named WP{WP}.BK1. The following message appears momentarily at the bottom of the WordPerfect screen:

*** Please Wait ***

When the message clears, the document has been backed up. Every 30 minutes thereafter, WordPerfect updates WP{WP}.BK1, provided that you have edited what is on screen during that time. WordPerfect deletes all temporary files when you exit it normally by using the EXIT (F7) key.

If you are a WordPerfect user who experiences frequent power failures in your office, or if you are a fast typist who can type many pages in a short period of time, consider indicating a shorter time interval than every 30 minutes—perhaps every 10 or 15 minutes (or even more frequently). While the operations of WordPerfect will be slowed down each time a document is backed up, a power or machine failure will cost you, at most, only 10 or 15 minutes of work.

But keep in mind that the Timed Backup feature is not a substitute for saving a document in a file on disk with a name of your choosing by using the SAVE (F10) or the EXIT (F7) key. (See Chapter 11 for more on saving documents to disk.) Because WordPerfect deletes the temporary files when you exit WordPerfect normally, Timed Backup is of value *only* in the case of a power or machine failure.

You can specify a directory in which timed backup files will be stored by using the Location of Auxiliary Files option on the Setup menu, described in a later section of this appendix, "Location of Auxiliary Files." If you do specify a directory, it will be indicated on the Backup screen next to the heading "Backup Directory." If you do not specify a directory, then the timed backup file is saved in the same directory as the one in which the WordPerfect program file (WP.EXE) is stored.

If you experience a power or machine failure when the Timed Backup feature is active, then the backup files remain on disk. When you then reload WordPerfect, the program will ask whether you wish to rename these files so that you can retrieve and work with them again. See the last section of Chapter 1 for more details, should you experience a power or a machine failure.

The second backup feature is Original Backup. Original Backup instructs WordPerfect to save the original file each time you replace it with the document on screen. The original copy is saved with the extension .BK! (and remains on disk even when you exit normally from WordPerfect). You activate the Original Backup option from the Backup screen (shown in Figure B-2) by selecting Original Document Backup (2 or O), and then typing **Y**. WordPerfect inserts the word "Yes" next to the heading "Original Document Backup." Then press ENTER to return to the Backup screen, or press EXIT (F7) to return to the Typing (or Reveal Codes) screen.

As an example of how Original Backup operates once activated, suppose that you type and save a document on the disk in drive B with the filename MEMO. Next, you edit the document and save it again with the same filename. When you save, WordPerfect prompts

Replace B:\MEMO? (Y/N) No

If you type **Y**, then the old version of MEMO will be saved under the name MEMO.BK!, and MEMO will be replaced with the new version on screen. The next time you edit and save the document, MEMO.BK! will be replaced with the contents of the file named MEMO, and then MEMO will again be replaced with the new version on screen.

Those of you who have used WordStar, which automatically backs up an original, are familiar with the advantage of the Original Backup option—it safeguards against inadvertently replacing a file.

Keep in mind that files that have the same name but a different extension share the same original backup file. For example, if you have files named MEMO.1 and MEMO.2, only one backup file will be created. Thus, if you use the Original Backup feature, consider naming all your documents with unique filenames (such as MEMO1. and MEMO2.) so that each can be assigned its own original backup file.

If you mistakenly replace a file when the Original Backup feature is active, you still have a copy of that replaced file on disk. You can retrieve the original backup file in the same way you retrieve other files. You can then resave that file with an extension other than .BK! Or you can first rename the file with an extension other than .BK! (see Chapter 13 for the method to rename files in WordPerfect). Then retrieve it as you would retrieve any other file.

Cursor Speed

Most keys on the computer keyboard repeat when they are held down. (Keys on the keyboard that commonly do not repeat when held down include CTRL, ALT, SHIFT, CAPS LOCK, and NUM LOCK.) By default, WordPerfect is set up to repeat 30 times for every one second that you hold a key down (30 characters per second), as shown in Figure B-1. Select Cursor Speed (2 or C) on the Setup menu, and WordPerfect allows you to increase or decrease the rate at which keys repeat. WordPerfect prompts, with the following menu:

Characters Per Second: **1** 15; **2** 20; **3** 30; **4** 40; **5** 50; **6** Normal: **0**

Choose a menu option to change the cursor speed, or choose Normal (6 or N) to return to your keyboard's normal cursor speed, which is usually ten characters per second. Moreover, if the Cursor Speed feature does not work properly on your computer, or if it conflicts with a TSR (Terminate and Stay Resident) program that you use, then select the Normal option to avoid any incompatibilities. Once you select an option, the Characters Per Second menu clears. You can then press ENTER or EXIT (F7) to return to the Typing screen.

You may wish to experiment with the Cursor Speed feature to see which setting you prefer. One way to do this is by using the cursor movement keys. For instance, at the default of 30 characters per second, position the cursor at the beginning of a sentence and press and hold the RIGHT ARROW key down until the cursor moves to the end of the sentence. Then change the cursor speed, and again move the cursor through the same sentence by using the RIGHT ARROW key. You'll quickly find the speed that is most comfortable for you. And you may find that faster isn't always better—because a faster cursor speed often results in overshooting the location where you want to position the cursor.

You should know that WordPerfect Corporation offers another product, named Repeat Performance, which allows for faster cursor operations for all of your software, and includes other features such as Adjustable Delay and Expanded Type Ahead Buffer. Check with WordPerfect Corporation for details.

Display

Select Display (3 or D) on the Setup menu and WordPerfect displays the screen shown in Figure B-3. On this screen you can alter how text and menus are exhibited on screen as you work in WordPerfect. The options available are as follows.

Automatically Format and Rewrite

The default setting is "Yes," meaning that WordPerfect will format the text on screen as you edit to abide by current margins, tabs, and so on. You can request that WordPerfect stop the automatic reformatting of text by selecting Automatically Format and Rewrite (1 or A) and then typing **N**, so that WordPerfect inserts

```
Setup: Display

     1 - Automatically Format and Rewrite     Yes

     2 - Colors/Fonts/Attributes

     3 - Display Document Comments            Yes

     4 - Filename on the Status Line          Yes

     5 - Graphics Screen Type                 IBM EGA 640x200 16 color

     6 - Hard Return Display Character

     7 - Menu Letter Display                  BOLD

     8 - Side-by-side Columns Display         Yes




Selection: 0
```

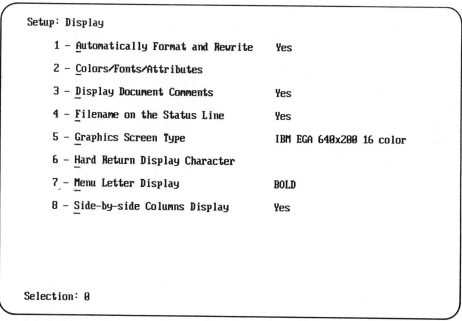

Figure B-3. *The Setup Display menu*

"No" next to this option; now WordPerfect will only format and rewrite text as you scroll through a document or when you press the SCREEN (CTRL + F3) key and select Rewrite (0 or R) or press ENTER.

Colors/Fonts/Attributes

WordPerfect supports numerous monitors and display cards, including: Monochrome, CGA, PC 3270, Black and White, EGA Color or Monochrome, VGA Color or Monochrome, 8514/A, MCGA, Hercules Graphics Card, Hercules Graphics Card Plus RamFont. You can change the characteristics, colors, and/or fonts by which normal text and text with attributes (such as boldfaced or superscripted text) appear on screen. The text can be displayed differently on the Doc 1 screen than on the Doc 2 screen. The choices available to you for displaying onscreen text depend on your computer monitor and display card. Select Colors/Fonts/Attributes (2 or C). Here are the basic monitors and the selections available to you:

Monochrome Monitors The Attributes screen appears, containing seven columns. The left column of this screen lists the possible attributes with which text might appear on screen: Normal (without any special attributes); Blocked (where text is within the boundaries of a phrase with **Block on** flashing); with one of the 16 size and appearance attributes found on the FONT (CTRL + F8) key (such as Underline, Strikeout, Bold, Double Underline, Small Caps, and so on); Bold & Underline (text that is both boldfaced and underlined at the same time); and Other Combinations (such as text that is underlined and in small caps at the same time or that is boldfaced and double underlined at the same time). The middle columns each indicate whether or not the capabilities of your monitor (Blink, Bold, Blocked, Underline, or Normal) should be activated for each of the attributes. The last column shows you a sample of the result of your selection for a particular attribute. Here's an example for three attributes on the Attributes screen:

Attribute	Blink	Bold	Blocked	Underline	Normal	Sample
Normal	N	N	N	N	Y	Sample
Underline	N	N	N	Y	N	Sample
Bold	N	Y	N	N	N	**Sample**

For each attribute, move the cursor across the appropriate row, to each capability, and type **Y** to turn on the capability or **N** to turn it off, or press the SPACEBAR to switch Y to N or N to Y. You can turn on more than one capability for an attribute; for instance, select both Blink and Bold. (You may not be able to turn on or off certain attributes which are reserved for your display card; WordPerfect will skip over attributes that you are unable to change.)

CGA/PC 3270/MCGA Monitors (This also applies to EGA monitors when you have insufficient memory on your display card to use the font capabilities or have EGA in a mode that displays more than 25 lines on your screen.) The Colors/Fonts screen appears, containing two options. Select Fast Text Display (2 or F) to determine whether you want WordPerfect to speed up text display. Then type **Y** or **N**. If you select "Yes" to activate fast text display, you may find that "snow" (static) appears on the Typing screen, in which case you will want to change this option to "No." (If the setting for this option is predefined as "N/A," then the setting cannot be changed for your monitor.)

Select Screen Colors (1 or S) to choose your monitor's colors for specific attributes. At the top of the screen, WordPerfect lists 16 colors that are available for display on your screen, along with their corresponding letters. Below this are four columns. The left column lists the possible attributes with which text might appear on screen—the same as for monochrome monitors (above). The middle two columns each indicate by letter the foreground and background colors that should be used for each of the attributes. The last column shows a sample of the result of your selection for a particular attribute.

Here's an example for three attributes on the screen (the samples are not shown here because this book does not display text in colors other than black):

Attribute	**Foreground**	**Background**	**Sample**
Normal	H	B	
Underline	H	A	
Bold	P	B	

For each attribute, move the cursor across the appropriate row and press a letter key to select a color for the screen's background and foreground. For example, you can select white as your foreground color and black as your background color for normal text, and light blue as your foreground color and black as your background color for underlined text. (You may not be able to turn on or off certain attributes which are reserved for your display card; WordPerfect will skip over attributes that you are unable to change.)

EGA/VGA Monitors The Colors/Fonts screen appears, containing six options, as shown in Figure B-4. Options 2 through 6 are your font options. Select one of these font options and an asterisk appears next to the selected option. (If you have the Hercules Graphics Card Plus RamFont, you can display 6 or 12 fonts, rather than only 1 font as on the EGA.) If an asterisk does not appear, then there is a problem in loading that font; copy all WordPerfect files ending with .FNT to the directory in which WP.EXE is located.

If you selected Font option 2 (Italics), 3 (Underline), or 4 (Small Caps), then you can choose to see one of these fonts and/or choose from eight colors.

If you selected Font option 5 (512 Characters), then you increase the number of displayable characters in the current font from 256 to 512 (which is useful if your documents frequently contain special characters, as described in Chapter 17), and you can choose from eight colors on screen.

If you selected Font option 6 (Normal Font Only), then no special fonts will

```
Setup: Colors/Fonts

     1 - Screen Colors

     2 - Italics Font, 8 Foreground Colors

    *3 - Underline Font, 8 Foreground Colors

     4 - Small Caps Font, 8 Foreground Colors

     5 - 512 Characters, 8 Foreground Colors

     6 - Normal Font Only, 16 Foreground Colors




Selection: 0
```

Figure B-4. The Colors/Fonts screen for EGA/VGA monitors

be shown on screen, but 16 colors are available to choose from.

Next, select Screen Colors (1 or S) to choose your monitor's fonts and colors for specific attributes—pertaining to the font option that you selected. At the top of the screen, WordPerfect lists eight colors (or 16 colors if you selected font option 6) that are available for display on your screen, along with their corresponding letters. Below this are five columns (or four columns if you selected font option 5 or 6). The left column lists the possible attributes with which text might appear on screen—the same as for monochrome monitors (above). The next column (which appears only if you selected font options 2, 3, or 4) tells whether the font you selected should be activated for each attribute. The following two columns each indicate, by letter, the foreground and background colors that should be used for each of the attributes. The last column shows a sample of the result of your selection for a particular attribute.

Here's an example for three attributes on the screen, assuming that you selected font option 2, 3, or 4 (the samples are not shown here because this book does not display text in colors other than black):

Attribute	**Font**	**Foreground**	**Background**	**Sample**
Normal	N	H	B	
Underline	Y	H	A	
Bold	N	P	B	

For each attribute, move the cursor across the appropriate row and type **Y** or **N** to indicate whether or not the font should be activated (not applicable if you selected font options 5 or 6), and then press a letter key to select a color for the screen's background and foreground. For instance, for normal text you can select no font, white as your foreground color, and black as your background color, and for underlined text, you can activate the font and select light blue as your foreground color, and black as your background color. (You may not be able to turn on or off certain attributes that are reserved for your display card; WordPerfect will skip over attributes that you are unable to change.)

Whatever type of monitor you use, once you choose how characters will be displayed on one document screen (that is, on either the Doc 1 or Doc 2 screen), press SWITCH (SHIFT + F3) to then assign characteristics to attributes on the other document screen. Repeat the same procedure as described above or, if you want the Doc 1 screen and Doc 2 screen to both display colors, fonts, and attributes in the same way, simply press the MOVE (CTRL + F4) key; the attributes are copied from the other document screen into the current one.

Finally, press EXIT (F7) to save your selections and to return to the Display menu.

Note: Remember that any changes you make affect the manner in which attributes are shown on the screen, but not how they appear on the printed page; see Chapter 7 for a discussion of how to change the manner in which attributes appear when printed.

Display Document Comments

The default setting is "Yes," meaning that when you insert comments in your text (as described in Chapter 3), WordPerfect will display the comment on screen in a double-line box. You can request that WordPerfect conceal comments by selecting Display Document Comments (3 or D) and typing **N**, so that WordPerfect inserts "No" for this option; now comments inserted in any of your documents will be hidden on the Typing screen, and you will know that a comment exists only when you see the code **[Comment]** on the Reveal Codes screen.

Filename on the Status Line

The default setting is "Yes," meaning that once you save a file to disk, the file's path and filename appear on the status line when that file is on screen. You can decide to suppress the filename by selecting Filename on the Status Line (4 or F) and typing **N**, so that WordPerfect displays "No" for this option.

Graphics Screen Type

WordPerfect automatically selects a graphics driver for your monitor and display card when you start the program. Figure B-3, for example, shows that WordPerfect has detected the following: an IBM EGA monitor, with 640 × 200 resolution and 16 colors available.

If WordPerfect has selected the wrong graphics driver or if you have a special situation, such as two monitors running on the same computer, then you can indicate a different option by selecting Graphics Screen Type (5 or G). WordPerfect displays a list of screen types. Position the cursor on the correct item and press

ENTER. Or, if the graphics screen type you use is not shown in this list, then you will need to copy the driver file for your graphics screen (with an extension of .WPD) from the Fonts/Graphics diskette to the directory where WP.EXE is located. Then return to the Display menu and select the Graphics Screen Type option.

Hard Return Display Character

WordPerfect assumes that you want a hard return displayed as a space on the Typing screen (in which case it is invisible, unless you switch to the Reveal Codes screen, where you can view the **[HRt]** codes). If you want a character other than a space to be displayed, select Hard Return Display Character (6 or H) and type the character you want to use, such as] or >. To have the hard return displayed as a shaded box on screen (■), press a function key. Or, to have the hard return displayed as a special character, such as ≫ or →, you can use the Compose feature (see Chapter 17) to insert that character on screen. The new display character is shown on the Display menu. If you change your mind and do not want a character to represent a hard return, then you can again select Hard Return Display Character (6 or H), and press the SPACEBAR.

Menu Letter Display

WordPerfect is designed with mnemonic menus, so that in addition to typing a number to activate a feature, you can instead type the mnemonic letter for that feature. WordPerfect assumes that you want the mnemonic letter displayed on screen in bold. However, you can choose to display the mnemonic with another attribute, such as underline (which is how mnemonic letters are displayed in this book so that they are easy to spot). Select Menu Letter Display (7 or M), and WordPerfect prompts with the following menu:

1 Size; 2 Appearance; 3 Normal: **0**

The choices on this menu are the same as the first three options on the Font menu, which appears when you press the FONT (CTRL + F8) key. Now you can select Size (1 or S) or Appearance (2 or A) to select a size or appearance attribute for the menu letter display. The attribute that you select is shown on the Display menu. Or select Normal (3 or N) if you want the mnemonic to display as normal text—implying that you plan to select all features with a number, rather than with the mnemonic. Your choice for how the mnemonic is displayed takes effect for both the Doc 1 and Doc 2 screens.

Side-by-Side Columns Display

The default setting is "Yes," meaning that the text columns you create with the Columns feature (as described in Chapter 19) are displayed side by side, as they appear on the printed page. You can decide to display each column on a separate page by selecting Side-by-side Columns Display (8 or S) and typing **N**, so that WordPerfect displays "No" for this option. This is useful for speeding up performance when editing documents that contain a large amount of text in column format.

Note: Even when columns are displayed on separate pages on screen, they still appear side by side on the printed page.

Fast Save (Unformatted)

As shown in Figure B-1, the default setting for option 4, Fast Save (unformatted), is "No," meaning that whenever you press SAVE (F10) or EXIT (F7) and store a document to disk, WordPerfect will save the document as formatted. Instead, you can request that WordPerfect save without formatting. Select Fast Save (unformatted) (4 or F) on the Setup menu and type **Y**, so that WordPerfect inserts "Yes" on the Setup menu; now WordPerfect will save the on-screen document to disk without formatting that document.

By activating the Fast Save option, you reduce the time it takes to save a document. But be aware that a document cannot be printed from disk unless it is formatted; a document can be printed from disk when Fast Save has been activated only if you press HOME, HOME, DOWN ARROW to format the document just before saving it. Otherwise, you must retrieve the document and print it from screen.

There are tradeoffs, therefore, in activating the Fast Save option. If you typically print documents from screen, consider activating the Fast Save option; this will speed up the process of saving. Just remember to press HOME, HOME, DOWN ARROW before saving documents that you wish to print from disk. On the other hand, if you typically print documents from disk, consider leaving the Fast Save option set as "No."

Initial Settings

Select Initial Settings (5 or I) on the Setup menu and WordPerfect displays the screen shown in Figure B-5. On this screen WordPerfect offers features to change format settings, as well as print and beep options. These options are as follows:

Beep Options

WordPerfect can sound a beep to alert you when one of the following messages appears on the status line: (1) an error message, such as **ERROR: File not found;**

```
Setup: Initial Settings

     1 - Beep Options

     2 - Date Format                        3 1, 4

     3 - Document Summary

     4 - Initial Codes

     5 - Repeat Value                       8

     6 - Table of Authorities









Selection: 0
```

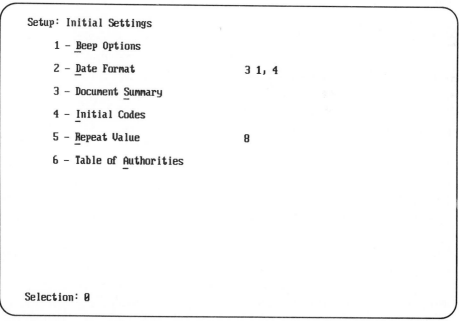

Figure B-5. The Setup Initial Settings menu

(2) the message that prompts for hyphenation, which begins **Position Hyphen; Press ESC . . .**; or (3) the message indicating that the search string was not found during a Search or Replace operation—which is * **Not Found** *.

When you select Beep Options (1 or B), a Setup Beep Options screen appears which indicates the current default settings. The default setting is for a beep to sound during hyphenation, but not on an error or search failure. Select an item from the Beep Options menu and type **Y** to turn on the option or **N** to turn it off. Then press ENTER to return to the Initial Settings screen, or press EXIT (F7) to return to the Typing screen.

Date Format

Chapter 8 describes the Date feature, which can automatically insert the current date (or time) for you. Figure B-5 shows that WordPerfect assumes that you want to display the date as "3 1, 4", where the number 3 represents the month as a word, the number 1 represents the day of the month, and the number 4 represents the year with all four digits shown—for example, May 5, 1989, or September 26, 1989.

You can change the default style for the date format by selecting Date Format (2 or D). The Date Format menu appears, on which you can make a change and then press ENTER or EXIT (F7) to return to the Initial Settings screen (refer to Chapter 8 for more on the Date Format menu).

Document Summary

As described in Chapter 11, WordPerfect provides the opportunity to create a document summary, which will be attached to a specific document when it is saved as a file on disk. You can decide on two default settings for document summaries: (1) whether a document summary form is automatically displayed when you press SAVE or EXIT to store a new document for the very first time (the default setting is "No"); and (2) the subject search text, which is the preselected phrase used by WordPerfect to find the subject of a document (the default is RE:).

To alter these settings, select Document Summary (3 or S). WordPerfect displays the Setup Document Summary menu. Select Create on Save/Exit (1 or C). Type **Y** to have WordPerfect prompt you for a document summary if one does not already exist as you press SAVE or EXIT. You may also select Subject Search Text (2 or S) and enter a search string, such as SUBJECT: or TOPIC--, that you commonly use to identify the subject of your document. (Be sure to refer to Chapter 11 for a fuller explanation of the Document Summary feature.)

Initial Codes

Every time you clear the screen and are ready to begin typing a new document, WordPerfect makes certain assumptions about how the new document should be formatted. For instance, the default left, right, top, and bottom margin settings are one inch. The default line spacing is single. The default justification is for justification on (meaning both the left and right margins will be justified). These initial settings can be changed *from document to document* by inserting format codes, as explained in Chapter 8 and other chapters.

But what if you find yourself changing a specific format setting in the same way *for every document?* You can alter that default permanently, changing the initial format codes to the ones you use most often. Then WordPerfect assumes the new default every time you begin to type a document.

As a general rule, don't change the Setup menu unless you find yourself altering a format setting in the same way for almost all of your documents.

To alter the default format settings, select Initial Codes (4 or I). WordPerfect displays the Setup Initial Codes screen, which is identical to a clear Reveal Codes screen. If the bottom window on screen is completely blank, this indicates that all the default settings as set up by WordPerfect Corporation are in effect (many of the initial format settings are listed in Chapter 8). If format codes are displayed, then you or another user have already altered some of the initial format settings.

To change any setting, insert format codes just as you would on the Typing screen for a specific document. For example, if you wish to change right justification from "On" to "Off" as the default, press FORMAT (SHIFT + F8), select Line (1 or L), select Justification (3 or J), type **N**, and press EXIT (F7)—just as you would to turn off justification in a specific document. If you want the margin defaults to change, press FORMAT (SHIFT + F8) and proceed to change margins as if in a document. Or, if you wish to alter WordPerfect's assumptions on footnote options (such as the spacing between each footnote), press FOOTNOTE (CTRL + F7), select Footnote (1 or F), select Options (4 or O), and when the Footnote Options screen appears, make any changes you desire—as you would in a document. The codes will display only on the bottom window on the screen (just as they appear only on the bottom window in the Reveal Codes screen within a document). Then press EXIT (F7) to return to the Initial Settings screen.

Once you change the default format settings, new settings will affect future documents—new documents that you create from that point on. Of course, any of the newly defined default settings can still be changed in a particular document; when you're typing a document and you use the Document Initial Settings option on the Format Menu, the default initial settings can be seen, edited, or eliminated for that one document.

But any change to the default format settings will have no effect on pre-existing documents. That's because an invisible document prefix (or packet of information) is saved with every document that you store on disk. The invisible packet includes those codes existing on the Document Initial Codes screen (as described in Chapter 8); unless altered, those codes are derived from the codes found on the Setup Initial Codes screen at the time the document is created. For example, suppose that you created and stored on disk one document using the default left/right margin settings of 1″. If you then use the Setup menu to alter the default to 2″, that first document will remain with margins of 1″.

Repeat Value

You can change the number of times that the ESC key repeats a keystroke. The ESC key is used to repeat a character, a cursor movement, or a macro. By default, when you press ESC, WordPerfect prompts

Repeat Value = 8

This means that the next keystroke you enter will be repeated eight times. If you wish, you can permanently change the default value for this feature by selecting Repeat Value (5 or R), typing a number, and pressing ENTER. (Be aware, however, that you can override the default setting of the repeat value for a specific working session when viewing the Typing or Reveal Codes screen by pressing ESC, typing a number, and pressing ENTER; see Chapter 3 for details.)

Table of Authorities

As described in Chapter 22, WordPerfect can generate a table of authorities for you. You can decide on three default settings that affect the style of table of authorities entries when generated: (1) whether a dot leader should precede the page location of each authority (the default settings is "Yes"); (2) whether to allow underlining in the generated table (the default setting is "No"); and (3) whether to insert blank lines between authorities (the default setting is "Yes").

To alter these settings, select Table of Authorities (6 or A). WordPerfect displays the Setup Table of Authorities menu. Select an option and type **Y** or **N**. (You can also change these settings for a specific document, rather than changing the default.) Refer to Chapter 22 for a more detailed explanation of the Table of Authorities feature.

Keyboard Layout

With the Keyboard Layout feature, you can create or edit a keyboard definition, where a keyboard definition specifies which key should be chosen to perform a certain task or feature. For instance, the original keyboard definition, as set up by WordPerfect Corporation, defines the F1 key as the CANCEL key, the ESC key to activate the Repeat Value feature, and the F3 key as the HELP key. You can set up your own keyboard definition whereby:

- A feature is activated by pressing a key of your choosing. For instance, you can reassign the F1 key as the HELP key.
- A special character is inserted on screen by pressing a key of your choosing. For instance, you can reassign CTRL + S to insert the legal section symbol (§). (Special characters are discussed in Chapter 17.)
- A macro is executed by pressing a key of your choosing. For instance, create a macro that automatically inserts a paragraph number when you press CTRL + P. (Macros are discussed in Chapter 27.)

Any key can be assigned to a feature, a special character, or a macro. And you can create many keyboard definitions. For example, you can create one keyboard definition that stores all your macros, and another that houses your special characters. Or create one keyboard definition that assigns features, special characters, and macros when you're working on legal documents, and another for book chapters. Each keyboard definition is saved on disk with the extension .WPK (which stands for WordPerfect Keyboard).

Select Keyboard Layout (6 or K) and WordPerfect displays the Setup Keyboard Layout screen. The top of the screen lists the names of any keyboard definitions that you have already created. The bottom shows the Keyboard Layout menu, as follows:

1 Select; **2** Delete; **3** Rename; **4** Create; **5** Edit; **6** Original; **N** Name Search: **1**

To create a new definition, you would choose Create (4 or C). WordPerfect prompts

Keyboard Filename:

Enter a name that is one to eight characters in length (using the same characters that are allowable when specifying a filename). The Keyboard Edit screen is displayed, as shown in Figure B-6 for a keyboard definition named LEGAL, with a new menu appearing at the bottom of the screen. Now you can begin to create a

```
Keyboard: Edit

  Name: LEGAL

  Key                 Description                                Macro




Key: 1 Edit; 2 Delete; 3 Move; 4 Create;  Macro: 5 Save; 6 Retrieve: 1
```

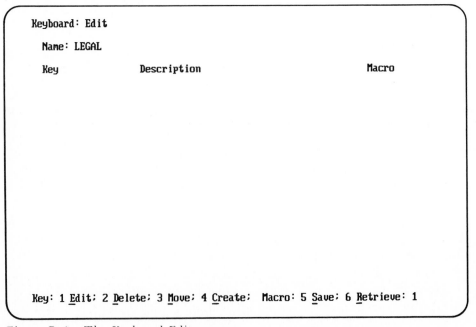

Figure B-6. The Keyboard Edit screen

definition, as follows:

1. Select Create (4 or C), and at the WordPerfect prompt, press a key to create a definition for that key. The Key Edit screen appears, as shown in Figure B-7 for the key CTRL + S (signified at the top of the screen as "Ctrl-S").

   The top of the Key Edit screen lists the name of the key being defined. Next is the "Description" heading. Finally, under the "Action" heading is a double-line box that contains only the keystroke for the key to be defined. Any keystroke other than a plain character (such as a, or A, or 3) is surrounded by curved brackets. For instance, {^S} signifies CTRL + S, {ALT F} signifies ALT + F, {Merge/Sort} signifies the MERGE/SORT (CTRL + F9) key, and {Del to EOL} signifies the DEL EOL (CTRL + END) key combination.

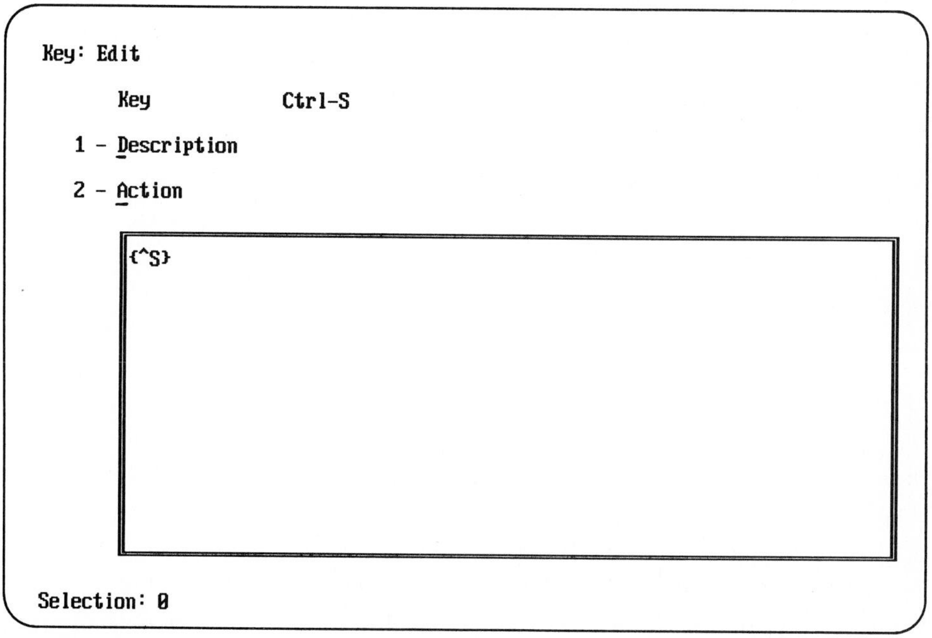

Figure B-7. The Key Edit screen

2. If you wish to insert a description of how you are about to reassign a key—which is highly recommended in case you later forget which task you assigned to that key—select Description (1 or D) and type a description of up to 39 characters. Then press EXIT (F7) or ENTER.
3. To insert the keystrokes that will define the key, select Action (2 or A). The cursor moves inside the Action box. You can press the DEL key to erase the keystroke that represents the key you are defining. Or you can press RIGHT ARROW to move past the keystroke, and press ENTER to move down a line.

   Now you can insert a character or a key name at the current cursor position by pressing that key. For instance, press COMPOSE (CTRL + 2) and type in the WordPerfect character number of the special character that you want to have defined for that key (as described in Chapter 17). Or press CENTER (SHIFT + F6) and WordPerfect inserts {Center}, to define that key as the new CENTER key.

   Or, if you plan to insert more than one keystroke, then you are essentially creating a macro; be sure to refer to the last section in Chapter 27 to learn the procedure for editing a macro and for using the Macro Programming Language, which operates on the Key Edit screen, as well as on the Macro Edit screen. (Certain key actions can be inserted only after you press CTRL + V or CTRL + F10; this, too, is discussed in the last section of Chapter 27.)
4. Press EXIT (F7) to leave the Action box.
5. Press EXIT (F7) to return to the Keyboard Edit screen. The screen now lists the key you just assigned, the description of that key's task, and, if that key performs as a macro, the macro number. (The macro number is a reference, in case you include the keystrokes when defining a macro.)
6. Repeat steps 1 through 5 for each key you wish to define.

From the Keyboard Edit menu, you can also edit or delete a key, move a key's task to a different key, or save the definition of a key to a file macro (which assigns that file an extension of .WPM so that it can be executed like a standard macro, as described in Chapter 27). Position the cursor on a key by using the arrow keys or the →SEARCH key and then press the key so that the cursor moves to that key. Now select an option from the bottom of the Keyboard Edit screen, such as Delete (2 or D), and follow the WordPerfect prompts.

In addition, you can assign a previously created file macro to a key from the Keyboard Edit screen. Select Retrieve (6 or R), press the key to which it will now be assigned, and then enter the name of the macro file. Now that macro can be executed either when the keyboard definition to which it is assigned is active, by pressing the assigned key, or when you use the standard macro execution procedure (described in Chapter 27).

Once you have created a keyboard definition, press EXIT (F7) to return to the Keyboard Layout screen. From here, you can create another keyboard definition by again following steps 1 through 6 above.

Once keyboard definitions have been created, other options on the Keyboard Layout menu allow you to activate a keyboard definition:

- **Name Search** Enables you to position the cursor on a keyboard definition without using the cursor movement keys. Choose N, Name Search, and type the beginning letters of the name of the keyboard definition you wish to select. The cursor moves to the keyboard definition name that matches the letters you type.
- **Select** Allows you to activate a specific keyboard. Position the cursor on the name of the keyboard definition you wish to select—either with the cursor movement keys or by selecting the Name Search option, and choose Select (1 or S) or simply press ENTER since 1 is the default option on the Keyboard Layout menu. The Setup menu returns to the screen, and the active keyboard definition is listed next to option 6.
- **Original** Allows you to select the original keyboard definition. Choose Original (6 or O). The Setup menu returns to the screen, with no keyboard definition listed next to option 6 (meaning that the original keyboard is active).

Note: You can also return to the original keyboard definition from the Typing or the Reveal Codes screen when another keyboard definition is currently active. Simply press CTRL + 6.

Other options on the Keyboard Layout menu enable you to edit a keyboard definition, as follows:

- **Delete** Enables you to delete a keyboard definition and, therefore, the assignments of all keys within that keyboard definition. Position the cursor on a keyboard definition name, select Delete (2 or D) and confirm the deletion by typing **Y**. The keyboard definition by that name (and with the extension .WPK) is erased from disk.

- **Rename** Allows you to rename a keyboard definition. Position the cursor on the keyboard definition name, select Rename (3 or R), and enter a new name.
- **Edit** Allows you to edit a keyboard definition. Position the cursor on a keyboard definition name and select Edit (5 or E). The Keyboard Edit screen (Figure B-6) appears for that feature. Now edit individual keys by positioning the cursor on a key and selecting an item from the menu at the bottom of the screen.

You can specify a directory in which keyboard definition files (as well as macro files) are stored by using the Location of Auxiliary Files option on the Setup menu, described in the following section of this appendix.

You should know that WordPerfect includes on the Conversion disk a number of keyboard definitions which you can use and/or edit as you like. These are shown on screen when you select the Keyboard Layout option after you insert the Conversion disk in drive B (floppy disk users) or specify where these files are housed by using the Location of Auxiliary Files option (hard disk users). The definitions included are

- **Alternate** This keyboard definition, stored on disk with the name ALTRNAT.WPK, moves the Help feature to F1, the Cancel feature to ESC, and the Repeat Value feature to F3 (so as to match more closely the keys assigned by other software packages you may use).
- **Enhanced** This keyboard definition, stored on disk with the name ENHANCED.WPK, reassigns more than ten keys. For instance, HOME, HOME, LEFT ARROW is reassigned to the HOME key, and HOME is assigned to the number 5 key.
- **Macros** This keyboard definition, stored on disk with the name MACROS.WPK, assigns a variety of macros to the ALT and CTRL keys, and illustrates some of the useful tasks you can perform by creating a macro, which is assigned to a specific key.

You may wish to examine these three predefined keyboard definitions before you begin to create your own definitions.

Be careful when creating a keyboard definition, so that as you redefine the task performed by a function key you don't lose a function that you need. For example, suppose that you are creating a keyboard definition to use when you type legal documents, and you assign the section symbol (§) to the F4 function key. In that case, when you activate that keyboard definition, you will no longer have access to the →Indent function. A better idea is to assign the section symbol to another key, such as CTRL + S or ALT + 1.

Note: Among the very few keys that cannot be assigned a task are CTRL + 2 and CTRL + 6, which have already been assigned tasks by WordPerfect Corporation. CTRL + 2 controls the Compose feature, as described in Chapter 17. CTRL + 6 returns WordPerfect to the original keyboard directly from the Typing or Reveal Codes screen, as described above.

Remember, too, that if you choose to activate a keyboard definition when you've assigned tasks to the ALT key plus a letter, such as ALT + S or ALT + A, then those tasks will be executed rather than the macros you may have created and stored under ALT + S or ALT + A. To solve this problem, you can either (1) choose to return to the original keyboard before pressing ALT + S or ALT + A, or (2) assign each macro to a key in that key definition.

You may find it handy to keep beside your desk a list of the keyboard definitions that you created and the keys assigned in those definitions. It is all too easy to forget which keys you assigned to which tasks. (To refresh your memory, you can return to the Keyboard Layout menu, position the cursor on the name of the keyboard definition you wish to review, and select the Edit option; a list of keys and their descriptions are displayed for you.)

Location of Auxiliary Files

Select Location of Auxiliary Files (7 or L) from the Setup menu and WordPerfect displays the menu shown in Figure B-8. On this menu, you specify where certain auxiliary files that WordPerfect uses are located on disk. (In most cases, if you do not specify a location for auxiliary files, WordPerfect assumes that these files are located in the default drive/directory or in the directory where the file WP.EXE is stored.) The options on the Location of Auxiliary Files menu include

- **Backup Directory** The directory in which you want your timed backup files (described previously in this chapter) to be stored by WordPerfect.
- **Hyphenation Module(s)** The directory in which WP{WP}EN.HYL is located. This file is an optional hyphenation dictionary that you can purchase separately from WordPerfect Corporation. (Refer to Chapter 8 for

```
Setup: Location of Auxiliary Files

     1 - Backup Directory

     2 - Hyphenation Module(s)

     3 - Keyboard/Macro Files

     4 - Main Dictionary(s)

     5 - Printer Files                    C:\WPER

     6 - Style Library Filename

     7 - Supplementary Dictionary(s)

     8 - Thesaurus




Selection: 0
```

Figure B-8. The Setup Location of Auxiliary Files menu

more on the optional hyphenation dictionary.) When you specify a default path for the hyphenation modules, the message "Hyphenation (C) Copyright Soft-Art Inc., 1988" appears momentarily.

- **Keyboard/Macro Files** The directory in which your keyboard files (with the extension .WPK), macro files (with the extension .WPM), and macro resource files (with the extension .MRS) are stored. Refer to Chapter 27 for more on the Macro feature, and to the preceding section of this appendix, "Keyboard Layout," for information on the Keyboard Layout feature.
- **Main Dictionary(s)** The directory in which the WP{WP}EN.LEX file (or another main dictionary file that you use, such as in another language) is located. This file contains the dictionary of words used to perform a spelling check of a document. See Chapter 16 for more on the Speller feature.
- **Printer Files** The directory in which files with the extension .PRS are located. These files are created for each printer that you define. WordPerfect

assumes that these files are stored in the same directory where WP.EXE is housed, unless you specify otherwise. The procedure for defining printers is found in Appendix A.

- **Style Library Filename** The path and filename for the file that acts as your style library. Note that this is the only option on the Location of Auxiliary Files menu for which you must indicate not only a directory, but also a specific filename. For instance, suppose that you wish to establish as your style library the file named STYLE.LIB, which is stored on the hard disk in the subdirectory \WPER. Then you would enter the following as the style library file: **C:\WPER\STYLE.LIB**. See Chapter 10 for more on the Styles feature.
- **Supplementary Dictionary(s)** The directory in which the WP{WP}EN.SUP file (and other supplementary dictionary files) are located. See Chapter 16 for information on the Speller feature.
- **Thesaurus** The directory in which the WP{WP}EN.THS file (or another thesaurus file that you use, such as in another language) is located. This file contains the thesaurus of words used when you press THESAURUS (ALT + F1). See Chapter 16 for details on the Thesaurus feature.

By specifying a location for your auxiliary files, you can arrange a hard disk's WordPerfect files into their own directories. For example, if you specify a keyboard/macro files directory, then whenever you create a keyboard definition or a macro, WordPerfect automatically stores the file in the directory that you specified. And when you activate a keyboard definition or invoke a macro, WordPerfect looks to that directory to find the definition or the macro. Therefore, you can keep all keyboard definitions and macros separate from your document files, and thus maintain a well-organized filing system.

Keep in mind that on the Location of Auxiliary Files menu you indicate a drive/directory for all items except for item 6, Style Library Filename, for which you indicate a drive/directory *and a filename.*

Units of Measure

Many WordPerfect features involve some type of measurement. WordPerfect allows you to display all measurements in inches, centimeters, points, or version 4.2 units (lines and columns).

WordPerfect assumes that you want measurements to be displayed in inches. For instance, margins and tab settings on the Line Format menu are shown in inches (such as 1″). When you change margins or tabs, WordPerfect assumes inches. And the format code inserted in the text also displays the measurement in inches, such as **[L/R Mar:2″,1.5″]**.

Further, WordPerfect assumes that you want the "Ln" and "Pos" indicators on the status line to display in inches, so that the status line may read

Doc 1 Pg 4 Ln 2.5″ Pos 1″

You can alter the way measurements are displayed and/or change the way the cursor position is displayed on the status line. Select Units of Measure (8 or U) on the Setup menu, and WordPerfect shows the menu illustrated in Figure B-9. Your unit-of-measurement options are

- **Inches indicated with ″** This is the default setting for both items.
- **Inches indicated with i** For example, if you select Status Line Display (2 or S) and type **i** to change the status line display, the status line then reads **Doc 1 Pg 4 Ln 2.5i Pos** 1i.
- **Centimeters** For example, if you select Status Line Display (2 or S) and type **c** to change the status line display, the status line then reads **Doc 1 Pg 4 Ln 6.36c Pos** 2.54c.
- **Points** This is a commonly used measurement in the publishing industry. For example, if you select Status Line Display (2 or S) and type **p** to change the status line display, the status line then reads **Doc 1 Pg 4 Ln 180.5p Pos** 72p.

  In WordPerfect, points equal 1/72 inch. You should know that in publishing, points equal 1/72.27 inch, a 0.4% difference which is small but nevertheless significant when doing precise work.
- **Version 4.2 units** In version 4.2, vertical measurements are represented as lines, and horizontal measurements as column positions. For example, if you select Status Line Display (2 or S) and type **u** to change the status line display, the status line then reads **Doc 1 Pg 4 Ln 10 Pos** 10.

  When you select version 4.2 units, the size of a line or column varies based on the size of the font you are using in your document. Also, should you decide to work with the status line in version 4.2 units, you must keep in mind that the "Ln" number indicates a distance from the top *margin,* while for the other units of measure it indicates a distance from the top *edge of the page.*

```
Setup: Units of Measure

     1 - Display and Entry of Numbers          "
          for Margins, Tabs, etc.

     2 - Status Line Display                   "


Legend:

     " = inches
     i = inches
     c = centimeters
     p = points
     u = WordPerfect 4.2 Units (Lines/Columns)







Selection: 0
```

Figure B-9. *The Setup Units of Measure menu*

No matter which measurement you decide to use as your default, you do not have to enter measurements in the selected unit. You can still enter a measurement in another unit of measure as long as it is followed by a letter to indicate the units—i or ″ for inches, c for centimeters, p for points, h for version 4.2 horizontal units, and v for version 4.2 vertical units.

For instance, suppose that you selected the display and entry of numbers to be in inches. You can indicate a left margin of 2.5c (centimeters), 90p (points), or 15h (version 4.2 horizontal units). WordPerfect will convert your entry into inches. If, instead, you simply enter **2**, then WordPerfect assumes that you are specifying two inches.

You may wish to change the unit of measure frequently, depending on the document you are working on. You may wish to switch into points, for example, when producing a newsletter, and to version 4.2 units for standard documents if you previously used version 4.2. You can also select the status line to have one unit of measure and the display and entry of numbers to have a different unit of measure.

C

Getting Additional Support

As you use WordPerfect and as your knowledge of WordPerfect expands, you will begin to move from the basic to the more advanced WordPerfect features. In doing so, you may bump up against a question specific to a particular document you are typing, or you may need help using a particular feature. Or perhaps you encounter a glitch when using WordPerfect with a particular piece of equipment. Be sure to check the index of this book, check your WordPerfect manual, and consult your co-workers and colleagues for answers. Also, try the sources of additional support listed below.

- The WordPerfect 5 package contains a workbook and a tutorial to help you learn the program. The WordPerfect Workbook is a book of 32 lessons under the headings of Fundamentals, Formatting Documents, Merging Documents, and Special Applications. If you wish to proceed with a lesson in the Workbook, you should load WordPerfect. Then, floppy disk users should place the Learning disk in drive B, while hard disk users should change the default to the directory on the hard disk in which the learning files are stored, which may be \WPER\LEARN or \WP50\LEARN if you installed WordPerfect as described in Appendix A. (Chapter 13 explains how to change the default directory from within WordPerfect.)

WordPerfect's on-line tutorial guides you through the basics, such as using the keyboard, naming files, formatting a document, and moving text—the same information as in the Fundamentals section in the Workbook—and through advanced features, such as merging with a file (Mail Merge) and working with tables of authorities. To access the tutorial, you must be in DOS, with the DOS prompt on screen. If you have loaded WordPerfect, exit the program by pressing the EXIT (F7) key.

Floppy disk users should place the WordPerfect 1 disk in drive A and the WordPerfect Learning disk in drive B. At the DOS prompt, type **B**: and press ENTER. Then type **LEARN** and press ENTER to access a special batch file for floppy disk users that starts the tutorial. Once the tutorial is loaded, WordPerfect will prompt you to replace the WordPerfect 1 disk with the WordPerfect 2 disk.

Hard disk users should change to the \WPER\LEARN directory (or to the directory in which the WordPerfect learning files are stored). For instance, type **CD \WPER\LEARN** and press ENTER. Then type **TUTOR** and press ENTER to start the tutorial.

Note to hard disk users: For the tutorial to operate correctly, you must have a path established that indicates where both the WordPerfect program file WP.EXE and the tutorial files are housed (see Appendix A for instructions on altering the AUTOEXEC.BAT file to insert the proper DOS PATH command).

- WordPerfect Corporation continually improves its product—even within months after the introduction of a new version. When minor changes are made for a version already on the market, the changes for new releases of that version are documented in two files on the Learning disk: README.WP, a WordPerfect document, and README, a DOS text file. Both files contain the same information.

  Check the list of files on your Learning disk or directory (you can press the LIST FILES (F5) key from within WordPerfect). If there's a file named README.WP, then print it out, just like you would any WordPerfect document, to read the special information pertaining to your particular release of WordPerfect 5. Or, when you're in DOS and the DOS prompt is on screen, you can use DOS commands to view the contents of the README file.

- Your computer dealer may be able to answer a question for you, especially if it relates to getting WordPerfect to work properly with your equipment.

- There are user groups devoted to your brand of computer. If you have an IBM PC, for example, there may be an IBM PC user group in your area, where you can meet other people who use WordPerfect and exchange information with them. User group names and addresses are usually listed in regional (or even national) computer magazines.

- There are user groups devoted to WordPerfect Corporation products. Like other computer user groups, WordPerfect user group names and addresses are listed in computer magazines.

  A well-regarded group is the WordPerfect Support Group, based in Baltimore, Maryland. This group produces a newsletter called *The Word-Perfectionist,* which is an excellent source for update information and tips on WordPerfect Corporation products. In addition, the WordPerfect Support Group operates an electronic mail bulletin board service (for those of you with a modem) through which members can share ideas and information. You can contact the group at the following address:

  WordPerfect Support Group
  P.O. Box 1577
  Baltimore, MD 21203

  To sign up for a subscription to *The WordPerfectionist,* call this toll-free number: 1 (800) USA-GROUP.

- WordPerfect Corporation's telephone support is frequently hailed as the best in the business. At last count, there were more than 200 people answering the telephones in the Customer Support Department—which represents over one-third of the entire WordPerfect Corporation staff—ready to answer your questions on WordPerfect with regard to installation, printers, or general items. Be sure to be at your computer when you call so that you can duplicate the problem, keystroke by keystroke, as you speak with the Customer Support representative.

  Customer Support representatives are extremely responsive once you get through to them, but you may be placed on hold during peak hours, which are 11:00 A.M. to 3:00 P.M. Mountain Standard Time. Once you are connected to WordPerfect Corporation, listen for a prerecorded message that will indicate the additional numbers to dial so that you are transferred to the proper support group. Soon, a friendly person will come on the line. If that person can't answer your question, he or she will usually find someone who can answer your question.

The customer-support, toll-free number (if you are within the United States, Puerto Rico, or the U.S. Virgin Islands) is

(800) 321-5906

Hours are 7:00 A.M. to 6:00 P.M. Mountain Standard Time on Monday through Friday and 8:00 A.M. to noon on Saturday.

There's another telephone number available if you are in an area in which the phone system does not support toll-free numbers (you will be charged for the call).

(801) 226-6800

Or you can write to WordPerfect Corporation. The address is

WordPerfect Corporation
Attention: Customer Support Department
1555 North Technology Way
Orem, UT 84057

When you write, include a full description of the equipment you use, the version and release date of your WordPerfect program, and the problem. (To determine the release date, from within WordPerfect press the HELP (F3) key and your software's release date will be displayed in the upper right-hand corner of the Help screen.)

Trademarks

Adobe™	Adobe Systems, Inc.
AutoCAD®	Autodesk, Inc.
Bitstream® Fontware™	Bitstream
CADAM®	CADAM
CBDS™	International Business Machines Corporation
CHART-MASTER®	Decision Resources, Inc./Ashton-Tate
dBASE®	Ashton-Tate
dBASE III®	Ashton-Tate
DESQview®	Quarterdeck Office Systems
Diablo®	Xerox Corporation
DIAGRAM-MASTER®	Decision Resources, Inc./Ashton-Tate
DisplayWrite™	International Business Machines Corporation
DisplayWrite 3™	International Business Machines Corporation
Dr Halo II™	IMSI
Enable™	The Software Group
Energraphics™	Enertronics Research, Incorporated
Epson®	Seiko Epson Corporation
Framework II®	Ashton-Tate
Freelance®	Lotus Development Corporation
GDDM™	International Business Machines Corporation
GEM®	Digital Research, Incorporated
Generic CADD™	Generic Software, Inc.
Genius™	DataMate
GPG™	International Business Machines Corporation
Graph-in-the-Box®	New England Software
Graphwriter™	Graphic Communications, Incorporated
Harvard™	Software Publishing Corporation
Helvetica®	Linotype Co.

Hercules®	Hercules Computer Technology
HP Graphics Gallery™	Hewlett-Packard Company
HP Scanning Gallery™	Hewlett-Packard Company
IBM®	International Business Machines Corporation
Javelin™	Emulex
LaserJet®	Hewlett-Packard Company
Lotus® 1-2-3®	Lotus Development Corporation
Mace Utilities®	Paul Mace Software, Inc.
Macintosh®	Apple Computer, Inc.
MacPaint®	Claris Corporation
MathCAD®	Mathsoft
MathPlan	WordPerfect Corporation
Microsoft®	Microsoft Corporation
MS-DOS®	Microsoft Corporation
MultiMate®	MultiMate International Corporation
NEC®	NEC Corporation
Okidata®	OKIDATA, and OKI AMERICA CO.
PC Paint Plus®	Mouse Systems
PC Paintbrush®	Z-Soft, Incorporated
Personal Computer XT™	International Business Machines Corporation
PFS:Professional Plan™	Software Publishing Corporation
PicturePaks™	Marketing Graphics Inc.
PlanPerfect™	WordPerfect Corporation
PostScript®	Adobe Systems, Inc.
Printmaster™	Leading Edge Products
Quattro®	Borland International, Inc.
QuietWriter®	International Business Machines Corporation
Repeat Performance™	Popular Demand
SIGN-MASTER®	Decision Resources, Inc./Ashton-Tate
SlideWrite Plus™	Advanced Graphics Software
SuperCalc®	Computer Associates International, Inc.
Symphony®	Lotus Development Corporation
The Norton Utilities®	Peter Norton Computing, Inc.
Times®	Linotype Co.
Topview®	International Business Machines Corporation
TWIN®	Mosaic Software, Inc.
VersaCAD®	T & N Systems
VP Planner®	Paperback Software International
WordPerfect®	WordPerfect Corporation
WordPerfect Library®	WordPerfect Corporation
WordStar®	MicroPro International Corporation

Index

The manuscript for this book was prepared and submitted to Osborne/McGraw-Hill in electronic form. The acquisitions editor for this project was Cynthia Hudson, the technical reviewers were Stuart Osser and Bill Usim, and the project editor was Dusty Bernard.
Text design uses Baskerville for text body and for display. Cover art by Bay Graphics Design Associates. Color separation by Phoenix Color Corp. Screens produced with InSet from Inset Systems, Inc. Book printed and bound by R.R. Donnelley & Sons Company, Crawfordsville, Indiana.